W9-BAE-637

Piano Duet Repertoire

Piano Duet Repertoire

*Music Originally Written for
One Piano, Four Hands*

Cameron McGraw

Indiana University Press • Bloomington and Indianapolis

This book was brought to publication with the
assistance of the generous donors to the
Indiana University Press Music Publishing Fund.

This book is a publication of

Indiana University Press
601 North Morton Street
Bloomington, IN 47404-3797 USA

http://www.indiana.edu/~iupress

Telephone orders 800-842-6796
Fax orders 812-855-7931
Orders by e-mail iuporder@indiana.edu

© 1981 by Cameron McGraw

Updated guide to publishers and distributors,
© 2001 by Indiana University Press

All rights reserved

No part of this book may be reproduced or utilized in any form or by
any means, electronic or mechanical, including photocopying and
recording, or by any information storage and retrieval system, without
permission in writing from the publisher. The Association of American
University Presses' Resolution on Permissions constitutes the only
exception to this prohibition.

The paper used in this publication meets the minimum requirements
of American National Standard for Information Sciences—
Permanence of Paper for Printed Library Materials, ANSI Z39.48-1984.

Manufactured in the United States of America

Library of Congress Cataloging-in-Publication Data

McGraw, Cameron.
Piano duet repertoire.
1. Piano music (4 hands)—Bibliography.
I. Title.
ML128.P3M2   016.7864'956   80-8097
ISBN 0-253-14766-2
ISBN 0-253-21461-0 (pbk.)

2 3 4 5 6 05 04 03 02 01

To Monroe Levin
Friend, Colleague, and Keyboard Companion

Contents

Preface

Music history, like Alice's Wonderland, is full of unexpected and often extraordinary curiosities—subplots of the principal story, by-products of major developments—which assume identities and purposes of their own. One of the most fascinating of these phenomena, which made its appearance in the cultural world of the late eighteenth century, was the rapid rise of the piano duet.

The astonishing growth and development of one piano, four hands, as an independent form of music making, its enormous popularity and consolidation as a social institution by a growing middle class, its flowering and expansion in the nineteenth century, and its current revival all attest to the tremendous appeal of this genre as a vital medium of musical expression. Yet the varied literature it has inspired has been largely neglected and, even to musicians, remains almost unknown.

The piano duet medium is unique because it is the only kind of musical encounter in which two people, using the full resources of a single instrument, effectively perform music originally written or especially arranged for that combination. In addition, it possesses a surprisingly abundant repertoire of remarkable diversity in both scope and function. As a purely pedagogical tool it is of unparalleled value in providing training in musicianship and ensemble playing, in sight reading, and in rhythmic control. And for serious study as well as for delightful diversion, it offers a distinctive literature of first-rate music at every level of technical proficiency.

The earliest examples of music written for two people at one keyboard, A Verse for two to play, by Nicholas Carlton, and A Fancy for two to play, by Thomas Tomkins, date from the early to mid-seventeenth century and belong to the tradition of the Elizabethan virginalist school. Written for the small harpsichord of the period with its range of only five and a half octaves, these pieces are amazingly effective, considering the restricted compass of their activity. But they stand as charming, unexplained isolates of the late English Renaissance, separated stylistically and spiritually from the next appearance of four-hand writing by an unaccountable gap of more than a century.

The second emergence of the four-hand medium occurred during the last forty years of the eighteenth century, with the appearance of Niccolò Jomelli's *Sonata*, Joseph Haydn's *The teacher and the pupil*, and the little *Sonata* (C), K.19d, by Mozart. Impetus was given to the movement somewhat later by the publication of Charles Burney's *Two sonatas or duets for two performers on one piano-forte or harpsichord*, which appeared in 1777, and, in response to apparent popularity, a sequel of two more sonatas in 1778. With the publication of Burney's works the art of four-hand writing was elevated to respectability: it had received the imprimatur of a well-known and highly esteemed musician and scholar and was thus no longer a novel curiosity.

The Preface to Dr. Burney's 1777 work is worth quoting in its entirety for some of the insights it provides into four-hand playing and into the performance of music in general:

As the following pieces are the first that have appeared in print it may be necessary to say something concerning their utility, and the manner of performing them.

That great and varied effects may be produced by *Duets upon Two keyed-Instruments*, has been proven by several ingenious compositions, some of which have been published in Germany; but the inconvenience of having two Harpsichords, or two Piano-Fortes, in the same room, and the short time they remain exactly in tune together, have prevented frequent trials, and even the cultivation of this species of music, notwithstanding all the advantages which, in other respects, it offers to musical students. The playing Duets by *two persons* upon *One instrument,* is, however, attended with nearly as many advantages, without the inconvenience of crowding a room, or of frequent or double tunings; and so extensive is the compass of keyed-instruments, that the most full and elaborate compositions must, if played by one person, leave many parts of the scale unemployed; which, perhaps, first suggested the idea of applying Pedals to the Organ. And though, at first, the near approach of the hands of the different performers may seem aukward [sic] and embarrassing, a little use and contrivance with respect to the manner of placing them, and the choice of fingers, will soon remove that difficulty.

Indeed, it frequently happens, that when there are two students upon the same keyed-instrument, in one house, they are in each other's way; however, by compositions of the following kind, they become reciprocally useful, and necessary companions in their musical exercises.

Besides the *Amusement* which such experiments will afford, they may be made subservient to two very useful purposes of *improvement*, as they will require a particular attention to *Time*, and to that clair-obscure which is produced by different degrees of *Piano* and *Forte*. Errors committed in the *Measure*, by either of the performers of these pieces, who may accelerate, retard, or otherwise break its proportions, will be sooner discovered, and consequently attended with more disagreeable effects, than if such errors were committed by a single player, unless the other give way, and conform to the mistakes that are made. And with respect to the *Pianos* and *Fortes*, each Performer should try to discover when he has the *Principal Melody* given to him, or when he is only to *accompany* that Melody; in order, either to make it more conspicuous, or merely to enrich its harmony. There is no fault in accompanying, so destructive of good melody, taste, and expression, as the vanity with which young and ignorant Performers are too frequently possessed, of becoming *Principals*, when they are only *Subalterns;* and of being heard, when they have nothing to say that merits particular attention. If the part which would afford the greatest pleasure to the hearer be suffocated, and rendered inaudible, by too full, and too loud an accompaniment, it is like throwing the capital figure of a piece into the back-ground, or degrading the master into a servant.

It is hoped, however, that the great strides which the executive part of Music, at least, makes toward perfection, in this metropolis, abounding at present in a greater number of capital performers, of almost every kind, than any other in Europe, will soon render such remarks as these useless; and that something analogous to *Perspective*, *Transparency*, and *Contrast* in painting, will be generally adopted in music, and be thought of nearly as much importance, and make as great a progress among its students, as they have lately done in the other art.

St.Martin's-street, Jan.1777

If Dr. Burney's contributions to early piano duet literature are somewhat lacking in musical inventiveness and excitement, they at least show the composer's sensitivity to some of the problems of four-hand writing in matters of textural variety and balance between the parts.

Mozart's youthful essay, the *Sonata* (C), K.19d, mentioned above, shows a highly musical if rather experimental approach to the keyboard duet, but his mature works reveal him to be one of the great masters of the four-hand art. His *Sonata* (F), K.497, is not only one of the finest masterpieces in piano literature but also one of Mozart's most profound and moving works.

Another of the early duet composers was Johann Christian Bach, the so-called London Bach, youngest son of Johann Sebastian. His three *Sonatas* (1778–1780) are elegant, refined, controlled pieces very much in the early style of his young friend and admirer, Wolfgang Mozart.

By the closing years of the eighteenth century, piano four-hand

music had become so well established that it was able to attract among
its enthusiastic contributors such diverse composers as Muzio Clementi,
Jan Ladislav Dussek, Ignace Pleyel, Giovanni Colizzi, Tommaso and
Giuseppe Giordani, Leopold Koželuh, and Beethoven. They, and other
composers writing before 1800, were careful to indicate in their titles
optional use of harpsichord or piano, even though the piano seemed to
be the preferred instrument of many of them. But by 1800 the word
"harpsichord" had all but disappeared from such titles, just as the instrument itself had vanished from the musical scene.

The nineteenth century was witness to a number of developments
that exerted a strong influence on the style and the function of piano
four-hand music. Through a series of improvements and alterations,
which included the extension of the keyboard to seven octaves and beyond and the expansion of its resonating capabilities by increasing the
size and tension of the strings, the early nineteenth-century piano was
gradually transformed into a full-toned instrument capable of respond-
ing expressively to every shade of dynamic subtlety and virtuosity
demanded of it. Thus reinforced, strengthened, and amplified, it established itself firmly as the preeminent musical instrument of the nineteenth century—a Romantic instrument that both inspired and helped
interpret the Romantic movement.

Coincidental with these gradual changes in the musical scene were
parallel developments in the character, quality, and structure of early
nineteenth-century society. One of the most significant of these was the
rise and consolidation of a growing and prosperous middle class, eager
for the cultivation of all the arts, but especially for participating in
home music making. Just as the piano became the popular instrument
of the era, piano duet playing came to be the favorite social and musical pastime in every affluent parlor.

For the reasons suggested by Dr. Burney in his Preface—limited
space and the need for frequent tunings—the one-piano, four-hand medium was obviously more popular for home entertainment than two-
piano playing, even as early as 1780, with the result that the piano duet
inclined toward the development of a chamber-music quality, but
more intimate and less spectacular than its sister art. This is not to suggest that the piano four-hand repertoire is lacking in music of virtuosity
and brilliance; on the contrary there is a significant body of works originally written for the medium that makes great technical demands on
both performers. An examination of the four-hand works of Schubert,
for instance, the most prolific of all duet composers, reveals a surprisingly broad variety of musical styles, from the thin-textured intimacy
of some of the *Polonaises* to the "orchestrated" brilliance of *Lebens-*

stürme, requiring great technical security and dynamic control to bring off a successful performance.

In response to the steadily increasing and seemingly insatiable public demand for piano duets, nineteenth-century publishers flooded the market with vast quantities of music that took advantage of the piano's expanded resources for sonorities, color, and dynamic effects, without measurably increasing the demands made upon the individual performers. A large part of this output appeared in the form of arrangements of music, either originally written for or associated with other media: marches, popular songs, dances, operatic arias, and the like, issued under a variety of titles such as "duettino," "rondino," "fantasia," "nocturne," and "pot-pourri."

Furthermore, there is an extensive body of piano four-hand literature, well known to piano students and music lovers, consisting of arrangements of Classical and Romantic compositions: symphonies and chamber music of Mozart, Haydn, Beethoven, Mendelssohn, Schumann, and Brahms; complete operas of Wagner and Verdi—all of them valuable sources of instruction and pleasure to the music amateur of pre-phonograph and -radio days. Many a young nineteenth-century musician first became acquainted with the great works of music literature through just such transcriptions. A quick glance at current publishers' catalogues indicates that a surprisingly large proportion of these works is still available in four-hand reductions, along with a healthy number of arrangements of twentieth-century orchestral works by Debussy, Richard Strauss, Max Reger, Schoenberg, Ravel, Stravinsky, and Hindemith.

It is interesting to note the lengths to which some tasteless merchants have been willing to go in order to take full advantage of the lucrative four-hand market. Since all music was fair game and every composition, great or small, was potentially marketable in some format, over-eager publishers occasionally pushed their enterprise to ludicrous extremes by issuing oddities such as piano-duet adaptations of some of Beethoven's piano sonatas (including Op.57 in F minor, the "Appassionata"), the Chopin *Nocturnes*, and even some of the latter's *Études*.

However, beyond the reductions, arrangements, adaptations, and curiosities lies a body of first-class and little-known works. Consisting of dances, sonatas, variations, concertos, character pieces, suites, preludes and fugues, teaching pieces, studies, accompaniments to choral and/or instrumental pieces, and even a full-length *Operetta without a text*, all these works were originally conceived for one piano, four hands. It is the purpose of this volume to present this repertoire to the

increasing number of music students, teachers, and music lovers interested in broadening their knowledge of piano duet literature, and to
the uninitiated, amateurs as well as professionals, to encourage them
to join the ranks of those piano duettists who have already discovered
this most amiable and rewarding way of making music.   .

Acknowledgments

This book has benefited from the efforts and talents of many people. The author is indebted to all these collaborators—musicologists, librarians, historians, musical amateurs, friends, and other contributors —whose assistance, counsel, and encouragement have helped bring this work to completion.

Recognition is due, first of all, to Professors Donald Grout and John Kirkpatrick, inspired musicians and teachers, whose memorable duet performances many years ago at Cornell University first opened the author's ears to the sounds and delights of four-hand music.

Special appreciation is also due the late Ernest Lubin, teacher, composer, and author of *The Piano Duet*, for his gracious support and warm interest.

For their invaluable help and practical suggestions, grateful acknowledgment is made to Douglas Townsend, musicologist and piano duet expert; Harold Samuel, Yale University School of Music Librarian; Robert Dumm, Catholic University; Richard Stevens, San Francisco; Helene Hoffmann and Paul Strickler, Philadelphia; and to the late Rita Benton, University of Iowa, for her kindness in making available a quantity of material on Pleyel's four-hand music.

I would like to thank the following for their assistance in locating or providing music and special bibliographical data: Naomi Donaldson, Ann Arbor; John Diercks, Hollins College; Jack Gottlieb, Hebrew Union College; Harold Moore, Cornell University; Gretchen Buehler, Devon, PA; Milton Salkind, San Francisco; the late Léon Leduc, Asnières, France; Ruth Zimmerman, Leipzig; David Lloyd, Philadelphia; the staff of the Music Library of the British Museum; Sam Dennison, Frederick Kent, and John Angell, librarians at the Free Library of Philadelphia; Ruth Bleecker and her staff at the Boston Public Library; the staff of the Music Division, Library of the Performing Arts, Lincoln Center, New York; the staff of the Music Library of the University of Pennsylvania, Philadelphia; the staff of the Music Division of the Library of Congress; R. E. Baré and Brian Martin of Allens Music, Melbourne; Kenzo Ito of Kawai Gakufu Co., Tokyo; and Shimpei Matsuoka, Zen-On Music Publishers, Tokyo.

Thanks are owed to the following national music information centers and their staffs for their generous contributions of catalogues and/ or copies of works by their native composers: Liv Lindberg, Society of Norwegian Composers; Thorkell Sigurbjörnsson, Iceland Music Information Centre; Per Olof Lundahl, Swedish Music Information Centre (STIM); H. A. Mutsaers, Canadian Music Centre (Toronto); Harald Goertz, Österreichische Gesellschaft für Musik; M. M. de Azarêdo Perdigão, Calouste Gulbenkian Foundation, Lisbon; Hans Steinbeck, Swiss Music Archives; Anna Van Steenberge, Centre Belge de Documentation Musicale; H. Barbu and A. Popa, Editura Muzicală a Uniunii Compozitorilor din R.S.R., Bucharest; and Jan Hanuš, Guild of Czechoslovak Composers.

A special word of thanks and appreciation is due to Philip Buehler, Drexel University, for his devoted interest and counsel, for reading the manuscript and making beneficial and practical suggestions, for providing a firm and dependable Secondo at the keyboard when it was needed, and for faithfully helping pilot the book through to its conclusion.

I should also like to express my gratitude to my colleagues, family, friends, and students for their patience and unflagging encouragement.

Errors and omissions are an unavoidable consequence of a reference work of this nature, and the author would be most grateful to have corrections and additions brought to his attention.

General Explanations

As its subtitle indicates, this book is limited to music originally written for one piano, four hands. Arrangements or adaptations from other media are excluded except in rare cases where the composers themselves have made the transcriptions or where such adaptations have long been considered part of the standard four-hand repertoire.

The piano duet repertoire is listed alphabetically by composer. Some or all of the following data are included:

1. Composer's surname followed by given name; birth and death dates.

2. Full title of composition followed in parentheses by titles of shorter pieces included under the main heading: e.g., *Three easy pieces* (March; Valse; Polka). An asterisk (*) preceding the title or publisher indicates the work was in print in 1978. Foreign titles, except those in French, German, or Italian, are given both in the original language and in their English translation; Russian titles are also transliterated.

3. Key signature. Major keys are given in capital letters (A♭), minor keys in lower case (a♭).

4. Opus number and date of composition. Opus numbers and series of pieces within a given opus are separated by a slash (/); movements of a work are indicated by lower-case roman numerals: e.g., Op.15/2/iii means Opus 15, number 2, third movement.

5. Place and date of publication; publisher's name. See Index of Publishers, p. xxiii, for works currently or recently in print, and reissues or new editions of older publications.

6. Location of item if in manuscript or no longer in print. Unfortunately it has not been possible to examine every work listed because only a relatively small number of compositions cited in late eighteenth-, nineteenth-, and early twentieth-century publishers' catalogues and

cumulative indexes are still extant. A large proportion of the present listings have disappeared, having been lost or destroyed. However, some unexpectedly rich sources of four-hand music—especially out-of-print, obscure, or unusual works—are contained in the collections of many European and American libraries, museums, national archives, and music information centers. Library code numbers (sigla) indicate locations where such items may be found; photocopying and microfilming services are often available at these sources. See Index of Library Locations. (Many vanished four-hand works, by the way, turn up in quite unexpected places. Enthusiasts and collectors should be encouraged to keep an eye out for them in second-hand bookshops, antique shops, small local libraries, auctions, and, of course, old piano benches and attic trunks.)

7. Descriptive comment, critical evaluation, or other annotation. Approximate grade is indicated in parentheses by the following abbreviations: A—Advanced; E—Elementary; I—Intermediate; L—Lower; U—Upper. Examples: (LE)—Lower Elementary; (UI)—Upper Intermediate; (UE-LI)—Upper Elementary to Lower Intermediate; (LA)—Lower Advanced. A single symbol, e.g., (E) or (LI), indicates that both the Secondo and Primo parts are at the same level of difficulty (in this case Elementary and Upper Intermediate). A difference in grade level between the two parts is designated by a slash (/): e.g., (I/E) means that the Secondo part is Intermediate and the Primo is Elementary.

Works in which one or both parts are restricted to a five-finger position are denoted by "5" added to the grade level: e.g., (I/E-5) is interpreted as Secondo at the Intermediate level, while Primo is Elementary and limited to five-finger span in both hands. (I/E-5) is also used to indicate those works, usually consisting of a series of short pieces, in which the easier part appears sometimes in the Primo and sometimes in the Secondo. The symbol (E-5), reduced from (E-5/E-5), denotes that *both* Primo and Secondo are in the five-finger position at the Elementary level.

Because the greatest portion of duet music was directed to a performing public of modest technical and musical resources, ungraded entries in this catalogue tend to lie within the Upper Elementary (UE) to Upper Intermediate (UI) range of difficulty. Titles themselves frequently offer a clue to the approximate difficulty of a work: *Grande sonate, Grand duo, Fantaisie brillante,* and similar descriptive names suggest music of greater technical demands than *Sonatina, Duettino,* and *Pièce caractéristique.*

A grade level, especially if it follows an entry without an accompanying annotation, is often the one given in the publisher's catalogue from which the citation was taken.

The terms *conservative* and *traditional* refer to the common-practice harmonic style cultivated in the eighteenth and nineteenth centuries and still very much in use today.

Instructional or Pedagogical music—sometimes called Teaching Pieces—can be roughly divided into three general, often overlapping, categories: etudes and technical exercises; pieces written for two performers at different levels, either teacher and pupil, or a beginning and a more advanced pupil; and teaching or recreational pieces for two students of equal proficiency.

The first category, etudes and technical exercises, is familiar to all piano students and is sparingly represented in four-hand literature by Carl Czerny, Henry Köhler, and Heinrich Wohlfahrt, the major contributors to the genre. Well known for their solo piano studies and exercises, these three pedagogues composed a corresponding, though smaller, body of instructional music designed as an aid in mastering some of the technical difficulties peculiar to piano duet playing. These works, together with similar efforts by other nineteenth- and twentieth-century composers, constitute a modest collection of exercises and short studies that serve a useful purpose in developing musicianship and a feeling for ensemble playing.

Greater in volume and certainly more absorbing musically than the preceding, is the popular repertoire of duets written for teacher and pupil, featuring one easy and one more-difficult part. Many variations in the distribution and difficulty of the individual parts occur throughout duet literature, but the arrangement most frequently encountered is that in which the Primo plays the easier part within the restricted range of five notes in each hand, while the Secondo part is given to the teacher or a more advanced pupil. A number of composers, intrigued by the architectural strictures of the five-note form, have lavished some of their finest and most imaginative efforts on this popular and effective genre, which seems to have been first developed, if not invented, by Antonio Diabelli.

The third category, teaching or recreational pieces, for two students of equal proficiency, is by far the largest, and has consistently maintained its appeal up to the present time. The best of these teaching pieces are well written, melodious, and attractively set in a variety of styles—traditional through contemporary. The individual parts are well distributed, and they are intended to divert as they instruct.

The term *Salon* describes a familiar type of second-rate music popular in the nineteenth and early twentieth centuries. Shallow, predictable, and mawkish at its worst, it is abundantly represented in four-hand as well as solo piano literature. Because of its dubious musical quality and because the bulk of it is material arranged from original two-hand versions, works of this type have been omitted from this listing. On the other hand, many of the less-known composers, as well as some of the more-familiar figures of the period, have contributed duets of substance and considerable interest, solidly crafted in polished, elegant salon style, and these works are included.

Sample Entry (fictitious)
with Explanations

Schmidt, Johann (1799–1860)

2 *Sonatinas* (C,db), Op.102 (1801). Leipzig: B&H, ca.1802; °NEd.1903. D-ddr:Bds–GB:Lbl–US:Wc, Op.102/2/iii. Instructional. (UE-LI/E-5)

The two Sonatinas are in the keys of C major and db minor, written in 1801, and published in Leipzig by Breitkopf & Härtel in 1802; a new edition by the same publisher was issued in 1903 and is still in print. The Sonatinas are in the collections of the (East) Berlin Staatsbibliothek and the British Museum; a copy at the Library of Congress is incomplete and contains only the third movement of the second Sonatina (db). Both Sonatinas are teaching pieces with the Secondo part written at the Upper Elementary level of difficulty while the less-difficult Primo part is set at the Elementary level in the five-finger position for both hands.

Abbreviations

°	work in print in 1978
(A)	Advanced
ACA	American Composers Alliance (American Composers Edition; Composers Facsimile Edition); see Index of Music Publishers.
ACE	American Composers Edition; see ACA.
AMC	American Music Center; see Index of Music Publishers.
AMP	Associated Music Publishers
arr.	arranged; arranger
B&H	Breitkopf and Härtel
BRD	Bundesrepublik Deutschland (West Germany)
CeBeDeM	Centre Belge de Documentation Musicale, Brussels; see Index of Music Publishers.
comp.	compiler
D.	refers to work by Schubert indexed in Otto Deutsch, *Schubert: Thematic Catalogue of All His Works in Chronological Order* (London: Dent, 1951).
DDR	Deutsche Demokratische Republik (East Germany)
(E)	Elementary
4H	four hands
(I)	Intermediate
K.	refers to work by Mozart indexed in Ludwig Köchel, *Chronologisch-thematisch Verzeichnis sämtlicher Tonwerke Wolfgang Amadeus Mozarts*, 3d. ed., revised by Alfred Einstein (Leipzig: B&H, 1937).
(L)	Lower
ms.	manuscript
n.d.	no date
NEd	new edition
NOTES	Quarterly Journal of the Music Library Association
Op.	opus
o.p.	out of print

OUP   Oxford University Press
2H   two hands
2P   two pianos
p.o.p.   permanently out of print
pub.   publisher, or published
PWM   Polskie Wydawnictwo Muzyczne (Polish Music Publishers); see Index of Music Publishers.
RISM   International Inventory of Musical Sources, published by the International Musicological Society and the International Association of Music Libraries: *Einzeldrücke von 1800*, A/I (Kassel: Bärenreiter, 1971–); *Recueils imprimés*, B/II (Munich: G.Henle, 1964).
SCE   William S. Newman, *The Sonata in the Classic Era* (Chapel Hill: University of North Carolina Press, 1963; 2nd ed., New York: W.W. Norton, 1972).
SSB   William S. Newman, *The Sonata since Beethoven* (Chapel Hill: University of North Carolina Press, 1969; 2d ed., New York: W.W. Norton, 1972).
(U)   Upper
UEd   Universal Edition
VEB   Volkseigener Vertrieb ("People's Own Industry"), used in the name of East German publishers.
w.o.n.   without opus number
WoO   refers to works without opus numbers by Beethoven in Georg Kinsky and Hans Holm, *Das Werk Beethovens, thematisch-bibliographisches Verzeichnis seiner sämmtlichen, vollendeten Kompositionen* (Munich-Duisberg: G. Henle, 1955).

Index of Parent Companies or U.S. Distributors of Music Publishers

[1]   **ALMA,** Inc. (Association for Latin-American Music and Art), 10985
        West Broward Blvd., Plantation, FL 33321,
        Website: www.alma-usa.com, E-mail: mail@alma-usa.com,
        Tel: 1-888-275-2562, Fax: (954) 915-9144

[2]   **Associated Music Publishers,** Inc., Music Sales Corp., 257 Park Avenue
        South, 20th Floor, New York, NY 10010, Website:
        www.musicsales.com, Tel: (212) 254-2100, Fax: (212) 254-2013

[3]   **Belmont** Music Publishers, P.O. Box 231, Pacific Palisades, CA 90272,
        Website: www.primenet.com/~belmus/, E-mail:
        belmus@primenet.com, Tel: (310) 454-1867, Fax: (310) 573-1925

[4]   **Boosey & Hawkes,** Inc., 35 East 21st Street, New York, NY 10010-6212,
        Website: www.ny.boosey.com, Tel: (212) 358-5300,
        Fax: (212) 358-5301

[5]   **Bourne** Publishing Company, 5 West 37th Street, 6th Floor, New York,
        NY 10018, Website: www.internationalmusicco.com,
        E-mail: bournemusic@worldnet.att.net, Tel: (212) 391-4300,
        Fax: (212) 391-4306

[6]   **Brodt** Music Co., *mailing address:* P.O. Box 9345, Charlotte, NC 28299,
        street address: 1906 Commonwealth Avenue, Charlotte, NC 28205,
        Website: www.brodtmusic.com, E-mail: orders@brodtmusic.com,
        Tel: (704) 332-2177 (local and international), Tel: 1-800-438-4129
        (U.S. and Canada), Fax: (704) 335-7215 (local and international),
        Fax: 1-800-446-0812 (U.S. and Canada)

[7]   **Broude** Brothers, 141 White Oaks Road, Williamstown, MA 01267-
        0547, E-mail: broude@sover.net, Tel: 1-800-525-8559,
        Tel: (413) 458-8131, Fax: (413) 458-5242

[8]   **Burt** & Company Discount Music Supply, P.O. Box 1145, Marlton, NJ
        08053, Website: www.burtnco.com, E-mail: burtnco@burtnco.com,
        Tel: (609) 983-6004 (local and international), Tel: 1-800-548-2878
        (U.S. & Canada) or 1-609-983-6004, Fax: (609) 983-6159 (local and
        international), Fax: 1-888-830-2525 (U.S. & Canada)
        or 1-609-983-6159

[9] **Concordia** Publishing House, 3558 South Jefferson Avenue, Saint Louis, MO 63118-3968, Website: www.cph.org (homepage), Website: www.cphmall.com (mall), E-mail: cphorder@cph.org (for orders), E-mail: jpkelley@cphnet.org (for information), Tel: 1-800-325-3040 (for orders), Tel: 1-800-325-3040, ext. 1055 or (314) 268-1055 (for information), Fax: (314) 268-1411

[10] **ECS** Publishing (parent company to E. C. Schirmer Music), 138 Ipswich Street, Boston, MA 02215, Website: www.ecspublishing.com, E-mail: office@ecspublishing.com, Tel: (617) 236-1935, Tel: 1-800-777-1919 (orders only)

[11] **Elkin Music International,** Inc., 16 NE 4th Street, Suite 140, Fort Lauderdale, FL 33301-3262, Website: www.elkinmusic.com, E-mail: timsloan@worldnet.att.net, Tel: (954) 522-3611, Fax: (954) 522-3609
In Europe: William **Elkin** Music Services, Elkin Music International Inc., Station Road Industrial Estate, Salhouse, Norwich NR13 6NS, England, E-mail: richard@elkinmusic.demon.co.uk, Tel: (44) (01603) 721302 (24 hours), Fax: (44) (01603) 721801

[12] Carl **Fischer**, Inc. (sells to dealers only), 65 Bleecker Street, New York, NY 10012, Website: www.carlfischer.com, E-mail: info@carlfischer.com, Tel: (212) 777-0900, Tel: 1-800-762-2328, Fax: (212) 477-6996

[13] The **FJH** Music Company, Inc., 2525 Davie Road, Suite 360, Fort Lauderdale, FL 33317-7424, Website: www.fjhmusic.com, E-mail: sales@fjhmusic.com (sales), E-mail: custserv@fjhmusic.com (customer service), Tel: 1-800-262-8744, Tel: (954) 382-6061, Fax: (954) 382-3073

[14] **Foreign Music** Distributors, 9 Elkay Drive, Chester, NY 10918, Fax: (914) 469-5817, (no phone orders)

[15] Mark **Foster** Music Co., *street address:* 28 East Springfield Avenue, Champaign, IL 61820, *mailing address:* Box 4012, Champaign, IL 61824-4012, Website: www.markfostermusic.com, E-mail: info@markfostermusic.com, Tel: 1-800-359-1386, Tel: (217) 398-2790, Fax: (217) 398-2791

[16] Neil A. **Kjos** Music Co., 4380 Jutland Drive, San Diego, CA 92117-0894, E-mail: email@kjos.com, Website: www.kjos.com, Tel: 1-800-854-1592, Tel: (619) 270-9800, Fax: (619) 270-3507

[17] Hal **Leonard** Publishing Corp., *street address:* 7777 West Bluemound Road, Milwaukee, WI 53213, *mailing address:* P.O. Box 13819, Milwaukee, WI 53213, Website: www.halleonard.com, E-mail: halinfo@halleonard.com, Tel: (414) 774-3630, Fax: (414) 774-3259

[18] **Magnamusic** Distributors, P.O. Box 338, Sharon, CT 06069, Website: www.magnamusic.com, E-mail: magnamusic@magnamusic.com, Tel: (203) 364-5431, Fax: (203) 364-5168

[19]   **MCA** Music Publishing, Universal Music Publishing Group, 2440
Sepulveda Boulevard, Suite 100, Los Angeles, CA 90064-1712,
Website: www.mcamusicpublishing.com, Tel: (310) 235-4700,
Fax: (310) 235-4905, (See Hal Leonard [17] for retail distribution,
permission to arrange or copy in the U.S.)

[20]   **MMB Music,** Inc., Contemporary Arts Building, 3526 Washington
Avenue, Saint Louis, MO 63103-1019, Website: www.mmbmusic.com,
E-mail: mmbmusic@mmbmusic.com, Tel: 1-800-543-3771 (U.S. and
Canada), Tel: 314-531-9635, Fax: 314-531-8384

[21]   **Music Sales** Corp., 257 Park Avenue South, 20th Floor, New York, NY
10010, Website: www.musicsales.com, Tel: (212) 254-2100,
Fax: (212) 254-2013

[22]   **Oxford** University Press, Inc., Order Department, 2001 Evans Road,
Cary, NC 27513, Website: www.oup-usa.org, Tel: 1-800-451-7556,
Fax: (919) 677-1303

[23]   J. W. **Pepper & Son,** Inc., P.O. Box 850, Valley Forge, PA 19482,
Website: www.jwpepper.com, Tel: 1-800-345-6296, Fax: 1-800-260-1482

[24]   C. F. **Peters** Corp., 373 Park Avenue South, New York, NY 10016,
Website: www.cfpeters-ny.com, E-mail: sales@cfpeters-ny.com,
Tel: (212) 686-4147, Fax: (212) 689-9412

[25]   **Plymouth** Music Company, Inc., 170 NE 33rd Street, Fort Lauderdale,
FL 33334, Tel: (954) 563-1844, Fax: (954) 563-9006

[26]   Theodore **Presser** Co., 1 Presser Place, Bryn Mawr, PA 19010-3490,
Website: www.presser.com, E-mail: retail@presser.com (retail),
E-mail: sales@presser.com (wholesale), Tel: (610) 525-3636,
Fax: (610) 527-7841

[27]   G. **Schirmer** Music Co., Music Sales Corp., 257 Park Avenue South,
20th Floor, New York, NY 10010, Website: www.schirmer.com,
E-mail: schirmer@schirmer.com, Tel: (212) 254-2100,
Fax: (212) 254-2013

[28]   **Shawnee** Press, Inc., P.O. Box 690, Delaware Water Gap, PA 18327-
1099, Website: www.shawneepress.com,
E-mail: shawneepress@noln.com, Tel: 1-800-962-8584 (orders),
Tel: (570) 476-0550, Fax: (570) 476-5247

[29]   **Warner Brothers** Publications, Inc., 15800 NW 48th Avenue, Miami, FL
33014, Website: www.warnerbrospublications.com,
Tel: 1-800-327-7643, Tel: (305) 620-1500 (orders),
Fax: (305) 621-4869 (sales dept.)

[30]   Current address or U.S. distributor unconfirmed. A music retailer may
be able to obtain scores for you.

[31]   No longer in business.

Index of Music Publishers

The [bracketed] number preceding the publisher's name refers to the number of the U.S. distributor or parent company in the preceding index.

Helios Music Edition (*superseded by* **Editio Helios**)
G. **Henle** USA. Inc. (G. **Henle** Verlag), P.O. Box 460127, Saint Louis, MO 63146, Website: www.henleusa.com, E-mail: musicpubs@msn.com, Tel: (314) 514-1791, Fax: (314) 514-1269
Éditions **Henn**, *street address:* 8, rue de Hesse, CH-1204 Geneva, Switzerland, *mailing address:* P.O. Box 5476, CH-1211 Geneva 11, Switzerland, E-mail: sidomusic@bluewin.ch, Tel: (41) 22 311 51 85, Fax: (41) 22 311 18 52

[30]   **Herelle**, Paris (*see* **Consortium Musical**)
[30]   **Heritage** Music Press
[26]   **Heugel** et Cie, Ravières, France
[30]   Edition **Heuwekemeijer**, Amsterdam, Netherlands
[30]   **Hinrichsen** Edition, London
[30]   Franz Anton **Hoffmeister**
[30]   Musikverlag Friedrich **Hofmeister**, Ubierstrasse 20, D-6238 Hofheim am Taunus, Germany
[30]   Friedrich **Hofmeister** Musikverlag, Karlstrasse 10, Postfach 147, Leipzig, Germany
[29]   **Hug & Co.**, Limmatquai 28-30, CH-8022 Zurich, Switzerland, Fax: (41) 1 269 41 41, Fax: (41) 1 269 41 06
[30]   **Iceland** Music Information Centre, Laufásvegur 40, Reykjavík, Iceland
[26]   **Impero** Verlag, Wilhelmshaven, Germany
[30]   Musikforlaget **Imudico**, Copenhagen
[5]   **International** Music Corp.
[30]   **Internationales** Musikinstitut Darmstadt, Informationscentral für zeitgenössische Musik, Darmstadt, Germany
[26]   **Israel** Music Institute, 144, Hayarkon Street, 63451 Tel Aviv, Israel, Website: www.aquanet.co.il/vip/imi, E-mail: 035245275@doar.net, Tel: (972) 3 527 0219, Tel: (972) 3 524 6475, Fax: (972) 3 524 5276
[26]   **Israeli** Music Publications Ltd., Tel Aviv, Israel
[26]   Éditions Jean **Jobert**, Paris, France
[30]   Éditions **Joubert**, 25, rue d'Hauteville, F-75010 Paris, France
[30]   P. **Jürgenson**, Moscow, Russia
[30]   Verlag C. F. **Kahnt**, in der Hofstatt 8, Lindau-Bodensee, Germany
[11]   Edwin F. **Kalmus** & Co., Inc., P.O. Box 5011, Boca Raton, FL 33431, Website: www.kalmus-music.com, E-mail: info@kalmus-music.com, Tel: (561) 241-6340 (Florida and international), Tel: 1-800-434-6340 (other U.S.), Fax: (561) 241-6347
[30]   **Kawai** Gakufu Co., Ltd., 321, 2-chome, Komagome, Toshima-ku, Tokyo
[30]   E. C. **Kerby** Ltd., 198 Davenport Road, Toronto, Ontario M5R 1J2, Canada

Index of Library Locations
and National Information Centers

D-brd:Gs   Göttingen: Niedersächsische Staats- und Universitätsbibli-
            othek
D-brd:Hch   Hamburg: Gymnasium Christianeum
D-brd:HEms Heidelberg: Musikwissenschaftliches Seminar der Universität
D-brd:Hhm   Hamburg: Harburg, Helmsmuseum
D-brd:HL   Haltenbergstetten: Schloss über Niederstetten (Baden-Würt-
            temberg), Fürst zu Hohenlohe-Jagstberg'sche Bibliothek
D-brd:Kl   Kassel: Murhard'sche Bibliothek der Stadt Kassel und Lan-
            desbibliothek
D-brd:KA   Karlsruhe: Badische Landesbibliothek, Musikabteilung
D-brd:KIl   Kiel: Schleswig-Holsteinische Landesbibliothek
D-brd:KIu   Kiel: Universitätsbibliothek
D-brd:KNh   Cologne: Staatliche Hochschule für Musik, Bibliothek
D-brd:KNmi Cologne: Musikwissenschaftliches Institut der Universität
D-brd:LB   Langenburg (Württemberg), Fürstlich Hohenlohe-Langen-
            burg'sche Schlossbibliothek
D-brd:LCH   Lich, near Giessen: Fürstlich Solms-Lich'sche Bibliothek
D-brd:LÜh   Lübeck: Bibliothek der Hansestadt Lübeck, Musikabteilung
D-brd:Mbs   Munich: Bayerische Staatsbibliothek, Musiksammlung
D-brd:MB   Marbach/Neckar: Schiller-Nationalmuseum, Deutsches Liter-
            aturarchiv, Musikaliensammlung
D-brd:MGs   Marburg/Lahn: Staatsarchiv und Archivschule
D-brd:Mmb   Munich: Städtische Musikbibliothek
D-brd:MT   Metten über Deggendorf (Bavaria): Abtei Metten, Bibliothek
D-brd:MÜs   Münster (Westfalen): Santini-Bibliothek
D-brd:MÜu   Münster (Westfalen): Universitätsbibliothek
D-brd:MZsch Mainz: Musikverlag B. Schott's Söhne, Verlagsarchiv
D-brd:Ngm   Nürnberg: Bibliothek des Germanischen National-Museums
D-brd:OF   Offenbach am Main: Verlagsarchiv André
D-brd:Rp   Regenburg (Bavaria): Proske—Musikbibliothek
D-brd:Rtt   Regensburg (Bavaria): Fürstlich Thurn und Taxissche Hof-
            bibliothek
D-brd:Sl   Stuttgart: Württembergische Landesbibliothek
D-brd:SPlb Speyer: Pfälzische Landesbibliothek
D-brd:Tmi   Tübingen: Musikwissenschaftliches Institut der Universität
D-brd:W   Wolfenbüttel (Niedersachsen): Herzog-August-Bibliothek,
            Musikabteilung
D-brd:WD   Wiesentheid (Bavaria): Musiksammlung des Grafen von
            Schönborn-Wiesentheid.

D-ddr—German Democratic Republic

D-ddr:BD   Brandenburg/Havel: Domstift, Bibliothek (Archiv der Kath-
            arinenkirche)
D-ddr:Bds   Berlin: Deutsche Staatsbibliothek, Musikabteilung
D-ddr:Dlb   Dresden: Sächsische Landesbibliothek, Musikabteilung
D-ddr:GOl   Gotha: Landesbibliothek
D-ddr:HAu   Halle/Saale: Universitäts- und Landesbibliothek Sachsen-An-
            halt, Musiksammlung

D-ddr:LEm Leipzig: Musikbibliothek der Stadt Leipzig (Musikbibliothek Peters and various collections in the Leipziger Stadtbibliothek)

D-ddr:LEu Leipzig: Universitätsbibliothek der Karl-Marx-Universität, Fachreferat Musik

D-ddr:SWl Schwerin: Mecklenburgische Landesbibliothek

D-ddr:WRl Weimar: Landeshauptarchiv, Bibliothek

D-ddr:WRtl Weimar: Thüringische Landesbibliothek, Musiksammlung

D-ddr:ZI Zittau: Stadt- und Kreisbibliothek "Christian-Wiese-Bibliothek"

DK—Denmark

DK:A Aarhus: Statsbiblioteket i Aarhus

DK:Kk Copenhagen: Det kongelige Bibliotek

DK:Kmk Copenhagen: Det kongelige danske Musikkonservatorium

DK:Kv Copenhagen: Københavns Universitets Musikvidenskabelige Institut

EIR—Ireland

EIR:Dn Dublin: National Library and Museum of Ireland

F—France

F:Pc Paris: Bibliothèque du Conservatoire national de musique (at Bibliothèque nationale)

F:Pn Paris: Bibliothèque nationale

F:Psg Paris: Bibliothèque Sainte-Geneviève

F:V Versailles: Bibliothèque municipale

GB—Great Britain

GB:BA Bath: Municipal Library

GB:Bp Birmingham: Public libraries

GB:Bu Birmingham: University of Birmingham, Music Library, Barber Institute of Fine Arts

GB:Ckc Cambridge: Rowe Music Library, King's College

GB:Cpl Cambridge: Pendlebury Library of Music

GB:Cu Cambridge: Cambridge University Library

GB:En Edinburgh: National Library of Scotland

GB:Er Edinburgh: Reid Music Library of the University of Edinburgh

GB:Gm Glasgow: Mitchell Library

GB:Gu Glasgow: Glasgow University Library

GB:Lam London: Royal Academy of Music

GB:Lbbc London: British Broadcasting Corporation Music Library

GB:Lbl London: British Library (British Museum)

GB:Lcm London: Royal College of Music

GB:LEc Leeds: Leeds Public Libraries, Music Department, Central Library

GB:Lmic London: British Music Information Centre

GB:Ltc London: Trinty College of Music

GB:LVp Liverpool: Public Libraries, Central Library

NL:Uim	Utrecht: Instituut voor Muziekwetenschap der Rijksuniversiteit

P—Portugal

P:La	Lisbon: Biblioteca do Palácio nacional de Ajuda

PL—Poland

PL:Kj	Kraków: Biblioteka Jagiellońska
PL:WRu	Wrocław: Biblioteka Uniwersytecka

S—Sweden

S:L	Lund: Universitetsbiblioteket
S:Sic	Stockholm: Swedish Music Information Center
S:Sk	Stockholm: Kungliga Biblioteket
S:Skma	Stockholm: Kungliga Musikaliska Akademiens Bibliotek
S:Sm	Stockholm: Musikhistoriska Museet, Biblioteket
S:Ssr	Stockholm: Sveriges Radio, Musikbiblioteket
S:St	Stockholm: Kungliga Teaterns Biblioteket
S:Uu	Uppsala: Universitetsbiblioteket

US—United States

US:AA	Ann Arbor: University of Michigan, Music Library
US:BE	Berkeley: University of California, Music Library
US:Bh	Boston: Harvard Musical Association
US:Bp	Boston: Boston Public Library, Music Department
US:BRp	Brooklyn, NY: Brooklyn Public Library
US:BU	Buffalo, NY: Buffalo and Erie County Public Library
US:CA	Cambridge, MA: Harvard University Music Libraries
US:CDs	Concord, NH: New Hampshire State Library
US:Cn	Chicago: Newberry Library
US:ECstarr	Eastchester, NY: Saul Starr private collection
US:I	Ithaca, NY: Cornell University Music Library
US:IO	Iowa City: University of Iowa Music Library
US:IObenton	Iowa City: Rita Benton private collection
US:NH	New Haven, CT: Yale University, The Library of the School of Music
US:NYamc	New York: American Music Center Library
US:NYhs	New York: New York Historical Society Library
US:NYp	New York: New York Public Library at Lincoln Center
US:PHf	Philadelphia: Free Library of Philadelphia, Music Department
US:PHu	Philadelphia: University of Pennsylvania Music Library
US:PRu	Princeton, NJ: Princeton University Library
US:PROu	Providence, RI: Brown University Libraries
US:Pu	Pittsburgh: University of Pittsburgh, Music Library
US:R	Rochester, NY: Sibley Music Library, Eastman School of Music
US:SFp	San Francisco: San Francisco Public Library, Music Division
US:Wc	Washington: Library of Congress, Music Division
US:WGw	Williamsburg, VA: Colonial Williamsburg Research Department, historical collection.

Piano Duet Repertoire

Abeille, Johann Christian Ludwig (1761–1838)

German pianist, court organist, director of music and conductor of the private orchestra of the Duke of Württemberg; composer of songs, stage entertainments, and piano music.

Grand concerto (D), Op.6. Offenbach: André [1793]. D-brd:HL,LB,OF—DK:Kmk—GB:Ckc. Written for harpsichord or piano with accompaniment of several instruments.

Sonate (C), Op.22. Heilbronn: Johann Amon, n.d. A:Wgm—D-brd:F,Sl. Despite an inclination toward excessive use of sequential passages and a general unevenness of quality, this two-movement sonata in classical style is a flowing work with attractive harmonies and lyrical melodies (one of which bears more than a passing resemblance to the theme of Mozart's A major Rondo for solo piano). The rhapsodic character of the second-movement variations is especially intriguing, with frequent, unexpected cadenzas and sudden changes of meter. (I)

Six walses, Book 1 (D,G,C,g,Bb,Eb); Book 2 (F,C,G,D,Eb,a); Book 3 (C,e,G, D,Bb,Eb). Leipzig: B&H, ca.1808. D-brd:B. Instructional pieces for beginning pianists. (LI)

Adam, Johann Ludwig (Louis) (1758–1848)

Sonate. Pub. and date missing. F:Pc.

Symphonie concertante (F), Op.5. Paris: Naderman et LeMenu [1787]. F:Pc. For piano or harpsichord.

Adams, Mrs. Crosby

American

Barcarolle, Op. 2/1. Chicago: Clayton Summy, 1897. GB:Lbl.

Three piano duets in unfamiliar keys for courageous beginners (Song without words; Peter Pan; Valse arabesque), Op.20. Boston/Leipzig: A.P. Schmidt 1907. GB:Lbl—US:Wc (Op.20/2 only).

Adams, James O.
English
A *duett for two performers on one pianoforte*. London: pub.missing [1820]. GB:Lbl.

Agafonnikov, Nikolai
Soviet composer.
Polka; Waltz; Russian dance (LI-I). In collection *Sbornik fortepiannikh*, N. Agafonnikov, ed.

Agay, Denes (1911–)
Hungarian-born American editor, arranger, educator, and composer.
*Dance toccata. New York: Sam Fox, 1962. Sparkling, idiomatically written show piece in effective contemporary idiom; not difficult. (LI)

Aggházy, Károly (1855–1918)
Hungarian pianist and composer of stage works, orchestral and chamber music, and piano pieces in Romantic style with strong Hungarian folk flavor.
Poèmes hongrois, Op.13. Berlin: Bote & Bock, 1887. GB:Lbl. Spirited, rhythmical set of pieces. (I).
Rondo all'ongarese; Marcia, Op.18. Berlin: Bote & Bock [1886]. GB:Lbl.

Agthe, Wilhelm Johann Albrecht (1790–1837)
German pianist and teacher; composed numerous piano works in traditional style, often pedagogical in purpose.
Trois grandes marches (E,a,f), Op.6. Leipzig: Peters, 1816. US:Wc. (I)
Trois marches (Eb,C,c), Op.3. Leipzig: B&H [1814]. US:NYp. Strong, rhythmic works in classical style. (I)

Aguilar, F.
Spanish composer
*Pitusines, four easy pieces. Madrid: Unión Musical Española, n.d.

Ahlberg, Tor (1913–)
Swedish pianist; has written pieces for orchestra, chamber groups, and piano.
Två Bagateller (Two bagatelles) (1938). Ms. photoprint. S:Sic.

Aitken, George
La mascarade, suite (Rendezvous; Danse; Le retour), Op.14. London: Leonard & Co., 1899. GB:Lbl.

Aitken, Hugh (1924–)
American teacher and composer.
*Four pieces, four hands (Arioso; Chorale; Canon; Song). Philadelphia: Elkan-Vogel, 1965. Very short pieces in mildly contemporary idiom; interesting sonorities and technical devices. (LI)

Akimenko, Feodor Stepanovich (1876–1945)
Russian composer; pupil of Balakirev and Rimsky-Korsakov; settled in France

in 1917. His 4H works show influence of French Impressionism and are idiomatically set with carefully balanced parts.

Quatre morceaux (Sur les Alpes, au printemps; Clair de lune sur les ruines du Forum Romanum; Au jardin de Luxembourg, les enfants; Sous les voûtes de Notre-Dame), Op.41. Moscow/Leipzig: Jurgenson, 1909. US: Wc. (I)

°*Six pièces ukraïniennes* (Dumka; Do tantzu; Piznia; Vessila; Listopad; Gretchaniki), Op.71. Paris: Salabert (Rouart Lerolle, 1925). US:NYp,Wc. (I)

Tableaux idylliques (Valse; Pastorale; Élégie: Danse rustique; Romanza), Op.62. Leipzig: Jul.Zimmermann [1914]. US:Wc. (I)

Albéniz, Isaac (1860–1909)

Spanish pianist and composer; student of Liszt. His works are written in a strongly Spanish nationalist idiom.

°*Aragón, fantasia.* Madrid: Unión Musical Española, 1921. Strongly rhythmical work in energetic Spanish style; attractive though not idiomatically set for 4H. The many doublings and frequent awkward collisions between the parts suggest a transcription, possibly by the composer, from an original 2H version. (I)

d'Albert, Eugen (1864–1932)

German pianist and composer of French descent and British birth; student of Liszt; brilliant pianist; wrote operas, choral works, chamber music, and piano compositions in late German Romantic style.

[12] *Walzer*, Op.6. Berlin: Bote & Bock, 1888. US:Wc. Ingratiating suite of lilting waltzes somewhat reminiscent of Brahms's *Liebeslieder* in style and polish; worth reviving. (I)

Albrechtsberger, Johann Georg (1736–1809)

Austrian theorist, teacher, and composer; much sought as teacher of counterpoint. It is said he thought very little of the musical talent of his most famous pupil, Beethoven.

Prélude et fugue (Bb). Vienna: S.A.Steiner [ca.1805, 1823?]. D-ddr:Bds–GB:Lbl–US:NYp. Short, thin-textured academic work in classical idiom; well distributed for both parts. (I)

Alexander, Haim (1915–)

Israeli teacher and composer.

Six Israeli dances (arr. by the composer). Tel Aviv: Israeli Music Publications, n.d.

Alexandrescu, Romeo (1902–)

Romanian composer and teacher.

°*Trei piese uşoare pentru pian la patra mîini* (Three easy pieces for piano four hands) (1957). Bucharest: Editura Muzicală, 1958. US:Wc. Charming little instructional pieces based on Romanian folk songs. (UE)

Alford, Edith

A day in the woods. London: Elkin & Co., 1917. GB:Lbl–US:Wc. Six short
   instructional pieces. (E-UE)

Alkan, Charles-Valentin (Morhange) (1813–1888)

French virtuoso pianist; greatly respected by Liszt, Chopin, and other contemporaries; composed a quantity of études, préludes, and other bravura
concert pieces.

**Bombardo-Carillon.* Paris: Gérard Billaudot, n.d. This work was also tran-
   scribed by the composer for two performers, four feet, on organ pedals or
   pedal piano. (UI-A)

**Finale,* Op.17. Paris: Gérard Billaudot [1842].

*Trois marches (Ab,Eb,Bb), Op.40. Paris: Billaudot, n.d. Rather long and
   technically demanding works containing the composer's characteristic
   writing: extended passage work, unexpected chromaticisms, and plenty of
   bombast. Fine textures alternate with thick chordal masses, always with
   enormous effect. (UI-A)

Allemande à trois, exécutée par Alexandre Casarti et ses deux soeurs, pour
   le pianoforte à deux et à quatre mains. Pub. missing, ca.1830. GB:Lbl.

Allende Sarón, Pedro Humberto (1885–1959)

Chilean violinist; teacher; and composer of symphonic and chamber music,
piano pieces, and violin works; active in folk music research.

Seis piezas (Six pieces) (Tempo di marcia; Minuetto; Gavotta; Corrente;
   Alemanda; Vals lento; Rigodón). Santiago de Chile: pub. by composer,
   1948. US:Wc. Charming, graceful suite of pieces in old forms. (I/E-5)

Alpert, Pauline

American

**March of the blues.* Melville, NY: Belwin, n.d. (E)

Amon, Johann Andreas (1763–1825)

German horn virtuoso, conductor, and prolific composer of operas, masses,
symphonies, chamber works, and piano music.

Sonate (F), Op.67. Mainz: Schott, ca.1815. D-brd:MZsch.

Sonate (Bb), Op.100/6. Bonn/Cologne: Simrock ca.1823. A:Wgm–US:Wc.
   Three-movement work, similar in style to Op.99, but longer and somewhat more difficult. (I-UI)

Deux sonates (C,Eb), Op.99. Offenbach: André ca.1823. US:NYp,Wc.
   Three-movement works of moderate length in late Classical style, with
   rhythmic vitality, interesting thematic development, and melodic charm;
   worth reviving. (I)

Six variations sur un air de Conradin Kreutzer . . . cinquième air varié, Op.
   119/5. Hannover: C.Bachmann, n.d. DK:Kk–I:M01.

Six walses (C,C,C,C,F,C), avec guitarre obligée, Op.52. Offenbach: André
   ca.1809. A:Wgm–D-brd:HEms,LCH.

[5]*Walzer* (F,F,F,C,A) (7th volume of waltzes), Op.87. Wallerstein: Johann Amon, n.d. D-brd:B.

Ancot, Jean (1799-1829)

Belgian pianist and prolific composer of violin pieces and piano works.
Favorite air with variations, Op.221. London: pub. by composer, 1824. GB: Lbl.

Anderberg, Carl-Olof (1914–1972)

Swedish conductor, author, and composer. His musical style evolved through serial techniques into an advanced, highly complex personal idiom.
Als hätte ich vier Hände, Op.60 (1967). Ms. S:Sic. Serious work of moderate length; dissonant; tightly organized structurally, with rhythmic complexities; technically demanding. (A)

Anderson, T.J., Jr.

Five portraits of two people (Canvas; Contemplations; Capriciousness). New York: ACA-CFE, n.d.

Andersson, Margit E.

Fyra små händer. För piano fyra händer (Four little hands, for piano four hands). Stockholm: Nordiska Musikförlaget; Copenhagen: Hansen, 1946. DK:A,Kk. (E)

Andersson, Richard (1851–1918)

Swedish pianist and pedagogue; pupil of Clara Schumann; professor at Stockholm Conservatory; composed songs and numerous piano pieces.
[12]*Schwedische Tänze* (d,Bb,Eb,g,e,G,f,c,Ab,C,a,E). Berlin: Simrock, 1881. GB:Lbl–US:Wc. Suite of Swedish folk dances, contrasting in character, tempo, and texture, skilfully and imaginatively set in Romantic tonal idiom. (I)

André, Johann Anton (1775–1842)

German pianist, violinist, teacher, businessman. His ingratiating 4H compositions are instructional in character and are written in a solid, Classical idiom. The majority were published by the composer himself, who took over his father's publishing house in Offenbach. Although these tidy, well-balanced works make only modest demands on the performers, they are rich in rhythmical vitality and melodic grace.
Conversations musicales (Marche[Eb], Valse[Eb]), Op.42. Offenbach: André [1818]. US:NYp,Wc. Short amiable works.
Six divertissements (C,F,D,G,Bb,d), Op.18. Offenbach: André [ca.1803]. US:Wc.
Drei divertissements (C,Eb,G), Op.19. Offenbach: André [1803]. D-brd:B.
Trois divertissements (C,a,F), Op.20. Offenbach: André [1803]. US:NYp.
　°NEd. Divertimento (a), Op.20/2, ed. Zeitlin and Goldberger. New York: Peters, 1961. °NEd. Divertimento (F) No.3, Op.20/3, in *Piano duets of the classical period*, ed. D. Townsend. Bryn Mawr:Presser, 1956.

The three sets of Divertissements, Opp.18,19, and 20, consist of charming, concise, one- and two-movement pieces; masterfully written; arranged in progressive difficulty; they should all be revived. (LI-I)

Trois marches (D,d,C), Op.28. Offenbach: André [1805]. A:Wgm. Brief, rhythmical, attractive. (LI-I)

Douze morceaux faciles, Op.44. Offenbach: André, n.d. D-brd:OF.

Sonate (C), Op.12. Offenbach: André [ca.1801]. GB:Lbl—US:Wc. (I)

Trois sonates (C,F,e),Op.46. Offenbach: André, 1821. US:Wc. (I)

Easy sonata (C), Op.56. Offenbach: André, n.d. A:Wgm—GB:Lbl. (I)

Six easy sonatinas (C,G,F,d,D,B♭), Op.45. Offenbach: André [1820]. US: PHf,Wc. °NEd. *Six easy sonatinas*, ed. Zeitlin and Goldberger. Evanston: Summy-Birchard, 1959. °Op.45/1 (C), in collection *Forty-four original piano duets*, ed. Eckard. Series of short, tuneful, workmanlike sonatinas. (LI)

Sonatina (C), Op.73. Offenbach: André, n.d. D-brd:OF.

Neun leichte Stücke (C,C,D,F,F,g,B♭,C,G), Op.72. Offenbach: André, n.d. D-ddr:Bds. Brief, melodious pieces in progressive difficulty with contrasts of rhythm and texture. (E-LI)

André, Julius (1808–1880)

German organist and pianist, son of Johann Anton; best known for his four-hand arrangements of Mozart's orchestral works.

Six morceaux amusants, Op.38. Offenbach: André [1864]. GB:Lbl.

Musikalischer Familienkreis, Suites I and II, Op.59; Suite III, Op.63; Suite IV, Op.64. Offenbach: André 1875–77. GB:Lbl.

Drei Polonaisen, Op.7. Offenbach: André, ca.1832. US:NYp,Wc.

Sonata (F). Offenbach: André, n.d. D-brd:OF.

Andriessen, Juriaan (1925–   )

Member of famous Dutch musical family; pianist and composer. His works, influenced by Stravinsky and the French school, include film scores, chamber music, concertos, orchestra pieces, and piano compositions.

°*Fantasie* (1962). Amsterdam: Donemus, 1962. US:NYp. Lively, sparkling work in mildly dissonant, open-textured idiom. (I)

°*Kathenka's music book* (five easy pieces). Amsterdam: Broekmans & Van Poppel, n.d. Short pieces written for one easy and one slightly more advanced part are so arranged that the exclusively white-note Primo blends with the attractive harmonies of the Secondo in a most refreshing way. (UE-LI/E-5)

Andriessen, Louis (1939–   )

Brother of Juriaan; studied with Berio. His style has been influenced by Cage, Stockhausen, and Stravinsky. He has also written for electronic improvisation groups.

°*Ittrospezione* No.1, 1961. Ms. NL:Ad.

Anon

A *favorite grand duett for two performers*. . . .composed by an eminent master in the stile of W.A.Mozart. [New York]: printed & sold at J. Hewitt's musical repository & library [1807–1810]. US:BU,PROu,Wc. This curiosity, capitalizing as it does on the name of a famous composer and on the guilelessness (or poor eyesight) of the innocent purchaser, is one of the respectable misrepresentations in the history of the music publishing business, which has had its share of piracy, deceptions, chicanery, frauds, and fast-money operators. A quick, uncritical glance at the title page leads one to believe that the composition is by Mozart; a careful scrutiny, however, reveals the fine print embedded in the decorative scrolls and flourishes. While the work is full of Classical melodic ideas and abounds in superficial references to Mozart's idiom, it would never be mistaken for the work of any eminent master, most assuredly not Mozart. (LI)

Anon. (late 18th century)

Sonata per dui in uno Clavicembalo (D). Leipzig: B&H, n.d. I:Bsf.

Anon. (late 18th century)

°*Sonatina* (C). In collection *Vermischte Handstücke*, ed. Kreutz. Short, single-movement work in classical style. (UE)

Anotta, Louise

°*Surprise*. Paris: Consortium Musical, n.d. (I)

Anschütz, J. A. (1772–1856)

German pianist and conductor; founder of music school in Coblenz.
Scherzo symphonique. Paris: Heugel, 1897. US:Wc. Brilliant, effective salon piece. (I)

Ansermet, Ernest (1883–1969)

Swiss conductor; founder of the Orchestre de la Suisse Romande; well known as interpreter of Stravinsky and twentieth-century French music.
Deuxième marche militaire. Lausanne: Foetisch Frères, n.d. CH:Zma.

Antalffy-Zsiross, Dezsö (Desider von) (1885–1945)

Hungarian organist; U.S. resident; wrote light opera, choral works, organ pieces, and piano pieces in Romantic style.
°*Hungarian suite* (Alla marcia; Scherzo; Serenata; Finale), Op.17. Boston: Boston Music Co., 1913. US:Wc. Attractive set of pieces in Hungarian style, well distributed for both parts. (UI-LA)

Anthiome, Eugène Jean-Baptiste (1836–1916)

French composer of chamber music and instructional piano pieces.
Deux duos enfantins (Valse sentimentale; Moments joyeux). Paris: A.Noël, n.d. °NEd. Moments joyeux. Paris: Consortium Musical, n.d. (LI)
Douze petites pièces (Berceuse; Aux bords du Nil; Fête au sérail; Barcarolle;

Marche de la patrouille; Chasse; Farandole; Valse; Mazurka; Galop; Boléro; Tarantelle). Paris: Michel et Rosen, 1887. GB:Lbl. (UE-LI/E-5)

Anthony, Bert R.

At the dancing school; Rob Roy. In collection *Playing Together for the Pianoforte.*

°*Salute to the colors.* Bryn Mawr: Presser, n.d.

Antiga, Jean

Do not forget me; Gavotte in ancient style; Impressions of Savoy; Souvenir of Spain. Boston: Oliver Ditson, 1910. GB:Lbl–US:Wc. (LI)

Applebaum, Stanley (1922–   )

American

°*Musical miniatures* (Barcarolle; Hop, skip and jump; Pastorale dance; Peasant dance; Reverie rondino). New York: Chappell, 1953. US:Wc. Short, useful, contrasting teaching pieces; occasional mild dissonance and unexpected harmonic shifts help maintain interest. (UE)

°*Doubleplay, ten miniatures* (Peasant dance; Rondino; Hop, skip and jump; Barcarolle; Reverie; Pastorale dance; Romanza; Space age polka; Interplay; Power plant). New York: Tetra Music Corp., 1977. This series incorporates the whole of *Musical miniatures* together with five new pieces; jazz elements, modality, and pentatonic scale passages add further color and variety; the entire group is well laid out for the keyboard. (UE-LI)

Arbeau, P.

°*Pavane pour Evelyn.* Paris: Choudens, n.d.

°*Ronde pour Jean-Claude.* Paris: Choudens, n.d.

Archer, Violet (1913–   )

Canadian, studied with Hindemith and Bartók; her works include orchestral and chamber music, choral pieces, and piano compositions.

°*Ten folk songs* (Book 1: The dancing top; Singing bells; In the woods; Gay is the rose; Music everywhere. Book 2: Pirate song; Paul Jones; Eskimo prayer; Cherry tree carol; The frog and the mouse) (1953). Toronto: BMI Canada Ltd., 1955. Group of Canadian folk songs of both French and English origin set in fastidious and inventive arrangements. (LI-I)

Arensky, Anton (1861–1906)

Russian; student of Rimsky-Korsakov; wrote in a lyrical style close to Tchaikowsky's.

°*Six pièces enfantines* (Conte; Le coucou; Les larmes; Valse; Berceuse; Fugue sur un thème russe), Op.34. Moscow: Jurgenson, 1894. NEd. Augener; °International; °MCA: *Six recital pieces,* ed. Mirovitch (Vol.3 of *The student pianist*); USSR State Publishers 1926. Charming, melodious, well-balanced suite of pieces in transparent-textured Romantic idiom. (LI-I)

Kindersuite, canons, Op.65. Leipzig: Jurgenson, 1904.

°*Twelve pieces* (Prelude; Gavotte; Ballade; Menuetto; Elegie; Consolation; Valse; Marche; Romance; Scherzo; Berceuse; Polka), Op.66. Moscow: Jurgenson [1903]. NEd. International, n.d. Carefully constructed works; tuneful; similar in style to Op.34, but somewhat more difficult. (I)

Arenson, Adolf

Menuet und Habanera. Leipzig: Schuberth, 1893. US:Wc. (LI)

d'Argenton, Antonin

La danse des ombres (Schattentanz) (Ab), Op.21. Leipzig: B&H, ca.1872. GB:Lbl.

Arizaga, Rodolfo (1926–   )

Argentine teacher, music critic, author, and composer; student of Nadia Boulanger and Messiaen. His early style was influenced by neo-Classicism and Spanish Impressionism, but he later developed his own eclectic idiom. *Serranillas de la infanza* (1957). Buenos Aires: Editorial Argentina de Música, n.d.

Arma, Paul, pseud. Imre Weisshaus (1905–   )

Hungarian pianist and composer; student of Bartók.
Pantomime, neuf petits morceaux. London: Goodwin & Tabb, 1956. GB:Lbl.

Armstrong, William Dawson (1868–1936)

American composer of operas, sacred works, and instructional piano music.
Paola and Francesca. New York: B&H, 1902. US:Wc. (UE)
Papillon, air de ballet. New York: B&H, 1904. US:Wc. (UE)
Suite de ballet (Entr'act; Valse lente; Scene in the garden; The Kermesse). Boston: A.P.Schmidt, 1895. US:Wc. Descriptive pieces in salon style. (I)

Arnell, Richard (1917–   )

British composer, student of John Ireland; writes in eclectic style with neo-Classical and Romantic affinities.

°*Sonatina*, Op.61. London: Schott, 1950. Dedicated to George Balanchine and intended as a ballet score. Four-movement work cast in a tonal idiom spiced with mild dissonance. The 21-bar introductory Andante movement leads into a bright Allegro, which in turn is followed by a contrasting Andante. The work ends in a bustling Presto. Rhythmically vigorous and melodically appealing, the entire Sonata is carefully written for the medium. (I-UI)

°*Two simple piano duets* (Thoughts; Second thoughts). London: Hinrichsen, 1961. Witty, refined, entertaining works in artful settings; attractive, useful teaching material. (UE)

Arnold, Carl (1794–1873)

German pianist and conductor; wrote church music, an opera, orchestral works, and piano pieces.

Rondo (D). Offenbach: André [ca.1818]. D-ddr:Bds.

Arnold, Malcolm (1921–)

English composer of film scores, ballets, instrumental sonatas; vivid orchestrator; writes in a direct style, often ironic and whimsical.

Concerto for pianoforte duet and orchestra. Pub. and date missing. Written for Paul Hamburger and Helen Pyke, piano 4H specialists. GB:Lmic.

Scottish dances. Pub. and date missing. GB:Lmic.

Arrieu, [Mme.] Claude (1903–)

French composer of operas, chamber works, incidental radio music, and piano pieces in neo-Classical idiom.

°*Suite pour Mélodyne* (Prologue; Dominos; Pic et dic et col et gram; Trois soldats; Romance dans paroles; Berceuse; Aubade à Mélodyne). Paris: Amphion, 1946. Delightful set of short, effective teaching pieces. (LI-I/E-UE)

Artaud, Émile

Marche nuptiale. Paris: Enoch, 1878. GB:Lbl.

Artsybushev, Nikolai (1858–1937)

Russian composer; member of nationalist school.

Pantalon. See *Badinage.*

Ashforth, Alden (1933–)

American composer

Big Bang. Ms., 1970. Available from composer, Music Department, UCLA, Los Angeles, CA 90007.

Ashton, Algernon (1859–1937)

English pianist and composer; German-trained; wrote chamber works and over 200 pieces for piano solo. His four-hand compositions, though rather long and often diffuse, are competently crafted in Romantic idiom with Brahmsian texture. The flowing style, frequently sparkling with brilliance, features abundant passage work, strong rhythms, and absorbing development of the fresh melodic ideas, some of which are of folk origin. (I-A)

Englische Tänze, Op.10. Berlin: Simrock, 1883. GB:Lbl,Lcm–US:Wc.

Irische Tänze, Op.26. Berlin: Simrock, 1885. GB:Lbl–US:Wc.

Marsch und Tarantella, Op.30. Berlin: Simrock, 1887. GB:Lbl–US:Wc.

Schottische Tänze, Op.18. Berlin: Simrock, 1885. GB:Lbl–US:Wc.

Serenade (Bb), Op.40. Berlin: Simrock, 1885. GB:Lbl–US:Wc.

Trauliche Zwiegespräche, Op.14. Leipzig: Siegel [1886]. GB:Lbl–US:Wc.

Asioli, Bonifazio (1769–1832)

Italian theorist, educator and composer. In addition to operas and a prodigious quantity of religious music, he wrote prolifically in late Classical style for instrumental combinations of all kinds; also wrote theory, harmony, and composition textbooks, and methods for playing the contrabass and the piano.

Capriccio (Bb) (Adagio; Allegro; Allegretto; Allegretto con variazioni; Larghissimo; Presto), Op.3. Zürich: Nägeli [ca.1803]. I:Nc,Mc. Long, sectional work, light in character; weakened by overabundant passage work and lack of melodic variety. (I)

Sonata, ms. GB:Lbl. Possibly one of the three sonatas Asioli is supposed to have written in 1777, at eight years of age, without any instruction.

Sonatine (G) (Allegretto only). Ms. I:MOe. Melodious, direct, unpretentious one-page work in ingratiating style. (E)

Asioli, Luigi (ca.1767–1815)

Italian tenor and composer, probably brother of Bonifazio. In 1804 he moved to London, where a number of works appeared under his name between 1805 and 1825. In comparing the solo sonatas of the two brothers, William Newman (SCE 299) finds strong similarities in style and idiom. He suggests that Luigi, whose musical reputation in London was already established, may have had at least one of Bonifazio's works published under his own (Luigi's) name. If this assumption is true, then the two duets below may well have been written by Bonifazio.

Andantino tacitino assai (G). Ms. I:MOe. Short, one-page movement in appealing style; well laid out for the medium. (UE-LI)

Sonata (Duetto) (f). London: Thomas Monzani, ca.1813. GB:Lbl–I:MOe– US:Wc. The three movements of this pleasant work in Classical mold are fluent and well balanced for both parts. Despite sections of arid passage work and weak thematic development, the composer's use of unexpected chromaticism in modulatory passages (foreshadowing later Romantic tendencies) and the overall rhythmic flow of the work help to sustain interest. (I)

Atterberg, Kurt (1887–1974)

Prolific Swedish composer of music in late Romantic style often containing folk material.

Rondeau rétrospectif. Ms. S:Sic. (A)

Attwood, Thomas (1765–1838)

English organist, pupil of Mozart, friend of Mendelssohn; wrote stage works, sacred compositions, solo songs, and many sonatas and lessons for piano.

March and waltz (Eb). Pub. missing, ca.1835. GB:Lbl.

d'Aubel, Henri

French

Six morceaux (3H and 4H) (Polka-Marche; Calinette; Danse tzigane; °Boute en train, galop; °Gardénia, polka mazurka; Marche des pantins). Paris: Leduc, 1887. GB:Lbl. (UE-LI/E-5)

Aubert, Louis (1877–1968)

French pianist and composer; studied with Fauré and Widor.

°*Feuille d'images,* cinq pièces enfantines (Confidence; Chanson de route;

Sérénade; Des pays lointains; La danse de l'ours de peluche). Paris: Durand, 1930. (E)

Auda, Alain
°*Pour les petites personnes;* première année, pièces faciles dans tous les tons. Paris: Chappell, 1973. GB:Lbl. (E-UE)

Aulin, Tor (1866–1914)
Swedish violinist, conductor, and composer; student of Scharwenka; wrote symphonic music, chamber music, and piano compositions.
Valse-caprice. Stockholm: Elkan & Schildknecht, Emil Carelius, n.d. S:Sic.

Auric, Georges (1899–   )
Youngest member of the French group "les Six"; studied with d'Indy. His melodious style shows influences of Stravinsky, Satie, and popular music. He has written film scores, incidental music, songs, chamber works, and piano pieces.
°*Cinq bagatelles* (Ouverture; Petite marche; Valse; Rêverie; Retraite). Paris: Heugel, 1926. Short pieces in light style, arranged by the composer from incidental theater music into attractive and effective teaching material. (UE-LI)

Austin, Ernest (1874–1947)
English businessman turned composer; wrote extensively in all musical forms. His piano duets are written in conservative nineteenth century idiom.
Campbells are coming. London: Lengnick, n.d. (I)
Gavotte and musette. London: Lengnick, n.d. (LI)
Lass of Richmond Hill. London: Lengnick, n.d. (LI)
Russian song and dance. London: Lengnick, n.d. (LI)
Sailor's hornpipe. London: Lengnick, n.d. (I)
St. Patrick was a gentleman. London: Lengnick, 1915. Brisk, catchy, rhythmical piece with folk-song character. (LI)

Babin, Victor (1908–1972)
Russian-born American pianist and composer; studied with Schnabel; performed in two-piano team with his wife, Vitya Vronsky; director of Cleveland Institute from 1961 until his death. He wrote orchestral and chamber music, two two-piano concertos, and many piano works.
David and Goliath, eleven Bible scenes for young and old, ed. and fingered by Vitya Vronsky (1. On the ancient hills under the clear wide sky; 2. David plays for King Saul; 3. David drives out Saul's evil spirit; 4. March of the Philistines; 5. Israel's lament; 6. Challenge of Goliath the giant; 7. David's battle and victory; 8. The flight of the Philistines; 9. Israelites' prayer of thanks; 10. The Israelites dance and rejoice; 11. End of the

story). London: Augener, 1951. GB:Lbl—US:Wc. Elegantly wrought series of descriptive tone pictures dextrously set in contemporary idiom. Though not excessively demanding, the work makes imaginative use of changing meters, imitations, polytonality, and free dissonance. There is rhythmical variety and excitement, and the textures in general remain thin and clear; at times the writing is widely spaced. The pieces are thoroughly pianistic and well balanced for both performers; the notes lie well under the hands, even in some tricky hand-crossing passages, and the total effect is captivating. (I-UI)

Bach, Johann Christian (1735-1782)

Eighteenth child and eleventh son of Johann Sebastian Bach. Popularly known as the "English" or "London" Bach, Johann Christian was one of the first contributors to the 4H medium. His sonatas, or duetti, are elegant, thin-textured works in two movements, written in the graceful, melodious "galant" style of the late eighteenth century.

°*Drei Sonaten* (C,A,F), Op.15/6, ca.1778, Op.18/5, ca.1780, Op.18/6, ca. 1780, ed. Weisman, Peters. Most familiar of Johann Christian's duets. °*Duetto* (C) (Sonata [No.1]). Kalmus. °*Duetto* (A) (Sonata [No.2]), Kalmus; Nagels Musik-Archiv. (I)

Duett 1 (D) [No.4], ca.1780; *Duett* 2 (G) [No.5], ca.1780. First published in *Four progressive lessons for the harpsichord or piano forte and two duetts, for two performers.* London: Longman & Broderip, ca.1780. F:Pn —GB:Lbl—US:AA,NH. °*Rondo* (second movement) of *Duett* 2. In collection *Style and interpretation*, vol.5, ed. H. Ferguson. Duetts 1 and 2 are similar in character to the first three Sonatas. (LI)

Six sonates à quatre mains (Eb,G,Bb,D,C,F). Ms. B:Bc. Brief three-movement works, also known as *lessons*; slighter and less difficult than the other duets. (LI)

Bach, Johann Christoph Friedrich (1732–1795)

Ninth son of Johann Sebastian; known as the "Bückeburg" Bach because of his activity at the court of that name.

°*Sonata*(A) (1786). NEd. Willi Hillemann, ed. Wilhelmshaven: Noetzel, 1960.

°*Sonata*(C) (1791). NEd. Willi Hillemann, ed. Wilhelmshaven: Noetzel 1969.

Both sonatas are three-movement works in Classical style, showing influence of Mozart and Carl Philipp Emanuel Bach; tuneful, antiphonal, light-textured, with frequent doublings. (LI-I)

Bach, Wilhelm Friedrich Ernst (1759–1845)

Son of Johann Christoph Friedrich and grandson of Johann Sebastian, Wilhelm Friedrich Ernst was the last male descendant of the J. S. Bach line. °*Andante* (a). In *Zwo Stücke für vier Hände*, ed. Alfred Kreutz, Schott.

D-ddr:SWl. Graceful, flowing piece in gently nostalgic mood; strongly contrasting middle section. (LI-I)

Divertimento per quattro mani [Allegro assai (F); Andante with Variations (F); Allegro moderato (Bb); Andante legato (Bb); Allegro fugato (Eb)]. Ms. GB:Lbl.

Das Dreyblatt (F) (Andante con moto) fürs Forte Piano und sechs Hände. GB:Lbl. Though this amusing work is written for three players at one piano and, strictly speaking, is beyond the scope of the present catalog, it is included here for its commentary on a social aspect of multiple performers at a single keyboard. In a note on the first page of the piece the composer writes: "The gentleman playing the middle part should sit a little further back than the two ladies on either side of him. Their arms should be held above his own. The restricted space makes it necessary for the three performers to sit somewhat closely together, the man in the middle playing the highest notes with his right hand, and the lowest notes with his left."

Duett (C), from *Five sonatas for the harpsichord or piano forte and one duett*. London: Napier, ca.1780. GB:Lbl. Short, lightweight, two-movement piece in graceful Classical style. (UE-LI)

Bache, Francis Edward (1833–1858)

English pianist and composer of two operas and works for piano.
Two little duets for his little brothers. London: Augener, 1909. GB:Lbl.

Bachmann, Georges (1864–1894)

°*Chanson Louis XV.* Paris. Consortium musical, n.d. (I)
Dix petites pièces symphoniques en forme d'études. Mainz: Schott [1885]. D-brd:MZsch.

Bachmann, Gottlob (1763–1840)

Sonate (C), Op.41. Bonn: Simrock [1803]. D-brd:B.

Bachmann, Father Sixtus (1754–ca.1818)

Austrian monk; organist and composer. As a consequence of a dispute with the publisher Hofmeister, in Vienna, Bachmann refused to permit his works to be published.
Sonatine. Ms. D-brd:Rp.

Bacon, Ernst (1898–   )

American conductor, pianist, critic; his compositions have American folk flavor and often feature folk tunes.
The battle of Jericho (for 2P or 4H). New York: American Music Editions, 1962. US:Wc.
°*The hootnanny* (Betty Anne; The Boston boy; The brave volunteer; Come in; Cripple Creek; Go to sleep, little child; Leather britches; Oyster River; The spire at Hancock, N.H.; Swannanoah). New York: Chappell, 1954.

US:Wc. Exceptionally fine and sensitive descriptive tone pictures of American scenes plus arrangements of dance tunes. (LI)

Sassafras (Wake up; Jockie and Jinnie; Garry Owen; Sassafras; Joshua Ebenezer Fry; The blue of heaven; The devil's kitchen). New York: Lawson-Gould, 1960. US:Wc. (I)

Badinage, Quadrille [6 pieces]. Pantalon by Nikolai Artsibushev; Été by Joseph Wihtol; Poule by Anatol Liadov; Trénis by Nikolai Sokolov; Pastourelle by Alexander Glazounov; and Finale by Nikolai Rimsky-Korsakov. Leipzig: M. Belaieff, 1891. GB:Lbl. Suite of short easy pieces, each one page long, in ABA form; written for diversion, in late Romantic idiom, by a group of Russian composers, very much in the manner of *Paraphrases.* (UE-LI)

Badings, Henk (1907–)

Dutch musician trained as engineer; director of Royal Conservatory at The Hague; has written in all musical forms in a balanced, neo-Classical idiom showing kinship with Hindemith's style.

°*Arcadia,* Book IV. Zehn kleine Stücke; Diskant im Fünfton-Umfang (Preludio; Punto d'organo; Intermezzo; Elegia; Tripla; Scherzo; Minuetto; Siciliano; Ballata; Finale). Mainz: Schott, 1951. Attractive set of pieces with contemporary flavor, elegantly written in chromatic-modal idiom. (UE-LI/E-5)

°*Arcadia,* Book V. Zehn kleine Stücke; Diskant auf zehn Tasten (Preludio; Sarabanda; Canzonetta; Elegia; Cinque fante di piche; Mazurka; Enigma; Illusion; Gioco; Rondo finale). Mainz: Schott, 1951. Similar in idiom and fastidious setting to Book IV, but more difficult. (I/UE-10 notes)

°*Arkadia VIII:* Kleine Klavierstücke vierhändig. Amsterdam: Donemus, 1965.

Balletto grottesco (1939). Vienna: UEd, n.d.

Bagge, Selmar (1823–1896)

German critic and teacher; wrote chamber music, a symphony, and piano pieces in Romantic style.

[13]*Walzer,* Op.15. Berlin: Simrock, 1883. GB:Lbl.

Baille, Gabriel

Les bords de l'Agli, Op.68. Paris: Brandus, ca.1870. GB:Lbl. Suite of salon waltzes in Viennese style. (LI)

Valse d'un fantôme, Op.73. Paris: Brandus, 1884. GB:Lbl.

Bainton, Edgar L. (1880–1956)

English piano teacher and composer; settled in Australia; wrote piano pieces in conservative style.

A dance. Melbourne: Allans, 1941. US:Wc. Short piece in Classical minuet style. (LI)

Miniature suite (Menuet; Barcarolle; English dance). London: Anglo-French Music Co., 1922. GB:Lbl—US:Wc. Character piece in traditional setting. (LI)

Baker, F.T.
American
°*Danse écossaise*. Philadelphia: Presser, n.d. (LI)

Balakirev, Mily (1837–1910)
Russian musician; leader of nationalist group of composers, "The Russian Five"; incorporated elements of Russian folk song into many of his works.

°*Seven legends* (The royal princess of Kraków; Kostriuk; Nikita Romanovich; Grisha Otrepiev; Vasili Okulievich; The brigand brothers and sisters; Birds and beasts). Bonn/Bad Godesberg: Robert Forberg-P.Jurgenson, Musikverlag, n.d. (reprint of original Jurgenson edition). Arrangement of Russian folk songs in appealing settings with strong harmonies. The major drawback is the frequency of hand collisions and other awkward passages, which strongly suggest an arrangement, possibly of an original version for voice and piano. (I)

°*On the Volga*. NEd. see *Complete Works* below.

°*Thirty Russian folk songs* (based on *Thirty songs of the Russian people*). Moscow: Jurgenson, 1898. NEd. see *Complete Works* below.

°*Suite* (c♯) (Polonaise; Chansonette sans paroles; Scherzo). Leipzig: Zimmerman, 1909. US:PHf,Wc. NEd. see *Complete Works* below. Somewhat demanding work; colorful Russian-style Scherzo is brilliant, fast, and exciting; Chansonette has contrapuntal texture. (UI)

°*Complete works of Balakirev*, ed. Sorokin. Moscow State Publishing House. All the above works are available in vol.3, part 1.

Baldenecker, Jean-Bernard (b.1791)
French musician.
Polonaise(D). Mainz: Schott, n.d.
Two sonatas, Op.9. Pub. and date missing.

Balkashin, Iuri A. (1923–1960)
Soviet composer.
Echo. In collection, *Sbornik fortepiannikh*, ed. N. Agafonnikov.

Barabino, P.
°*Eres amable*, mazurca. Buenos Aires: Ricordi, n.d.
°*Felicidad infantil*, polca. Buenos Aires: Ricordi, n.d.
°*Gabriela*, mazurca. Buenos Aires: Ricordi, n.d.
°*María Luisa*, mazurca. Buenos Aires: Ricordi, n.d.
°*El recreo*, vals. Buenos Aires: Ricordi, n.d.

Barbedette, Hippolyte-LaRochelle (1827–1901)
French author of monographs on Beethoven, Chopin, and Weber; wrote chamber music and piano pieces in Romantic style.

°*Divertissement hongrois*, Op.107. Paris: Hamelle, ca. 1860.

°*Divertissement italien*, Op.108. Paris: Hamelle, n.d.

°*Polonaise*, Op.59. Paris: Hamelle, n.d.

°*Valses*, Op.123. Paris: Hamelle, n.d.

Barber, Samuel (1910–)

American composer; his style is traditional European Romantic, lyrical, and expressive, with strong neo-Classical influence.

°*Souvenirs*, ballet suite, Op.28 (Waltz; Schottische; Pas de deux; Two-step; Hesitation-Tango; Galop)(1952). New York: Schirmer, 1954. Delightful suite of popular dances evoking the atmosphere of the pre-World War I era; full of nostalgia and charm; technically demanding in part. (UI-A)

Barblan, Otto (1860–1943)

Swiss organist, conductor, and composer; wrote cantatas, organ pieces, part songs, and piano works in late Romantic style.

Zwei Walzer (C). Pub. by composer, n.d. °*Walzer No.1* (C), first printing in *Musik-Beilage zur neuen Musik-Zeitung*, ca.1902. CH:Zma. Short one-page waltz in Viennese style.

Barbour, Florence Newell (1867–1946)

American concert pianist; composed choral works, songs, and piano pieces in conservative idiom.

Rambles in musicland. Boston: A.P.Schmidt, n.d.; London: Lengnick, 1912. GB:Lbl—US:Wc. Attractive instructional pieces. (I)

Treasure Island, six duets. Boston: A.P.Schmidt, 1915. GB:Lbl—US:Wc.

Bardac, Raoul

French composer; son of Debussy's second wife, Emma Bardac.

Petite suite majeure (Prélude; Valse; Polka; En jouant; Finale). Paris: Durand, 1914. US:Wc. Charming group of pieces in early French Impressionistic harmonic language. (I-UI)

Bargiel, Woldemar (1828–1897)

German teacher and musician; half-brother of Clara Schumann; wrote orchestral works, chamber music, and piano pieces.

Gigue (c). Vienna: Haslinger, 1864. GB:Lbl.

Suite (C). Op.7 (Allemande; Courante; Sarabande; Air; Gigue). Leipzig: B&H[1860]. GB:Lbl—US:PHf,Wc. Serious work in Romantic style, somewhat in the manner of Robert Schumann; well written, with melodic and harmonic interest, though wanting in inspiration. (I)

Drei Tänze (Ländler; Menuett; Springtanz), Op.24. Leipzig: Rieter-Biedermann, 1864; London: Augener, 1907. GB:Lbl.

Barlow, Fred

°*Plaisir de jouer: quatre pièces* (La petite biche; Berceuse pour Yves; Le noble éléphant à son jeune fils; Valse pour Claude). Paris: Lemoine, 1957. (E)

Barlow, Sybil

*The sad little spinner, from Two scenes from a fairy tale. London: Winthrop Rogers (Boosey), 1937. Short lyrical piece with irregular phrase lengths; well-balanced parts. (E)

Barnes, Archie Fairbairn

Duo giocoso. London: Augener, 1951. US:Wc. Bright, rhythmical work. (LI)

Holiday sketches; seven duets (At the seaside; Swimming; Tramping; Fishing; Boating; Over the rocks; Cliff-climbing). London: Augener, n.d. (UE)

Barth, Richard (1850–1923)

German violinist and conductor; student of Joachim; close friend of Brahms whose strong influence is felt in his music: string quartets, violin pieces and piano works.

Stimmungen und Regungen, Op.16. Berlin: Simrock, 1903. US:Wc. Pleasant suite of waltzes. (LI)

Barth, Rudolf

Vier Märsche, Op.4. Leipzig: Rieter-Biedermann, 1871. GB:Lbl.

Barthe, A.

Pays basque, esquisses musicales (Passacaille; Marche espagnole; Menuet de l'Infante; Chanson basquoise; Le chevrier; Gitanika). Paris: Leduc, 1898. US:Wc. Engaging, coloristic, evocative pieces with Spanish flavor. (I)

Barthelémon, François Hippolyte (1741–1808)

Irish-French violinist, conductor, and composer; wrote operas, orchestral music, and chamber works.

Three favorite duets. New York: Peter Erben [organist of St.George's Chapel] [1807–1812]. US:CA,ECstarr.

Bartholomée, Pierre

*Invention premier double. Brussels: Schott Frères, 1969.

Bartlett, Homer N. (1845–1920)

American pianist, organist; composed sacred music, songs, and many short works for piano in late Romantic style.

Kuma Saka (founded on Japanese themes), Op.218. New York: Schirmer, 1907. US:Wc. Atmospheric piece using pentatonic and oriental scales. (I)

Bartoccini, Mario

Villanella e canzone. In collection Album di Musica Moderna, vol.I.

Bartoš, Jan Zdeněk (1908–   )

Prolific Czech composer of patriotic cantatas, chamber works, and educational music influenced by native folk songs.

*Malý oznamovatel (The little announcer). Prague: Artia, n.d. (E-UE)

Basili (Basily), Francesco (1767–1850)

Italian conductor; wrote symphonies in the style of Haydn, sacred music, and piano pieces.

Fuga(e). Milan: Ricordi, n.d. A:Wgm—I:Mc,Bc.

Bassot, Nanine (1901–   )

°*Première suite de pièces enfantines* (Grave; Choral; L'insouciant; Complainte; Les cloches; Marche; Romance; La moqueuse; Berceuse; Pâques; Appel de clairon). Paris: Heugel, 1953. Excellent little pieces; imaginative use of simple harmonic materials. (UE-LI/E-5 to span of octave)

°*Deuxième suite de pièces enfantines* (En flânant; Un pauvre petit; Le petit navire; Seconde berceuse; Haut les couleurs!; Prière; Chansonette; Pluie; Espagne; Bourrée; Histoire des brigands). Paris: Heugel, 1955. Engaging suite of short pieces inventively written, containing unexpected harmonies, irregular phrase lengths, and rhythmic interest. (UE-LI/E)

Bastien, Jane Smisor

American pianist, teacher, author, and composer of instructional piano music.

°*Duets for fun* (*Music through the piano* series), Book I (Alligator blues; John Brown; The fairy tale waltz; Lazy Mary; Little Indian princess; Mexican clap hands dance; Marching moon men; Jingle bells). Park Ridge, IL: General Words and Music, 1968.

°*Duets for fun*, Book II (Dog-gone blues; Red rock; Petite tango; Misty bells; Country gardens; Greensleeves; Battle hymn of the Republic). Park Ridge, IL: General Words and Music, 1971.

Books I and II both contain tasteful folk-song arrangements together with original pieces in capable instructional style. (E-UE)

Battman, Jacques Louis (1818–1889)

French organist; wrote theoretical works; composed church music and piano pieces in Romantic style.

°*Simple mélodie*, Op.429/4. Paris: Hamelle, n.d.

°*Le départ*, Op.429/6. Paris: Hamelle, n.d.

Bauer, L.

°*Très pressé*. Paris: Consortium musical, n.d. (LI)

Baum, Alfred (1904–   )

Swiss composer

Sieben Klavierstücke nach Negro Spirituals (Good-by, Mother; By an' by; Don't let your watch run down; Get thee behind me Satan; Deep river; Heaven; Things about comin' my way). Ms., 1967. CH:Zma. Compact, artful arrangements in traditional jazz style. (LI)

Baumann, Herbert (1925–   )

German conductor; studied with Boris Blacher and Celibidache; has written numerous stage works, film and television scores, orchestral and chamber music, and instrumental pieces.

°*Musik für Klavier zu vier Händen* (Toccata; Intermezzo; Variationen) (1950). Halle: S.Mitteldeutscher Verlag, 1950. Bright, energetic suite in neo-Hindemith idiom. Quartal harmony is the foundation of the work, and is used throughout the three movements. (I)

Baumer, Cecil

°*Five duets for young fingers* (The story; Sailor's song; Tea party: Melody; Polka). London: Ascherberg, Hopwood & Crew, 1965. GB:Lbl. Tuneful melodies in traditional idiom. (LI)

Bavicchi, John (1922–)

American

°*A duet dozen.* New York: OUP, 1975. Fascinating, bright pieces, ranging in length from six to twenty measures, admirably set for young players in contemporary tonal idiom featuring unconventional use of triads and scale fragments, surprise resolutions and rhythmic turns. (UE)

Beach, Mrs. H.H.A. (Amy Marcy Cheney) (1867–1944)

Pianist and first American woman to achieve reputation as a serious composer; wrote a symphony, piano concerto, chamber music, choral works, and piano pieces in late Romantic style with strong Brahmsian influence.

Suite. Pub. and date missing.

Summer dreams, six duets (The brownies; Robin redbreast; Twilight; Katydids; Elfin tarantelle; Good-night), Op.47. Boston: Arthur Schmidt, 1901. US:Wc. Ably crafted set of descriptive pieces; carefully balanced for both partners. (UE-LI)

Variations on a Balkan theme, Op.60. Pub. and date missing.

Beale, William George Frederick (1784–1854)

English organist and composer of glees, madrigals, and piano pieces.

Divertimento for two performers on one pianoforte. London: Pub. missing, 1846. GB:Lbl.

Beaumont, Paul, pseud. Edward Sydney Smith

English composer of salon pieces.

Bal des poupées, six danses très faciles (Grotte ancienne; Valse mignonne; Polka mazurka; Galop; Polka; Mazurka). London: Lengnick, 1905. GB: Lbl.

Bergers et bergères, gavotte. London: Ashdown, n.d. GB:Lbl.

Bluette. London: Ashdown, n.d. GB:Lbl.

Carnaval-Galop. London: Ashdown, n.d. GB:Lbl.

Menuet moderne. London: Ashdown, n.d. GB:Lbl.

Paquerette, mélodie. London: Ashdown, n.d. GB:Lbl.

Beauvarlet- Charpentier, Jean-Jacques (1734–1794)

French organist and composer; works include organ music, two concertos, music for harpsichord, and collections of piano sonatas.

Airs variés pour clavecin ou forte-piano (1. Les amours d'été; 2. Mon petit coeur; 3. Des bergères du hameau; 4. L'ariette du jour de Cecil [par un bieau jour]), oeuvre 14. Paris: LeDuc, 1782). D-ddr:Bds—F:Pc. Four sets of variations on French popular melodies, all following the same structural formula. The note values in the passage work increase in each succeeding variation, while the underlying ostinato-like patterns (rhythmic, melodic, and harmonic) remain unchanged. Variation 3 is the most successful and has a great deal of charm. (UE-LI)

Beck, Christian Friedrich (late 18th century)

Active in the last quarter of the eighteenth century. His four-hand works are attractive, melodious pieces in the Classical tradition. Although the writing is occasionally blemished by an overabundance of sequential repetitions, the style on the whole is clean and economical.

Six menuets (G,F,Bb,Eb,G,C). Heilbronn: Amon, 1793; Vienna: Hoffmeister, 1794. B:Bc. °*Menuet* (G), No.5. In collection *Vermischte Handstücke*, ed. Kreutz. (UE-LI)

Six pièces faciles (Allegretto[F]; Walzer [C]; Allegretto[G]; Marsch[C]; Walzer[F]; Andante rondo [Eb]). Mainz: Schott, 179[?]. A:Wgm. (UE-LI)

Sonata (Bb), from *Deux sonates pour le clavecin l'une à quatre mains et l'autre accompagnée d'un violon*. Speier: Bossler, 1789. D-ddr:Dlb. (LI-I)

Beck, Thomas (1899–1963)

Norwegian composer

Dansar frå Gudbrandsdal (Dances from Gudbrandsdal), Op.24. Oslo: Musikk-Huset A/S, 1946 (Noreg-Edition No.38). N:Onk. Well-fashioned settings of three Norwegian folk dances in Romantic harmonic style showing the influence of Grieg. (I-UI)

Becker, D.G.

Six sonatinas (C,a,G,F,G,Bb), Op.30. Offenbach: André, 1871. D-brd:OF.

Beckwith, John (1927–   )

Canadian composer, teacher, music critic; has written in many styles; influenced by Satie, Ravel, Hindemith, Ives, and Stravinsky; has also used serial and collage techniques. Works include orchestral and chamber compositions, concertos, choral music, and pieces for other instrumental combinations.

Music for dancing, seven pieces (Prelude; First pantomime; Waltz; Second pantomime; Polka; Dance for two; Round dance), 1948. Ms. C:Tcmc. Attractive, elegantly set pieces in polished lean-textured style. (I)

Becucci, Ernesto (1845–1905)

Italian composer of sacred music and songs; best known for his piano pieces of light character.

°*Una giornata di vacanza*, quattro piccoli pezzi, Op.194. Milan: Carisch, 1909.

Petits fleurs, danses faciles. Milan: Carisch & Jänichen, 1909.

Tre piccole ricreazioni (Sorrisi; Carezze; Baci), Op.280. Milan: Ricordi, 1902. US:Wc. Amiable pieces in instructional style. (UE/E-5)

Precipitevolissimevolemente, galop, Op.266. Milan: Ricordi, 1900. Jovial salon piece. (I)

Bečvařovsky (Beczwarzowsky), Antonín Felix (1754–1823)

Czech composer; spent much of his life in Germany as organist and teacher. His four-hand sonatas and sonatinas are charming, solidly constructed works in refined classical style; many of them are in single movements.

Vier leichte Sonaten (No.1 [G], ?No.2 [F], No.3 [F]). Braunschweig: G.M. Meyer. A:Wgm.

Vier leichte Sonatinen (No.3 [G], No.4 [D]). Braunschweig: G.M.Meyer, n.d. US:Wc.

Leichte Sonatine (F). Braunschweig: G.M.Meyer, n.d. US:Wc.

Nouvelle sonatine instructive et progressive [G]. Berlin: Schlesinger, ca. 1812. D-brd:Mbs.

°*Leichte Sonatine für Anfänger.* In collection *Album of four-hand works by old Czech masters*, ed. Kleinová, Fišerová, and Müllerová. (UE-LI)

Beebe, Edward J.

°*Twenty fingers* (Casual encounter; Courtly caper; Gay episode; Miniature parade; Reluctant waltz; Sagebrush serenade; Summer doldrums; Twenty fingers). Westbury, NY: Pro-Art, 1968. Set of useful instructional duets featuring a variety of technical and musical problems. (LI-I)

Beecke, Ignaz von (1733–1803)

German army captain and amateur musician; friend of Haydn, Mozart, Gluck, and Jomelli; brilliant pianist who developed his own approach to piano technique; composed operas, cantatas, orchestral and chamber works, songs, and piano pieces in Classical style.

Sonate. Pub. and date missing. A:Wgm.

Zwei Sonaten (Bb,F). D-brd: Bibliothek Öttingen-Wallerstein. Friedrich Munter draws special attention to these two sonatas for their fine handling of four-hand ensemble writing, their richly organized structure and melodic invention, and their effective ornamentation. ("Ignaz von Beecke [1733–1803] und seine Instrumentalkompositionen," *Zeitschrift für Musikwissenschaft* 4 [1921–22].)

Beer, Max Josef (1851–1908)

Austrian pianist and composer; works include an opera, a cantata, and piano pieces.

Abendfeier, drei Phantasiestücke, Op.16. Leipzig: B&H, 1878. GB:Lbl.

Haidebilder aus Ungarn, drei Stücke mit Benutzung ungarischer National-Melodien, Op.19. Berlin: Ries & Erler, 1878. GB:Lbl.

Was sich der Wald erzählt, fünf lose Blätter, Op.23. Leipzig: Forberg, 1879. GB:Lbl.

Beeson, Jack (1921–   )

American composer; studied with Bartók; has written operas, orchestral and band music, and instrumental works.

*Round and round, seven easy duets. New York: OUP, 1970. 1. Round and round: double canon at the octave. 2. Accidents: canon at the tenth. 3. First tangle: canon at the third in contrary motion. 4. Simple Simon's song: double canon at the ninth. 5. Second tangle: bitonal combination of the Lydian mode on F major and Gb major. 6. Musical chairs. 7. Round and round again: double canon at the octave; inversion of Round and round. Charming pieces fascinatingly set in linear style illustrating various type of canons; attractive music, interesting introduction to traditional contrapuntal techniques. (UE-LI)

Beethoven, Kaspar (1774–1815)

Brother of Ludwig.

According to Robert Eitner, there is a manuscript in possession of the publisher Artaria and Co. in Vienna entitled *Clavir vor vier Hände par Caspar Beethoven*, consisting of a sonata in three movements in the composer's autograph (*Biographisch-Bibliographisches Quellenlexikon der Musiker und Musikgelehrten . . .* , 10 vols. [Leipzig: B&H, 1898–1904]).

Beethoven, Ludwig van (1770–1827)

Beethoven did not lavish his greatest efforts on the piano duet medium, but the four-hand works he left behind—a relatively minor portion of his total output—all bear the strong and unmistakable imprint of the master. With the exception of the *Grosse Fuge*, Op.134 (arranged by the composer from the original string quartet), Beethoven's piano duets are genial, light-hearted works of great charm and good-natured humor, and are well worth investigating.

Beethoven's complete four-hand works (exclusive of Op.134) are available in *International, *Kalmus, *Peters, and *Universal editions. (The Peters edition is published in two forms: as a single volume; and in two volumes, with Op.6 and Op.45 in vol.I, and the two sets of variations in vol.II.) The *Henle edition contains the complete works, including Op.134.

*Grosse Fuge (Bb), Op.134 (1826). Henle. Arranged by the composer from the original finale of the String Quartet, Op.130 (and later published separately as Op.133). This long, difficult, and agonizingly unpianistic musical curiosity is interesting for its value as a study score of the original and for the insights it provides into the composer's techniques in transcribing his own music from one medium to another. (A)

Six variations on the song "Ich denke dein" (D) (1800), Wo074. This set of sensitive and inventive variations, based on an original song to a text by Goethe, is lighter and somewhat less difficult than the Count Waldstein variations. (I)

Sonata (D), Op.6 (1797). *Bèrben; *Durand; *Consortium Musical;

*Schott. Two-movement work in the composer's early style; bright, vigorous Allegro followed by a flowing Rondo. (I)

Three marches (C,Eb,D), Op.45 (1804). Strong, mature works, with rhythmic drive, hints of orchestral color, and waggish touches here and there; among the finest in the genre. (I-UI)

March (C), Op.45/1 and Gavotte (F) [by Koželuh]. Schott.

Variations on a theme by Count Waldstein (C) (1794), Wo069. The eight imaginative variations and coda are deftly set; contrasting in character, mood, and technical demands. Terminates in a humorous coda with alternating fast and slow sections. (I-UI)

Works Wrongly Attributed to Beethoven:

*[9] *Deutsche Tänze*, ed. Bittner. Leipzig: Peters, 1939. Edited from the music book of an amateur, dating from about 1815, these pieces have never been associated with Beethoven's name despite the assertion by the editor that they are "unmistakably marked with Beethoven's art." They must be regarded as stemming from the pen of an unknown composer.

Gavotte (F), arranged from ballet music by Leopold Koželuh, q.v.

Behr, Franz (1837–1898)

Prolific composer of salon pieces and pedagogical material; following is a partial list of his four-hand works.

L'Alerte, Op.512. Pub. and date missing. US:Wc.

Arabesques, huit morceaux de salon. Vienna: Goll, n.d. US:Wc.

Bilder aus Ungarn, charakteristische Tonstücke. Braunschweig: Litolff, ca. 1877. GB:Lbl.

Birthday gavotte. London: Ashdown, 1890. GB:Lbl.

Two brilliant duets (Hungarian dance; Turkish march). London: Hammond, 1910. GB:Lbl.

Commencement march. New York: Schirmer, 1889. US:Wc. (UE-LI/E-5)

Csárdás-Album, nach ungarischen Volksliedern. Leipzig: Peters, ca.1879. GB:Lbl–US:PHf,Wc. Nine pieces reminiscent of Brahms's *Hungarian dances*. (UI-A)

*[6] *Danses hongroises*, Op.401. NEd. Enoch. GB:Lbl.

Dors, chérie; berceuse. Leipzig: Hatzfeld, 1893. US:Wc.

Etelka, csárdás, Op.415/3. Leipzig: Forberg, n.d. GB:Lbl.

Festklänge, Walzer. Dresden: Brauer, 1890. US:PHf. (UE-LI/E-5)

Fest-Ouvertüre. Milan: Carisch, n.d. US:Wc.

Gitanella, habañera. Leipzig: Hatzfeld, 1893. US:Wc.

Jadis, Chanson-gavotte. Leipzig: Hatzfeld, 1893. US:Wc.

Marche sultane. Pub. and date missing. US:Wc.

Quatre morceaux de salon, Op.592. Leipzig: Forberg, 1889. GB:Lbl–US: PHf,Wc. (I)

Le Postillon d'Amour, Op.221/2. NEd. Hamelle, n.d. US:Wc. (LI)

°*Il primo sogno*, sei pezzi facilissimi (Ninna-nanna; Mattitino d'estate; Arrivederci; Amaranto; Cuoricino mio; Mormorio della sera). Milan: Carisch, n.d. (UE)

La revue. Pub. and date missing. US:Wc.

°*Romance*. Paris: Consortium Musical, n.d. (I)

°*Slavische und ungarische Volksweisen*, Op.379. Paris: Hamelle, n.d. (LI)

Zwei Stücke, Op.328. Leipzig: Forberg, 1875. GB:Lbl. (UE-LI/E-7)

°*À toute brise*. Paris: Consortium Musical, n.d. (E)

Ungarische Lieder und Tänze, Op.392. Leipzig: Forberg, 1877. GB:Lbl.

Ungarische Tänze. Braunschweig: Litolff; Boston: A.P. Schmidt, 1879. US: Wc.

°*À vos souhaits*. Paris: Consortium Musical, n.d. (E)

Zigeunerweisen. Leipzig: B&H, ca.1877. GB:Lbl.

Behrmann, Heinrich

Four pianoforte duets (When swallows homeward turn; Daffodil days; Song of springtime; Merrymakers' dance). London: Ashdown, 1909. GB:Lbl–US:Wc. Short instructional pieces. (UE)

Belchamber, Eileen, arr.

°*Four little hands*, fifty easy piano duets; nursery songs, folk songs, and Christmas carols. New York: Chappell, n.d. Delightful, useful collection of folk songs in fastidious arrangements. (E)

Beliczay, Gyula von (1835–1893)

Hungarian pedagogue and composer. Works include choral, symphonic, and chamber music; songs; and piano pieces.

Drei Stücke im ungarischen Stil, Op.22. Leipzig: B&H, 1880. GB:Lbl.

Bella, Rudolf (1890–)

Czech-born Austrian professor and choir director; Swiss resident.

Fünf Stücke. Leipzig: Weinberger, 1921. CH:Zma. (UE-LI/E-5)

Bellecour, M.

°*Petite suite, très facile*. Paris: Hamelle, 1908. (E)

Bellenot, Philippe (1860–1928)

French choirmaster at St. Sulpice; wrote operas, masses, motets, and piano music.

°*Berceuse*. Paris: Consortium Musical, n.d. (LI)

Belletti, —

°*Six little character pieces*. Bologna: Bongiovanni, n.d. (LI)

Bellisario, Angelo

°*Acquario*, tre pezzi facili. Ancona: Bèrben, 1973. Three melodious, well-balanced pieces, attractively set in tonal, mildly dissonant idiom. (LI-I)

°*Smarties*. Ancona: Bèrben, 1978. Pleasant, short work in mildly contempo-

porary idiom. Two bright, sharply rhythmical Allegros with ostinato figures frame a tranquil Adagio middle section. (LI-I)

Benda, Friedrich Wilhelm Heinrich (1745–1814)
Member of German musical family of Czech origin; pianist and composer of
operas, oratorios, concertos, chamber music, and piano works.
Sonate, Op.6. Berlin/Amsterdam: J.J. Hummel, ca.1799. B:Bc—CS:Bm—
GB:Ckc—US:Wc.

Bendel, Franz (1833–1874)
Czech pianist and teacher; student of Liszt. His piano music is written in
refined salon style.
Deutsche Märchenbilder, Op.135. New York: Schirmer, 1908. US:Wc. De-
scriptive pieces in light style. (I)
Kinder-Ball, sechs kleine Charakterstücke (Polonaise; Walzer; Menuetto;
Polka; Mazurka; Française), Op.4. Leipzig: J.Schuberth, 1860. US:NYp,
PHf,Wc. Tuneful, carefully written instructional pieces. (I)
Ländliche Bilder, sechs Charakterstücke, Op.70. Leipzig: Cranz, 1874. In
collection *Oesterle's graded four-hand collection*, vol.4. (I)
Tarantella, Op.56. Leipzig: Kahnt, ca.1865. US:PHf.

Bendl, Karel (1838–1897)
Czech conductor and composer; wrote in a national musical style close to
that of Smetana and Dvořák.
°*Z dětského světa* (From the children's world), ten melodious pieces
(1884). NEd. Prague: Artia, n.d.

Benjamin, Arthur (1893–1960)
Australian pianist, teacher, and composer; taught at Royal College of Music;
wrote operas, songs, chamber music, and piano pieces.
Suite in C. London: OUP, 1925. GB:Lbl,Lcm.

Bennett, Richard Rodney (1936–   )
English pianist and composer; student of Boulez; uses serial techniques.
Capriccio. London: UEd, 1968. Bright, animated, atonal work. The brilliantly and cleanly scored single movement has a contrasting slower middle part. It features mirror writing and antiphonal sections. Concludes
with a startling and effective double glissando with each part beginning
simultaneously on two adjacent notes: the Primo ascending from Gb and
F to the top, and the Secondo descending from the neighboring D♯ and E
to the bottom of the keyboard. (A)

Bennett, Sir William Sterndale (1816–1875)
English pianist and composer; student of Mendelssohn and friend of Schumann; professor of music at Cambridge University. He wrote in graceful
early Romantic style, influenced by Mendelssohn, and, to some extent, by
Schumann.

Three diversions (A,E,a), Op.17. Leipzig: Kistner, ca.1839; NEd. London: Augener, 1885. US:Wc. Moderately long, carefully constructed pieces in elegant style; worth reviving. (I)

Beñser, J.B. (late 18th century)

English conductor and pianist.

A first sett of three divertimentos in two parts, Op.3. London: Pub. by the composer, ca.1791. GB:Lbl.

Five sonatas and one duetto, Op.5. London: pub. by the composer, n.d. GB: Lbl.

Berardi, Gaston

Valses hongroises. Brussels: pub. missing, 1880. GB:Lbl.

Berens, Hermann (1826–1880)

Swedish pianist and composer of German origin; court conductor in Stockholm; wrote operas, incidental music, songs, and many pieces and studies for piano.

Autumn song; Gnomes; In the twilight. In collection *Thirty-two graded pieces for piano duet.* (LI-I)

Gesellschafts-Quartets for violin, cello, and 4H, No.1, Op.23, 1852; No.2 (D), Op.48, 1856; No.3 (e), Op.72, 1863; No.4 (f), Op.80, 1869. Leipzig: Cranz. D-brd:B.

[27] *Melodische Uebungsstücke,* Op.62. Hamburg: Cranz, 1861. NEd. °Kalmus; Peters. GB:Lbl. (UE-LI/E-5)

Berger, Ludwig (1777–1839)

German musician, student of Clementi; famous as Mendelssohn's piano teacher.

Presto (D), Op.44. Leipzig: Hofmeister, n.d. NEd. 184[?] D-brd:B. Dashing, bright scherzo in Classical idiom; forceful. (LI)

Rondeau (e), Op.47. Leipzig: Hofmeister, n.d. D-brd:B. Moderately long work; competently written in sturdy, though colorless, style. (LI)

Sonata (g), Op.15 (1805). Berlin: Laue, ca.1825. NEd. Leipzig: Hofmeister, ca.1844. A:Wgm. Three-movement sonata in skilled Classical style, probably intended as a pedagogical work. A pleasant, fluent, light-textured piece with attractive melodies, harmonic richness, and rhythmic activity. The work demonstrates the composer's skill in the manipulation and development of his thematic material. However, despite these virtues, the Sonata lacks the inner fire and drive of an inspired hand and tends toward the kind of flatness that inspired Walter Georgii to remark that the piece "tastes like bread which the baker forgot to salt" (*Klaviermusik* [Zürich-Freiburg: Atlantis Verlag, 1950]). (LI-I)

Berkeley, Lennox (1903–)

English composer of operas, songs, film music, orchestral and choral works, and piano pieces. His style is lyrical and very approachable, influenced to some extent by Stravinsky and the modern French school.

•*Sonatina*, Op.39. London: Chester, 1954. Tightly constructed neo-Classical work in frequently dissonant tonal idiom. Texture of the three contrasting movements—Allegro, Andante and Allegro—is clear, often linear. Rhythmically brisk, well fashioned for duet and enjoyable to play. (I-UI)

•*Palm Court Waltz*. London: Chester, 1976. Nostalgic, evocative concert waltz in turn-of-the-century style with a few contemporary twists; melodious, appealing. (I)

Berkovich, I.J.

Soviet musician; has composed many pedagogical works for piano.

Ten pieces, Op.30. Moscow: Musfond, 1956. •No.6, Ukrainian dancing song; •No.9, Romanze, and •No.10, March, in collection •*Brother and sister*, ed. Goldstein.

•*Variations on a Russian folk song* (a). In collection *Russian music for the young pianist*, vol.4, ed. Zeitlin and Goldberger. Ingratiating, well-balanced work in conservative style. (UE-LI)

Berlin, Boris, pseud. Lawrence London (1907–)

Rosemary skating waltz. Oakland, Ont.: The Frederick Harris Music Co., Ltd., 1952. US:Wc.

Bernard, Georges

•*Souvenirs d'enfance* (Câlinerie; Dans les prés fleuris; Défilé des soldats de carton; Flocons de neige; Gai réveil; Premier sourire), Op.306. Paris: Gallet, n.d. The six pieces are issued separately by the current publisher, Consortium Musical, Paris. (UE-LI/E-5)

Berners, Lord Gerald Tyrwhitt (1883–1950)

English composer, painter, author, and diplomat; studied in Vienna and Dresden. His works, humorous and often parodistic, include one opera, ballets, film music, orchestral and vocal compositions, and piano pieces.

•[3] *Valses bourgeoises* (Valse brillante; Valse caprice; Strauss, Strauss et Straus) (1917). London: Chester, 1919. Entertaining set of witty, satirical waltzes, well written for the medium; technically demanding in part. (I-UI)

Berr, José (1874–1947)

Swiss pedagogue and composer, of German origin; wrote choral music, songs, and piano music.

•*Suite nocturne*, Op.86 (1942). Pub. by composer, n.d. CH:Zma.

Bertini, Henry (1798–1876)

In addition to writing a quantity of popular fantasies on operatic themes, which appeared in both piano solo and duet versions, Bertini was a prolific composer of instructional and salon music. His piano duet études were issued in groups of 25 pieces arranged in progressive order of difficulty. Although these studies are written in an outworn musical idiom, they are nonetheless useful in working out some of the rhythmical and technical problems of ensemble playing.

[25] *Études*, Op.97. Leipzig: B&H, ca.1833. GB:Lbl–US:NYp,PHf,Wc.

[25] *Études*, Op.100. Pub. and date missing. US:NYp.

[25] *Études*, Op.135, livre 6. Mainz: Schott [1842].

[25] *Études*, Op.149, livre 2. Mainz: Schott, n.d. US:NYp.

[25] *Études*, Op.150, livre 3. Mainz: Schott, n.d. US:NYp.

[25] *Études*, Op.160, livre 1 (L'art de la mesure). Mainz: Schott, n.d. US: Bp,NYp.

Mother and daughter, four easy pretty duets. Boston: Nathan Richardson, n.d. GB:Lbl. (E)

Motor race. In collection *Thirty-two graded pieces for piano duet*. (LI)

Rondino (A), Op.77. Leipzig: B&H, ca.1830.

Variations brillantes sur un thème original. Leipzig: Kistner, ca.1830.

Berwald, Franz (1796–1868)

Swedish violinist and composer; studied in Germany. His works—operas, symphonies, chamber music, and piano compositions—were little appreciated in his lifetime, but he is now regarded as Sweden's most significant Romantic composer.

En landtlig Bröllopsfest (A rustic wedding). Stockholm: Elkan, 1844. S:Sic.

Minnen af norska fjällen (Recollections of Norwegian mountains). Stockholm: Elkan, n.d. S:Sic.

Bessem, Saar (1907–)

Dutch pedagogue; specializes in writing music for children.

°Danssuite naar oud-Hollandse Kinderwijzen (Dance suite on old Dutch children's songs). Amsterdam: Donemus, 1948.

Besthoff, Mabel

American composer of instructional piano music.

°The bass singer; °The choir singer; °Dainty toes; °Dancing Dolores; °Happy hop toads; On the way to Dream Town; Song of the carillon bells; °Tired hikers; The toy band parade; °The young piano prodigy. Belwin-Mills, 1947. (UE)

Betts, Lorne (1918–)

Canadian musician; studied with Hunter Johnson, Krenek, Roy Harris, and Alan Rawsthorne. He writes in a basically tonal style using occasional dissonance and polytonality.

Suite breve (Parade; En sourdine; Rondeau), 1967. Ms. C:Tcmc. Short set of light, good-humored pieces; pompous fanfare, dreamy interlude, and bright, rhythmical finale. (I-UI)

Beyschlag, Adolf (1845–1914)

German conductor; wrote songs and piano pieces.

Sechs Tänze in Canonform, Op.2. Mainz: Schott, 1873. GB:Lbl.

Bhatia, Vanraj (1927–   )

Indian composer, born in Bombay; studied at Royal Academy of Music.

°*Indian nursery* (Rain; My cat; Cat and mouse; Myself; We are soldiers; We are toys; More rain). London: Novello, 1956. Charming suite of descriptive pieces employing East Indian melodic ideas in a basically conventional harmonic idiom; well balanced for both performers. (LI)

Bibl, Rudolf (1832–1902)

Viennese organ virtuoso; composed liturgical music, organ pieces, and works for piano.

Suite (G) (Allegro moderato; Waltz; Romance; Gavotte; Fugue), Op.62. New York: E. Schuberth, 1888. US:Wc. Agreeable set of pieces in well-fashioned salon style; the fugal finale is especially impressive. (UI)

Biederman, August Julius (1825–1907)

German-American musician.

À la chasse (US:PHf,Wc); *Alla marcia*, Op.90; *Columbus march*, Op.26 (US:PHf,Wc); *Dancing waves*, Op.82; *A dream*, Op.79; *La gondola*, Op.88; °*Impromptu*, Op.81, in collection *Popular duets*, Book 1, comp. Fraemke; °*A little jewel*, Op.87; *Mélodie*, Op.28 (US:PHf,Wc); *The village blacksmith*, Op.80. New York: G. Schirmer; Leipzig: Dieckman, ca. 1890. Instructional pieces. (LI-I)

Biehl, Albert (1833–1892)

Prolific composer of piano methods and instructional material for both 2H and 4H.

Sonatine (G), Op.74. Braunschweig: Bauer, 1879. GB:Lbl. (UE-LI/E-8)
Quatre sonatines mélodiques et instructives (C,G,C,G), Op.104. Hamburg: Cranz, 1884. GB:Lbl.

Bierey, Gottlob Benedikt (1772–1840)

German theater director and composer; successor to Weber as Kapellmeister at Breslau. Wrote operas, operettas, cantatas, and orchestral and chamber music.

Deux sonates faciles (G,C). Leipzig: B&H, ca.1808. A:Wgm. Appealing, short instructional works in Classical style. Each Sonata is in three contrasting movements; open-textured, flowing, melodious, with rhythmical interest. (UE)

Biggs, John (1932–   )

La mort. Ms. US:NYamc.

Bihl, Rudolf

Concert waltz, Op.60. New York: Schuberth, 1888. US:Wc. Large-scale work in salon idiom; brilliant in part. (I-LA)

Bihler, Gregor
Variations pour le clavecin ou forté-piano (Journal de musique pour les Dames, No.43). Offenbach: André, 1795. D-brd:OF.

Bilbro, Mathilde
°*At the circus.* Cincinnati: Willis, n.d. (UE)

°*By the sea.* Boston: Boston Music Co, n.d. (UE)

°*Eight recollections.* Cincinnati: Willis, n.d. (E-UE)

°*Flame vine.* Cincinnati: Williams, n.d. (UE)

°*Marche militaire.* Cincinnati: Willis, n.d.

°*Our first duet book.* Bryn Mawr: Presser, n.d. (UE-LI)

°*Piano duets for two young people.* Cincinnati: Willis, n.d.; Melbourne: Allans, n.d. (E)

°*Two young students,* first grade piano duets (If only rain would stop; Waltz of the kewpies; Peter Pan polka; Going to the picture show; Marching in the parade; Waltz of the Christmas dolls; Naughty little goblins; Jolly club girls; Little broken-winged robin; At the gypsy camp). Philadelphia: Hatch Music Co., 1917. US:PHf. (E)

Billi, Vincenzo (1869–1938)
Italian conductor; wrote pieces of popular character and instructional piano music.

°*The happy age,* six little pieces on five notes (The little sharpshooter, march; With full sails, barcarole; On green meadows, dance; Village bells; The first sorrow; The little geisha, Japanese dance). Milan: Ricordi, n.d. (UE-LI/E-5)

°*La festa della mamma.* Florence: Forlivesi, n.d.

°*Children's paradise,* six easy pieces (Happy dreams, lullaby; Pinocchio in war, march; Among the roses, Boston-waltz; The fisherman's song; The wandering musician; Chinese drummer, dance), Op.337. Milan: Ricordi, n.d. (UE-LI/E-5)

°*Pattaglia giapponese.* Florence: Forlivesi, n.d.

Binet, Frédéric
°*Pour déchiffrer,* Op.44. Paris: Durand, n.d. US:Wc. Twenty short, varied pieces arranged in progressive order of difficulty and set in contrasting musical forms. Rhythmical, pianistic, and ensemble problems are stressed. (E-UI)

Binkerd, Gordon (1916–   )
American composer of symphonies, ensemble works, and piano pieces.

°*And viva sweet love,* for men's voices and 4H. New York: Boosey & Hawkes, 1970. GB:Lbl.

Bird, Arthur (1856–1923)
American pianist; studied with Liszt; spent most of his life abroad; composed in late Romantic style.

Amerikanische Weisen (Rondes américaines)(D,F,G), Op.23. Breslau: Hainauer, 1887. GB:Lbl—US:Wc. Suite of waltzes, more Viennese in style than American. The music is tastefully fashioned. (UI)

Ballet music, Op.13. Breslau: Hainauer/New York: G.Schirmer, 1886. GB: Lbl—US:Wc. Elegant, unpretentious work. (UI)

Drei charakteristische Märsche (F,f,C), Op.11. Breslau: Hainauer/New York: Schirmer, 1887. GB:Lbl—US:Wc. Strong, vigorous, rhythmical. (UI)

Introduction and fugue (d), Op.16. Breslau: Hainauer/New York:Schirmer, 1887. GB:Lbl—US:Wc. Masterfully written, large-scale work, brilliant in part; worth investigating. (UI-A)

Eine Karneval-Szene, Op.5. Breslau: Hainauer, n.d. GB:Lbl.

Erste kleine Suite (F) (Marschmässig; Ziemlich schnell; Langsam; Mässig schnell), Op.4. Breslau: Hainauer, 1885. US:Wc.

Zwei Poesien (A,g), Op.25. Breslau: Hainauer/New York:Schirmer, 1888. US:Wc.

Bishop, Dorothy

°*Ani-Mated scale duets*. New York: Carl Fischer, 1977.

°*A folk holiday* (This old man; Vidalita; Bridge of Avignon; Minka; Frog went a-courting; Mayday carol; In Baia town; Weggis fair; Greensleeves; Roselil; Pat-a-pan; Sweet Betsy of Pike; Night herding song; Kolyada). New York: Carl Fischer, 1959. Fluent arrangements of folk songs in traditional idiom, neatly set for 4H. (UE-LI)

Bitsch, Marcel (1921–)

French author and composer; along with orchestral, chamber, and piano music, he has also written harmony textbooks.

°*Pastourelles*, dix pièces enfantines (1ᵉʳ Album: Berceuse; Hornpipe; Choral; Claire fontaine; Le jeu du sapin. 2ème Album: Aurore; Laendler; Pastorale; Harmonies municipales; Nocturne). Paris: Leduc, 1956. Ingeniously set, effective pieces in polished French style; mild dissonances and surprise harmonies add pungency. (UE-LI)

Bizet, Georges (1838–1875)

Illustrious French composer of operas (*Carmen* and *The Pearl-fishers*), incidental music to *L'Arlésienne*, a symphony, choral works, and piano pieces.

Jeux d'enfants (Children's games), Op.22 (1872). °Durand; °Hug; °International; °Kalmus; °Peters; °Schirmer; °Bèrben, Op.22/2 only. One of the most engaging works in the entire four-hand repertoire, this set of pieces contains some of the composer's finest and most sensitive writing. It is perhaps more familiar in its orchestral transcriptions. In its original form the suite was ingeniously designed for the duet medium and consists of twelve colorful, imaginative tone pictures warmly describing various children's games and activities. Each piece is a gem of workmanship and musical effect, and offers a refreshing interpretive experience to both performers. A basic repertoire item for every four-hand team; demands exceptional delicacy of touch and dynamic control. 1. L'Escarpolette (The swing). While arpeggios rise quietly from the Secondo bass and respond in descending cascades in the Primo, a fervent sweeping melody in Secondo describes the movement of the swing as it slowly accelerates, climbing higher and higher, gradually loses momentum, and finally returns to rest where it began. (I-UI) 2. La toupie (The top). The unsteady progress of the top is depicted as it whirs along steadily at first, weakens and begins to falter, recovers only to stagger again, and finally wobbles off drunkenly before flopping down. (I-UI) 3. La poupée (The doll). Gentle, lyrical lullaby. (I) 4. Les chevaux de bois (Merry-go-round). Strongly accented, galloping scherzo. (UI) 5. Le volant (Badminton). The shuttle-cock bounces back and forth between the players with rapid, smoothly floating chromatic passages. (UI) 6. Trompette et tambour (Bugler and drummer). Little march with strong percussive beats and trumpet flourishes; triplet figures and dotted rhythms predominate; after an imitative middle section the sound begins to die away as the marchers move into the distance. (UI) 7. Les bulles de savon (Soap bubbles). An undulating melody in the Primo right hand bounces its way capriciously through the piece like the fragile, erratic flight of a bobbing soap bubble as the Secondo pursues with a feathery light chordal accompaniment. (I-UI) 8. Les quatre coins (Puss-in-the-corner). One of the most delightful, and difficult, pieces of the suite; bright and colorful, propelled by a strong, rhythmic motive; fugal development; exciting climaxes; some thorny technical problems. (UI-LA) 9. Colin-maillard (Blindman's buff). The music follows the blindfolded child as he unsteadily gropes his way; he stumbles, recovers his footing, and after several unsuccessful lunges, finally catches his quarry. (I) 10. Saute-mouton (Leap frog). Light, capering triplet figure hops up and down the keyboard from low bass to high treble with constant hand-crossing. (UI) 11. Petit mari, petite femme (Playing house). Lyrical, sentimental theme (with hints of *L'Arlésienne* to come) describes this warm-hearted domestic scene: the husband and wife have a mild disagreement followed by a tender, happy reconciliation. (LI-I) 12. Le bal (The ball). Rousing, lively dance; exhilarating, impetuous, full of spirit. (UI-LA)

Blake, Dorothy Gaynor (1893–)

American teacher and pianist; composer of songs and piano teaching pieces. The following works are published by Willis Music Co., Cincinnati; single titles marked (°) within collections are also published separately:

°*The camel*, 1960. Primo melody with oriental flavor against ostinato figure in Secondo. (E)

°*Companions at the keyboard* (°Spring dance; °Christmas chimes; °Wooden

shoe dance; °In Seville, Spanish dance; °Our republic, march; °Down the River), 1929. Tuneful, attractive pieces in instructional style. (E-5).
°*Indian braves*, 1926. (E)
°*My clock.* (E)
°*Tunes for two* (°The Japanese toy man; °Trailing moon vine; °The quick step; °The clock man; °The sunrise trail; °Row, brother, row!; °The maid in green; °The old-time fiddler), 1929. (E-5)

Blake, Jessie
°*Eight duets for beginners.* London: Boosey & Hawkes, n.d. (E-UE)

Bloch, André (1873–1960)
°*Six petites pièces pittoresques* (Marche militaire; Danse des poupées; Sur la montagne; Songe d'orient; Humoresque; Fantaisie joyeuse). Paris: Enoch, n.d. (UE-LI)

Blomberg, Erik (1922–   )
Swedish
Fyra händer på ett piano (Four hands at one piano) (1970). Ms. S:Sic. Craggy serial work; linear, spare textured, rhythmically complex. (UI-A)

Blumenthal, Sandro (1874–   )
Piccolo suite (A). Leipzig: Hofmeister, 1907. US:Wc. Salon music. (I-UI)

Boccosi, Bio
°*Tarantella.* Ancona/Milan: Bèrben, n.d.

Bödecker, Louis (1845–1899)
Ernstes Gedenken, Op.27. Leipzig: Rieter-Biedermann, 1885. GB:Lbl.
Frühlings-Idylle, Phantasie (C), Op.16. Leipzig: Rieter-Biedermann, 1882. GB:Lbl–US:Wc. Salon piece. (I)
Sonatina (A), Op.26. Leipzig:Rieter-Biedermann, 1885. GB:Lbl.

Bodenhoff, Harold
Bagatellen, neun Clavierstücke (Praeludium; Valse lente; Larghetto; Intermezzo; Rokoko; Humoresque; Valse noble; Polka bohême; Polonaise), Op.7. Leipzig/Boston: A.P.Schmidt, 1908. GB:Lbl.

Boëllmann, Léon (1862–1897)
Alsatian · organist; successful composer of orchestral and chamber music, organ pieces, and piano works.
°*Scènes du moyen-âge* (Ronde de la nuit; La veillée; Le tournoi). Paris: Salabert, n.d.

Bohdanovicz, Basilius von (1754–ca.1815)
Musikalische Familie für Klavier, from *Daphnis et Philis* with "Adieu à quatre mains," 1798. Pub. missing. A:Wgm.

Böhm, Johann Christian (late 18th century)
Wechselgesang mit vierhändiger Klavier-Begleitung in Part. und Stimmen vom 6.VII.1798. Ms. D-ddr:Bds.

Bohm, Karl (1844–   )

German composer of pedagogical music.

Aus der Brautzeit, Walzer, Op.270. Breslau: Hainauer, 1881. US:Wc. Suite of three tuneful waltzes in salon style. (LI)

Blonde Locken, Walzer, Op.208. Pub. and date missing. In collection *Popular duets*, ed. Fraemcke. Salon piece. (LI)

Two duets (Allegro brillante; Rondo in C), Op.217. London: Hammond, 1911. GB:Lbl.

A fanfare, military rondo, Op.303. Berlin: Simrock, 187[?]. In collection *Exhibition pieces for four hands*, and in Ditson, Presser, and Schirmer editions. GB:Lbl.

Le fanfare des Uhlans, galop militaire, Op.213. Berlin: Simrock, 1883; New York: °Schirmer. Popular salon piece of the late nineteenth century. (I-UI)

Geburtstags-Musik, moderne Suite (Marsch; Wiegenlied; Zwischenspiel; Walzer und Finale), Op.250. Breslau: Hainauer/New York: Schirmer, 1881. US:NYp,Wc. Pleasant group of pieces in salon style. (I)

Kindersonate (F), Op.108. Berlin: Simrock, 1873. GB:Lbl. (UE-LI)

Rondo in militarischen Stile, Op.333a. Breslau: Hainauer, 1886. GB:Lbl.

[2] *Sonatas* (D,G), Op.84/1, 2. Leipzig: Rühle, 1874; New York: Schirmer, 1889, 1892. GB:Lbl. Salon pieces in serious vein; more difficult than Op. 391. (I)

Sonate (F), No.3, Op.317. Berlin: Simrock, 1884. GB:Lbl. (LI-I)

Zwei Sonaten (G,D), Op.391. Berlin: Simrock, 1884. US:Wc. Instructional sonatas. (LI-I)

Tanzskizzen, Op.305. Leipzig: Hainauer, 1884. GB:Lbl. Twelve pieces in salon style; demanding in part; effectively scored. (I-UI)

Tarantella. London: Lengnick, 1913. GB:Lbl.

Waltz, Op.207. In collection *Oesterle's graded four-hand collection*, vol.II. (UE-LI)

Bois, Rob du (1934–   )

Dutch composer of music for solo instruments, orchestra, ensembles; makes use of contemporary techniques and unusual playing devices.

°*Deuxième série de rondeaux*, pour piano à quatre mains et deux instruments à percussion ad lib. (glass chimes; petite caisse avec deux baguettes de bois) (1964). Amsterdam: Donemus, 1967. US:NYp. Each of the nine rondeaux in this set involves the solution of a different technical or stylistic problem. The idiom is current, atonal, pointillistic, frequently aleatory. (A)

Boisard, Victor

°*Berceuse*. Paris: Consortium Musical, n.d. (E)

°*Gavotte*. Paris: Consortium Musical, n.d. (LI)

°*Marche militaire*. Paris: Consortium Musical, n.d. (LI)
°*Prière du soir*. Paris: Consortium Musical, n.d. (LI)

Boisdeffre, Charles-Henri René de (1838–1906)

French composer of orchestral, chamber, and instrumental works in elegant salon style.

°*Marche religieuse*, Op.14. Paris: Hamelle, n.d.
°*Quatre petites pièces faciles* (Ronde champêtre; Sérénade; Bébé et sa grand'maman, berceuse; Les cloches du village, carillon), Op.69. Paris: Hamelle, n.d. (LI)
°*Suite* (Prélude, en forme de danse; Air de ballet; Orientale; Valse), Op.44. Paris: Hamelle, ca.1904. (UI)
°*Suite lorraine* (Les bords de la Moselle; Le chant des bergers; Idylle; La fête au village lorrain), Op.92. Paris: Hamelle, 1899.

Boldemann, Laci (1921–1969)

Swedish composer of Finnish descent; wrote operas, symphonic music, choral works, songs, and piano pieces.

Liten svit på egna barnvisor (Little suite on original children's songs), Op.16 (1960). Stockholm: Nordiska musikförlaget [1961]. S:Sic—US:Wc. Charming group of short pieces in mildly contemporary idiom. (I-LA)

Bonawitz, Johann Heinrich (1839–1917)

German pianist, conductor, and teacher; wrote operas, religious music, chamber and orchestral works, and piano pieces.

Divertissement, Op.17. London: R.Cocks (Augener), 1894. GB:Lbl.
Two impromptus, Op.4. London: Cocks, 1894. GB:Lbl.
Tänze, Op.3. Vienna: Kratochwill, 1877. GB:Lbl.

Bonis, Mélanie (1858–1937)

French composer of salon and instructional music.

°*Les gitanes*, valse espagnole. Paris: Hamelle, n.d.
Suite en forme de valses (Ballabile; Valse lente; Danse sacrée; Scherzo-valse; Interlude; Bacchanale). Paris: Leduc, 1898. US:Wc. Attractive set of waltzes in various styles and tempi. (LI-I)

Bordes, Charles (1863–1909)

French musical scholar, teacher, organist, and composer; founder of the Schola Cantorum in Paris. He devoted his life to the revival of polyphonic sacred and secular music. Composed liturgical works, orchestral and chamber music, and piano pieces.

°*Divertissement sur un thème béarnais*. Paris: Herelle, 1924.
°*Euskal Herria*. Paris: Salabert, n.d.

Bornhardt, Johann Heinrich Carl (1774–1840)

Sechs kleine Sonatinen für angehende Spieler. Leipzig: B&H, 1825. A:Wgm.

Borodin, Alexander (1833–1887)

Brilliant and productive member of the "Russian Five" group of nationalist composers, Borodin shared his interest in music with an equally successful career as a professor of chemistry. His musical compositions include orchestral and chamber works, operas, songs, and piano pieces.

°*Marche funèbre*, see *Paraphrases.*

°*Mazurka*, see *Paraphrases.*

Pièce (Eb) (1879). Incomplete unpub. ms. USSR:Lsc.

°*Polka*, see *Paraphrases.*

°*Polka* (d) ("Hélène") (1843). Moscow: Musgiz, n.d.; ms. in USSR:Lit. In collection *Russian music for the young pianist*, vol.6, eds. Zeitlin and Goldberger. Short, tuneful, bright, rhythmical piece in lightweight style; an arrangement by the composer of a 2H piece he wrote for the object of a boyhood crush. (LI-I)

°*Requiem*, see *Paraphrases.*

Tarantella (D) (1862). Moscow: Musgiz, 1938. US:Wc.

Borris, Siegfried (1906–)

Aufzug (Frühlings Gesellen), Divertimento und Sonatine. Berlin: Sirius-Verlag, 1950. D-brd:DSim.

Bortkievich, Sergei Edvardovich (1877–1952)

Russian emigré composer; wrote orchestral, chamber, and piano music in refined Romantic style.

Russische Tänze, Op.18. Leipzig: Kistner & Siegel, 1898, 1914. GB:Lbl–US:Wc.

Russische Weisen und Tänze, Op.31. Leipzig/Milan: Rahter, 1926. GB:Lbl–US:Wc. Appealing arrangements of Russian folk tunes. (I)

Bortz, Alfred (1882–1969)

German teacher and composer; wrote opera, orchestral music, choral works, and piano pieces.

Sonata(a), Op.22. Berlin: Simrock, 1920. US:PHf,Wc. Effectively written three-movement work in conservative idiom; useful teaching material. (I-UI)

Boscovich, Alexander Uriah (1907–1964)

Israeli composer of Romanian origin; his style incorporates many elements of Near Eastern folk music.

°*Semitic Suite*. Tel Aviv: Israeli Music Publications, 1958. Set of colorful, descriptive, character pieces with vivid folk flavor inspired by Israeli dances; also exists in 2P and orchestra versions. (I-UI)

Bossi, Marco Enrico (1861–1925)

Italian organist; wrote orchestral and chamber music, operas, organ works, and piano pieces in Romantic style.

Suite de valses, Op.93. Leipzig: Rieter-Biedermann, 1894; Peters, 1918. US: PHf. Bright set of waltzes in Viennese style. (I)

Bottenberg, Wolfgang (1930–)

Canadian of German descent; cultivates dissonant tonal style.

Three English carols (God rest you merry, gentlemen; The holly and the ivy; Good King Wenceslas) (1963). Cincinnati: Westwood Press, n.d.

Bouchard, Remi G.
Canadian musician.

Ode for piano duet. Waterloo, Ont: Waterloo Music, 1976. Brief, tuneful, but naively written and structurally weak. (LI)

Boucherit-Lefaure, M.
Mikou et son ours, petit amusement pour la transformation de rhythme (Berceuse; Valse; Sérénade; Bourrée). Paris: Lemoine, n.d. (E)

Bourgault-Decoudray, Louis Albert (1840–1910)
French composer of operas, cantatas, chamber music, and piano pieces.
Le carnaval d'Athènes, danses grecques. Paris: Choudens, 187[?]. US:Wc.

Bourges, Jean Maurice (1812–1881)
French composer, critic, editor; composed songs, an opera, piano pieces, and chamber music.
Quatre pièces (Cortège-ballet; Les noces d'or; Musette tambourin; Tertullia). Paris: pub. missing, ca.1884. GB:Lbl.
Six pièces de caractère (Premier fragment de ballet; Deuxième fragment de ballet; Marche-cortège pour une féerie; Procession des pénitents; Marche; Marche noble). Paris: pub.missing, ca.1884. GB:Lbl.

Boutron, M.
Jour de fête, pièce très facile pour deux élèves. Paris: Lemoine, n.d. (E)

Boutry, H.
Tabatière de musique. Paris: Salabert, n.d.

Bowen, York (1884–1961)
English pianist, violinist, horn player; composed orchestral music, concertos, viola pieces, and piano works in fastidious Romantic idiom.
Four pieces (Prelude; Humoresque; Serenade; Dance tune), Op.90. London: OUP, 1930. GB:Lbbc.
Suite (Prelude; Dance; Nocturne), Op.52. London: Stainer & Bell, 1919. US:Wc. (I-UI)
Suite No.2 (Allegro; Barcarolle; Moto perpetuo), Op.71. London: Stainer & Bell, 1923. US:Wc. Serious, engaging work; vigorous allegro; affecting barcarolle; brilliant moto perpetuo. (I-LA)

Boyd, Anne (1946–   )
Australian composer, resident in England.
Rain on Castle Island, for SSS (or SSA), percussion and piano 4H; text by Kitahara Hakuso. London: Novello, 1970. (No.28 in *Musical Times,* supplement Nov. 1970.) Short work in advanced idiom; Primo limited to glissandos played by fingernail crossing strings; Secondo plays similarly on lower strings with occasional plucking. (A)

Boyle, Harrison (1953–)

American; cultivates eclectic, basically tonal, style.

Two Ecclesiastical Scherzi, Op.27. Ms. US: NYamc. Commissioned by Howard Levitsky and Jeffrey Eschleman, piano duettists. Hymn-tune fragments, a waltz, and jazz elements, together with echoes of Stravinsky and Messiaen, are present in the two movements of this gently parodistic work: The Transmogrification of St. Francis and St. Vitus Dance. (A)

Songs of Religion (1. What Tomas said in a pub, poem by James Stephens [1978]; 2. The war prayer, text by Mark Twain), for baritone and piano 4H, Op.22. AMC Ms. [1976].

Braal, Andries de (1909–)

Small rondo (1973). Amsterdam: Donemus, 1973. NL:Ad.

Brahms, Johannes (1833–1897)

Like Beethoven before him, Brahms made a comparatively small contribution to the four-hand repertoire, but he brought to the medium the full measure of his inventive genius, rigorous self-criticism, and solid craftsmanship.

Hungarian dances (1858 and earlier) (Book 1: g,d,F,f,f♯,Db,A,a,e,E; Book 2: a,d,D,d,Bb,f,f♯,D,b,e,e). NEds. °B&H; °Consortium Musical; °Durand; °Hansen (Book 2 only); °Henle; °International; °Kalmus; °Peters; °Ricordi; °Schirmer; °Schott; °Bèrben (No.5 only). Possibly Brahms's most popular compositions, these 21 piano-duet settings of original melodies patterned after Magyar and gypsy tunes have been arranged for innumerable instrumental combinations. (I-A)

Eleven Ländler, arranged for 4H from Schubert's 2H Ländler, D.366. See Schubert.

[18] *Liebeslieder waltzes,* Op.52 (1869); [15] *New Liebeslieder waltzes,* Op.65 (1875). NEds: °B&H (Op.52a and Op.65a only); °Peters; °Simrock; °UEd. These ingratiating waltzes were originally written for vocal quartet with 4H accompaniment and sound best in that arrangement, although all of Op.52 and part of Op.65 are performable as 4H solos. Both sets also exist as Op.52a and Op.65a, in Brahms's own arrangement for 4H solo; less effective than the originals. (UI-A)

Variations on a theme by Robert Schumann (Eb), Op.23 (1861). NEds: °B&H; °International; °Peters; °Simrock. Based on a theme that Schumann, in his final delirium, imagined had been dictated to him by Schubert and Mendelssohn. This profound and poetic set of variations was Brahms's personal tribute to his friend. With its rich harmonic and melodic variety and its frequent references to orchestral effects, it is one of the great masterpieces of the 4H literature. (A)

[16] *Waltzes,* Op.39 (1865) (B,E,g♯,e,E,C♯,c♯,Bb,d,G,b,E,B,g♯,Ab,c♯). NEds: °B&H; °Henle; °International; °Kalmus; °Peters; °Schirmer; °Schott. Suite of Viennese waltzes with occasional touches of Hungarian flavor; also arranged by the composer in a simplified edition. (I-LA)

*Complete works, Breitkopf und Härtel critical edition of 1884–1897, vol. 4; available in reprint by Dover Publications, New York. Complete one-volume edition of Brahms's 4H works (exclusive of the arrangements of Schubert's Ländler).

Braithwaite, Sam Hartly (1883–1947)
English teacher and composer.

Chopinesque. London: Augener, n.d. GB:Lbl. (I-UI)

Pastorale. London: Augener, 1937. GB:Lbl. (I-UI)

Prelude in the style of the eighteenth century. London: Augener, 1937. GB: Lbl–US:NYp. Long, brisk, restless work in Classical idiom with an abundance of passage work and a thickening of the basically linear texture as the piece moves forward; the parts are well laid out. (I-UI)

Brandse, Wim (1933–)
Double dutch. New York: Schirmer, 1977.

Brant, Henry (1913–)
Canadian-born American; studied with Riegger and Antheil. In his compositions he has made use of "controlled improvisation" for easy performance of complex textures; also experiments with unusual instruments and sound effects.

Ceremony, triple concerto for violin, oboe, soprano, alto, tenor, bass, divided orchestra, and 4H (1954). Pub. and date missing. US:NYamc.

Brehme, Hans (1904–1957)
German pianist; wrote in Reger-Hindemith idiom.

Gavotte (g#) and Musette. In collection *Spielbuch Zeitgenössische Originalkompositionen.* Tuneful dances in conservative style with harmonic and rhythmic interest; textures incline to be overdense. (I)

Bremner, Ernst J.
Deuxième suite (d) (Praeludium; Tanz; Intermezzo; Alla siciliana; Scherzo finale). Paris: A. Bourlant-Ladam, 1906. US:Wc. Work in salon style. (UI)

Brendler, Frans Frederik Edward (1800–1831)
Swedish flutist; friend of the composer Geïjer.

Sonatine (C). Stockholm: Eberling, 1830. S:Sic.

Bresgen, Cesar (1913–)
Austrian composer who derives his musical style from the melody and rhythms of old German folk songs.

Kuckuckssuite (G). In collection *Spielbuch Zeitgenössische Originalkompositionen.* Light, playful set of pieces in three short movements.

Bréville, Pierre de (1861–1949)
Procession (from *Album pour Enfants*). Paris: Édition mutuelle (Salabert), 1912. US:Wc.

Brings, Alan (1934–)
American composer; student of Otto Luening, Gardner Read, and Roger Sessions.
Passacaglia, Interlude and Fugue. US:NYamc.
Variations on a solemn theme. Ms., 1975. US:NYamc. Slow-moving, linear
work in modal idiom. Because of the unvarying texture and the subtlety
of its harmonic and rhythmic fluctuations, the piece tends to sound static;
it nonetheless has a certain charm and appeal. (UE-LI)

Brink, Jules ten (1838–1889)
Six pieces. Paris: pub.missing, ca.1881. GB:Lbl.

Briquet, Marc (1896–)
Swiss composer.
Nyam-nyam (burlesque). Pub. by composer. CH:Zma.

Britten, Benjamin (1913–1975)
°*Noye's Fludde,* Op.59, for solo voices, string quartet, amateur string orchestra, recorders, bugles, percussion, and 4H (1957). London: Hawkes & Son,
1958. (Piano parts LI-I)

Broaddus, Helen
°*Tulip time.* Cincinnati: Willis Music Co., 1936. Instructional piece.

Brockt, Johannes (1901–)
Austrian conductor, musicologist, and composer.
°*Piccoli pezzi contrapuntistici,* Op.37. Vienna: Doblinger, 1946. US:Wc.

Brodersen, Viggo
Drei stücke, Op.39. Leipzig: Steingräber, 1923. US:Wc.

Brown, Rayner (1912–)
American; church organist; has written orchestral and chamber music, organ
pieces, and piano compositions.
°*Variations.* Los Angeles: Western International Music Co., 1970.

Bruce, M. Campbell
°*Divertissements.* London: Curwen, n.d. (I)
°*Matelotte, masque and tarantelle.* London: Curwen, 1953. (I)
°*Tinker tailor.* London: Curwen, n.d. (E)

Bruch, Max (1838–1920)
German conductor and composer; best known for his first Violin Concerto;
also wrote symphonies, operas, choral works, and chamber music in German
Romantic idiom.
Capriccio, Op.2. Leipzig: Kistner & Siegel, 1858. GB:Lbl. (I)
Swedish dances, Op.63. Bonn: Simrock, n.d. GB:Lbl. Also exists in versions
for solo piano and for violin and piano.

Brück, Julius (1859–   )

[12] *Danses hongroises*, Op.13. Budapest: Bárd, ca.1897. US:NYp. Settings of Hungarian tunes in traditional style. (I)

Bruckner, Anton (1824–1896)

°*Three little pieces* (1852–54). NEds: °OUP; °Schott. Written when the composer was a piano teacher. These short pieces have a simple charm and directness. (E)

°*Quadrille* (1854). NEd. Magdeburg: Heinrichshofen, 1944. The three amiable, flowing pieces in this somewhat more difficult set of duets have been partially reconstructed from the composer's original score by the editor, Heinrich Lemacher, the first page of Secondo and the last page of Primo parts having been lost. (I)

Bruguier (Brughier), David

Three duetts, Op.7. London: pub. missing, ca.1820. GB:Lbl.

First sett of three favorite Duetts, Op.3. London: pub.missing, ca.1826. GB: Lbl.

Brüll, Ignaz (1846–1907)

Austrian pianist and composer; friend of Brahms; wrote in late Romantic style.

Bretonische Melodien, Op.45. Pub. and date missing.

Brunner, Christian Traugott (1792–1874)

German organist and conductor; prolific composer of salon pieces and instructional music for piano.

Les joyeux, Op.237. London: pub.missing, ca.1852. GB:Lbl.

Le petit bouquet, six rondeaux mignons. Mainz: Schott, ca.1868. GB:Lbl.

Sonatine (F) im Umfang von fünf Tönen, Op.336. Magdeburg: Heinrichshofen, 1859. GB:Lbl. (UE/E-5)

[3] *Sonatinen* (G,F,D), Op.465. Berlin: Bote & Bock, 1866. GB:Lbl.

Bruzdowicz, Joanna

°*Esitanza*. Paris: Choudens, n.d.

Bryan, Charles Faulkner (1911–1955)

°*Folk fun for four hands*. Glen Rock, NJ: J.Fischer, 1952.

Buée, A. Quintin

Three sonatas, the third for two performers (Bb). London: printed for the composer, ca.1800. GB:Ob,Cu—US:Wc.

Buesser, Fritz

Suisse et Alsace, trois valses caractéristiques. Paris: pub.missing, ca.1861 GB:Lbl.

Bugbee, L.A.

°*Dance of the Fairy Queen*. Philadelphia: Presser, n.d. (E)

Bülow, Hans von (1830–1894)

German pianist, music editor, conductor; disciple of Liszt and Wagner; also champion of Brahms; wrote symphonic works, songs, and piano pieces.
Humoristische Quadrille über Motive aus Berlioz Cellini. Berlin: Schlesinger, n.d.

Burchett, E.C.

Seven piano duets for beginners. Melbourne: Allans Music, 1951. AU:Samc.

Bürgel, Konstantin (b.1837–)

Variationen über ein eigenes Thema (d), Op.30. Mainz: Schott, 1879. D-brd:MZsch.

Burghardt, Hans-Georg (1909–)

German pianist, musicologist, professor at Martin-Luther University, Jena. He has written piano concertos, sonatas, symphonic and chamber works, an opera, choruses, and keyboard pieces.

•*Sonate,* Op.98 (1963). Leipzig: VEB Peters, 1967. Brilliant, intense, three-movement work in chromatic, neo-Classical idiom. The first movement features fugal development of the thematic material; the tranquil Romantic second movement is an ingenious exercise in bitonality; the work concludes with a bright, scherzo-like finale. Except for a few fortissimo climaxes muddied by thick doublings in the Secondo part, the textures throughout are generally thin and clean. The writing is well balanced for both parts. (I-UI)

Burgmein, J. (pseud. Guilio Ricordi)

Carnaval vénitien, suite mignonne (Florinda; Rosaura; Colombine; Le Seigneur Arlequin). Miland: Ricordi, 1897. US:Bp. Suite in salon style, beautifully printed and illustrated, and elegantly bound. (I)

Burgmüller, Friedrich (1806–1874)

German composer of pedagogical music and light salon pieces.
Easy duets for master and pupil. London: pub. missing, 1863. GB:Lbl.
La fête au couvent, quadrille. Mainz: Schott, n.d. US:NYp.

Burnam, Edna Mae

•*Changing places.* Cincinnati: Willis Music Co., n.d. (E)
•*A dozen piano duets.* Cincinnati: Willis Music Co., 1957. Instructional pieces. (LI)
•*Rounds for reading,* twenty pieces. Cincinnati: Willis Music Co., n.d.

Burney, Charles (1726–1814)

Dr. Burney, the famous English historian, chronicler, and composer, wrote two sets of four duet sonatas, which, as he states in his introduction to the first series, were the first of their kind to be published in England. If interest in these works is more historical than musical, it is because of their inclination toward excessive length and their lack of a well-defined musical character. However, they are nonetheless skilfully written, melodious compositions, competently arranged for the medium, and they contain many passages of charm and beauty. (I)

Four sonatas or duets for two performers on one piano forte or harpsichord (F,D,Bb,C). London: R. Bremner, 1777. B:Bc—F:Pc—GB:Cu,Ckc,Lbl, Ltc—I:Fn—US:CA,NH,PRu,R,Wc,WGw. °Sonata(F) [No.1], ed. Rowley. London: Schott, 1952.

A second set of four sonatas or duets. . . . (Eb,G,D,F). London: R.Bremner [1778]. B:Bc—D-ddr:SWl—GB:Cu,Lbl,Lcm—I:Fn—US:BRp,BU,NH,R, Wc,WGw. *Sonata* (Eb) [No.1]. In collection *Piano duets of the classical period.*

Burney, Charles Rousseau (1747–1819)
Nephew of Dr. Charles Burney.

A duett [Eb] *for two performers.* London: Broderip & Wilkinson, n.d. DK:Kv —US:Wc.

Four sonatas and a duet [Eb] *for two performers.* London: pub. by composer, ca.1795. B:Bs—GB:Lbl.

Two sonatas and a duet [a] *for two performers,* Opera 2. London: pub. by composer, ca.1800. GB:Ckc,Lbl,Lcm.

The two four-hand sonatas (Eb,a) are two-movement works in Classical style. Both are musically weak and often with poorly balanced parts, a condition offset somewhat by their appealing melodies. (UE-LI)

Burns, Felix
°*Flowers in the forest.* Cincinnati: Willis Music Co., n.d. (UE-LI)

Burty, Marc
Gais loisirs, six duos très faciles (Canzonetta; Brimborion; Sérénade en mer; Pas d'armes; Kermesse; Retour du pêcheur). Paris: Consortium Musical (Colombier), 1888. GB:Lbl.

Busch, Adolf (1891–1952)
German-born violinist, composer; took Swiss nationality as protest against Nazism; member of famous musical family; founder of Busch String Quartet; colleague of son-in-law, Rudolf Serkin. His musical style was influenced by Reger.

Thema und Variationen. Ms. CH:Zma.

Busoni, Feruccio (1866–1924)
Prodigious pianist and teacher; influential composer of Italian-German background; cultivated eclectic, polyphonic, anti-Romantic style, blending Italian grace and Teutonic intellectualism; important influence on Hindemith, Toch, Casella, and Malipiero.

°*Finnish folk tunes,* Op.27. NEd. New York: Peters, 1953. Two moderately long settings of Finnish folk songs, skilfully arranged for the medium in the composer's distinctive idiom. (UI)

Büsser, Henri (1872–1973)

French conductor, teacher, organist, and composer of operas, symphonic and chamber music, organ pieces, and piano works.

*Marche de fête. Paris: Durand, n.d.

*Petite suite, divertissement Watteau. Paris: Durand, 1897. (I)

Butler, N.C.

A *duet for two performers*, in which is introduced the favorite air *Sweet passion of love* and the popular dance *The recovery*. London: Skillern, ca. 1820. US:Wc.

Butler, Thomas Hamly (1762–1823)

English musician; studied in Italy with Piccinni; wrote theater music and piano pieces.

Amo amas, a rondo for two performers. London: Longman & Broderip, ca. 1789; Glasgow: J.Aird, ca.1795. US:BE,NYp. Amusing arrangement of the popular song *The Frog and the Mouse*. (I)

Butterley, Nigel (1935–   )

Australian composer; cultivates advanced techniques including serial writing. His choral works often have religious context.

Toccata [No.18], 1955. Ms. AU:Samc.

Buzzi-Peccia, Arturo (1854–1943)

Italian song composer; also wrote an opera, symphonic and chamber music, and piano pieces in light style.

Les rendez-vous, suite galante (Timide; Calant; Amoureux; Joyeux). New York: Schirmer, 1921. US:Wc. Well-written salon pieces. (I)

Voyage de noces, suite intime (En voyage; Enfin seuls!!; Douce intimité; Sur le gazon; Petite réception au château). New York: Schirmer, 1922. US: Wc. Salon pieces. (I)

Byrd, William (1543–1623)

A *battle or no battle*, in *Musica Britannia*, vol.XIX. London: Stainer & Bell, 1963. This delightful curiosity by the distinguished Elizabethan composer is in the form of divisions on a ground. Strictly speaking, it is a three-hand piece, but is included here because of its historical interest as one of the earliest examples of keyboard duets. The Primo has the major responsibility in the work while the Secondo plays only the ground bass line, which in many instances coincides with the bass line of the Primo. (I)

Calderara, —

*Ninna-nanna della bambola. Bologna: F. Bongiovanni, n.d.

Calkin, Jean Baptiste (1827–1905)

English pianist, organist, choirmaster, teacher; composed liturgical works, chamber music, organ pieces, and instructional piano music.

Hommage à Mozart, morceau symphonique. London: pub.missing, 1880. GB:Lbl.

Mélodies gracieuses, six duettinos, Op.11. London: pub.missing, 1854. GB: Lbl.

Les vivandières, marche, Op.41. London: pub.missing, 1866. GB:Lbl.

Calvini, A.

°La chasse aux gazelles, Op.11. Philadelphia: Presser, n.d. (LI)

Camidge, John (1790–1859)

Member of famous family of Yorkshire musicians; his father, grandfather, son, and grandson were organists of York Minster.

Grande march, duett. London: pub.missing, ca.1815. GB:Lbl.

Campbell, Colin Macleod (1890–1953)

British composer and conductor; wrote operas, children's ballet, and piano works.

°Legend. London: Curwen, 1950. US:Wc. Imaginative teaching piece featuring modal melodies and unusual harmonies. (E-LI)

Moon fairies. London: Paxton, 1932. US:Wc. Mood piece; dreamlike and inviting. (LI)

Campbell, Henry (1926–)

American; studied with Burrill Phillips and Bernard Rogers; has written orchestral and chamber music, choral works, and piano pieces.

°First piano duets. Glen Rock, NJ: J.Fischer, 1966. Thirteen short, varied instructional pieces, resourcefully written at the very beginning level. (LE)

Sonata. Ms., ca.1960. Available from composer, Montana State University, Bozeman, MT 59715. Three-movement work in dissonant, Bartókian idiom. (A)

Capanna, Alessandro, OFM (1814–1892)

Le quattro stagioni, il parco lieto in primavera, grand divertimento serale. Turin: F.Blanchi, n.d. I:Bsf.

Caplet, André (1878–1925)

French conductor and composer; friend of Debussy. He wrote orchestral music, sacred works, chamber music, and piano pieces in a refined and sensitive idiom.

Pour les enfants bien sages: un tas de petites choses (Une petite berceuse; Une petite danse slovaque; Une petite barcarolle; Une petite marche bien française; Un petit truc embêtant). Paris: Durand, 1925. This charming suite is both fascinating as duet material and intriguing as a compositional tour-de-force. The Primo part of all the pieces is written entirely within a five white-note span (C–G) in both hands, while the Secondo changes key signatures for each piece. (I-UI/E-5)

Capuis, Matilde

°*Bozzetti* (Sketches) (Variazioni; Canone; Pastorale; Divertimento; Corale; Toccata). Milan: Edizioni Curci, 1969. Short, bright teaching pieces, admirably set for the medium. (UE-LI)

Caracciolo, Eduardo

Fantasia di concerto. Milan: pub.missing, 1872. GB:Lbl.

Carell, Rainer

°*Rhythmische Fantasie,* from *Moderne Rhythmen,* IV. Leipzig/Berlin: Harth Musik Verlag, 1970. Waltz, Foxtrot, and Carioca are three of the forms employed in this cheerful work set in a 1950s jazz idiom. (I-UI)

Carlton, Nicholas (17th century)

°*A verse for two to play on one virginall or organ,* see *Elizabethan Keyboard Duets.*

Carman, Marius

°*Joyeux postillon.* Paris: Lemoine, n.d. (I)
°*Marche des petits marsouins.* Paris: Lemoine, n.d. (UE)

Carmichael, John

Puppet show, suite (Puppet overture; Marionette waltz; Sacha the Hungarian gypsy; Parade of the puppet ponies; Lullaby of the sleeping doll; Finale). London: Augener, 1959. GB:Lbl–US:Wc. Fresh, light, airy, descriptive music in popular style; the writing suggests a transcription. (I)

Carmichael, Mary Grant (1851–1935)

British pianist; composed an operetta, song cycle, and piano pieces.
Five waltzes for two performers. London: pub.missing, 1878. GB:Lbl.

Carr, Benjamin (1768–1831)

English-born music publisher, arranger, and composer; He emigrated to America with his father and brother and established flourishing music stores in Baltimore, Philadelphia, and New York, where they printed music of European as well as American composers. He wrote operas, incidental music, and piano pieces.
Two duetts, Op.3. Baltimore: J. Carr; Philadelphia: Willig; New York: J. Hewitt, ca.1804. US:Wc.
Sonata, duett for two harpsichord [*sic*] (Eb). Ms. US:Wc. In large part this curious, naive little work can be performed quite comfortably on a single keyboard. (LI)

Carre, John F.

Whitecaps. New York: J.Fischer, n.d. US:NYamc.

Carse, Adam (1878–1958)

English teacher and writer on music; wrote orchestral pieces, chamber works, and educational music.

°*A little concert* (36 pieces in two books). London: Augener, 1914. GB: Lbl. (E)

Progressive duets (three volumes). London: Augener, 1913. GB:Lbl. Melodious, carefully scored pieces in traditional idiom. Book 1 (UE-5); Book 2 (LI); Book 3 (I).

°*Tunes for two* (Jumping frog; Two voices; A rustic dance; A step behind; Fair exchange; Waltz; Turn about; Dance; Upstairs and downstairs; Goodnight). London: Augener, 1925. GB:Lbl. Appealing set of pieces in conventional style. (E)

Variations on a theme (a). London: Joseph Williams, 1919. US:Wc. Solid, well-written, organically developed set of variations; interest is sustained throughout. (LI)

Three waltzes. London: Augener, 1912. GB:Lbl. (LI)

Carter, Charles Thomas (1734–1804)

Irish organist and composer of musical comedies, songs, and harpsichord sonatas.

Two favourite duets (C,G) *and a sonata* (F). London: Printed for S.A. & P. Thompson, ca.1780. US:NYp. Short works in thin, Haydnesque style; somewhat lacking in melodic freshness, but having an unsophisticated charm of their own. (LI)

A new invention, for one performer, or two performers on the same harpsichord; La chanson de Mi Lord Malbroug, and some variations. London: pub. by the composer, n.d. GB:Gu,Lbl,Ob.

Caryll, Ivan, pseud. Felix Tilkin (1861–1921)

Belgian-American composer; made his career in England and U.S. as composer of operettas and musical comedies.

°*La valse du prince.* London: Chappell, n.d.

Casarti, Alexandre, arr.

See *Allemande à trois*

Casella, Alfredo (1883–1947)

Italian composer and pianist. His compositions reflect a variety of influences, from Mahler to Debussy, from Romanticism to neo-Classicism and beyond. Many of his works are touched with irony.

Fox-trot (1920). Vienna: UEd, 1922. US:Bp,Wc. An excellent, absorbing study in early jazz; occasionally dissonant. (UI-A)

°*Pagine di guerra,* Op.25 (1915–1918) (Nel Belgio: sfilata di artiglieria pesante tedesca; In Francia: devanti alle rovine della cattedrale de Reims; In Russia: carica di cavalleria cosacca; In Alsazia: croci di legne). London: Chester, 1922. Descriptive musical pictures, transcribed by the composer from his short orchestral pieces, suggested by filmed incidents from World War I; intended to convey in startling musical language the brutality, violence, and horror of modern warfare. (A)

°*Pupazzetti,* cinque musiche per marionette (Marcietta; Berceuse; Serenata; Notturnino; Polka), Op.27. London: Chester, 1921. Masterfully written pieces of great charm and sense of fantasy, cast in moderately dissonant, coloristic, pungent harmonic idiom. Also in version for nine instruments. (UI-A)

Casimiro da Silva, Joaquim (1808–1862)

Portuguese composer of sacred and stage music, and piano works.
Sonata. Ms. Calouste Gulbenkian Foundation, Lisbon, Portugal.

Cassadó, Gaspar (1897–1966)

Spanish cellist and composer; pupil of Casals. His compositions reflect the influence of Ravel and Falla.
°*Hispania.* Paris: Salabert, n.d.

Ceiller (Ceillier), Laurent (1887–1925)

French composer; published collection of Breton songs; also wrote instrumental works.
Pièces pour Anne-Marie; six petites pièces pour de grands enfants (Entrée; Chanson pour danser en ronde; Penser; Intermède; Lied; Scène). Paris: Durand, 1912. US:Bp. Engaging group of pieces; interest and activity in both parts. (I)

Chabrier, Emmanuel (1841–1894)

French composer, pianist, conductor; wrote one opera, orchestral works, and piano compositions. His melodious and carefully fashioned works are direct and alive, and they lean toward lightness and humor.
°*Cortège burlesque* (oeuvre posthume). Paris: Costallat, 1923. Lively, bright, merry work in the style of a vivacious Gallic polka; delightful to play. (I-UI)
°*Souvenirs de Munich,* quadrille sur les principaux motifs de *Tristan et Yseult* de Wagner. Paris: Chabrier, 1911 (Éditions Musicales Transatlantiques). Entertaining, cleverly written, high-spirited quadrilles on themes from Wagner's *Tristan und Isolde* with strong Gallic flavor. Written by a minor composer out of respect and admiration for a major one. Not altogether successful pianistically or always of equal interest for both partners, but amusing nevertheless; cf. Fauré-Messager *Souvenirs de Bayreuth.* (UI)
°*Trois valses romantiques.* Paris: Enoch, n.d.

Chadwick, George W. (1854–1931)

American composer and teacher. Though German-trained, he is considered a pioneer in establishing a distinctively American kind of symphonic composition. His style was conservative, late Romantic, and his works include

operas, choral and orchestral compositions, chamber music, and pieces for piano and organ.
°*Cricket and the bumblebee.* Melville, NY: Belwin-Mills, n.d.

Chagrin, Francis, pseud. Alexander Paucker (1905–1972)

Romanian-born composer, lived in England; studied with Dukas and Boulanger; works include piano concerto, film music, orchestral suites, chamber music, and piano pieces.
Aquarelles (portraits of children). London: Augener, 1951. GB:Lbl. (LI)
°*Six duets.* London: Novello, 1968.

Chaminade, Cécile (1857–1944)

French composer and pianist; student of Godard. She wrote opera, ballet, orchestral suites, and light piano pieces in salon style.
°*Six pièces romantiques* (Primavera; La chaise à porteurs; Idylle arabe; Sérénade d'automne; Danse hindoue; Rigaudon), Op.55. Paris: Enoch, n.d.

Chanaud, J.

Danses savoyards (Le chalet des fonds; Le Lac de Gers; La bourgeoise; Le criou). Paris: pub. by composer, 1913. US:Wc. Light, winsome descriptive pieces, together with dances of the Savoy. (I)

Charles-Henry, —

°*Trois plus trois,* petites pièces faciles pour le piano-jazz (Strut-slow; The just average; Lime tree slow; Invention de blanc; Negro baby; It is claering [sic] up). Paris: Lemoine, n.d. (UE)

Charles-René, —

°*Reflets du nord* (Fête flamande; Paysage, nuit d'hiver; Marche agreste; Le lutin d'Argyll; Fête polonaise). Paris: Lemoine, n.d. (LI-I)
°*Trois valses caprices* (Dans la plaine; Dans les bois; Dans l'espace). Paris: Lemoine, n.d.

Charpentier, Jean Jacques Beauvarlot

See Beauvarlot-Charpentier

Chavagnat, Édouard

°*Les débuts de Fanfan,* récréations faciles (Le carillon; La balançoire; Petit Guignol; La boîte à musique; Petits chevaux de bois; Le régiment qui passe). Paris: Enoch, n.d. (UE-LI)

Chernov, A.

Soviet musician.
Negritanskaia melodia (Negro melody) (UE-LI). In collection *Sbornik Fortepiannikh,* N. Agafonnikov, ed.

Cheslock, Louis (1899–   )

English-born American violinist and composer. He has written operas, orchestral and choral music, and chamber works.

Rhapsody in red and white. Ms. Available from composer, Peabody Conservatory of Music, Baltimore, MD 21202

Chesneau, C.

°*Les Kosaks de l'Ukraine.* Paris: Enoch, n.d.

Choisy, Laure

°*Cinq petites pièces enfantines* (Le petit enfant triste; Berceuse de la poupée; Pierrot à la promenade; [missing]; En passant près de la vieille église). Geneva: Henn, 1918. Compact, attractive set of pieces; expressive, contrasting in style and mood. (UE-LI/E)

Chopin, Frédéric (1810–1849)

°*Variations sur un air national de Moore* (D) (ca.1826), ed. and with reconstruction of lost pages by Jan Ekier. Warsaw: Ars Polonia, 1965. One of the several partially reconstructed pieces of the 4H literature, this recently discovered curiosity is an early work, dating from the composer's sixteenth year. Except for the lost *Variations* (f) and Chopin's own 4H arrangement (Op.15) of his *Grand Duo for Pianoforte and Cello,* this is the composer's only 4H work, and in it he lavishes most of the pianistic interest on the Primo part. It abounds in characteristic Chopinesque scale and arpeggio passage work, while the Secondo is largely confined to accompanying figures. The reconstruction is convincing and the editing scholarly. (I-UI/UI-LA)

Chrétien, Hedwige

Balancelle, petite valse. Paris: Evette & Schaeffer, successeurs au Buffet-Crampon & Cie, 1923. US:Wc. Simple, effective little piece. (LE)
°*Pastels.* Paris: Rouart, 1929.

Christmann, Johann Friedrich (1752–1817)

Recueil de douze marches pour le pianoforte contenant aussi deux à quatre mains, Op.3. Offenbach: André, n.d. D-brd:Mbs,OF.

Chvála, Emanuel (1851–1924)

Czech music critic and composer of songs, chamber music, orchestral works, and piano pieces.
Obrázky z babičky (Pictures from grandmother). Prague: Mojmir Urbánek, 1902. CS:Pchf.
Kirchfesttag. Prague: Urbánek, n.d. CS:Pchf.
Veseloherní pochod (comic march). Prague: Urbánek, n.d. CS:Pchf.
Z jarních dojmu (Impressions of springtime). Prague: Urbánek, n.d. CS:Pchf.

Chwatal, Franz Xaver (1808–1879)

German music teacher and composer of instructional pieces for piano.
Première grande sonate (C), Op.15. Leipzig: Schuberth & Niemeyer, n.d. US:PHf. Well scored; parts carefully distributed, but lacking in musical substance. (I-LA)

Cibulka, Matthäus Aloys (1770–ca.1810)

Allemandes faciles. Leipzig: Kühnel, Bureau de musique, ca.1813. D-brd: MB.

Claasen, Arthur (1859–1920)

German conductor and composer, lived in U.S.; wrote orchestral and choral works, songs, and piano pieces.

Zwei Ländler (f,G), Op.38. Leipzig: Siegel, 1900. US:Wc. Salon pieces. (I)

Clark, Mary Elizabeth

American pianist, educator, and composer.

°*Alpen dance*. Boulder, CO: Myklas Press, 1977. Pleasant teaching piece in ländler style. (E-UE)

°*Three Spanish dances* (Sevillanas; Jota Navarra; Fandango). Boulder, CO: Myklas Press, 1976. Attractive arrangements of Spanish folk melodies. (UE-LI)

Clarke, Hugh Archibald (1839–1927)

Canadian-born American organist and teacher; wrote oratorios, orchestral music, songs, and piano pieces.

Romanza; Sonatina (C). Boston: Oliver Ditson, n.d. US:Wc.

Clarke, Lucia

°*Jazz duet I, II, III*. Boulder, CO: Myklas Press, 1977. Bright, attractive pieces. (LI)

Claussmann, Aloÿs

Alsace, six valses, Op.25. Versailles: Vernède, n.d. GB:Lbl.

Clavers, R.

°*Quatre pièces faciles* (Joyeux carillon; Mélodie; Vieux refrain; La ronde improvisée). Paris: Lemoine, n.d. (UE)

Clementi, Muzio (1752–1832)

Clementi's four-hand works are worthy counterparts of his more familiar piano solo compositions. Classical in idiom, their difficulty ranges from moderately easy to intermediate, and they are rewarding both pianistically and musically. In addition to the three Rondos and seven Sonatas (the latter arranged here in chronological order and with the composer's own opus numbers), Clementi left manuscripts of a number of small four-hand pieces that he called *Duettini*. Originally written for his daughter Cecilia Susanna, these late works are shorter and easier than his major duet compositions. According to Pietro Spada, in the introduction to his edition of *Tre Pezzi*, the *Duettini* were conceived as a series of six works but were never finished as a group. The *Duettino* (C), Tyson WO24, alone exists in complete three-movement form, while only the first and second movements of the *Duettino* (G), Tyson WO25, and unfinished sketches of a third survive, together with assorted pieces that appear to be single movements and fragments of the projected series. Both *Duettini* (C,G) and three of the shorter pieces have been published in modern editions listed below. Tyson catalogue numbers (Alan Tyson, *Thematic catalogue of the works of Muzio Clementi* [Tutzing: Hans Schneider, 1969]) are furnished for supplementary identification. Titles of individual Sonata movements are also given in the following list, along with numberings and order of the Sonatas that differ from Clementi's. Two editions in which such disagreements appear are cited below with abbreviations: OC indicates *Oeuvres complettes de Muzio Clementi* (Leipzig: B&H, 1804–19); and ZG refers to *Muzio Clementi, six sonatas*, ed. Zeitlin and Goldberger (New York: Schirmer, 1960).

Allegro (C), Tyson WO26. US:Wc (as "Duettino 2").

Allegro (Chasse) (C), Tyson WO27. US:Wc (as "chasse Duettino 1, M.C.").

Allegro (C), Tyson WO28. GB:Lbl (Ms.34007, "Duettino sei per pianoforte di M. Clementi").

°NEd. *Tre pezzi* (dai "Duettini") [Tyson WO26,28,27], ed. Pietro Spada. Milan: Bèrben, 1972. (UE-LI)

Duettino No.1 (Allegro [C]; Alla negra: Allegretto moderato [F]; Allegro [C]), Tyson WO24. GB:Lbl–US:Wc.

Duettino No.2 (Allegro vivace [G]; Masurka; Andante con moto [C]; Allegretto vivace [G]), Tyson WO25. GB:Lbl–US:Wc.

°NEd. *Two duettinos*, Tyson WO24,25, ed. Pietro Spada. New York: Schirmer, 1972. (UE-LI)

°NEd. *Tre duettini*, Tyson WO24 only, ed. Franco Margola. Padua: Zanibon, 1969. (UE-LI)

Troix rondeaux agréables (G,C,G), Op.41. Bonn: Simrock, ca.1798. °NEd. *Three rondos*, ed. Townsend. New York: Schirmer, 1967. (LI-I)

Sonata (C), Op.3/1 (Allegro spiritoso; Rondo presto) 1779. OC-IV/4; ZG:4 (Op.16/1).

Sonata (Eb), Op.3/2 (Allegro maestoso; Andante, tempo di menuetto), 1779. OC-IV/5; ZG:5 (Op.16/2).

Sonata (G), Op.3/3 (Allegro; Rondo allegretto), 1779. OC-IV/6; ZG:6 (Op.16/3).

Sonata (C), Op.6 (Allegro assai; Larghetto con moto; Presto), 1780–81. OC-XII/8.

Sonata (C), Op.14/1 (Allegretto; Adagio; Allegro), 1786. OC-IV/1; ZG:1 (Op.14/1).

Sonata (F), Op.14/2 (Allegro; Allegro assai), 1786. OC-IV/2; ZG:2 (Op. 14/2).

Sonata (Bb), Op.14/3 (Allegro; Adagio; Rondo allegro), 1786. OC-IV/3; ZG:3 (Op.14/3).

Editions of Clementi's Four-hand Sonatas:

°*Six sonatas*, ed. Zeitlin and Goldberger. New York: Schirmer, 1960. Complete except for Op.6.

°[4] *Sonatas*, Op.14/3; Op.3/1,2; Op.6 °Kalmus; °Peters.

Sonata (C), Op.14/1. In collection *Piano duets of the classical period*, ed. D. Townsend.

°*Sonata* [G], Op.3/3, Allegro only. In collection *Style and interpretation*, vol.5, ed. H. Ferguson.

°*Sonata* (C), Op.6, Allegro assai only. In collections *Classical album*, G. Schirmer; and *Pianoforte album*, C.F.Peters.

Clough-Leighter
See Leighter

Cobb, Hazel

°*Piano duets*. Chicago: Chart Music, 1959. Short pedagogical pieces; careful and effective writing. (E-UE)

°*Playing together* (Hot cross buns; Waltz for two; Children's march; Fiesta; Temple bells; Heel and toe; Vesper bells; Chinese clown; Peasant dance; Dance for Dmitri; Ancient Irish tune). New York: Harold Flammer, 1962. Delightful set of pieces; well weighted for both parts. (E-LI)

°*Spirit of the U.S.A.* (F). Cincinnati: Willis Music Co., n.d. (UE-LI)

Coenen, Louis (1856–1905)
Dutch pianist and composer; student of Liszt.

Sonata (Eb). Amsterdam: Alsbach, 1902. US:Wc. Large-scale, four-movement work in Wagnerian harmonic idiom; well distributed for both partners, but somewhat dry and academic. (A)

Coerne, Louis Adolphe (1870–1921)
American conductor and composer, trained in Germany. He wrote operas, symphonic pieces, chamber music, and piano compositions in late Romantic style.

Three duets for young pianists (A fairy tale; The music lesson; Under the apple blossoms), Op.153. New York: Schirmer, 1922. US:Bp. (E-UE)

Four-hand recreations (Pussy willows; Little shepherdess; May morning; Pearls; Love's raptures), Op.136. Philadelphia: Presser, 1919. US:Bp,Wc. Instructional pieces. (UE-I/E-5)

Three piano pieces (La gaciosa; Autumn gold; Birthday song), Op.158. Boston: Oliver Ditson, 1921. US:Bp. Light salon pieces. (UE-LI/E)

Concone, Joseph (Giuseppe) (1801–1861)
Italian singing master, pianist, and composer; best known for his solfège exercises and instructional music for piano.

°*1er livre*, quinze études élémentaires, Op.46. °NEd. Paris: Consortium Musical (Gallet), 1923.

°*2ème livre*, quinze études dialoguées, Op.38. °NEd. Consortium Musical, n.d.

Consalvo, Tommaso (late 18th century)
Due sonatines (C,D), per uso della Signorina D. Carolina Hipman. Ms. I:Mc.

Sonatina (C). Ms. I:Mc.

These Sonatinas are short, single-movement pieces in thin Classical style; pedagogical in purpose. (UE)

Conus (Konjus), Georgii Eduardovich (1862–1933)

Russian composer; studied with Arensky and Taneiev. His works include orchestral and chamber music, ballets, and piano compositions written in late Romantic style.

Morceaux (Valse; Nocturne; Sérénade), Op.16. Moscow: Jurgenson, n.d. US:Wc. Easy, flowing, salon pieces. (UE-I)

Trois pièces sur des thèmes populaires slaves, Op.41. Moscow: Jurgenson, 1913. US:Wc. Tasteful arrangements of Russian folk songs. (I)

Converse, Frederick Shepherd (1871–1940)

American composer; studied with Rheinberger. His works include four operas; six symphonies; other orchestral works, including *Flivver ten million* (which celebrates the manufacture of the ten-millionth Ford car); chamber music; and piano pieces. His style ranges from academic Classicism to Romanticism.

Valzer poetici, Op.5. Boston: Miles & Thompson, 1896. US:Wc. Suite of waltzes in Brahmsian style; serious, skilfully constructed, grateful for the medium. (I)

Coolwijk (Coolwyk), Dennis H.

°*Puck* (Petit chanson de Puck; Litanie; Chanson russe et trepak; Arietta; Berceuse; Sérénade; Valse lente; Loure; Petite danse russe; und zum Schluss ein Wiener Walzer). Utrecht: Wagenaar, n.d. Engaging suite of short pieces in conservative idiom with French Impressionistic color. (I)

Corigliano, [Domenico, Marchese] di Rignano

Sinfonia per pianoforte a quattro mani. Naples: G.Gerard, n.d. I:Nc.

Cork, Cyril

Four hands adventuring. London: H. Freeman, 1962. US:Wc. Set in a non-adventurous idiom, these instructional pieces are well constructed and give both parts an equal work-out. (LI)

Corticelli, Gaetano (1804–1840)

[2] *Polonese* (C,A). Ms. I:Bc.

Coulpied-Sevestre, G.

°*Choral à quatre mains.* In collection *Pour mes petits amis, premier livre, courts préludes à deux et quatre mains.* Paris: Consortium Musical, n.d. (UE)

°*Des grosses notes pour quatre petites mains;* six pièces très faciles. Paris: Consortium Musical, n.d. (E)

°*Marche nuptiale.* In collection *Silence, je vais jouer, courts préludes à deux et quatre mains.* Paris: Consortium musical, n.d.

Cramer, Johann Baptist (1771–1858)

Famous German pianist, pedagogue, and composer; student of Clementi.

He combined a career as successful concert pianist with that of composer; best known for his piano studies and other pedagogical compositions.

Grande sonate No.2 (G), Op.33. Leipzig: B&H, 1817. US:Bp.

Sérénade favorite. Brussels: H. Messemaeckers, n.d. US:Wc. Salon piece. (I)

Sonata (Eb), Op.27. Leipzig: B&H, ca.1810. US:Wc.

Cramer's duet sonatas, Opp.27,33, and 88, are large-scale three-movement works in Classical style. Despite their general aridity and lack of any marked stylistic individuality, they are masterfully laid out for both parts and are thoroughly pianistic. (I-UI)

Cramm, Helen J.

Five juvenile dances (Peek-a-boo waltz; Dame Trot's dance; Grandmother's polka; Dutch doll's dance; Promenade, two step). Philadelphia: Presser, 1925. Instructional pieces. (E)

Cras, Jean (1879–1932)

French composer and naval officer. He wrote in a lyrical and expressive style. His compositions range from orchestral and chamber music to choral pieces and piano works.

Âmes d'enfants (Pures; Naïves; Mystérieuses). Paris: Senart, 1922. US:Wc. Three charming, warm, atmospheric tone-pictures about young people but not intended for them to play. The music describes different aspects of the child's soul. Impressive, affecting. (I-LA)

Crèvecoeur, Louis de

Amphitrite errante (Matin sur la mer Égée; Iris danse sur les flots; Le bacchanale passe au loin des îles; Vois, petite mère, les trirèmes), suite brève. Paris: Demets, 1922. US:Wc. Light, pleasant group of pieces on Greek mythological subjects. (LI)

Cristiani, Stefano (1768?–ca.1825)

Born in Italy, resided in New York and Philadelphia.

Sonata (C). Philadelphia: pub. by the composer, ca.1819. US:PHf,Wc. Bright, cheerful, two-movement work in lightweight, often clumsily fashioned, Classical style. (UE-LI)

Croisez, A.

Carnaval de Venise. Paris: Consortium Musical, n.d.

Les chasseurs au rendez-vous. Paris: Consortium Musical, n.d. (UE-LI)

Souvenir des Alpes. Paris: Consortium Musical, n.d. (UE-LI)

Crotch, Dr. William (1775–1847)

English child-prodigy organist and composer; wrote sacred choral music, glees, fugues, and piano pieces.

March and waltz for two performers on the piano forte. Ms., 1833. D-brd:B.

Cui, César Antonovich (1835–1918)

Russian musician of French descent; member of nationalist group of composers known as "The Five." His works include ten operas, orchestral and chamber compositions, and piano pieces.

Ten pieces on five notes, Op.74 (1906). Moscow: State Publishing House, 1929. US:Wc. The short, moderately easy pieces in this volume are imaginative and artful, with unusual harmonies and especially felicitous writing for both parts. (I/E-5)

Scherzo (F), Op.1. St.Petersburg: Bessel & Co., 1857.

Scherzo à la Schumann, Op.2. St.Petersburg: Bessel, 1857.

°*Valse*, see *Paraphrases*.

°[24] *Variations and finale* (with Liadov and Rimsky-Korsakov), see *Paraphrases*.

Cumming, Richard (1928–)

American composer; studied with Ernest Bloch, Schoenberg, and Sessions.

°*Holidays* (Prelude; Sarabande; March; Waltz-Musette; Lullaby). New York: Boosey & Hawkes, 1962. Short, attractive, straightforward pieces, with abundant rhythmic interest and harmonic color; make only the simplest demands on both partners. (UE-LI)

Cundick, Robert (1926–)

Epsom Esq. Sonos Music Resources, n.d. US:NYamc.

°*Prelude and Fugue*. New York: Carl Fischer, 1973. Serious work of moderate length and difficulty in modal, contemporary idiom. Slow introductory Prelude followed by animated Fugue. The texture is open, and the sound is refreshingly new. (I)

Cursch-Bühren, Franz Theodor (1859–1908)

German conductor and editor; wrote symphonic and choral pieces, piano works, and Singspiele, including one entitled *Emol As* [e minor, a flat], a satire on Richard Strauss's *Salome* (spelled backwards).

Bihary Janos, csárdás; Hungarian dance. London: Augener, 1904. US:Wc. Brilliant dance in Hungarian style commemorating the gypsy chief Bihary Janos. (I)

Curwin, Clifford

°*Six French nursery songs* (La boulangère; La mère Michel; Do-do, l'enfant, do-do; Nous n'irons plus au bois; Il était un petit navire; Monsieur de la palisse). London: Chester, 1952. Clever, compact, folk-song settings. (I-UI)

Cury, E.

°*Ecole élémentaire de la mesure*. Paris: Enoch, n.d. No.9 of *Ecole moderne du piano*.

°*Études faciles et mélodiques*. Paris: Enoch, n.d. No.10 of *Ecole moderne du piano*.

Cuscinà, Alfredo (1881–1955)

Italian composer of melodious operettas and light piano pieces.

Carezza di mamma; Laguna d'argento; Sfogliando la margherita; I soldatini; Il valzer del cucù. Milan: Edizioni Curci, 1953. US:Wc. Little, unpretentious instructional works in simple tonal language. (UE)

Czerny, Carl (1791–1857)

One of the most prolific composers of all times, with a total of well over a thousand published works to his credit, Czerny is best known for his contributions to pedagogical literature for piano solo: studies, instructional methods, and the like. Less familiar and only slightly less voluminous was the composer's output of piano duet material consisting of nocturnes, rondos, dances, fantasies, thèmes variés, and études. Unfortunately much of Czerny's music, solo and duet alike, is of mediocre quality, but here and there in this run-of-the-mill assortment of music may be found a number of superior items. These, together with salon pieces and instructional works, are included in the following selected list of the composer's four-hand works.

Allegro affetuoso, Op.137. Leipzig: Peters, 1827. GB:Lcm–US:Bp. Brilliant display piece of moderate length in pedestrian style with thunderous bravura finale. (UI-LA)

Le chiron musical (Vol.1: Dix exercises faciles; Vol.2: Premier sonatine facile; Vol.3: Deuxième sonatine facile), Op.277. Halle: H.Helmuth, n.d. US:Wc (Vol.3 only). Pedagogical work. (I)

Concerto (C) for piano 4H and orchestra, Op.153. Leipzig: Kistner, 1831. GB:Lbl.

[42] *Études progressives et brillantes,* Op.495. Bonn: Simrock; Paris: Costallat, ca.1845. US:PHf. Exercises stressing ensemble and rhythmic problems. (LI-LA)

Grande sonate (f), Op.178. Leipzig: Kistner, 1829. GB:Lbl.

Grand rondeau brillant, Op.254. Vienna: Trentsensky (Cappi), 1832. A: Wgm,Wn.

Grande sonate brillante (c), Op.10. Hamburg: Cranz, 1821. GB:Lcm. Considered the composer's finest 4H sonata. (UI-LA)

Introduction et variations brillantes sur un thème original, Op.106. Paris: Schlesinger, n.d. B:Bc (Ms.).

Introduction et variations faciles sur une valse de Gallenberg, Op.87. Leipzig: Kistner, ca.1825. A:Wst. (LI)

[3] *Leichte Sonatinen* (C,F,–), Op.156. Vienna: Diabelli, 1828. US:Wc. Short instructional sonatas. (I)

Ouverture caractéristique et brillant, Op.54. Leipzig: Kistner, 1824. GB:Lbl.

Praktische Taktschule, 44 leichte Uebungsstücke in fortschreitender Ordnung für Anfänger und vorgerückte Schüler, Op.824. Offenbach: André, n.d. *NEd. Heugel; Schirmer: *Practical method for playing in correct time.*

Presto caratteristico, Op.24. Hamburg: Cranz, n.d. US:Wc. Brilliant salon piece. (I-LA)

Rondeau brillant (B♭), Op.321. Hamburg: Schuberth, n.d. US:NYp. Brilliant, long, rather busy salon piece. (I)

Deuxième rondo brillant, Op.23, Paris: Schlesinger, n.d. GB:Lcm.

Troisième rondo brillant, Op.102. Paris: Schlesinger, 1826. US:Wc. Salon piece; technically demanding. (LI-A)

Sonate militaire brillante (C), Op.119. Hamburg: Cranz, n.d. D-ddr:Bds.

Sonate pastorale (F), Op.121. Hamburg: Cranz, 1826. GB:Lbl–US:Wc. Instructional work. (I)

Sonate sentimentale (G), Op.120. Hamburg: Cranz, n.d. GB:Lbl–US:Wc. (I-LA)

Sonatina (f♯), *à la Scarlatti*, Op.788. Pub. and date missing.

Deux sonatines brillantes (G), Op.50/1. Amsterdam: Theune, n.d. [no record of Op.50/2]. US:Wc. °NEd. Sonatine (G), Op.50/1, ed. D. Townsend. New York: Sam Fox, 1963; °Sonatine, Op.50/1. Ancona: Bèrben, n.d. One of Czerny's most graceful works: succinct, bright, cheerful, ingratiating; well arranged for both parts. (I)

Première sonatine facile, in vol.2 of *Le Chiron musical*.

Deuxième sonatine facile, in vol.3 of *Le Chiron musical*.

Trois sonatines faciles instructives, Op.158. Leipzig: Kistner, 1830. US:Wc. Instructional pieces. (I)

Souvenir à Schönbrunn, seconde grande marche, Op.250. London: Wessel, ca.1835. GB:Lbl.

Uebungsstücke, Op.239. Leipzig: Peters, 1886. US:Wc.

Czerný, Joseph (1785–1842)

Introduzione e Rondo (D), Op.38. Vienna: Cappi, 1824. A:Wgm–CS:PLm.

Sonatine, Op.47. Vienna: Eder, 1825. A:Wgm.

Variations sur un thème favorit de Rovelli. Vienna: Eder, 1826. A:Wgm.

Dacci, Giusto (1840–1915)

Italian teacher, author of theory textbooks. He wrote sacred music, instrumental works, and piano pieces.

Six petits morceaux (Scherzo improvisé; Romance sans paroles; Menuet; Alla marcia; Gavotte; Galopade). Milan: Carisch & Jänichen, 1908. US: Wc. Charming instructional pieces; whimsical; effective. (I)

Dahl, A.

°*Danse hongroise*, Op.26. Paris: Hamelle, n.d.

Dahl, Ingolf (1912–1970)

American composer of German origin. He wrote chamber music and orchestral works in a contrapuntal, freely dissonant idiom.

Four intervals (1969). Unpub., arr. by composer from original version for string quartet.

Rondo (1938). Unpub.

Dalberg, Johann Friedrich Hugo, Freiherr von (1760–1812)
German musical dilettante; pianist, author of treatises on music. He composed cantatas, songs, chamber music, and piano works in late Classical style.

Fantaisie, Op.26. Offenbach: André, 1807. D-brd:OF.

Grande sonate (Eb). Mainz: Schott, 1792. A:Wgm–B:Bc–D-brd:F.

Sonata (for piano 5H), Op.19. Bonn: Simrock, 1803. CS:Bm–D-brd:Bhm–D-ddr:BD,GOl–GB:Lbl–US:Wc.

Sonata (Bb), Op.24. Bonn: Simrock, 1805. CS:Bm–D-brd:Mbs.

Sonata (C), Op.9/3. Offenbach: André, 1794. CH:Bu–US:AA.

Sonata (e). Augsburg: J.C.Gombart, 1793. A:Wgm–B:Bc–CH:EN–D-brd: Mbs, KNmi.

Variations, Op.18. Mainz: Karl Zulehner (Schott), n.d. CS:Bm–D-ddr:HAu.

Dale, Joseph (1750–1821)
London music publisher and organist. He composed keyboard sonatas and arranged vocal airs.

Three favorite duetts (C,G,F), Op.7. London: pub. by the composer, ca. 1785. GB:Lbl,Ob–US:Wc.

A second sett of three favorite duetts (C,G,F), Op.10. London: pub. by the composer, ca.1791. GB:Lbl,Ob–US:Wc. Short, instructional works in thin Classical style. (UE-LI)

Damase, Jean-Michel (1928–)
French pianist and composer of a piano concerto, a ballet, orchestral works, piano pieces, and music for harp.

°Drominiana, trois pièces pour piano à quatre mains. Paris: Editions Musicales Transatlantiques, 1977. Diverting, light, effervescent work in French neo-Classical style with traces of jazz and Poulenc in the harmonic idiom. The slow, stately introduction in French overture manner with iambic dotted notes is followed by a gracefully flowing middle movement with a pastorale quality. The third movement, a brilliant allegro vivo with passage work and changing meters, provides a bravura ending. Excellent recital finale. (I-LA)

Damcke, Berthold (1812–1875)
German cellist and teacher; friend of Berlioz. He revised and edited two of Gluck's operas, and wrote oratorios, songs, and piano pieces.

°Sonatine sur les cinq notes de la gamme (C). Leipzig: B&H, 1876. °NEd. Paris: Hamelle, n.d. US:Wc. Instructional piece. (UE/E-5)

Damiani, F.

A duet for two performers, Op.13. London: pub. by the composer, ca.1800. GB:Lbl.

Dandelot, Georges (1895–1975)
French composer; studied with Widor, Dukas, and Roussel. His works in-

clude operas, orchestral and chamber music, concertos, and piano pieces.

*Six chants populaires bretons. Paris: Senart, n.d.

Danzi, Franz (1763–1826)

German composer of Italian descent; composed Singspiele, comic operas, and orchestral and chamber music. He was a forerunner of Weber and Romanticism, though his roots and musical education lay in the pre-Classic school at Mannheim.

Pièces détachées (F,D,A), Op.11. Munich: Falter, 1802. CH:BEl–D-brd: Mbs–I:PAc–US:CA. Rambling pieces, though nonetheless intriguing for their melodic variety, textural interest, and rhythmic strength. Especially noteworthy is Danzi's skill in manipulating thematic development through imitation and other contrapuntal devices, and there is a foreshadowing of later compositional techniques in his handling of modulation and chromaticism. (I)

Sonate (Bb), Op.9. Leipzig: B&H, 1806. A:Wgm–D-brd:Bhm,Mbs–S:Sm, Uu–YU:ZHa.

Sonata (C), Op.2. Munich: Falter, 1797. A:Wgm,Wst–D-brd:Mbs,MT, Ngm–F:Pc–GB:Lbl–I:PAc–US:Wc,NYp. Serious, three-movement work in Classical idiom featuring broad, expressive melodies, dextrous thematic development, and careful attention to the balance between parts. Startling modulations are not uncommon. The theme and variations of the slow movement are especially captivating. (I)

Sonata (Eb). Paris: Nadermann, n.d. D-brd:MNba.

Darcieux, Francisque

*Carillons; *Chantons. Paris: Consortium Musical, n.d. (LI)

*Dansons; *Dormons. Paris: Consortium Musical, n.d. (UE)

*Les pélerins de St-Odile. Paris: Consortium Musical, n.d. (I)

Dargomyzhski, Aleksandr S. (1813–1869)

Russian composer; pioneer in the nationalist school; associated with "The Five" though not a member himself. He composed operas, orchestra pieces, vocal works, and piano compositions.

Fantaisie sur des airs finois. St.Petersburg: Bessel, 1881.

Tarantelle slave. Moscow: Jurgenson, 1867. US:Bp,NYp,Wc. Tuneful work in which the main performing burden falls on the Primo part. The very easy Secondo consists of two notes throughout and is described in one edition as being written for a performer who "does not even play the piano" (cf. Igor Stravinsky, Three easy pieces). (LE/I-UI)

Davico, Vincenzo (1889–1969)

French composer; studied with Reger. He composed several operas, orchestral and chamber music, and songs.

Tre piccoli pezzi (Barcarola; Serenata; Pastorale). Paris: Rouart, Lerolle, 1925. US:Wc. Atmospheric pieces in Impressionistic style. (UI-LA)

Davies, Evan
°*In hanging gardens.* Cincinnati: Willis, n.d.

Davy, John (1763–1824)
A favorite duett in which is introduced the favorite air of Fal lal la. London: Lavenu, n.d. GB:Bu.

Debussy, Claude (1862–1918)
°*Six épigraphes antiques* (Pour invoquer Pan; Pour un tombeau sans nom; Pour que la nuit soit propice; Pour la danseuse aux crotales; Pour l'Égyptienne; Pour remercier le pluie au matin) (1914). Paris: °Durand, 1915; NEd. °Broekmans & VanPoppel. Subtle, mature works from the composer's final years. Their Impressionistic color and delicacy, evocative of pagan rituals, demand sensitive musicianship and refined interpretive skill. (UI-A)

°*Marche écossaise sur un thème populaire* (The Earl of Ross March) (1891). Paris: Fromont (°Jobert), 1903; °NEd. Leipzig: Peters, n.d. US:NYp,Wc. Commissioned by a Scottish general to commemorate his forbears and originally titled *Marche des anciens comtes de Ross dédiée à leur descendant, le général Meredith Read, Grand-croix de l'Ordre du Rédempteur,* this curiosity is a medley of Scottish airs outfitted with early Debussian harmony and the master's touch. It was later orchestrated by the composer. (I-UI)

°*Petite suite* (En bateau; Cortège; Menuet; Ballet) (1889). Paris: Durand, 1904. NEd. °Broekmans & VanPoppel; °International; °Hug; °Schirmer; °UMP. Issued separately: Menuet, °UMP; En bateau, °UMP. The four pieces in this familiar suite, suavely written in the composer's pre-Impressionistic style, are tuneful and challenging for both parts. (I)

Symphonie (b), ed. Zhilyaev. Moscow: Ogiz (Musgiz), 1933. US:Bp. Duet arrangement of the symphony made from the composer's own autograph. A student work, it was written between 1880 and 1882, during Debussy's sojourn in Russian with Mme. von Meck, and was probably never orchestrated. (A)

Dechelle, Jean
°*Pour endormir la 'tite soeur.* Paris: Consortium Musical, n.d. (UE)

DeCoursey, Ralph
°*The blue pagoda.* New York: Schirmer, 1966. Quiet, contemplative, atmospheric piece in alternating 4/4 and 5/4; pentatonic. (LI)

Dedieu-Peters, —
°*Trois petits préludes.* Paris: Salabert, n.d.

Degen, Helmut (1911–)
German musicologist and teacher. He has written extensively for orchestra, chorus, chamber ensembles, voice, and solo instruments.

Sonata über In Dulci Jubilo. Heidelberg: Müller, 1950. D-brd:DSim.

Delannoy, Marcel (1898–1962)

French composer, formerly painter and architect; mainly self-taught in music. His works include operas, ballets, symphonies, chamber music, and songs.

°*Bourrée*. Paris: Heugel, 1928. See *L'Éventail de Jeanne*. (A)

Delden, Lex van (1919–)

Dutch composer of orchestral and chamber works, operas, children's ballets, and choral music.

°*Bartókiana* (with fifth hand). Op.61. Amsterdam: Donemus, 1958.

Delibes, Léo (1836–1891)

French organist, chorus master at Paris Opéra; composer of ballets *Sylvia* and *Coppélia*, and of the opera *Lakmé*.

Intermezzo. Paris: Heugel, 1892. US:Wc. Salon piece. (I)

Dello Joio, Norman (1913–)

American composer, pianist, and organist; studied with Hindemith and writes in lyrical neo-Classical style; also interested in Catholic liturgical music.

°*Christmas music*. New York: Edward Marks Co., 1968. Attractive, skillfully written set of pieces based on Christmas carols. (I)

°*Family album* (Family meeting; Play time; Story time; Prayer time; Bed time). New York: Edward Marks Co., 1962. (UE)

°*Five images* (Cortège; Promenade; Day dreams; The ballerina; The dancing sergeant). New York: Edward Marks, 1967. (LI-I)

Written for the composer's own children, *Family album* and *Five images* each consist of five charming compositions set in a conservative contemporary harmonic idiom. They are melodious and have considerable interest for both parts.

°*Stage parodies*, piano suite (The actor; The writer; The singer; The dancer). New York: Associated Music Publishers, 1975. Entertaining descriptive pieces in mildly contemporary idiom; unpretentious; effective. (LI-I)

Delmas, Marc (1885–1935)

French composer; works include symphonic poem, operas, chamber music, and piano pieces.

°*Quatre pièces féeriques* (La fée des neiges; Lavandières; Sylphes; Korrigans), Op.258. Paris: Gallet, 1926. (I)

Delsignore, C.

[6] *Croquis* (Schizzi). Mainz: Schott, n.d. GB:Lbl. Tuneful salon pieces. (I)

Del Tredici, David (1937–)

American pianist and composer. He has written pieces for orchestra, for a variety of instrumental combinations, often with amplification, and for piano.

°*Scherzo* (1960). New York: Boosey & Hawkes, 1975. Commissioned by Milton and Peggy Salkind. Brilliant, rhythmically complex, serial work in a single movement with contrasting sections: two glittering, rapid outer sections enclosing a lyrical, middle part. (A)

DeLulli, A.

°*Chopsticks waltz*. Philadelphia: Presser, n.d.

Delvincourt, Claude (1888–1954)

French composer of stage and orchestral works, choral pieces, chamber music, and piano compositions. He wrote in elegant French style in which elements of neo-Classicism, mild dissonance, and Impressionism are used in conventional harmonic idiom.

°*Images pour les contes du temps passé* (Le petit chaperon rouge; Le chat botté; Barbe-bleue; Riquet à la houppe; La belle au bois dormant; Le petit poucet). Paris: Leduc, 1935. Winsome set of evocative, sensitive tone-poems based on fairy tales. (I/UE-LI)

Demar, Johann Sebastian (1763–1832)

Bavarian organist and music publisher.

Grande sonate. Heilbronn: Johann Ammon, n.d. I:Nc.

Demarest, Anne Shannon

°*Bouncing balls*. Boulder, CO: Myklas Press, 1978. (UE-LI)
°*Caprice*. Boulder, CO: Myklas Press, 1978. (UE-LI)
°*Simoon*. Boulder, CO: Myklas Press, 1975. Mood piece with eastern Mediterranean flavor; oriental atmosphere is produced by Phrygian scale patterns and rhythmic ostinati. (UE)

Demarquez, Suzanne (1899–   )

French critic and composer. Her works, often with an ironic touch, include compositions for orchestra, chamber ensemble, and piano.

Barcarolle. Paris: Salabert, 1939, 1941.

°*Twenty little pieces* (supplement No. 1 to *Le petit clavier* by Morhange-Motchane). Paris: Salabert, n.d.

Demharter, Joseph (late 18th century)

Adagio et rondo pour pianoforte à quatre mains concertans avec flûte et violon, Op.4. Augsburg: Gombart, ca.1819. B:Bc. Work of moderate length requiring flute and violin for proper performance; except when playing the concerted sections, the piano functions mainly as an accompaniment. Classical in idiom, the music is thin and lacking in variety. (LI)

Demuth, Norman (1898–1968)

English musician strongly influenced by French composers from Franck to Roussel. His works include operas, ballets, incidental and film music, choral pieces, chamber and orchestral works, and piano compositions.

Sonatina (1954). London: Joseph Williams, 1956. US:Wc. Agreeable, sunny, three-movement work in compact neo-Classical style; parts well balanced for both performers. (UI-A)

Waltz for two: for pupil and teacher. London: Joseph Williams, 1958. (LI/UE)

Denisov, Edison (1929–   )

Soviet composer of avant-garde works with strong influence of Russian folk music; uses serial techniques and electronic resources.

Three pieces (1967). Ms. Commissioned by Milton and Peggy Salkind. Available from composer, Union of Soviet Composers, Moscow, USSR. Short works in advanced style. (A)

De Pablo, Luis (1930–   )

Spanish composer; uses principally serial and aleatory techniques.

Movil II, pour un piano et deux pianistes. Paris: Musique contemporaine, 1968. US:Wc.

Désánfalva, Anne Gyïka de

[6] *Allemandes.* Vienna: Cappi, 183[?]. A:Wst.

Desentis, — (end of 18th century)

Sonate (E♭). Paris: Boyer, n.d. *Journal de pièces de clavecin,* 4ème année, No.40. F:Pn. Amiable, two-movement work in late Classical style; well-balanced parts compensate somewhat for general harmonic and melodic superficiality. (I)

Desormery, Jean-Baptiste-Léopold-Bastien (b.1772)

French pianist and composer of piano pieces.

Sonate (G), Op.2. Ms. F:Pc. Large-scale, three-movement, loosely constructed work in Classical idiom. Strong melodies and unusual harmonic and melodic features are diminished by monotonous motivic repetition and arid development sections. (I)

Diabelli, Anton (1781–1858)

The four-hand production of this publisher and minor composer, who furnished the theme for Beethoven's famous piano variations, is good solid music in the Classical, didactic tradition. The fact that these duets are currently available in many editions is witness to their usefulness and durability as teaching material. Most of them offer few technical or interpretive problems beyond the intermediate level.

°[28] *Melodious pieces in progressive order for pupil and teacher* (*Melodische Uebungsstücke*), Op.149. (UE-LI/LE-UE-5). NEd. °Artia; °VEB B&H; °Carisch; °Consortium Musical; °Durand; °Carl Fischer; °Heugel; °Kalmus; °Lemoine; °Peters; °PWM; °Ricordi; °Schirmer; °UEd.

Military rondo (D), Op.152. Vienna: Diabelli, n.d. NEd. °Kalmus. (I)

Pleasures of youth (*Jugendfreuden*), six sonatinas (C,G,F,D,A,F) for pupil and teacher, Op.163. Vienna: Diabelli, 183[?]. (LI/UE-5) NEd. °Artia; °VEB B&H; °Carisch; °Consortium Musical; °Durand; °Heugel; °Kalmus; °Lemoine; °PWM; °Ricordi; °Schirmer; °UEd.

Deux sonates (*Sonatines*) (C,G), Op.24. (LI)

Sonata (Sonatina) (F), Op.32. (LI)
Sonata (Sonatina) (D), Op.33. (LI)
Sonata (Sonatina) (C), Op.37. (LI)
Sonata (Bb), Op.38. (LI-I)
Sonata (Sonatina) (C), Op.54. (LI)
Sonata (Sonatina) (a), Op.58. (LI)
Sonata (Sonatina) (F), Op.60. (LI)
Sonata (F), Op.73. (LI-I)
Deux sonates mignonnes (Sonatines) (C,G), Op.150; also listed with *Military rondo* (Op.152), as *Trois sonates amiables*, Op.152. Vienna: Diabelli, n.d. US:Wc.
Sonate (G), Sehnsucht nach dem Frühling, Op.156. Vienna: Diabelli, 1834. US:NYp,Wc. (I)
Sonate (C) ("Résolution"), Op.158. Vienna: Diabelli, 1834. US:Wc. (I)
[7] *Sonatinen* (F,G,C,Bb,D,G,a), Op.168. Leipzig: B&H, n.d.
Tanzlust der Jugend, Walzer, Op.164. Hamburg: Cranz, n.d. (I/E-5)
Sonata Collections:
°*Five sonatinas*, Opp.24, 54, 58, 60. °VEB B&H; °Durand; °Lemoine; °Consortium Musical; °Heugel; °Kalmus; °Peters; °Presser; °Ricordi; °Schirmer.
°*Three sonatas*, Opp.32, 33, 37. °Kalmus; °Lemoine; °Omega; °Peters.
°*Two sonatas,* Opp.38, 73. °Kalmus; °Peters; °Ricordi.
°*Five sonatas*, Opp.32, 33, 37, 38, 73. °Heugel; °Ricordi.
°*Deux sonatines mignonnes* (C,G), Op.150; *Rondo militaire*, Op.152. °VEB B&H; °Lemoine; °Peters.

Dichler, Josef (1912–)

Austrian pianist and pedagogue; has written textbooks, articles on piano performance, and piano pieces.
°*Drei Kinderszenen* (Praeludium; Berceuse; Bolero) (1950). Vienna: Doblinger, 1956. Instructional pieces cast in contemporary harmonic idiom, which cleverly incorporates scale patterns and other technical devices into the fabric of the music in a delightfully whimsical and unobtrusive way. (I)

Dickinson, Peter (1934–)

English composer and organist; studied at Cambridge and Juilliard.
°*Five forgeries*. London: Novello, 1964. Warm-hearted, humorous, well-written satires imitating the styles of Poulenc, Hindemith, Delius, Stravinsky, and Bartók. (I)

Diény, Amy

°*Chanson et contes*, [40] pièces faciles et progressives. Paris: Consortium Musical, n.d. (I/E)

Diercks, John (1927–)

American pianist and composer. He writes in a lyrical, rhythmically active, frequently dissonant, tonal idiom.

°*The bee caresses the flower as the elephant destroys the stable* (1956). Hamilton, OH: C.A.P., n.d. Pentatonic work with oriental color; requires plucking and strumming of strings inside partially prepared piano. (LI-I)

°*Two Israeli dances* (1959). Ms. available through composer, Hollins College, VA 24020. Bright, vigorous dances with strong rhythmic drive and Middle Eastern flavor. (UE-LI)

°*Moon spell* (1959). Ms. available through composer, Hollins College, VA 24020. Impressionistic mood piece; haunting, atmospheric. (LI-I)

°*Suite No.1* (March; Dance; Song; Finale). New York: MCA Music,1972. Attractive set of pieces, bright and playful in character; exceptionally effective for the amount of technique required for performance; thin textures with contemporary sounds; light dissonance. Well worth investigating. (UE-LI)

°*Toccata* (1959). Ms. available through composer, Hollins College, VA 24020. Forceful, brilliant, exciting work featuring ostinati; open-textured; bustling rhythms. (I-UI)

Dietrich, Albert Hermann (1829–1908)

German composer; friend of Schumann and Brahms. His opera, *Robin Hood*, and his orchestral, chamber, choral, and piano works reflect his close association with the two masters.

Sonate (G), Op.19. Leipzig: Rieter-Biedermann, 1870. US:Wc. Tasteful, competent work in Romantic style. (UI-LA)

Dietrich, Karl (1927–)

German composer.

°*Variationen über ein Thema aus der Sonate für Violoncello und Klavier Op.119 von Sergej Prokofjew*. Berlin (DDR): Verlag Neue Musik, 1973. Cast in dissonant tonal idiom, these effective variations display a variety of moods and instrumental color through the use of string plucking, tone clusters, and strong rhythmic activity. (A)

Dietrichstein, Count Moritz von (1775–1864)

Viennese court conductor, self-educated in music; composer of part-songs, hymns, and piano pieces, including many German dances, a form he especially cultivated in his four-hand works.

[12] *Deutsche Tänze und zwölf Trios* (C,G,D,Bb,F,A,D,G,C,Eb,G,C). Vienna: Mechetti, 1819. A:Wst–D-ddr:Dlb.

[12] *Deutsche Tänze und zwölf Trios* (D,G,D,A,C,F,Bb,Eb,G,C,A,D). Vienna: S.A. Steiner, n.d. D-ddr:Dlb.

[12] *Deutsche Tänze und zwölf Trios* (Eb,G,D,Bb,F,A,D,G,C,F,Bb,Eb). Vienna: Mechetti, 1819. D-ddr:Dlb.

Dijk, Jan van (1918–)

Dutch composer, student of Pijper. His individual style shows contemporary French influences.

°*Ordre*. Amsterdam: Donemus, 1953.

*Trois pastorales. Amsterdam: Donemus, 1969.

*Sonatina (1956). Amsterdam: Donemus, 1957. Short, playful two-movement work in dissonant style; thin textured for the most part with a few rhythmic complexities. (I)

Dittenhaver, Sarah Louise (1901–)

American composer of piano music for the young.

*The children's parade (G). Cincinnati: Willis Music Co., 1950. Jolly brisk tune with activity in both parts; effective. (UE)

*Let's play duets (Up the winding stairs; Frère Jacques; Billy hurt his knee; Gay dancers; In seven-league boots; Lullaby; Off to the circus; On the mountain; Rain at night; Sailing out to sea; Smooth flying). Bryn Mawr: Oliver Ditson, 1947. Short, instructional pieces in traditional style; noteworthy for imaginative writing and flashes of descriptive color. (E-UE)

Dobrowolski, Andzej (1921–)

Children's suite (1955). Warsaw: Ars Polonia, 1957.

Dobrzynski, I.F. (1807–1867)

Polish pianist and conductor; composed orchestral and chamber works, and piano pieces.

Rondo alla polacca, Op.6. Leipzig: Hofmeister, n.d. DK:Kk.

Dodgson, Stephen (1924–)

English composer; works include symphonic and chamber music.

*Gavotte. London: Curwen, 1954. US:Wc. Short piece in traditional style. (LI)

*Hill-Billy. London: Curwen, 1953. US:Wc. Rollicking instructional piece. (I)

Dohnányi, Ernő (Ernst) von (1877–1960)

Hungarian pianist and composer of operas, symphonic and chamber music, and many piano works. His musical style is related to Brahms and German Romanticism rather than to the nationalist movement of Bartók and Kodály.

*Walzer, Op.3. Vienna: Doblinger, 1906. *NEd. London: Arcadia Music Pub.Co. US:NYp,Wc. Suite of lilting concert waltzes in Viennese style; vigorous, tuneful, idiomatically scored; urbane. (I)

Doige, Catharine

*Seven up (Platform rocker; Caribbean caper; Aaron aardvark; Bells; Parallel bars; Mad cap polka; I'm a cat). Westbury, NY: Pro-Art, 1965, Series of instructional pieces in popular jazz idiom. (LI-I/E-UE)

Donaldson, Molly

*Piano partners (the young pianist or adult beginner with the advanced pianist). Bryn Mawr: Presser, 1951. US:Wc.

Donatoni, Franco (1927–)

Italian teacher and composer; studied with Pizzetti. He has written ballet, symphonic, chamber, and piano music; and evolved his own advanced style influenced by Bartók, Schoenberg, and Cage.

Duetto per clavicembalo (1975). Pub. and date missing.

Donizetti, Gaetano (1797–1848)

°*Tre Pezzi* (Marcia lugubre; Polacca; Larghetto), ed. Carlo Pestalozza. Milan: Ricordi, 1971. Delightful pieces by the famous opera composer, dating from his student days. They reveal an astonishingly sensitive musical talent and imagination. (UE-LI)

°[4] *Sonate*, ed. Douglas Townsend. Toronto: E.C.Kerby, Ltd., 1974. The four one-movement works in this fascinating collection also date from the composer's student days (1816–1821). Carefully edited, and bound in a handsome edition, these charming sonatas are full of fresh, youthful sparkle and melodic grace, and they are rewarding to play. (LI-I)

Donovan, Richard (1891–1970)

American organist, teacher, and conductor; wrote in freely dissonant harmonic idiom.

Fantasy on American folk ballads, for male chorus, 4H, and orchestra. Glen Rock, NJ: J. Fischer, 1940.

Doppler, Károly (1825–1900)

Hungarian flutist, conductor, and composer. He wrote opera, songs, flute pieces, and piano music.

Csardas (C). In *Album for Piano Duet*, ed. Vácsi. Short, bright work with lively Hungarian flavor. (UE-LI)

Dorn, Heinrich Ludwig Egmont (1804–1892)

German conductor and opera composer; also wrote cantatas, symphonies, and piano pieces.

Thema und Variationen (A), Erinnerung an der Königin Weinberg, Op.97. Berlin: Bote & Bock, 1865. US:Wc. There are many charming and imaginative moments in this otherwise predictable set of variations cast in Romantic style. (I)

Dörumsgaard, Arne (1921–)

Norwegian composer of piano pieces and songs in tightly constructed, moderately contemporary idiom.

Det syng um land (Song of the land). Oslo: Musikk-Huset, 1944. N:Onk. Simple, direct, appealing settings of eight Norwegian folk songs. (UE-LI)

Douglas, Martin

°*Dan the piccolo man*. New York: Belwin, 1946. Instructional piece. (E)

Draeske, Felix (1835–1913)

German composer of piano works, operas, chamber music, and orchestral compositions.

[6] *Kanonische Räthsel*, Op.42. Leipzig: Kistner, 1888. US:Wc. Puzzle

canons, ably set for 4H; should provide entertainment and satisfaction to students who enjoy riddles. (I)

[18] *Kanons zu sechs, sieben, und acht Stimmen,* Op.37. Leipzig: Kistner, 1882. US:Wc. Less successful than Op.42, these canons are admirable as contrapuntal tours-de-force, but they are musically unexciting and not especially grateful for the 4H medium. (LI-I)

Dring, Madeleine (1923–   )

°*Four duets* (May morning; Little waltz; The evening star; Morris dance). London: Joseph Weinberger, 1964. Melodious pieces equally weighted for both players. (UE-LI)

°*Three for two* (Country dance; The quiet pool; Hobby horse). London: Joseph Weinberger, 1970. Tuneful, pleasant teaching pieces. (UE)

Drischner, Max

Sonnen-Hymnus: passacaglia (E). Tübingen: C.L. Schultheiss, 1955. US: Wc. Long, Baroque-style work. (I)

Drozdov, Anatolii Nikolaevich (1883–1956)

Soviet pianist, teacher, musicologist, and conductor.

°*Three pieces on folk themes* (Estonian waltz; Polka; Lingering) (1949). Moscow, Leningrad: State Music Publishers, 1951. Attractive, well-balanced settings of folk songs. (LI)

Dubois, Théodore (1837–1924)

French organist, teacher, and composer; director of Paris Conservatoire. His music is written in conservative Romantic idiom.

Dix esquisses. Paris: Heugel, 1912. US:Wc. Short pieces in flowing, agreeable style. (LI)

Duboscq, Claude

Pour jouer avec la bien-aimée, trois ressouvenirs. Paris: Demets, 1922. US: Wc. Well-written and effective suite; demands interpretive sophistica-tion. (I)

Ducasse, Roger

See Roger-Ducasse

Duke, Henry

°*Flight of swallows,* seven easy sketches (Flight of swallows; Gliding; Country ramble; Horses and hounds; Swans on the lake; Making hay; Tramping). London: Forsyth, 1966. Amiable set of short, attractive teach-ing pieces. (UE)

°*Tuneful tunes for two,* [12] easy duets for young pianists. London: Forsyth, 1962. (E-UE)

Dunayevskii, Isaak (1900–1955)

Soviet composer of operettas, ballets, film music, mass-songs, chamber music, and piano music. His style is lyrical and popular, conforming to the conserva-tive compositional principles of the Stalinist era.

Galop (I). In collection *Sbornik fortepiannikh*, ed. N.Agafonnikov.

Duncombe, William

English musician.

The favorite air of God Save the King with variations. Kensington: pub. by composer, ca.1790. GB:Gu,Lbl,Ob.

Dungan, Olive (1903–   )

Dance of the fleas. Bryn Mawr: Oliver Ditson, n.d. (UE)

Dancing on skates. Bryn Mawr: Oliver Ditson, 1955. Lilting waltz in attractive instructional style. (UE)

Hop-toads. New York: Schroeder & Gunther, 1966. Gay little teaching piece. (E)

Red-nosed clown. Bryn Mawr: Oliver Ditson, n.d. Well-balanced piece in traditional idiom. (UE)

Seminole campfire. Bryn Mawr: Oliver Ditson, 1952. Teaching piece with Indian flavor. (E)

Dunhill, Thomas Frederick (1877–1946)

English composer of operettas, ballets, cantatas, and piano pieces in conservative Classical idiom.

Four-hand fancies. London: Curwen, n.d. (I)

Side by side series, Book III (Trumpet and drum; A pastoral dance; The bambino dances; Faun's dance). London: Ashdown, n.d. (LI)

Dupin, Paul (1865–1949)

Prolific French composer of great originality; largely self-taught; composed effectively in a variety of styles.

Le beau jardin (La pelouse aux maronniers; La pièce d'eau aux petits poissons rouges; Aubade au poulailler; D'où l'on voit la vieille église) (1911). Paris: Durand, 1912. US:Wc. Suite of light, descriptive pieces in pleasant style. (I)

L'offrande à la danse; danse de caractère (1913). Paris: Durand, 1921. US: Wc. Curiously attractive work featuring frequent changes of tempo and textures, spasmodic fragmentary melodies, and wavering tonal centers. (I-UI)

DuPlessis, Hubert (1922–   )

South African musician; studied at Royal Academy of Music, London. He composes in a highly concentrated tonal idiom, which is linear, often dissonant, but refined and controlled.

Prelude, fugue and postlude, Op.17. London: Novello, 1958.

Sonata, Op.10 (1951). London: Novello, 1954. Large-scale work in three contrasting movements: Dissonant, contrapuntal, featuring tritone. Concludes with brilliant passacaglia and fugue. (A)

Durey, Louis (1888–1979)

French composer, strongly influenced by Satie, and one-time member of "les Six." After World War II he became a *progressist*, writing music of mass appeal in accordance with Communist "progressive art." His works include chamber music, songs, opera, and piano pieces.

Deux pièces (Carillons [1916]; Neige [1918]), Op.7. Paris: La Sirène (Salabert), 1921. US:Wc. Subtle, descriptive, coloristic pieces tending toward Debussian Impressionism; require advanced pianism. (A)

Dusautoy, J.

°*Tarantelle*, Op.15. Paris: Hamelle, n.d.

Dušek (Duschek), František (Franz) Xaver (1731–1799)

Dušek (Duschek in German orthography) is often confused with his compatriot Johann Ladislaus Dussek (Dusík in Czech), who was thirty years his junior. Dušek's four-hand works are appealingly written in a fluent, melodious, Classical idiom, and are well balanced technically and musically for each partner. He was a friend of Mozart and his compositions show many similarities to the latter's style. The following works are numbered chronologically according to the catalogue of the composer's works included in Václav Jan Sykora, *František Xaver Dušek, život a dílo* (František Xaver Dušek, Life and Works) (Prague: Statní Nakladatelství Krásné Literatury, Hudby a Umení, 1958).

Andantino con variazioni (C), Sýkora 23. Pub. and date missing. CS:Pk (contemporary copy).

Menuetto (C), Sýkora 24. Pub. and date missing.

II Sonates (C,Eb) *pour le fortepiano ou clavecin*, Sýkora 24, 26. Vienna: Hoffmeister, ca.1788. A:Sca,Wn—CS:K.Pnm—D-brd:Es—D-ddr;Dlb—US: NYp. (LI-I)

Sonata (G), Sýkora 27. [Vienna]: pub. by the composer, ca.1792. B:Bc— CS:Pnm. °NEd. Third movement (Allegretto scherzando) only in *Album of four-hand compositions of old Czech masters*, eds. Kleinová, Fišerová, and Müllerová.

Sonata (C), Sýkora 28. Pub. and date missing. Contemporary copy, property of Dr. Ant. Němec. CS:Pchf.

Sonata (C), Sýkora 29. Pub. and date missing. Contemporary copy, property of Dr. Ant. Němec. CS:Pchf.

Divertimento (G), Sýkora 30. Pub. and date missing. Contemporary copy, property of Dr. Ant. Němec. CS:Pchf.

Andante con variazioni (Eb), Sýkora 31. Pub. and date missing. Contemporary copy, property of Dr. Ant. Němec. CS:Pchf.

Dussek (Dusík), Johann Ladislaus (1760–1812)

Dussek (Dusík in modern Czech spelling) was Czech by birth, a background he shared not only with Viennese composers Leopold Koželuh and Jan Vaňhal but also with Frántišek Dušek (Duschek), whose name is confusingly similar, especially in older spellings. A contemporary of Mozart, Haydn, and

Beethoven, Dussek anticipated many of the trends and characteristics of the Romantic era. His four-hand sonatas, like his other piano works, are full of inventive writing, featuring striking harmonic relationships, remote modulations, and fanciful dissonances, together with a colorful, often ornate, melodic style that foreshadows the innovations of Chopin and Schumann.

Most of Dussek's four-hand compositions are contained in Vols. IV, VII, and IX of the twelve-volume collection, *Oeuvres de J. L. Dussek*, Leipzig: B&H, 1813–37, available at the following library locations: A:Wn—B:Bc—CS:Pu—DK:A—D-brd:Mbs—D-ddr:SWl. Locations of individual works in both the *Oeuvres de J.L. Dussek* (DuCE) and its reprint (New York: DaCapo Press, n.d.) are indicated by volume numbers as, for example: DuCE VII/DaCapo IV.

The following list of Dussek's 4H works gives bibliographical information for a single edition (often the first) of each composition, together with its library location; other editions of the work are not identified individually but are grouped together along with their library locations. Complete details on all editions of Dussek's 4H works may be found in RISM:A/I and B/I, and in Howard Allen Craw, "A Biography and Thematic Catalog of the Works of J.L. Dussek (1760–1812)," diss., University of Southern California, 1964. In addition to supplying full bibliographical data on the composer's duets, the latter work also provides a catalogue number (Craw) for each work in the list, which is chronologically arranged.

Sonata (Grand Overture) (C), Op.32 (Craw 144). [London & Edinburgh]: Corri, Dussek & Co., ca.1796. DuCE VII/DaCapo IV. GB:Cu,Lbl,Lcm, Ob—US:Bp,Wc. In other editions as *Duo* or *Grand duo*: B:Bc—CH: Bchristen—CS:Bm—D-brd:Bhm,LB,LÜh,Mbs,W—D-ddr:Bds,SWl—F:Pn—GB:Cu,Lbl,Lcm,Ob—I:Tci—S:L,Skma—US:Bp,NH,SFp,Wc—USSR:Lsc, Ml.

Sonata (Duo) (C), Op.48 (Craw 186). [Paris]: Érard, ca.1801. DuCE VII/DaCapo IV. CH:SO—D-ddr:Bds—US:Wc. In other editions: B:Bc—CS: Bm,Bu,BRnm—D-brd:Bhm,BNba,LÜh,Mbs,W—D-ddr:LEm,WRtl—EIR: Dn—GB:Lbl—S:L,Skma,Sm—US:CA,NH,NYp,PHf—USSR:Ml.

Waltz (G) (Craw 191). Altona: L. Rudolphus, ca.1804. D-brd:LÜh—DK: Kk—S:Skma. In other editions: US:Wc.

°*Sonate posthume* (C) (Craw 207). "A New Sonata for two performers. . . . Last Year Expressly Composed in Berlin for Pio Cianchettini of London seven years old, Who in his recent Tour of the continent was Honoured by the first Professors & Conoisseurs with the Surname of Mozart Britannicus, By his Uncle." London: Cianchettini & Sperati, 1806. B:Bc—EIR:Dn—GB: Lbl. °NEd. ed. J. Ligtelijn. Amsterdam: Heuwekemeijer, 1957.

Trois fugues à la camera (D,g,F), Op.64 (Craw 227,228,229). Leipzig: B&H, 1808. DuCE IX/DaCapo V. A:Wgm—B:Bc—CH:Zz—CS:Bm—D-brd:BHm,LÜh,Mbs—D-ddr:BD—GB:Ckc—S:Skma—US:NYp—USSR:Ml.

°*Sonatas for one piano four hands* (C,F,Bb), Op.67 (Craw 230,231,232). As *Trois sonates progressives*, Op.67. Paris: Pleyel, 1809. °NEd. Zeitlin and Goldberger, eds. Philadelphia: Elkan Vogel, 1961. US:Wc.

Grande sonate (Eb), Op.72 (Craw 239). Leipzig: B&H, 1810,1815. DuCE IX/DaCapo V. A:Wgm—CS:Bm—D-brd:LÜh—GB:Lbl—S:Skma—US:Wc.

Grande sonate (Bb), Op.74 (Craw 234). Leipzig: B&H, 1811;1814;1823. °NEd. Zanibon, 1978. DuCE VII/DaCapo IV. CS:Bm,Bu—D-brd:Bhm, BNba,LÜh,Mbs,W—I:Nc—S:Skma—US:NH. Other editions: D-brd:LB, LÜh—S:Skma—US:Wc. This work is an arrangement of *Trois duos concertantes pour la harpe et le piano forte*, Op.69/II.

Grande sonate (F), Op.73 (Craw 243). Leipzig: B&H, 1813. CS:Bm,BRnm —DK:A—S:Skma. This work is an arrangement of *Trois duos concertantes pour la harpe et le piano forte piano*, Op.69/III.

Duvernoy, Jean-Baptiste (1802–1880)

French composer of instructional piano music and studies.

°*L'Émulation*, vingt petites pièces, Op.314. Milan: Ricordi, n.d.

Petit dialogue, Op.106. Leipzig: B&H, n.d. US:Wc. Instructional piece based on a French folk song. (LI)

Dvořák, Antonín (1841–1904)

Dvořák, like Schubert, had a special relationship with the piano duet: both composers seemed more at ease writing for four hands than for piano solo. Perhaps it was because they found the latter too restrictive in range and sonority to express their large-scale orchestral concepts. Whatever the reason, they put some of their best efforts into composing duets. Dvořák's output of four-hand music, while not as voluminous as Schubert's, is nonetheless remarkable for its consistently high quality. The *Slavonic Dances* are some of the finest works in the entire repertoire.

From the Bohemian forests (*Ze Šumavy*), Op.68 (1884). °NEd. Prague: Artia, 1955. Commissioned by the composer's publisher, Simrock, in Berlin as a sequel to the successful *Legends*, Op.59, and the first set of *Slavonic Dances*, Op.46, these six descriptive character pieces of Bohemian country life are impeccably scored and filled with the some ingenuity of melody and rhythm as Dvořák's other 4H works. If they are somewhat uneven in inspiration, they are all varied in mood and character, and, like their predecessors, reflect the composer's close identification with Czech folk song. 1. The spinning room: lively, active. 2. Walpurgisnacht: vivid, bustling portrait of a traditional folk carnival. 3. In wait: dramatic. 4. By the dark lake, and 5. Silent woods; the two gems of the suite; poetic, lyrical, sensitive tone paintings. 6. From troubled times: wild, almost orchestral. (UI-LA)

Legends, Op.59 (1881). °NEd. Prague: Artia, ca.1955; °Simrock. Less familiar, but similar in inspiration and character to the *Slavonic Dances*, the *Legends* are exquisitely set for the medium. Because they are somewhat easier to play they make an admirable introduction to Dvořák's 4H works, offering the same variety of color, texture, and endless melodic freshness that characterizes all of Dvořák's music. The first three pieces, 1. Allegretto non troppo (d), 2. Molto moderato (G), and 3. Allegro giusto (g) are bright and cheerful, close to the *Slavonic Dances* in style. 4. Molto maestoso (C) is more sober, its marchlike sections alternating with quiet, rapid, scale passages; and 5. Allegro giusto (Ab) ends the first book in a serious vein. 6. Allegro con moto (c♯) opens the second book with broad, spacious lines. 7. is a lovely Allegretto grazioso (A); 8. Un poco allegretto e grazioso quasi Andantino (F), a gentle pastorale. The work concludes with two quiet, dancelike movements full of the spirit of Czech folk song, 9. Andante con moto (D) and 10. Andante (bb). (I-UI)

Three men's choruses, Op.43, for male voices and piano four hands (1877–78). °NEd. Prague: Artia, n.d.

Slavonic dances, Op.46 (1878), Op.72 (1886). Both sets are available in the following editions: °Artia, °VEB B&H, °Hamelle, °International, °Schirmer, °Schott, °Simrock. Masterfully written in their original 4H form, though perhaps better known in orchestral transcription, these melodious, rhythmical works range in mood from dreamlike simplicity to fiery brilliance and are enjoyable—often exhilarating—to play. Op.46, 1. Presto (C): bustling furiant tempo; 2. Allegretto scherzando (e): amiable melody alternating with faster sections; 3. Allegretto scherzando (D): simple, direct, flowing; 4. Tempo di Menuetto (F): graceful, deliberate, restrained; 5. Allegro vivace (A): rhythmical; impetuous; 6. Poco allegro (Ab): moderately paced polka; 7. Allegro assai (c): bright folk melody with rapid figurations; 8. Presto (g): sparkling, driving furiant. Op.72, 1. Molto vivace (B): brilliant, with slower middle section; 2. Allegretto grazioso (e): full of longing and sadness, most familiar in arrangements; 3. Allegro (F): fast, bumptious, interesting chromatic middle section; 4. Allegretto grazioso (Db): unusual harmonies, almost Impressionistic, moves with quiet grace; 5. Poco adagio (bb); bold, swaggering slow section followed by vivace, scintillating ending; 6. Moderato, quasi Menuetto (Bb): tranquil; 7. Presto (C): fiery, brilliant; 8. Lento grazioso, quasi tempo di valse (Ab): quiet, subdued. (UI-A)

The following works were not originally written for piano duet but were published in effective and appealing 4H versions, possibly arranged by the composer:

Polonaise (Eb) (1879). °NEd. Peters, n.d. Originally scored for orchestra. Only the 4H version of this sparkling, difficult work remains. (UI-A)

Écossaises (Schottische Tänze), Op.41 (1879). In collection *Piano duets of the masters.* Short, charming, melodious, evocative pieces in Czech idiom, modeled after Beethoven's works of the same name. (LI)

Silhouettes, Op.8 (1880). 12 pieces of varying length similar in character to

Op.41. (I)
Further Editions of Dvořák's Four-Hand Works:

°Antonín Dvořák: *Kritische Gesamtausgabe*, ed. Otakar Šourek. Prague: Artia, 1956– . Complete 4H works.

°*Selected pieces: Legends*, Op.59/4,5,8,10; *From the Bohemian forests*, Op. 68/5, 6; *Slavonic dances*, Op.46/1,2,8; Op.72/2,4,8. Peters.

°*Slavonic dance*, Op.72/2. Ancona: Bèrben, n.d.

Dvorkin, Judith (1930–)

°*Two pairs of shoes*. Bryn Mawr: Presser, n.d. (E)

Eberl, Anton (1765–1807)

Popular Austrian musician, friend of Gluck and Mozart; brilliant concert pianist and composer. His works are written in late Classical style with some pre-Romantic traits.

Caprice et rondo (C), Op.42. Vienna: Bureau des Arts et d'Industrie, 1804. A:Wn–CH:E–CS:Bm. Long, repetitious work with modest structural and melodic interest; marred by weak development of thematic materials. (I)

Polonaise (Bb), Op.19. Vienna: Bureau des Arts et d'Industrie, ca.1801. A:Wgm,Wn–CH:BEl–CS:Bm–D-ddr:LEm. Other editions in US:Bp, Wc.

Polonaise (D), Op.24. Vienna: Weigl, ca.1803. CS:Pnm. Other editions in A:Wn–CH:BEl–D-ddr:Bds,GOl,ZI–DK:Kk–GB:Lbl–US:Wc.

Deux sonates (C,F), Op.7. St.Petersburg: Gerstenberg & Dittmar; Vienna: Bureau des Arts et d'Industrie, Weigl. A:Wgm,Wn,Wst–CS:Bu,Pk–D-ddr:Dlb,WRtl. Rather short, three-movement works in compact, tuneful, Classical style; well balanced, but lightweight in content. (LI-I)

Ebers, Carl Friedrich (1770–1836)

German composer of symphonies, operas, cantatas. He incurred wrath of Weber when he made unauthorized arrangement of the latter's clarinet quintet as a piano sonata.

Douze petites pièces (C,C,F,C,C,C,F,C,C,C,Eb,Eb), Op.6. Brunswick: Au magasin de musique à la Höhe, 1796. B:Bc. Short, two- and three-part pieces in a variety of Classical dance forms in thin harmonic idiom; parts are not always carefully balanced. (I)

Eckardt, Gustav R.

Grande marche (g). New York: William Hall, 1863. US:Wc. Brilliant salon pieces; interesting and well balanced for both parts. (I)

Edwards, C.

°*March of the Magi kings*. Cincinnati: Willis Music Co., n.d. (E)

Eggeling, Georg (b.1866)

German teacher and composer of instructional and salon music for piano.

La capricieuse, valse (D), Op.120. Boston: A.P.Schmidt, 1906. US:Wc. (LI)

Festival march (Bb), Op.212. Philadelphia: Presser, 1924. US:Wc. (I)

Folk dance, Op.220. Philadelphia: Presser, 1925. US:Wc. (I)

Hunting song, Op.173. Boston: A.P.Schmidt, 1911. US:Wc. (I)

Marche militaire. Boston: A.P.Schmidt, 1922. US:Wc. (UE-LI)

Minka, mazurka brillante. Boston: A.P.Schmidt, 1924. US:Wc. (LI)

Souvenir de Pesth (f), Op.113. Boston: A.P.Schmidt, 1906. US:Wc. Display piece in salon style. (UI)

Ungarischer Tanz, No.1 (g), Op.108. Boston:A.P.Schmidt, 1905. US:Wc. Salon piece in Hungarian style with balanced parts and considerable rhythmic interest. (I)

Eggert, Joachim (1780–1813)

German-born Swedish organist and conductor. He wrote operas, symphonies, cantatas, and chamber music in Classical style showing traits of early German Romanticism.

Variationen auf ein schwedisches Volkslied, 1815. Ms. S:Skma (in C. Schwencke, *Oeuvres*, Cah. 5, 6). Seven variations and a finale in classical style; diverting in spite of routine passage work and harmonies. (I)

Eiges, Konstantin Romanovich (1875–1950)

Lëgkie variatsii (Easy variations). Moscow: State Music Publishers, 1938. US:Wc. Charming, inventive set of five variations in conventional harmonic idiom; well distributed for both parts; deserves to be reprinted. (UE)

°*Elizabethan Keyboard Duets* (Nicholas Carlton: *A verse for two to play*; Thomas Tomkins: *A fancy for two to play*), ed. Frank Dawes. London: Schott, 1949. °*For two to play* (Nicholas Carlton: *A verse for two to play*; Thomas Tomkins: *A fancy for two to play*), ed. Franzpeter Goebels. Kassel: Nagels Verlag, 1973. The earliest-known pieces for two performers at one keyboard, these two duets date from the early seventeenth or possibly late sixteenth century. They are fine examples of the English *fancy*, a form of polyphonic composition similar to the continental *ricercare*, which in some respects anticipated the fugue and was much cultivated by the English virginalist composers. Nicholas Carlton's *A verse* is an *In Nomine*, a type of fancy of vocal motet origin, often written for viols or virginals and based on a plainsong melody, *Gloria tibi Trinitas*. Fugal themes are developed around the cantus firmus, which extends from the beginning to the end of the piece. The Tomkins piece is shorter and freer in form than the Carlton work. Fugal entrances, sometimes overlapping, are developed imitatively without a central cantus firmus and, later, antiphonally. (I)

Ellen, Barbara

°*Dance suite now.* Boulder, CO: Myklas Press, 1978. (UE-LI)

°*The giant and the cricket.* Boulder, CO: Myklas Press, 1977.

°*Parakeets.* Boulder, CO: Myklas Press, 1977.

There is interest and activity for both parts in these three appealing little pieces. (UE)

°*Ski slope.* Boulder, CO: Myklas Press, 1975. Short, lively teaching piece; antiphonal scale passages. Optional parts for rhythm sticks. (E)

Elliott, Robert (1932–   )

English composer; studied at Royal College of Music and Royal Manchester College of Music.

°*Fantasie sur un motif de sarabande,* Op.3. London: Novello, 1957. US: NYp,Wc. Rather short, but effective, slow-moving work in placid modal linear idiom; parts are well distributed; a pleasant work. (UE-LI)

Elsner, Ksawery Józef (Joseph Xaver) (1768–1854)

Polish conductor and composer of German origin; teacher of Chopin at Warsaw Conservatory. He wrote operas, sacred music, piano pieces, orchestral works, and chamber music.

Cinq polonaises (only C,f,G for 4H). Leipzig: Kühnel, 1807. A:Wgm. Bracing, vigorous settings in Classical style with interesting chromaticisms; Two of the polonaises are reworkings of operatic themes. (I-UI)

Emery, Stephen Albert (1841–1891)

American teacher, critic, and author. He composed church music, songs, and piano pieces.

Apfelblüthen Walzer (Apple-blossom waltzes), Op.14. Boston: A.P.Schmidt, 1868; Chicago: Henry Tolman, ca.1868. US:Wc. Suite of five waltzes in salon style. (I)

An evening at home, eight easy four hand pieces (Before the fire; A story of the war; The sister plays; The mother's story; Children and kittens; The sleeping boy; Evening song; Quiet rest), Op.26. Boston: White, Smith & Perry, 1870. US:Bp,Wc. Short instructional pieces. (UE-LI/E-5)

Enckhausen, Heinrich (1799–1885)

German organist; composed an opera, sacred music, and many instructional works for piano.

°*Instructive melodische Tonstücke,* Op.84. Eisleben: Kuhnt, 1852. NEd. *Ecole de piano,* collection de morceaux mélodiques et progressives, Op.84. °Durand; °Hamelle; °Heugel.

°*Vingt petits morceaux,* faciles et progressifs, Op.72. Paris: Hamelle, n.d. (UE-LI/E-5)

°*Sonatas* (C,F), Op.71. Paris: Hamelle, 1848.

Variations brillantes sur un thème original, Op.27. Offenbach: André, n.d.

US:Wc. Salon piece; abundance of scales and passages work with little thematic development. (I)

Variations faciles et brillantes sur un air autrichien (G), Op.33. Offenbach: André, 1878. US:NYp,Wc. Similar in style and idiom to Op.27, but somewhat easier. (UE-LI)

Variations sur l'air favori suisse "Steh' nur auf, du lieber Schweizerbue", Op.42. Pub. and date missing. US:Wc.

Enesco, Georges (1882–1955)

Romanian-born violinist and composer. He wrote in a strongly individual post-Romantic style that incorporated Romanian folk elements.

°*Aubade*. Paris: Enoch, n.d.

Engelmann, H.

°*Four-hand album for the pianoforte*. Philadelphia: Presser, 1917.

Enke, Heinrich (1811–1859)

°*Sechs melodische Uebungsstücke* (Romanze; Hongroise; Andante cantabile; Polonaise; Tarantella; Polka), Op.6. Leipzig: °VEB Peters, 1957; °Ricordi.

°*Six pièces mélodiques* (Barcarolle; Berceuse; Galop; Romance; Valse; Marche funèbre), Op.8. Leipzig: °VEB Peters, 1957; °Ricordi.

Both Op.6 and Op.8 are well-written, attractive instructional pieces; useful teaching material. (UE-LI/E-5)

Enslin, Philipp

Marche (C). Offenbach: André, n.d. D-brd:Mbs.

Erb, Joseph Marie (1860–1944)

French composer and teacher. He wrote operas, symphonic and sacred music, chamber works, and piano pieces.

°*Six pièces*, Op.6. Paris: Hamelle, n.d.

Erdmannsdörfer, Max (1848–1905)

Bavarian conductor and teacher. He wrote choral works, chamber music, and piano pieces.

Nordseebilder nach Heines Liederzyklus Die Nordsee, Op.15. Berlin: Ries & Erler, 1873.

Erich, F.

When Johnny comes marching home. Boston: A.P.Schmidt, 1927. US:Wc. Instructional piece; not an arrangement of the famous Civil War tune. (LI)

Esch, Louis von (late 18th century)

Echos & air sylphes, a grand duo. London: Broderip and Wilkinson, n.d. J:Tma.

Impromptu duo. London: Broderip & Wilkinson, ca.1800. DK:Kk—GB:Cu, Lbl,Ob.

A military divertimento. London: Broderip & Wilkinson, n.d. GB:Ckc,Ob–
J:Tma.

*Il passo tempo, containing Un petit délassement, Pastorale & Rondo à la
Savoyard.* London: Preston, ca.1781–89. J:Tma–S:Uu–US:Wc. Cheerful
suite of short pieces in thin Classical idiom; melodies are trite, and the
harmony is shallow. (I)

Esipoff, Stepán

Forest flowers, six easy duets for young players (Au revoir; Dancing on the
green; Harvest song; Legend; Lullaby; Sunshine). Boston: Oliver Ditson,
1907. US:PHf.

Essex, Timothy

Twelve dances, as duetts for two performers (Gary Owen; College hornpipe;
Drops of brandy; Sir David Hunter Blair's reel; La Dansomanie; Lady
Mary Ramsay; Go to the devil and shake yourself; Mrs. Casey; Madame
del Caro's hornpipe; Moll in the wad; The new rigg'd ship; Irish washer-
woman). London: G.Walker, 17[??]. GB:Lbl–US:Bp,Wc. Easy arrangements of late eighteenth-century popular dance tunes. (E-LI)

A duett for two performers, Op.2. London: pub. by the composer, n.d.
US:Bp.

A grand duett, for two performers on one pianoforte with accompaniment for
two flutes, Op.9. London: Birchall,Broderip & Wilkinson, n.d. US:Bp.

L'Éventail de Jeanne (Jeanne's fan). A ballet for which various movements
of the music were contributed by respected French composers of the day.
Half the pieces in this cooperative production appeared as piano solos,
the remaining five—by Marcel Delannoy, Pierre Ferroud, Maurice Ravel,
Albert Roussel, and Florent Schmitt—were for 4H. The ballet was performed privately in 1927 using the piano accompaniments. Because of
certain awkward and unpianistic passages, some of the 4H pieces appear
to be sketches for an orchestration of the work that was made after 1927.
All five of the 4H pieces are listed in the Heugel catalog as transcriptions.

Ewing, Montague (1890–1957)

°Amid the tulips. Bryn Mawr: Presser, n.d. (UE-LI)

Three cameos (Airs and graces; Porcelain people; Tambouretta). London:
Francis, Day & Hunter, 1949. US:Wc. Graceful, well-balanced little instructional pieces. (UE-LI)

Royal suite (Command performance; Ghosts of the palace ballroom; A naval
occasion). Melbourne: Allans, 1953. US:Wc. Short, pleasant instructional
pieces. (LI)

Ezell, Helen Ingle (1903–   )

°We two. Boston: Boston Music Co., n.d.

Fabrizi, Vincenzo (b.ca.1765)

Sonata (C). Ms. I:Mc. Two-movement instructional work, crudely written; static harmony. (UE-LI)

Falbe, H.

Deux valses (Eb,F). Copenhagen: C.C.Lose, n.d. US:Wc. Short pieces in early Romantic style. (UE)

Six écossaises. Christiana (Olso): H.T. Winther, n.d. US:Wc. Suite of short, sixteen-measure dances in light Schubertian style. (UE)

Faning, Eaton (1850–1927)

English choral conductor. He wrote operettas, orchestral and chamber music, piano pieces, and choral works.

Festival march. London: Joseph Williams, 1917. US:Wc. Instructional work, carefully weighted for both parts. (LI)

Farina, Guido (1903–)

Italian composer of operas, an oratorio, and orchestral and chamber music.

°*Sei piccole composizioni*. Milan: Zerboni, 1952.

Farjeon, Harry (1878–1948)

English; composed piano concerto, operettas, piano pieces, and songs.

Three duets. London: OUP, 1925. US:Wc. Engaging, well-crafted works; musically interesting and satisfying; parts carefully balanced; touches of Impressionistic harmony. (UE-LI)

Two Italian sketches (On the water; On the road). London: Paxton, 1928. GB:Lbl–US:Wc. Somewhat more difficult than *Three Duets* but equally well constructed, with rhythmic and harmonic variety throughout. (I)

Farquhar, David (1928–)

New Zealand musician and teacher; studied in England. He has written orchestral and chamber works, choral pieces, and piano music in an expressive, frequently dissonant, tonal idiom.

°*Anniversary duets* (Preamble; Ground; Waltz; Americana; Bells; Barn dance) (1959–60). Wellington, N.Z.: Price Milburn & Co., 1973. Engaging series of pieces originally written for the composer's wife, a beginner on the piano; artfully set with effective use of modal color, dissonance, and polytonality. (UE-LI/E-5)

Farrenc, Jeanne Louise (1804–1875)

French pianist; professor at the Conservatoire; composed symphonies, overtures, chamber music, and piano works.

Air martial des Capuletti, Op.29. Pub. and date missing. F:Pn.

Fasanotti, Filippo (1821–1884)

Andante e allegro; Omaggio all'arte. Op.132. Padua: Pietro Prosperini, n.d. I:Bsf.

Fauré, Gabriel (1845–1924)

Influential French composer; teacher of Ravel and Florent Schmitt. His idiom is characterized by balance, delicacy, restraint, and fastidious attention to detail.

°*Dolly*, Op.56 (1893–1896). Paris: Hamelle; International. Popular suite of pieces of refined and elegant expression; charmingly set for the medium in Fauré's characteristic harmonic and melodic language; one of the treasures of the repertoire. The inspiration for the music was Dolly Bardac, young daughter of Mme Emma Bardac, for whom Fauré wrote the song cycle *La Bonne Chanson*. Described as a captivating and very feminine little blond child, she is the same Dolly who gained fame as the stepdaughter of Debussy—his beloved "Chou-chou"—when Mme Bardac became the composer's second wife several years later. The suite opens with a dreamy, tranquil Berceuse, artless in its simplicity. The unexpected rhythmical leaps and feints of the next piece, together with the title itself, Mi-a-ou, suggest the frolicking of a lively cat. But Marguerite Long, pianist and friend of both the composer and the Bardac family, strongly contradicts this notion in her book *Au piano avec Fauré* (Paris: Julliard, 1963), asserting instead that Mi-a-ou is in fact the nickname Dolly gave to her older brother, Raoul Bardac, of whom the piece is a kind of musical portrait. Raoul himself was a musician and studied with both Fauré and Debussy. Le jardin de Dolly, the third piece, is a fanciful walk into an enchanted dream garden; and the animated, graceful Kitty-valse, which follows, is described by Long, despite its title, as the whirling leaps and turns of a favorite dog. The affecting Tendresse is subtle and delicate with shifting tonal centers, so characteristic of Fauré's style. The final work, Pas espagnol, is light and gay in character, with pulsating Spanish rhythms and more than a touch of Chabrier. Long indicates that this work is the musical expression of a bronze equestrian statue by Frémiet, Fauré's father-in-law. The ornament, which stood on a mantlepiece in Mme Bardac's residence, was greatly admired by the young Dolly. (I-UI)

Fauré, Gabriel and André Messager

°*Souvenirs de Bayreuth;* fantaisie en forme de quadrille sur les thèmes favoris de l'Anneau du Niebelung de R. Wagner (1880). Paris: Costallat, 1930. For Wagnerophiles, Wagnerophobes, and everyone who enjoys a somewhat erudite, inside spoof on themes from *Der Ring des Nibelungen*, this collaborative effort by two composers of quite different backgrounds should prove to be a diverting and playful romp. (UI-LA)

Febel, Reinhard

Kaleidoskop 1 und 2 für Klavier zu vier Händen. Celle: Moeck, 1979.

Federer, Ralph

°*Lonely dancer.* Bryn Mawr: Presser, n.d. (I)

°*The scarlet cape.* Bryn Mawr: Presser, 1949. US:Wc. Display piece in Spanish style with lively beguine, tango, and rumba rhythms; effective. (I)

Fedrigotti, Johann

Introduction, walses et coda. Vienna: Mechetti, 1822. A:Wst. Lightweight waltzes preceded by florid introduction. (LI-I)

Feinberg, Samuel E. (1890–1962)

Russian pianist and composer; influenced by Skriabin and Russian folk music.

°*Chuvash melody* (g). In collection *Brother and Sister,* ed. Goldstein. Graceful setting of Soviet ethnic folk song. (UE-LI)

Felber, Rudolf

°[10] *Slovakische Tänze mit Benutzung slovakischer Volksliedmelodien komponirt.* Mainz: Schott, n.d. (I)

Felciano, Richard (1930–)

American composer; studied with Milhaud and Dallapiccola; teaches at University of California, Berkeley, where he is co-director of the university electronic music studio. One of the most highly esteemed American composers of the past twenty years, he has been cited for his originality, the elegance of his sonorities, and his exceptional talent in combining the utterances of conventional orchestral instruments with electronic sounds.

°*Gravities* (1965). Boston: E.C. Schirmer, 1974. Commissioned by Milton and Peggy Salkind. Pointillistic; avant-garde. "The piece evolves by subjecting its musical ideas to forces of attraction and repulsion in terms of each of the compositional materials involved: duration, harmony, dynamics, and texture. Contrast is achieved through stasis. Dance gestures and certain aural images of electronic music are in evidence. . . . The four-hand medium is exploited through the simultaneous use of wide registers and the employment of overlapping rhythms and dense textural blocks not otherwise available" (from the preface). (A)

Feldman, Morton (1926–)

American composer; studied with Riegger and Stefan Wolpe. His style has been influenced by John Cage. Feldman has evolved a spare idiom based on exploration of new kinds of sound.

°*Piano four-hands* (1958). New York: C.F. Peters, 1962. Avant-garde work in traditional notation; aleatoric indications; features muted, slow-moving single sounds. (A)

Felton, James (1927–)

American composer, author, and music critic.

Hommage à "les Six" (1962). Ms. Available from composer, *Philadelphia Bulletin,* Philadelphia, PA 19104.

Fernandez, Oscar L. (1897–1948)

Brazilian musician; wrote in harmonically conservative idiom influenced by the folklore of his country.

*The fantastic horseman. New York: Peer International, 1945.

Ferrari, Giacomo Gotifredo (1763–1842)

Italian musician; settled in London, where he taught singing. He wrote operas, ballets, songs, and pieces for piano, harp, and flute.

Twelve Recreations, Op.36. London: Robert Birchall, n.d. A:Wn.

Ferrari, Giorgio (1925–   )

Italian violinist; has written opera, ballet, orchestral and chamber music, songs, and piano pieces.

*Divertimento. Padua: Zanibon, 1969.

Ferraria, Luigi Ernesto (1855–1933)

[24] Intermezzi ritmici. Milan: Ricordi, 1932. US:NYp. Short pieces in conservative style presenting a variety of rhythmic and ensemble problems; useful to all students of 4H playing. (I)

Ferrell, Billie

American musician; has written instructional music for piano.

*Bom-bom-boogie. Boulder, CO: Myklas Press, 1975. Traditional boogie with syncopations and dotted rhythms; features an optional part for one player performing on bongos or home-made drums. (UE)

*The ghost wind. Boulder, CO: Myklas Press, 1973. A repeated chromatic motive in the Primo part against chordal bass and scale passages in the Secondo provides the eerie quality suggested by the title. (UE)

Ferroud, Pierre-Octave (1900–1936)

French composer of symphony, opera, and piano solos in a lyrical popular idiom influenced by Ravel and Florent Schmitt.

*Marche, from L'Éventail de Jeanne. Paris: Heugel, 1927. Saucy, gently dissonant; tongue-in-cheek. (I)

*Sérénade (Berceuse; Pavane; Spiritual). Paris: Durand, 1927. Attractive pieces in Impressionistic style; well-distributed parts; requires subtlety and sensitive musicianship for adequate performance. (I)

Ferté, Armand (1882–1973)

Distinguished French pianist and teacher; among his compositions are instructional works for piano.

*Dialogues (Marche; Menuet; Quiétude; Valse). Brussels: Schott Frères, 1958. Attractive instructional pieces in fastidious conservative idiom. (I/E)

*Cinq notes; petit recueil pour piano de courtes pièces très faciles. Paris: Éditions musicales transatlantiques, n.d.

Fétis, François-Joseph (1784–1871)

Musicologist, teacher, author; best known for his writings on music literature, history, and theory. He composed seven operas, symphonies, chamber
music, and sacred works.

Sextet for piano 4H, two violins, viola, and cello (Bb), Op.5. Paris: Michel
Ozy, 1819; Paris: Brandus, n.d. NEd. Mainz: Schott, 1864. GB:Lbl. One
of the few works in this form in the 4H literature.

Fiala, George (1922–)

Canadian organist, pianist, and teacher of Ukrainian origin; studied in Kiev,
Berlin, and Brussels with Jongen. He writes in neo-Classical, dissonant, sometimes polytonal idiom.

°*Dance.* Toronto: BMI Canada, 1958. Short, appealing work in modal
idiom; well written for both partners. (LI-I/UE)

Fíbich, Zdeněk (1850–1900)

Czech-born pianist, critic, and composer; received early musical training in
Germany and France. He cultivated a meticulous cosmopolitan musical
idiom—lyrical and highly personal—showing influences of Schumann, Liszt,
Wagner, and his teacher, Dvořák. He wrote operas, orchestral and chamber
music, songs, and piano compositions.

Ciacona a Impromptu, Op.25 (1885). Prague: Urbánek, 1886. US:Wc.
Solid, serious works in Romantic idiom; carefully arranged for both partners. (I)

°*Dětem;* vyber přednesovych skladeb pro klavir na dvě a čtyři ruce (For
children; selection of elementary pieces for piano solo and four hands),
collected and edited by Věra Koubková. Prague: Artia, 1960. US:Wc. The
five duets in this collection (Nos. 12, 13, 14, 15, 16) are short, effective
pieces in folk style, admirably written for the medium. (LI)

Fugato a kolo vil (Fugato and canon), Op.24 (1885). Prague: Urbánek,
1886. US:Wc. Contrapuntal works effectively set. (UI-A)

Maličkosti (Mignons) (Waltz; One thousand and one nights; [untitled];
Rococo, gavotte), Op.19 (1870–1872). Prague: Urbánek, 1884. US:Wc.
Short, engaging character pieces. (LI)

Maličkosti (Bagatelles) (March; Against the storm; Confidence; At the theatre), Op.48. Prague: Urbánek, 1896. US:Wc. Descriptive and mood
pieces; short, attractive. (I-UI)

Nálady, dojmy a upomínky (Moods, impressions and recollections,. Prague:
Urbánek, 1910. US:Wc. Set of winsome, musically rewarding pieces. (UI)

°*Skladbičky a cvičeny* (Little pieces and studies). Prague: Artia, 1956.
(UE-LI)

°*Sonata* (Bb), Op.28 (1886). Prague: Urbánek, 1887. °NEd. Prague: Artia,
1964. GB:Lbl–US:Wc. Large-scale, three-movement work dedicated to

the composer's teacher, Dvořák. Graceful, melodious, polished; technically demanding in part; well worth reviving. (UI-A)

Vigiliae; deux morceaux caractéristiques, Op.20. Prague: Urbánek, 1886. US:Wc. Refined, attractive work; also written for orchestra, but better known and perhaps more successful in the 4H version. (I)

°*Zlatý věk; hudební drobotiny* (Golden age; children's pieces) (March, Barcarola; Tyrolienne; Courante; Mazurka; Song without words; Waltz; Elegie; Dumka; Gigue; Polka; Festive procession), Op.22. Prague: Urbánek, 1886. °NEd. Prague: Artia, n.d. US:Wc. Amiable character pieces and dances with strong Czech folk song influence. (I)

Fichandler, William (1886-   )

°*Fun for four-hands*. Cincinnati: Willis Music Co., 1960. Ten short pieces, tuneful, attractive, well-balanced; occasional linear texture. (UE-LI/ E-UE)

°*Six duets* (Harvest dance; Rhumba rhythm; Pastorale; Spinning; Roundelay; Canoeing at Twilight). New York: Chappell, 1956. Gay, bright teaching pieces; contrasting in mood and color. (I)

Ficher, Jacobo (1896–1978)

Russian-born Argentine violinist and conductor; became established in Buenos Aires in 1923. He composed carefully constructed orchestral works, chamber music, and piano pieces in a lyrical, often chromatic and dissonant, tonal idiom; made frequent use of Hebrew and Argentine folk melodies.

Preludio, siciliano y fuga, Op.111 (1969). Ms. Available from Editorial Argentina de Música, Defensa 320, Buenos Aires, Argentina. Bold, large-scale work employing Classical structures; contrapuntal, with contrasts of texture and effective use of instrumental color; brilliant in part. (A)

Field, John (1782–1837)

Irish composer; brilliant concert pianist; studied with Clementi; settled in St. Petersburg. His most important works are 18 piano Nocturnes, a form and style he invented and which Chopin developed. The abbreviation HOP, used below, refers to the catalogue numbers of Field's compositions in Cecil Hopkinson, *A Bibliographical Thematic Catalog of the Works of John Field, 1782–1837* (London: printed for the author, 1961).

Air russe varié, "How have I grieved you." Moscow: C. F. Schildbach, 1803–10. HOP 10A. US:Wc.

Duet on a favorite Russian air. Munich: Aibl; London: Clementi, Banger, Collard, Davis & Collard, n.d. HOP 10B. US:NYp.

Variations sur l'air russe "Chem tebia ia ogorchila". Offenbach: André, n.d. GB:Lbl–US:Wc.

There are many editions (others by B&H, Artaria, Niemeyer, Peters, Simrock) of the same work, a short, pleasant set of variations on a Russian folk melody with occasional touches of Slavic color. (LI-I)

Andante (c). Contemporary ms. (tiré de la Gazette Musicale). US:Wc.

Grande valse (a). St-Petersbourg: Dalmas, ca.1812–13; as *Grande valse de rondeau*: Offenbach: André, ca.1823. GB:Lbl,Lcm—US:NYp,Wc. Long repetitious work; Primo more active than Secondo. (I)

°*Nine nocturnes*, arr. for 4H by Franz Liszt. °NEd. reprint by Musical Scope Publishers. US:Bp. Though officially beyond the range of this catalogue, these charming arrangements of a selection of Field Nocturnes are listed here because they are outstanding examples of the art of transcribing from one medium to another. In reworking the originals, Liszt has produced a series of ingeniously orchestrated and subtly balanced duets, every bit as interesting as if they were original 4H works. (I)

Rondeau (G). Bonn: Simrock, 1819. HOP 43. GB:Lcm.

Fiévet, Paul (1892–)

French composer of symphonies, a ballet, an operetta, choral pieces, chamber works, and piano music in conservative style.

°*La journée d'un petit enfant bien sage; six petites pièces*. Paris: Eschig, 1927.

Finkbeiner, Reinhold (1929–)

Drei zahme Klavierstückchen (Übermütig; Langsam und monoton; Rumba) (1948). Wiesbaden: B&H, 1957. US:Wc. Charming, entertaining pieces in mildly dissonant idiom. (I)

Finke, Fidelio F. (1891–1968)

German-Czech composer; attended Prague Conservatory and later taught there. He wrote choral and orchestral works, chamber music, and piano pieces. His style shows the influence of Brahms, Reger, Hindemith, and Schoenberg.

°[10] *Stücke für Lehrer und Schüler* (Langsam; Langsam; Passacaglia; Sehr langsam; Langsam; Lustig; Langsam aber fliessend; Gondellied; Marionettentanz; Ich fahr' dahin). Vienna: UEd, 1936. °NEd. Leipzig: VEB B&H, 1969. Designed for pupil and teacher (or advanced student). Effective short pieces cast in conservative tonal idiom with frequent dissonances and pungent harmonies; five of the pieces are tasteful settings of folk songs. (I/E-UE)

Firnhaber, J.C.

Sonata, Op.3, from *Six Sonates pour le clavecin, et un duo pour quatre mains*. Frankfurt: W.N. Haueisen, n.d. A:Wgm.

Firnkees, G.

°*Klavierspiel vierhändig*. Wolfenbüttel: Möseler, n.d.

Fischer, Émile (1872–)

Czech musician; student of Dvořák; wrote symphonies and chamber music.

°*Lili*. Paris: Consortium Musical, n.d. (LI)

°*Perles roses.* Paris: Consortium Musical, n.d. (I)
°*Les petites marquises.* Paris: Consortium Musical, n.d. (E)

Fischer, E. von

Andantino und Scherzo, Op.1. Leipzig: Bosworth, 1905. US:Wc. Graceful, flowing work for teacher and pupil. (I/E-5)

Fischer, Michael Gotthard (1773–1829)

German organist and conductor; composed organ works, symphonies, concertos, chamber music, songs, and piano works.
Sonate (C), Op.12. Leipzig: B&H, 1809. D-brd:B.

Flegl, Václav (1876–1951)

Czech teacher and organist; composed orchestral and vocal works; wrote piano methods and numerous piano pieces.
°*Čtyři ruce zmohou více* (Four hands can do more). Prague: Supraphon, n.d.

Fleischmann, Johann Friedrich (1766–1798)

German composer of operas, symphonies, songs, and piano music.
Sonate (G), Op.2. Offenbach: André, 1796. D-brd:Bhm,LB—US:Wc. Structurally weak and meandering four-movement work in Classical style; rescued to some extent by occasional imaginative melodic ideas and attractive harmonic passages. (I)

Florentine, S.

°*Sunbeam frolic.* Cincinnati: Willis Music Co., n.d. (UE)

Florschütz, Eucharius (ca.1757–ca.1820)

Grande sonate (Eb) [No.1]. Leipzig: Hoffmeister & Kühnel, ca.1803. A: Wgm—D-brd:B,FLs—D-ddr:GOl,HAu—DK:Kk—S:L,Sk—US:Wc.
Grande sonate (F), No.2. Leipzig: Kühnel, 1804. A:Wgm—D-ddr:GOl,HAu —DK:Kk—I:Nc—US:Wc.
Grande sonate (A), oeuvre III. Leipzig: Kühnel, ca.1812. A:Wgm—CH:E.
The three-movement sonatas by this obscure eighteenth-century composer are written in Classical style and are characterized by assertive melodic ideas, conventional harmonic language colored by antiphonal writing, occasional chromaticism, and an unexpected kind of major–minor tonal fluctuation reminiscent of Schubert. The predominantly homophonic character of the music is interrupted by frequent sections of linear texture—the first movement of the Sonata in Eb, for instance, includes a fully developed fugato. But the eloquence and sensitivity of the hauntingly beautiful slow movements hardly compensate for the overall inclination of the sonatas toward repetitive passage work and harmonic redundancy. (I)

Flothuis, Marius (1914–)

Dutch composer, largely self-taught. He writes in a lyrical, expressive style showing influences of Monteverde, Debussy, and Bartók.

°*Valses nobles*, Op.52. Amsterdam: Donemus, 1954. Suite of six connected waltzes in the Schubertian tradition; cast in a neo-Romantic, chromatic, harmonic idiom. (UI-LA)

°*Valses sentimentales*, Op.21. Amsterdam: Donemus, 1944. (I)

Flotow, Friedrich, Freiherr von (1812–1883)

German nobleman; French-trained composer of over 25 operas (*Martha* and *Alessandro Stradella* among the best known), ballets, chamber music, and piano pieces.

[6] *Etüden* (C,a,G,e,D,b), Op.15. Rostock: Wessel, 1873. GB:Lbl. Series of melodious 4H studies featuring problems of ensemble, dynamics, and rhythm. (I)

Fly, Leslie (1902–)

English musician; composer of instructional music for piano.

°*Cornerstones*. London: Forsyth, n.d. (UE-LI)

°*Forest themes* (Cranham Woods; Bowland Forest; New Forest). London: Forsyth, 1971. Attractive little descriptive pieces, carefully written in conservative style. (UE-LI/E in octaves throughout)

°*Four in hand*. London: Forsyth, n.d. (UE)

°*A trio of duets* (May day revel; Chinese dance; Fiesta). London: Forsyth, 1968. Set of short, appealing, instructional pieces. (UE-I)

Fodor, Carolus Antonius (1768–1846)

Dutch conductor; composed concertos, sonatas, symphonies, chamber music, and piano pieces.

Simphonie, Op.16. Berlin: J.J. Hummel; Amsterdam: Grand magazin de musique, n.d. US:Cn.

Sonate (D), Op.1. Offenbach: André, 1783. D-brd:OF–D-ddr:Dlb. Sonata in Classical idiom using the figures, motivic structures, and general architectural apparatus of the period with little ingenuity, imagination, or manipulative skill. Some of the writing in the Secondo part tends to be too low to be effective, especially in antiphonal sections; entire work is limited in harmonic and melodic interest. (I)

Sonate (C), Op.9. Berlin: J.J. Hummel; Amsterdam: Grand magazin de musique, n.d. D-brd:Bhm.

Fogg, Eric (1903–1939)

English conductor and organist. He wrote choral works, songs, church music, and piano pieces.

Four pieces, Op.44. London: Bosworth, 1920. US:Wc. Amusing set of short compositions; light-hearted, pleasant. (I)

Foote, Arthur (1853–1937)

American organist and composer; studied with John Knowles Paine at Harvard. He wrote cantatas, orchestral suites, and organ and piano works in a fastidious, noninnovative style—Classical in form, Romantic in harmonic language.

Drei Clavierstücke (Air; Intermezzo; Gavotte), Op.21. Boston: A.P.Schmidt, 1891. US:Wc. Suite of engaging pieces of excellent craftsmanship and musical merit; adapted by composer from suite for string orchestra. (I)

Twelve duets on five notes (Zwölf kleine Stücke). Boston/Leipzig: A.P. Schmidt, 1891. "Reverie" and "Waltz" in collection *Duets of early American music,* ed. Anne McClenny and Maurice Hinson. (UE-LI/E-5)

Six pianoforte duets (Church bells; Graceful dance; At night; The maypole; A solemn march; The swing). Boston: A.P.Schmidt, 1905. US:Wc.

The two suites above consist of short easy pieces, skilfully designed, providing excellent balance between the parts; effective. (UE-LI)

Forchhammer, Theophil (1847–1923)

Swiss organist and composer of organ and piano pieces.

Sonate (G) (1872). Unpub. ms. CH:Zma.

Ford, Charles Edgar (b.1881)

English organist and composer; settled in Australia. His compositions include sacred music, songs, organ works, and piano pieces written in conservative style.

Country fair. Melbourne: Allans Music, 1952. US:Wc.

Puck. Melbourne: Allans Music, 1950. US:Wc. Fresh little pieces in English "country dance" idiom; well written for both parts. (UE-LI)

Fornerod, Aloys (1890–1965)

Swiss musician.

Deux pièces (Romance; Bergère), Op.45 (1963). Ms. CH:Zma.

Forsman, John Väinö (1924–   ) and Rovsing Olsen

Danish of Finnish extraction; writes in expressive neo-Classical style.

Alfestykker (Elf-pieces). Copenhagen: Hansen, 1956. US:Wc. Four short, witty pieces. The imaginative music is fresh and up-to-date; has metric changes, occasional dissonance, and surprising harmonic twists. (UE-LI)

Förster, Alban (1849–1916)

German violinist and teacher. He wrote symphonies, chamber music, songs, and instructional piano music in light, conservative style.

Für die Jugend, Sonatinen (C,F,G), Op.76. Mainz: Schott, 1883. GB:Lbl.

Für die Jugend, sechs leichte Vortragsstücke, Op.97. Leipzig: B&H, 1886. GB:Lbl. (UE-LI/E-5)

Original-Compositionen (Salon; Walzer; Alpen-Idylle; Blumengeflüster; Auf der Wanderschaft; Chanson d'amour; Barcarole). Mainz: Schott, 1908. GB:Lbl–US:Wc. Salon pieces. (LI)

Waldes-Visionen, Tonbild in Scherzo-form, Op.31. Leipzig: Kistner & Siegel, 1876. GB:Lbl. (UI)

[10] *Walzer,* Op.45. Leipzig: Kistner, 1878. GB:Lbl. (I)

Förster, Emmanuel Alois (1748–1823)

German theorist, teacher, and composer; published practical textbook on figured bass. His 48 string quartets, models of their kind, enjoyed such a reputation in Vienna that Beethoven went to him for lessons in quartet composition. Förster also wrote organ and piano works.

Sonata (Bb), Op.23 (or 24). Vienna: Bureau des arts et d'industrie, 1803. D-ddr:BD,GOl,ZI—I:PAc—A:Wgm. Large-scale, three-movement work in classical style, competently written for the medium; the strong thematic ideas are well developed and the harmonic framework solidly fashioned. (I)

Förster, Josef Bohuslav (1859–1951)

Czech music critic and teacher. In addition to seven operas and a large quantity of symphonic music, he wrote chamber works, choral pieces, and piano compositions.

Lyrische Stücke, Op.33. Prague: Urbánek, 1902.

Viola odorata; Rosa mystica. Prague: Urbánek, 188[?]. US:NYp. Short pieces in light style with Czech folk flavor. (LI-I)

°For two to play. See *Elizabethan Keyboard Duets.*

Foster, Jean

°Side by side series, Book X (Everyday duets; [25] easy pieces). London: Ashdown, n.d. (E)

Fraenzel [Fränzl], Ferdinand (1770–1833)

German violinist and conductor; composed orchestral and chamber music, operas, songs, and piano pieces.

Favorite variations for two performers. New York: W.Dubois, ca.1820. US: Wc. Charming, naive set of variations on a simple tune; set in Classical style. (LI-I)

Françaix, Alfred (b.1880)

French composer, father of Jean.

°Nos vieilles chansons. Paris: Senart, n.d.

Françaix, Jean (1912–)

French pianist and composer. His works, which manifest the influence of Stravinsky, are characterized by a French spirit of clarity, wit, spontaneity, and Classical restraint.

°Napoléon, suite. Paris: Éditions Musicales Transatlantiques; Mainz: Schott, 1956. US:Wc. Sixteen short, light, amusing pieces. (I)

°Quinze portraits d'enfants d'Auguste Renoir, transposés pour piano à quatre mains à l'usage des jeunes élèves. Paris: Éditions Musicales Transatlantiques, 1971. The short pieces in this artfully and sensitively crafted collection are based on children's portraits by Auguste Renoir. The harmonic

idiom is crisply French, and each piece is accompanied by a picture whose title also supplies the title of the music. (I/E-LI)

Franck, César (1822–1890)

The composer's four-hand compositions, dating from an early period, show influences of Beethoven, Schubert, Méhul, and Weber.

Polka (1848). London: M.S.M. Music Publishers, 1977. When the composer's young and vivacious wife entreated her newly wedded husband to learn to dance, the reluctant Franck compromised by writing a polka. Exhibiting few of the stylistic characteristics of the mature composer, this bright, unventuresome work, which also exists in a piano solo version, is typical of its period, and was probably intended to be performed with his bride. (LI-I)

Premier duo sur le God Save the King, Op.4 (1842). Hamburg: Schuberth, 1846. US:Wc. Brilliant, difficult, showy fantasy on the familiar theme featuring passage work, repeated notes, rapid arpeggios, and other demanding technical effects. (UI-A)

Franck, Richard (1858–1938)

Works of this German pianist and teacher include orchestral and chamber music, choral compositions, and piano pieces.

[10] *Progressiv geordnete Salonstücke*, Op.62. Berlin: Otto Wernthal, 1901. US:Wc. Short salon pieces. (E-I)

Drei Stücke in Kanonform, Op.11. Magdeburg: Heinrichshofen, 1886. GB: Lbl.

Francmesnil, Roger de (1884–1921)

French pianist and composer of chamber music, orchestral works, songs, and piano pieces.

Quatre petites pièces (Berceuse; Souvenir; Prélude, Le bon vieux temps). Paris: Mathot, n.d.

Franco, Johan H.G. (1908–   )

Dutch composer, resident in U.S. He has written symphonic, chamber, and piano pieces.

Hymn, 1940. Ms. US:Wc. Short work dedicated to Helen and Karl Ulrich Schnabel, piano-duettists. Linear, with some dissonance. (UI)

Frank, Alan (1910–   )

English editor, writer on music, and composer.

March. London: OUP, 1936. US:NYp,Wc. Bouncy, whimsical work with piquant harmonies and jazz rhythms. (I)

Franke, Theodore

Russian intermezzo. Bryn Mawr: Presser, n.d. (UE-LI)

Frick, Philipp Joseph (1740–1798)

Organist and pianist of German origin; also played the glass harmonica.

Duett for two performers on one Pianoforte (D), Op.4. London: pub. by composer, n.d. GB:Lbl.

A *duett for two performers on one Pianoforte with or without additional keys*. London/Edinburgh: Corri, Dussek & Co., 1796. GB:Lbl.

Fricker, Peter Racine (1920–)

English composer; writes in dissonant idiom influenced by Bartók, serial techniques, and jazz.

°*Nocturne and Scherzo*, Op.23. London: Schott, 1958. Fluent, serious work in linear, dissonant idiom: evocative Nocturne; fast, vivid, rhythmical Scherzo. Effectively set for both partners. (A)

Frid, Géza (1904–1978)

Hungarian-born resident of Holland; student of Bartók and Kodály; concert pianist. His works include choral and orchestral compositions, chamber music, and piano pieces.

°*Kermesse à Charleroi*, Op.44a. Amsterdam: Donemus, 1953; New York: Southern Music Pub., 1964. Bright, pulsating work describing the excitement, bustle, and exuberance of a low-country outdoor festival; effective show-piece. (UI-A)

°[4] *Schetsen*, Op.72b. Amsterdam: Donemus, 1969.

Fried, Oskar (1871–1941)

German conductor, student of Humperdinck. He wrote orchestral and choral works, chamber music, and piano compositions.

[7] *Leichte Stücke* (Kleines Fantasiestück; Soldatenliedchen; Venezianer Gondellied; An der Mühle; Menuett; Auf zur Jagd; Kleiner Walzer), Op.6. Berlin: Bote & Bock, 1901. US:Wc. Melodious, fluent pieces in salon style. (I-UI/UE-LI)

Friedman, Ignaz (1882–1948)

Polish-born concert pianist; composed extensively for piano and small ensembles.

[5] *Walzer*, Op.51. Vienna: UEd, 1912. US:Wc. Suite of energetic, often brilliant waltzes, in melodious and rhythmical Viennese style; well fashioned for the medium. (I/UI-A)

Friml, Rudolf (1879–1972)

Czech composer and pianist; lived in U.S. Like his successful operettas *Rose Marie* and *The Vagabond King*, his piano music is light and melodious.

°*Musical adventures for four little hands* (Wishing moon; In magic land; Chatterbox; Blue fairy; Foxy kitten). Cincinnati: Willis Music Co., 1925. Short, attractive teaching pieces. (LI/E-5)

Frischknecht, Hans Eugen (1939–)

Swiss musician.

Für zwei (1970). Ms. CH:Zma. Atonal work without barlines or rhythmic notation; structural features include tone clusters and aleatory elements; avant-garde. Two versions: 4H and 2P. (A)

Frölich, Franz Joseph (1780–1862)

In addition to liturgical music, an opera, and orchestral works, this Bavarian conductor wrote one of the few four-hand concertos.

Concerto for piano four hands and orchestra (D). Bonn: Simrock, ca.1814. A:Wgm–B:Bc.

Sonaten (G,F). Bonn: Simrock, ca.1814. A:Wgm.

Sonate (C). Leipzig: B&H, ca.1815. A:Wgm.

Frölich, Friedrich Theodor (1803–1836)

Swiss composer of popular songs and piano pieces.

Fugen (1832). Ms. CH:Zma.

Ouverture (E♭) (1833). Ms. CH:Zma.

Frommel, Gerhard (1906–   )

German composer and teacher. He has written symphonies, chamber music, and piano pieces.

°*Impromptu* (E♭). In collection *Spielbuch, zeitgenössische Originalkompositionen.* Traditional harmonic and melodic patterns; sly modulations add color to this pleasant work. (I)

Frontini, F. Paolo (1860–1939)

Composer and teacher; wrote songs and piano pieces.

°*Pezzettini facili in ordine progressivo.* Milan: Carisch, n.d. (UE-LI)

Frugatta, Giuseppe (1860–1933)

[12] *Interludii.* Milan: Ricordi, 1921. US:Wc. Suite of engaging pieces; unusual musically and pedagogically in their graceful presentation of rhythmical and technical problems. (UE-I)

Fuchs, Albert (1858–1910)

Swiss-born conductor, teacher, and composer.

[12] *Kleine Walzer,* Op.9. Leipzig: Fritzsch, 1884. GB:Lbl. Attractive suite of waltzes in a variety of keys. (UE-LI)

Ungarische Suite, Op.12. Vienna: Gutmann, 1883. US:Wc. Salon pieces in Hungarian style. (I)

Fuchs, Robert (1847–1927)

Viennese teacher and member of Brahms's circle; his instructional works for piano, four hands, are especially noteworthy for their ingratiating charm and originality, and for the great sensitivity the composer demonstrated in his resourceful handling of the subtleties of piano duet writing.

Frühlingsstimmen, [12] kleine Stücke, Op.1. Vienna: Doblinger, 1872. US: Wc. Short, effective works in melodious Schumannesque style. (UE-LI).

In der Dämmerstunde, [10] Skizzen, Op.38. Berlin: Simrock, 1885. GB:Lbl. Amiable group of pieces in Romantic style. (UE-LI)

Miniaturen, [24] kurze und leichte Clavierstücke, Op.44. Berlin: Simrock, 1887. GB:Lbl. Evocative, lyrical, handsomely shaped little compositions. (LI-I)

Miniaturen, [16] kurze und leichte Clavierstücke, Op.93. Vienna: Robitschek, 1911. US:Wc. Series of short refined works, similar in character to Op.44. (LI)

[5] *Stücke*, Op.4. Leipzig: Kistner, 1872. GB:Lbl—US:Wc. Similar in style and idiom to Op.1, but slightly more difficult. (I)

[6] *Stücke*, Op.7. Leipzig: Kistner, 1872. GB:Lbl—US:Wc. Similar to Op.4.

Variationen (d), Op.10. Leipzig: Kistner, 1875. US:Wc. Intriguing set of variations ranging from easy to brilliant; attractive, rewarding; require technical facility. (UI-A)

[24] *Walzer*, Op.25. Leipzig: Kistner, 1880. US:Wc. (I)

[12] *Walzer*, Op.90. Vienna: Robitschek, 1910. US:Wc.

Op.25 and Op.90 are effective sets of amiable, lilting Viennese waltzes. (LI-I)

[20] *Wiener Walzer*, Op.42. Berlin: Simrock, 1886. GB:Lbl—US:Wc. Exceptionally fine, elegantly fashioned chain of waltzes set in a variety of keys in Brahmsian style. (I)

Fulton, Norman (1909–)

English composer of film and radio music, as well as orchestral and chamber works, songs, and piano pieces.

°*Dance miniatures*, Op.33. London: OUP, 1965. Set I: Menuet; Hornpipe (UE/E); Set II: Tarantella; Rumba (UE-LI/UE); Set III: Polonaise; Tango (I/UE-LI); Set IV: Waltz; Hungarian Dance. Attractice pieces arranged in progressive order of difficulty; solidly and imaginatively set in conservative harmonic idiom. (I)

Fumagalli, Disma (1826–1893)

Valzer, Op.314. Milan: Ricordi. n.d. GB:Lbl. Salon waltzes. (I)

Fuss, Johann Evangelist (1777–1819)

Andante (G). Vienna: Cappi, 1808. A:Wgm.

Gabler, Christoph August (1767–1839)

German pianist and composer.

Notturno (E♭) [with four-voice chorus for the first movement], Op.47. Leipzig: Peters, ca.1826. A:Wgm,Wn—D-brd:B—D-ddr:Dlb—I:PAc. Large-scale, five-movement work (Marcia; Menuetto; Larghetto cantabile; Polonaise; Andante con variazioni) in Classical idiom. The writing is pianistic, ranging from ponderous, thick chords in the March to lighter figurations in the variations. Although the thematic development lacks inventiveness and tends toward the routine, the melodies are agreeably tuneful and the whole is well balanced for both partners. (I)

Ouverture (A), Op.44. Leipzig: Peters, ca.1818. D-brd:B—S:Sm—I:PAc—US:PHf.

Drei Polonaisen (Bb,G,C), Op.30. Leipzig: B&H, 1805. A:M—D-brd:B, Bhm,LÜh—D-ddr:BD.

Drei Polonaisen (D,Eb,C), Op.32. Leipzig: B&H, 1810. A:Wn—I:PAc—S: Sm.

Rondeau en forme de walse (Bb), Op.52. Leipzig: Peters, ca.1821. A:Wgm—I:PAc.

Serenade (C), Op.4. Leipzig: Hilscher, 1796. B:Bc. Four-movement work based on dance forms (Marcia; Minuetto; Polonaise: Englische Tanz). Thin fare for the most part, with a few touches of imaginative writing notably in the fourth movement. (I)

Sonate (F), Op.22. Leipzig: B&H, 1802. A:Wn—D-brd:B—D-ddr:HAu.

Die Spinnerin, alla polacca (Bb), Op.43. Leipzig: B&H, ca.1819. US:Wc. Diffuse polonaise in lightweight Classical style, with harmonic and melodic touches suggestive of Weber. (I)

Variations sur an air russe (a), Op.33. Leipzig: B&H, 1810. A:Wgm—D-brd: B—I:PAc.

Walzer. Leipzig: C.F. Lehmann, ca.1799. D-ddr:LEm.

Gade, Niels Wilhelm (1817–1890)

Danish composer of opera, choral works, symphonies, chamber music, and piano pieces; his style was influenced by Mendelssohn and Schumann.

Tre Karakteerstykker (Three character pieces in march form), Op.18. Copenhagen: Hansen, ca.1849; Peters, ca.1850. DK:A,Kk—GB:Lbl—US:Bp, NYcu,PHf,Wc. (I)

Nordiske Tonebilleder, Fantasien (Norwegian tone pictures, fantasies), Op.4. Copenhagen: C.C.Lose & Delbancos, ca.1841; Hansen, 1843; Augener, 1882. US:NYp,Wc. Three charming pieces in Romantic style with Nordic folk flavor; there is strong individuality in the composer's melodic and harmonic idiom. (I)

Gaertner, Marie-Thérèse

French teacher and composer of music for children.

°Concertino (G), pour piano à quatre mains et percussion. Paris: Leduc, 1969. Charming, tuneful, effective work featuring simple variations on a lively theme through carefully designed modifications of mode, rhythm, tempo, and meter. The ensemble is not difficult to work out with percussion. Enjoyable to play and to hear; excellent concert piece. (UE-LI)

Gál, Hans (1890–)

Austrian musicologist and composer; Scottish resident; his compositions are written in neo-Romantic style.

Three marionettes (Pantalone; Columbina; Arlecchino), Op.74. London: Augener, 1960. GB:Lbl—US:NYp,Wc. Full-textured, descriptive pieces in tonal idiom with piquant harmonies and strong rhythms. (LI-I)

Serbische Weisen, Op.3 (1916). Vienna: UEd., 1919. US:Wc. Suite of six Serbian folk songs in tasteful settings. (I)

Galaverni, I.

°*La festa del Babbo,* sei pezzettini facili (Augurio mattutino; Fiori e doni; Raccontino; Scampagnata; Pranzo di gala; Si danza). Milan: Carisch, n.d. (LI-I)

°*I piccoli concertisti,* quattro pezzi di media difficoltà. Milan: Carisch, n.d. (LI-I)

Galimberti, Giuseppe (1851–1909)

Italian composer of operettas and instrumental pieces of light character.

[8] *Schizzi campestri* (Al mattino; La valletta; Il molino; Nella chiesa; Sul lago; Godimento di perca; Canto del Boseginolo; La calma della sera). Milan: Carisch & Jänichen, 1905. US:Wc. Easy pedagogical pieces; good balance between parts. (UE-LI)

Galluzzi, Giuseppe (1861–1936)

Italian teacher and composer of instructional pieces for piano.

°*A rotta di collo,* galop. Milan: Carisch, n.d.

°*Il primo concerto del giovane pianista.* [32] Pezzettini melodici. 6 vols. Milan: Carisch, n.d. (UE-LI/E-5)

°*Ricreazioni,* [24] piccoli pezzi melodici, 2 vols. Milan: Ricordi, 1918; 1925. (UE-LI/E-5)

Gandini, Alessandro (1807–1871)

Italian court conductor and opera composer.

°*Six sonatines* (C,D,G,F,A,D). NEd. Paris: Gallet, 1931. (UE-LI/E)

Gänsbacher, Johann Baptist (1778–1844)

Austrian conductor. His compositions are written in Classical style with early Romantic elements: chromaticism and unusual modulations.

Divertimento (G), Op.20. Vienna: Artaria, ca.1818. A:Wgm.

Divertissement (Eb), Op.29. Vienna: Artaria, 1821. A:Wgm. This four-movement work is similar to Op.20 in three movements: both are long, rambling, amiable pieces and light in character. Although some of the melodic ideas and their development are unexceptional, they are handled competently. (I)

Six variations sur l'air Ist denn Liebe ein Verbrechen (A), Op.9. Bonn: Simrock; Leipzig: Kühnel, 1809. A:Wgm—D-brd:Mbs—D-ddr:Dlb. Unpretentious, expressive, sure-handed writing. (I)

Ganschals, Carl

Big notes; Cheer up; Comic song; Hussar's galop; In double time; March; Rustic dance. In collection *Duet playing,* ed. Leo Podolsky. (E)

Gárdonyi, Zoltán
[15] *Hungarian folk songs*. Budapest: Zeneműkiadó Vállalat, n.d.

Garrow, Louise
American composer of piano music for children.
°*Caribbean moonlight*. Melville, NY: Belwin, 1971. Rhythmic tune with calypso flavor featuring syncopation. (LI)
°*Easy for two* (Playing games; Moonlight serenade; Cherry pie; Little lost lamb; Swing time; Boogie blues; Away we go; Princess Red Wing; Thanksgiving is here; Santa's reindeer). New York: Schroeder & Gunther, 1955. Simple tunes, active in both parts; printed in large notes. (E)
°*March of the animals*. Melville, NY: Belwin, n.d. (LE)
°*Sailor's polka*. New York: Schroeder & Gunther, 1961. Lively, bright, well-balanced teaching piece. (E-UE)
°*Wee wooden shoes*. New York: Schroeder & Gunther, 1957. (UE)

Garścia, Janina
°*Graj ze mną na cztery ręce* (Let's play a piano duet) (Vol.I: Echo; The drum; Lullaby; Tarantella; Kitten and mouse. Vol.II: A country melody; Kujawiak; Our paths shall never meet; Maciek; Brigands' dance), Op.37. °Kraków: PWM, 1968 (Vol.I), 1971 (Vol.II); °Amsterdam: Broekmans & Van Poppel, n.d. The delightful little pieces in this two-volume set are nicely arranged for both parts. The writing is idiomatic with some modal flavor and tone painting. The books are beautifully laid out and are provided with charming illustrations. (E-LI)

Garztecka, Irena
°*Kolej* (A train ride). In collection *Drobiazgi* II, ed. Raube. (LI)
°*Taniec muszek* (Dance of the young flies). In collection *Drobiazgi* II, ed. Raube. (LI)

Gaynor, Jessie L. (1863–1921)
American composer of songs and piano pieces for children.
°*Miniature duets* (The merry-go round; A little duet; The gypsies; The waltzing mice; Peasant dance; A little waltz; Night song; Voyage of the rocking chair). Philadelphia: Presser, n.d.

Geijer, Erik Gustaf (1783–1847)
Swedish historian, philosopher, theologian, poet, and composer. His relatively small output of music shows the influence of Haydn and Mozart along with later stylistic tendencies resembling those of Schumann.
Sonata (f) (Dubbel Sonate) (1819). Stockholm: C. Müller, 1820. S:Uu.
Dubbel sonata (Eb) (1819). Ms. S:Sic,Uu.
Both these three-movement "double" sonatas are of exceptional interest for their advanced use of chromaticism and extraordinary harmonic relationships. They have both Classical and Romantic affinities in structure and

style. Despite some awkward writing, they are charming representatives of the medium and should be reprinted. (I)

Geiser, Walther (1897–)

Swiss musician.

Pastorale, Op.20 (1947). Pub. by the composer. CH:Zma.

Geist, K.

°*Seven Mari folk songs and dances*, Op.14. Moscow: State Publishing House, n.d.

Geister, Karl

La comédie (Pantalon; Arlequin; Colombine; Pierrot; Scaramouche). Paris: Durand, 1910. US:Wc. Teaching pieces. (E-UE)

La fête à ma tante. Paris: Durand, 1911. US:Wc. Teaching piece. (UE-LI/ E-5)

Gemmingen, Eberhard Friedrich, Freiherr von (1726–1791)

Trois sonates (Eb,C,F), Op.1. Offenbach: André, 1786. GB:Lbl–S:Skma. Short three-movement works in lightweight, watery, Classical style by a dilettante nobleman. (LI-I)

Gentil, M.L.

°*Six courtes pièces pour les jeunes enfants* (Prélude; Clair matin; Petite ronde; Petite valse; Choral; Petit berger). Paris: Lemoine, 1936. US: NYp. Charming suite of descriptive teaching pieces. (LI/E)

Genzmer, Harald (1909–)

German composer and teacher. He writes in neo-Classical style influenced by Hindemith. Among his works are concertos, orchestral pieces, chamber music, and piano compositions.

°*Sonata* (D). Leipzig: Litolff, 1943. Attractive, melodious, ingratiating, compact work in linear setting. The work begins with a fast-paced bright allegro; moves into a quiet, flowing middle movement; and ends with a lively finale, in which the staccato theme, treated fugally at first, moves to a brilliant climax and subsides quietly with the theme in inversion at the end. Effective and grateful for both performers. (I-UI)

°*Spielbuch*, 2 vols. Mainz: Schott, 1942–43. Effective sets of pieces in the same polished idiom as the *Sonata*. (Vol.1: I/E-5; Vol.2: I/UE-LI)

Spielmusiken, for violins, recorders, and four hands. Pub. and date missing. D-brd:DSim.

George, Jon

American composer of music for children.

°*Cowboy song.* Evanston, IL: Summy-Birchard, 1970. Short, melodious tune. (UE/E)

°*Kaleidoscope duets*, five books. New York: Alfred Music Pub., 1973–74. Tuneful well-balanced duets for two equal performers; the idiom is conservative and refined; carefully balanced for both performers. (LE-LI)

°*Play time two;* eight elementary piano solos and five duets. Evanston, IL: Summy-Birchard, 1971. The five winsome duets in this collection are easy for the student and a bit more difficult for the teacher. (UE-LI/E)

°*Two at one piano,* Books I, II, III. Evanston, IL: Summy-Birchard, 1969–76. These three volumes include pieces in folk-song style—some plaintive, some rollicking—and in a variety of other styles; excellent ensemble fare for young pianists. (E-LI)

German, Edward (1862–1936)

English composer, violinist, and theater conductor; cultivated a light, tuneful, and theatrically effective style.

Four pianoforte duets (Humoresque; Reverie; Valse fantastique; Caprice). London: Ashdown, 1925. GB:Lbl.

Tarantella. London: Ashdown, n.d. US:Wc. Light salon music. (LI)

Gernsheim, Friedrich (1839–1916)

German pianist, composer, and conductor. He wrote instrumental and vocal works in eclectic style.

Tanzstücke (Alla mazurka; All'ongarese; Walzer; All'ongarese), Op.30. Mainz: Schott, 1873. US:Wc. (I-UI)

Tongedichte (Angelus; Auf der Piazzetta; Ballade; Weihe der Nacht; Tanz), Op.67. Leipzig: Rieter-Biedermann, 1901. Collection of descriptive and mood pieces in Romantic style. (I-LA)

Gevaert, François-Auguste (1828–1908)

Belgian historian, theorist, teacher, and composer.

Gran fantasia para piano a cuatro manos sobre motivos españoles (Grand fantasy for piano four hands on Spanish motives). B:Bc. Madrid: Salazar, n.d. Medley of Spanish folk and dance tunes in salon idiom. (I)

Geyer, Johann Egidius (ca.1760–1808)

German lawyer and musical dilettante.

Six petites pièces, pour ceux qui sont encore des écoliers. Brunswick: Pub. missing, 1800. °NEd. Andante (F) and Andante grazioso (G) in collection *Vermischte Handstücke,* ed. Kreutz. Short, melodious works in Classical style; principal interest is in Primo part. (UE-LI)

Walzer, Liv. 2. Leipzig: C.F. Lehmann, ca.1799. D-brd:LB—D-ddr:HAu.

Ghiel, T.F. de

Sonata concertante (D), for two violins, two French horns, double bass, and piano 4H. Mainz: Schott, n.d. D:brd:Mbs. A trifling work, this curiosity was composed for and dedicated by a first lieutenant to his commanding officer, Baron de Zweyer, general and chief commandant of Frankfurt. It is doubtful whether the five added instruments contributed materially to the total effect of this thin, derivative, and unvaried work, or whether they are merely an adventitious ornament. In any case, if the

Concerto pleased the Baron, and incidentally earned the composer a promotion, it really didn't matter. (I)

Giasson, Paul E.

American musician.

°*The carriage trade*. New York: General Music, 1964. (LI-I)

°*The cuckoo bird*. New York: General Music, 1963. This work and the one above are amiable, rhythmic, melodious pieces in the popular style of a soft-shoe dance. (LI-I)

°*Dance of the Christmas goose*. New York: Harold Flammer, 1965. Lively, witty piece with rhythmical drive. (LI-I)

°*Little ballerina*. New York: Harold Flammer, 1964. Spirited waltz. (UE-LI)

°*Three play-full piano duets*. New York: General Music, 1969. Entertaining, bright, cleverly written pieces of moderate length, evocative of light popular music. (I-UI)

°*The puppet parade*. New York: Harold Flammer, 1964. Dashing, rhythmical march tune spiced up with occasional blue notes. (LI)

°*A sleigh bell serenade*. New York: General Music, n.d.

°*Waltz for a rainy afternoon*. New York: Harold Flammer, 1965. Slow, wistful waltz tune in popular-music style. (LI)

Gieseking, Walter (1895–1956)

German pianist; outstanding interpreter of Chopin and French Impressionist composers as well as the German Classicists. His compositions include songs, chamber music, and piano works.

Spiel um ein Kinderlied. Berlin: Johannes Oertel, 1948. US:Wc. Charming set of variations on "Ah, vous dirai-je, Maman," ingeniously worked out in effective, mildly contemporary style. (I-UI)

Gigout, Eugène (1844–1925)

French organist and composer; studied with Saint-Saëns. He wrote organ music, sacred choruses, and piano pieces.

°*Caprice-ballet*. Paris: Hamelle, n.d.

°*Fantaisie scolastique*. Paris: Hamelle, n.d.

°*Pièce symphonique*. Paris: Hamelle, ca.1900.

Gilbert, Anthony (1934–)

English; has written an opera, music for small orchestra, and works for various instrumental combinations. He writes in serial idiom; often makes use of electronic devices.

°*Sonata* No.2, Op.8 (1966–67). London: Schott, 1969. US:Wc. Avant-garde; pointillistic, complex work in four movements: Strophe I, Strophe II, Jamboree I, and Jamboree II. The score calls for fist and forearm clusters, string plucking inside the piano, and cloth and metal string mutes. Conventional notation is supplemented by indications for harmonics, unusual pedalings, and other special effects. Extremely difficult. (A)

Gilbert, Gladys V.

Picture tales. London: Stainer & Bell, 1921. US:Wc. Short, easy teaching pieces in simple harmonic style. (UE)

Gilbert, Henry Franklin Belknap (1868–1928)

American composer; pupil of MacDowell; made use of Creole, Negro, and American Indian melodies. His works include ballet music, choral and orchestral works, songs, and piano compositions; his style is vigorous and spontaneous.

°*Three American dances* (Uncle Remus; Delphine; Br'er Rabbit). Boston: Boston Music Co., 1919. US:Bp,NYp,Wc. Inspired by the Uncle Remus stories. The three pieces in this set vary in mood but they all flow along gracefully in catchy, syncopated, ragtime rhythms, strikingly reminiscent of Scott Joplin's rags. These works are very much in the tradition of the 4H Creole dances by the nineteenth-century American composer Louis Moreau Gottschalk. They are infused with folk feeling, extensive modal flavor, and an irrepressible beat. (I-UI)

Gilchrist, William Wallace (1846–1916)

American organist; composed choral music, songs, symphonies, and piano works.

Une petite suite (Alla marcia; Mélodie; Styrienne; Fughetta). Boston: A.P. Schmidt, 1885. US:Wc. Salon-style suite concluding with well-constructed and spirited little fugue. (I-UI)

Gildon, John

A favorite duet (Bb), Op.14. London: J. Balls, ca.1818. US:NYp.

A grand duett, Op.12. London: J.Balls, ca.1818. US:NYp.

Both duets, Op.14 in two movements and Op.12 in three, are cast in a naive, uneventful Classical idiom with charming melodies but weak thematic development.

Gilse, Jan van (1881–1944)

Dutch composer and conductor; wrote symphonic works, choral pieces, songs, chamber music, and piano pieces.

°*Variaties over een St.Nicolaasliedje* (Variations on a St. Nicholas song). Middelburg: Noske, 1910; Amsterdam: Alsbach, n.d. °NEd. Donemus, n.d.

Ginneken, Jaap van (1913–1973)

Dutch sound technician and composer; has written symphonies, string quartets, piano concertos, and piano pieces.

Scène à deux. Amsterdam: Donemus, 1944. NL:Ad.

Giordani, Tommaso (ca.1730–1806)

Italian composer; worked in London and Dublin. He composed or wrote sections of more than fifty operas; also wrote songs and instrumental works.

A duetto for two performers on one pianoforte or harpsichord (C). London: John Preston, ca.1785. GB:Bp,Gu,Lbl,Ob.

Four favorite duettinos for two performers . . . (C,G,D,Bb). London: John
Preston, ca.1785. GB:Ckc,Lbl. NEd. Duettino No.3 (D), in collection
Piano Duets of the Classical Period, ed. Townsend.

*A first sett of three duetts for two performers on one piano forte or harpsi-
chord* (C,D,Bb). London: S. Babb, ca.1780. GB:Lbl—US:NYp,R,Wc.
Also published as *Trois sonates* . . . , Op.9. Berlin: Hummel, 1783. A:Wgm
—B:Bc—F:Pn—NL:DHgm—USSR:Mk.

*A second sett of three duetts for two performers on one piano forte or harp-
sichord* (G,Eb,F). London: S.Babb, ca.1780. CH:Fcu—GB:Lbl—US:NYp,
Wc.

These six pleasant two-movement sonatas, appearing in two sets of three
duets each, are set in a Classical idiom. They are reminiscent of J.C.
Bach's *Duettini* in conception, style, and texture, with an abundance of
Alberti bass accompaniments, antiphonal thematic development, and extensive use of sixths and tenths between the parts. The first movements
are in sonata-allegro form, followed by shorter and lighter movements
consisting of dance forms and themes with variations. (I)

Trois sonates à quatre main [sic] *sur un clavecin ou forte piano* (Bb,C,F).
Paris: Sieber, n.d. S:Skma.

Girnatis, Walter (1894–   )

Polish-born German composer of symphonies, concertos, cantatas, church
music, radio operas, and piano pieces.

°Kleine Suite, from *Musik zu einem Handpuppenspiel* (Listiges Vorspiel;
Romanze; Kleiner Tanz; Burleske). In collection *Spielbuch, zeitgenössische Originalkompositionen*. Bright, cheerful work in traditional harmonic setting, with angular rhythms and contrasts in mood. (I)

Glazunov, Alexandre (1865–1936)

Russian composer, settled in Paris; wrote symphonies, concertos, ballets,
songs, and piano pieces in Romantic style, uninfluenced by Russian nationalist elements.

Pastourelle. See *Badinage*.

Glière, Reinhold (1875–1956)

Russian composer; pupil of Arensky, Tanayev, and Ippolitov-Ivanov. He
wrote prolifically in late Romantic style, often with Russian folk influences.
His music is well crafted and has strong dramatic quality.

[24] *Easy pieces*, Op.38. Moscow: Jurgenson, 1909. NEd. Moscow: State
Publishing House, n.d. US:PHf,Wc. Book I: Prelude; Waltz; Impromptu;
Menuet; Popular song; Mazurka. Book II: Albumleaf; Moment musicale;
Elegy; Melody; Lullaby; Scherzo. Book III: Regret; Restlessness; Lyrical
moment; Fairy tale; Orientale; Sketch. Book IV: Reverie; Arabesque;
Intermezzo; Song; Sad thoughts; Tarantella. Engaging series of short,
sensitive pieces, masterfully set for 4H; should be reprinted. (LI)

[12] *Pieces* (—; —; Sketch; Lament; Etude; Shepherd song; Arabesque;

Dreaming; Mazurka; Fughetta; Scherzo; Orientale), Op.48. Moscow: Jurgenson, 1911. US:Wc (missing first two pieces). °Op.48/5, 11 (Etude and Scherzo), in collection *Eighteen Original Piano Duets*, ed. Balogh. °Op.48/4 (Lament), in *Russian Music for the Young Pianist*, Vol.5, ed. Zeitlin and Goldberger (New York: MCA, 1969). A second set of exceptionally fine pieces, similar in style and character to Op.38. (LI)

Glinka, Mikhail (1804–1857)

Considered to be the first Russian nationalist composer, Glinka wrote in a clear, post-Classical musical idiom making frequent use of native thematic material. His four-hand works are only a fraction of his total output. They consist mainly of short, lively pieces in popular dance forms (Trots de Cavalerie, Polka, and Galop). They show stylistic consistency and capable writing for the two parts.

°*Capriccio sur des thèmes russes* (1934). Moscow: Jurgenson, 1904. US: NYp,PHf,Wc. Long, repetitious, and episodic. (I-LA)

°*Impromptu en galop* (Bb) on the Barcarolle from Donizetti's *L'Elisir d'Amore* (1832). (I)

°*Polka* (Bb) (1852). Moscow: Jurgenson, 1904. (I-UI)

°*Trot de cavalerie* (C) (1829–30). Moscow: Jurgenson, 1878. US:NYp,PHf. (I)

°*Trot de cavalerie* (G) (1829–30). Moscow: Jurgenson, 1878. (I)

M. Glinka Polnoye Sobranie-Sochinenii (Glinka's Complete Works), vol.5. Moscow: State Music Publishing House, 1957. Contains Glinka's complete 4H works.

Glover, David Carr (1925–   )

American musical pedagogue and composer of piano teaching materials.

°*Blow that bugle.* Melville, NY: Belwin, 1971. Short piece, based on bugle call, in jazz idiom with syncopation. (LE)

°*Clap it boogie.* New York: Schroeder & Gunther, 1951. Instructional work in boogie style. (UE-LI)

°*Clowns.* Melville, NY: Belwin, 1969. Light, bouncy teaching piece. (UE)

°*Donkey with a sombrero.* Melville, NY: Belwin, 1969. Latin rhythms are featured in this bright little piece. (UE)

Hayride boogie. New York: Charles Hansen, 1961.

°*Piano duets*, Level I, II, IV. Melville, NY: Belwin, 1971. Arrangements and original pieces in easy, flowing, predictable style. (UE)

°*Waltz.* Melville, NY: Belwin, 1971. Simple melody and accompaniment; evenly balanced parts. (LE)

Gnesin, Mikhail Fabianovich (1883–1957)

Russian composer; studied with Rimsky-Korsakov and Liadov. He wrote many works with Jewish associations, including operas, orchestral suites, and chamber music. Gnesin also composed songs, folk-song arrangements, and piano works. His style is lyrical and Romantic, with Hebrew and other folk influences.

Detiam, malen'kaia siuita (For children, little suite) (Spring dance; Oriental dance I; Oriental dance II; Song of the knight of old; Lullaby; Ballet waltz), Op.27. Moscow: State Music Publishing House, 1919. US:Wc. Delightful suite of pieces with Russian flavor; shows excellent craftsmanship and sensitivity for the 4H medium. (LI-UI)

Malenkie p'esy (Little pieces) (Swan lake; Waltz; Red Ridinghood; Dance), Op.29. Moscow: State Music Publishing House, 1940. US:Wc. Short, colorful, tone pictures from Andersen's fairy tales. (I-UI)

Pesni i tantsi adygeiskikh Cherkesov (Songs and dances of the Adygei Circassians) (Meramuk; Zezhuako; Kazhra; Song of the flood; Song of the Adygei youth), Op.53. Moscow: State Music Publishing House, 1941. US:Wc. Exotic, atmospheric settings of Circassian folk melodies. (I)

Piat' pesen narodov SSSR (Five folk songs of the USSR) (Sar kaiak; Siudov, siudov; Kolektivse vania eri; Biulbiul em; Melody of the Crimean Tartars), Op.54. Moscow: State Music Publishing House, 1939. US:Wc. Effective folk-song settings, some with vivid oriental coloring. (I)

Variations on an "Orah," Op.35. Jerusalem: Jibne Ed., n.d.

Gnesina, Yelena Fabianova (1874–1967)
Soviet pianist and teacher; wrote pedagogical music.

[2] *P'esy* (Pieces) (Patty cake; March). Moscow: State Music Publishing House, 1929; also in *Izbrannye detskie p'esy dlia fortepiano,* ed. Z. Finkelshtein (Moscow: State Music Publishing House, 1963). US:NYp. (UE-LI)

Godard, Benjamin (1849–1895)
French composer of operas, stage music, orchestral music, choral and chamber works, and piano pieces written in light salon style.

°Contes de la veillée, six morceaux (Conte pastorale; Conte amusant; Conte triste; Conte burlesque; Conte surnaturel; Conte de chevalerie), Op.67. Paris: Durand, 1882. US:Wc. Character pieces, artfully set. (I)

Carnaval, six morceaux (Columbine, polketta; Marguerite, valse; Pierrot, galop; Española, habañera; Fleurette, mazurka; Scaramouche, galop). Berlin/Leipzig: Simrock, 1893. US:Wc.

Quatre morceaux caractéristiques et très faciles, Op.115. Leipzig: Forberg, n.d.; London: Ashdown, n.d. US:Wc. (I)

Godowsky, Leopold (1870–1938)
Polish-born American pianist and composer. He wrote concert studies and piano pieces, and transcribed many famous orchestral works into virtuoso piano compositions and performed them.

Miniatures. New York: Carl Fischer, 1918. US:Bp, PHf. *First Suite:* In church; At night; Lullaby; Rustic dance. *Second Suite:* Arietta; Sarabande;

Cradle song; Baratelle (valsette). *Third Suite:* Prelude (The organ point); Chorale; Hymn; Epilogue (Retrospect for l.h. alone). *Ancient Dances:* First minuet (C); Second minuet (G); °Rigaudon; Gavotte; Bourrée; Siciliana; Irish jig. *Modern Dances:* Polka; Tyrolean (Ländler), Valse élégiaque; °Tarantella (Italy); °Csárdás (Hungary); Mazurka (Chopin-esque); Polonaise. *Miscellaneous Pieces:* Serenade; The miller's song; °Meditation; °Pastorale (Angelus); °The exercise; °Processional march; Scherzo; Arabian chant (Orientale); Albumblatt (Intermezzo); °Funeral march; Plaintive melody; Ballade; °Nocturne; °Barcarolle; °Humoresque; Toccatina; Impromptu (In days of yore); °The scholar (fughetta); The hunter's call (Woodland mood); Military march. °*Modern Dances* was reprinted by PWM.

A *Key to the Miniatures of Leopold Godowsky*, containing a brief analysis and description of each of the 46 pieces in the series, was at one time available from Carl Fischer. This exceptionally fine collection, comprising three suites of four pieces each, fourteen dances (ancient and modern), and twenty miscellaneous works, forms an impressive array of refined, dextrously fashioned 4H works cast in a variety of styles, forms, and musical idioms. From the point of view of sound structure and interplay of the two parts, the series represents one of the most successful essays made by any composer into the highly restricting field of writing effectively for the Primo in a five-note span, with a more difficult Secondo part. (I-UI/ E-UE-5)

Goedicke, Aleksandr Federovich (1877–1957)

Russian pianist, teacher, and composer of operas, orchestral and chamber music, piano pieces, and folk-song arrangements.

Six pièces (°Valse; °Barcarolle; Marche; °Berceuse; Sérénade; Gavotte), Op.12. Moscow: State Music Publishing House, 1928. US:NYp,Wc. Charming, melodious, solidly crafted pieces in effective Romantic idiom; first-class teaching material. (LI-I)

Goethel (Göthel), Ernst

Nocturne (Kanon in der Terzdecime), Op.5. Leipzig: Kahnt, 1905. US:Bp, Wc. Musical oddity; canon at the thirteenth (upper sixth) written in such a way that both players read from the same two lines of music, the Primo in the G clef, and the Secondo in the F clef. Appropriate signals indicate entries of the canon; works out well and effectively with a few rhythmical problems. (I-UI)

Goetz, Hermann (1840–1876)

German composer of two operas, symphonic and choral works, chamber music, and piano compositions; his premature death cut short a promising career.

°*Sonata* (g), Op.17 (1865–1866). Leipzig: Kistner, 1878. °NEd. Munich-

Gräfelfing: Verlag Walter Wollenweber, 1970 (in the series *Unbekannte Werke der Klassik und Romantik*); °Amadeus, 1976. Lyrical, fluent, and imaginative three-movement work, regarded as one of the finest 4H sonatas of the nineteenth century. An exemplary work for the medium in its harmonic and contrapuntal interest, clarity of texture, and sensitively balanced parts. Shows the influence of Mendelssohn rather than Schumann. Lies well under the hands. (UI-A)

Goldmark, Karl (1830–1915)

Viennese composer of Hungarian origin; best known for his *Rustic Wedding Symphony*. Other works include operas, chamber music, and piano pieces. His music, often overly sentimental, is characterized by melodic invention and artful manipulation of thematic materials.

°*Drei Stücke*, Op.12. Budapest: Editio Musica, 1956 (Rózsavölgyi, 1891). A:Wgm. Pieces of contrasting color and mood in Romantic style: Pastorale; marchlike Polonaise; assertive Finale. The texture of all three· pieces suggests orchestral origin. (I-UI)

Tänze, Op.22. Mainz: Schott, 1876. US:Wc.

Goldner, Wilhelm (1839–1907)

A minor composer in the Romantic tradition, Goldner concentrated his efforts on four-hand composition, and produced a quantity of attractive, flowing pieces that demonstrated great dexterity and inventiveness. His thirteen suites, resembling sonatas in style and form, are especially remarkable for their craftsmanship and richness of sound.

Danse russe, Op.43. St. Louis: Balmer & Weber, 1886. US:Wc. (I)

°*Première sonatine* (C). Paris: Lemoine, n.d. (UE)

°*Deuxième sonatine* (C). Paris: Lemoine, n.d. (E)

°*Troisième sonatine* (g). Paris: Lemoine, n.d. (UE)

°*Quatrième sonatine* (F). Paris: Lemoine, n.d. (LI)

Suite hébraïque sur des vieux chants du synagogue (F) (Melodie am Gesetzgebungsfest [Shavuoth]; Dankgesang am Befreiungsfest [Al horishonim]; Lied am Makkabäerfest [Channukah]; Kol Nidrei), Op.64. Leipzig: Schuberth, 1905. US:Wc.

Suite mélodique (Bb), Op.63. Leipzig: Schuberth, 1904. US:Wc.

Suite moderne No.1 (D), Op.38. Leipzig: Schuberth, 1875. US:PHf (LI-I)

Suite moderne No.2 (C), Op.39. Leipzig: Schuberth, 1876. US:Wc.

Suite moderne No.3 (G), Op.40. Leipzig: Schuberth, 1877; Boston: Boston Music Co., 1917. US:Bp,PHf,Wc.

Suite moderne No.6 (G), Op.49. Leipzig: Schuberth, 1887. US:Bp.

Suite nuptiale (D) (*Hochzeitsmusik*) (Cortège; Chant de la fiancée; Ronde de la fiancée; Nocturne), Op.65. Leipzig: Schuberth, 1906. US:Wc.

Suite pittoresque (c), Op.59. Leipzig: Schuberth, 1898. US:Wc.

Suite romantique (a), Op.61. Leipzig: Schuberth, 1901. US:Wc.

Waldscenen, suite caractéristique (E♭) (Unter den Bäumen; Dianens Jagdzug; Auf einsamen Wegen; Runde der Berggeister), Op.58. Leipzig: Schuberth, 1897. US:Wc.

Goldstein, Michael
Soviet music editor and composer.
°*Fröhlicher Tanz.* In collection *Brother and Sister,* ed. Goldstein. Vigorous, amiable work, with some tricky passage work for the Primo. (UE-LI)

Gómis, José Ramón
Alma de España. Madrid: Unión Musical Española, 1956. US:Wc. Jota in light salon style. (I)

Goolkasian, Dianne
°*Tarantella.* Brighton, MA: Carousel Publishing Co., 1972.

Gottlieb, Jack (1930–)
American composer of songs, synagogue music, and orchestral and vocal works.
The silent flickers, twelve diversions for piano four hands (1967) (Opening titles; .The heroine's face emerges out of the rose;. The softshoe vamp; Cheek-to-cheek with the chic sheik; The chase; The old homestead; The royal hunt [variations: a. Fanfare; b. Horses and hounds; c. Fall of the stag; d. The groaning board; e. Processional]; March of the suffragettes; Dalliance and intrigue at the masked ball; Barbershop quartet; Speak easy to the pink lady; Into the sunset; The end?). Ms. Available from composer, Hebrew Union College, 40 W. 68 St., New York, NY 10023. Evocative, amusing satire on the music and situations of the silent films. The style is tonal and mildly dissonant, with a strong jazz flavor. Frequent awkwardness in the setting of the two parts suggests an origin in some other medium, possibly orchestral. (UI-A)

Gottschalk, Louis Moreau (1829–1869)
One of the most dazzling and romantic figures of the American musical world of the mid-nineteenth century, Gottschalk was a brilliant ·virtuoso pianist with a flamboyant style and a flair for dramatic programming. As a composer he wrote for piano solo and for orchestra, and contributed to the four-hand repertoire with numerous arrangements of solo piano works along with the following original duets. The abbreviation CCat refers to the catalog number of the composer's works listed in *The Centennial Catalogue of the Published and Unpublished Compositions of Louis Moreau Gottschalk* (New York: Prepared for *Stereo Review* by Robert Offergeld, 1970).
La Gallina, Op.53 (1863), CCat 100. Boston: Oliver Ditson, 1865.
Ojos criollos, Op.37 (1859), CCat 184. New York: William Hall, 1859.
Radieuse (Grande valse de concert) (ca.1859), CCat 217. Boston: Oliver Ditson, 1865. First published under the pseudonym of "Seven Octaves."

Réponds-moi, Op.50 (1859), CCat 225. New York: William Hall, 1864.
°*The Piano Works of Louis Moreau Gottschalk*, ed. Vera Brodsky Lawrence
(New York: Arno Press and New York Times, 1969) contains reprints
of the above works. The three Cuban dances, La Gallina, Ojos criollos,
and Réponds-moi, are strongly spiced with Creole flavor and syncopated
rhythms and reflect the composer's fascination with Caribbean folk music
and dance. They also represent a genre of piano duet concert music in
which the moderately difficult Secondo supplied the foundation for the
brilliant, often technically demanding, Primo. This novel form was ideally
suited to Gottschalk's frequent concert tours of the Western hemisphere in
the mid-nineteenth century. It added a touch of variety to his solo pro-
grams; with a local pianist supplying the basic rhythmic and harmonic
support in the relatively unspectacular Secondo part, the composer would
continue to dazzle his audiences, this time with glittering displays of pyrotechnics in the upper register of the instrument. (I-UI/A)

Gounod, Charles (1818–1893)

French composer of the successful opera *Faust;* also wrote symphonic and
liturgical music, songs, and piano pieces.

Andante. Ms. Copy furnished by David R. Reed, Muhlenberg College.
Short, melodious piece in flowing Romantic style. (LI)

L'angélus, melody. London: Augener, n.d. GB:Lbl.

Menuet (g). London: Augener, 1858. GB:Lbl.

Gouvy, Théodore (1819–1898)

French choral and symphonic composer; studied in Berlin. He wrote chamber
music, and many piano pieces.

Sonata (d), Op.36. Paris: Richault (Costallat), 1862. US:Wc.

Sonata (c), Op.49. Paris: Richault (Costallat), 1868. US:Wc.

Sonata (F), Op.51. Paris: Richault (Costallat), 1868. US:Wc.
The three sonatas, Op.36, 49, and 51, are well-written melodious works in
dry instructional style. (I-UI)

Variations sur un thème original (Db), Op.52. Vienna: Doblinger, 1869.
US:Wc. Bright, attractive; somewhat demanding technically, especially
in Primo. (I)

Variations sur une chanson française (c), Op.57. Paris: Costallat, 1873. US:
Wc.

Grädener, Hermann (1844–1929)

Chamber works, piano pieces, operas, and orchestral compositions are included in the output of this German conductor-composer.

Trois impromptus (e,f♯,D), Op.2. Hamburg: Fritz Schuberth, 1868. US:Wc.
Bustling, engaging works, dextrously set for the medium. (I)

Graeff, Johann Georg (late 18th–early 19th century)

Three duets (C,F,D), Op.12. London: Longman, Clementi & Co., ca.1799.
GB:Cu,Lbl,Ob.

A favorite duet (G), Op.14. London: Clementi, Banger, Hyde, Collard & Davis, n.d. US:PHu.

Graf (Graaf), Christian Ernst (ca. 1726–ca.1804)

German-born composer, resident of The Hague.

Dix petites pièces aisées, Op.30. The Hague: pub.missing, n.d. DK:Kmk.

II Sonates, Op.29. The Hague: pub.missing, n.d.; Berlin: Hummel, 1797. DK:Kmk–B:Bc–NL:DHgm,At.

Graham, Robert (1912–   )

American.

°*Fiddle tune*. Philadelphia: Elkan-Vogel, 1961. (E)

°*Maverick trail*. Philadelphia: Elkan-Vogel, 1961. (E)

°*Shepherd's suite*. Philadelphia: Elkan-Vogel, 1967. (LI)

The composer exploits the limited resources of elementary 4H pianism with taste and imagination in these smartly crafted works.

Grainger, Percy Aldridge (1882–1961)

Australian-born pianist; U.S. citizen; studied with Busoni. He collected and edited English folk music and wrote choral and orchestral works, chamber music, and piano pieces.

°*Let's dance gay in green meadow; 'Neath the mould shall never dancer's tread go.* Faeroe Island dance folk song, collected by Hjalmar Thuren, set for one piano twosome (1946). London: Faber Music Ltd., 1967. Diverting curiosity; one of the composer's last manuscripts. Parts are of equal difficulty and move with great rapidity. (A)

Grammann, Carl (1844–1897)

German operatic composer; also wrote symphonies, chamber music, and piano works in conservative idiom.

Walzer, Op.25. Berlin: Ries & Erler, 1875. US:Wc. Suite of waltzes in salon style. (I)

Granados, Enrique (1867–1916)

Spanish composer, pianist, and conductor. He wrote operas, orchestral works, and piano pieces in the Spanish nationalist idiom.

Dos marchas militares. Barcelona: Sociedad Anónima Casa Dotesio, n.d. US: Wc. Two pleasant marches of moderate length, with vivid Spanish color. (I)

Granier, H.

°*Suite villageoise* (Entrée villageoise; Mélancolie; Valse ballet; Saltarelle). Paris: Lemoine, 1908. (I)

Gratia, Louis-Émile

°*Le chant du coucou*. Paris: Consortium Musical, n.d. (E)

Graves, John (1916–   )

English composer; studied at Royal College of Music.

Four springtime pieces. London: Novello, 1954. (UE-LI/E-5)

Graves, Richard Harding (1926–   )

Saucy jig. London: Augener, 1955. GB:Lbl–US:Wc. Bright, lively, happy teaching piece. (UE-LI)

Slavonic dance. London: Augener, 1960. US:Wc. Bustling, rhythmical. (UE-LI)

Gray, Donald

Over the hills. London: Boosey & Hawkes, n.d. (E)

Graziani, Louis

Piccoli pianisti. Florence: A. Forlivesi, n.d.

Graziani-Walter, Carlo (1851–1927)

Italo-Belgian composer of very popular instructional piano music.

Danza orientale, Op.166. Milan: Carisch, n.d.

Diavoletti, galop. Op.167. Milan: Carisch, n.d.

Marcia festiva. Milan: Carisch, n.d.

Raccolta di cinque suonatine sulle cinque note (Preghiera del mattino; L'addio; La partenza; Sul lago; Il ritorno), Op.102. Milan: Lucca, n.d. GB:Lbl. (UE-LI/E-5)

Greer, Jesse (1896–   )

Farmerette. New York: Belwin, n.d.

Greim, Helen A.

Dutch dance. New York: Carl Fischer, 1934. Short, attractive teaching piece. (UE)

Jig. New York: Carl Fischer, 1936. Bright, melodious teaching piece. (E)

Mazurka. New York: Carl Fischer, 1936. Instructional work with strong rhythmical drive. (E)

Twilight. New York: Carl Fischer, 1934. Easy arpeggios are featured in this tuneful piece. (UE-LI)

Gretchaninoff, Alexander (1864–1956)

Russian composer; pupil of Rimsky-Korsakov; U.S. resident. He wrote operas, liturgical music, symphonies, songs and piano works; cultivated a German post-Romantic style.

On the green meadow (On the green meadow; Mother's song; Ballad; Lost in the woods; On a walk; Spring morning; Fairy tale; In the village; In the mountains; Serenade), Op.99. New York: MCA, 1945; *Schott Ed. (Auf grüner Wiese), 1926; Moscow: *State Publishing House, 1952. Exceptionally well-written and attractive suite of well-balanced pieces; frequently reprinted in anthologies. (UE-LI)

Grieg, Edvard (1843–1907)

Norwegian composer of Scottish ancestry. In addition to his famous *Piano Concerto, Peer Gynt Suite,* and *Holberg Suite,* he wrote choral works, songs,

Norwegian folk-music arrangements, and many piano pieces, much of which is of strong nationalist character.

°*Norwegian dances* (d,G,A,D), Op.35 (1881). °Peters, °Schott, °Bèrben (Op.35/2 only), °Schirmer (Op.35/3 only). Charming dances, full of Norwegian folk flavor; familiar in their orchestral transcription, but most effective in original duet form. (UI-A)

°[2] *Waltz Caprices*, Op.37 (1883). °Peters. Graceful, lyrical, light-textured waltzes; technically demanding in part; well worth investigating. (UI/UI-A)

°*Fantasy* (D), Op.11. Augener; Peters. Arr. from *En Fantasi* (1860), concert overture for orchestra.

°[2] *Symphonic pieces* (Ab,c), Op.14. Peters. Arr. from two movements of unpublished symphony (1863). (UI)

Opp. 11 and 14 are transcriptions frequently found in anthologies.

Griffis, Elliot (1893–)
American composer of orchestral and chamber works.

Tunes for two, three and four hands; a book of duets for a beginner and an experienced player. Flushing, NY: D.L. Schroeder, 1943. US:NYp. A motley collection of pieces consisting of folk-song arrangements, little etudes, and original melodies; well worth looking into. (UE-LI/E)

Griffiths, David
°*The little cuckoo.* London: Curwen, n.d. (UE)

Grimaldi, François
Joujoux, six petits morceaux, Op.109. Leipzig: Kistner, n.d. (LI)

Petits bijoux, six morceaux (Valse lente; Sérénade de Pierrot; Mazurka sans gêne; Galop pour rire; Promenade sérieuse; Marche des cadets), Op.120. Boston: A.P. Schmidt, 1893. US:Wc. Short instructional pieces for teacher and pupil. (UE-LI/E-5)

Petits cadeaux, morceaux (Valse gaie; Mazurka amusante; En avant! marche), Op.53. Boston: A.P.Schmidt, 1893. US:Wc. Teaching pieces. (UE-LI/E-5)

Grimm, Julius Otto (1827–1903)
German pianist and composer; friend of Brahms. He wrote piano music and orchestral works.

Zwei Scherzi (b,g), Op.4. Leipzig: B&H, 1853. US:Wc. Brisk, energetic character pieces in salon style. (I)

Grinfeld, G.
Soviet musician.

°*Estonian folk dance* (c). In collection *Brother and Sister,* ed. Goldstein. Graceful arrangement of Soviet ethnic melody. (UE)

Groot, Cor de (1914–)
Dutch pianist and composer.

°*Printemps*. Amsterdam: Donemus, 1961. NL:Ad.
Suite '9' (1974). Amsterdam: Donemus, 1974. NL:Ad.

Grove, Roger (d.1978)

American composer.

°*Couples only*. Chicago: Summy-Birchard, 1976. Attractive, lively teaching piece for early beginners. (UE)

°*Doubletalk*. New York: Carl Fischer, 1973. Sparkling little work with rhythmic excitement and melodic vigor. (E)

°*Together time*. Buffalo: Montgomery Music, 1969. Effective setting of simple melody with accompaniment. (E)

Groven, Eivind (1901–)

Norwegian composer and folk-song scholar; his compositions have been influenced by Norwegian folk music.
Lengsel og dåd (Dreams and deeds), ballad. Ms. N:Onk.

Gruber, Josef

°*A.B.C.* [50] Melodických cvičení pro čtyři ruce (Fifty melodious exercises for four hands). Prague: Artia, ca.1958. US:Wc.

Grund, Friedrich Wilhelm (1791–1874)

German cellist, conductor, and composer. His works include operas, sacred compositions, and orchestral and chamber music.
Grande polonaise (C), Op.14. Leipzig: Peters, 1820. US:Wc. Strong, assertive work in Classical style; capably written for the medium. (I)
Sonata (D), Op.10. Hamburg: Böhme, 1818. US:NYp.

Gump, Richard (pseud. Dr. Fritz Guckenheimer) (1906–)

Fantasia, 1955. Commissioned by Milton and Peggy Salkind. Available from composer, 250 Post St., San Francisco, CA 94108.

Gurlitt, Cornelius (1820–1901)

German pianist, organist and composer of attractive, useful educational piano music.

°*Der Anfänger*, [22] leichte, melodische Uebungsstücke, Op.211. Mainz: Schott, n.d. Resourceful set of instructional pieces arranged in progressive order of difficulty. (UE-LI/E-5)

Bunte Blätter, [12] kleine Tonstücke, Op.163. London: Augener, 1888. (UE-LI)

°[12] *Feuillets d'album* (Albumblätter), Op.147. Mainz: Schott, n.d. Instructional pieces skilfully set in salon style. (UE-LI)

Grateful tasks (Erholungsstunden) (on five notes), Op.102. London: Augener; Mainz: Schott, ca.1880. GB:Lbl. Collection of 26 inviting teaching pieces in all major and minor keys, arranged in progressive order of difficulty. (UE-LI/E-5)

Der Kindergarten, Op.179. Mainz: Schott, 1911; London: Augener, n.d. US:Wc. 34 descriptive pieces in tasteful salon style. (UE-LI)

Kleine Blumenstücke, [20] leichte melodische Tonstücke, Op.178. Leipzig: A.P.Schmidt, 1891. US:Wc. Collection of pleasant teaching pieces. (UE-LI)

Melodische Stücke, Op.81. Leipzig: Forberg, 1876. (UE-LI/E-5)

Präludien und Choräle zur Häuslichen Erbauung, Op.28. Leipzig: B&H, 1866.

Rhythmische Studien, Op.75. Hamburg: Cranz, n.d. GB:Lbl. Twelve instructional pieces adroitly laid out for 4H in various keys and meters, in progressive order of difficulty. (UE-LI)

Eighteen short pieces, Op.136. London: Augener, 1891. GB:Lbl. (E-5/ UE-LI)

Six sonatinas (C,F,d,Eb,c,A), Op.124. London: Augener, 1883, 1891, 1908. GB:Lbl. Instructional works in progressive order of difficulty. (UE-LI)

Drei Sonatinen (F,a,C), Op.57. Hamburg: Cranz, 1873, 1903.

Drei Sonatinen (A,C,b), Op.69. Hamburg: Cranz, 1875, 1903.

Drei Sonatinen (F,a,F), Op.149. Mainz: Schott, 1891.

°*Heiterer Gurlitt* (collection of selected works), ed. Walter Frickert. Leipzig: VEB Peters, 1965. Contains: Op.81/3,8; Op.136/4,5,6; Op.147/14, 15; Op.178/7,9,10,11,12,13; Op.179/2; Op.211/1.

Gutchë, Gene (pseud. of Romeo E. Gutsche) (1907–   )

German-born American composer; works include symphonic and choral music, concertos, chamber works, and piano compositions; uses serial and microtonal techniques.

°*Gemini,* concerto for piano four-hands and orchestra, Op.41 (1965). Unpub. Score and parts may be rented from Galaxy Music Corp. and through the Edwin A. Fleisher Music Collection of PHf. A tape (No.302) is also available from the Fleisher Collection. Commissioned by the University of Minnesota and first performed by the Minnesota Orchestra, Leopold Sipe, conductor, and Victoria Markowski and Frank Cedrone, pianists. *Gemini* is a large-scale symphonic work inspired by the 1965 astronauts' space walk. It is divided into three movements: 1. 9 . . . 8 . . . 7 . . . 6 . . . 5 . . . 4 . . . 3 . . . 2 . . . 1 . . . zero; 2. Walk into space; 3. Earthbound. The composer uses free treatment of serial technique and has scored the concerto for full orchestra with amplified effects. Contemporary critics cite the work's similarity to compositions by Bartók, Stravinsky, and Ives. (A)

Haarklou, Johannes (1847–1925)

Norwegian conductor and composer; his works are written in Romantic style influenced by Norwegian folk song.

Preludium et Fuga, Op.1. Oslo: Warmuth, c/o Norsk Musik-Forlag, n.d.

N:Onk. Serious, moderately long, academic work in fluent contrapuntal style. (UI)

Hahn, Reynaldo (1875–1947)

Venezuelan-born French composer and conductor. He wrote operas, operettas, and stage music. His piano works, songs, and chamber music are written in elegant conservative French style.

Sept berceuses (Berceuse des jours sans nuages; Berceuse pour la veille de Noël; Berceuse pour les enfants de marins; Berceuse des soins d'automne; "Selfiana", berceuse créole; Berceuse pensive [for three hands]; Berceuse tendre). Paris: Heugel, 1904. US:Bp. Masterfully set in placid, refined harmonic style, partly linear and imitative. (I)

Pièce en forme d'aria et bergerie. Paris: Heugel, 1896. US:Wc. Attractive work in direct, unaffected style. (I)

Trois préludes sur des airs irlandais (The little red lark; My love's an arbutus; The willow tree). Paris: Heugel, 1894. US:Wc. Dedicated to the Irish-French composer Augusta Holmès and based on Irish melodies from the collection of Sir Charles Villiers Stanford. These felicitous pieces are pleasant and haunting instructional works. (UE)

Variations puériles sur une mélodie de Reinecke. Paris: Heugel, 1905.

Haieff, Alexei (1914–   )

Russian-born American composer of orchestral and chamber music, ballets, choral pieces, and piano works in neo-Classical style influenced by Stravinsky.

Business as usual, suite (1936). Pub. and date missing.

Sarabande (1941). Pub. and date missing.

Information on these works is available from the composer, c/o Chappell & Co., Inc., 609 Fifth Ave., New York, NY 10017.

Haigh, Thomas (1769–1808)

English violinist, pianist, and composer; studied with Haydn. He wrote violin concerto, songs, chamber music, and instructional piano works in Classical style.

Three duets for two performers, Op.42. London: C. Mitchell, n.d. GB:Lbl. (UE-LI)

Three duettinos, Op.28. London: Lewis Lavenu, ca.1805–11. GB:Lbl.

Two duetts (Bb, Eb). London: Longman & Broderip, n.d. GB:Lbl.

Three duetts with favorite airs, Op.5. London: Preston, 1794.

Three easy duets, Op.7. London: Preston, ca.1797. GB:Lbl–H:Bn.

A favorite duett (Bb), in which is introduced the Portugueze [*sic*] hymn of the Nativity. London: Preston, ca.1800. C:Tu–GB:Cu,Lbl.

Håkanson, Knut (1887–1929)

Swedish composer and conductor; wrote in late Romantic style with strong Swedish folk-song influence.

°*Divertimento* (Marcia; Scherzo; Arioso; Rondo [Polska]), Op.31 (1927). Ms. S:Sic. Suite of graceful dances, carefully balanced between the parts. (I)

°*Svensk suite* No. 2. (Gånglåt; Vals; Intermezzo; Polska), Op.27 (1925). Ms. S:Sic.

Halm, Anton (1789–1872)

Austrian piano teacher and composer; close friend of Beethoven. He wrcte liturgical pieces, chamber music, and piano works.

Grandes variations brillantes sur un thème original, Op.48. Vienna: Witzendorf (Cappi), 1822. A:Wgm.

Trois marches héroïques (E♭,C,C), Op.45. Vienna: Mechetti, 1822. A:Wst. Large-scale works, well written for the medium, but arid and lacking in inspiration. (I).

Haney, Ray (1921–)

Rockin' and drinkin' music for bartenders only. Norwood Music Co., 1961. US:Wc. Soft-shoe jazz piece. (I)

Hanuš, Jan (1915–)

Czech composer of operas, symphonies, chamber music, and piano works.

°*Polní kviti*, lidové písně, tance a koledy (Meadow flowers, popular songs and dances). Prague: Panton, 1968. Collection of Czech folk songs, dances, and carols in tasteful, imaginative settings. (E-UE-5)

Harris, Cuthbert

°*Nine easy duets.* London: Warren and Phillips, 1930. (UE)

°*Hornpipe and jig.* Melbourne: Allan & Co., n.d. (UE-LI)

°*Jolly sailor boy.* Melbourne: Allan & Co., n.d. (UE-LI)

Three Norwegian dances. London: Warren and Phillips, 1927. US:Wc. Short instructional pieces in conservative style. (UE)

Harris, William H. (1883–1973)

English organist and composer of church music and piano pieces in conservative style.

°*The Windsor dances* (Castle walls; Down by the river; At a canter). London: Novello, 1939. Descriptive pieces of moderate length; attractively set for the medium. (LI)

Harteck, Lutz

°*Twenty fingers* (Little mosaic) (Corrida; Little dream; Valsette; Rumbina) (1955). Zürich: Eulenburg, 1957. This engaging work with its four charming pieces was commissioned by Radio Zürich. Written with an easier Primo part, the pieces are set in popular, tuneful style. They lie well for the hands and comfortably satisfy the specifications of the commission, which called for "an original composition for piano four hands, entertaining in the best sense and yet instructive, not too difficult technically yet interesting harmonically and rhythmically; the purpose of the work being to fulfill the wish of many music amateurs, teachers, and pupils, both the young in years and the young in heart, to play something different from the 'customary' four hand compositions." (I/UE-LI)

Hartmann, Johann Peter Emil (1805–1900)

One of the leaders of the Danish school of composers. He wrote operas, symphonic poems on Nordic subjects, and choral works.

Petit rondeau, Op.4 (1826). Copenhagen: Hansen. NEd. 1888. US:Wc. Ingenuous, pleasant work. It may be identical with a composition variously listed as a 4H arrangement by the composer of an early unpublished 2H piano sonata, Op.4; or an original 4H sonatina, Op.4, or a movement of the latter. (I)

Harvey, Vivien (1917–   )

°*Birds of a feather*, ten easy pieces. New York: Ricordi, 1952. US:Wc. (UE)

Häser, August Ferdinand (1779–1844)

German conductor and teacher. He wrote liturgical music, operas, orchestral pieces, and instructional piano music.

Ländler, Op.22. Hanover: Bachmann, 1826. A:Wgm. (I)

Polonaise (Bb), Op.23. Hanover: Bachmann, 1826. A:Wgm. Moderately long work in early Romantic style. (I)

Haslinger, Tobias (1787–1842)

Viennese music publisher; friend of Beethoven.

Sonatines faciles et agréables (C,G). Vienna: Haslinger, n.d. A:Wst. Instructional pieces in thin Classical idiom. (UE-LI)

Hasse, C.F.

Sonate, Op.1. Leipzig: B&H [1802]. PL:WRu.

Hässler, Johann Wilhelm (1747–1822)

German pianist and organist; skilled composer of piano works. His earlier pieces are set in late Baroque style, his later ones in high Classical idiom.

Sonata (c), No.6 of vol.2 of *Leichte Sonaten*. Erfurth: pub. by composer, 1787. NEds. in collection *Sonaten für Liebhaber*, Walter Frickert, ed. Mainz: Schott, n.d.; and in *Zwei Sonaten für Klavier zu drei Händen und zu vier Händen*, ed. Martin Glöder (Hanover: A.Nagel, 1928 [Nagel's Musik-Archiv, Nr.19]).

Sonata (C), for three hands, No.6 of vol.1 of *Leichte Sonaten*. Erfurth: pub. by composer, 1787. NEd. see *Zwei Sonaten für Klavier zu drei Händen. . . .* ed. Martin Glöder, above.

Written in a genial and sure-handed Classical idiom, the above sonatas are two out of the seven the composer wrote for piano, three- and four-hands. The two-movement 4H work opens with a slow, serious adagio featuring dotted rhythms and is followed by a brisk allegro. Both sonatas are sensitively set with contrapuntal interest and harmonic inventiveness. (LI-I)

Hastetter, Ernst

Eine kleine Krippenmusik, for three violins (or two violins and viola), cello ad lib., and piano 4H. Munich: Hieber, 1951. D-brd:DSim.

Hauer, Josef Matthias (1883–1959)

Austrian composer who arrived at his own technique of twelve-tone writing independently of Schoenberg and apparently some time before him, around 1912. His works are structurally complex, dissonant, both chordal and linear. They tend to be tightly compacted and dense, staying within a narrow, limited range in both parts.

°*Echte gewachsene naturbelassene Zwölftonmusik* (February 1959). Vienna: Fortissimo, 1959. US:Wc.

°*Hausmusik* (Sept.1958). Vienna: Fortissimo, 1958. GB:Lbl.

°*Labyrinthischer Tanz* (1952). Vienna: UEd., 1953. GB:Lbl–US:Wc. (I-UI)

Nomos, Op.1, for two pianos or piano 4H. Vienna: Josef Eberle, 1912.

°*Zwölftonspiel* (tone-row by Ernst Hartmann; January 1947). Vienna: Fortissimo, n.d.

°*Zwölftonspiel* for piano 4H and accordion (March 1955). Pub. missing.

°*Zwölftonspiel* (May 1955). Vienna: Fortissimo, n.d.

°*Zwölftonspiel* (1956). Vienna: Fortissimo, 1956. US:Wc. (I)

°*Zwölftonspiel* (July 1956). Vienna: Fortissimo, n.d.

°*Zwölftonspiel* for two violins, viola, cello, and piano 4H (April 1957). Vienna: Fortissimo, n.d.

°*Zwölftonspiel* (July 1957). Vienna: Fortissimo, n.d.

°*Zwölftonspiel* for violin, cello, accordion, and piano 4H (October 1957). Vienna: Fortissimo, n.d.

Haufrecht, Herbert (1909–   )

°*3 Duos*. New York: ACE, n.d. (UE-LI)

°*From the ground up*. New York: ACE, n.d. (UE-LI)

Haupt, Lois von

°*Twelve very first duets for two young pianists*. New York: Carl Fischer, n.d. Elementary instructional pieces. (E-5)

Havelaar, Louis F.

Walse. Rotterdam: L. Coenen, 1836. US:Wc (No.1 and 3 only). Attractive, trim instructional pieces. (UE)

Havlíček, Ilja (1927–   )

Czech editor and musician; has published folk music, dances, songs, and instrumental works featuring native Czech elements.

°*Zahrajme si do tance* (Let's play for dancing). Prague: Artia, 1960. Seventeen Czech dances in charming settings; parts are well balanced. (UE-LI)

Haydn, Franz Joseph (1732–1809)

°*Il maestro e lo scolare*, theme and variations (1778), Hob.XVIIa,1. Available singly from °Schott, and probably others, and in many collections, including °*Classical Album,* Schirmer; °*Pianoforte Album,* Peters; °*Teacher and Student,* ed. Lubin, Amsco Music. One of the most famous works in the duet repertoire, this teaching piece by the great Viennese master makes excellent sight-reading and study material for pianists of every age. Its sudden notational shifts give even an experienced pianist some amusing jolts, and it tests the technical skills of developing pianists with warmth and grace. The teacher (Secondo part) introduces the piece with a phrase that is immediately repeated, note for note, two octaves higher by the student (Primo part). The teacher then plays a second phrase, the student imitates it, and so on. This antiphonal technique, interspersed with sections in which the two parts play together, continues throughout the seven variations with gradually increasing note values and rhythmic complexity. Effective teaching material and delightful entertainment. (UE-LI)

°*Partita* (F) (Allegro; Menuet and Trio) (1778), Hob.XVIIa,2. Included in the following collections: °*Eleven Piano Duets by the Masters,* ed. Zeitlin and Goldberger; °*Piano Duets of the Classical Period,* ed. Douglas Townsend; °*Sonaten für Liebhaber,* ed. Frickert; and °*Style and Interpretation,* vol.V, ed. Howard Ferguson. Somewhat less difficult than *Il maestro e lo scolare,* this pleasant two-movement work is a relatively recent addition to the repertoire, and a welcome one. (I)

Hedges, Anthony

Hornpipe rondo. London: Elkin, 1958. US:Wc. Bright little teaching piece. (UE)

°*Tweedle-dum and Tweedle-dee* (White rabbit; Tweedle-dum and Tweedle-dee; Alice; Caucus race; Queen of hearts; Mock turtle). London: British and Continental Music, 1968. The six pieces of this enchanting suite are based on episodes from *Alice in Wonderland* and are written in a modern harmonic idiom. There is strong emphasis on a variety of rhythmic patterns and considerable linear texture, featuring the canon and other contrapuntal devices. (UE-LI/E-5)

Heiden, Bernhard (1910–)

German-born American composer. He has written chamber and orchestral works, choral music, incidental stage music, and piano pieces in a clear, linear style showing the influence of Hindemith, with whom he studied.

°*Sonata* (1946). New York: Associated Music, 1953. Large-scale work in three movements: Allegro moderato, rapid Ostinato; slow-paced Fantasia-Variations; and a brilliant Vivace, in which the two partners play the same fast passages in different octaves. The music is effectively set in strongly individual neo-Classical style. (A)

Heinrich, Anthony Philip (Anton Philipp) (1781–1861)

American violinist and composer of Czech origin; composed large-scale patriotic, often descriptive orchestral music; frequently used Indian themes; important figure in the musical life of early New York.

The four-pawed kitten dance. A mewsical jest for the piano-forte, purr-formed with eclaw at the Cat-caton Street assemblies, by Miss Cat-herine Grimalkin and her talon-ted sister. This capriccio with a feline purr-ora-tion, is dedi-cat-ed to all mewsical cat-alogues by A.P. Heinrich. London: Clementi, Collard & Collard, ca.1830. US:Wc.

Heins, Carl

°*Flying doves,* galop. Philadelphia: Presser, n.d. (UE)

°*Happy games.* In collection *Duet Playing,* Vol.3, ed. Podolsky. Instructional piece. (UE)

Heintz, Karl

Duo mignon (C), Op.29. Offenbach: André, 1871. D-brd:OF.

Hekker, W.J.C.

°*Pavane Médicis XVIe siècle* (C). Paris: Gallet, n.d. (E-LI/E)

Heller, Stephen (1813–1888)

Hungarian pianist and teacher; his piano works are written in refined and elegant salon style.

°*Six valses,* Op.152. Leipzig: Kistner, 1883; Paris: °Hamelle, n.d.

Helps, Robert (1928–   )

American pianist, teacher, and composer. His works include orchestral and chamber music, vocal compositions, and piano pieces.

°*Saccade.* New York: Peters, 1969. Commissioned by Milton and Peggy Sal-kind. One-movement, atonal work; develops through the use of melodic and harmonic elements rising out of the opening incisive, craggy, four-bar theme. The strongly accented off-beat grace notes tied to the initial chords of the theme and played against the on-beat bass notes suggest a possible explanation for the title: In string terminology, *saccadé* means "jerked" or sharply accented, derived from the French equitation term describing a sudden, sharp reining-in of the horse. The piece is pianistic and lies well for both partners. (A)

Helyer, Marjorie

°*Contrasts,* eight pieces (Gay dance; Cradle song; The lake; Minuet; Ga-votte; Homage to Bach; Song of the Isles; A lively tune). London: No-vello, 1958. (LI)

°*Two dance duets.* London: Novello, n.d. (I)

°*Holiday sketches* (On the river; At sea). London: Novello, 1957. Melodi-ous pieces of moderate length set in a pleasant, effective traditional style. (UE-LI)

°*Nimble fingers,* fourteen very easy duets for little pianists. London: No-vello, n.d. (E)

*Side by side, Book XX (Acrobats; A sunny day; Waltz; Chinese dance; March; Clowns; Russian dance; Goodnight). London: Ashdown, n.d.

*Two's company (The trumpeters; At the ballet; Lavender and lace; A pleasant day; Ländler; Hornpipe; The musical box; On the river). London: Novello, 1958.

Hemberger, Johann August (late 18th century)
Deux symphonies, Op.15. Paris: Boyer, Mme leMenu, n.d. I:Pac.

Hemmer, Eugene (1929–)
American teacher and composer; writes in a basically tonal style.

Remembrance of things present (Promenade; Our Lady of the Angels; Beachnik tango; Sea crystals; Pacific Pan; Sunsets and wine; Venice West: Hora!). Cincinnati: Spire Editions, 1961. US:Wc. Appealing suite of pieces describing some points of interest in southern California. (UI-LA)

Hemmerlein, Joseph (late 18th century)
German pianist and composer of symphonies, piano concertos, chamber works, and piano compositions.

Sonate (F), No.33 du Journal de musique pour les Dames. Offenbach: André, ca.1790. B:Bc–D-brd:LB,Mbs–GB:Lbl. Charming, light, three-movement work in Classical idiom. Delicate, supple melodies with both parts sharing interest. (I)

Sonate (Op.8b), No.58 du Journal de pièces de clavecin par différens auteurs. Paris: Boyer, LeMenu, n.d. I:Tci–S:Skma.

Hengeveld, Gerard (1910–)
Dutch composer; has written a piano concerto, sonatas, film music, and folk-song arrangements.

*Ten folk and rhythmical dances (Hongaarse dans, czardas; Spaanse dans; Rumba; Noorse dans; Quick fox; Irish jigg; Poolse dans; Valse triste; Rumba cubana; Foxtrot). Amsterdam: Broekmans & VanPoppel, 1962. (I/E-5)

*Little suite. Amsterdam: Broekmans & VanPoppel, n.d.

*Ten rhythmical dances (Waltz; Rumba; Tango; Slow foxtrot; Paso doble; March; Quick foxtrot; Samba; Boogie woogie; Berceuse). Amsterdam: Broekmans & VanPoppel, 1960. This set of dances and its companion piece, Ten folk and rhythmical dances above, are compact and felicitous works in popular style. The composer succeeds in making these short, melodious dances interesting and appealing, in spite of the restricted range of the Primo performer. Useful teaching material. (I/E-5)

Henkel, Michael (1780–1851)
German organist and prolific composer of church music, school songs, organ works, and piano pieces.

Der Lehrer und der Schüler, 24 pièces, Op.42. Offenbach: André, n.d. D-brd:OF.

Six petites pieses [sic], No.6. Imprimé par M. Engel à Fulde, n.d. US:PHf. Charming little curiosities from the early nineteenth century. (I)

Sonata (G), Op.16. Bonn: Simrock, ca.1821. A:Wgm. Despite some accomplished writing for both parts, including intricate hand-crossing and some surprise shifts in harmony, this four-movement work in pallid Classical style generally lacks imagination. (I)

Hennessy, Swan (1866–1929)

Irish-born musician; lived in Paris and Switzerland. He composed a quantity of graceful melodious piano pieces, many with Celtic elements as well as chamber music.

Petite suite irlandaise d'après des airs anciens de la collection Petrie. Paris: E. Demets, 1909. US:Wc. Fine settings of old Irish tunes with ingenious treatment of modal material. (I)

Henselt, Adolf von (1814–1889)

Bavarian pianist and teacher. His piano works include a concerto, studies, and many pieces.

Kanon. Leipzig: Rahter, n.d.

Petites pièces (L'Innocence; Petite pièce). St.Petersburg: Bernard, 1877.

Herford, —

Melodies in two. New York: E.B. Marks, n.d.

Heron, William

Three progressive duets, Op.3. London: James Cooper, n.d. GB:Lbl.

Herrmann, Kurt (1900–1975)

German piano pedagogue; published a variety of works on piano teaching.

Dance sketches. Zürich: Hug, 1966. Pleasant suite of short pieces ably set for the medium. Contains waltzes, tangos, fox-trots, blues. (LI/E-5)

Tschechische Volkstänze und Lieder. Leipzig: VEB Peters, 1956. Collection of twenty short folk tunes in attractive settings. (UE-LI/UE)

Herz, Henri (1806–1887)

Austrian pianist and composer; settled in Paris. He wrote eight piano concertos and other piano music, much of it in shallow virtuoso style.

Variations sur l'air Au Clair de la Lune, Op.4. Paris: Henry Lemoine, n.d. US:Wc. Brilliant, technically demanding set of variations in florid style; thin in substance. (A)

[12] *Walses brillantes,* Op.26. Leipzig: F. Hofmeister, n.d. US:Wc. Delightful group of short waltzes (possibly arranged from solo piano pieces). The Primo part sustains most of the interest with the Secondo playing the accompaniment. (LI)

Herz, Jacques Simon (1794–1880)

Pianist and composer; his piano works are similar in character and quality to those of his brother, Henri.

Trois polonaises (Eb,d,C), Op.15. Leipzig: Kistner, ca.1826. US:Wc. Brilliant pieces in florid Romantic style. (I)

Herzogenberg, Heinrich von (1843–1900)

Herzogenberg's contributions to the four-hand literature are skilful, somewhat academic works written in an attractive style strongly influenced by his good friend Brahms. (LI-LA)

Allotria, [6] Stücke, Op.33. Leipzig: Rieter-Biedermann, 1882. US:Wc. (I)

Variationen über ein Thema von Johannes Brahms (a), Op.23. Leipzig: Rieter-Biedermann, 1876. US:Wc. (I)

Variationen (Bb), Op.85. Leipzig: Rieter-Biedermann, 1896. US:Wc. (I)

Variationen (d), Op.86. Leipzig: Rieter-Biedermann, 1896. US:Wc. (I)

Walzer, zweite Folge, Op.83. Leipzig: Rieter-Biedermann, 1896. US:Wc.

Hess, Willy (1906–)

Swiss musicologist and bassoonist; Beethoven specialist; also composer.

°[12] *Kleine Tonstücke*, Op.43. Milan: Ricordi, n.d. (LI-I)

Hessenberg, Kurt (1908–)

German composer; his style is neo-Classical and contrapuntal with free dissonance.

Fantasie, Op.19. Heidelberg: Müller, 1942.

°*Partita capricciosa* (Preambulo; Notturno; Fughetta; Nenia; Scherzo; Serenata; Danza con variazioni [Tanz mir nicht meiner Jungfer Käthen]), Op.91. Cologne: Hans Gerig, 1973. Attractive suite of contrasting pieces. Somewhat long (38 pages) but written with a light and sensitive touch. Good concert fare. (I-UI)

°*Sonata* (c), Op.34/1. Mainz: Schott, 1950. (I)

Variationen über ein eigenes Kinderlied, Op.34/2 (1944). Mainz: Schott, 1951. US:Wc. Engaging work, worth looking into. (I)

Heuschkel, Johann Peter (1773–1853)

German organist and oboist; teacher of Weber; wrote vocal and instrumental music.

Six pièces faciles, Op.12. Mainz: Schott, n.d. D-ddr:Bds.

Trois sonatines. Mainz: Schott, 1819. GB:Lbl.

Hier, Ethel Glenn (1889–)

American composer of chamber and orchestral music, songs, and piano pieces; studied with Ernest Bloch.

Carolina Christmas. US:NYamc.

Hiller, Ferdinand (1811–1885)

German pianist, conductor, teacher, and composer. He wrote operas, orchestral music, and piano works in Romantic style strongly influenced by Mendelssohn.

Leichte Serenade (Praeludium und Scherzo; Variationen und Intermezzo;

Reverie und Finale), Op.128. Leipzig: Kistner, 1867. US:Wc. Amiable, flowing suite. (I-LA)

Operette ohne Text (Ouvertüre; Romanze des Mädchens; Polterarie; Jäger-chor und Ensemble; Romanze des Jünglings; Duettino; Trinklied mit Chor; Marsch; Terzetti; Frauenchor; Tanz; Schlussgesang), Op.106. Leip-zig: Rieter-Biedermann, 1874; Augener, 1882. US:Wc. This is a full-length operetta without a text, a diverting suite of pieces, from Overture to the Closing Song finale. Though a bit overlong and faded, it still has many touches of graceful and expressive writing for both parts—an enter-tainment worth reviving. (I-LA)

Thema und Variationen (b), Op.124. Leipzig: Rieter-Biedermann, 1870. US:Wc. Pleasing, well-written set of variations. (UI-LA)

Himmel, Friedrich Heinrich (1765–1814)

German pianist; successful opera and instrumental composer.

Écossaise pour piano à quatre mains ou deux pianos. Berlin: Hummel, n.d. US:Wc.

Favorit Polonaise. Berlin: Lischke, n.d. D-ddr:Bds.

Sonate (Eb), oeuvre posthume. Berlin: Lischke, n.d. S:Skma.

Hind, John

°*Summer song.* London: Curwen, n.d. (UE)

Hindemith, Paul (1895–1963)

Influential German composer; wrote prolifically in all forms. His linear style owes much to Reger and Busoni. He used Classical structures and free har-monic relationships; developed Gebrauchsmusik (functional music).

°*Sonata* (1938). Mainz: Schott, 1939. A significant contribution to 4H liter-ature. Large-scale work in three movements: I. Moderately fast and flow-ing; II. Brilliant, moody scherzo; III. Quietly moving lyrical section with contrasting rapid middle section followed by a return of the lyrical melody treated fugally and ending peacefully. One of the composer's most in-spired works. It demands secure technique and musicianship together with a sensitivity for tonal balance. (A)

Hlucháň, Jan (1890–1959)

Czech composer; wrote pedagogical works and instructional piano pieces with folk-song influence.

°*Zahrajme si čtyřručně* (Let's play four hands). Prague: Supraphon, n.d.

Hoddinott, Alun (1929–)

Welsh teacher and composer. He has written for orchestra, chorus, organ, chamber ensembles, and piano.

°*The silver swimmer*, for mixed chorus and piano 4H (1973). London: OUP, 1975.

Høffding, Finn (1899–   ). See Birgitta Nordenfelt.
Danish composer in "European modernist" tradition, with influences of Carl Nielsen, Bartók, and Hindemith observable in his music.

Hoffman, Miss J.
Three duets, the first for two harpsichords, the other two for two performers on one pianoforte. London: printed for the composer, 1795. GB:Gu,Lbl, Ob.
Six duetts for two performers on one piano-forte. London: pub. by composer, ca.1798. GB:LBl,Ob.

Hoffmann, Phillipp Carl
Variations pour le clavecin, Op.3. Offenbach: André, ca.1794. CS:KRa.

Hoffmeister, Franz Anton (1754–1812)
Viennese church musician and publisher; established Bureau de Musique, now C.F. Peters, in Leipzig in 1800. He composed prolifically in all forms; wrote in Classical style.
Six allemandes (D,G,C,F,Bb,G), Op.69. Leipzig: Kühnel, ca.1810. US:NYp.
Trois marches. Bonn: Simrock, 1808. D-brd:B—D-ddr:Bds.
Polonaise en rondeau. Bonn: Simrock, ca.1809. D-brd:B—DK:Kv—US:Wc.
The three titles above are routine works demonstrating a mastery of the 4H medium while at times displaying some unexpected and exceptionally sensitive harmonic effects. (I-UI)
Rondeau alla polacca. Vienna: Chemische Druckerei, n.d. A:Wgm,Wn.
Variations et deux rondeaux (one for piano 4H). Pub. and date missing. A:Wgm.

Hofmann, Heinrich (1842–1902)
A prolific composer in the Schumann tradition, Hofmann wrote a quantity of attractive, tuneful, polished four-hand pieces. While much of this music tends toward the salon in style, it is always effective and eminently playable.
Am Rhein, vier Skizzen (Ausfahrt; Rhein-Nixen; Am Lurleyfels; Winzerfest), Op.43. Leipzig: Peters, 1880. US:PHf. (I-UI)
°*Aus alter Zeit;* [7] Stücke in freier Bearbeitung. Berlin: Ries & Erler, 1879; London: Novello, n.d.; Paris: Hamelle as *Souvenirs d'Autrefois* (Française; Italienne; Bourrée de J.S. Bach; Suédoise; Italienne; Bohémienne; Française), n.d.
°*Aus meinem Tagebuch* (Auf dem Wasser; Den Bach entlang; Die Nachtigall singt; In der Haideschenke; Jagdscene; Letztes Geleit; Plauderei; Reigen; Schneeflocken; Unter der Dorflinde; Wandervöglein; Zum Abschied), Op.46. Berlin: Ries & Erler, n.d.; °NEd. of No.4 only as *Danza campestre,* ed. G. Rosati (Ancona/Milan: Bèrben, 1974). Descriptive suite in Romantic style. (I-UI)

[3] *Charakterstücke in leichten Spielart* (Fughetta; Menuett; Festmarsch), Op.10. Berlin: Simrock, n.d. GB:Lbl.

[3] *Charakterstücke* (Reigen; Nächtlicher Zug; Tanzlied), Op.35. Leipzig: B&H, 1876. GB:Lbl—US:Wc. Pleasant flowing pieces in light style. (I)

[6] *Charakterstücke* (Tscherkessen-Marsch; Elegie; Scherzo; In der Schmiede; Menuett; Finale), Op.70. Leipzig: B&H, 1884. GB:Lbl.

Ekkehard, Skizzen nach Jos. Viktor von Scheffels gleichnamiger Dichtung, Op.57. Leipzig: B&H, 1882; London: Novello, n.d. GB:Lbl—US:Wc.

°[3] *Genre-Bilder in leichten Spielart* (Marsch; Spinnlied; Bauerntanz), Op.3. Berlin: Simrock, n.d.; London: Witt, n.d. as *Three characteristic pieces;* Paris: °Hamelle, n.d. as *Trois tableaux de genre* (morceaux faciles), Op.3. GB:Lbl. (I)

Hungarian rhapsody. Cincinnati: John Church, 1890. GB:Lbl. (I)

[3] *Intermezzi* (E,C,G), Op.66. Breslau: Hainauer, 1883. GB:Lbl. (I)

Italienische Liebesnovelle, sechs Stücke (Einleitung; Barcarole; Ständchen; Zwiegespräch; Carnavalscene; Hochzeitzug), Op.19. Leipzig: B&H, 1864; 1924; London: Novello, n.d. GB:Lbl—US:Bp,PHf,Wc. Attractive pieces in sure-handed duet setting. (I-UI)

Kirmess-Suite, Genrebilder (In der Laube; In der Schaubude; Ankunft der Gäste; Ländler; Trinklied; Indischer Tanz; Schwertertanz; Chinesen; Herkules), Op.102. Berlin: Challier, 1890; London: Novello, n.d. US:Wc. (I)

[6] *Klavierstücke nach Scheffels Trompeter von Säkkingen,* Op.52. Leipzig: B&H, 1880. US:Wc. (I-UI)

[7] *Ländler* (G,b,Gb,Bb,f,A,g), Op.23. Berlin: Ries & Erler, 1875; London: Witt, n.d. GB:Lbl—US:Wc.

Liebesfrühling, fünf Stücke nach Dichtungen Friedrich Rückerts, Op.29. Berlin: Ries & Erler, 1875. GB:Lbl. (I-UI)

Minnespiel, eleven waltzes for soprano, alto, tenor and bass, and piano 4H accompaniment, Op.42. Berlin: Erler, 1878. GB:Lbl, see *11 Walzer,* Op. 42a.

Neue ungarische Tänze. Berlin: Ries & Erler, 1875; Paris: Durand, 1884; London: Novello, n.d. GB:Lbl.

Norwegische Lieder und Tänze. Berlin: Ries & Erler, 1875; London: Novello, 1875. GB:Lbl.

Romantische Suite (Eb) (Frölishe Jagd; Elfenreigen; Zigeuner; Burgfräulein; Landsknechte; Minnesänger; Auf dem Söller; Festlicher Zug), Op. 120. Leipzig: B&H, 1896. US:Wc.

Russische Lieder und Tänze. Berlin: Ries & Erler, 1880. GB:Lbl. Tasteful settings of Russian folk songs. (I-UI)

2 Serenaden (c,G), Op.54. Leipzig: B&H, 1881. GB:Lbl—US:Wc.

Silhouetten aus Ungarn, vier Stücke mit Benutzung ungarischer National-Melodien. Berlin: Ries & Erler, 1876. GB:Lbl.

Drei Sonaten (c,F,G) in kleiner Form, Op.86. Leipzig: B&H, 1887. GB:Lbl.

Melodious, flowing instructional pieces with well-balanced parts; useful teaching material. (LI-I)

Steppenbilder, drei Clavierstücke mit Benutzung russischer Volkslieder, Op. 39. Berlin: Ries & Erler, 1877. GB:Lbl–US:Wc. (UI)

4 Stücke (Festmarsch; Melodie; Abendgesang; Gavotte), Op.76. Berlin: Challier, 1885. GB:Lbl. (UI)

Ungarische Tänze. Berlin: Ries & Erler, n.d. US:Wc.

Waldmärchen, ein Zyklus (Der Falkner; Rast an der Quelle; Beim Meister Schmied; Waldtraut; Zigeuner; Beim Einslieder; Irrlichter; Geständnis), Op.79. Leipzig: B&H, 1886, 1897. GB:Lbl–US:PHf.

11 Walzer, Op.42a. Berlin: H.Erler, 1878. GB:Lbl–US:PHf,Wc. (I). See *Minnespiel*, Op.42.

Walzer und Kosakenmarsch, Op.13. Berlin: Bote & Bock, 1873. London: Witt, n.d. GB:Lbl. (I-UI)

Hofmann, Karl

Parisian dances (Danses parisiennes). Berlin: Schlesinger, 1884; London: B.F.Wood, 1910. US:Wc. Twelve lively pieces in a light, merry mood. (I)

Hokanson, Margaret (1893–)

°*On the mountain* (G). Cincinnati: Willis, n.d. Instructional piece. (E)

Holder, Joseph William (1765–1832)

English organist and composer of choral and piano music.

A favorite duett, Op.10. London: Goulding, Phipps & D'Almaine, 1799. GB: Lbl.

Hollander, —

°*My first duets*. New York: Edward B. Marks, n.d.

Holländer, Alexis (1840–1924)

German conductor and teacher; wrote piano works and chamber music.

Deutsche Tänze, Op.54. Berlin: Schlesinger, 1898. US:Wc. Suite of dances, primarily waltzes, in fastidious salon style. (I)

Höller, Karl (1907–)

German composer; has written choral and orchestral works, concertos, chamber music and piano compositions. His eclectic style ranges from French impressionism and early Stravinsky to Hindemith's linear polyphony and German neo-romanticism.

°*Kleine Sonate* (b), Op.32/1, from *Zwei kleine Sonaten*, Op.32 (b,G). Leipzig: Litolff, 1943; also complete in °*Spielbuch, zeitgenössische Originalkompositionen.* (*Kleine Sonate* (G), Op.32/2 reported p.o.p., 1976.) Appealing, skilfully set, three-movement work in clear-textured, mildly dissonant, tonal idiom. The first movement, marked Lightly and Playfully, is written in Classical sonata-allegro form. The contrasting middle movement, Slowly and Expressively, has a tender, lyrical melody supported by chromatically shifting chords. The Very Fast and Lively finale is bright, joyful, and impetuous. (I)

Hollfelder, Waldram

°*Kleiner Tiergarten*, for children's choir, piano 4H and percussion, after texts by Franz Bauer. Lippstadt: Kistner & Siegel, 1962.

Holloway, Jack

Fantasy (1957). Ms. Commissioned by Milton and Peggy Salkind.

Holmes, George Augustus (b.1861)

English pedagogue and composer. He wrote manuals on piano and harmony instruction and composed piano pieces.

Six characteristic duets. London: Joseph Williams, 1892. US:Wc. Instructional pieces, carefully balanced for both parts. (UE-LI)

Holst, Matthias von

Atalanta, a duet for two performers on one piano forte (Siciliano pastorale; Allegro; Andantino; Allegro). London: G.Walker, ca.1805. GB:Lbl. Short work in thin Classical style, weak in thematic interest and development. (UE)

Hook, James (1746–1827)

The four-hand works of this English composer are instructional in nature; but unfortunately their bright melodic ideas and buoyancy are often weighed down by an excess of scales, Albert basses, passage work, and similar pedagogical impedimenta. (UE-LI)

A duett for two performers, Op.85. London: Bland & Weller, 1797. GB:Lbl.

A duetto for two performers (F), Op.44. London: J. Preston, 1781. GB:Lbl.

Two English, two Irish, two Scotch, and two Welsh airs, arranged as duetts, Op.83. London: Bland & Weller, 1798. GB:Lbl.

Three favorite duetts (G,C,D), Op.82. London: Bland & Weller, 1797. GB: Lbl,Ob.

Hope, Brian·

°*Three Elizabethan pictures*. London: Novello, n.d.

Hopkins, H.P.

°*Little brown bunny*. Bryn Mawr: Presser, n.d. (E-UE)

Hopp, Hippolyt (1869–1919)

Czech teacher and conductor; his compositions were influenced by Czech folk music.

°*Dětem pro radost* (For children's pleasure). Prague: Supraphon, n.d.

Horder, Mervyn Horder, Baron (1910–   )

°*Three open-air waltzes* (Fun fair waltz; Swing waltz; Sailors on shore). London: Hinrichsen, 1961. US:Wc. Likable set of bustling, lilting waltzes. (UE-LI)

°*Punchinello dance*. New York: Carl Fischer, 1961. US:Wc. Curiously diverting little piece in spite of unevenly balanced parts and a lack of strong harmonic and melodic direction. (LI)

°*Theme and variations*. New York: Carl Fischer, 1960. US:Wc. Five variations on an original theme; the setting is somewhat naïve and amateurish, but there are enough flashes of interest to keep one going. (I)

°*A travelogue* (On the journey; Scotland [Eightsome reel]; France [Champagne waltz]; Switzerland [Mountains and valleys]; Russian [Gopak]; Greece [Klephtiko]; Italy [Tarantella]). London: Hinrichsen, 1960. Suite of short, light, descriptive pieces. (UE-LI)

°*Travelogue II*, another suite (On the journey; England [Barn dance]; Ireland [Jig]; Spain [Tango]; Norway [Sailor's dance]; Poland [Polonaise]; Hungary [Czardas]. London: Hinrichsen, 1961. Descriptive pieces, slightly more difficult than the preceding suite. (LI-I)

Horne, Elsie

Instructional pieces. (LI)

°*Country dance* (Come lasses and lads). London: Chappell, n.d.

°*Three duets* (Allegretto; Sarabande; Scherzino). London: Chappell, n.d.

°*Theme and variations* (a). London: Chappell, n.d.

°*Valse caprice* (b). London: Murdoch and Murdoch, 1923. US:Wc.

Horneman, Emil (1841–1906)

Danish teacher; composed an opera, orchestral works, songs, and piano music.

Album for fire Haender, lette Smaastykker (Album for four hands, short pieces). Copenhagen: Hansen, 188[?]. US:NYp. Simple arrangements of Danish folk songs and other tunes. (LI/E)

Femtonige Smaastykker (Short pieces in five notes). Copenhagen: Hanson, 188[?]. US:NYp. Sixteen short melodious instructional pieces encompassing a variety of technical and rhythmical problems. (LI/E-5)

Hornstein, Robert von (1833–1890)

German composer; friend of Wagner and Schopenhauer. He wrote operas, ballet, songs, and piano works.

Sonata (E♭), Op.10. Mainz: Schott, 1860. D-brd:MZsch.

Horr, Peter (b.1800)

Polonaise (A), Op.14. Offenbach: André, n.d. US:Wc. Short instructional piece. (I)

Sonate (G), Op.12. Offenbach: André, ca.1831. US:Wc. Short, two-movement work in thin Mendelssohnian idiom. (I)

Horváth, Géza

Hungarian dance, Op.2. Philadelphia: Presser, n.d. US:Wc. (I)

Hungarian national dance, Op.115. Philadelphia: Presser, n.d. US:Wc. Salon piece. (I)

Three short pianoforte duets, Op.91. London: Augener, 1907; Mainz: Schott, 1911. US:Wc. Salon pieces. (I)

Slavonic sketches, Op.139. London: Augener, 1913. US:Wc. (I)

Hovhaness, Alan (1911–   )

American composer of Armenian descent. His works, often rhapsodical and mystical, are expressive, Classical in design, and strongly influenced by the color and timbres of Middle Eastern and oriental music. He frequently uses exotic modes and stylistic approaches to Eastern music.

°*Child in the garden*, Op.168. New York: Peters, 1961. Short, quiet, expressive work in modal idiom using ostinati and other repeated patterns to produce a misty, atmospheric tone color. (LI-I)

°*Ko-ola-u* for two pianos four hands, Op.136. New York: Peters, 1963. Sensitive, refined, haunting mood piece. It is not uncommon for 4H works written for one piano to be performed on two pianos, for the players' comfort and convenience, though the sound is not the same. Performing a two-piano work on one piano is usually physically impossible because of the overlapping of the parts. The present work in an exception: although it is a two-piano four-hand work, it is written in such a way that it can also be comfortably and effectively executed by two performers on one piano. (I)

Howard, Samuel (1710–1782)

English organist and composer; pupil of Pepusch. He wrote songs, cantatas, stage works, and instrumental compositions.

Three duetts for two performers on the same instrument, Op.2. London: pub. and date missing. GB:Lbl.

Hoyt, Reed (1947–   )

American composer.

Enclosure (1967). Ms. Available from composer, Newcomb College (Tulane University), New Orleans, LA 70118. Spare texture, post-Webern pointillistic style. (A)

Hrachowetz, Ignaz

Valses réveillantes, Op.20. Vienna: Jos. Czerný (Cappi), 1830. A:Wgm.

Huber, Hans (1852–1921)

Highly esteemed by his contemporaries, Huber was a versatile and prolific composer who developed a sure-handed, eclectic musical style, revealing influences of Schumann, Brahms, and Liszt. While the musical content of some of his works tends toward superficiality, the best of his four-hand compositions are technically refined, attractive, and well laid out for the duet medium.

Aus den Alpen, Episoden (Suite) (Bb). Berlin: Simrock, 1909. CH:Zma.

Aus Goethe's West-östlichen Divan, 8 Stücke, Op.41. Leipzig: Kistner, 1877. US:Wc. (I)

Gita Gowinda, eine Idylle, Op.95. Berlin/Leipzig: A.Fürstner, 1887. US:Wc. (I-UI)

5 *Humoresken nach Dichtungen von Jos. Victor Scheffel*, Op.24. Leipzig: Kistner, 1877. US:Wc. (I)

Im Winter, Suite (G), Op.76. Leipzig: Forberg, 1884. US:Wc. (UI-LA)

Italienisches Album, Phantasien (Prolog; Barcarole; Wiegenlied; Serenade; Auf dem Corso; Am Meere; Canzonetta; Tarantella; Epilog), Op.62. Leipzig: B&H, 1881. US:Wc.

Kindergarten, Op.108. Leipzig: Siegel, 1886. US:Wc. (LI-I)

15 *Ländler vom Luzerner See*, Op.11. Vienna: Bösendorfer, 1884.

Ländliche Suite (Frühling im Lande; Im Kornfeld [Liebesgespräch]; Im Herbst [Winzerleben]; Hochzeitsmarsch), Op.73. Berlin: Bote & Bock, 1884. US:Wc. (I-UI)

Märchenerzählungen, Vortragsstudien, Op.16. Leipzig: B&H, 1876. US:Wc. (I)

6 *Militärmärsche*. Ms. CH:Bu.

Die Nachtigall, Märchen von Rudolf Keltenborn, ca.1880. Ms. CH:Bu.

Präludien und Fugen (C,eb,Bb,c,F,e,G,d,D,b,a,C#), Op.100. Breslau: Hainauer, 1888. US:Wc. (A)

Romanzen-Cyklus nach Heine, Op.15. Leipzig: B&H, 1876. CH:Zma—US: Wc. (I)

Schweizer Lieder und Tänze. Leipzig: Forberg, 1886. CH:Zma.

Serenade (E), Op.55. Berlin: Ries & Erler, 1879. CH:Zma—US:Wc.

Suite (C) (Praeludium; Gavotte; Romanze; Menuet; [missing]), Op.57. Mainz: Schott, 1880. CH:Zma—US:Wc. (I-LA)

Variationen über einen Walzer von Johannes Brahms (A), Op.71. Leipzig: B&H, 1884. CH:Zma. (I-UI)

Vom Luzernersee, 10 Ländler, Op.47. Zürich: Hug, 1879. CH:Zma—US: PHf,Wc. (UI-LA)

Walzer, for violin, cello and piano four-hands, Op.27. Leipzig: Rieter-Biedermann, 1878. CH:Zma.

Walzer, Op.59. Leipzig: Peters, 1880. CH:Zma.

Hudson, —

°*Commencement grand march*. New York: Sam Fox, n.d.

Hull, Anne

°*Ancient ballad*. New York: OUP, 1964. Short, appealing modal piece based on a Flemish tune; linear, with imitation. (E)

Humbert, G. Frank

°*Contrasts* (Valse; Barcarolle; March). London: Schott, 1951. Also published as *Zu Zweien*, Mainz: Schott. Tuneful, imaginative teaching pieces. (UE)

Falling leaves; Dream song. In collection *Thirty-two graded pieces for piano duet*.

Hummel, Johann Nepomuk (1778–1837)

German composer, friend and associate of Haydn, Mozart, and Beethoven. Hummel wrote skilfully and idiomatically for piano four-hands. Because of his exploration into expanded formal structures and his use of unusual harmonic relationships and new pianistic devices—techniques later exploited by Chopin and Schumann—he is often regarded as a transitional figure between the Classic and Romantic eras. His solid craftsmanship and the dramatic quality of his music gained Hummel the deep respect of his contemporaries, who often compared him to Beethoven. Unfortunately, subsequent generations have not sustained this high opinion of the composer; while his music has vitality and brilliance, it tends to be thematically weak and lacking in depth. Yet it still has great charm and character of its own, and deserves to be performed and heard. The following list of Hummel's four-hand works has been compiled from publishers' catalogues and library inventories, supplemented by data from Dieter Zimmerschied, *Thematisches Verzeichnis der Werke von Johann Nepomuk Hummel* (Hofheim am Taunus: Friedrich Hofmeister, 1971) and from Joel Sachs, "A Checklist of the works of Johann Nepomuk Hummel" *Notes* 30 (1974):735–54. The abbreviation *CC* refers to the series *Collection complète des oeuvres de J.N. Hummel, pour le Piano-Forte, revue, corrigée et publiée par J.P. Pixis*, Société pour la publication de musique classique et moderne. Paris: M. Schlesinger [182?].

Sonate . . . Marche et Rondeau (Eb), Op.51. Vienna: pub. by composer (1811–15). A:Wn—CS:Pu—D-ddr:WR1—H:Bn—US:Wc. In *CC* and other editions: A:Gk,Wgm,Wn—CH:BE1—CS:Pu—D-brd:B,K1,Mbs,W—D-ddr:Bds,WR1—H:Bn—N:Oum—US:NYp,PHf,R—USSR:Lsc. (I-UI)

Six waltzes with trios followed by a great battle (Six waltzes for the Apollo Saal), Op.91. Vienna: Steiner, ca.1821. In *CC* and other editions: A:Gk, Wn—D-brd:Mbs,W—DK:Kk—PL:Kj—US:NYp,Wc. Originally written for orchestra; the 4H version is the second of seven arrangements for various instrumental combinations. (I-UI)

Grande sonate (Ab), Op.92. Vienna: Cappi & Diabelli; Leipzig: Peters, ca. 1821. A:Gk,Wgm,Wn — CS:Pu — D-ddr:Bds — GB:Lbl — US:NYp,Wc — USSR:Lsc. In *CC* and other editions: A:Gk,Wgm—B:Br—CH:BE1—CS: BRnm — D-brd:K1,Mbs,Sl — D-ddr:Bds,LEu — DK:Kk — GB:Mp — H:Bn —N:Oum—NL:Uim—PL:Kj—US:NYp,R,Wc—USSR:Lsc. °NEd. Andante sostenuto (third movement) only. Ancona: Bèrben, 1976. (I-UI)

Nocturne (F), with two horns ad lib., Op.99 (1822). Leipzig: Peters, ca. 1824. A:Wgm,Wn—D-brd:K1,Mbs,MÜs—D-ddr:Bds,Dlb,WRtl—NL:At—S:Uu—US:NYp. In *CC* and other editions: A:Gk,Wn—CH:Bu—CS:BRnm — D-brd:K1,Mbs,Sl,W — D-ddr:Bds — DK:Kk — F:Pc — GB:Mp — I:Nc — N:Oum—PL:Kj—US:NYp,Wc. (I-UI)

Variations on a Tyrolean air (F) [Op.118/2]. In collection °*Eleven Duets by the Masters*, ed. Zeitlin and Goldberger. This work was originally written for voice with orchestral accompaniment and entitled *Air à la Tiro-lienne avec Variations*, Op.118. The 4H arrangement was published simultaneously by Haslinger in Vienna.

Rondo agréable. London: R. Cocks (The beauties of Hummel, No.26), ca. 1831. A 4H arrangement of *La Galante*, rondeau agréable pour le piano seul, Op.120, transposed to G. US:NYp. (I)

Hünten, Franz (1793–1878)

French-trained piano teacher of German origin. Hünten was a prolific composer of salon-style pieces, including many florid arrangements and transcriptions of opera tunes, popular melodies, and folk songs, some of which are to be found in the following selected list. Although Hünten's music is idiomatically written for four hands, much of it is barren and outmoded.

Marche militaire (A), Op.37. Leipzig: Peters, 1828. US:PHf,Wc. (I)

Polonaise brillante (E), Op.16. Berlin: Paez, 1827. US:Wc. (I)

Swiss air with variations (F), Op.32. Mainz: Schott, 1827, 1833. US:PHf, Wc. (I)

Variations militaires sur la Marche d'Alexandre (A), Op.12. Berlin: Paez, 1825. US:NYp,PHf (the latter has copy titled *Fall of Paris with variations*). (I)

Variations militaires (Thème français) (F), Op.47. Leipzig: Peters, 1829. US:Wc. (I)

Variations (Thème tyrolien), Op.27. Mainz: Schott, 1827. US:PHf. (I)

Husa, Karel (1921–)

Czech composer of orchestral pieces, chamber works, and piano compositions. He writes in tonal, lyrical, neo-Classical idiom, showing influences of Nadia Boulanger, Honegger, Bartók, and Kodály.

°Eight easy duets (Overture; Rondo; Melancholy song; Solemn procession; Elegy; Little scherzo; Evening; Slovak dance), 1955. Mainz: Schott, 1958. Short, light, inviting pieces, skilfully set in Czech folk-song idiom with strong rhythmic echoes of Bartók, lie effectively for both partners. (LI-I)

Hüttenbrenner, Josef Anselm (1794–1868)

Austrian contemporary and fellow student of Schubert; friend of Beethoven; prolific composer in all forms.

Six valses avec trios (Bb,Eb,C,Bb,Eb,C), Op.3. Vienna: Cappi, 1826. A:Wst. Suite of short, pleasant, tuneful dances, in lightweight Schubertian style. (LI)

Hyson, Winifred

°Fantasy on three English folksongs. Park Ridge, IL: General Words and Music, 1970, 1976.

°Eight light-hearted variations on The Jolly Miller. Park Ridge, IL: General Words and Music, 1970, 1976.

The capably arranged folk-song settings and the ingratiating set of variations are fine additions to the repertoire of attractive, well-balanced teaching material. (UE-LI)

Imbrie, Andrew (1921–   )

American composer and teacher; student of Roger Sessions; uses serial techniques. He has written orchestral, choral, chamber, and piano works.

°*Concerto for piano duet and orchestra* (1955–56). Delaware Water Gap: Shawnee Press, n.d. Commissioned by Milton and Peggy Salkind.

d'Indy, Vincent (1851–1931)

French composer of orchestral, operatic, chamber, and piano works in a style strongly influenced by his teacher César Franck.

°*Sept chants de terroir sur des thèmes de divers pays* (Noël Nouvelet à Cassis en Provence—petites filles provençales; Rigaudon sur la place de Lachamp-Raphaël [Hauts plateaux vivarois], danseurs cévenols; Seguidilla à l'alameda de Séville, guitarreros; Yonkina sur le port de Yokohama, Japon, matelots japonais; Chanson de plein vent, au bord de la rivière [Forêt de Pavlovsk] chanteur russe, accompagnateur polonais; Aubade devant la Madone des tre campanelle [Campagne romaine], Zampagnari; Tarantelle sur le bateau de Capri [Golfe de Naples], pitres napolitains), Op.73. Paris: Rouart-Lerolle, 1919. Effectively written, often brilliant, tone pictures based on popular national themes. (UI-A)

Inghelbrecht, Désiré-Émile (1880–1965)

French conductor; composed ballets, choral and orchestral works, chamber music, and piano pieces. He wrote in a clear, expressive, often lyrical, French idiom.

°*La nursery.* Paris: Salabert (Vols.1,2,4,5,6), 1907–1932; Leduc (Vol.3), 1920. This delightful and effective six-volume series is a most useful contribution to piano 4H literature. It contains elegant and resourceful arrangements of 36 French folk songs. Though expressly written for teacher and pupil, the entire series should be of exceptional value to all pianists of modest technical proficiency, children and adults alike, in particular to those in search of attractive, sophisticated music of considerable interpretive variety, written for one slightly advanced and one less experienced pianist. (UE-LI/I)

Isaacs, Leon

°*L'amour de moi.* London: Curwen, n.d. (I)
°*William Taylor.* London: Curwen, n.d. (I)

Ísólfsson, Páll (1893–1974)

Icelandic organist, editor, music critic; director of Reykjavík Conservatory. He wrote choral, orchestral, organ, and piano compositions.

Two heroic songs. [Reykjavík, Iceland]: Helgafell, n.d. IS:Rmic. Solemn, heavy, somewhat thick-textured works in Nordic style; orchestral in character. (UI)

Ivanov-Radkevich, Nikolaï Pavlovich (1904–)

Russian composer; studied with Glière. He has written ballets, chamber music, symphonies, and piano works.

°*Five pictures of Russian nature* (Spring in the fields; Arrival of the birds; In the thick forest; In the glade; Birches in autumn). Moscow: State Music Publishing House, 1950. Pleasant series of tone pictures set in conservative Russian folk-song idiom. (LI)

Shest' p'es dlia nachinaiushchykh (Six pieces for beginners) (March; Lullaby; Gavotte; Waltz; Sad song; Dance), 1946. Moscow: State Music Publishing House, 1948. US:NYp. Short melodious pieces in traditional idiom. (E-UE)

Ivey, Jean Eichelberger (1923–)

American pianist and composer; uses serial techniques and electronic resources.

°*Parade.* New York: Lee Roberts Music Pub., 1965. Attractive melodious twelve-tone work; musical interest is evenly divided between the parts. (LI)

– Jacob, Maxime (Dom Clément Jacob OSB) (1906–)

French composer, pupil of Milhaud; has written a comic opera, orchestral music, songs, and piano pieces.

°*Sérénade.* Paris: Jobert, 1928.

Jacobi, Frederick (1891–1952)

American conductor and composer; student of Bloch. Many of his works made use of Indian music.

Variation on El Hibne Hagalile, holograph. US:Wc.

Jacobi, Wolfgang (1894–)

German teacher and composer; author of theory textbooks. He writes in neo-Classical style.

4 Klavierstücke für Ursi (Menuet; Walzer; Kleine Romanze; Walzer). Munich: Max Hieber, 1954. US:Wc. Witty, lively pieces in mildly contemporary idiom. (I)

Jacobson, Maurice (1896–1976)

English pianist, composer, publisher, and pedagogue. His works, written in conservative style, include ballet, orchestral, choral, and chamber music as well as many piano pieces.

°*Beginner and teacher* (album). London: Curwen, n.d. (UE-LI/E)

°*Heart's ease.* London: Curwen, 1944. Pleasant, melodious teaching piece. (E)

°*Lonely mill.* London: Curwen, n.d.

°*Mosaic.* London: Curwen, 1949. US:Wc. Rambling; mildly dissonant. (UI)

Jadassohn, Salomon (1831–1902)

German teacher and composer; wrote textbooks on music theory. A master contrapuntist, he made frequent use of the canon form in all his musical works. Though carefully written, they tend to be dry and scholarly.

Die [6] *leichtesten Stücke* (Vorspiel; Ländler; Kavatine; Marsch; Polonaise; Walzer), Op.99. Leipzig: Forberg, 1888. GB:Lbl. Set of deftly crafted instructional pieces, arranged in progressive order of difficulty. (UE-I/ E-5)

Sextett (G), for 2 violins, viola, cello, and piano four hands, Op.100. Leipzig: Kistner, 1888. US:Wc.

Jadin, Hyacinthe (1769–1802)

French pianist; wrote concertos, chamber works, and a quantity of piano music.

Duo. Paris: Magazin de musique, n.d. F:Pc–US:PHf. Sonata in thin Classical style. (I)

Jadin, Louis Emmanuel (1768–1853)

Brother of Hyacinthe; composed chamber and piano music in Classical style.

Trois sonates, Op.2. Paris: L.E.Jadin, Mlle Rivet; Versailles: Jadin. F:Pc (2 copies);Pn. *Sonate* (Eb) only. Offenbach: André, ca.1796. D-brd: OF.

Jambor, Agi

Hungarian-born American pianist, harpsichordist, musicologist, and teacher.

°*Three pieces* (Bagpipe; Berceuse; This terrible minor scale). Philadelphia: Elkan-Vogel, 1965. Delightful set of whimsical pieces; descriptive, gently satirical. (LE-LI)

Jambor, Eugen

Souvenirs d'enfance, Op.35. Offenbach: André, 1897. US:Wc. Eleven instructional pieces, well-balanced parts. (LI)

Janáček, Leoš (1854–1928)

Czech composer of operas, liturgical works, song cycles, chamber music, and piano pieces. From study of his native Moravian folk song and speech he evolved a strikingly original musical style, influenced somewhat by French Impressionism.

Národní tance na Moravě (National dances of Moravia), in collaboration with L. Bakešová and X. Běhálková. Book 1 (1891), Book 2 (1891), Book 3 (1893). Brno: pub. missing, 1891–93. CS:Pchf.

Jaques-Dalcroze, Émile (1865–1950)

Swiss educator and composer; inventor of Eurythmics. He wrote pedagogical compositions, orchestral suites, choral works, chamber music, and piano pieces.

°*Allegretto commodo.* Lausanne: Foetisch Frères, n.d. CH:Zma.

°*Canzonetta,* Op.11. Paris: Rouart Lerolle, n.d. CH:Zma.

Danse romande, Op.68. Lausanne: Foetisch, n.d. CH:Zma—US:Wc. Amiable little dance in salon style. (LI)

Valse badine, Op.4. Paris: E.Baudoux, ca.1890. US:Wc.

Járdányi, Pál (1920–1966)

Hungarian folklorist and writer on music; his compositions show strong folk-song influence.

°*Bolgár ritmusok* (Bulgarian rhythms). Budapest: Editio musica, 1956,1964. Group of ingeniously crafted, largely black-note pieces, each one featuring a different metrical pattern; strongly reminiscent of Bartók in style and harmonic idiom. (I)

°*Hungarian folk song* ("Érik a szolo"), from °*Piano Duets by Hungarian Composers,* Book I, in the collection °*Album for Piano Duet,* ed. Váczi. Bright setting of national melody with strong rhythmical drive; parts effectively distributed. (UE-LI)

Jarratt, Arthur

Á la polonaise. London: Ashdown, n.d. GB:Lbl. Instructional piece. (I)

Jelinek, Hanns (1901–   )

Viennese student of Schoenberg and Berg. He writes in twelve-tone technique.

°*Zwölftonfibel;* Zwölf mal zwölf sehr leichte bis mittelschwere Übungen und Spielstücke nebst allerlei Varianten und Tonleitern im Zwölfton (for three and four hands). Wolfenbüttel: Möseler, 1953.

Jelinek, Stanislav (1945–   )

Czech composer.

Small suite (1973). Cited in *Music News from Prague,* No.3, Spring 1973. CS:Pchf.

Jelmoli, Hans (1877–1936)

Swiss pianist, conductor, and composer.

Variationen über ein schottisches Volkslied, Op.12. Zürich-Leipzig: Hug, 1914. CH:Zma.

Jemnitz, Sándor (Alexander) (1890–1963)

Hungarian conductor, composer, and writer on music; pupil of Reger and Schoenberg. His music is written in a complex atonal, contrapuntal idiom with traces of Hungarian folk influence.

°*Leaping dance* (1956). Budapest: Editio Musica, 1958. Short piece in folk style; activity in both parts. (UE-LI)

Jenkins, Cora W.

°*Down the shady path.* Cincinnati: Willis, 1936. Instructional. (E)

°*In the morning early.* Cincinnati: Willis, n.d. Instructional. (UE)

°*The strolling players.* Cincinnati: Willis, n.d. Instructional. (UE)

Jensen, Adolph (1837–1879)

German pianist and composer; student of Liszt. He wrote in lyrical, late Romantic salon idiom.

°*Abendmusik,* Op.59. Breslau: Hainauer, 1877. °NEd. Leipzig: Peters, 1952. US:PHf,Wc. Six charming, well-written pieces in refined style. (I)

°*Hochzeitsmusik* (Festzug; Brautgesang; Reigen; Notturno), Op.45. Breslau: Hainauer, 1873. NEd. Leipzig: Peters, 1952. US:PHf,Wc. Attractive, melodious salon pieces. (I)

Drei Idyllen, Op.43. Breslau: Hainauer, n.d. US:Wc. Flowing, graceful pieces. (I-UI)

Drei Klavierstücke (Scherzo; Wiegenlied; Pastorale), Op.18. Leipzig-Hamburg: Schuberth, 1864; London: Augener, 1886. GB:Lbl–US:Wc. Neatly crafted, lyrical works in fresh Romantic idiom. (I)

Ländliche Fest-Musik. Berlin: Ries & Erler, 1882. US:Wc. (I)

Lebensbilder (Im Rittersaal; Am Brunnen; Soldatenmarsch; Sommerlust; Zigeunerkonzert; Letzter Gang), Op.60. Breslau: Hainauer, 1877. US: Wc. Melodious descriptive pieces, dextrously set. (I)

Zwei Stücke (In der Rosenlaube; Holländertanz), Op.65. Leipzig: B&H, n.d. US:Wc. Tuneful, well-balanced works; somewhat demanding. (UI-LA)

Silhouetten, sechs Klavierstücke. Breslau: Hainauer, 1877. US:Wc. (I)

Jensen, Joyce

Sonata (1961). Ms. Large-scale dissonant work. US:Wc.

Jerea, Hilda (1916–)

Romanian composer.

°*Douăsprece mici piese pentru pian la patru mîini* (Twelve little pieces for piano four hands) (1963). Bucharest: Uniunii Compozitorilor din R.S.R. (Editura Muzicală), 1964. Short pieces beautifully set for two equal performers; linear in character with a strong intriguing modal flavor of Romanian folk music. (UE-LI)

Jersild, Jørgen (1913–)

Danish teacher, author, and composer; writes in moderately contemporary style influenced by French Classicism.

°*Duo concertante;* eighteen short piano pieces (Ouverture alla marcia; Con sentimento; The doll's piano; Little trumpet melody; Marionettes; Pastorale; Andantino; Triplets in a minor key; Quick end; Minuetto; To Daniel Gottlob Türk; Romance; Mit Schmerz; Signor Alberti; The cream goat; Its kid; Mrs. Andersen's cycling tour; Final galop). Copenhagen:

Hansen, 1956. Mild dissonance, changing meters, polytonality, and knocking on the piano case are some of the 20th-century techniques used in this exceptionally appealing and useful set of short pieces, some of which are for three hands. The Secondo part is frequently asked to play over the Primo, and vice versa. (LI-I/E)

Jindřich, Jindřich (1876–1967)

Czech composer and collector of his country's folk songs, many of which he arranged for solo voice, chorus, and piano.

°*Dva chodské tance* (Two dances from the Chod district). Prague: Artia, 1960. US:Wc. Capable settings of two folk melodies. (LI)

°*Národní písně a tance* (Popular songs and dances). Prague: Artia, 1960. US:Wc. Czech folk dances and popular melodies in fresh arrangements. (I)

Johnson, Thomas A. (1908–   )

English pianist and composer of piano music in conservative style; also writes on musical subjects.

°*Country pedlar*. London: Curwen, n.d. (E)

°*Gavotte*. London: Curwen, n.d. (LI)

°*Lady of Brazil*, a samba. London: Curwen, 1955. US:Wc. Lively, pulsating showpiece in popular Latin American rhythm with predictable harmonies. (I)

°*Partners* (Three graded albums): Vol.I: You and I, 35 tuneful duets (VE). Vol.II: Together we play (E-UE). Vol.III: Melody-making for two, 20 tuneful duets (LI). London: Hinrichsen, 1965. Short melodious pieces, designed for sight-reading and ensemble practice.

°*Polka*. London: Curwen, n.d. (LI)

°*Rumba*. London: Curwen, 1950. US:Wc. (I)

°*Scherzino*. In collection *Pianoforte album, original compositions*, Vol.II. Bright, pleasant work in traditional style. (LI)

A suite of five easy duets (Melody; Spanish dance; Italian dance, Tarantella; French dance, Minuet; Russian dance). London: Lengnick, 1948. US:Wc. Useful, melodious teaching pieces. (LI)

°*Summer bells*. London: Curwen, n.d. (E)

Tango. London: Bosworth, 1968. US:Wc. Instructional piece in Argentine dance style. (LI)

Water play. London: Leonard, Gould & Bottler, 1955. US:Wc. Attractive arpeggio study. (LI)

Johnston, Peter F., arr.

°*Three Scottish folk tunes*. New York: OUP, n.d.

Jomelli, Niccolò (1714–1774)

Italian composer of oratorios, 50 operas, church music, and instrumental pieces.

Sonata per clavicembalo a quattro mani (ca.1760). Pub. and date missing.
B:Bc. One of the earliest 4H works; written for harpsichord. Short, three-
movement work in early Classical sonata form. Active inner parts; heavily
ornamented. (LI)

Jones, Kelsey (1922–   )

American-born Canadian. Jones has written chamber opera, orchestral works,
chamber and choral music, and piano compositions. His style is tonal with
some free dissonance and liberal use of contrapuntal textures.

Theme and variations (1961). Ms. C:Tcmc. Strong, assertive set of variations in harmonically rich idiom, with textural, rhythmic, and dynamic
contrasts. (I-UI)

Jongen, Joseph (1873–1953)

Belgian composer; wrote in all musical forms in a style deriving from César
Franck and French Impressionism.

°*Cocass-March; Petite berceuse; Divertissement*, Op.129, 1949. Brussels:
CeBeDeM, 1965. US:Wc.

°*Fantaisie sur deux Noëls wallons*, Op.24, 1902. Paris: Durand, n.d. (UI-LA)

°*Intermezzo piccolo*, Op.136bis, 1950. Brussels: CeBeDeM, n.d. US:Wc.
Short work in Impressionist style. (LI)

°*Jeux d'enfants*, Op.120, 1941. Brussels: CeBeDeM. US:Wc. Three amiable,
effectively written pieces; well distributed for both parts. (LI-I)

Pages intimes (Il était une fois; Dansez; Mizelle; Le bon cheval), Op.55,
1917. London: Chester, 1919. US:Wc. Charming, artfully constructed little
pieces. (UE-LI)

Jordan, Royland (1915–   )

The ice fairy. Brighton: H. Freeman, 1953. US:Wc. Instructional piece. (LE)

Sparkling waves. Brighton: H. Freeman, 1953. US:Wc. Instructional piece.
(E)

Josif, Enriko (1924– ,   )

Isaček (A piece), for narrator, soprano, and piano 4H (1954). Pub. and
date missing. D-brd:DSim.

Joubert, John (1927–   )

South African composer, living in England; his musical idiom is tonal, clear
in texture, and eclectic in style.

°*Divertimento*, Op.2, 1951. London: Novello, 1953. US:Wc. Delightful,
four-movement work in sparkling, polished style; idiomatic for the medium.
(I)

Joyner, Beryl

°*In sunny fields* (G). Cincinnati: Willis, n.d. (E)

Judd, Percy

English composer.

Four character studies (The saucy sailor; The shepherd; The lonely maiden;

The vagabond). London: Elkin, 1948. US:Wc. Bright, lively pieces in English folk-song style. (UE)

Jung, Siegfried

Zwei Vortragsstücke im Orgelpunkt (Pastorale; Weihnachtsidylle), Op.11. Magdeburg: Heinrichshofen, 1909.

Juon, Paul (1872–1940)

Russian-born composer, settled in Germany; his style is late Romantic strongly influenced by Brahms.

Aus alter Zeit, suite (Sonata alla Bourrée; Minuetto; Ciacona; Tambourin; Gavotte), Op.67. Leipzig: Leuckhart, 1920. US:Bp. Charming pieces in 18th-century style. (I)

Tanzrhythmen: Books I,II, Op.14, 1901; Books III,IV,V, Op.24, 1904; Books VI,VII, Op.41, 1908. Berlin: Lienau. US:Wc. The three sets of this work constitute an unusually ingenious group of pieces. Handsomely crafted and effectively organized, they emphasize rhythmic aspects of the music through the use of a variety of metrical patterns. There are unexpected groupings and juxtapositions, and irregular and variable meters. The style is stiff and academic at times, but is attractive and interesting for both partners. (UI-A)

Just, Johannes August (ca.1745–ca.1800)

German opera and instrumental composer active in London and Holland.

Six divertissements (Divertimentos) (D,A,F,Bb,C,Eb), Op.12. Berlin: Hummel, ca.1781; Paris: Sieber, n.d.; London: Bland, ca.1785. °NEd. *Two little sonatas* (No.5[C] and 6[Eb]), ed. Willi Hillemann. Mainz: Schott, 1951. B:Bc—CH:Bchristen,Bu—D-ddr:Dlb—F:Pc—GB:Lbl—NL:Uim—S:Skma—PL:WRu—US:NYp,Wc (No.1,2,3). Short, two-movement works in fastidious high Classic style; compact, light-textured, inviting. (UE-LI)

Kabeláč, Miloslav (1908–   )

Czech composer of orchestral, choral, and chamber music as well as instructional pieces for piano.

°*Malá suita* (Little suite), Op.42. Prague: Panton, 1962. Five-movement work in mildly contemporary idiom; chromaticism; changing meters, occasional rhythmic problems. (LI-I)

Kadosa, Pál (1903–   )

Hungarian composer, influenced by Bartók, Kodály, and Hungarian folk music, and to some extent by Stravinsky and Hindemith. His music is characterized by percussive rhythms, free metric organization, and contrapuntal textures.

°*Six bagatelles*. Budapest: Editio Musica, 1964. US:Wc. Short, polished attractive pieces featuring dissonance and mild atonality in a Bartokian idiom. (LI)

Kis szvit (Little suite), Op.49c. Budapest: Editio Musica, 1958. US:Wc. Three pleasant short pieces with Hungarian flavor; the sometimes unidiomatic distribution of the parts suggests orchestral origin. (LI).

May song. Budapest: Editio Musica, 1957. Also in collection *Album for Piano Duet,* ed. Váczi. Charming setting of Hungarian folk melody with delicate texture and balance between parts. (UE-LI)

Kaegi, Werner (1926–)

Ariadne in Zürich (Ballettsuite, 1956). Zürich: Astoria-Verlag. CH:Zma.

Kahn, Marvin (1915–1969)

Two for the show. New York: Mills, n.d.

Kahn, Robert (1865–1951)

German teacher, conductor, and composer of choral and instrumental works.

Am See, sechs kleine Stücke, Op.13. Leipzig: Leuckart, 1891. US:PHf. Salon pieces. (LI)

Kalkbrenner, Friedrich (1785–1849)

German pianist, performer, and teacher; settled in Paris. He composed four piano concertos, works for piano and chamber ensembles, and many piano compositions.

Sonata (C), Op.3. Paris: Sieber, ca.1815. US:Wc. (I)

Sonata (F), Op.76 (79). London: Clementi, ca.1826. US:Wc. Tidy, serious, well-constructed work in early Romantic idiom; lies well and provides considerable contrapuntal activity for both partners. (UI-LA)

Sonate (Bb), Op.80. Leipzig: B&H, 1826. US:Wc.

Deux walses ou marches à pas redoublé (D,G), Op.40. Leipzig: Kistner, ca. 1824; Leipzig: B&H, ca.1827. US:Wc. Lightweight marches in triple meter. (I)

Kalliwoda, Johann Wenzel (1801–1866)

Czech violinist and composer of instrumental music in salon style.

Trois grandes marches (Eb,C,D), Op.26. Leipzig: B&H, 1835. US:Wc. Stirring, energetic works. (I)

Deux grandes valses (valses célèbres), Op.27 (C), Op.169 (G). Leipzig: Peters, 1858. Melodious waltzes in lightweight style. (UE-LI)

Recreation, Op.123. Leipzig: Peters, ca.1843. US:Wc. Broad, expansive work; possibly a trancription from the original orchestral version. (I)

Deux valses (D,A), Op.39. Leipzig: Peters, 1834. US.NYp.

Kaminskii, Dmitrii Romanovich (1907–)

Dve p'esy (Two pieces) (First snow; At the circus). Leningrad: State Music Publishing House, n.d. US:Wc. Felicitous little pieces with piquant harmonies. (LI)

Kanne, Friedrich August (1788–1833)

German editor; composed operas, symphonies, masses, and piano music.
Grande sonate, Op.31. Vienna: Haslinger, n.d. D-ddr:Bds.

Kaplan, Robert Barnett (1924–)

°*Andante con variazione;* theme and ten variations, Op.33. Boston: Branden Press, 1971. There are some grateful moments in this work with pleasant and effective sounds, but for the most part it is poorly written and unnecessarily fussy. Frequent hand collisions make comfortable performance difficult. (I)

Karel, Rudolf (1880–1945)

Czech composer; pupil of Dvořák.
Slavisches Scherzo-Capriccio, Op.6. Berlin: Simrock, 1911. US:Wc. Serious work in chromatic, tonal idiom, reminiscent of Reger. The setting suggests a transcription from orchestra. (I)

Karg-Elert, Sigfrid (1877–1933)

German composer of organ and harmonium works, symphonies, chamber music, songs, and piano pieces in an often extravagant but always expressive and original style.
Walzer-Capricen, Op.16. Leipzig: Friedrich Hofmeister, 1904. US:Wc. Solid, melodious, resourceful works tending toward thick textures; chromatic; difficult key signatures. (LI)

Karlsen, Kjell Mörk (1947–)

Norwegian organist and oboist. His early compositions were inspired by medieval, renaissance, and baroque music; his recent works have been more experimental.
°*Musikk for firhendig klaver* (Music for four hands) (Dialog; Dans [Dance]; Improvisasjon over en norske folkevise [Improvisation on a Norwegian folk song]). Ms. N:Onk. Short, three-movement work in dissonant idiom. (UI-A)

Karp, David

American teacher and prolific composer of instructional piano pieces, for the most part in conservative style.
°*An ancient land.* Melville, NY: Pro-Art, 1975. (UE-LI)
°*The Arkansas swinger.* Melville, NY: Pro-Art, 1974. (I)
°*Clouds.* Melville, NY: Pro-Art, n.d. (LI)
°*Day dreams.* Melville, NY: Pro-Art, 1975. (UE-LI)
°*Emerald polka.* Buffalo: Montgomery Music, 1969. Short; well balanced for both partners. (E)
°*Evening nocturne.* Minneapolis: Schmitt, Hall & McCreary, 1973. Tranquil mood piece. (UE)
°*Fifth Avenue parade.* Melville, NY: Pro-Art, n.d. (UE)
°*Fun for two.* Melville, NY: Pro-Art, 1970. Short, rhythmical dance. (LE)

°*Holiday polka.* Melville, NY: Pro-Art, 1971. (LE)

°*Holiday time.* Melville, NY: Pro-Art, n.d. (UE)

°*Israeli dance.* Melville, NY: Pro-Art, n.d. Bright, lively dance in hora rhythm. (LI)

°*Jon Peter polka.* Minneapolis: Schmitt, Hall & McCreary, 1973. Brisk dance with a German-band flavor. (E)

°*Junior duets* (Blues in the right; Sleigh ride; Song without words; Galloping horses; The fairy princess; Pioneer dance; Kangaroo boogie; Martian march). Melville, NY: Pro-Art, 1972. Appealing suite of tuneful pieces. (E-UE)

°*Lydian landscape.* Minneapolis: Schmitt, Hall & McCreary, 1974. Short piece in Lydian mode. (E)

°*Marta's mazurka.* Cincinnati: Willis, 1971. Attractive, effective teaching piece. (E)

°*Merry merry dance.* Melville, NY: Pro-Art, n.d. (UE-LI)

°*Modes for two.* (Cuban dance; A sad tale; Flying high; A walk in the forest; Daydreaming; Cuckoo clock blues; A pleasant memory; Ski slope; Farewell). Delaware Water Gap: Shawnee Press, 1976. The nine short pieces in this unusually fine and original collection exploit a number of technical devices, modal patterns, and rhythmic problems. Traditional sounds are combined with contemporary compositional practices in a most attractive way. (LI)

°*Nightfall.* New York: Lee Roberts, 1969. Quiet, atmospheric piece in 5/4 meter with appealing sonorities. (UE)

°*Peace pipe.* Melville, NY: Pro-Art, 1975. (UE-LI)

°*Perky panda.* Melville, NY: Pro-Art, n.d. (E)

°*Ride of the Indians.* Minneapolis: Schmitt, Hall & McCreary, 1973. Teaching piece with conventional Indian motifs of pulsating rhythms, open fifths, and pentatonic scales. (E)

°*Rocky Mountain dance.* Melville, NY: Pro-Art, n.d. (E-UE)

°*Rocky Mountain waltz.* Buffalo: Montgomery Music, n.d. (UE)

°*Seconds on the march.* Minneapolis: Schmitt, Hall & McCreary, 1973. The interval of a second is featured in this rousing teaching piece. (E)

°*Sleigh ride.* Minneapolis: Schmitt, Hall & McCreary, 1973. Boisterous, rhythmical teaching piece. (E)

°*Snow is falling.* Minneapolis: Schmitt, Hall & McCreary, 1974. Delicate, refined Impressionistic mood piece; imaginative and well written; one of the composer's finest. (E)

°*Spacemen on parade.* Minneapolis: Schmitt, Hall & McCreary, 1973. (E)

°*Tango jubilate.* Melville, NY: Pro-Art, 1974. (UE-LI)

°*Trumpet parade.* Melville, NY: Pro-Art, 1972. (E-UE)

°*Waltzing bobcats.* Buffalo: Montgomery Music, n.d. (UE)

Kasemets, Udo (1919–)

Estonian-born Canadian music critic and composer; often uses serial and other advanced techniques.

°*Squares* (1962). Don Mills, Ontario: Berandol Music, 1969. One page avant-garde work in aleatoric style. (A)

Kasschau, Howard

American pianist, teacher, and composer.

°*East side, west side.* New York: Schroeder & Gunther, n.d. (UE)

Kauer, Ferdinand (1751–1831)

Austrian composer of stage music, operettas, and vocal and instrumental works.

12 Hongroises (C,a,F,D,A,e,C,Eb,Bb,g,G,D), Op.20. Vienna: Koželuch, 1791. A:Wgm. Series of very short pieces in Classical style with an overlay of Hungarian rhythmic and harmonic flavor. (LI)

Kauffmann, Leo Justinius (1901–1944)

Alsatian composer of operas, radio music, and instrumental compositions.

°*Bagatelle* (G). In collection *Spielbuch, zeitgenössische Originalkompositionen.* Bright, tuneful scherzo with a touch of Gallic gaiety; contrapuntal interest and careful balance between the parts. (I)

Kaun, Hugo (1863–1932)

German teacher and prolific composer.

Six compositions (Menuet; In distant land; Mazurka; In peaceful vale; Festival procession; Waltz), Op.18. New York: Schuberth, 1890. US:Wc. Salon pieces. (I)

Kay, Ulysses (1917–)

American composer of ballets, choral and orchestral music, chamber works, and organ and piano pieces. His style is lyrical and harmonically sensitive, with a predilection for contrapuntal textures.

°*Two short pieces* (Prelude; Moto perpetuo). New York: Ricordi, 1962. Charming compositions in mildly contemporary idiom. The first piece is a study in arpeggiated eleventh and thirteenth chords; the second an essay in rhythm using five-note patterns in an animated tempo. The Secondo part is somewhat easier in Moto perpetuo than in Prelude. (UE-LI)

Keats, F.

°*Dance of the rosebuds.* Philadelphia: Presser, n.d. (UE)

Keenan, Gertrude

°*Off to Donegal and back.* New York: Carl Fischer, 1934.

°*Prancing pony.* New York: Carl Fischer, 1935.

These two works have an Irish touch. Both are also available in collection *Four hands at the keyboard.* (UE)

Kéler-Béla, A. (pseud. of Albert von Keler) (1820–1882)
Soldatenleben, militärisches Tonbild, Op.62. Mainz: Schott, n.d. US:Wc.
Salon piece. (I)

Keller, Lue Alice
°*Garden things,* ten big-note piano duets. Boston: Boston Music Co., n.d.
(UE-LI)
°*Vacation time* (12 pieces). Boston: Boston Music Co., n.d. (UE-LI)

Keller, Oswin (1885–1961)
5 *Klavierstücke für Vortrag und Unterricht.* Hamburg: Cranz, 1934.

Kellner, Johann Christoph (1736–1803)
German theorist, organist, and composer of organ and piano pieces.
2 *Fugen* (G,D) (for organ or piano four hands). Leipzig: B&H, 1795. B:Bc
—CH:SO—D-brd:KTl—D-ddr:BD,HAu—GB:Ckc,Lbl. Academic works in
Bach contrapuntal style; better suited for organ, for which they were no
doubt written. (I)

Kelly, Frederick Septimus (1881–1916)
Australian pianist and composer; killed in World War I.
Waltz-Pageant, Op.11A (1905–1912). London: Schott, 1913. US:Wc. Com-
petent work in serious vein; cast in chromatic tonal idiom. (UI)

Kennaway, Lamont
°*Downstream;* °*Interrupted serenade.* London: Hinrichsen, 1967. Short,
bland, uneventful pieces. Also exist in other instrumentations. (I)

Kennedy-Fraser, Marjorie (1857–1930)
Scots tunes (Book II of *Scots Suites*). London: Paterson's Publishers, 1949.
US:Wc. Attractive arrangements of three Scottish melodies; Primo part
more interesting than largely accompanying Secondo. (I)

Kerpen, Hugo Franz Alexander Karl von (1749–1802)
German musical dilettante.
Sonate (F), Op.4. Mainz: Schott, ca.1798. D-brd:LB,MZsch.

Kessler, Michael
American composer.
°*Prelude, waltz and march.* Philadelphia: Elkan-Vogel, 1956. Bright con-
temporary sounds; parts well distributed. (LI)

Ketterer, Ella
°*Partners at the keyboard,* 10 duets. Bryn Mawr: Presser, n.d. (I)
°*Share the fun* (10 pieces). Bryn Mawr: Presser, n.d. (UE)
°*Side by side* (10 pieces). Bryn Mawr: Presser, 1940. (E)

Keuning, Hans P.
°*The Hobbits.* Hilversum (Holland): Harmonia Ed., ca.1973. NL:Ad.

Kevan, G. Alexander (1908–   )
°*An old-fashioned ballroom.* Melville, NY: Pro-Art, n.d. (E)

°*Peg leg Pete*. Melville, NY: Pro-Art, n.d. Rollicking melody with strong Secondo accompaniment. (UE-LI)

°*Tinkling bells*. Melville, NY: Pro-Art, n.d. (UE)

Keys, Helen Day

Nine little playtime duets (°Happy and gay; °Parade; °Pixie's dance; In the sunshine; Come and play with me; Stepping lightly; In the hammock; Twilight; Sleeping time). Cincinnati: Willis, 1921. Pieces marked ° available in single copies. (E)

Khadzhiev, Parashkev (1912–   ), and Aleksandŭr Raichev

Khadzhiev is a Bulgarian teacher and composer. His works include orchestral and chamber music, arrangements of Bulgarian folk songs, and theatre music.

Piesi za piano na chetiri rŭtse (Pieces for piano four hands) (Rodino; Kozarcheta and Tsigankata Rubiya by Khadzhiev; Theme and variations, by Raichev). Sofia: Dŭrzhavno izdatelstvo "Nauka i Izkustvo" (State publishing house of science and art), 1959. US:Wc. Solid, refreshing works, capably fashioned in mildly contemporary style colored by the modes and rhythms of Balkan folk song. (I)

Khrennikov, Tikhon (1913–   )

Soviet composer; influential as president of Union of Composers, a political position of much influence in dictating acceptable styles of composition according to socialist doctrine. He writes in a bland, eclectic, conservative style based to a great extent on folk materials.

°*Two by two*, fifteen pieces (The maidens' song; Little toccata; Friendship waltz; A jolly clown; Snow flurries; Homeland; Russian dance; Processional; Dramatic sketch; Nocturne; March of the comrades; Distant chimes; Dithyramb; Pantomime; Galop fantastique). New York: Schirmer, 1976. Series of pleasant, melodious pieces arranged in progressive order of difficulty; varied in character and style, with some cautious dissonance. (UE-I)

Kiel, Friedrich (1821–1885)

German composer and teacher; he wrote in traditional style.

Vier Humoresken, Op.42 (1865). Berlin: Simrock, 1866. °Paris: Hamelle, n.d. as *Humoresque*, Op.42. US:NYp,Wc. Compact, well-written works. (I)

Ländler, Op.66. Berlin: Bote & Bock, 1876. US:PHf,Wc. Two volumes of light, flowing Austrian dances. (I)

Zwei Sonatinen (kleine Sonaten) (D,F), Op.6 (1850). Leipzig: Peters, 1857, 1868. US:Wc. Short, lightweight pedagogical works. (LI-I)

Variationen über ein eigenes Thema (a), Op.23, 1861. US:NYp,Wc. Serious, skilfully written work in dry Brahmsian idiom. (I-LA)

10 Walzer, Vol.1, Op.47, 1866. Berlin: Simrock, 1867; London: Augener, 1909. US:Wc.

10 Walzer, Vol.2, Op.48. Berlin: Simrock, 1867; London: Augener, 1910. US:Wc. Opp.47 and 48 are attractive suites of connected waltzes in the style of the Brahms *Liebeslieder.*

Kienzl, Wilhelm (1857–1941)

Austrian composer; associate of Liszt; also friend of Wagner, whose compositional principles he adopted in his operas, songs, and piano pieces.

Tanzbilder, zwölf Stücke in Tanzform, Op.41. Berlin: Ries & Erler, 1892. US:Wc.

30 Tanzweisen, Op.21. Berlin: Ries & Erler, 1881. US:Wc.

King, Janet

°*Sea pictures;* eight duets. London: M.S.M. Publications, 1977. (E)

King, Matthew Peter (1773–1823)

English composer of stage works, solo songs, and numerous piano pieces.

A grand duett for two performers, Op.8 [9?]. London: Longman & Broderip, ca.1797. GB:Lbl,Ob. Three-movement instructional work in routine Classical style. (LI)

Kingman, Dan

°*Four miniatures for young pianists* (Follow the leader; Black and white; Whistling tune; Sand castles). Los Angeles: Western International Music Co., 1962. Teaching pieces of unusual merit: imaginative, absorbing, gracefully set. (E)

Kinkel, G.

Le pianiste imprévu, galop burlesque, Op.39. Mainz: Schott, 1882. (La première partie peut être exécutée par une personne qui n'a jamais étudié le piano). D-brd:MZsch. (UE-LI/LE)

Kinscella, Hazel Gertrude (1895–1960)

American musicologist and composer; wrote extensively on music in America. Her compositions include choral and piano works.

Ten little duets (Village dance; Evening song; A jolly time; The merry shepherd; At twilight; Marching on; Playing tag; Ghosts; Lullaby; [missing]). New York: Schirmer, 1922. US:Bp. (E)

Kirby-Mason, Barbara, arr.

°*Eight Jamaican folk-songs.* London: OUP, 1970. Dextrously set arrangements of rhythmical songs; interest in both parts. (E)

Kirchner, Fritz (1840–1907)

German composer of instructional piano music and salon pieces.

À toutes voiles, Op.322. London: Pitt & Hatzfeld, 1890. US:Wc. (I)

Auf Flügeln der Liebe, Galop, Op.721. Leipzig: Kieslers Musikverlag, 1898. US:Wc. (I)

Danses allemandes, Op.280. London: Pitt & Hatzfeld, 1891. US:Wc. (LI-I)

Danses anglaises, Op.269. London: Pitt & Hatzfeld, 1891. US:Wc. (I)

Danses espagnoles, Op.282. London: Pitt & Hatzfeld, 1891. US:Wc. (I)

Danses françaises, Op.255. London: Pitt & Hatzfeld, 1893. US:Wc. (I)

En traîneau, Op.1013. London: Augener, n.d. US:Wc. (I)

Galop brillant (Meereswagen), Op.900. London: Augener, 1901. US:Wc. (I)

Nouvelles danses françaises, Op.290. London: Pitt & Hatzfeld, 1890. US:Wc. (I)

Scènes rustiques, Op.323. London: Augener, n.d. US:Wc. (I)

Sonatine (G), Op.225. Leipzig: Kistner & Siegel, 1888. US:Wc. (I)

Tone sketches, Op.986. London: Augener, 1904. US:Wc. (I)

Kirchner, Theodor (1823–1903)

German organist, conductor, teacher, composer; friend of Mendelssohn and Schumann, who influenced the style of his carefully fashioned piano pieces. Kirchner also wrote choral works, chamber music, organ pieces, and songs.

Albumblätter, Op.7. Leipzig: Hofmeister, 1856. "Elegie" in collection *Meister der Romantik.* GB:Lbl has Op.7/2,5,6.

2 Märsche, Op.94. Greiz: Willy von Franquet, 1890. US:Wc. (I)

12 original compositionen, Op.57. Leipzig: Peters, 1881. GB:Lbl–US:Wc. Well-shaped, melodious pieces. (I)

Sechs Walzer (G,g,Eb,Ab,Eb,G), Op.104. Leipzig: Leuckhart, 1894. US: Wc. Elegant set of graceful waltzes. (LI-I)

Kirkman (Kirchman), Jacob (?–ca.1799)

German-born English harpsichord and piano maker; organist. He wrote organ and piano pieces.

A duett for two performers. London: Birchall & Andrews, ca.1785. GB:Lcm –US:Wc.

Four duetts, three for two performers on one harpsichord or pianoforte (G,Eb,C), and one for harpsichord and pianoforte, Op.2. London: I. Blundell, ca. 1790; London: Longman & Broderip, ca.1785. GB:Ckc,Lbl. Two-movement works set in pallid Classical style; weak melodically and harmonically. (I)

Four progressive duettinos (G,F,C,A), Op.16. London: Birchall, ca.1795. GB:Lbl. Short melodious instructional pieces in two movements; undistinguished but pleasant. (UE-LI)

Two sonatas and one duet for two performers, Op.5. London: Preston, ca. 1785. US:Bp.

Kjaer, Vilfred (1906–1968)

Danish pianist, pedagogue, and composer.

°*Af tidens danserytmer* (Of the dance rhythms of time). Copenhagen: Hansen, n.d.

Kjerulf, Halfdan (1815–1868)

Norwegian composer; wrote in Romantic style imbued with Norwegian folk flavor.

Fandango. Oslo: Warmuth (Norsk Musik-Forlag), 1886. N:Onk. (I)
Marsch (c), Op.21. Berlin: Simon; Stockholm: Hirsch, 1876. N:Onk. (I)
Polonaise (C), Op.13. Berlin: Simon, 1876. N:Onk. (I)
Rondino (F), Op.22. Berlin: Simon, 1876; Stockholm: Hirsch, 1869. N:Onk. (I)

Klebe, Giselher Wolfgang (1925–)

German composer; his early neo-Classical style has developed into an advanced serial idiom. He has also written electronic music. His works include operas, chamber and symphonic music, and piano compositions.

Szene, for four solo violins, tutti violins, and piano four hands. Pub. missing, 1954. Available from composer, Detmolder Musikakademie, Detmold, Nordrhein-Westfalen, West Germany.

Kleffel, Arno (1840–1913)

German conductor and critic; composer of incidental music, chamber and choral works, lieder, and piano pieces.

Walzer- und Ländler-Album, Op.21. Berlin: Simon, 1876; NEd.1911. US: PHf,Wc. Assortment of various dances in late-Romantic idiom. (LI-I)

Kleinheinz, Franz Xavier (1765–1832)

German conductor and composer of operas, sacred music, and instrumental works.

Grande sonate (d), Op.12. Vienna: Bureau d'Arts et d'Industrie, 1803. A:Wgm–D-ddr:Bds–US:Wc. Three-movement work in broad Classical style. Despite appealing melodies and strong harmony it is weak in thematic development and lacks excitement. (I)

Kleinmichel, Richard (1846–1901)

German conductor, teacher, and composer of instructional piano music.

Grande valse brillante (Eb). Hamburg: Berens, ca.1867. US:NYp. (I)

Klerk, Albert de (1917–)

Aria with variations. Ms. NL:Ad.

Klink, Waldemar (1894–)

German choral conductor; has specialized in writing children's choral music.

°*Kleines Lob der grossen Stadt,* Jugend-Kantate mit Texten von Waldemar Klink (in three versions). Version III: for Chorus with percussion and piano 4H. Lippstadt: Kistner & Siegel, ca.1964.

Knight, Colin (1913–)

°*March of the shearers.* Melbourne: Allans Music, 1967.
°*Summer tide.* Melbourne: Allans Music, 1969.

Knischek (Knĕžek; Knieschek), Wenceslaus (Václav) (1743–1806)

Czech bassoonist; composed cantatas and piano pieces.

Sonata (G). Regensburg: Daisenberger, ca.1800. D-brd:Mbs—GB:Lbl.

Knittelmair, Peter Lambert (1769–1845)

Six allemandes (D,A,F,D,Bb,Eb). Munich: Falter, n.d. D-brd:Mbs. Pleasant, lightweight dances with trios; Schubertian in character, form, and harmonic idiom. (LI)

Trois marches. Munich: Falter, ca.1818. D-brd:Mbs—D-ddr:Bds—GB:Lbl.

Knorr, Ernst Lothar von (1896–1973)

German violinist and composer of choral works, concertos, chamber music, organ pieces, school music, and piano pieces.

°*Introduktion und Allegro.* In collection *Spielbuch, zeitgenössische Original-kompositionen.* Broad, serious introduction, with more than a touch of Hindemith, leads to fast 12/8 staccato section in mainly linear movement, then back to the reprise of the introduction. (I-UI)

Knorr, Iwan (1853–1916)

German-born Russian teacher; composer of choral, orchestral, and piano music in salon style.

Vier Walzer, Op.9. Leipzig: B&H, 1868. US:Wc (Op.9/1 only).

The following works of Iwan Knorr were published under the pseudonym of J.O.Armand:

6 leichte Stücke, Op.9. Leipzig: B&H, 1890. US:Wc.

10 Phantasiestücke, Op.20. Leipzig: B&H, 1905. US:Wc. (I)

Knox, Isabel

°*My first duets,* sixteen little duets. Melbourne: Allans, n.d. (UE)

Koch, Frederick (1927–)

American teacher and composer. He has written orchestral, chamber, and choral works, and instructional piano music of high quality.

°*Four dance episodes.* New York: Carl Fischer, 1974. (I)

°*Golliwog's dance.* Boston: Boston Music Co., 1963. Angular, syncopated work in contemporary idiom. (UE-LI)

°*It takes two,* six pieces. New York: General Music, 1969. Effective mood pieces featuring changing meters, whole-tone and pentatonic scales, and tone clusters. (I)

°*Skateboard fun.* New York: Galaxy Music, n.d.; also in *Contemporary collection of Cleveland composers,* I.

Kochan, Günther (1930–)

German teacher; composer of TV and film music, opera, cantatas, symphonic works, piano concerto, and piano pieces.

°*Elf kleine Stücke* (Moderato; Lento; Allegretto scherzando; Abendlied [Andante]; Kleine Ballade [Andante con moto]; Thema und [8] Variationen; Allegretto grazioso; Elegie [Adagio]; Andantino; Moderato; Capriccio [Allegro molto]), Op.20, 1958. Leipzig: Litolff, 1962. Unusually attractive and absorbing set of little pieces, shaped with delicacy and refinement by a sensitive craftsman. They are succinct and trim, and are cast in a spare, linear, contemporary, tonal language. Dissonance, modality, changing meters, and tonal ambiguity are employed with sophistication, restraint, and telling effect. (UE-I)

Koechlin, Charles (1867–1951)

French critic, author, and composer of orchestral and chamber works, songs, and piano pieces in an individual, original, eclectic idiom based on Classical forms.

Quatre sonatines françaises, Op.60 (1925). London: OUP, 1927. US:Wc. Delightful, clean-textured, often witty pieces in mildly contemporary idiom. Contrapuntal; cool and elegantly molded. Require secure musicianship; deserve to be reprinted. (I-UI)

Köhler, Ernst (1799–1847)

German organist and pianist; wrote symphonic and sacred music and instructional pieces.

Trois rondos (F,Eb,A). Leipzig: B&H, ca.1824. D-ddr:Bds. Short teaching pieces. (LI)

Köhler, Gottlob Heinrich (Henry) (1765–1833)

German flutist; prolific composer of instructional piano music. His sonatas and other pieces, like those of his namesake, Louis Köhler, have long been regarded as useful pedagogical material despite their musical aridity.

Introduction et polonaise pour flûte et piano à quatre mains, Op.121. Hamburg: Böhme, ca.1812. B:Bc.

Trois petites sonates, 12ème collection, liv. 1–3. Leipzig: Hofmeister, ca.1819. D-brd:BFd (Sonate No.2).

Sonate (C), Op.57. Mainz: Schott, ca.1810. D-ddr:Bds.

Sonate (F), Op.69. Bonn: Simrock, ca.1810. CH:Bchristen–D-brd:B,Mbs– D-ddr:Bds–S:Skma.

Sonate (G), Op.88. Mainz: Schott, ca.1810. D-brd:MZsch–D-ddr:Bds.

Sonate facile (D), Op.14. Bonn: Simrock, ca.1819. D-brd:B–D-ddr:Bds.

Sonatina (F), Op.139. Mainz: Schott, ca.1822. D-ddr:Bds.

Polonaise (C). Hamburg: Böhme, n.d. S:Skma.

Quatre walzes et deux écossaises (C,G), Op.47. Bonn: Simrock, ca.1807. CH: Bchristen–D-brd:B–DK:Kmk.

Six walzes. Berlin: J.J.Hummel, ca.1806. Hamburg: Böhme; Leipzig: Peters; Vienna: Mollo, ca.1806. S:Skma.

Six walzes, Op.67, livre II(IV). Leipzig: Hofmeister, ca.1812. D-brd:BFb (No.II)–DK:Kmk (No.IV).

Kohn, Karl (1926–   )

Viennese-born American pianist and conductor; cultivates serial, aleatory, and avant-garde techniques.

°*Castles and Kings*, a suite for children. New York: Carl Fischer, 1965. Charming, well laid out for both partners. The composer makes use of tonal idiom with mild dissonance in some of the pieces, and of total serialization in others. Unusual sonorities; challenging. (I)

°*Recreations* (1968). New York: Carl Fischer, 1973. Long, complex work in twelve-tone idiom. (UI-LA)

Kolinsky, Mieczyslaw

°*First piano duets*, seven easy pieces (On the ferris wheel; Cinderella; On the hobby horse; Hush-a-bye; Spanish dance; Once upon a time; Arabian dance). New York: Schirmer, 1965. The attractive music in this unusual collection is tuneful and artfully set for both partners. (E-5)

°*Three pieces* (Around the maypole; At the court of Old King Cole; By the campfire). New York: Carl Fischer, 1954. Pieces also published separately. Delightful, short, effective compositions ingeniously written in single-line texture. (E-5)

Kölling, Carl

Teacher and pupil, thirty melodious study pieces, Op.366. Philadelphia: Presser, 1902. US:PHf. (UE-LI/E-5)

Kollman, August Friedrich (1756–1829)

German-born English organist and theorist.

Twelve analyzed fugues, with double counterpoints in all intervals, for two performers on one pianoforte or organ, Op.10. London: pub. by composer, 1822. A:Wgm—CH:Zjacobi—GB:Gu.

Piece. Pub. and date missing. GB:Lbl.

Komma, Karl Michael (1913–)

German-Czech composer of cantatas, songs, piano pieces, and organ concertos.

Deutsche Tänze aus dem Kuhländchen, Op.8a. Reichenberg: E. Ullmann, n.d. US:Wc. German dances in effective 4H settings. (I)

König, Gustav, Jr.

6 Melodische Uebungsstücke, Op.9. Offenbach: André, n.d. (UE-LI/E-5)

Sonatine instructive, Op.8. Hamburg: Cranz, n.d.

Kopelent, Marek (1932–)

Czech composer; has written orchestral pieces, chamber works, children's music, and piano pieces.

°*Zkratky* (10 short pieces). Prague: Artia, 1963. Attractive set of refined little teaching pieces. (E)

Koppel, Herman D. See Birgitta Nordenfelt.

Dane of Polish origin; writes in conservative idiom in the tradition of Nielsen.

Korda, Viktor (1900–)

°*Aus Österreich*, Volkstänze. Vienna: Doblinger, n.d.

Körner, Gotthilf Wilhelm (1809–1865)

German music publisher; wrote many organ and piano pieces.

Fuga, Allegro con spirito (C). Ms. Written for Joseph Emmer, 19 March 1859. US:Wc. Academic four-voice fugue. (LI)

Kosteck, Gregory (1937–   )

American teacher and composer; employs advanced compositional techniques.

°*Music for piano duo* (on a note-row by Alban Berg) (1969). Ms. photocopy available from Rochester Music Photo Copy Co., Inc., Maiden Lane, Sodus Point, NY 14555. Divided into short sections: Introduction, Duologue, Signiture [sic], Masqurade [sic], and Epitaph. Based on a theme from Alban Berg's *Violin Concerto*. The texture is spare with pointillistic flashes of color and sparkle. Rhythmic vitality, widely spaced sonorities, and carefully controlled use of the pedal add to the effectiveness of this trim and concise work. (A)

Kotchetow, Nikolai Razumnikovich (b.1864)

Russian critic and composer.

Suite russe (Prélude; Rêverie; Conte; Berceuse; Rondo), Op.32. Moscow: Jurgenson, 1914. US:Wc. Colorful settings of Russian folk tunes. (I)

Kotzwara (Kočzwara), Franz (ca.1750–1791)

Czech musician, resident of London; wrote the popular *Battle of Prague* and other works for piano.

A *duett for two performers*, No.3. Amsterdam: Hummel, ca.1790; London: Blanc, ca.1790. GB:Lbl.

Kountz, Richard (1896–1950)

American composer of choral works, organ pieces, and piano compositions.

°*The sleigh*, à la russe. New York: Schirmer, n.d.

Koželuh (Kozeluch), Leopold (1748–1818)

Czech composer of the Viennese school; contemporary of Vaňhal. In his day Koželuh enjoyed even greater popularity than did Mozart or Haydn. He succeeded Mozart, after the latter's death, in his post at the Austrian court in 1792, and composed prolifically in all forms. In spite of its lightweight character, Koželuh's four-hand music is agreeable, well written, and melodious, and the repertoire contains many attractive compositions especially useful for the intermediate pianist.

The following consolidated catalogue of Koželuh's four-hand compositions has been copiously supplemented with data provided in Milan Poštolka's study of the composer and his works, *Leopold Koželuh, život a dílo* (Prague: Státní Hudební Vydavatelství, 1964) and additional details from RISM. Works are listed by form (Sonata, Concerto, etc.) according to Poštolka's chronological numbering system. As many as 25 different editions of a single work may exist, issued by a variety of publishers and often under several titles. However, full listings below are limited to first editions and modern editions in print. Library locations, on the other hand, are provided for all editions, both listed and unlisted. (For full details on other editions see RISM or Poštolka.)

Sonata (F), Op.4. Poštolka XI:1. Vienna: Artaria, 1781. A:Wgm,Wn,Wst—BR:Rn—CH:E—D-brd:KIl—D-ddr:Dlb,SWl—I:PAc—US:Pu,Wc. Other editions published under the titles *Duett; Sonatina; Sonata*, Op.4; or *Sonata*, Op.11: A:Wn—B:Bc—CS:Pnm,Pr—D-brd:B—F:V—GB:Lbl—I:PAc—J:Tma —S:Skma,St—US:NH,NYp,Wc.

Trois sonates, dont la troisième est à quatre mains (B♭), Op.8. Poštolka XI: 2. Vienna: Torricella, 1784; Vienna: Magazin Kozeluch, 1784. B:Bc—CS: Pk—D-brd:Mbs,Sl—D-ddr:SWl—GB:Lbl—US:Wc. Other editions published as *Duett*, Op.8; *Duo*, Op.9; *Sonata*, Op.12; or *Sonata*, Op.13: A:ST, Wn—B:Bc—BR:Rn—CH:E—CS:KRa,Pnm,Pu—D-brd:Bhm—D-ddr:Dlb—GB:Cu—I:Vc—US:Wc.

Sonata (F), Op.10. Poštolka XI:3. Vienna: Torricella, 1784. CS:Pnm—D-brd: KIl. °NEd. First and third movements only (listed as Adagio and Rondo from *Duo*, Op.19), No. 11 and 12 in *Album of four hand compositions by old Czech masters*, ed. Kleinová, Fišerová, and·Müllerová. Other editions published as *Duett*, Op.22; *Duo*, Op.19; or *Sonata*, Op.10, Op.13, or Op.19: A:LIm,ST,Wgm,Wn,Wst—B:Bc—BR:Rn—CH:Bchristen,Bu—CS: KRa,Pk,Pnm,Pr,Pu,PLm — D-brd:B,BNba,BNu,F,Mbs,Mmb,Rp — D-ddr: Dlb,SWl,WRtl — F:Pc,V — GB:Cu,Lbl — I:Mc,MOe,Nc — NL:DHgm — S:Sk,Skma,Ssr—US:Bp,NH,NYp,PHf,PHu,Wc.

Sonata (B♭), Op.29. Poštolka XI:4. Vienna: Kozeluch (Magazin), 1789. A: Wgm—CS:Pnm—D-brd:HEms—I:PAc,Tn—US:Wc—YU:Zs. Other editions published as *Duett; Duo;* or *Sonata*, Op.29 or Op.19: A:Wgm,Wn—B:Bc—BR:Rn — CH:Bn — CS:Bm,K,Pk,Pnm,TRE—D-brd:B — D-ddr:Dlb — GB: Lbl,Lcm,Cu,Ob,Er—N:Ou—NL:Uim—US:PHf,PHu.

Trois sonates (C,F,D). Poštolka XI:5,6,7. Kassel: Wöhler, ca.1803. CS:Pnm, Pu—D-brd:LÜh—D-ddr:LEm. °NEd. *Sonata* (C) (Poštolka XI:5) complete: Nos.13,14,15 in *Album of four hand compositions by old Czech masters*, eds. Kleinová, Fišerová, and Müllerová. Other editions published as *Trois sonates*, Op.12; *Trois sonates*, Op.13; *Leichte Sonate Werk* 10; or *Sonatine* No.9: A:Wn—CS:Pnm—D-brd:Hch,Hhm,HEms,KIu,OF—D-ddr:LEm,SWl—DK:Kk—F:Pc,Pn—N:Ou—S:Skma,Sm,Uu—US:Cn,Wc.

Concerto (B♭) *a quattro mani per il clavicembalo ô fortepiano*, violino 1, violino 2, due oboi ô flauti, due corni (B♭), due viole obl. e basso. Poštolka IV:8. Leipzig: B&H, 1787. °NEd. (piano score) Zanibon, 1978 (orchestra score and parts available). B:Bc—CS:Pnm.

Poštolka XXIV:1,IV 22 (*Gavotte*)(F), 18 (*Marzia lugubre*), III 17 (*Allegro*)(B♭) [ca.1794]. These three pieces were originally ascribed to Mozart and so indicated in Köchel's *Verzeichnis*. Later they were attributed to Beethoven by Saint-Foix, Jack Werner, and Harold Bauer (in 1920 Bauer published a new 4H edition of the *Gavotte* as a work by Beethoven, and later he recorded it in a 2H version). Otto Deutsch ("Kozeluch Ritrovata," *Music and Letters*, January 1945) finally identified the three pieces correctly as excerpts from Koželuh's *La Ritrovata Figlia de Ottone II* (Poštolka XXIV:1), produced in Vienna in 1794. (A piano reduction of the score is located in GB:Lbl under the title *Musica del Ballo intitolato La Ritrovata Figlia di Otone ii*, Op.39 [London: Lavenu and Mitchell, n.d.].) The arranger of the 4H adaptations of these works is unknown. The °*Gavotte*, erroneously listed under Beethoven's authorship, appears in the collection *Easy Original Piano Duets*, ed. Zeitlin and Goldberger.

Kraehenbuehl, David

American pianist and composer; studied with Hindemith; has written extensively for children.

°*Bugler's holiday*. Evanston, IL: Summy-Birchard, 1969. (UE-LI)

°*A Christmas canzona*, 1966. Princeton, NJ: National Keyboard Arts Associates, 1972. Five contrasting variants of a Christmas melody. Each section features a different pianistic device. The partners share equal responsibility, and the writing is ingratiating and effective. (UE)

Concert for the mysteries (II) for two pianists at one piano, and orchestra. Pub. and date missing.

°*Grand march*. Evanston, IL: Summy-Birchard Co., 1969. (LI)

°*Lowlands* (canonic variations on a sailor's lament). Princeton, NJ: National Keyboard Arts Associates, 1972. A clever and engaging contrapuntal setting of a modal folk melody featuring different kinds of canons divided between the two performers. (UE-LI)

°*Rodent reel*. Evanston, IL: Summy-Birchard, 1969. (E)

°*When Johnny comes marching home*. Evanston, IL: Summy-Birchard, 1969. (LI)

The two preceding duets, together with *Bugler's holiday*, are attractive and skilfully written. The musical language is polished, colorful, and appealingly up to date.

Kraemer, C.

°*Etta waltz*. Cincinnati: Willis, n.d. (E)

Kramer, Duane (1939–)

American composer and music engraver; his works include many pieces for young pianists.

°*Take a chance*. Boulder, CO: Myklas Press, 1973. Amusing piece in aleatoric technique involving clapping, whistling, singing (and shouting), and a variety of keyboard activities. Interesting, attractive, imaginative writing. Performance instructions are clearly indicated; the piece may be played as a solo or against a pre-recorded tape of the other part. (LI-I)

°*Trichroism* (Prologue; Vermilion; Indigo; Aureolin). Boulder, CO: Myklas Press, 1974. The title of this intriguing work is taken from the optical phenomenon of a single prism, which reflects various colors in three different directions. It features quartal harmony and chromaticism and uses contrasting, often vague, tonal relationships. (UE-LI)

Krasev, Mikhail Ivanovich (1897–1954)

Soviet composer of children's music, operettas, choruses, stage works, and various instrumental pieces.

V *Kryme* (In Crimea) (Cavernous town; Morning in the mountains), Op.3. Moscow: State Music Publishing House, 1926. US:NYp. Agreeable, short settings of two Soviet ethnic folk songs (Turkish and Tatar); well-balanced parts. (I)

Kraus, Ernst

Trois sonatines (a,C,F). Prague: Urbánek, 1912. US:Wc. Pedagogical works; considerable thematic variety within limited range. (UE-LI)

Krause, Anton (1834–1907)

German pianist, conductor, and composer. He wrote choral works and pedagogical piano music.

2 Instruktive Sonaten (F,g), Op.20. Leipzig: B&H, 1869. US:Wc. (UE-LI/E-5)

Serenade (Eb), Op.6. Leipzig: B&H, 1858. US:Wc. (LI)

Krause, Franz (1889–)

Passacaglia, Op.27. Kassel: pub. by composer, 1963. US:Wc. Weighty composition of large proportions; well developed; ends in fugue. (UI-A)

Krehl, Stephan (1864–1924)

German theory teacher and author; wrote music theory texts and instructional piano music.

Slovenische Tänze, Op.9. Leipzig: B&H, 1894. US:Wc.

Krenek, Ernst (1900–)

Austrian-born composer, resident in U.S. Atonality, jazz, serial techniques, electronics, and musico-mathematics have all played a part in the development of his style.

°*Hausmusik*. Seven pieces for the days of the week. Kassel: Bärenreiter, 1959. No.1 is for piano 4H.

Krentzlin, Richard (1864–1956)

German piano pedagogue and composer of instructional pieces for piano.

°*In Schubert's day*, Op.109. Philadelphia: Presser, 1929. (UE-LI)

Minuet favori, Op.43. Berlin: Krentzlin; Boston: A.P.Schmidt, 1913. US:Wc. (I)

Kreutzer, Konradin (1780–1849)

German Kapellmeister. He composed operas, an oratorio, theater music, and instructional piano music.

Trois marches. Vienna: Diabelli, ca.1826. A:Wgm.

2 Romanzen. Pub. missing, ca.1826. A:Wgm.

Rondeau brillant, Op.68. Vienna: Diabelli, ca.1826. A:Wgm—I:Mc.

Sonatine en fantaisie (A), Op.25. Mainz: Schott, ca.1821. A:Wgm.

Sonatine en fantaisie (C), Op.61. Leipzig: Kistner, ca.1824. A:Wgm.

Křička, Jaroslav (1882–1969)

Czech teacher and conductor. He composed operas, orchestral works, song cycles, chamber music, and piano pieces and is especially noted for his children's pieces for voice and piano.

°*Šest ukolébavky se snazším prvním hlasem* (Six lullabies with an easier primo part) (Lenka; Madlenka; Jolanka; Vendalka; Vitoušek; Janko), rev. Karel Šolc (1962–1964). Prague: Panton, 1967. Engaging little mood pieces in Czech folk idiom. (UE-LI/E)

Krieger, Edino (1928–   )

Brazilian composer of chamber, orchestral, and piano works. In his early period he used serial techniques, but later he adopted the neo-Classical idiom.

°*Sonata.* New York: Peer International, 1971. Moderately short, single-movement work in tonal idiom with Brazilian folk flavor. Triadic with some quartal harmony; transparent linear writing leads into richly textured climaxes. Well written for the medium; appealing and flowing; delightful to play. (I-UI)

Kroeger, Ernest R. (1862–1934)

American organist, pianist, educator, and composer.

Danse caractéristique, No.1. St.Louis: Kunkel Bros., 1884. US:PHf,Wc.

March of the Amazons. St.Louis: Kunkel Bros., 1883. US:Wc. Salon piece. (LI)

Suite de valses. St. Louis: Kunkel Bros., 1885. US:Wc. Lively, well-constructed set of tuneful waltzes in salon style. (UI)

Krollmann, N.A.

Sonatina facile et brillante (F), Op.24. NEd. Leipzig: Hofmeister, 1864. US:PHf,Wc. Instructional work. (I)

Kronke, Emil

German pianist and composer; his four-hand works are instructional in character.

Three characteristic pieces. Philadelphia: Presser, 1922. US:Wc. (LI)

From far and near; five duets, Op.66. Boston: A.P.Schmidt, 1912. US:Wc. (LI)

°*Kleine Suite* (Polonaise; Walzer; Marsch; Lied ohne Worte; Ungarisch; Tarantelle), Op.88. Leipzig: Leuckart, 1912; NEd., 1953. US:Wc. (UE-LI/E-5)

Moments du bal, Op.15. Leipzig: Steingräber, 1907. US:Wc. (LI)

Two pieces (Cossack dance; Tarantella). Philadelphia: Presser, 1914. US: Wc. (LI)

Krufft, Nikolaus, Freiherr von (1779–1818)

Grosse Sonate (E♭). Vienna: Mechetti, 1813; Berlin: Schlesinger. A:Wst– D-ddr: Bds.

Marche (E♭). Vienna: Bureau, 1802; Haslinger, 1826. D-ddr:Bds.

Krug, Arnold (1849–1904)

German composer and conductor. He wrote symphonic and chamber music, concertos, and instructional pieces for piano.

Double blossoms, ten melodious pieces, Op.114. London: Augener, 1902. US:Wc. Salon pieces. (UE-LI)

Five pieces, Op.117. London: Augener, 1903. US:Wc. Teaching pieces. (UE-LI)

Kücken, Friedrich Wilhelm (1810–1882)

German composer of piano music in salon style.

Introduction et polonaise brillante, Op.4. Hamburg: Schuberth, ca.1852. US:NYp. (LI-I)

Küffner (Kiefner), Johann Jakob Paul (1727–1786)

Sonate (G), avec l'accompagnement de deux violons, deux cors, et cello, point obligés, Op.2. Regensburg: pub. by composer [Gramm], n.d. D-brd:B (complete), Rtt (Ms.)–F:Pc.

Kuhlau, Friedrich (1786–1832)

German flutist and composer; settled in Denmark. He wrote operas, piano concertos, and chamber music, but is best known for his flute pieces and piano sonatinas.

Adagio et rondeau (A♭), Op.124. Copenhagen: Lose, n.d. US:NYp. Moderately long work in the composer's well-balanced, Classical idiom, a style that also characterizes his more familiar solo sonatinas. The parts are carefully distributed, the melodies are appealing, and the rhythm is interesting throughout. (I-UI)

Trois airs variés (Air des fées; Non più andrai; Air suisse), Op.114. Leipzig: Peters, ca.1829. US:Wc. These three works follow a similar format: Introduction, five or six variations, and a brilliant coda. The burden lies principally with the Primo part, which abounds in florid passage work and pyrotechnics, while the Secondo is restricted to chordal accompaniment. The air varié was a genre common in the period, and Kuhlau does rather better than most at it. (I/I-UI)

Allegro pathétique (c), Op.123. Copenhagen: Lose, n.d. US:NYp,Wc. Long, dramatic work with contrasting chordal and linear passages; also contains fugal sections. (UI)

Trois rondos agréables (D,C,F), Op.70. Hamburg: Cranz, ca.1826. US:PHf, Wc. Works of moderate length with the Primo the more difficult and active part. Music tends to be repetitious, with excessive passage work. (I/I-UI)

Trois rondeaux (Air autrichien: Air militaire anglais; Galopade bourgeois), Op.111. Paris: Farrenc, n.d. US:PHf,Wc. Similar to preceding work in structure. Passage work in both parts, but predominantly a Primo piece. (I/I-UI)

Sonatine (F), Op.17. Copenhagen: Lose, n.d. US:PHf. Attractive work in the style of the composer's 2H sonatinas; not difficult; useful. (UE-LI)

°*Six sonatinas*, Op.44 (G,C,F) and Op.66 (F,C,G). NEd. °Consortium Musical; °Heugel; °Peters; °Ricordi. These melodious, skilfully set pieces form an important and useful contribution to 4H literature. They may be favorably compared with Clementi's duet sonatas for their musical and pedagogical value. (I-UI)

Kühner, Conrad (1851–1909)

Pianist, teacher; composer of pedagogical works for piano.

Schule des vierhändigen Klavierspiels. (Original compositions in classical and modern style arranged in order of increasing difficulty from elementary level on.) 12 vols. Leipzig: B&H, 1899.

Kuhnert (Kunnerth), Rudolf

Deutsche Tänze aus dem Sudetenland. Leipzig: B&H, 1924. US:NYp.

Kunitz, Sharon Lohse

°*The crickets came to dance.* Boulder, CO: Myklas Press, 1977. (E)

Kurka, Robert (1921–1957)

American composer of Czech background. His works include symphonic and chamber music, a choral piece, piano compositions, and an opera, *The Good Soldier Schweik*, completed just before his death.

Dance suite (Prelude; Furiant; Polka; Waltz; Finale), Op.29. New York: Weintraub Music, 1965. Commissioned by Milton and Peggy Salkind. Polished, beautifully crafted suite with a strong Czech flavor. The work is cast in a highly individual, frequently dissonant, tonal idiom. Carefully balanced for both partners; a valuable addition to the repertoire. (I-LA)

Kurtág, György (1926–   )

Hungarian teacher and pianist. His musical style has been influenced by Kadosa, Milhaud, and Messiaen, with whom he studied. He has written choral works, chamber music, a violin concerto, and piano pieces.

°*Suite* (C). Budapest: Editio Musica, 1956.

Labey, Marcel (1875–1968) and Charlotte Sohy (1887–1955)

Labey was French conductor and composer of orchestral and chamber works. He also wrote piano pieces in Romantic style influenced by his teacher, d'Indy.

°Quatre pièces faciles (Pour Monique; Pour Elaine; Pour Philippe; Pour France). Paris: Rouart-Lerolle, n.d. (LI/UE)

Lacerda, Osvaldo Costa de (1927–   )

Brasiliana No.4. São Paulo-Rio de Janeiro: Irmãos Vitale, 1968.

Lachner, Franz (1803–1890)

Viennese musician, friend of Schubert. His pedagogical music for piano includes a quantity of deftly and idiomatically written 4H pieces. The majority tend to be dry, colorless works but they are nonetheless useful for ensemble and sight-reading practice.

Grande Sonate (d), Op.39. Vienna: Diabelli, 1832. US:Wc.

Grosse Sonate (c), Op.20. Vienna: Leidesdorf, 1827. US:Wc. Opp.20 and 39 are large-scale, well-written compositions; technically challenging, but lacking in inspiration. (UI)

Tre scherzi, Op.26. Vienna: Leidesdorf, 1829. US:Wc. Carefully written compositions, with occasional bright moments. (I)

Variationen (e), Op.138. Mainz: Schott, 1868. US:Wc. Perfunctory work of moderate length; neatly written for both partners. (I)

Lack, Théodore (1846–1921)

French piano prodigy and composer of elegant salon music.

°Impressions de voyage. Paris: Lemoine, 1911.

Lacôme d'Estalenx, Paul-Jean-Jacques (1838–1920)

French composer of operettas, religious works, songs, orchestral and chamber music, and piano pieces.

La douce maison, scènes familiales (La maison active; Bercelonnette; Conte d'hiver; La leçon de danse, petite valse; Le tennis, scherzo). Paris: Costallat, 1908. US:Wc.

Les Pyrénées, suite. Paris: Enoch, 1899. US:Wc.

Ladmirault, Paul (1877–1944)

French composer of piano works, operas, and sacred and orchestral music. His style is refined and lyrical with strong associations with Breton folk music.

Dan lullaby. London: OUP, 1927. GB:Lbl–US:Wc. Gentle, tranquil work in Romantic idiom with some Impressionistic sonorities. (LI)

Musiques rustiques, suite (Fantaisie sur deux "rounds" camoëlais; Tro Cornouailles; Final sur deux thèmes vannetais). Paris: Demets, 1906. US:Wc. Pleasant, skilful settings of Breton folk melodies. (LI-I)

Rhapsodie gaëlique (Les Campbells arrivent; Danse des fées; Nocturne; Limerick Pibroch; Chanson écossaise; Fantaisie sur une contredanse populaire). Paris: O. Bouwens van der Boijen & Co., 1909; Leduc, 1922. US:

Wc. Appealing, skilled settings of Celtic melodies from various sources—Scottish, Irish, and Breton. (I-UI)

°*Suite bretonne* (Chant des bugale-noz; Chanson populaire, thème du XIIème siècle). Paris: Salabert, n.d.

°*Valse mignonne.* Paris: Consortium Musical, n.d. (UE)

Variations sur des airs de Biniou trécorois (tirés du recueil de Quellien). Paris: Demets (Max Eschig), 1906. US:Wc. Attractive settings of five Breton melodies; worth reviving. (I)

Ladukhin, Nikolai Mikhailovich (1860–1918)

Russian composer of sacred pieces, chamber works, music for children, and solfeggio books.

Répertoire enfantin, recueil de pièces (Conte; Réveil; Cigales; Cortège). Moscow: Jurgenson, ca.1913. US:NYp. Short, instructional piece with Russian folk-song flavor. (E)

Ladurner, Ignaz Anton (1766–1839)

Austrian teacher and composer; settled in France. He wrote operas, chamber works, and piano compositions.

Sonate (F), Op.2. Paris: Boyer, 1793. B:Bc—F:V. Strong, two-movement work with contrasting sections, well-developed themes, and textural variety. Rhythmic and harmonic interest is sustained throughout. (I)

Sonate, Op.6. Paris: Naderman, ca.1804. D-brd:Mbs.

Sonate (C), Op.12. Paris: Naderman, ca.1800. US:Wc.

Laemmerhirt, G.

Deux sonates faciles, Op.2. Leipzig: B&H, 1798. A contemporary review describes these two sonatas as melodious and well set, and emphasizes their qualities as fine study pieces for the beginning student. D-brd:BE. (UE-LI)

Lahmer, Ruel (1912–)

Canadian-American composer; student of Roy Harris; works include orchestral and choral pieces and chamber music.

Passacaglia and fugue for clarinet and piano duet, 1949. Pub. missing. US: NYamc.

Lake, Genevieve

°*Czech dance* (e). New York: Carl Fischer, 1948. Pleasing folk-song arrangement. (UE)

°*You and who* (two marches + two waltzes). New York: Schirmer, 1969. Instructional pieces without octaves; activity in both parts. (E-UE)

Lambert, Cecily

A droll tale. Boston: Boston Music Co., n.d. US:NYamc.

°*A duet a day* (Helston flora dance; March of the three kings; Agincourt song; Parado de Valldemosa; Trumpet and drum; Elizabethan dances;

Acrobats). London: Forsyth, 1968. Effective collection including original pieces and arrangements of folk songs. (UE-LI)

March with bells. Boston: Boston Music Co. US:NYamc.

Lambert, Constant (1905–1951)

English conductor and composer, strongly influenced by jazz. His works include ballets, film music, choral and orchestral compositions, chamber music, and piano pieces.

°*Trois pièces nègres pour les touches blanches* (Aubade; Siesta; Nocturne) (1949). London: OUP, 1950. US:PHf,Wc. Ingenious, witty set of pieces introduced with a sly touch of Satie-esque puckishness in its antithetical title. Using pandiatonicism as a tonal basis the composer has formed all the melodies, chords, and clusters exclusively from white notes. The work has a jazz and West Indian Creole flavor with rhythmic variety, a unique modal quality, and fascinating tone color. (I)

Lambert, George Jackson (1794–1880)

English composer and organist.

Duett for two performers (D). London: Rutter & McCarthy, ca.1815. GB: Lbl. Short, two-movement instructional work in sonata form. (UE-LI)

LaMontaine, John (1920–   )

American composer; has written an opera, orchestral and chamber music, songs, and piano pieces in refined neo-Classical style.

°*Sonata,* Op.25. Philadelphia: Elkan-Vogel, 1967. Brilliant three-movement work (grave, ponderous Preamble; light, busy Scherzo; and brilliant concluding Fugue). Uses full resources of the keyboard. Tonal style influenced by 20th-century French neo-Classicism and to some extent by Hindemith's linear polyphony. This work is rewarding concert fare, requiring advanced pianism. (A)

La Motte Fouqué, Friedrich, Baron von (1874–1944)

6 Deutsche Tänze, Op.33. Wolfenbüttel: Verlag für musikalische Kultur und Wissenschaft, 1936. In Vol.6 *Deutsche Hausmusik der Gegenwart,* 1. Reihe, Instrumentalmusik. US:NYp.

Deutsche Tänze, zweite Folge, Op.39. Wolfenbüttel: Verlag für musikalische Kultur und Wissenschaft, 1938. US:NYp.

These two sets of dances are arranged in frequently chromatic, traditional harmonic idiom. The use of occasional changing meters appears to be more decorative than functional. (I-UI)

Lancen, Serge (1922–   )

French composer of ballets, concertos, chamber pieces, and orchestral works.

°*Cubana.* London: Hinrichsen, 1955. In collection *Pianoforte album, original compositions,* Vol.II. Moderately paced work in Latin American rhythmic patterns; set in traditional harmonic structure. (LI)

Lanchbery, J.
°The little red fox. London: Curwen, 1953. (I)

Landry, Albert
°*Un concert lilliputien*, Op.144. Paris: Gallet, n.d. (UE-LI/E-5)
°*Mariée du village*, fête paysanne, Op.216. Paris: Leduc, n.d. (I)
°*Trois petites pièces* (Soir-rose; Clochettes villageoises; Bal d'enfants). Paris: Durand, 1911. US:Wc. Instructional pieces. (UE-LI/E-UE)
°*Trottez menu*, Op.142. Paris: Gallet, n.d. (UE)

Lang, Hans (1897–1968)
German composer and teacher; wrote choral works, songs, and instrumental pieces for children.
°*Kleine Maienkonzert*, Musik über alte Frühlingslieder (G). In collection *Spielbuch, zeitgenössische Originalkompositionen*. Attractive, tasteful arrangements in traditional idiom of three German folk songs celebrating the coming of spring. (LI)

Lang, Johann Georg (1724–ca.1800)
Bohemian composer; trained in Italy; resident in Darmstadt.
Quatre grandes sonates, dont l'une [G] est à quatre mains avec l'accompagnement d'un violon et violoncelle, Op.7. Offenbach: André, ca.1783. CH: Zz—D-brd:AD,LB—D-ddr:Dlb,SWl—GB:Lbl. Despite some weaknesses in craftsmanship and inventiveness, this is an engaging work in Classical style with interesting antiphonal effects, fresh harmonies, and lyrical melodies. (I)

Lang, Walter (1896–)
Swiss pianist; has written chamber music and piano works.
°*Ferientage*, Op.64. Zürich: Amadeus, 1976. (UE-LI)

Lange, Samuel de, Jr. (1840–1911)
Dutch organist, conductor, and teacher. He wrote choral and organ works, chamber music, and piano compositions.
Sonata (e), Op.33. Cologne: J.F. Weber (Tonger), 1881. US:Wc. Serious three-movement work, structurally sound, but written in a dry, academic conventional idiom, rooted in Mendelssohn. (LI-UI)

Lannoy, Eduard, Freiherr von (1787–1853)
Austro-Belgian conductor; composed operas, orchestral and chamber music, and piano works.
Trois grandes marches, Op.8. Vienna: Mollo, 1820. A:Wgm.

Lanz, Johann Michael (fl. late 18th century)
Sonata (F), Op.5. Brunswick: Musikalische Magazin auf der Höhe, 1796; Zürich: Nägeli, 1796. B:Bc—S:Skma. Short two-movement work in Classical style with pleasant melodies, simple harmonies, and well-balanced

writing for both parts. Contains little or no thematic development. (UE-LI)

Lanza, Alcides (1929–   )

Argentine pianist and composer currently residing in U.S.; uses advanced compositional techniques, especially electronic.

°*Plectros (1962-II)* for one or two pianos, 1962. Buenos Aires: Barry, 1963. The tonal experiments of John Cage come to mind in this avant-garde work featuring unconventional use of the piano. Detailed instructions by the composer call for, among other things, striking the piano with the fist or palm of the hand, plucking the strings with fingernail or plectrum, or striking them with drumsticks.

Laparra, Raoul (1876–1943)

French composer of operas, an orchestral suite, and piano pieces with striking Spanish and Basque influence.

°*Lore dantzariak* (Les fleurs qui dansent), morceaux (Prélude: réveil des fleurs au matin; Arrosa-Gorreia, la rose rouge; Iatsia-Pherdia, la fougère; Belhar-Chuta, la lavande; Othia, le genêt épineux; Ansuna, l'ortie; Elhorri Churia, l'aubépine; Lili Ezteiak, les noces du lierre et de l'aubépine; Chira Ostua, le lierre; Guilharria, la bruyère; Sorguin Orracia, le chardon). Paris: Enoch, 1927. US:Wc. Pleasant settings of folk-like melodies, possibly Basque, describing various flowers and plants of the Basque region. Rhythmic and harmonic interest with free use of changing meters and unusual phrasing. (LI-I)

Last, Joan

English pianist and pedagogue.

°*6 Pantomime pictures.* London: OUP, n.d. (LI)

°*Two and a piano;* a series of easy duets in five sets. London: OUP, 1960. Instructional pieces: simple melodies in traditional style, well arranged, useful. (E-LI)

LaTombelle, Fernand de (1854–1928)

French organist, student of Saint-Saëns; wrote organ and piano pieces, choral works, and chamber music.

°*Bourrée* (E), from *Bourrées et Montagnardes.* Paris: Hamelle, n.d.

°*Montagnarde* (d), from *Bourrées et Montagnardes.* Paris: Hamelle, n.d.

°*Prélude pour un conte de fées.* Paris: Hérelle, 1924. (LI-I)

Latour, Francis Tatton (1766–1837)

Divertissement sur un thème de Pleyel. Offenbach: André, ca.1822. US:Wc. *A duett in which is introduced the air of O Dolce Concento with variations.* Rotterdam: Steup, n.d.; Boston: Graupner, n.d.; The Hague: Weygand, n.d.; Philadelphia: Willig, n.d. US:Bp,Wc. Work in pallid style of Haydn imitators; larded with passage work and sequences; lacks musical substance. (LI-I)

Duo sur l'air de la Flûte Enchantée. Paris: Pacini, n.d. GB:Lbl–US:PHf. (I)
Duo sur l'air tyrolien et hongrois, No.6. Bonn: Simrock, n.d. US:NYp,Wc.
Original duett, Op.6. London: Bland & Weller, ca.1795. US:NYp.

Laub, Vaša (1860–   )
Slavisches Märchen (Slovanská pohádka), Op.16. Breslau: Hainauer, 1893. US:Wc. Salon pieces. (I)

Lauber, Joseph (1864–1952)
Swiss conductor and composer. He wrote orchestral, choral, and chamber music.
Humoresque. Op.36. Geneva: Henn, n.d. CH:Zma.

Lavagnino, Angelo Francesco (1909–   )
°*Le danze antiche* (Minuetto; Gavotta; Giga). Milan: Carisch, n.d.
°*I giochi* (Alle signore; La trottola; Alla guerra). Milan: Carisch, n.d.
°*Incontri con Gesù* (È nato Gesù Bambino; La notte della Befana; L'agnellino di Pasqua). Milan: Carisch, n.d.
°*La passeggiate* (Al bosco dei mughetti; Al convento delle suore azzurre; Al vecchio mulino). Milan: Carisch, n.d.

Lawson, —
°*Rose petals.* Philadelphia: Presser, n.d.

Lazarus, Gustave (1861–1920)
°*Marche funèbre.* Paris: Salabert, n.d.

Lazzari, Sylvio (1857–1944)
French composer, student of César Franck.
Rhapsodie hongroise. Paris: Leduc, 1903. US:Wc. Salon piece. (I)

Leduc, Alphonse (1804–1868)
Founder of Paris publishing house of A. Leduc; prolific composer of songs and piano salon pieces.
Golden bell. St.Louis: Balmer & Weber, 1887. US:Wc. (LI)

Lee, Ernest Markham (1874–1956)
English pianist, organist, and writer on music. His compositions include sacred works and many carefully written instructional pieces for piano.
°*Alice in wonderland;* twelve easy duets. (Set I: The White Rabbit whisks along; Alice gets smaller and smaller; Alice gets bigger and bigger; Resting against a buttercup; The Cheshire Cat; Off with his head. Set II: The March Hare and the Mad Hatter; In the beautiful garden; Doleful Mock Turtle; The Lobster quadrille; Sleepy Dormouse; Will you, won't you.) London: Anglo-French Music Co. (OUP), 1923. GB:Lbl. Captivating suite of instructional pieces in practiced musical style: melodious, restrained, polished. (UE-LI)
°*Celandine.* London: Curwen, n.d. (LE)

Diversions (In the sunshine; Silks and satins; Slavonic dance; Tarantella). London: Chappell, 1930. GB:Lbl. Attractive teaching pieces. (UE)

°*First duets* (Chatterboxes; Dance; Evensong; Four-part harmony; Merry-makers; Valse). London: Chappell, n.d.

°*Folk song*. Melbourne: Allans Music, 1966.

In the meadows. London: Lengnick, n.d. In *Path of Progress*, ed. Rowley. (UE-LI)

In Switzerland. London: Lengnick, n.d. In *Royal Road*, ed. Moy. (E-UE)

Irish tune. London: Lengnick, 1924. In *Path of Progress*, ed. Rowley. Vivacious, high-spirited gigue in folk-song idiom. (I)

Little Jack Horner. London: Lengnick, n.d. In *Path of Progress*, ed. Rowley. (E)

°*Merry dance*. London: Curwen, n.d. (UE)

Nigger dance. London: Lengnick, 1919. In *Path of Progress*, ed. Rowley. Bright, rhythmic, cheerful. (LI)

Norwegian dance. London: Lengnick. In *The Royal Road*, ed. Moy. (UE-LI)

Oranges and lemons. London: Lengnick, n.d. In *The Royal Road*, ed. Moy. (E)

O where is my little dog gone. London: Lengnick, n.d. In *The Royal Road*, ed. Moy. (E)

°*Peasant dance*. Melbourne: Allans Music, 1966.

Prelude, Romance and Irish tune. London: Lengnick, 1924. GB:Lbl—US: Wc. Engaging group of descriptive pieces well distributed for both parts; effective. (LI-I)

°*Procession*. London: Winthrop Rogers, n.d. Stately, somewhat pompous, march in the style of Elgar; well balanced for both parts. (LI)

°*Six progressive duets*. Melbourne: Allans Music, n.d.

°*Reel*. London: Curwen, 1949. US:Wc. Gay, bouncy, teaching piece. (UE-LI)

Romance. London: Lengnick, n.d. In *The Royal Road*, ed. Moy. (I)

°*Sailor's dance*. Melbourne: Allans Music, 1966.

Step by step, Ten easy and progressive duets (Valse; The patrol; Dream time; Gavotte; March; Bagpipes; Yo! heave ho!; Reverie; Mazurka; Polka). London: International Music Co., 1927. GB:Lbl. (E-UE/E-1,2,3, 4,5)

°*Tarantella*. London: Curwen, 1949. US:Wc. Rhythmical, bright. (UE-LI)

Tunes for two players (Gavotte; A quiet time; Valse triste; In Russian style; Country tune; Sleepy head; Minuet; March). London: International Music Co., 1926. GB:Lbl. (UE/E-5)

Lee, Noël (1924–)

American pianist and composer; resides in Paris. He has written ballet, orchestral, and chamber music, song cycles, and piano pieces. He cultivates a neo-Classical style.

Diversions (1958). Available from composer, 4, Villa Laugier, 75017 Paris, France.

Lee, Peter

A conversation piece for two persons to sing and play together on one harpsichord or pianoforte. London: printed for composer, ca.1790. GB:Gu,Lbl, Ob.

Lefébure-Wély, Louis James Alfred (1817–1869)

French organist; composed liturgical works and piano music in salon style.

École concertante (1ère série: Scherzo pastorale; Berceuse; Marche; Thème varié; Andante; Scherzo-chasse. 2ème série: Scherzo symphonique; Rêverie; Presto; Andantino; Boléro; Scherzo poste), Op.85. Mainz: Schott, ca.1856. US:Wc. (I)

Lefebvre, Charles Édouard (1843–1917)

French composer of operas, church music, orchestral and chamber works, and piano pieces. His four-hand works are salon in style.

Andantino, Op.15. Paris: Mackal & Noël (Heugel), n.d. US:Wc. (LI)
Ballade. Paris: Salabert, n.d. (LI)
Menuet, Op.2. Paris: Mackal & Noël, n.d. US:Wc. (LI)
Prélude dramatique et intermède, Op.33. Paris: Noël, 1898. US:Wc. (I)

Lefeld, Jerzy (1898–   )

Polish pianist and teacher; has written symphonic, chamber, and piano works in conservative style.

Dzwony (The bells). In collection *Drobiazgi*, Vol.I, ed. Raube. (UE-LI)
Marsz (March); *Toccatina; *Wariacje na temat ludowy* (Variations on a folk theme). In collection *Drobiazgi*, Vol.II, ed. Raube. (I)

Lefevre, Armand

Je danse. Paris: Consortium Musical, n.d. (UE-LI)

LeGallienne, Dorian (1915–1963)

Australian music critic; wrote theater and orchestral music, chamber and choral works, and piano pieces in traditional style. Much of his music remains unpublished.

Sonatina (1941). Ms. AU:Samc.

LeGrand, E.

Trois petites esquisses (Causerie matinale; Petite retraite; Berceuse). Paris: Salabert, n.d. (I)

Leidesdorf, Maximilian Joseph (1787–1840)

Pianist and guitarist; friend of Schubert and Beethoven.

Grande sonate brillante (Eb), Op.44. Leipzig: B&H, 1816. US:Wc. Large-scale, forceful, effective work, but rambling in style and lacking in melodic interest and harmonic variety. (I-UI)

Trois marches avec trios, Op.46. Vienna: Cappi, ca.1816. A:Wn.

Trois polonaises, Op.57 (c), Op.58 (D), Op.59 (G). Vienna: Mechetti, 1817. A:Wgm (Opp.57, 59), Wn (Op.58). Well-balanced pieces; elementary harmonies; unexceptional melodies. (I)

Le rendez-vows, adagio, Op.68. Vienna: Cappi, 1818. A:Wgm.

Rondeau (Eb), Op.69. Vienna: Maisch, 1818. A:Wgm.

6 Scherzi capricciosi. Vienna: Mechetti, 1817. A:Wgm.

Sonatine (C), Op.103. Vienna: Cappi, 1819. A:Wn.

Leighter, Henry Clough (Clough-Leighter, Henry) (1874–1956)

American organist, teacher, and composer of choral, orchestral, and chamber works, and piano pieces in salon style.

Four novelettes. Boston: Boston Music Co., 1911. US:Wc. (I-UI)

Leitert, George (1852–1901)

German pianist, pupil of Liszt.

7 Walzer, Op.36. Leipzig: Seitz (Forberg), 1875. US:PHf. Salon pieces. (UE-LI)

Lemacher, Heinrich (1891–1966)

German composer of orchestral and choral works, chamber and piano music, and songs, many of them for use by amateur performers. He wrote in Neoclassical, often linear, style.

Duisdorfer Kirmes, Op.115. Cologne: Gerig, 1954. US:Wc. Diverting set of five pieces set with humor and a light touch. (UE-LI)

°*Leuzbacher Tänze,* Op.114. Wilhelmshafen: Noetzel, 1958. US:Wc. Suite of light, buoyant dances in crisp modern idiom. (I)

Lemoine, Henry (1786–1854)

French piano teacher and music publisher; composed educational piano works.

Bagatelle [No.1] *sur une mazurka et une valse favorites.* Mainz: Schott, ca. 1845. US:Wc. (I)

Divertissement, Op.30. Liége: Muraille, n.d. US:Wc. (I)

Lenel, Ludwig

German-born American teacher and composer-in-residence at Muhlenberg College, Allentown, PA 18104.

Variations suite (1972); two sets of variations on *Schnellpolka* (Act III, Scene 3) from Alban Berg's *Wozzeck,* and on H. Neusiedler's *Der Judentanz.* Ms. Available from composer. Large-scale work in frequently complex but always vivid contemporary idiom that achieves its effect through rhythmic, harmonic, and textural variety and through the clarity of the 4H setting. The composer's choice of his two themes—written 400 years apart and exceptional music for their own times—is a masterful touch. (A)

Lenormand, René (1846–1932)

French composer and writer on music; works include an opera, orchestral pieces, chamber music, songs, and piano compositions.

°*Divertissement américain*, Op.12. Paris: Hamelle, n.d.

°*Introduction et allegro*, Op.10. Paris: Hamelle, n.d.

°*Six morceaux*, Op.9. Paris: Hamelle, n.d.

°*La Nouba Medjenneba*, fantaisie, Op.19. Paris: Hamelle, n.d.

Lentz (Lenz), Heinrich Gerhard von (ca.1764–1839)

Polish-German teacher and pianist; wrote a self-instruction manual on piano tuning. He composed songs, piano pieces, chamber music, and symphonies.

Sonata (F), Op.2. Paris: Boyer, n.d. Two-movement work in Classical style. Although it has some promising bright melodies, they are scantily developed, and the structure is overburdened with heavy reliance on parallelism (sixths and tenths between the parts), sequential passages, and antiphonal effects. (LI-I)

Lessel, Franz (Franciszek) (1780–1838)

Polish composer; studied with Haydn. He published numerous piano works in Classical style.

Fugue (d), Op.11. Leipzig: B&H, 1812. D-brd:B.

Lesur, Daniel (1908–   )

French organist and pianist. He has written choral and orchestral works, chamber music, songs, organ pieces, and piano compositions in a lyrical and refined idiom.

°*Le bouquet de Béatrice* (Le joli laurier; Voici le mois de mai; La marjolaine; Gentil coquelicot; Giroflé, girofla), 1947. Paris: Durand, 1949. Enchanting suite of short pieces based on traditional children's melodies; elegantly written and effective. (UE-I)

Letnaň, Július

°*Our little games;* short instructional pieces. Prague: Panton, n.d.

Letorey, Omer (1873–1938)

French composer of operas and instrumental works.

Pantomime des quatre médecins; fantaisie dans le style de Lulli, 1919. Paris: Demets, 1920. US:Wc. Short piece in 18th-century style. (LI)

Liadov, Anatole (1885–1914)

Russian composer. His piano works especially show the influence of Chopin and Schumann, while his symphonic poems and other compositions are in Russian nationalist style.

°*Cortège triomphale;* °*Galop;* °*Gigue.* See *Paraphrases.*

Poule. See *Badinage.*

°*Valse.* See *Paraphrases.*

°*24 Variations and Finale* (with César Cui and Rimsky-Korsakov). See *Paraphrases.*

Lichner, Heinrich (1829–1898)

German; prolific composer of pedagogical works and salon pieces, a selection of which is listed below.

Aus der Jugendzeit, 12 leichte und melodische Tonstücke, Op.85. Berlin: Challier, 1871. US:Wc has Op.85/5; *Dancing on the lawn*, Philadelphia: Presser, 1899. Salon music. (LI)

Vier Rondos (C,F,D,d), Op.182. Leipzig: Kistner & Siegel, 1878. US:PHf, Wc. Salon pieces. (LI)

Der Sommernachtsball, 6 leichte Tänze, Op.229. Leipzig: Kistner & Siegel, 1882. US:Wc has Polonaise, Op.229/1.

Lichtenthal, Peter (1780–1853)

Austrian musical amateur; wrote ballets, church music, songs, chamber works, and piano pieces.

Sei marce a quattro mani (D,F,A,C,Eb,G), Milan: Ricordi, n.d. A:Wgm—I:Mc. Composed for and dedicated to Signora Costanza Casella, a nine-year-old piano virtuoso. These marches with trios are set in a pleasing harmonic idiom; they are fluent and melodious, with contrapuntal interest. (LI)

Lickl, Carl Georg (1801–1877)

Viennese composer; son of Johann Georg.

Rondo alla polacca (Ab), Op.42. Vienna: Jos. Czerný, ca.1830. A:Wgm.

Lickl, Johann Georg (1769–1843)

Viennese piano teacher. He wrote stage music, operettas, church music, chamber works, and piano pieces.

Sonata (c), Op.16. Vienna: Musikalisches Magazin, ca.1795. A:Wgm.

Sonata (D), Op.3. Vienna: Cappi, ca.1807. A:Wgm—I:Bsf—US:Wc. Well-balanced, three-movement work in Classical style. Appealing melodic ideas and harmonic variety; no innovations, but worth investigating. (I)

Lidholm, Ingvar (1921–   ). See Birgitta Nordenfelt.

Swedish conductor and composer of orchestral and chamber music, choral works, and piano pieces.

Lieth, Lenore

Dance of the toys, Op.41/1. Philadelphia: Presser, 1926. US:Wc. Instructional piece. (UE-LI)

Liftl, Franz J.

In the woodland mill. Philadelphia: Presser, 1915. US:Wc. Instructional piece, well balanced for both partners. (LI)

Lighthill, Norman

In the lead. Philadelphia: Presser, 1921. US:Wc. Instructional piece. (LI)

Lind, Gustave

The silent mere, three impressions (Once upon a time; The woodnymph;

Moonrise). London: Augener, 1912, 1923. GB:Lbl. Carefully written instructional pieces. (LI-I)

Lindberg, Oskar (1887–1955)

Swedish organist; composed orchestral and choral works, songs, and piano pieces in neo-Romantic style.

Hymn och Marsch. Ms. S:Sic.

Lindeman, Ludvig Mathias (1812–1887)

Norwegian composer and organist; active collector and publisher of Norwegian folk music.

Variations on Gubben Noah (1839). Ms. N:Onk. Charming, ingratiating work in early Romantic style. (I)

Lindeman, Peter (1858–1930)

Norwegian composer and teacher, son of Ludvig Mathias.

Suite over Norske Fjeldmelodier (Suite on Norwegian mountain tunes), Op.15. Oslo: Norsk Notestik & Forlag, n.d. N:Onk.

Liste, Anton (1774–1832)

German pianist, teacher and conductor; composed piano music in early Romantic style.

Grande sonate (B♭), Op.2. Leipzig: B&H, ca.1809. US:Wc. Long, serious work, brilliant at times; competently set for the medium but lightweight and uneven in musical content. (UI)

Liszt, Franz (1811–1886)

Liszt's contributions to the four-hand repertoire are minor and, except for one original duet, are arrangements of his orchestral works or four-hand versions of pieces for piano solo.

Festpolonaise. Pub. missing, 1876. Included in the supplement to the biography by A. Göllreich, *Franz Liszt* (Berlin, 1908); available at one time at US:NYp. Lubin states that this work is the composer's only original piano duet and was composed in honor of the marriage of Princess Marie of Saxony.

Grand galop chromatique, Op.12. Pub.missing, 1838. US:Bp. Arranged by the composer himself from the 2H version. This exciting, irrepressible, superbly written bravura piece is full of energy and drive. (A)

Grande valse de bravura (B♭), Op.6. Leipzig: Schuberth, 1844. US:NYcu, Wc. Brilliant virtuoso piece similar in character to Op.12, and, like it, arranged from the original solo version. (UI-A)

Nine nocturnes. See John Field.

Prelude, 1880. See *Paraphrases.*

Weihnachtsbaum, 12 Klavierstücke (Psallite; O heilige Nacht; Die Hirten an der Krippe; Adeste Fideles; Scherzoso; Carillon; Schlummerlied; Altes provençalisches Weinachtslied; Abendglocken; Ehemals; Ungarisch; Polnisch). Berlin: Fürstner, 1882. US:Wc. This 4H setting of the original solo version is a charming work, full of warmth and tenderness. The writing is well balanced and masterfully conceived for the medium, with special emphasis on textural diversity. The composer has taken account of the full resources of the keyboard with brilliant sonorities and massed tonal effects missing in the solo version. (UI-A)

Liubarskii, N.

6 P'es na temy ukrainskikh narodnych pesen (6 pieces on themes of Ukrainian popular songs). Moscow: State Music Publishing House, 1939. US: Wc. Tasteful folk song settings; parts well distributed. (UE)

Liviabella, Lino (1902–1964)

Italian composer of operas, symphonic poems, chamber music, and piano pieces.

Riderella; fiaba musicale (Il ruscello; La fuga del mare; La città azzuro; Il pianto di Riderella; La pietà del sole; Il ruscello). Milan: Suvini-Zerboni, 1949. US:NYp,Wc. Delightful suite of pieces in contemporary, often astringent, harmonic idiom; published in an elegant edition with attractive color illustrations. (I/I-UI)

Suite giocattolo, quadretti pianistici per bambini piccolissimi (La gocciolina; Il tamburino; Valzer; Cucù; La campane, omaggio a Mussorgsky; Capricetto finale), 1952. Milan: Suvini-Zerboni, 1953. US:NYp. A collection of diverting little pieces in a refreshing idiom. The composer takes seriously his title "for very little children" and includes one three-hand piece for which the child is held on the parent's or teacher's lap in order to play the very easy inner part (the Cucù) while the older performer plays the outer voices. (LI-I/LE-E)

Loam, Arthur S. (1892–   )

°*Bushland suite,* 2 vols. Melbourne: Allans Music, 1955.

Lobachēv, Grigorii Grigorevich (1888–1953)

Russian composer of songs, chamber music, works for massed chorus and orchestra on Soviet themes, and pedogogical compositions.

Seven songs of different peoples (Uzbek; Kirghiz; Don region; Bashkir; Ukrainian; Georgian; Bashkir dance), Op.20. Moscow: State Music Publishing House, 1926. US:NYp. Melodies from various Soviet ethnic groups in agreeable, skilful arrangements. (UE/E-5)

Loebner, Roland

Tanzstücke (Carioca; Fandango). Cologne: Gerig, 1958. From Neue Reihe No.6, *Blätter für Spielmusik,* ed. Hugo Wolfram Schmidt. US:Wc. Witty, amiable pieces in a light vein in mildly contemporary idiom. (E-UE)

Loeschhorn, Albert (1819–1905)

German pianist, teacher, and composer of pieces and instructional materials for piano.

°*10 Kinderstücke*, Op.182. Leipzig: Peters, 1883. (UE-LI/E-5)
°*12 Tonbilder*, Op.51. Leipzig: Peters, 1859. NEd. °Kalmus; °Ricordi.
(UE-LI)

Loewe, Carl (1796–1869)
German organist, pianist, conductor, and writer on music; wrote ballads, operas, oratorios, and piano music in early Romantic style.
Grosse Duo, Op.18. Berlin: Trautwein, n.d. US:Wc. Large-scale sonata in three movements; well set for piano 4H. The musical style is strongly influenced by Beethoven, but is thinner and lacks well-defined character.

Logier, Johann Bernhard (1777–1846)
German pianist and teacher; settled in Dublin; composed choral works and piano pieces in drawing-room style.
Introduction, fugue et deux canons, Op.18. Berlin: Logier, n.d. A:Wgm—GB:Lbl. Serious work of uneven quality in thin Classical style; at times brilliant, often academically dry and pedantic, but of special interest because of its ingenious contrapuntal manipulation and effective 4H setting. (UI)

Lomon, Ruth
°*Soundings*. Washington, DC: Arsis Press, 1975. Avant-garde work; calls for mallets on strings, clusters, unusual pedalings; special notation. (A)

Longmire, John
°*Six dance duets*. London: Forsyth, 1968. (UE-LI)

Longo, Alessandro (1864–1945)
Italian pianist and musicologist; composed chamber music and piano works in conservative style.
Piccola suite, Op.38/1 (A), 2 (D), 3 (b), 4 (F), 5 (Bb), 6 (G). Milan: Ricordi, 1903. US:Wc. Pedagogical in purpose, these six three-movement suites serve as introductions to various musical forms. They are set in traditional language by the well-known Scarlatti scholar and cataloguer. Well written for piano 4H. (UE-LI)
Serenade, Op.10. Leipzig: Kistner, 1894. US:Wc. Well-written salon music. (I)

Loomis, Harvey Worthington (1865–1930)
American composer, student of Dvořák. He wrote finely crafted operas, cantatas, children's songs, and piano pieces.
After the lesson; twenty-four miniature piano lyrics in duet form for teacher and youngest pupils, Op.75. Boston: C. C. Birchard, 1902. US:Bp,NYp. Instructional pieces. (UE-LI/LE-E)
The young musicians, Op.81. New York: Witmark, 1909. US:NYp. Instructional pieces in traditional idiom arranged in progressive order of difficulty. (UE-LI)

Lopez de la Rosa, Horacio (1933–)

Argentine composer of theater music, choral and chamber works, organ and piano pieces. The following works are available from Editorial Argentina de Música.

Divertimento, 1962. For piano 2H and 4H. Ms.

Sonata, 1960. For piano 2H and 4H. Ms.

Tempi, 1962. For piano 2H and 4H. Ms.

Louis, Nicolas

Six *méditations musicales* (Ā Henri Herz; Ā Mendelssohn; Ā Bertini; Ā Thalberg; Ā Chopin; Ā Liszt), Op.100. Mainz: Schott, ca.1840; Paris: Meissonnier, ca.1840. US:Bp,Wc. Light, superficial musical curiosity; series of pieces in the style of different composers. (I)

Trois mélodies italiennes variées, Op.109. Mainz: Schott, n.d. US:Bp,Wc. Instructional pieces. (I)

Variations brillantes sur un thème original, Op.60. Paris: Lemoine, n.d. US: Bp. Florid variations in salon style. (UI-A)

Variations brillantes sur un thème original (A). Bonn: Simrock, 1842. US: Bp. Brilliant demanding work in salon style. (UI-A)

Lovell, Joan

°*Scherzino*. London: Galaxy, n.d. (E)

°*Twos and threes:* duets and trios for one piano. London: Elkin, 1960; London: Novello, n.d.

Lovelock, William (1899–)

°*Short sketches*. Melbourne: Allans Music, 1963.

°*Suite* (Prelude; Fugue; Arabesque; Waltz). Melbourne: Allans Music, 1958. US:Wc. Pleasing works contrasting in mood and style; attractive teaching material. (I)

Løvenskjold (Lövenskiold), Hermann Severin (1815–1870)

Norwegian organist; composed ballets, operas, orchestral works, chamber music, and piano compositions.

Quatre impromptus caractéristiques en forme de scherzos, Op.8. Vienna: Diabelli, 1839. US:Wc. Long, three-part pieces, more like waltzes than scherzi, in conservative Mendelssohnian idiom with some surprising modulations and chromaticisms. (I)

Sonatine (G), Op.27. Hamburg: Kreisler, 1860. DK:Kk.

Löw, Josef (1834–1886)

Czech pianist; composer of a quantity of popular, instructional piano pieces and studies, a selection of which is listed below.

6 *Charakteristische Tonstücke*, Op.318. Bremen: Praeger, 1878. US:Wc.

Charakteristische Vortrags-Stücke, Op.414. Bremen: Fischer, 1881. US:Wc. (UE-LI/E-5)

Geburtstagsklänge, Bilder in Tönen, 30 kleine charakteristische Stücke, Op.

191. Stuttgart: Stümer, n.d.; Philadelphia: Presser, 1910. US:PHf.

3 *Instruktive charakteristische Tonstücke*, Op.563. Leipzig: A.P.Schmidt, 1892. US:Wc. (UE-LI/E-5)

Ländliche Bilder, Op.150. Brunswick Litolff, 1877. US:PHf. (UE-LI/E-5)

4 *National-Tänze*, Op.570. Leipzig: A.P.Schmidt, 1892. US:Wc. (UE-LI)

6 *Rhythmisch-melodische Tonstücke*, Op.330. Leipzig: Rieter-Biedermann, 1878. US:Wc. (UE-LI)

Scenen aus dem Orient, Op.583. Leipzig: A.P.Schmidt, n.d. US:Wc. (UE-LI)

Sei ruhig, mein Gemüth (In sweet repose), Op.562. Boston/Leipzig: A.P. Schmidt, 1892. US:Wc. (LI)

°Teacher and pupil, a practical course of four-hand playing. New York: Schirmer, n.d.; Kalmus. Settings of 65 folk songs, operatic excerpts, national songs, and the like, arranged in progressive order of difficulty. (I/E-5 to UE)

Lubin, Ernest (1916–1978)

American teacher, critic, author, and composer; influential figure in the revival of interest in four-hand music through his book, *The Piano Duet*.

Theme and variations (d). Boston: A.P.Schmidt, 1955. US:Wc. Short, ingratiating set of variations on an original theme, skilfully set for four hands. (LI-I)

Łuciuk, Juliusz (1927–)

Polish composer; studied in Poland and in France; his works include choral and orchestral compositions, piano pieces, songs, and chamber music.

°Mini-Opus (Bagatelle; Legend; Scherzino; Cradle song; Toccatina; Imitation; Structure), 1971. Kraków: PWM, 1972. Exceptionally attractive suite of short pieces in polished, imaginative, mildly contemporary tonal idiom. The textures are generally thin, often single lines, and melodic fragments appear antiphonally. Chromaticism and clusters are used occasionally. Rewarding teaching fare. (UE-LI)

Luening, Otto (1900–)

American teacher and conductor; has composed an opera, orchestral works, and many pieces using tape recorder.

°The bells of Bellagio. New York: Peters, 1973. While two people can play this vibrant, sonorous, well-crafted contrapuntal work with great effect, it is most tellingly performed by three players at one, two, or three pianos. (I)

Lutoslawski, Witold (1913–)

Polish composer of orchestral works, children's songs, choral music, and piano pieces. In recent years he has used electronic and serial techniques.

°Zasłyszana melodyjka (A tune I once heard). In collection *Drobiazgi*, Vol. II, ed. Raube. (I)

Luzzatto, Fr.

°*Les deux soeurs,* 12 morceaux caractéristiques faciles. Paris: Hamelle, n.d.

Lybbert, Donald (1923–   )

American composer and teacher. He writes in a contemporary idiom using serial techniques and complex rhythmical devices.

°*Movement.* New York: Peters, 1967. US:Wc. Variously described in reviews as "pungent," "eccentric," "taut," "finely wrought," and even "well-intentioned." This six-minute atonal composition contrasts two brilliant Allegro intrepido outer movements with a brief, delicate Lento middle section. Wide leaps, tremolos, trills, repeated ostinato-like figures, harmonics, grace notes, and glissandi are some of the effects employed in this intricate work, which makes considerable demands on both performers. (A)

Lysberg (Bovy-Lysberg), Charles Samuel de (1821–1873)

Swiss pianist, pupil of Chopin; teacher at Geneva Conservatory. He composed a comic opera and a quantity of piano music in salon style.

°*La baladine, caprice,* Op.51. Paris: Lemoine, n.d. US:I,Bp. Brilliant, exhilarating, impetuous caprice; technically demanding in part. (UI-LA)

°*Valse brillante,* Op.22. Paris: Richault, n.d.; °Hamelle.

McBride, Robert (1911–   )

American composer of theater works, music for dance, chamber and orchestral compositions, and piano pieces. His idiom is tonal, strongly influenced by jazz.

°*Easy five;* student/teacher. New York: ACE, n.d. (E)

°*Folk tunes.* New York: ACE, n.d. (UE-LI)

°*Vocalise for chorus and piano four hands* (1959). New York: ACE, n.d.

MacCluskey, James Thomas (1931–   )

View on a theme by Effinger. Pub. missing, 1954. US:Wc. (I)

MacDowell, Edward A. (1861–1908)

American composer, trained in Germany and France; taught at Columbia University. He was most successful in his short piano pieces, somewhat in the style of Grieg. He also wrote orchestral works, piano concertos, études, songs. His style derives from German Romanticism with touches of French Impressionism.

°*Moon pictures* (The Hindu maiden; Story of the stork; In Tyrol; The swan; Visit of the bears), Op.21 (1884–1885). Breslau: Hainauer, 1886; New York: Schirmer, 1886. US:NYcu,Wc. Based on the stories from Hans Christian Andersen's *Picture-book without pictures,* the five descriptive pieces of this pleasing suite are set in the composer's lyrical, often saccharine, but practiced early musical idiom. (I-UI)

Three poems (Night by the sea; A tale from knightly times; Ballade), Op.
20. Breslau: Hainauer, 1885; New York: Schirmer, 1905. US:Bp,PHf,Wc.
Character pieces in bold, expressive, often thick-textured Romantic style;
require interpretive subtlety to bring off well. (I-LA)

MacFarren, Walter (1826–1905)

English pianist, conductor, and teacher. He wrote symphonic and choral
music, songs, and piano works.
Sonata (e). Pub.missing, ca.1850. GB:Lam.

McGrath, Joseph G.

On the see-saw. Philadelphia: Presser, 1920. US:Wc. Instructional piece.
(UE-LI)
Pieces of eight, Op.86. Boston: McLaughlin & Reilly, 1964. US:Wc. Suite of
melodious teaching pieces. (UE)

McGraw, Cameron (1919–   )

American teacher, composer, and piano-duettist. He has written choral and
instrumental music, and piano pieces for young people in traditional style.
°*Two pieces* (Pastorale; Country dance). Boston: Boston Music, 1964.
(UE)

MacGregor, Helen

°*Singing in the moonlight*. Cincinnati: Willis Music, n.d. (E)

McIntyre, Edwin Vaile

°*The meadowlark*. Cincinnati: Willis Music, n.d. Teaching piece. (UE-LI)
°*A sail boat*. Boston: Boston Music, n.d. Instructional piece. (E)
°*Sunshine and laughter*, six four-hand recreations (Good morning; Marching
on; Galloping along; Skipping together; Summer holidays; Merry little
dancers), Op.66. Cincinnati: Willis, 1925. Attractive teaching pieces.
(UE-LI)

McSween, Frances H.

°*My shadow*. Melville, NY: Pro-Art, 1961. Instructional piece featuring imitation. (UE-LI)

Madeline, Georgette

°*Pour mes petits amis*. Paris: Salabert, n.d.

Makarov, E.

°*Who is faster?* In collection *Brother and Sister*. Bustling, happy little
teaching piece. (UE)

Maklakov, V.

Medved' na progulke (The bear is out for a walk). In collection *Sbornik
fortepiannikh*, ed. Agafonnikov. (UE-LI)

Maler, Wilhelm (pseud. of Christoph Tucher) (1902–1976)

German teacher, author of harmony text. His compositions include chamber music, orchestral works, dances, and piano pieces in neo-Hindemithian idiom.

°*Sonate* (D). Heidelberg: Süddeutscher Musikverlag (Willy Müller), 1946.

Malipiero, Gian Francesco (1882–1973)

Italian composer of operas, symphonies, chamber music, songs, and piano music. His early style was influenced by the modes, but his later style became more dissonant.

Impressioni dal vero, IIa parte (Colloquio di Campana; I cipressi il vento; Baldoria campestre). London: Chester, 1924. US:Wc.

°*Pause del silencio.* Bologna: Bongiovanni, n.d.

Mamlok, Ursula Lewis (Lewis-Mamlok, Ursula) (1928–   )

°*Bells.* Bryn Mawr: Presser, 1956.

Mana-Zucca (pseud. of Augusta Zuckerman) (1890–   )

American pianist, singer, and composer of songs and piano pieces in popular style.

°7 *Four-hand fancies* (Fun; Bees; Petals; Breezes; Bubbles; Sunshine; Play), Op.285. Bryn Mawr: Presser, 1973. Short set of bright instructional pieces. The music is well laid out and predictable. (UE-LI)

°*Joking.* New York: Schirmer, 1960. Instructional .piece. (LE)

Silver stars, Op.264/1. Boston: McLaughlin & Reilly, 1964. Instructional piece. (E)

°*Three little ducks.* New York: Schirmer, 1960. Instructional piece. (LE)

Mancuso, Sylvia

°*Sleigh bells.* Melville, NY: Belwin, n.d. Simple single-line melody in Primo part with chordal accompaniment in Secondo, the latter provided by David Carr Glover. (UE-LI)

Manenti, Luigi

Italian organist and teacher. He has written stage works, orchestral and chamber music, organ pieces, and numerous piano compositions.

Primi colloqui (Galante; Patetico; Scherzoso) (1958). Milan: Curci, 1959. US:Wc. Amiable suite in light, graceful, flowing style. (UE-LI)

Manevich, A.

Pokhodnaia pesnia kitaiskikh soldat (Marching song of the Chinese soldiers). In collection *Sbornik fortepiannikh,* ed. Agafonnikov. (UE-LI)

Marez Oyens, Tera de

Ballade grotesque, for chorus and piano four hands. Amsterdam: Donemus, ca.1973. NL:Ad.

Margola, Franco (1908–   )

Italian composer; has written orchestral and piano music in lyrical style.

°*Three pieces.* Bologna: Bongiovanni, n.d.

Marinuzzi, Gino, Jr. (1920–)

Italian conductor; has written piano pieces, orchestral and chamber music, and film scores.

°*Divertimento su un tema popolare Fra Martino campanaro.* Milan: Carisch, n.d.

Marschner, Heinrich (1795–1861)

German composer of Romantic operas, songs, choruses, orchestral works, and piano pieces. His four-hand works are set in early Romantic style strongly influenced by Weber; although well written, they tend to be perfunctory.

Divertissement, Op.17. Leipzig: Hofmeister, 1822. D-brd:B.

Rondo scherzando (C), Op.81. Leipzig: Schuberth & Niemeyer, 1840; NEd. 1881; Litolff, 1892. US:Wc. Well-balanced work in early Romantic style. (I)

Tre scherzi (Ab,g,C), Op.28. Leipzig: Probst, ca.1823. GB:Lbl.

Marsh, John (1752–1828)

Two new fugues (C). Pub. missing, ca.1780; NEd. Magdeburg: Heinrichshofen, 1944. GB:Lbl.

Martin, Frank (1890–1974)

Swiss composer and pianist. His early colorful and intense Impressionistic style was superseded by a highly individual use of serial techniques.

Pavane couleur de temps. Geneva: Henn, 1920. CH:Zma. Adagietto movement transcribed by the composer from his own string quintet. Thin textured, tending toward linear writing; traditional harmonic idiom. (I)

Martin, Georges

°*Amazones au bois,* fantaisie. Paris: Hamelle, n.d.

Martin, Hazel

°*Peppermint polka.* Melville, NY: Belwin, n.d. (UE-LI)

°*Pineapple polka.* New York: Mills, 1955. Teaching piece emphasizing double thirds. Vigorous, rhythmical, bright. Principal interest is in Primo. (LI)

°*Tango moderne.* New York: Mills, 1961. Teaching piece with Spanish flavor and rhythms. (LI)

°*Tune time for two,* eight modern duets. New York: Mills, 1962. Set of instructional pieces featuring jazz and boogie-woogie rhythms. (I)

Martin, Robert Charles

°*L'A.B.C. du quatre mains,* Op.123. Paris: Durand, n.d. Suite of pleasant instructional pieces. (I/UE)

°*Entre grands et petits* (Petite fleur de ces champs; Les cigales; Cornemuse; Menuet alsacien; Pastourelle; La capricieuse; Chasse), Op.61. Paris: Durand, 1914. Teaching pieces. (UE)

Marx, Karl (1897–)

German composer of orchestral and chamber works, concertos, and music for young people.

°*Sonatine* (E), Op.48/5. Kassel: Bärenreiter, 1952. US:Wc. Compact, airy work in refined neo-Classical tonal idiom with free dissonance. The opening movement is a bright, dancelike Allegro. The broad, flowing Andante poco sostenuto features a repeated ostinato figure accompanied by shifting harmonies. Using an inversion of the first movement as its principal subject, the Allegro vivace e giocoso finale ends the work in the spirited way it began. The texture is spare and linear, with considerable contrapuntal interest; quartal harmony is frequently used. (I)

Mašek (Maschek), Vincenc (1755–1831)

Czech composer, studied with Dušek. He wrote church music, operas, cantatas, orchestral works, chamber music, and piano pieces in Classical style.
Concertino for four hands, two clarinets, two flutes, two horns, two bassoons, and strings. Leipzig: B&H, ca.1802. D-brd:B.
Sonate. Leipzig: B&H, 1802. CS:Pk.
Walzes, quadrilles et anglaises. Paris: Cochet, n.d. CH:Bchristen.

Masetti, Enzo (1893–   )

Italian composer of film music, instrumental works, and stage music.
°*Una copanna, un bimbo, una stella.* Bologna: Bongiovanni, 1931. US:NYp.
Short, atmospheric Christmas pieces emphasizing bell sonorities. (UE)
Nei giardini di villa Strà. In collection *Album di Musica Moderna*, Vol.I.

Mason, Daniel Gregory (1873–1953)

Member of distinguished American musical family; educator and composer.
He wrote in conservative style influenced by German Romanticism.
Birthday waltzes, Op.2. Boston: E.C.Schirmer, 1932. Pleasant series of carefully crafted pieces. US:Bp. (I)

Mason, William (1829–1908)

Pianist and teacher, son of Lowell Mason and uncle of Daniel Gregory. He studied with Moscheles and Liszt and wrote in refined nineteenth-century style.
Badinage, amusement, Op.27 (1869). Boston: Koppitz, Prüfer & Co., 1870. US:Wc. Lively, appealing, well constructed, scherzo-like. (LI)
Teacher and pupil, eight duos for instruction and recreation (°Malbrook; Charming little valley; Mary had a little lamb; Life let us cherish; Baby, bye, here is a fly; °The honest old miller; Buy a broom; Waltz from *Der Freischütz*), Op.26. New York: Pond & Co. (1869)–1897. US:Bp. °*Malbrook* and °*The honest old miller* in collection *Duets of Early American Music*, ed. Anne McClenny and Maurice Hinson, David Carr Glover Library (Melville, NY: Belwin-Mills, 1971). (LI-I/UE)

Massenet, Jules (1842–1912)

French composer; best known for his operas. He also wrote instrumental music in an elegant, melodious salon idiom.
Année passée, suite de douze pièces (1er. livre, Après-midi d'été: À l'ombre;

Dans les blés; Grand soleil. 2ème livre, Jours d'automne: Feuilles jaunies;
Deux novembre; Joyeuse chasse. 3ème livre, Soirs d'hiver: Noël; En son-
geant; On valsait. 4ème livre, Matins de printemps: Les premiers nids;
Lilas; Paques). Paris: Heugel, 1897. US:Wc. (I-UI)
*Première suite, trois pièces (F), Op.11. Paris: Durand, 1882.
Scènes de bal (Entrée des masques; Première danse; Promenade au clair de
lune; Deuxième danse; Causerie sentimentale; Troisième danse; Marche-
finale), Op.17. Paris: Heugel, 1865. US:Wc. (I-UI)

Masséus, Jan (1913–)

Dutch composer; student of Badings and Pijper. He writes in mildly contemporary style; also uses electronic techniques.
*Confetti, moderne dansen. Hilversum: Harmonia, 1969. NL:Ad.
*Gezelle liederen, for soprano, alto, piano 4H, and percussion (1955). Pub.
missing. NL:Ad.
*Helicon suite. Amsterdam: Donemus, 1952. NL:Ad.
*Zoölogical impressions (The aquarium; Sea anemones; The camel; The
chameleon; The snake; Monkeys at play), Op.24. Amsterdam: Donemus,
1954. Short descriptive tone pictures in French Impressionistic harmonic
idiom, capably set for the medium. (I-UI)

Mater, Eduardo (1942–)

Improvisaciones No.1, for string quartet and piano 4H (1964). Pub. and
date missing. D-brd: DSim.

Maul, Octavio

Cirandinha. Rio de Janeiro: Arthur Napoleão, 1957. US:Wc. Instructional
piece. (E)

Maxfield, Richard Vance (1927–1969)

American composer and teacher. He wrote an opera, a ballet, and instrumental works and used serial and electronic techniques.
Six little pieces, Op.17 (1952). Facsimile of Ms. US:NYp. Short pieces in
serial style, contrasting in character and mood. (A)

Maxson, Frederick (1862–1934)

American organist; composer of anthems, songs, organ works, and piano
pieces.
5 Melodious duets, Op.7. Boston: A.P.Schmidt, 1890. US:Wc. Instructional
pieces. (E-5/UE-LI)

Mayer, Carl (1799–1862)

German pianist and prolific composer of educational piano pieces; student of
John Field.
Arabesques, 12 morceaux élégants, Op.207. US:Wc. Salon pieces. (I)
Notturno, No.3. Paris: Richault, n.d. US:Wc. Salon piece. (I)

Maykapar, Samuel (1867–1938)

Russian pianist, pedagogue and author of articles on music. He was important in the development of Soviet children's piano literature.

°*First steps; 16 easy duets,* Op.29. New York: Leeds, 1948. Appealing, melodious pieces carefully constructed in a variety of meters, with rhythmic interest and harmonic vitality. Especially useful and effective for the young pianist. (UE-LI/E)

Mayseder, Joseph (1789–1863)

Viennese violinist, composer, and teacher. He wrote violin pieces, chamber music, religious works, and piano compositions in Romantic style.

Krönungs-Rondo, Op.49. Vienna: Haslinger, ca.1831. US:Wc.

Mayuzumi, Toshiro (1929–   )

Avant-garde Japanese composer. He has written electronic, orchestral, chamber, and piano music.

°*Sphenogrammes,* for flute, alto sax, marimba, violin, cello, voice, and piano 4H (1950). New York: Peters, n.d. (A)

Mazzinghi, Joseph (1765–1844)

English teacher, organist, and piano pedagogue; pupil of J.C. Bach. He composed operas, glees, vocal works, and over 70 piano sonatas.

Air tyrolien varié über Wenn ich in der Früh aufsteh'. Berlin: Schlesinger, n.d. D-brd:B.

Three duets, Op.35. London: Goulding, Phipps & D'Almaine, n.d. C:Tu.

Two sonatas, Op.27. London: G. Goulding, ca.1798. GB:En,Lbl.

Two sonatas, Op.57. Pub. and date missing. GB:Lbl.

Meale, Richard (1932–   )

Australian pianist, conductor, and teacher. He has written works for orchestra, chamber groups, chorus, and piano in an advanced style incorporating serial, aleatory and other contemporary techniques.

Sinfonia for piano four hands and strings (1959). Pub. and date missing. AU:Samc. (A)

Mederitsch, Johann (Georg Anton) Gallus (1752–1835)

Viennese composer of light operas and piano pieces in Classical style.

Sonate facile. Vienna: Träg, 1813.

Mehegan, John

American composer, author, teacher, and jazz specialist.

°*Jazz caper.* New York: Sam Fox, 1965.

°*Vienna woodshed.* New York: Sam Fox, 1965. This work and *Jazz caper* are intellectualized jazz pieces featuring characteristic figures, rhythms, ostinati, and harmonies. They are cheerful and pleasant. The Primo plays the melody in octaves while the Secondo part accompanies with chordal figures. (I)

Melartin, Erkki (1875–1937)

Finnish pianist and composer of orchestral and chamber music, an opera, and piano pieces.

Marionettes, suite (Entrée des marionettes; Pas de deux; Sérénade; Capriccio; Duo amoureux; Cortège et sorties de marionettes), Op.1. Helsingfors (Helsinki): K.F.Wasenius, ca.1900. US:Wc. Salon pieces. (I-UI)

Mendelssohn, Felix (1809–1847)

Since Mendelssohn and his sister, Fanny, both excellent pianists, were frequent performers of duets at family concerts throughout their younger days, it seems surprising that the composer's output of duet music was so meager. Mendelssohn's original contributions to the duet medium include *Allegro brillant,* Op.92, *Andante and variations,* Op.83, and the unpublished *Fantasia.* In addition the composer made a small number of four-hand arrangements of his own orchestral works, which are listed below. Both Op.92 and 83 are available in °International, °Kalmus, °Peters, and °Schirmer editions.

°*Allegro brillant* (E), Op.92 (1841). Somewhat shorter than Op.83, this concise work is a bravura piece, one of the real virtuoso compositions of the 4H repertoire. Technically and physically difficult, with rapid scale and arpeggio passages, brilliant antiphonal sections, and a dazzling impetuous coda. Requires control of dynamics, delicacy of touch, and sweeping velocity for successful execution. (A)

°*Andante and variations* (Bb), Op.83 (1841). Published after the composer's death, and erroneously listed as Op.83a, this work also appeared in a piano solo version, arranged by Mendelssohn and published as Op.83. It is a large-scale composition, fastidiously scored with Classical restraint and overflowing with the composer's characteristic melodic invention. Impeccably set for the medium, each variation exploits a fresh musical idea. The entire work is technically demanding, especially the brilliant finale. (A)

Fantasia (d) (1824). Ms. D-ddr:Bds. This fresh, youthful work, written when the composer was 15, tends to be diffuse and overlong, but it contains many passages of great beauty. Its harmonic and melodic style, sometimes naive and undeveloped but always of a strongly defined character, bears the imprint of the more mature Mendelssohn. (UI-LA)

Midsummer night's dream, incidental music, arr. by the composer. Peters, ca.1880. The 4H arrangement of the Overture of this early orchestral work was performed by Felix and Fanny in November 1826, but it is not clear whether the duet setting of the remaining sections of the incidental music were also completed at the same time. At any rate, the full-length score was eventually published by Peters, only to be superseded ca.1895 by a new edition transcribed by Richard Kleinmichel. A comparison of the two versions reveals the brilliance of Mendelssohn's creative genius in transforming his own compositions from orchestral to keyboard music, to the detriment of Kleinmichel's pedestrian transcriptions of the same work.

Mendelssohn's arrangements are more pianistic and capture the subtle spirit of the original with refinement and poetry. (UI-LA)

Overture (g). Ms. Cited by Eric Werner in his review of "Das Problem Mendelssohn," *Notes* 33 (1976):281–84, as a 4H work of "consummate polyphony that has no peer before Reger." According to Werner, the Overture appears to be a more complex and ambitious arrangement of the composer's own Symphony No.XII (g) (Leipzig: Deutsche Verlag für Musik, 1967, in *Leipzig Ausgabe der Werken Felix Mendelssohn Bartholdys*, Serie I, Band I).

Overture to the opera *Das Heimkehr aus der Fremde* ("Son and Stranger"), Op.89 (1829). Ernest Lubin asserted that this early work was originally written as a piano duet, possibly as a preliminary sketch for subsequent orchestration. An arrangement by Richard Kleinmichel appears in an edition of Mendelssohn's Overtures published by Peters, ca.1895.

See also Ignaz Moscheles.

Mérigot, F.

°*Grande marche*. Paris: Durand, n.d. (E)
°*Pour deux tout petits*. Paris: Durand, n.d. (E)

Merikanto, Oskar (1868–1924)

Finnish organist, pianist, conductor, and musicologist. He wrote operas, organ works, piano music, and songs in Romantic style with Finnish folk-song influence.

°*Valse mélancolique*. Helsinki: Frazer, n.d.

Merrill, Mary B.

°*First robin*. New York: Schroeder & Gunther, 1941. (UE)

Messager, André. See Gabriel Fauré

Messemaeckers, Henri (1778–1864)

Dutch, Brussels-based composer of operas, chamber music, and piano pieces.

Marche triomphale suivie d'une valse. Pub. and date missing. US:Wc. Works in light Schubertian style. (LI)

Metis, Frank

°*Pop/rock sketches*. New York: Piedmont Music, 1972. Likable, effective pieces in thin-textured, simplified rock style. (LI)

Metzner, A.

°*Loisirs du jeune âge*. Paris: Consortium musical, n.d.

Six sonatines caractéristiques (Enfantine [G]; Champêtre [F]; Sérénade [D]; Romantique [A]; Vénitienne [C]; Militaire [Bb]). Paris: Leduc, 1912. US:Wc. Instructional pieces. (UE-LI)

Meunier, Gérard

°*Deux pièces* (Pierre et Pierrette; Berceuse pour Jean). Paris: Consortium musical, n.d. (UE-LI)

Meyer, Nett (Nett-Meyer)

°*Bibliothèque rose en musique*, recueil (Ronde des petites filles modèles; Complainte des deux nigauds; La promenade de Cadichon; La noce des Montonet). Paris: Consortium musical, n.d. (LI)

Meyer-Helmund, Erik (1861–1932)

Russian-born German singer; composed songs, operas, a ballet, and piano pieces.

Walzer (G), Op.14. Hamburg: Rahter, ca.1885; Schirmer, 1905. US:Wc. Salon piece. (I)

Meyer-Olbersleben, Max (1850–1927)

German pianist and conductor, student of Liszt; composed in Romantic style.

Drei Dichtungen (Lyrisch; Episch; Drammatisch), Op.25. Leipzig: Otto Forberg, 1886. US:Wc has Op.25/2 and 3 only, by Carl Fischer, New York. Salon pieces. (I)

Micheuz, Georges

°*Boléro*. Paris: Consortium Musical, n.d. (I)

Midgley, Charles W.

Dance in the minors, suite. Sacramento: pub. missing, 1964. Reprod. from holograph. US:Wc. Four instructional pieces. (UI)

Mieg, Peter (1906–   )

Swiss pianist, critic; studied with Frank Martin. His decidedly individual musical style tends to be linear and polyphonic, influenced to some extent by Bartók and Stravinsky.

5 Mouvements (1947). Ms. CH:Zma.

Duo (1947). Pub. by composer. CH:Zma.

°*La passeggiata* (1968). Geneva: Ed.Henn, 1969. CH:Zma. In three movements (fast, slow, fast), tonal. Frequent use of alternating scale; variety of textures: linear and chordal; unusual notation of accidentals. Brilliant presto finale. (UI-A)

Migot, Georges (1891–1976)

French writer on music, talented painter, and composer. He wrote orchestral and chamber music, stage works, and piano pieces.

Danse de Bérénice. Paris: Leduc, 1953.

Miles, — (early 19th century)

Sonata. London: Lavenu, n.d. B:Bc.

Miles, Walter E. (1885–1961)

°*Sparklets*. New York: Sam Fox, n.d.

°*The water bug*. New York: Sam Fox, n.d.

Milford, Robin (1903–1960)

English composer, pupil of Vaughan Williams and Holst; works include a violin concerto, choral and chamber music, songs, and piano pieces.

°*Lullaby*. London: OUP, 1941. Slow, languid pieces subtitled "for Hubert

Foss, in memory of a bicycle ride that never took place"; parts of the song "A bicycle built for two" are dextrously incorporated into the piece with playful effect. (UE-LI)

°*Two easy duets* (Mr. Ben Jonson's pleasure; Mr. John Peel passes by). London: OUP, 1930. (UE-LI)

Milhaud, Darius (1892–1974)

Prolific French composer of orchestral and chamber music as well as vocal, organ and piano pieces. He wrote in an individual style often lyrical, often banal, incorporating a variety of techniques and influences: polytonality, jazz, folk song, Jewish chant, and polyphony.

°*Enfantines* (Fumée; Fête de Bordeaux; Fête de Montmartre). Paris: Eschig, 1928. US:NYp. Charming, short, bouncy pieces transcribed and recast by the composer from songs set to words by Jean Cocteau. (LI-I/UE)

Millico, Gioseffo (1739–1802)

Duett; March. Pub. and date missing. D-brd:Rp.

Milligan, Ralph

°*Together we two.* Boston: Boston Music, 1969. Seven folk-song arrangements in traditional style. (UE-LI)

Millot, —

Quatre sonatas et deux duos à quatre mains pour le clavecin ou le forte piano, Op.1. Paris: Leduc, ca.1784. D-brd:KA.

Modona, —

°*Waltz on two notes.* Florence: Forlivesi, n.d.

Mokrejs, John (1875–1968)

American composer of Czech descent. He wrote an opera, chamber music, and a quantity of teaching pieces for piano.

Bohemian folk songs, Op.12. Chicago: Clayton F. Summy, 1908. US:PHf. Sprightly settings of Czech and Slovak folk songs. (I)

Möller, Johann Gottfried

Sonata, Op.7. Gotha: Angermeyer et Co., ca.1797. D-ddr: GOl.

Monnikendam, Marius (1896–)

Dutch composer, student of d'Indy. His works are influenced by Orff and Honegger, and are in a contemporary idiom featuring polytonality and fragmentary thematic material.

°*Sonate biblique.* Amsterdam: Donemus, 1967. NL:Ad.

Montanaro, Ettore

Pezzi liriche, 12 espressioni (Corteo umoristico; Serenata di primavera; Voce del ruscello; Festina grottesco; Dolce lagune; Sorrisi; Per i viali; La preghiera; Salmerie; Parata di Lilliput; Sensazioni africane; La danza). Milan: Ricordi, 1937. US:Wc. (I)

°*Scenes from childhood.* Milan: Ricordi, n.d. (Belwin).

Morganti, Giovanni

Suite. Milan: Ricordi, 1884.

Mortari, Virgilio (1902–)

Italian pianist and composer, studied with Pizzetti. His works demonstrate a clarity of style, touches of humor, and frequent influences of folk melody.

°*Le favole e le danze dei vecchi tempi;* 6 pezzi facilissimi da antiche musiche per il liuto (Paesana; Canzone triste; Balletto; La caccia; Villanella; Cortesia). Milan: Carisch, n.d. (E-UE)

Marcetta. In collection *Album di Musica Moderna,* vol.1.

Mortelmans, Lodewyk (1868–1952)

Belgian composer, famous for his Flemish songs. He also wrote orchestral and choral works, children's cantatas, and piano pieces.

°*In de kindertuin;* bloemkransendans (Jardin d'enfants). Antwerp: Metropolis, 1954. Short teaching piece in traditional idiom. (LI)

Moscheles, Ignaz (1794–1870)

The Bohemian-born Moscheles, friend of Beethoven and lifelong promoter of his music, was himself a talented and skilled composer. But except for a series of technical exercises for the piano, his music is rarely heard today. Although it is carefully written and often engaging, it lacks the kind of musical substance that insures survival. Moscheles' works for four hands are skilfully written. They tend to be hollow and banal, but they are not without a certain amiable charm and occasional flashes of musical interest.

La belle union, rondo brillant (E♭), Op.76. Leipzig: Kistner, ca.1828. GB: Lbl–US:NYp,Wc.

Three characteristic duets (The little prattler; Evening thoughts; The boy's travels on his rocking horse), Op.142. London: Novello, n.d.; Hamburg: Cranz, 1868; Leipzig: Kistner, ca.1866. GB:Lbl. (UE-LI)

Les contrastes, grand duo, Op.115. Leipzig: Kistner, ca.1847. Transcribed by the composer from the original version for two pianos eight hands. US: NYp has original version only.

Domestic life (Familienleben), twelve progressive characteristic duets, dedicated to Moscheles' grandchildren (Brother and sister; Affection; Altercation; Grandfather's dance; Elegy; A fugal waltz; The harper's ballad; Grandmother at her spinning wheel; Soldier's life; Serenade; Quickstep; Canon alla tarantella), Op.140. London: Novello, n.d.; Leipzig: Kistner, 1867. GB:Lbl–US:PHf. (I)

Grande sonate (E♭), Op.47. Vienna: Artaria, 1819; Hamburg: Cranz, 1847, 1853. GB:Lbl,Lcm–US:NYp,PHf,Wc. Large-scale work in practiced but lightweight idiom. It was popular in its day and met with enormous success when it was performed by the composer with Mendelssohn, Chopin, and others. (UI-A)

Grande sonate symphonique (b) (1845), Op.112. Berlin: Lienau, 1846; Leipzig: Kistner, 1846. GB:Lbl.

Hommage à Haendel, grand duet, Op.92. London: pub. and date missing. US:NYp,Wc.

Humoristische Variationen, Scherzo und Festmarsch, Op.128. Leipzig: Kistner & Siegel, 1858. US:Wc. (UI-LA)

Lied im Volkston, Original-Thema mit Variationen, Op.139. Leipzig: Gebauer, 1864. US:Wc.

Two little duets for pianoforte students (March; Scherzo), Op.141. London: Novello, n.d. GB:Lbl. (UE-LI/E-5)

Trois marches héroïques (C,a,A), Op.31. Vienna: Spina (Mechetti),1815. GB:Lbl–US:Wc. (LI-I)

Polonaise brillante (F). Hamburg: Böhme, n.d. US:Wc. (I)

Romance et tarantelle brillante, composée pour sa fille Émilie, Op.101. Leipzig: Hofmeister, 1842. US:Wc. Fiery work in virtuoso style. (UI-A)

Rondo brillant (A), Op.30. Offenbach: André, ca.1825; Vienna: Spina, n.d. A:Wn,Wst,Wgm–GB:Lbl,Lcm–US:Wc. Brioso piece with abundant passage work. (I-UI)

Sonata (E), No.3 (1850–1851), Op.121. Leipzig: Kistner, 1853. US:Wc. (UI-LA). Also published for piano 2H with violin or cello.

59 Tägliche Studien über die harmonisierten Scalen, Op.107. Leipzig: Kistner, n.d.; London: Cramer, as *Daily studies on harmonised scales.* °NEd. 10 selected studies (6 in C; 1 in G; 1 in a; 2 in D), in collection *Teacher and student*, ed. Lubin. GB:Lbl–US:Bp. Scales in various rhythms accompanied by more difficult harmonized part; pleasant music for enlivening the study of scales. (E/LI)

Triumphmarsch (D), Op.10. Vienna: Spina (Mechetti), 1815. A:Wn–GB: Lbl–US:Wc. (I-UI)

Six valses avec trios, Op.33. Vienna: Artaria, n.d.; Hamburg: Cranz, n.d. London: Falkner's Opera Music Warehouse, n.d.; GB:Lcm–US:NYp,Wc. GB:Lbl has *Three waltzes with trios* (g,e,C). Pleasant melodious teaching pieces. (UE-LI)

Moscheles, Ignaz and Felix Mendelssohn

Variations brillantes sur une marche bohémienne tirée de l'opéra Preciosa de Weber. Paris: M. Schlesinger, 1834; Leipzig: Kistner, 1833. US:Wc. This delightful curiosity, one of the small number of collaborative efforts in the annals of musical composition, was put together by two important musicians of the early Romantic period: the lesser-known Moscheles, highly regarded in his day as a pianist and composer, and his student, the famous Felix Mendelssohn. This brilliant display piece, in the genre of the "thèmes variés" of the period, was scored first for two pianos and orchestra and assigned opus number 87b. It was successfully recast into a virtually new and independent composition—a fresh, absorbing, and effective setting for piano duet. In addition to its four variations, the work has a long introduction and dazzling finale. Moscheles' contributions (Variations 3 and 4) may not be up to Mendelssohn's in ingenuity and luster, but the music overall is still charming, and, considering its dual authorship, it is surprisingly consistent and well balanced. (UI-A)

Moss, Lawrence (1927–)

American teacher and composer. His works include orchestral and chamber music, two operas, songs, and piano compositions.

°*Omaggio*. Philadelphia: Elkan-Vogel, 1967. The 4H medium has historically been a vehicle for the performance of a literature that has been predominantly chamberlike. While exceptions abound, duet music is generally more intimate, and, partly because of the strictures of the keyboard and sitting space, more scaled down than its sister art, two-piano literature. In the present short work the composer offers an unexpected and entertaining departure from usual duet writing: he builds into it a visual dimension as well. Although not rivaling the spectacular, extroverted display of two-piano playing, it does afford each performer the unusual opportunity to play both the Primo and Secondo parts, at different times, without interrupting the continuity of the music. Shortly after the music is under way the Primo partner abandons his place at the keyboard and goes to the rear of the piano (a free-standing grand, of course) in order to pluck the bass strings. The Secondo partner continues playing and moves into the Primo's place. Primo then takes the Secondo position and continues to play while Secondo goes to the rear of the piano to pluck the strings. Finally, Primo slides back into his original position, as Secondo, returning from the rear, resumes his place, each partner having made a complete circuit of the instrument. As for the music itself, the composer uses an unconventional "spatial notation," substituting a series of large dots below the staff in place of bar lines to represent time intervals. The piece has a delicate, Impressionistic quality and is cast in an avant-garde idiom characterized by flashes of tone color—provided by cascades of 32nd-note passages in wide leaps—and sudden contrasts of pitch and dynamics. In addition to calling for the resonating of strings both with fingers and with a metal object, the score also features free improvisation, harmonics, and unusual pedalings. A clue to the object of the composer's homage can be found in two short quotations from Mozart: the key signatures of his six string quartets dedicated to Haydn (g,d,Eb,Bb,a,c) and, later, the first theme of the Sonata (Bb) for piano four hands, K.358. Appealing concert fare for two advanced pianists. (A)

Moszkowski, Moritz (1854–1925)

Polish pianist, teacher, and composer. Some of his four-hand works are well known, others are relatively obscure, but all deserve to be looked into.

Though many of them tend toward the salon style, they represent solid craftsmanship and are interesting for their fresh melodic invention and for their gratifying use of the piano duet medium.

Album espagnol (G,D,f♯,D), Op.21. Breslau: Hainauer, 1878. US:NYp, PHf,Wc. (I)

Deutsche Reigen (Rondes allemandes), 5 Stücke, Op.25. Breslau: Hainauer, 1880. US:Wc. (I-LA)

From foreign parts (Aus aller Herren Ländern), six characteristic pieces (Russia [a]; Germany [F]; Spain [A]; Poland [E]; Italy [A]; Hungary [D]), Op.23. London: Augener, 1880; Breslau: Hainauer, 1879; New York: Schirmer, n.d. US:Bp,PHf,Wc. (UI)

Kaleidoskop, 7 Miniaturbilder, Op.74. Leipzig: Peters, 1905. US:PHf,Wc. Especially attractive suite. (UI)

°*Le maître et l'élève*, 8 morceaux (Prologue; Moment musical; Mélodie; Air de ballet; Arabesque; Berceuse; Valse; Tarantelle). Paris: Enoch, n.d. (E-5/UE-LI)

Deux morceaux (Cortège; Gavotte), Op.43. Leipzig: Peters, 1887. US:Wc. (I-UI)

°*New Spanish dances* (Eb,a,F [Habañera]). Leipzig: Peters, 1900. °NEd. 1954. US:Wc. (I-UI)

°*Polish folk dances* (Polnische Tänze) (Krakowiak; Mazurkas [E,G]; Polonaise), Op.55. Leipzig: Peters, 1895; NEd. 1953. US:Wc. (I-UI)

°*Spanish dances* (C,g,A,Bb,D), Op.12. Berlin: Simon; Leipzig: Peters, 1976, °NEd. 1953; Milan: °Ricordi, n.d.; New York: °Schirmer, n.d.; °Peters, issued separately, Op.12/1,2,3,5. (I-UI)

3 *Stücke* (Polonaise; Walzer; Ungarischer Tanz), Op.11. Breslau: Hainauer, 1876. US:Wc. (UI)

4 *Vierhändige Klavierstücke* (Kindermarsch; Humoreske; Tarantelle; Spinnerlied), Op.33. Breslau: Hainauer, 1887. US:Wc. (I-UI)

°5 *Walzer* (A,a,E,G,D), Op.8. Berlin: Simon, n.d.; Leipzig: °Peters, 1876; New York: Schirmer, 1895; London: Augener, n.d. US:PHf,Wc. (I)

Mottl, Felix (1856–1911)

Austrian conductor and opera producer; wrote operas, chamber music, songs, and piano music.

°*Österreichische Tänze*. Leipzig: Peters, 1899. (LI)

Moy, Edgar

English composer of instructional piano music.

Berceuse. London: Lengnick, n.d. In collection *The royal road*, ed. Moy, Bk.1.

Bucolique. In collection *Thirty-two graded pieces for piano duet*.

Carillon. London: Lengnick, n.d. In collection *The Royal Road*, ed. Moy, Bk.1.

Chanson. In collections *Thirty-two graded pieces for piano duet* and *Path of progress*, ed. Rowley, Bk.1.

Marche miniature. In collection *Thirty-two graded pieces for piano duet.*

Roundelay. In collection *Path of progress*, ed. Rowley, Bk.2. (E)

Four scenes (Ondine; By a lakeside; Marionettes; On the march). London: OUP, 1927. Engaging short pieces in pleasant lyrical style. GB:Lbl. (LI)

Valse. In collection *Path of Progress*, ed. Rowley, Bk.1. (E)

Valsette. In collection *Thirty-two graded pieces for piano duet.* (UE)

Moyer, Ebbie

°*The Angelus* (C). Cincinnati: Willis, 1933. Short teaching piece; exceptionally saccharine. (UE)

Mozart, Wolfgang Amadeus (1756–1791)

Mozart had a special fondness for the duet medium, which no doubt derived from his many childhood concert appearances with his sister, Nannerl. His remarkable mastery of the techniques of four-hand writing reflects the same kind of comprehensive genius that made him equally at home in all musical forms. From his very first piano-duet works, so full of youthful buoyancy and promise, to the refinement and profundity of the great *Sonata* (F), K.497, one of the major masterpieces of the four-hand repertoire, his abundant harmonic variety, melodic grace, and matchless inspiration are always present.

Mozart's 4H works are complete in editions by °Wiener-Urtext and °Henle-Verlag. The Augener, °International, °Kalmus, °Peters and °Schirmer editions of the collected works are missing *Sonata* (C), K.19d, and *Sonata* (G), K.357. The °*Neue Mozart Ausgabe* (Bärenreiter, IX/24/2) is complete except for *Fantasies*, K.594 and K.608, and *Fugue* K.401.

Andante and variations (G), K.501 (1786). Flowing, delicate, amiable set of five variations that Alfred Einstein has suggested may be the final movement of the unfinished *Sonata* (G), K.357. The partners alternate as soloists as the simple theme is developed and elaborated. A thoroughly ingratiating work. Also in collection °*Style and interpretation*, vol.5; and in single edition by °Ricordi.

Fantasy I (f) (Ein Stück für ein Orgelwerk in einer Uhr), K.594 .(1790). Originally written on commission for a musical instrument called "an organ in a clock," this work and the following one have long been part of the 4H repertoire, possibly because they were first scored on four staves and were therefore taken by publishers to be duets. Little seems to be known about the mechanical clock-organ or the owner (or possibly inventor) of it, but in a letter to his wife, Mozart revealed his distaste at having to write for a mechanical contrivance of such limited musical capabilities, noting, however, that he would be glad when the work for his "watchmaker" was completed, because he would then be able to "slip a few ducats into the hands of my dear little wife." But he must have quickly overcome his initial reluctance, for these two pieces represent some of his most inspired writing. *Fantasy* I consists of a stately, placid Adagio; a rapid, contrapuntal Allegro; and a return to the Adagio. (UI-LA)

Fantasy II (f) (Ein Orgelstück für eine Uhr), K.608 (1791). Brilliant and imaginative work showing Mozart at the height of his musical genius. Opens with a bright, affirmative Allegro in dotted notes that leads into a brilliant fugue concluding with echoes of the opening theme. The lovely sustained Andante middle section leads back into a more complex version of the first fugue. The work ends with further references to the introductory dotted-note theme. The influence on Schubert is especially noticeable in the latter's *Fantasy* (f), Op.103, D.940. *Fantasy* II has been transcribed for other instruments, but is perhaps best known in its version as an organ piece.

It should be noted that the arrangement of the two *Fantasies*, K.594 and K.608, in the Henle-Verlag and Wiener-Urtext editions are close to the original scoring: thinner in texture, with fewer doublings, but at the same time somewhat more awkward to play than the smoother, more opulently pianistic, arrangements of the other editions. A version of *Fantasy* II, K.608, arranged for both one- and two-piano four hands by Paul Badura-Skoda, and published by Schirmer in 1974 under the title *Fantasy for mechanical organ*, differs substantially from the other editions. In an effort to approach the textural contrasts so characteristic of Mozart's 4H writing, Badura-Skoda has in effect re-orchestrated many portions of the work by rearranging the parts and by adding or eliminating doublings. He has enhanced the practical value of the edition by supplying fingers and copious suggestions for dynamics and phrasing, along with many useful editorial observations.

Fugue (g), K.401 (1782). Although this solidly fashioned work is unmistakably scored for four hands, it is not known whether it was intended as a duet piece, a movement of a string quartet, or a contrapuntal exercise. It remained unfinished until the last eight bars were completed by Abbé Maximilian Stadler, composer, musical scholar, and friend of Mozart. Available separately: °Ricordi.

Sonata (Bb), K.358 (186c) (1774). Joyful, lively work, often coupled in collections with the slightly more difficult *Sonata* (D), K.381. Bright Allegro, with an unusually long coda and truncated development section; lyrical Adagio; Molto Presto, dashing finale, with some tricky antiphonal solo sections in parallel tenths. (I)

Sonata (C), K.19d (1765). One of Mozart's earliest 4H compositions, written during a visit to London in 1765. The manuscript was lost and did not reappear until 1921, when a copy was found in the archives of the Bibliothèque Nationale in Paris; later an English edition came to light and was published by OUP in 1952. The sonata is in three movements—Allegro, Menuetto and Trio, and Rondo allegretto—and shows great skill in duet writing. Occasional hand collisions and other awkward passages suggest that Mozart may have had the two-manual harpsichord in mind when he composed the work. It is fresh, fluent, and imaginative—a significant achievement for a nine-year-old. (LI-I) In collection *Eleven piano duets by the masters*, ed. Zeitlin and Goldberger. Also available separately: *OUP, ed. Howard Ferguson; *Schott.

Sonata (C), K.521 (1787). The last duet by the composer; a mature work. Rather lighter in character than *Sonata* (F), K.497, while at the same time more demanding pianistically. In its brilliant passage work and strong suggestions of tutti versus solo sections, the entire sonata comes close to Mozart's concerto style. The first movement is a bold, assertive Allegro; the second is a melodious Andante with an agitated middle section; and the Allegretto finale is a placid, amiable rondo. (A)

Sonata (D), K.381 (123a) (1772). Often paired in anthologies with the somewhat easier *Sonata* (Bb), K.358, this is a sparkling, cheerful three-movement work: brilliant Allegro, tranquil Andante, and breathless finale Allegro molto. Clear, idiomatic writing. (I-UI) Available separately: *Schott; *Artia (Prague).

Sonata (F), K.497 (1786). Majestic, noble; mature Mozart, ranking with his greatest orchestral and chamber compositions in structural mastery and musical depth. The first movement begins with a slow Adagio introduction of 29 bars, containing some exquisite modulations and sonorities, and then progresses into an Allegro di molto, featuring a six-bar principal theme that alternates between the registers of the two pianists, a technique the composer uses in other portions of the sonata. The Andante is serious and tranquil, with some intricate passages of imitative writing. The Allegro finale, with its strong eleven-bar theme and haunting chromatic transitional melody of various guises, is an expansive and handsomely worked-out rondo. (A)

Sonata (G), K.357 (497a) (1786). Unfinished two-movement work completed from sketches in 1853 by Julius André, son of Johann André, the music publisher, who had purchased the manuscripts together with other autographs from Mozart's widow in 1799. André's tasteful and imaginative reconstruction has added very little new music, except for an 18-bar extension of the first movement development section and an 8-bar coda at the end of the Andante, both of which make ingenious use of Mozart's thematic material. André also completed the first movement, which was broken off at the beginning of the development, by repeating as a recapitulation the exposition section with a few minor alterations. The bold, energetic themes, surprise modulations, and tight construction of the Allegro are on a par with the best of Mozart's 4H writing. The Andante is thinner in quality, but the placid, antiphonal theme and variations, treated with a light touch, and its agitato middle section have moments of great charm. (UI)

Mozart, in the style of. See Anon.

Muczynski, Robert (1929–   )

American composer; works include orchestral, chamber, and piano compositions.

°*American songs*, 2 vols. New York: AMP, 1960. Fastidious, exceptionally inventive arrangements of American folk songs; solid, well balanced, with considerable linear interest. (I)

Mühling, Heinrich Leberecht August (1786–1847)

Grande nocturne (Eb) (Marche; Rondoletto; Larghetto; Menuetto; Variation et coda), Op.29. Leipzig: Kistner, n.d. D-ddr:Bds. The movements are well worked out and carefully balanced, but shallow in content. (I)

Mul, Jan (1911–1971)

Dutch organist, critic, and composer; wrote in a personal idiom influenced by the French school.

°*Concert voor piano vierhandig* (1962). Amsterdam: Donemus, 1962. NL: Ad—US:NYp. Attractive three-movement work for piano 4H and orchestra in mildly dissonant idiom. (UI-A)

Mulder, Herman (1898–1959)

Dutch theorist; composed orchestral, sacred, and instrumental works with strong contrapuntal textures.

°*Fantasie*, Op.61. Amsterdam: Donemus, 1945. NL:Ad.

°*Vier stukken* (Four pieces), Op.158. Amsterdam: Donemus, 1968. NL:Ad.

Mullen, Frederick

2ème Duo de concert. London: Ashdown, 1911.

Hispania, duo. London: Ashdown, 1913. US:Wc. Instructional piece. (I)

In the cotton fields. London: Ashdown, 1913. US:Wc. Instructional. (I)

A Madrid festival. Cincinnati: John Church, 1906. US:Wc. Instructional. (I)

Marche des vainqueurs. London: Ashdown, 1902. US:Wc. Instructional. (I)

Müller, Christian Heinrich (1734–1782)

German organist; composed church music and a few piano works.

Drey Sonaten fürs Clavier, als Doppelstücke für zwo Personen mit vier Händen (D,G,Bb). Berlin: Friedrich Wilhelm Bernstiel, 1782. B:Bc—GB:Lbl —US:Wc. The three sonatas in this group are among the earliest published works for four hands, and are the only compositions published during the composer's lifetime. They are attractive three-movement pieces in early Classical style, sensitively arranged for the medium in spare, thin-textured idiom. (UE-LI)

Müller, Karl Friedrich (1797–1873)

Ã la Pologne, divertissemens gentils, Op.48. Berlin: pub. by composer, ca. 1837. US:Wc. Salon music. (I)

Grand rondeau brillant, Op.50. Berlin: pub. by composer, n.d. US:Wc. Salon piece. (I)

Rondeau turc original, avec accompagnement d'un tambourin et triangle ad lib., Op.64. Berlin: pub. by composer. US:Wc. Salon music. (LI-I)

Müller, Sigfrid Walther (1905–1946)

German teacher and composer of symphonic and chamber works, music for organ, and piano pieces; died in Soviet prison camp.

Festmusik (Passacaglia und Fuge) (C), Op.25. Leipzig: B&H, 1929. US: Wc. Large-scale work in refined neo-Classical idiom. (I)

Müller-Reuter, Theodor (1858–1919)

German conductor, teacher, and composer of operas, choruses, and piano pieces.

Im Ballsaal (Polonaise; Menuett; Promenade; Walzer; Intermezzo; Polka), Op.25. Krefeld: Schuckert, 1903. US:Wc. Salon music. (I-UI)

Müller von Kulm, Walther (1899–   )

Swiss composer of stage works, orchestral and chamber music, choral pieces, and piano compositions.

Praeludium und Fuge, Op.51 (1944). Pub. by composer. CH:Zma.

Drei Stücke, Op.16 (1927; revised 1961). Ms. CH:Zma. Brisk Allegro; chorale-like Adagio in 5/4 meter with quartal harmony; dashing Allegro giocoso with sections of imitation. The idiom is tonal, chromatic, and frequently linear. (UI)

Mumma, Gordon (1935–   )

American composer; employs electronic and aleatory procedures. He has written music for and performed with the Merce Cunningham Dance Company.

°*Medium size mograph 1963 for cybersonically modified piano with two pianists*. Don Mills, Ontario: BMI Canada, 1969. US:Wc. Avant-garde work involving electronically altered piano and tape; advanced notation. (A)

°*Small size mograph* (1964). Don Mills, Ontario; BMI Canada, 1967. US: Bp. Short, highly refined and concentrated work in advanced style. featuring slowly shifting sonorities made up of adjacent chromatic tones arranged in widely spaced chords. Conventional staff notation is used with special indications for appoggiaturas and held notes; the composer suggests "moderate tempo and dynamics throughout." Not difficult once the system is made clear. Lasts about 1 minute 45 seconds. (UI)

Münchhausen, Adolph, Baron von (1756–1811)

German diplomat and gifted musical amateur.

Sonate (C), Op.3. Paris: Chez Cesar, ca.1793. GB:Lbl.

2 Sonates (G,Eb), Op.2. Paris: Chez Cesar, ca.1793. F:Pc,Pn—GB:Lbl. Elegant, tuneful, flowing; skilfully written for the medium despite thinness of material. (I)

Munn, William (1902–   )

°*March of the tiny soldiers*. Cincinnati: Willis, n.d.

Murray, Mila

°*Theme and variations*. New York: Lee Roberts, 1972. Seven colorful variations on a theme. Changing meters. Resourcefully set for the medium. (UE-LI)

Musgrave, Thea (1928–   )

Scottish composer; currently teaching at University of California, Santa Barbara. Her works include choral and orchestral pieces, ballets, operas, chamber music, and piano compositions.

°*Excursions*, eight duets (Driving in the highlands; The road hog; Learner-driver; The drunken driver; The Sunday driver; Roadside repairs; Fog on the motorway; Backseat driver). London: Chester, 1966. Exceptionally fine and entertaining suite of pieces in contemporary idiom, centered around the events, problems, and crises encountered in an auto tour of Great Britain. The work is so arranged that the easier part has an opportunity to play half the pieces in the Primo position (Nos.5–8) and half in the Secondo (Nos.1–4), as the music explores assorted pianistic tricks with humor and great effectiveness. (UI/UE)

Mussorgsky, Modest (1839–1881)

Well-known Russian composer of the operas *Boris Godunov*, *Khovanchina*, and *Fair at Sorochinsk*; orchestral and choral works; songs; and piano pieces.

°*Allegro and scherzo*, from *Sonata* (C) (1860). In collections *Eighteen original piano duets*, ed. Balogh, and *Modest Petrovich Musorgsky Sämtliche Werke*, ed. Lamm, Vol.VIII,9 (Vienna: UEd, 1928–1939). The only extant movements of a projected 4H sonata, the melodious if somewhat rambling Allegro and the bright, rhythmical Scherzo show many of the inventive qualities of the more mature Mussorgsky. (I)

Myklegård, Åge (1904–   )

Norwegian organist and composer.

Little dances (Spring dance; Tempo di valse; Intermezzo; Norwegian; Finale). Leipzig: Hofmeister, 1928. N:Onk. Suite in dextrous salon style with strong Norwegian folk flavor and influence of Grieg. (UI)

Nagan, Zvi Herbert (1912–   )

Israeli composer of chamber music and piano compositions.

°*Seven pieces* (Song; Canon; Waltz; Chorale; March; [missing]; [missing]) (1964). Tel Aviv: Israel Music Institute, 1968. US:Bp,Wc. Short pieces based on tone row; narrow compass; sharp dissonances avoided. (I)

Nagy, Maryanne

*Danza españa. New York: Lee Roberts, 1970. Vigorous, rhythmical rumba. Carefully balanced activity between parts. Exciting, brilliant, very effective. (I)

*Double or nothing duets. Chicago: Creative Keyboard Publications, 1977.

*Finger puppets. Chappaqua, NY: Lee Roberts, 1968. US:Wc. Attractive piece in contemporary idiom. (E)

*From the color wheel. Chappaqua, NY: Lee Roberts, 1968. US:Wc. Charming work in up-to-date style. (UE)

*Hey Pedro. New York: Lee Roberts, 1972. Tuneful, strongly rhythmical, with Latin American flavor. (UE-LI)

*Magic mandarins. New York: Lee Roberts, 1970. Well-written black-note pentatonic piece. (UE-LI)

*Party polka. New York: Lee Roberts, n.d. Bright, lively, well-balanced teaching piece. (E)

Nakada, Yoshinao (1923–   )

Japanese musician.

*One piano four hands (Twinkle, twinkle little star; Our shoes squeak; Song of cradle; Play with me, Mama; The letter; Polish! polish!; The school of killies; The train running). Tokyo: Onga-ku no Tomo, n.d. (E-LI)

*Songs of woodpecker. Tokyo: Kawai Gakufu Co., 1969.

Nazarova, T.

*Khakassian folk dance, in collection Brother and Sister. Short folk song from Soviet Siberia in tasteful four-hand setting. (UE-LI)

Neal, Heinrich (1870–1940)

German teacher and composer, son of the American painter David Neal. He wrote a quantity of piano music, including studies, sonatas, and children's pieces.

Adagio mit Variationen (C), Op.62. Heidelberg: Verlag von Neal, 1916; Leipzig: Hug, 1910. US:Wc. Rambling work in late-Romantic style. (LI-I)

Neefe, Christian Gottlob (1748–1798)

Conductor and organist; Beethoven's teacher. He composed operas and Singspiele, choral and orchestral works, and piano pieces.

Six pièces d'une execution facile tirées de l'opéra Die Zauberflöte (G,Eb,Bb, G,F,C). Bonn: Simrock, 1793. D-brd:Mbs. *Vermischte Handstücke, ed. Kreutz, has No.4 only. Graceful arrangements of melodies from Mozart's opera, capably set for four hands. (LI)

Neruda, Franz (1843–1915)

Czech cellist and conductor; lived in Copenhagen. His works blend Czech elements with Nordic influences.

České tance (Czech dances) (E,C,D), Op.73. Prague: Urbánek, 1906. US: Wc. Resourceful settings of Czech folk melodies. (I)

Neumann, František (Franz) (1874–1929)

Czech conductor, notably of first performances of Janáček's operas. He wrote ballets, operas, cantatas, chamber music, and piano pieces in eclectic style.

°*16 Vierhändige Klavierstücke zum Unterricht für Anfänger*, Op.1. Leipzig: B&H, 1858; °NEd. Wiesbaden: B&H, 1948. Progressive pieces for beginning pianist and teacher in traditional idiom; proficiently set; useful. (I/E-LI)

Nevin, Ethelbert (1862–1901)

American composer; studied in Germany with Klindworth and von Bülow. He wrote songs and piano pieces in a lyrical, sentimental idiom.

Three pieces (Valse caprice; Country dance; Mazurka), Op.6. Boston: Boston Music, 1890; Mainz: Schott, 1893. US:PHf,Wc. Well-crafted salon pieces. (I)

Wynken, Blynken and Nod, for solo and chorus of mixed voices and piano four-hand accompaniment. Pub.missing, 1889.

Nevin, Mark

American composer of instructional piano music.

°*Three jazz duets*. Melville, NY: Belwin, 1966. Conventional pieces using boogie and jazz rhythms. Melody in octaves in Primo part; Secondo relegated to chordal accompaniment. (LI-I)

°*Little majorette*. Melville, NY: Belwin-Mills, n.d.

°*Five swingy duets* (Jazz holiday; Swing it slow; Swincopation; Swing those scales; Nocturne in swing). New York: Schroeder & Gunther, 1969. Collection of pieces in jazz idiom of 1940s. Primo plays melody in octaves; Secondo accompanies. (I)

Newton, Ernest

°*Maytime and playtime*; five easy duets. London: Paxton, 1921. (UE-LI/E-5)

Nicholl, Horace Wadham (1848–1922)

English organist, lived in U.S. He composed organ pieces, choral and orchestral works, chamber music, and piano pieces.

8 Characteristic pieces, Op.23. New York: E. Schuberth, 1889. US:NYp,Wc. (LI)

Nicholls, Heller

Tambouritza, Op.20. Boston: B.F.Wood, 1922. US:Wc. Salon piece in Spanish style. (LI)

Nickson, Noel John (1919–   )

Australian teacher and composer.

°*Playing together*. Melbourne: Allans Music, 1963.

Nicodé, Jean Louis (1853–1919)

German-Polish pianist, conductor, and teacher. He wrote symphonic and chamber music, songs, and piano works in traditional idiom.

Eine Ballszene, Walzer, Op.26. London: Augener, 1883; Leipzig: B&H, 1883. US:PHf,Wc. Lively salon waltz. (I)

Bilder aus dem Süden, 6 Characterstücke (Bolero; Maurisches Tanzlied; Serenade; Andalusienne; Provençalisches Märchen; In der Taberna), Op. 29. Leipzig, 1886, 1892. US:Bp,PHf,Wc. Salon music. (I)

Miscellen (Impromptu quasi scherzo; Walzer; Volkslied; Ein Stimmungsbild), Op.7. Leipzig: B&H, 1876. US:PHf,Wc. Salon music. (I)

Scherzo fantastique (e), Op.16 (1877). Berlin: Bote & Bock, 1878; New York: Schirmer, 1905. US:PHf,Wc. Long, serious, bravura piece, skilfully set in salon style. (LI-UI).

Walzer-Kapricen, Op.10. Leipzig: B&H, 1877; London: Augener, n.d. US: PHf,Wc. Suite of waltzes in refined salon idiom. The style and structure are reminiscent of the Brahms *Liebeslieder* Waltzes; unusual bits of chromaticism; deft handling of materials. (I-UI)

Nicolai, Johann Georg (1720–1788)

Sonate. Ms. B:Bc.

Nicolai, Valentin (late 18th cent.)

Four grand sonatas (F,Bb,Eb,C), Op.9. London: Preston, ca.1795; Longman & Broderip, ca.1790. GB:Lbl—US:NYp,Wc. Tuneful though weak and insipid works in Classical style; thin, with excessive passage work. (LI-I)

Nicolai's celebrated rondos from Opera III (Duetto I, II, III). London: Dale, n.d. US:Wc, in collection "Ayre."

Nicolai, Willem Fr. Gerard (1829–1896)

6 *Charakterstücke*, Op.3. The Hague: Weygand & Beuster, ca.1856. US: Wc. Instructional pieces. (LI)

Niehaus, Manfred

Einige Anweisungen für die Millellage, for electric guitar, viola, and piano with two players, 1969. Pub.missing. D-brd:DSim.

Nieland, Jan (1903–)

Dutch organist; has written church music and instructional piano works.

°*For the youth*. Amsterdam: Broeckmans & VanPoppel, n.d.

Niemann, Walter (1876–1953)

German pianist and musicologist; wrote chamber music and piano works.

°*Kocheler Ländler*, Op.135b. Leipzig: Peters, 1934. Group of waltzes, arranged from the original 2H version, Op.135a.

Nietzsche, Friedrich (1844–1900)

German philosopher, poet, and amateur composer. At first he was an ardent supporter of Wagner but turned against him to become a partisan of Bizet.

Musical works include songs, choral and orchestral pieces, and piano compositions. The works listed below are in the Nietzsche-Archiv, Weimar, DDR.

Fantasie. Ms. Reported by Ganzer & Kusche in *Vierhändig* (Munich: Heimeran, 1937) to be full of spirit.

Hymnus an die Freundschaft, for chorus and piano 4H (1874). Ms. Orchestrated by Nietzsche's friend Peter Gast as *Manfred-Meditation,* 1872.

Monodie (1872). Ms. Written on the occasion of the wedding of G. Monod.

Noel, Henri

°*Adaptar al tiempo* (Follow the beat). New York: Schroeder & Gunther, 1967. Short piece in Latin American style. Secondo has rhythmic bass with accompanying chords; Primo melody in octaves between the hands. (?)

°*Cauencia.* Melville, NY: Pro-Art, 1968. Bright melodious piece with catchy Latin rhythm. (LI/UE-in octaves)

°*Pare!* (Stop!). New York: Lee Roberts, 1965. Syncopated melody and strong rhythmic drive; well arranged for both parts. (LI)

Nofka, R.

°*Bobolink.* Cincinnati: Willis, n.d. (E)

°*Home dreams.* Cincinnati: Willis, n.d. (E)

Noona, Walter

American composer and music educator.

°*El diablo cojuelo.* Melville, NY: Belwin-Mills, 1969. Brilliant piece in Flamenco style featuring repeated chords, strong rhythms, occasional changing meters; effective. (I)

°*Stamp on it!* Melville, NY: Belwin-Mills, 1969. Exciting, noisy boogie piece with a few rhythmic complexities. (LI)

°*Waltz semplice.* Melville, NY: Belwin-Mills, 1969. (UE-LI)

°*Duet performer,* vol.4. of *Mainstreams in Ensemble* series (Little boy blues; Dorian sleighride; That's the way it goes; Valencia; The all-American home-town band). Dayton, OH: The Heritage Music Press, 1977. Group of tuneful, bright teaching pieces. (UE-LI)

Nops, Margory

°*Twenty fingers.* London: Forsyth, n.d. (UE-LI)

Nordenfelt, Birgitta (1909–   ) and Finn Höffding

Swedish music pedagogue.

Via nova; ny vej til ny musik (New road to new music). Copenhagen: Musikforlaget Imudico, 1952. US:Wc. A singular approach to piano study containing ten charming original 4H works by contemporary composers: Nos.9 (Fughetta),20, 23, 26, 29 by Herman D. Koppel; No.30 by Ingvar Lidholm; Nos.2, 5, 8, 10 in "Prima vista" section presumably by the author-compilers, Nordenfelt and Höffding. (UE-LI)

Norman, Ludvig (1831–1885)

Swedish conductor, teacher and composer; wrote songs, piano pieces, and chamber and orchestral music.

Resebilder (Travel pictures), 6 karakterstycken (six character pieces) (Reselust [Pleasure of travel]; Öfver Insjön [Near Insjön]; Genom skogen [Through the forest]; Hägring [Mirage]; I regnväder [In rainy weather]; I säker hamm [In a safe harbor]), Op.52. Stockholm: Julius Bagge, 1878; Leipzig: Kistner, 1885; Leipzig: Forberg, 1885. S:Sic–US:Wc. Pleasant suite in well-balanced Romantic style. (I-UI)

3 Stücke, Op.7. (1851). Leipzig: Kistner & Siegel, 1858. S:Sic.

Norre, Dorkas (1911–   )

Swedish musician.

Andantino, and *Alla marcia* (1965). Ms. S:Sic.

Sju små kulisser (Seven little scenes) (1970). Ms. S:Sic. Short, instructional pieces in traditional harmonic style. Optional parts for rhythm instruments are supplied. (UE-LI)

Nottebohm, Gustav (1817–1882)

German writer and musicologist; Beethoven specialist; intimate of Schumann and Mendelssohn.

Variationen über ein Thema [Sarabande] von J.S. Bach (d). Leipzig: B&H, 1865. US:Wc.

Novák, Vítěslav (1870–1949)

Pupil of Dvořák. His compositions are written in Romantic style with strong folk influences of his native Czechoslovakia. They include operas, ballets, works for chorus and orchestra, symphonic pieces, concertos, chamber music, and piano pieces.

Dvě balady na slova lidové poesie moravské (Two ballads on texts of popular Moravian poetry) for mixed chorus and piano 4H, Op.19. Prague: Chadím, n.d. CS:Pchf.

Drei böhmische Tänze (Polka; Sousedská; Furiant), Op.15 (1897). Berlin: Simrock, 1898. US:Wc. Vigorous, rhythmical dances with folk flavor. (UI)

In der Tatra, Op.26. Vienna: UEd, n.d. CS:Pchf.

Mein Mai, 4 Stücke, Op.20. Prague: Urbánek e synove, 1902. CS:Pchf.

Nürnberg, Hermann

4 Charakteristische Stücke, Op.354. Leipzig: Leuckart, 1890. US:Wc. Instructional pieces. (LI)

Nuyten, J-Michael

Twenty fingers; seven modern dances (Wambach boogie; Walk and whistle; Rock waltz; Fiësta; Rain play; Going to a party; Big Bill's boogie) (1973). Hilversum (Holland): Harmonia-Ed., 1974. Despite its Dutch origin, the jolly music in this collection is American in spirit and style with attractive pieces in boogie, rock, and other jazz forms. Useful and effective. (UE)

O'Brien, Eugene (1945–)

American composer; studied with Bernd Alois Zimmermann, John Eaton, and Iannis Xenakis. His works include a cello concerto and music for chamber ensemble and orchestra.

°*Ambages* (1972). New York: Schirmer, 1975. A prefatory note from the composer states that "In *Ambages* the composer has attempted a short four-hand piano work in which each part is of equal importance and difficulty. The thematic material is shared and developed identically by both players, reaching a point of great textural complexity in the last half of the piece and returning, at the close, to a treatment similar to the beginning. Many of the rhythmic motives have been worked out in canon." Intense serial work; motives consist of repeated notes grouped in shifting rhythmical patterns; rapid tempo; requires advanced pianism. (A)

Ochs, Siegfried (1858–1929)

German choral conductor and writer on music. His compositions include a comic opera, choral arrangements of folk songs, and piano pieces.

°'S *kommt ein Vogel geflogen*, im Stile älterer und neuere Meister humoristisch bearbeitet. Heidelberg: Süddeutscher Musikverlag (Willy Müller), 1954. (UE-LI)

Oesten, Max

Divertissement. Cleveland: S.Brainerd, n.d. US:PHf.

Oesten, Theodor (1813–1870)

German instrumentalist and teacher; composed instructional piano works and a quantity of light, sentimental pieces in salon style.

Volks-Harfe, 12 Divertissements über deutsche Volkslieder, Op.82. Bonn: Simrock, ca.1852. US:PHf, Wc.

Ó Gallchobhair (O'Gallagher), Éamonn (1906–)

Irish music critic, editor, and conductor. He has written operas; choral and orchestral music; and works for radio, films, and dance.

Díséad piano, ceithre lámh (Piano for two, four hands) (Baile'n doire, Allegro con moto; Fáinne geal an lae, Allegro). Baile Átha Cliath (Dublin): Oifig an tSoláthair (Stationer's Office), n.d. US:Wc. Charming settings of two Irish melodies. (UE-LI)

Ogiński, Michał Kleofas, Prince (1765–1833)

Polish nobleman, diplomat, writer, musical amateur, and fervent patriot. He composed music with strong national folk flavor.

Polonaise favorite (F). Vienna: Cappi, ca.1823; Offenbach: André, ca.1820. A:Wst—US:NYp. Short work in early Romantic style. (I)

Ogle, Louise Godfrey

°*Winding brook.* New York: Schroeder & Gunther, n.d. Instructional piece. (UE-LI)

Oldenburg, Elizabeth

°*Country fair.* Philadelphia: Elkan-Vogel, n.d. Instructional piece. (LI)

°*Cuckoo, cuckoo.* Boston: Boston Music, 1956. Very easy teaching piece. (LE)

°*Woodland frolic.* Boston: Boston Music, 1954. Instructional work. (E-UE)

Oldroyd, George (1886–1951)

English organist; composed church music, organ pieces, songs, and piano works in conservative style.

Miniature suite (Tip-toe dance; Sarabande; Scherzino; Lullaby). London: Elkin, 1914. US:Wc. Inviting suite of short instructional pieces. (UE-LI)

Olsen, Ole (1850–1927)

Norwegian organist and composer of operas, choral works, chamber and orchestral music, and piano pieces.

Scherzo (G), Op.2. Christiana (Olso): Warmuth, ca.1878. N:Onk.

Olson, Lynn Freeman

American composer and pedagogue. He has written numerous instructional piano pieces of high quality and has collaborated on a piano method.

°*The ash grove.* New York: Carl Fischer, 1971. Tasteful arrangement of the well-known Welsh folk song; interest in both parts. (UE)

O'Neill, Norman (1875–1934)

English conductor and teacher; successful composer of incidental music to stage works, choral and orchestral compositions, songs, chamber music, and piano pieces.

All fours. London: OUP, 1930. Attractive, well-written teaching pieces. GB: Lbl. (UE-LI)

Onslow, George (1784–1853)

French musical amateur of English-French noble ancestry (grandson of Lord Onslow); studied in London with Dussek and Cramer, and in Paris with Reicha. He spent most of his life at his family estate in Clermont-Ferrand, except for a few winter months each year in Paris to try out his chamber music. His compositions are of strongly individual and well-defined character, and include 34 string quintets; 36 string quartets; 6 piano trios; 4 symphonies; and violin, cello, and piano sonatas. The two sonatas listed below are exceptionally fine works, representing one of the high points of piano four-hand sonata composition in the first half of the nineteenth century. Fresh and inventive, they are especially noteworthy for their fastidious structure, contrapuntal ingenuity, and unusual resolutions. They are well distributed for four hands and demand sure-handed technique and sensitive pianism. Well worth investigating.

°*Sonata* (e), Op.7. Paris: Pleyel, ca.1815. NEd. reprint in series *Unbekannte Werke der Klassik und Romantik* (München-Gräfelfing: Verlag Walter Wollenweber, 1970). The opening Allegro espressivo has a soaring theme in the Primo against the propulsive energy of an agitato triplet figure in the Secondo accompaniment. The Romanza is lyrical with a contrasting, darker middle section with dotted notes. The Finale Agitato is fast-paced, brilliant, and exciting. (UI-A)

°*Sonata* (f), Op.22. Leipzig: B&H, ca.1820. NEd. reprint in series *Unbekannte Werke der Klassik und Romantik* (München-Gräfelfing: Verlag Walter Wollenweber, 1971). The first movement, Allegro moderato e patetico, opens with dramatic, fervent theme accompanied by a striking, chromatic rising and falling 16th-note motive in the Secondo. The second movement, Minuetto, moderato, is restrained, tinged with sadness, and gently moving—a minuet in form only. A short Largo, with dotted notes and some extraordinary modulations, leads into the animated Finale: Allegro espressivo. (UI-A)

Pièces inédites, found ca.1972 at the Château (now Musée) d'Aulteribe by Carl de Nys and Helen Salome, who performed them on a program, "Hommage à George Onslow," Châteaux en Auvergne, Château de Valprivas, 22 Sept.1974.

Oosterzee, Cornélie van (1863–1943)

Dutch composer of operas, chamber music, songs, orchestral works, and piano pieces.

6 Leichte Stücke (Lenzesmorgen; Malaiisches Wiegenlied; Geburtstag; Weihnachten; Javanischer Tanz; Puppenball), Op.55. Middelburg: A.A. Noske, ca.1904. US:Wc. Instructional pieces in neat, refined traditional style. (UE-LI)

Orban, Marcel (b.1884)

Belgian; composed orchestral pieces, chamber music, songs, and piano works.

°*Pour les petits*, six pièces faciles. Paris: Rouart, n.d.

Ore, Harry (b.1885)

°*Albumleaf*. London: Curwen, n.d. (I)

°*Three Latvian folk songs*, Op.27. London: Curwen, 1958. US:Wc. Resourceful, well-crafted re-creations of Baltic folk-song material; attractive and carefully balanced. (I)

°*Old Russian polka*. London: Curwen, n.d. (I)

Orem, Preston Ware (1865–1938)

American composer, organist, and critic; wrote a variety of works in late-Romantic salon style.

Romanze (D). Philadelphia: R.C.Schirmer, 1889. US:PHf. (I)
Valse brillante. New York: Schirmer, 1889. US:Wc. (I)

Ornstein, Leo (1895–)

Russian-born American composer and pianist. He made frequent concert tours in the U.S. and Europe, often performing his own compositions. His works, which include orchestral, chamber, and piano pieces, are written in a strikingly dissonant, often strident, idiom that earned him the title of "enfant terrible of modern music."

Two improvisations (Berceuse triste; Valse buffon), Op.95 (1921). Ms. US:NH has holograph.

Pièce pour piano, Op.19/1 (1913). Ms. US:NH has holograph.

Seeing Russia with teacher; ten descriptive duets. New York: Schirmer, 1925. US:NH, NYp. Imaginative, colorful, descriptive pieces written in the composer's nonconformist, "futuristic" idiom. Although the style is no longer as shocking as it may have been to 1925 ears, it is nonetheless pungent and vividly chromatic. Contains early use of tone clusters. (I/E-5)

Orr, Mrs. M. Gascoigne

Old Spanish dance. Boston: Miles & Thompson, 1892. US:PHf,Wc. Salon piece. (I)

Orthel, Léon (1905–)

Dutch pianist and composer of works in neo-Classical style.

°*Five small pieces*, Op.47 (1963). Amsterdam: Donemus, 1974. Short, attractive works effectively set in polished, economical style with 20th-century French influences and faint suggestions of Stravinsky. (LI-I/LE-E)

Osborne, George Alexander (1806–1893)

Irish-born English pianist, composer, and teacher; wrote chamber music and piano pieces.

Duo (Gb), Op.69. Mainz: Schott, 1850. D-brd:MZsch.

Oscar, J.C.

Souvenir de [sic] *amitié*. New York: Pond, 1865. US:Wc. Salon waltz. (LI-I)

Oser, Hans (1895–1953)

Liederbuch für Regina. Zürich: Hug, 1940. CH:Zma.

Osieck, Hans (1910–)

Dutch composer. His orchestral works, chamber music, and piano pieces are written in an eclectic idiom, influenced by his extensive travels.

°*Acht korte karakterschetsen* (Eight short character sketches) (1950). Amsterdam: Donemus, 1950.

Suite concertante, for piano 4H and orchestra. Pub. and date missing. NL: Ad.

Otto, Ernst Julius (1804–1877)

German conductor; composed oratorios, operas, songs, and instructional piano music.

3 *Leichte Rondos* (Auf dem Wasser; Im Freien; Auf den Bergen). Leipzig: Merseburger, ca.1852. US:Wc. (LI-I)

d'Ourville, Léon

Soirées musicales, eighteen pieces. (Book I: Spring; Rustic dance; In the garden; Polonaise; Reaper's song; Gondolina; The lake; Hunting song. °Book II: Slumber song; Swing song; Gavotte; Hungarian; Cavatine; Spinning song; The mill; Styrian; The smithy; Valse-impromptu.) New York: Carl Fischer, 1910 (Book I, p.o.p). US:PHf,Wc. Facile, light, instructional pieces (LI-I)

Owen, Harold (1931–   )

°*Metropolitan bas cantata*, for chorus and piano 4H (1960). Los Angeles: Western International Music Co., n.d.

Pace, Robert

American pianist and piano pedagogue.

°*Blue mice*. New York: Lee Roberts, 1976.

°*Drifting*. New York: Lee Roberts, 1976.

°*The farmer left the dell*. New York: Lee Roberts, 1976.

°*Marching*. New York: Lee Roberts, 1976.

Paciorkiewicz, Tadeusz

°*Melodia*; °*Sygnałk* (Signals); °*Żołnierzyki* (Toy soldiers). In collection *Drobiazgi* I, ed. Raube. (LI)

Paderewski, Ignace (1860–1941)

Polish pianist and statesman. He composed an opera, a symphony, chamber music, and many piano pieces in late-Romantic style.

Tatra-Album, Tänze und Lieder des polnischen Volkes aus Zakopane, Op.12. Berlin: Ries & Erler, 1884; London: Augener, 1922. US:Wc. Varied settings of Polish folk melodies arranged by the composer from the 2H version; well-written, appealing teaching material; worth reviving. (LI-I)

Pain, Eva

°*Fancy dress scales*. London: Curwen, 1964. (UE-LI/E)

°*Five finger farm*. London: Curwen, n.d. (LE)

Paladilhe, Émile (1844–1926)

French composer of operas, a symphony, sacred music, songs, and piano pieces in traditional style.

°*Marche en fête*. Paris: Enoch, n.d.

Palester, Roman (1907–   )

Polish composer; often uses serial techniques. His works show the influence of Stravinsky and Szymanowsky.

Sonatina (1940). Kraków: PWM (Ars Polonia), 1946. US:NYp. Effective work in taut, dissonant idiom; carefully balanced. (A)

Palmer, Robert (1915–   )

American composer and teacher; Professor of Music at Cornell University; studied with Howard Hanson, Roy Harris, and Aaron Copland. Palmer's frequently dissonant musical style, which makes free use of traditional formal structures, is characterized by rhythmic vigor and dramatic intensity, and is instantly recognizable. His compositions include orchestral, choral, and chamber music, and sonatas and shorter works for piano.

°Sonata (1952; rev. 1957). New York: Southern Music, 1969. Dedicated to Monroe Levin and Cameron McGraw, piano-duettists. Strong, energetic, large-scale work in three movements with lyrical passages contrasting with sections of sombre harmonic density. Textural variety ranges from thin, transparent counterpoint to vivid, jagged polychords. Ostinato figures and the alternating scale are used extensively throughout. In the first movement, Allegro molto marcato, the principal theme is bold and driving; restless, irregular rhythmic patterns predominate except in the more tranquil, grazioso sections; and there is close canonic overlapping with piling up of sonorities. The second movement, Largo e sostenuto, is weighty, solemn, intense, and slow-moving, with fugal development in the contrasting middle section. The principal theme of the finale, Allegro vivo, in a rapid 12/8, is introduced canonically; the second theme is flowing and tranquil; the development culminates in a section of great rhythmic and dynamic complexity with thick textures; and an exhilarating coda concludes the work. The parts are carefully balanced and masterfully engineered; an effective work, exciting to listen to and to play. (A)

Palschau, Johann Gottfried (Godfrey?) Wilhelm (ca.1742–1813)

German piano virtuoso; spent time in London and Copenhagen, eventually moving to St. Petersburg, where he became associated with the court.

Air varié (g), Op.1. St. Petersburg: Sprewitz, ca.1796. B:Bc. An attractive theme is developed pianistically and with imagination in spare contrapuntal texture in this charming short set of four variations. (LI-I)

Panormo, F

A duet (F) . . . in a familiar stile for juvenile performers, Op.2. London: G. Walker, n.d. US:Wc, in collection "Ayre." Very short three-movement instructional work, strongly derivative of Haydn; melodious and pianistic in spite of crudities in the setting. (UE-LI)

Papineau-Couture, Jean (1916–   )

Canadian composer; studied with Nadia Boulanger and at the New England Conservatory. His style is influenced by Stravinsky and the 20th-century

French school. He has written stage works, chamber and orchestral compositions, and piano pieces.

°*Rondo* (1945). New York: Peer International, 1960. US:Bp,Wc. Attractive work in neo-Classical idiom; spare-textured, linear, some dissonance, changing meters; well balanced. (UI)

°*Paraphrases*, 24 variations and 17 small pieces on a simple theme, dedicated to small pianists capable of executing the theme with one finger of each hand: 1. Twenty-four variations and finale (Cui, Liadov, Rimsky-Korsakov); 2. Prélude (Liszt); 3. Polka (Borodin); 4. Marche funèbre (Borodin); 5. Valse (Liadov); 6. Berceuse (Rimsky-Korsakov); 7. Galop (Liadov); 8. Gigue (Liadov); 9. Fughetta on B-A-C-H (Rimsky-Korsakov); 10. Tarantella (Rimsky-Korsakov); 11. Menuetto (Rimsky-Korsakov); 12. Valse (Cui); 13. Requiem (Borodin); 14. Carillon (Rimsky-Korsakov); 15. Mazurka (Borodin); 16. Fugue grotesque (Rimsky-Korsakov); 17. Cortège triomphale (Liadov); 18. Bigarrures, petit supplément (Sherbachëv). NEd. arranged and annotated by Alexandre Tcherepnine. Bonn: M.P. Belaieff, 1959. The fascination of this curiosity, a communal compositional frolic by a group of prominent Russian musicians of the late 19th century, lies less in performing these artfully devised works than in what they reveal about the harmonic and melodic ingenuity of the various contributors. Selection of the internationally famous *Chopsticks* as the ostinato theme seems to have been made by Rimsky-Korsakov, the instigator of this caper. Its use, however, as the unvarying cantus firmus, always in the exposed Primo part of all 41 pieces, makes serious performance of more than a few at a time a tedious undertaking, since the 19th-century Russian version of *Chopsticks* is as relentlessly monotonous as its contemporary American counterpart. All the same, this is diverting material for browsing, sight-reading, or recreation—a delightful tour-de-force by composers at play. (I-UI/LE)

Parfrey, Raymond

°*Steel band*. Minneapolis: Schmitt, Hall & McCreary, 1973. Syncopation and Caribbean flavor are featured in this pleasant teaching piece. (UE-LI)

°*Woodland stroll*. Minneapolis: Schmitt, Hall & McCreary, 1973. Pleasant little instructional piece; flowing, appealing. (UE-LI)

Paribeni, Giolio Cesare (b.1881)

Italian teacher, music critic; composed orchestral and chamber music, choral works, and piano pieces.

Sei piccoli pezzi. Magenta: A.Drago, 1947. US:NYp. Group of short, melodious pieces in pleasant traditional idiom. (UE-LI/E-5)

Parker, Henry (1842–1917)

English voice teacher and composer of operas, choral and orchestral pieces, songs, and piano music.

Three short duets. London: Lamborn Cock, n.d. GB:Lbl. Teaching pieces (LI-I)

Parmentier, Théodore
°7 *Canons d'un genre particulier.* Paris: Hamelle, 1878.

Parodi, Renato (1899–1974)
Italian teacher and composer of piano, chamber, symphonic, and choral music.

Danza (in forma di fuga). In collection *Album di Musica Moderna*, vol.II.

Parry, C. Hubert H. (1848–1918)
English composer and writer on music. He wrote an opera, oratorios, orchestral and liturgical works, chamber music, and piano pieces.

Sonata (f), Op.20 (1865). Ms. GB:Lcm.

Parusinov, Aleksei Vasilevich
Soviet musician.

Desiat' kirgizskikh melodii (Ten Kirghiz melodies), Op.15. Moscow: State Publishing House, 1928. US:NYp,PHf,Wc. Soviet folk melodies in imaginative arrangements. (LI-I)

Pasfield, William Reginald
°3 *Miniatures.* London: Ashdown, 1962.

Passy, (Ludvig Anton) Edvard (1789–1870)
Swedish pianist and teacher; studied with John Field in St.Petersburg; wrote piano concertos, church music, piano pieces, songs, and organ works.

Sonata. Pub. and date missing. S:Skma.

Patachich, Ivan (1922–)
Hungarian composer; has written film and stage music, choral and orchestral pieces, chamber works, and piano compositions.

°*Gay song.* In collections *Piano duets by Hungarian composers,* ed. Szelényi; and *Album for Piano Duet,* ed. Váczi. Bright, lively folk-song setting; sparkling, rhythmical. (UE-LI)

Patzinger, Felix
Kinderspiel, 8 leichte Stücke. Leipzig/Vienna: Schuberthaus-Verlag, 1909. US:Wc. Entertaining instructional pieces. (I/E)

Pauer, Max (1866–1945)
Austrian pianist and teacher; composed a number of piano pieces in salon style.

3 *Klavierstücke,* Op.10. London: Augener, 1896. US:Wc. (I)
Presto à la tarantelle, Op.2. Mainz: Schott, 1912. D-brd: MZsch. (UI)
Walzer, Op.12. Mainz: Schott, n.d. D-brd:MZsch. (I-UI)

Payer, Jérôme (Hieronymus) (1787–1845)
Austrian organist and conductor; composed operas, liturgical and chamber music, organ works, and piano pieces.

Deutsches Rondo, Thema aus "Barbier de Sevilla," Op.40. Vienna: Mollo, 1820. A:Wgm.

12 Walzer samt Coda, Op.47. Vienna: Maisch, ca.1820. A:Wgm.

Peck, Russell (1945–)

American composer; studied at the Eastman School of Music and the University of Michigan.

The cat's meow. Ms. Available from composer, Indianapolis Symphony Orchestra, Indianapolis, IN 46208. Bright, rhythmical, bustling work in jazz idiom featuring tone clusters, dissonance, and changing meters; effective. (UI)

Pelemans, Willem (1901–)

Flemish music critic; his musical works are written in late-Romantic idiom.

Sonate (1961). Brussels: Maurer, n.d. B:Bcdm.

Pelz, William

•*Bells, bells, bells* (Chimes in the tower; The little music box; Sleigh bells). New York: Century Music, 1963. Short descriptive instructional pieces. (UE)

Pensel, Johann

4 Marches, Op.10. Vienna: Cappi, ca.1821. A:Wn,Wgm.

6 Walses (D), No.4. Vienna: Cappi, 1818. A:Wn. Suite of Viennese waltzes in Schubertian style. (LI)

Pentland, Barbara (1912–)

Canadian composer; studied with Wagenaar, Jacobi, and Copland. Her works include symphonic and chamber music, choral pieces, and piano compositions. She uses serial techniques for the most part.

•*Two Canadian folk-songs* (Je le mène bien, mon dévidoir; A la claire fontaine). Ms. C:Tcmc. Four-voice arrangements of French Canadian melodies in modal, often dissonant, tonal idiom. The strongly linear texture of both pieces leans heavily on contrapuntal techniques, including imitation, inversion, and canonic writing. (LI)

Three piano duets on pictures by Paul Klee (I. Small fool in trance, after Klee's "Kleiner Narr in Trance"; II. Surfaces in tension, after Klee's "Verspannte Flächen"; III. Fish magic, after Klee's "Fischzauber") (1958). Ms. C:Tcmc. Short serial works; thin-textured, linear. (UI-LA)

•*Puppet show.* Toronto: BMI Canada, 1965. Remarkable little piece; single-line melody; spare texture; fascinating introduction to serial techniques. (UE-LI)

Percheron, Suzanne

•*Diorama,* six pièces faciles (Pardon en Bretagne; Carillon; Berceuse scandinave; Fête provençale; Valse viennoise; Valse orientale). Paris: Gallet, n.d. (UE)

•*Six estampes anglaises* (Perdu dans le brouillard jaune; Les fifres du roi;

Dans le sentier des fées; Danse de la petite Greenaway; Le chant du ruis-selet; Carillon de Westminster). Paris: Gallet, 1920.

Perdew, Ruth (1912–)

American teacher and composer. The following works are an exceptionally fine group of instructional pieces.

°*Breezy boogie.* Boulder, CO: Myklas Press, 1973. Amusing, attractive piece with contemporary sounds; chromatic melody, tone clusters; well balanced. (E-UE)

°*Dorian dance.* Boulder, CO: Myklas Press, 1972. Melody in dorian mode in Primo supported by rhythmic accompaniment in Secondo; unusual tonal combinations; effective. (E)

°*Penguin chatter.* Boulder, CO: Myklas Press, 1972. Short piece featuring polytonality; unconventional sonorities. (E)

°*Whistle tune.* Boulder, CO: Myklas Press, 1977. Jolly, good-humored piece; mainly pentatonic. (E)

Perrachio, Luigi (b.1883)

Italian lawyer, pianist, teacher, and composer of orchestral, chamber, choral, liturgical, and piano music.

Scherzetto. In collection *Album di Musica Moderna,* vol.II.

Persichetti, Vincent (1915–)

American composer and teacher; has written orchestral and chamber music, choral and organ works, and many piano compositions. His style, often eclectic, is tightly organized, melodic, freely dissonant, and occasionally polytonal. His idiomatic writing is noteworthy in his piano works, which have especially felicitous settings.

°*Appalachian Christmas carols* (after John Jacob Niles) (Down in yon forests; The cherry tree; The seven joys of Mary; Jesus, Jesus, rest your head; Jesus born in Beth'ny; Lulle lullay; Jesus, the Christ is born). Bryn Mawr: Elkan-Vogel, 1975. Sensitive, elegantly arranged group of folk songs. (LI-I)

°*Concerto for piano, four-hands,* Op.56 (1952). Philadelphia: Elkan-Vogel, 1954. Commissioned by the Pittsburgh International Contemporary Music Festival and performed there by the composer and his wife, Dorothea, on 29 Nov. 1952. This large-scale, single-movement work in five thematically related sections—Lento, Andante, Presto, Larghissimo, Coda—ingeniously exploits the full resources of the keyboard through the development of a single motive. In the first two sections, the theme is slowly expanded with the addition of new material with hints of faster tempi; here and in other sections of the work, inventive use of harmonics and sostenuto pedal provide coloristic effects. With the third section, Presto, the theme erupts into exuberant 16th-note passages, with rhythmic excitement and flashes of orchestral brilliance. The slowly accelerating Coda ends the work at a breath-taking tempo in a series of luminous sonorities. The work is technically demanding for both performers. (A)

°*Serenade* No.8, Op.62. Philadelphia: Elkan-Vogel, 1956. Amiable, melodious work in four short movements, gracefully written in polished contemporary idiom. (LI)

Pesse, Maurice

°*C'est une petite sérénade*. Paris: Consortium musical, n.d. (UE)

°*Concerto enfantin*. Paris: Consortium musical, n.d. (LI)

°*Douce flânerie*. Paris: Consortium musical, n.d. (LI)

°*12 Petites pièces, classées progressivement*. Paris: Durand, n.d. (UE-LI/ E-5)

°*Un tout petit rien*. Paris: Consortium musical, n.d. (LI)

Peterson-Berger, Olof Wilhelm (1867–1942)

Swedish critic and composer; his works are largely based ón Swedish folk song.

Vikingsbalk (Viking law), marsch (1893). Stockholm: Elkan & Schildknecht, Emil Carelius, n.d. S:Sic.

Petit, P.

°*6 Petites pièces*. Paris: Gérard Billaudot, n.d.

Petrassi, Goffredo (1904–   )

Italian composer of operas; ballets; film scores; orchestral, choral, and chamber music; and piano compositions. He writes in a clear harmonic and formal style with later influences of serial techniques.

Siciliana and *Marcia*. In collection *Album di Musica Moderna*, vol.II.

Petrová, Elena

Czech musician.

Inspiration (1973). Pub. missing. CS:Pchf.

Pfeffinger, Philipp Jacob (1765–1821)

German musician and teacher; lived in London and Paris. He wrote orchestral and chamber works, and a quantity of piano pieces.

Sonate concertante (c), Op.16. Paris: Richault, n.d. D-ddr:Dlb. Scale passages and Alberti bass figures in alternating solos between the two partners characterize the antiphonal substance of this somewhat weak and repetitious work in Classical style. (I-UI)

Pfeiffer, Georges-Jean (1835–1908)

French pianist; composed orchestral works, operas, chamber music, and piano pieces.

°*Suite*, Op.89. Paris: Hamelle, ca.1870.

Pfeiffer, Jean-Michel (fl. late 18th cent.)

Obscure composer, possibly of German origin, who appears to have been active in Venice. In addition to his four-hand works he published sonatas for two violins and a keyboard method.

°*Il maestro e lo scolare, o sonata* (C). Mannheim: Heckel, n.d.; Munich: Falter, ca.1789. °NEd. Amsterdam: A.J. Heuwekemeijer, 1960. B:Bc–GB:Lbl–D-brd:Mbs. Short, three-movement work in light Classical style. (E)

Sonata, Op.1. London: J. Bland, ca.1795. No.10 of a series *A duett for two performers on one harpsichord or piano-forte composed by the following emminent* [sic] *composers. . . .*" GB:Lbl.

Philip, Achille (b.1878)

French organist and teacher; his compositions include orchestral and choral music, songs, chamber works, and piano pieces.

°*10 Leichte Klavierstücke.* Cologne: Gerig, 1956.

Philipp, Franz (1890–   )

°*Sonate*, Op.50. Heidelberg: Süddeutscher Musikverlag (W.Müller), 1945.

Philipp, Isidor (1863–1958)

Hungarian-born French pianist and teacher; composed piano exercises, studies, and pieces.

°*Trois bluettes* (Valse mignonne; Berceuse; Danse hongroise). Paris: Hamelle, n.d. GB:Lbl. Inventive, fanciful set of teaching pieces set with skill and taste for young pianists. (LI-I)

Phillips, Burrill (1907–   )

American composer and teacher; writes in neo-Classical style.

°*Serenade.* New York: Southern Music, 1963. Suite of four pieces skilfully written for 4H in free-flowing, ingratiating style; dedicated to Dorothea and Vincent Persichetti. (UI-A)

Phillips, Leslie

°*Siesta.* New York: Galaxy Music, 1964. Dreamy mood piece in languid 7/4; Spanish flavor. (LI-I)

Piccioli, Giuseppe (1905–1961)

Italian pianist and teacher; author of books on piano literature. He composed a piano concerto, a ballet, symphonic and chamber music, and piano pieces in traditional style.

Due miniature (Petite valse; Storiella). Bologna: Bongiovanni, 1935. US: NYp. (I)

Pavana et minuetto. Bologna: Bongiovanni, 1939. US:NYp.

Pierce, Alexandra

Antares (1974). Ms. Atmospheric tone picture in spare pointillistic style; effective and not too difficult. US:NYamc.

Pieroni, Leopoldo

°*Album of little pieces.* Florence: Forlivesi, n.d.

Pijper, Willem (1894–1947)

Dutch critic, educator, and one of the dominant figures in 20th-century Dutch music. In his works he used polytonality, linear counterpoint, and polyrhythms.

Op den Weefstoel, for four-part chorus, wind instruments, and piano 4H (1918). Amsterdam: Donemus, 1950. NL:Ad.

Pike, Eleanor Franklin

°*Country dance*, Op.34. London: Ashdown, n.d.

°*Early days suite*, Op.39. London: Ashdown, n.d.

°*Five pianoforte duets*, Op.33. London: Ashdown, 1962. Original pieces and folk-song arrangements, competently set in conservative idiom. (UE-LI)

°*The princess dances*, Op.8/2. London: Ashdown, 1954. Bright, happy little waltz. (UE)

°*The spinning wheel*. London: Ashdown, n.d.

°*Springtime in the woods*, Op.14. London: Ashdown, n.d. (UE)

°*Valse mazurka*. London: Ashdown, n.d. (UE)

Pilling, Dorothy

°*Pageantry pieces*. London: Forsyth, n.d. (UE-LI)

°*Rural rhythms* (Hornpipe; Folk-song; Pastorale; Bourrée). London: Forsyth, 1936. Agreeable, flowing, melodic pieces in traditional idiom; well balanced. (LI-I)

Pillney, Karl Hermann (1896–)

°*Alt-Wien*, Walzer nach Lanner frei bearbeitet. Vienna: Böhm, 1926; Doblinger, 1967.

Weihnachtliche Hausmusik. Wiesbaden: B&H, 1952. US:Wc. Appealing arrangements of five German Christmas songs. (UE-LI)

Pilz, Eduard

6 *Klavierstücke*, Op.11. Leipzig: Pabst, 1913. US:Wc. Salon music. (LI)

Piovano, Antonio

°*Invenzioni, su motivi popolari abruzzesi* (Ninna nanna; Invito alla danza; L'addio; Serenata; Contadino stanco; Danza sull'aia). Ancona/Milan: Bèrben, 1975. A similarity in format binds these six pieces together. Ostinato figures and repeated patterns are used extensively; there are small rhythmical complexities; and a web of dissonance encloses the tonal Italian folk melodies on which the pieces are based. A fascinating group of pieces offering some new and refreshing sounds. (I)

Piozzi, Gabriele (18th cent.)

Three duets and three canzonets, Op.6. London: pub. by the composer, n.d. GB:Lbl.

Pitfield, Thomas Baron (1903–)

English poet, artist, designer, and prolific composer of choral and instrumental works.

°*Minors*, dance suite (Gaillard; Sarabande; Sinister dance; Rigaudon). London: J.B. Cramer, 1965. Chromaticism, irregular rhythmic groupings, and unusual meters characterize this group of pieces. The setting is effective, but not always grateful for the performers. (I)

°*Two-way tunes*. London: Elkin, n.d. (E)

Pixis, Johann Peter (1788–1874)

German pianist and composer of operas and works for piano, including a concerto, sonatas, and salon pieces.

Amusement pour le carnaval, valses élégantes (Eb). Vienna: J. Cappi, ca. 1824. A:Wst. Suite of connected waltzes in tuneful Schubertian style. (UE-LI)

Trois marches, Op.6. Vienna: J. Cappi, ca.1813. A:Wn.

Trois marches (F,D,bb), Op.22. Vienna: Mechetti, ca.1816. A:Wn. Attractive melodic ideas and unexpected chromaticisms, but lackluster on the whole. (UE-LI)

Soirées des muses, 2 quadrilles de contredanses. Leipzig: Kistner, n.d. US: Wc.

Variations sur "La Fiancée suisse," Op.114. Paris: Schlesinger, n.d. US:Wc. Salon. (I)

6 Walzer mit Trios (Eb,G,C,F,d,Bb). Vienna: Cappi, ca.1818. A:Wgm,Wn—US:NYp,Wc. Charming set of Viennese waltzes; brief and effective. (LI)

Pizzini, Carlo Alberto (1905–)

Italian composer, student of Respighi; has written works for orchestra, chamber ensembles, voice, and piano.

°*C'era un re que aveva tre figlie*. Milan: Ricordi, 1944.

°*Serafino*. Milan: Ricordi, 1935.

Plachý, Wenzel (1785–1858)

Three characteristic marches (Eb,C,eb), Op.9. Vienna: Haslinger, n.d.; London: T. Boosey & Co., n.d. GB:Lbl. Routine works in thin Classical style. Perhaps it is only a coincidence that the first march is strikingly similar to Beethoven's March, Op.45/1, in rhythmic pattern, melody, and formal design. (I)

Erholungen auf dem Wege zu Parnass, Op.44/1–6. Vienna: Joseph Czerný, ca.1827. A:Wgm (Nos.1,2,3,4,6); Wn (No.5 only)

Notturno (C), Op.20. Brunswick: Spehr, n.d. US:Wc. Salon piece. (I)

Pleskow, Raoul (1931–)

Viennese-born American composer; teaches at C.W. Post College. He has written orchestral and chamber music, songs, and piano pieces.

°*Three pieces*, ca.1968. ACA photocopy. Works of moderate length in advanced serial idiom. (A)

Pleyel, Ignace (1757–1831)

Austrian, student of Haydn. A successful piano manufacturer and a prolific composer, Pleyel was one of the most popular and frequently published mu-

sicians of his time. He wrote a quantity of unpretentious, moderately difficult (LI-I), melodious four-hand works in Classical style, most of which are
out of print. Rita Benton, Pleyel scholar and cataloguer, has demonstrated
that they are all arrangements of Pleyel's own chamber music. The justifi-
cation for listing them here is that they have long been regarded as original
piano duets because of the skill and sensitivity with which the composer set
them for the four-hand medium.

The sources of the following condensed list of editions are Benton, *Ignace
Pleyel: A Thematic Catalogue of His Compositions* (New York: Pendragon
Press, 1977), additional material from Benton, and data in RISM. The works
are listed in the order of their appearance in the Benton catalogue, which
includes a comprehensive inventory of editions of Pleyel's four-hand pieces,
their sources, and their library locations. They are arranged in six groups,
according to the original form of the pieces from which the four-hand versions were derived. A three-digit number identifies the original composition;
e.g., Ben 272 is a string quintet, Ben 301 a string quartet. The four-digit
number in parentheses preceding the Ben number refers to the particular
edition of the four-hand version. Thus the complete catalogue number Ben
(2541) 272 designates the Dresden edition of the four-hand arrangement
of the string quintet that was the source of *Sonate à quatre mains.*

Originally String Quintets:

Deux sonates à quatre mains, Ben(2541) 271 (Eb), 272 (g). Dresden, ca.
1790. CS:KRa—D-ddr:LEm,Hau—DK:A—GB:CKc,Lbl—I:OS—US:Wc.

Originally String Quartets:

Three duetts for the piano or harpsichord, Ben(6402) 301/i,iii (C), 304
(Bb), 310/i,iii,iv (Bb), adapted by F. Tomich. London: Longman & Broderip, 1789. D-brd:B—GB:Cu,Lbl,Ob. Other four-hand editions and their
locations: Ben (301): A:Wst—D-brd:B,WD—I:Bc,OS; Ben (304): D-brd:
Tmi—D-ddr:HAu—I:PAc—NL:Uim.

Two duets for two performers on one piano forte, Ben(6401) 332/ii (G),
137/iv [originally a symphony]. London: Lavenu, ca.1800. GB:Lbl.

Quatuor de Mr. Pleyel arrangé en sonate, Ben(3373) 340 (G), Étrennes
pour les dames, livre 8ième. Offenbach: André, 1789. CH:Bu—D-brd:AD,
Bhm,LB,MT,OF.

Quatuor arrangé en sonate . . . , par F. Frackman, Ben(3582) 355 (e). St.
Petersburg: Gerstenberg, 1793–95. D-brd:MÜu.

Originally Trios for Keyboard, Flute or Violin, and Cello:

A favorite duet for the pianoforte selected from the six sonatas, Ben(4426)
431 (C), 432 (G), 433 (Bb), 434 (A), 435 (e), 436 (D). London:
Clementi, Banger, Hyde, Collard and Davis, 1801–1806. GB:Cu (No.2)—
US:PHu (Nos.2–4), Wc.

Originally Violin Duos:

Trois sonates à quatre mains, Ben(5109–11) 513 (Bb), 514 (D), 515 (A).
Nos.35–36 Journal de musique pour les dames. Offenbach: André, 1789.

B:Bc—D-brd:Bhm,LB,OF—GB:Lhaas—S:L,Skma,Sm—US:BE. Locations
of other four-hand editions of Ben 513, 514, 515: CH:Bchristen,EN—CS:K
— D-brd:Mbs — D-ddr:WRtl — GB:Cu,En,Lbl,Ob — I:Fn,OS,PAc,VEc —
—US:IObenton, NYp,Wc.

Trois sonates à quatre mains, Ben(5111.3) 516 (F), 517 (c), 518 (e). 4ème
livre de sonates. Offenbach: André, 1791. CH:E—D-brd:Rp—D-ddr:WRtl
—NL:Uim. Locations of other four-hand editions of Ben 516, 517, 518:
A:Wgm — CH:EN,SA — D-brd:OF — DK:Kk — H:Bn — I:OS,VIb — US:
IObenton,R,Wc.

°*Sonata,* Ben(5220) 520 (g), ed. Zeitlin and Goldberger. New York: Peters,
1961. US:NYp.

Trois sonates à quatre mains, Ben(5185) 519 (C), 520 (g), 521 (A), 2ème
livre de sonates. Offenbach: André, 1790. B:Bc—DK:A—I:PAc—NL:At—
S:Sks. Locations of other 4H editions of Ben 519, 520, 521: A:Wgm—CH:
EN—GB:Cu,Lcm,LVp,Ob—US:Bp,NYp,R.

Trois sonates à quatre mains, Ben(5187) 522 (Bb), 523 (G), 524 (d), 3ème
livre. Offenbach: André, 1791. CH:E—D-brd:Bhm—D-ddr:WRtl—S:Sm.
Locations of other four-hand editions of Ben 522, 523, 524: A:Wgm,Wn,
Wst — B:Bc — BR:Rn — CH:SO — CS:Pnm — D-brd:B,Tmi — GB:Lbl —
I:Mc—NL:At—US:IObenton,R.

Originally Violin or Violin and Viola Duos:

Sonate à quatre mains, Op.71, Ben(5268) 528 (Eb). Offenbach: André,
1805. D-brd:MÜu,OF—NL:DHgm—S:Skma. Locations of other four-hand
editions of Ben 528: D-brd:B (as Op.69),KNh—DK:Kv (as Op.69)—N:
Ou (as Op.69)—NL:At (as Op.69)—US:Wc.

Sonate à quatre mains . . . XXX . . . oeuvre 47ème, Ben(5306) 530 (Bb).
Offenbach: André, 1797. D-brd:Rp—DK:A,Kk—S:Skma,Sm. Location of
other four-hand editions of Ben 530: A:Wgm, Wst—D-brd:B,KNh—D-ddr:
WRtl—F:Pn—GB:Cu,Lbl,LVp,Ob—I:Mc—N:Ou.

Poisot, Charles-Émile (1822–1904)

French pianist and composer of operas, a cantata, church music, and piano
pieces.

°*Fantaisie sur le Déserteur de Monsigny.* Paris: Hamelle, n.d.

Poldini, Ede (Eduard) (1869–1957)

Hungarian composer of operas and piano pieces of light character.

Au lac. Breslau: Hainauer; New York: Schirmer, 1896. US:Wc. (I)

En bohémien. Breslau: Hainauer; New York: Schirmer, 1896. US:Wc. (I)

Festandacht und Jubelwalzer, Op.50. Breslau: Hainauer, n.d. US:Wc. (I/E-
5-UE)

5 *Genrestücke,* Op.12. Breslau: Hainauer, 1896. US:Wc. (I)

3 *Morceaux.* Breslau: Hainauer, 1913. US:Wc. Instructional pieces. (LI)

°6 *Morceaux pittoresques,* Op.7. Budapest: Editio Musica, 1956. Sparkling
set of attractive teaching pieces. (UE-LI)

Musikalische Bilder für die Jugend, Clavierstücke in leichter Spielart, Op.16. Breslau: Hainauer, 1896. US:Wc. Instructional pieces. (UE-LI)

Poole, Clifford

°*Clapping song.* Cincinnati: Willis, 1965. Melodic fragments alternate with rhythmical hand-clapping in this effective little piece. (E)

°*Conga.* Cincinnati: Willis, n.d. Bright, rhythmical teaching piece. (E)

°*Waltz.* Cincinnati: Willis, 1965. Tschaikowsky-style waltz; conventional harmonies; balanced parts. (UE)

Portnoff, Mischa (1901–)

American composer and teacher of Russian background; studied in Berlin and Stockholm. He has written a piano concerto and music for piano solo and two pianos.

°*Singing duets.* Evanston, IL: Summy-Birchard, 1966. Attractive settings of 11 folk songs; well balanced. (UE)

Poser, Hans (1917–1969)

German teacher; composed choral and stage works, a TV opera, chamber music, and piano pieces.

°*Kleine Suite,* Op.13/1. Hamburg: Hans Sikorski, 1951. US:Wc. Short work in polished neo-Classical idiom. (UI)

°*Sonate,* Op.17 (1954). Hamburg: Sikorski, 1962. US:NYp,Wc. Conventional sonata form is the structural framework of this attractive, predominantly linear work: quartal harmony is also featured. (I)

Poulenc, Francis (1899–1963)

French pianist and composer; member of "les Six." He composed operas, ballets, concertos, sacred and choral works, chamber music, song cycles, and piano pieces.

°*Sonate* (1918). London: Chester, 1919. Sparkling, witty, clear-textured work in three short movements with contrasting moods of mock bombast, saucy dissonance, and melodious naïveté. Modéré: fast, martellato chords contrast with slower lyrical section. Rustique: a gently-moving pandiatonic pastorale. Final: begins with a fast scalar melody, introduces thematic materials from the first and second movements in a long accelerando-crescendo, and ends with the first theme. Delightfully fresh, rewarding fare. (I-UI)

Powell, Laurence (1899–)

English-born American teacher, conductor, and music critic. He has written choral and orchestral works, chamber music, and piano pieces.

°*Fourteen American folk tunes.* Boston: Boston Music, 1961. Graceful arrangements of some lesser-known folk songs. (I)

Pozzoli, Ettore (1873–1957)

Italian pianist, teacher, and author of pedagogical works and theory textbooks. His compositions include choral, chamber, orchestral, and piano works.

°*10 Piccoli pezzi caratteristici.* Milan: Ricordi, 1959. Charming descriptive pieces; tuneful with rhythmic variety. (UE-LI/E-5)

°*Smiles of childhood* (Sorrisi infantili), 23 little pieces. Milan: Ricordi, 1948; 1968. Short, melodious pieces appealingly set for the medium in compact traditional idiom. (LI/E-5)

Preobrajenska, V. (1926–   )

Polinchinelle (1976). Ms. Short, dissonant, two-voice piece with dynamic variety and drive; the constantly fluctuating Secondo rhythmic ostinato supports a contrasting single-line melody in the Primo. US:NYamc. (UI)

Prinz, Leonhard

Pantomime, five duets (Overture; Elf and dwarf; Dream of the good fairy; Sorcerer; Finale). London: Augener, 1936. US:Wc. Instructional pieces. (UE-LI)

Procházka, Ludwig (1837–1888)

Czech jurist and municipal officer, champion of Smetana. He composed Czech songs, arrangements of folk songs, and piano pieces.

Slavische Reigen. Berlin: Ries & Erler, 1887. CS:Pchf.

Prochazka, Rudolf, Freiherr von (1864–1936)

German-Czech lawyer, musician, and writer on music; studied with Fibich. His works include symphonic, choral, and chamber music; songs; and piano pieces.

Deutsch-böhmische Reigen, Op.26. Pub. and date missing. CS:Pchf.

Procter, Alice McElroy (1915–   )

American pianist and composer; studied at Smith College and the Eastman School of Music. She has written a number of excellent teaching pieces for piano.

°*Fun for two,* six pieces. Philadelphia: Elkan-Vogel, 1954. Exceptionally fine pieces for young pianists (four original and two folk-song arrangements), attractively set for piano 4H. (E-UE)

°*Happy go lucky.* London: OUP, n.d. (UE)

°*Holiday bells.* Philadelphia: Elkan-Vogel, 1954. Short teaching piece with interesting sonorities written in a refreshing style. (UE-LI)

°*Lullaby.* Philadelphia: Elkan-Vogel, 1951. Gentle piece in well-balanced, graceful idiom. (UE-LI)

°*March of the moon men.* Philadelphia. Elkan-Vogel, 1965.

°*On the road.* Philadelphia: Elkan-Vogel, 1965. This piece and the preceding one are excellent teaching material; short and to the point, they are sensitively written, tuneful, and have abundant rhythmic and harmonic interest. (UE-LI)

Song for Kathleen. Philadelphia: Elkan-Vogel, 1955. (UE)

°*Two dance pieces* (Squares tonight; Swing tune). Philadelphia: Elkan-Vogel, 1957. (UE)

°*Village dance*. Philadelphia: Elkan-Vogel, 1955. (UE)

Prószyński, Stanislaw

°*Pacynki* (Glove puppets). In collection *Drobiazgi*, vol.I, ed. Raube. (LI)

Puccini, Giacomo (1858–1924)

Minuets. Pub. and date missing. I:Li.

Pütz, Eduard

Frohes Musizieren, 6 kleine Stücke. Celle i. Hanover: Moeck, 1947. D-brd: DSim.

Quinet, Marcel (1915–1971)

Belgian composer of choral, orchestral, and chamber music.

°*Cinq miniatures* (1964). Brussels: CeBeDeM, 1965. US:NYp,Wc. Five short, thin-textured pieces in mildly contemporary idiom; moods range from serious to capricious and bouncy; delightful fare. (I)

Quintin Buée, A.

Three sonatas for the pianoforte, the third for two performers on one instrument. London: Hodsoll, printed for composer, ca.1797. GB:Lbl.

Rachmaninov, Sergei (1873–1943)

Russian composer, pianist, and conductor. His orchestral and piano music—concertos and pieces—have been popular for many years; but he also wrote songs, chamber works, and choral music. *Six Pieces*, Op.11, are the composer's major essay into four-hand writing; although not performed as frequently as the more familiar *Suites* for two pianos, they are solidly written in the composer's Romantic, and thoroughly pianistic, style.

°*Six pieces* (Six morceaux), Op.11 (ca.1893). Moscow: Gutheil, 1894; °State Music Publishing House (Muzyka), 1968; New York: °Boosey & Hawkes, 1947, 1976; °International Music, 1956. The gently swaying Barcarolle begins quietly with thin textures and gradually builds to a powerful climax as Secondo plays heavy chords against rippling 16th-note sextolets in Primo; the original theme returns; and the piece ends quietly. 2. The dazzling Scherzo must be played prestissimo for the most effective performance. 3. A simple folk tune introduces Russian Theme; the tune is varied and developed, growing in volume and intensity with rapid accompanying figures in Secondo, and gradually subsiding into a final simple statement of the theme at the end. 4. A rhythmical Waltz. 5. A melodious Romance. 6. Slava (Glory) is based on an old Russian liturgical chant and recalls the glitter and drama of Mussorgsky's opera *Boris Godunov*, in which the same melody is used with very powerful effect. Here the chant is treated in free variation form, growing from a simple melody with thin accompaniment into increasingly faster rhythmic patterns. At the end the piece bursts into a brilliant pianistic display as the chant is thunderously intoned in massive chords like the resounding echoes of a chorus of church bells. (I-LA)

°*Polka* (E♭) (In two versions, the second with trumpet). Moscow: Jurgenson, n.d., Musgiz, 1950, in Rachmaninov *Works for Four Hands and Six Hands;* New York: Carl Fischer, 1938.

°*Romance* (G) (1891). Moscow: Musgiz, 1950, in Rachmaninov *Works for Four Hands and Six Hands;* in collection *Russian Music for Young Pianists,* ed. Zeitlin and Goldberger. Pleasant, flowing work; clear-textured, simple, direct; not written in the composer's more familiar mature style. (UI)

Rack, J.G.

Grande marche, Op.16. Vienna: Cappi, ca.1810. A:Wgm.

Trois marches, Op.17. Vienna: chés [*sic*] l'auteur, n.d. A:Wgm.

Radecke, Robert (1830–1911)

German violinist, pianist, organist, teacher, and conductor. He composed an opera, symphonic and chamber music, piano pieces, songs, and choruses.

Allegro appassionato (f), Op.6. Leipzig: B&H, 1852. US:Wc. Serious work in strong Romantic vein; brilliant in part; effective and rewarding when performed with dash and style. (UI-A)

Raff, Joachim (1822–1882)

Swiss-born disciple of Liszt; prolific composer of symphonies, piano works, chamber music, and operas, written in a technically facile, refined salon style.

Aus dem Tanzsalon, Fantasietänze (Präludium; Quadrille; Walzer; Galopp; Ländler; Polka; Ungarischer; Mazurka; Spanish [Jaleo]; Tarantella; Polonaise; Russisch), Op.174. Leipzig: Ries & Erler, 1872. US:Wc. Attractive, competently written drawing-room pieces. (UI-A)

Humoreske in Walzerform (D), Op.159. Berlin: Bote & Bock, 1879. US:Wc. Extended waltz with contrasting brio section. (UI)

Marche brillante, Op.132. Leipzig: Hofmeister, n.d. US:Wc. (I)

Reisebilder, 10 Stücke, Op.160. Leipzig: Kistner & Siegel, 1871, 1875. US:Wc. Descriptive pieces in elegant salon style. (I)

°*12 Morceaux de salon* (Nina; Les faucheurs; Les batelières de Brienz; Wanda; Promenade au bord du ruisseau; Les fileuses; Les commères; Alison; Festpracht; Autrefois; Sous le saule du levant; Fischerinnen von Procida, Tarantella), Op.82. Leipzig: Peters, n.d.; Paris: Durand, n.d., °Hamelle. GB:Lcm—US:PHf,Wc. Attractive, well-balanced pieces. (I)

Totentanz (*Danse macabre*), 2. Humoreske in Walzerform, Op.181. Leipzig: Siegel, n.d. US:Wc. Long, discursive tone poem, related to Liszt in style and in philosophical content. (I)

Raichev, Aleksandur (1922–   )

Bulgarian conductor and pedagogue. He has composed extensively for children; his music is strongly influenced by Balkan rhythms.

Theme and variations. See Parashkev Khadjiev.

Raiger, Frédéric

Sonata (E♭), Op.8. Vienna: Witzendorf, ca.1815. A:Wgm.

Sonata (F), Op.14. Vienna: Witzendorf, ca.1821. A:Wgm.

Rakov, Nikolai Petrovich (1908–   )

Russian composer, studied with Glière. He has written orchestral and chamber music and piano pieces.

°*Three pieces* (Mazurka; Melody; Russian dance). Moscow: State Publishing House, n.d. (Leeds).

Protiazhnaia. In collection *Ansambli v Chetyri Ruki.*

Randhartiger, Benedikt (1802–1893)

Austrian composer; friend of Schubert. He wrote masses, motets, symphonies, songs, chamber music, and piano works.

Variations, avec accompagnement de deux cors, Op.11. Vienna: Maisch, 1827. A:Wgm.

Ránki, György (1907–   )

Hungarian composer. Folk and jazz elements are important influences in his works, which include cantatas, songs, orchestral pieces, chamber music, and piano works.

°*Two Hungarian folk songs* (*Ludas játék; Kapuvári verbunk*). Budapest: Editio Musica, 1958. Pleasant, rhythmical folk-song settings. (UE-LI)

Raphael, Günther (1903–1960)

German musician who cultivated a neo-Classical, contrapuntal idiom. He was principally an orchestral composer, but he also wrote choral, chamber, and piano works.

Romantische Tanzbilder, 10 Walzer, Op.10. Leipzig: Peters, 1925. US:Wc. °*Walzer* (B), Op.10/?, in collection *Leipziger Klaviermusik aus Vergangenheit und Gegenwart,* Peters Ed.; °*Walzer,* Op.10/4 in collection, *Spielbuch zeitgenössische Originalkompositionen.*

Raphling, Sam (1910–   )

American pianist and teacher; has written orchestral and chamber music and numerous piano works.

°*Four-hand sonata.* New York: General Music Publishing Co., 1970. Four short movements: Lively, Moderately slow; Slow-expressive; Fast and Joyful. Written in an angular, dissonant, thin-textured idiom; exploits pitch and dynamic contrasts. (I-UI)

°*Two by two.* New York: General Music Publishing Co., n.d.

Rausch, Frederick (1755–1823)

German-born American musician and music publisher.

Sonatina. New York: G. Gilfert & Co., ca.1794. US:Bp,PROu. Short movement in rough-edged Classical style. The work is of historical interest on account of its early publication in the U.S. (UE-LI)

Räusche, J.L.F.

Trois pièces faciles (G,A,C), Op.3. Hamburg: Böhme, n.d. D-brd:F.

Rauzzini, Venanzio Matteo (1746–1810)

Italian castrato, settled in England; teacher and composer. He wrote stage and vocal works, cantatas, chamber music, and piano pieces. Except for occasional sections of repetitious passage work and weak thematic development, the four-hand sonatas below are attractive, skilfully fashioned pieces in Classical style, containing tuneful melodies, rhythmic vitality, and abundant antiphonal writing.

Three grand duets for two performers on one piano-forte or harpsichord (F,D,C), Op.12. London: Beardmore & Birchall, ca.1782. GB:LEc—US: NYp. As *Trois grands duo,* Op.12. Paris: De Roullede, n.d. F:Pc.

Three sonatas (C,Bb,F) *and a duet* (Eb) *for the harpsichord or piano forte,* Op.15. London: Birchall & Andrews, ca.1783. GB:Lbl. As *Three sonatas and a duet,* Op.15. London: John Bland, n.d. GB:Ckc. As *A favourite duett for the harpsichord or piano-forte,* Op.15. London: Goulding & Co., ca.1800. GB:Lbl—US:Wc. As *Sonata . . . No.34 du Journal de musique pour les dames.* Offenbach: André, n.d. B:Bc—CH:Bu,Zz—D-brd:Bhm, F,LB.

Ravel, Maurice (1875–1937)

°*Fanfare.* Paris: Heugel, 1927. Opening movement of the ballet *L'Eventail de Jeanne* (q.v.). Bright, humorous. Bitonality adds a restless, astringent character. To indicate mock pomposity, one section of the piece is marked *Wagneramente.* (UI)

°*Frontispice,* pour S.P. 503 *Le Poème du Vardar* de R. Canudo (1918). Paris: Salabert, 1975. Very short (15 measures) Impressionistic mood piece using exotic scales, ostinati, and coloristic effects to evoke images found in Canudo's poem on which the work is based; a fifth hand is required in part. (A)

°*Ma mère l'oye* (Mother Goose Suite) (1908). Paris: Durand, 1910. Well known in its orchestral version, this is one of the choicest works of the piano 4H repertoire. The five pieces of this enchanting suite are based on French nursery tales and are set in the composer's refined and elegant style. They were originally written by Ravel for two talented children of his acquaintance, who later performed them, but they are hardly children's pieces, requiring sophisticated and subtle pianism, great dynamic control and sensitivity, and considerable dexterity for effective performance. 1. Pavane de la Belle au bois dormant: slow and thin-textured; describes the calm, unearthly quiet of Beauty lying asleep in the enchanted forest. 2. Petit Poucet: the composer has prefaced the piece with the story of the French Tom Thumb or Hop-o'-my-thumb: Lost in the forest he discovers that the birds have eaten the crumbs he had left behind so that he could find his way out. As the music describes the slow, halting progress of Petit Poucet, groping his way through the deep, dark woods, it moves steadily up and down in parallel thirds, with imitations of chirping birds in the trees overhead. A sunny, pianissimo C-major chord, high on the keyboard, ends the perilous journey successfully. (I) 3. Laideronnette, Impératrice des Pagodes: introduces an oriental atmosphere as it describes the story of the Empress of the Pagodas (in this case, tiny people, not buildings) stepping into her bath to the accompániment of all the pagodas playing an assortment of little instruments fashioned from nut shells. The music is entirely set in the black-note pentatonic scale, with Chinese bell and gong effects, and is technically demanding. (UI-LA) 4. Les entretiens de la Belle et de la Bête: moderately paced waltz tells the familiar story of Beauty and the Beast. The music closely follows the French text above the score as it describes the conversations between Beauty and the Beast in a most ingratiating and poignant way. The Beast, in a deep, though muted, roar in Secondo, pleads with Beauty for her hand; in a graceful Primo melody Beauty responds sweetly, but negatively; the Beast, in misery, pursues, and Beauty, finally overcome by pity, accepts his proposal, whereupon a sudden glissando in the Primo ends the magic spell. The Beast is turned into a handsome prince, and all ends happily. (I-UI) 5. Le jardin féerique: brief finale; a musical portrait of the enchanted garden. Beginning with a slow, serious theme elegantly set in smoothly flowing four-part harmony, the music gradually leads into a section of glittering, arpeggiated chords high on the keyboard; the first theme returns, grows with increasing volume and intensity until it explodes in a flash of brilliant pianistic color, with glissandi high in the Primo part and suggestions of trumpet flourishes and ringing bells in the Secondo. (UI)

Ravizé, A.

Choix de vieilles chansons (harmonisées). Paris: Durand, n.d. (UE)

Rawsthorne, Alan (1905–1971)

English pianist and composer; wrote mainly instrumental music in contrapuntal neo-Classical idiom, influenced by Hindemith.

*The creel, suite for piano duet, after Izaak Walton (1940). London: OUP, 1941. Strong, vivid, often witty set of four single-page descriptive pieces based on quotations from Izaac Walton's The Compleat Angler. Dissonant, with some atonality. The mighty pike is the tyrant of the fresh water: regal, majestic, in broad French-overture style. The sprat; a fish that is ever in motion: a nimble, dashing, roguish canon between the two partners. The carp is the queen of rivers; a stately, a good, and a very subtil fish: quiet, lyrical, restrained. The leap or summersault of the salmon: sparkling, dotted-note rhythms. (I-UI)

Raymond, Joseph
*Having fun. Melville, NY: Belwin, n.d.

Read, Edward
*Cinderella waltz. London: Novello, n.d.
*Wild rose waltz. Cincinnati: Willis, 1914.

Read, Gardner (1913–   )
American musician, teacher, writer on music, and composer of symphonic, piano, and organ music. His eclectic musical style shows Romantic, neo-Classical, Impressionistic, and folk influences; also uses polyharmonies, polytonality, and dissonance.
*The little soldiers, Op.95a. Glen Rock, NJ: J. Fischer, 1964.
*The toy parade. Glen Rock, NJ: J. Fischer, 1964. These two pieces are bright, attractive works in colorful, contemporary harmonic idiom. (UE-LI)

Rebe, Louise Christine (d.1979)
American pianist, teacher, and composer of instructional piano music.
*Salute to America. Cincinnati: Willis, n.d. (E)

Rebikov, Vladimir (1866–1920)
Russian composer of operas, ballets, orchestral suites, and piano pieces. He used the whole-tone scale, unresolved dissonances, and other advanced techniques in a basically Tchaikowskian harmonic idiom.
Petite suite (Valse; Danse des myosotis; Tarantelle; Danse orientale; Mazurka), Op.30. Moscow: Jurgenson, 1905.· US:NYp. Pleasant suite of moderately long pieces in late Romantic style. (I)

Reda, Siegfried (1916–1969)
*12 Minnelieder (four for piano four-hands). Kassel: Bärenreiter, n.d. (UE)

Reger, Max (1873–1916)
Reger's four-hand works, like the rest of his music, are, for the most part, Classical in inspiration and form, strongly influenced by Brahms, and written in a post-Wagnerian, at times highly complex, harmonic idiom. The composer brings to his duets a fertile musical imagination and enormous contrapuntal skill, along with a predilection for thick, opulent textures, which become intensified through his use of constantly shifting modulations and fussy convoluted chromaticism. While some of the early works, such as Opp. 10 and 22, have a graceful open-air charm about them, reminiscent of the

Liebeslieder Waltzes, Op.9 already suggests, in its solid writing for both parts, the direction toward the dense, often murky, style of Opp.58 and 94.
°*Werke für Klavier vierhändig*, vol.13 of *Max Reger Sämtlige Werke*. Bonn: Max-Reger-Institut (Elas Reger Stiftung), 1954–71. Complete 4H works.
°*Max Reger: Walzer-Capricen, Deutsche Tänze und andere Stücke*, ed. W. Fricker. Leipzig: Peters, n.d.
°*6 Burlesken*, Op.58 (1901). Berlin: Simrock, 1902; Leipzig: Peters, 1928. Chromatic, thick-textured, technically demanding; the playfulness of these pieces tends toward the ponderous and heavy-footed. (A)
°*20 Deutsche Tänze*, Op.10 (1893). London: Augener, 1894; Mainz: Schott, 1910.
5 Pièces pittoresques, Op.34 (1899). Leipzig: Aibl, 1899; Vienna: UEd, 1904, 1912, 1913. Long descriptive pieces, varying in mood from light-hearted and sportive to intense and serious. (A)
Introduction and passacaglia. Leipzig: B&H, n.d. Large-scale baroque works, originally for organ, but transcribed by the composer for 4H. (I-UI)
°*6 Stücke*, Op.94 (1906). Leipzig: Peters, 1906; NEd. 1943. (A)
°*3 Walzer*, Op.22 (1898). Leipzig: Aibl, 1899; Vienna: UEd., 1899, 1904, 1913. Set of charming waltzes in Brahmsian style, but more chromatic; thinner-textured and less complex contrapuntally than Opp.9, 10, 34, and 58.
12 Walzer-Capricen, Op.9 (1892). London: Augener, 1894; Mainz:Schott, 1910. (A)

Regner, Hermann
°*Klangspiele;* miniature concert for piano 4H and seven melodic percussion instruments. Wolfenbüttel: Möseler, n.d. (Belwin-Mills).

Rein, Walter (1893–1955)
German composer; made a speciality of writing choral music for children; also composed chamber music and piano pieces.
°*Spielbuch*. Zürich: Pelikan, 1953. (I)

Reinecke, Carl (1824–1910)
German composer of orchestral pieces, concertos, chamber music, operas, and piano music in Romantic style showing the influence of Mendelssohn and Schumann.
Geistliche Hausmusik; Die schönsten Choräle, Op.186. Leipzig: Forberg, n.d. US:Wc. Series of chorales and chorale-preludes in the style of Bach. (LI-I)
Improvisata über eine Gavotte von Gluck, Op.125. Leipzig: Peters, 1873. I:Bc—US:Wc. Tasteful, artfully constructed set of free variations on the well-known Gluck melody; written in refined and effective Romantic idiom, also in two-piano transcription by the composer. (I-UI)
10 Kleine Phantasien über deutsche Kinderlieder, Op.181. Leipzig: B&H,

1886. US:NYp,Wc. Short, easy pieces in Mendelssohnian style based on German folk songs. (UE-LI)

Musik zu Andersen's Märchen von Schweinehirten, Op.286. Leipzig: B&H, ca.1910. US:NYp,Wc. Tuneful, cleanly written pieces in effective salon style. (I)

Musik zum Märchen vom Nussknacker und Mausekönig, Op.46. Leipzig: B&H, 1866; New York: Schirmer, n.d. US:Bp. Descriptive music after an E.T.A. Hoffmann fairy tale; imaginative tone painting. (I-UI)

Sonate (a), Op.35. Brunswick: Litolff, 1854. US:Wc. Long, three-movement work; abundant passage work; rather lacking in solid thematic and harmonic material. (I-A)

3 Sonates miniatures (A,G,b), Op.213. London: Augener, ca.1901. US:PHf, Wc. Tuneful pieces in instructional style; lie well for both parts. (LI)

12 Studien in canonischer Weise, Op.130. Leipzig: Eulenberg, 1874. US: Wc. Duet settings of various types of canons; written in Mendelssohnian idiom. (UE-LI)

Variationen über eine Sarabande von J.S. Bach (a), Op.24. Hamburg: Schuberth, 1852; NEd.1874. US:PHf,Wc. Dextrously fashioned set of variations in refined salon style. (I)

°*12 Clavierstücke*, Op.54. Bonn: Simrock, 1857; London: Augener, 1875; Paris: °Hamelle, n.d. US:PHf,Wc. Instructional pieces. (UE-LI/E-5)

Von der Wiege bis zum Grabe, eine Zyklus von 16 Fantasiestücken, Op.202. Leipzig: Zimmerman, 1888. US:Wc. Suite of descriptive pieces in salon style. (UI)

Zu Klein's Zenobia, dramatische Fantasiestücke, Op.194. Leipzig: B&H, 1887. US:Wc. Salon pieces. (I-LA)

Reinhard, August (1831–1912)

German composer. His works include a sonata, a trio, and other compositions for the harmonium as well as organ and piano pieces.

Phantasie über den Namen BACH, Op.78. Leipzig: Kahnt, 1904; London: Novello, n.d. US:Wc. Extended work in traditional harmonic idiom on the theme B♭,A,C,B; frequently chromatic. (I)

Reisden, J.

6 Walzer, Op.2. Linz: Akademische Kunst- und Buchhandlung, n.d. A: Wgm.

Reisenauer, Alfred (1863–1907)

German composer; student of Liszt. In addition to over 100 songs, he wrote many piano pieces.

Reisebilder, 5 Stücke, Op.14. Hamburg: Sikorski, 1905. US:Wc. Descriptive pieces in traditional harmonic idiom. (I)

Reissiger, Friedrich August (1809–1883)

Conductor, organist, and composer who settled in Norway. He wrote male quartets, chamber music, and piano pieces.

Norske national og folkmelodier (Norwegian national and folk melodies).
Kristiana (Oslo): Warmuth, ca.1875. US:NYp.

Reissiger, Karl Gottlieb (1798–1859)

German teacher and conductor; successor to Weber as court musician at
Dresden; prolific composer of works in facile, popular idiom.

Introduction et polonaise (G), Op.32. Bonn: Simrock, ca.1824, US:NYp.

3 *Marches brillantes*, Op.11. Pub. and date missing. US:Wc. Salon pieces.
   (I)

Relfe, John (1763–1837)

English composer and teacher. He wrote theory textbooks, a cantata, songs,
and piano pieces.

Two duetts for the harpsichord, Op.3. London: pub. by composer, 1786.
GB:Gu.

The favorite glee of Care thou Canker. Adapted as a duett, with accompany-
ments for two performers on one harpsichord or piano. London: Preston,
n.d. GB:Lbl.

A *set of grand lessons* (Eb,D,A,C,Bb,D) *for the harpsichord or piano-forte*,
for two performers on one instrument in different stiles of composition.
London: Longman & Broderip, ca.1790. US:PHu.

Renner, André

Sarabanda de la Duchesse de Bourgogne, Op.26. Paris: F. Durdilly; Ch.
Hayet, 1920. US:Wc. Dance piece in 18th-century style. (UI)

Respighi, Ottorino (1879–1936)

Italian composer, conductor, teacher, and editor; pupil of Rimsky-Korsakov
and Max Bruch. He is best known for his vividly pictorial orchestral works.
He cultivated a neo-modal style with Romantic and Impressionistic harmonic
language and Classical form.

°6 *Little pieces* (1926). Hamburg/London: D. Rahter, 1926. Although
these pieces do not have the familiar harmonic and stylistic imprint of
Respighi the orchestrator, they are remarkable in their structure and pianistic color. As artful settings of piano duet music for young people, they
are some of the finest and most sensitive pieces in the literature. They are
masterfully constructed for one relatively easy and one more difficult part
and use a variety of key signatures, meters, and technical devices. The first
three pieces, the lyrical Romanza; the energetic, boisterous Sicilian hunting song, with its tarantella-like rhythmical drive; and the flowing, gentle
Armenian song all require the Primo to play mostly single-line melodies or
with hands an octave apart. Merry Christmas everywhere, the gem of the
suite, is a bright, joyful piece containing some extraordinarily effective
writing of bell sonorities. Two Scottish folk melodies, strongly pentatonic,
are used consecutively in the winsome Scottish Airs. The work ends in
mini-virtuoso style with a brisk march, The little highlanders, which adds

dotted notes, including the Scotch snap, and 16th-note passages, and concludes with a brilliant accelerando. (LI-I/UE-LI)

Suite della tabacchiera; musical joke for wind instruments and piano four hands on decorated themes on a snuffbox belonging to Count Chigi-Saracini (Nov. 30, 1930, Siena, Sala "micat in vertice"). I:Sac.

Reuther, Carl

At close of day. Boston: A.P.Schmidt, 1916. US:Wc. Six short instructional pieces. (LI)

Nacht-klänge (Canzonetta; Valse mignonne; Barcarole; Tarantelle). Breslau: Hainauer, 1911. US:Wc. Instructional pieces. (LI)

Reynolds, Verne (1926–)

American horn player and composer. His works include a violin concerto, a quintet for woodwind quintet and piano, a sonata for horn and piano, and numerous chamber works using brass, woodwinds, and percussion.

°*Graphics,* for trombone and piano 4H (1976). New York: Carl Fischer, 1977.

Xenoliths, for flute and piano 4H (1977). Mc. available from composer, Eastman School of Music, Rochester, NY 14606.

Rheinberger, Joseph (1839–1901)

German organist, pianist, conductor, teacher, and composer. His works include organ pieces, operas, church music, orchestral and chamber music, songs, and piano pieces written in a highly contrapuntal Romantic style derived from Beethoven, Schumann, and Brahms.

°*Aus der Ferientagen* (En vacances) (Allegro moderato; Allegretto; Tempo di marcia; Adagio marcato e moderato [Fugue]), Op.72. Bremen: Praeger & Meier, ca.1875; Paris: °Hamelle, n.d. US:Wc. Attractive, descriptive works in late-Romantic harmonic idiom. (UI)

Grosse Sonate (c), Op.122. Leipzig: Forberg, 1881. US:Wc. Resourcefully fashioned four-movement work, well scored for piano 4H and cast in broadly conceived lines; contrapuntally active with harmonic and melodic interest; worth reviving. (UI-A)

Tarantelle, Op.13. Leipzig: Kistner & Siegel, 1867; London: Augener, 1886; Paris: Hamelle, n.d. US:Wc. Brilliant work with vigorous rhythmical energy and harmonic variety. (UI)

Rheineck, Christoph (1748–1797)

3 *Kleine Sonaten.* Pub. and date missing. D-brd:MGs.

Rhené-Baton (pseud. of René Baton) (1879–1940)

French composer of songs, orchestral music, an opera, and piano music.

°*En vacances,* 6 pièces (Dans le bois; Au village; Légende; Au trot des mules; Promenade; Danse paysanne), Op.38. Paris: Durand, 1925. (UE)

Richardson, Alan (1904–)

Scottish pianist and composer of piano pieces in post-Romantic style.

°*Improvisation on a nursery tune* (1930). London: Winthrop Rogers, 1937. Delightful, rhapsodic variations on a children's folk song in up-to-date, frequently chromatic, idiom; well laid out for both parts. (I)

Richter, Carl

Chop sticks. New York: Bourne, 1957. US:Wc. Arrangement of familiar melody. (UE-LI)

Richter, Ernst Friedrich (1808–1879)

German theorist, teacher, and composer. In addition to textbooks on harmony, counterpoint, and fugue, he wrote oratorios, choral and chamber music, organ pieces, and piano works.

Variationen über ein Original-Thema (D), Op.34. Leipzig: Kistner & Siegel, 1867. US:Wc. Trim, well-fashioned series of variations in Mendelssohnian style. (I)

Richter, Georg Friedrich

2 *Sonates* (Bb,Eb) *et un duo* (F) *à quatre mains pour le clavecin ou·le forte piano,* Op.6. Paris: pub. and date missing. D-ddr:WRtl.

Ricordi, Giulio (1840–1912)

Italian music publisher, skilled draftsman, and composer of elegant salon music.

Le livre des histoires, suite de 9 contes musicaux, par J. Burgmein [pseud]; poésie de Paul Solanges. Milan: Ricordi, 1888. US:NYp.

Le livre des sérénades; 15 morceaux caractéristiques, par J. Burgmein [pseud]. Milan: Ricordi, ca.1888. US:Bp,NYp,Wc. Elegantly bound and illustrated little book of salon pieces with accompanying poems by Paul Solanges and fine color illustrations by A. Edel. (UI-A)

Le roman de Pierrot et de Pierrette; historiettes musicales par J. Burgmein [pseud]. Milan: Ricordi, 1892. US:NYp.

Rosette (Roosje), légende hollandaise (d'après Bellamy); suite dramatique de J. Burgmein [pseud]. Milan: Ricordi, ca.1892. US:NYp.

Ridley, S.C.

°5 *Petits morceaux.* Melbourne: Allans Music, n.d.

Rieder, Hélène

6 *Pièces,* pour un bon pianiste et un autre qui le deviendra. Lausanne: Foetisch, 1957. (I/E)

Rieff, Georg Joseph von (b.ca.1760)

Sonata, Op.3. Offenbach: André, 1796. D-brd:OF.

Rieger, Gottfried (b.1764)

3 *Sonatines très-faciles* (C,F,G), Op.19. Vienna: Witzendorf, 1822. A:Wgm.

Rieger, J.N. (1787–1828)

Grande sonate, Op.2. Paris: Sieber, n.d.

Sonata, Op.1. Berlin: Paez, ca.1824.

Riegger, Wallingford (1885–1961)

American conductor and composer. He wrote music for the dance, chamber music, choral and orchestral works, and piano pieces. His style, derived from modified serial techniques, is lyrical, austere, and dissonant.

°*The cry*, dance for Hanya Holm (1935). New York: Peer International, 1953; AMP.

°*Evocation*, dance for Martha Graham (1933). New York: Peer International, 1953; AMP.

°*New dance for piano four hands and percussion*, for Doris Humphrey (1936). New York: Peer International, 1953; AMP.

These three works, written as accompaniments to modern dances, are set in a free, occasionally dissonant, idiom, with great rhythmic vitality and dramatic contrasts. (UI-A)

Riem, Wilhelm Friedrich (1779–1857)

German pianist and organist. His works include an oratorio, chamber music, and organ and piano pieces written in early Romantic style.

Rondeau (A), Op.36. Leipzig: Peters; Hamburg: Cranz, ca.1822. US:NYp, Wc. Piece in early salon style. (I)

Deux rondeaux (Ab,A), Op.24. Leipzig: Peters (Kühnel), ca.1809. US:Wc. (I)

Sonate facile (G), Op.23. Leipzig: Peters (Kühnel), ca.1808. A:Wgm. Short, two-movement work; flowing; tightly constructed. (I)

Ries, Ferdinand (1784–1838)

Friend, student, and close associate of Beethoven; prolific and exceedingly popular composer whose music demonstrates many traits linking him with the Romantic movement. His craftsmanship and sure-handed, sympathetic writing for the piano are reflected in his four-hand works, but in his effort to please the public taste, the quality of his duets is weakened by an abundance of empty passage work and mediocre musical materials.

Deux airs favoris nationaux de Moore variés (Air portugais [Eb]; Air national [F]), Op.108. Paris: Richault, ca.1809. US:Wc.

Grande marche triomphale. Paris: Richault, n.d.; Leipzig: Peters, ca.1814. US:Wc.

Trois grandes marches (D,a,c). Op.12. Leipzig: Peters, ca.1814. US:NYp, Wc.

3 Grandes marches (Eb,c,Bb), Liv.2, Op.22. Bonn: Simrock, ca.1818; Hamburg: Cranz; Vienna: Mollo. A:Wgm—US:Wc.

Introduction et (cinquième) polonaise, Op.176. Leipzig: Schuberth, n.d. US:Wc.

Introduction et variations (Allemande à trois) (F), Op.155/1. Frankfurt: Dunst; Leipzig: Hofmeister, n.d.; Paris: Richault, n.d. US:Wc.

Introduction et variations sur l'air allemand "Gute Nacht" (Bb), Op.155/2. Bonn: Simrock, ca.1833. US:Wc.

Première polonaise (C), Op.41. Leipzig: Peters, ca.1812; Offenbach: André,
ca.1812; Vienna: Diabelli, ca.1812. US:Wc. (I)

Seconde polonaise (Bb), Op.93. Vienna: Diabelli, ca.1826. US:Wc. (I-UI)

Troisième polonaise (Eb), Op.138. Hamburg: Cranz, ca.1825. US:Wc.

Quatrième polonaise (D), Op.140. Leipzig: Peters, n.d. Work of grand proportions but meager contents. (I)

Sonata (Bb), Op.47. Leipzig: Peters, 1818; Vienna: Mollo, 1818. US:PHf.
Solidly constructed work in Beethoven idiom; structurally imposing, but
lacking in thematic development and harmonic resourcefulness; appealing, nonetheless, for its directness and pleasant melodies. (I)

Variations sur un air russe (Eb), Op.14. Leipzig: Peters, n.d.; Vienna: Mollo,
1818. A:Wgm—US:Wc.

Říhofský, Adalbert (1871–1950)

Czech organist and choirmaster. He wrote orchestral and choral music,
chamber works, and pieces for organ and piano.

Album pro mladež (Album for the young), Vol.1 (Mazurka; Melodie; Tänz-
chen; Elegie; Marsch; Ein Märchen; Am Abend), Op.22, 1906; Vol.2
(Lied; Polka; Romanza; Serenade; Walzer; Erinnerung), Op.28, 1909.
Prague: Mojmír Urbánek. CS:Pchf.

Rimsky-Korsakov, Nikolai (1844–1908)

Member of Russian nationalist group of composers; one-time naval officer.
He composed operas, symphonies, and overtures—all distinguished by brilliant orchestration—as well as chamber music, songs, and piano pieces. His
students include Glazunov, Prokofiev, Respighi, and Stravinsky.

°Berceuse; °Carillon; °Fughetta; °Fugue on B-A-C-H; °Minuet; °Taran-
telle; °24 variations and finale (with Cui and Liadov). See *Paraphrases*.

Rinck, Johann Christian Heinrich (1770–1846)

German organist, teacher, and composer. He wrote organ pieces, sacred
choral works, chamber music, and many pedagogical piano compositions.

3 *Divertissements*, Op.35, cah.1. Offenbach: André, ca.1816. US:NYp.

3 *Divertissements*, Op.36, cah.2. Offenbach: André, ca.1816. US:PHf.

3 *Divertissements*, Op.41, cah.3. Mainz: Schott, n.d. US:NYp. Opp.35,36,
and 41 are short, pleasing instructional pieces. (LI-I)

Sonate (F), Op.50. Offenbach: André, ca.1817. US:NYp.

Uebungsstücke für die ersten Anfänger im Klavierspielen, Op.60 (for both
two hands and four hands). Linz: Friedrich Emmanuel Eurich, ca.1821.
A:Wgm.

12 *Valses*, Opp.27 and 28. Offenbach: André, ca.1809. US:Wc has Op.27,
Six Valses. Charming set of graceful waltzes. (UE)

Riotte, Philipp Jakob (1776–1856)

German conductor and composer of a large number of stage works—operas,
pantomimes, ballets, incidental music, operettas—as well as a symphony,

chamber music, and piano compositions. He wrote in a fluent, early Romantic style.

Polonaise (G), Op.43. Vienna: Mechetti, ca.1810. A:Wst. Bright, rather long, and repetitious work in traditional idiom; melody largely confined to the Primo, with the Secondo providing the chordal accompaniment. (I)

Thème (canon) avec variations (Eb), Op.23. Leipzig: B&H, n.d. D-ddr:Bds. Set of carefully worked-out variations in practised, through dry and academic, contrapuntal style. The theme is first introduced canonically, then treated in various nonlinear ways; the work terminates in a weighty fugue using the canon theme as subject. (I-UI)

Ristad, Eloise

°*Leprechauns at play.* Boulder, CO: Myklas Press, 1975. Unexpected harmonies, fragmentary melodic patterns, and irregular phrase lengths characterize this short piece. It also comes with a well-constructed, catchy part for rhythm instruments. (UE)

Robertson, Frances C.

Five melodious and instructive pieces (Happy thoughts; Always merry; Valentine waltz; Moonlight dance; Ethiopian dance), Op.45. Philadelphia: Presser, 1903. US:Wc. Instructional pieces. (UE-LI)

Robinson, Anne

Six little duets (°Little march; °Waltzing; °Lullaby; °Polka petite; °Minuet; °Little clog dance). Cincinnati: Willis, 1952 (issued in single copies only). Instructional pieces. (UE/E-5)

Robinson, William E.

°*Oompah polka.* Melville, NY: Belwin-Mills, 1960. Bright lively dance in traditional idiom. (UE)

°*Rondo.* Cincinnati: Willis, 1952. Short piece in 18th-century Classical style. (UE)

Rochberg, George (1918–   )

American composer; professor of composition at University of Pennsylvania. He has written orchestral, chamber, and piano music in a highly organized serial idiom. More recently he has cultivated a neo-Romantic style.

°*Book of contrapuntal pieces for keyboard instruments.* Bryn Mawr: Theodore Presser, 1981. No.11, 4-part canon (1946); No.12, 7 chorales treated canonically (Ach wie nuchtig, ach wie flüchtig; Jesus Christus, unser Heiland; Straf mich nicht in deinem Zorn; Wie bist du, Seele?; Nun sich der Tag [with contrary motion canon]; Kommt Seelen dieser Tag; In dulce Jubilo) (1946); No.20, Fugue for four hands one piano, transcribed by the composer from his String Quartet No.4 (1977). Impressive collection of 49 contrapuntal exercises including inventions, fugues, preludes, fughettas, and canons, 9 of which were written for one piano 4H, the remainder for solo piano, two pianos 4H, and two pianos 8H. In his preface the composer writes: "The reason for gathering these studies in the art of counterpoint embracing the canon, invertible counterpoint, and the fugue is not complicated: I wanted to make available in one volume the bulk of my early efforts in this ancient and demanding craft so that 1) they could be performed by amateur or professional musicians for their own delectation (whether in private or in public); and 2) they could be used as stimulation and encouragement to my own students and other young, aspiring composers." These pieces are as delightful to play as they are rewarding to study for their contrapuntal brilliance and ingenuity. (I-UI)

Rodgers, Irene

°A *first duet book for little Jacks and Jills*. New York: Schirmer, 1951. Useful, pleasant teaching pieces in traditional idiom. (E)

°A *second duet book for little Jacks and Jills*. New York: Schirmer, 1957. Slightly more advanced continuation of the preceding book. (UE)

Rodrigo, Joaquín (1902–)

Spanish composer. His style, though shaped by study in Paris with Dukas, is strongly Spanish in character.

°*Gran marcha de los subsecretarios* (ca.1941). Madrid: Unión Musical Española, 1962. US:Wc. Imposing, energetic, somewhat pompous march with Spanish flavor.

Roesgen-Champion, Mme Marguerite (1894–1976)

Swiss harpsichordist. Her compositions include symphonic works, concertos for various instruments, and piano pieces.

°*Conte bleu et or; 5 pièces* (Marche royale; Le prince amoureux; La belle fileuse; Le maître à danser; Le mariage). Paris: Lemoine, 1936. Descriptive pieces in salon style. (I)

Rogalsky, Theodor (1901–1954)

°*Two dances for winds, percussion and piano four hands* (1925). Bucharest: Editura Muzicală a Uniunii Compozitorilor din R.P.R.

Roger-Ducasse, Jean (1873–1954)

French composer whose orchestral works, motets, chamber music, and piano pieces are written in an elegant French style in the tradition of Fauré, with a tendency toward polyphonic writing.

°*Études pour un commençant* (1916–1917). Paris: Durand, 1918. Three-volume collection of engaging pieces arranged in progressive order of difficulty, with increasing harmonic and rhythmic complexity. (E-I)

°*Petite suite* (Souvenance; Berceuse; Claironnerie) (1899). Paris: Enoch, 1904; Durand, 1911. Polished, charming set of pieces in light style. (I-UI)

Rogers, Elizabeth E.

°*The adventures of primo and secondo*. New York: Heritage Music Publishing Co. (Century), 1953.

°*One plus one*. New York: Heritage Music Publishing Co. (Century), 1958. Ten little teaching pieces, charmingly set, featuring dialogues between the parts. (LE)

Rogers, James (1857–1940)

American organist, critic, and composer of sacred music, organ pieces, and piano works.

°*Alpine song*. Cincinnati: Willis, 1918. Instructional piece in bland harmonic style with yodeling repartee. (UE-LI)

Rohde, Wilhelm (1856–1928)

German pianist, violinist, and teacher; lived in Chicago and Boston for many years. He wrote orchestral, chamber, and piano pieces.

Aus jungen Tagen, 6 Stücke, Op.19. Berlin: Vieweg, 1908. US:Wc. Instructional pieces. (I)

Rohm, Johann Huldreich (late 18th cent.)

Sonate (1788). Ms. US:Wc. Short, three-movement composition in pallid Classical style; early work for the medium in a primitive setting. (LI)

Rohwer, Jens (1914–)

German teacher and composer of music for children. He has also written works for orchestra, oratorios, and instrumental compositions.

°*Kleine Serenade*. Wilhelmshaven: Heinrichshofen, ca.1954. D-brd:DSim—US:Wc. Gently moving piece in tranquil mood; mildly contemporary idiom with frequent rhythmic changes. (UE-LI)

Rolfe, Walter (1880–1944)

°*America first*. Philadelphia: Presser, n.d.

Rollino, Joseph and Paul Sheftel

°*Festivities*, for four hands (or two people). New York: Carl Fischer, 1973. Ten short merry tunes introducing various technical devices in a witty and artful way. (E)

°*Further festivities*. New York: Carl Fischer, 1976. A continuation of the preceding; exploits more complex rhythmical and technical devices while still retaining the same attractive format. (UE-LI)

Roloff, Alex

Russian dances. London: Augener, 1916. US:Wc. Teaching pieces. (LI-I)

Valses mignonnes. London: Augener, 1916. US:Wc. Teaching pieces. (UE-LI)

Romili, Alessandro

Tarantella. Boston: Oliver Ditson, 1897. US:Wc. Salon étude.(I)

Romita, E.

°*Piccolo zoo*, 5 pezzi (No.5, I gattini vanno a nanna, is for 4H, the remainder are for 2H). Milan: Carisch. n.d. (E)

Röntgen, Johannes (1898–1969)

°*Feestelijke ouverture.* Amsterdam: Donemus, 1956. NL:Ad.
°*Passacaglia en gigue.* Amsterdam: Donemus, 1952. NL:Ad.

Ropartz, Joseph Guy (1864–1955)

Breton-French conductor and composer. He wrote symphonies, liturgical works, chamber music, and piano pieces.
°*Dix petites pièces.* Paris: Rouart, n.d.

Roques, Léon

Marche des Mousquetaires. Paris: Durand, n.d. US:Wc. Charming march in bold style. (LI)

Rose, Alfred

12 Aquarellen, Op.22. Magdeburg: Heinrichshofen, 1908. US:Wc. Short, instructional pieces. (UE-LI/E-5)

Rosegger, Sepp

°*Aus der Waldheimat,* steirische Ländlersuite. Vienna: S. Stanberg (Doblinger), ca.1944. US:Wc. Tasteful settings of Austrian ländler. (I)

Rosellen, Henri (1811–1876)

French pianist and composer of pedagogical music for piano.
L'aérienne, valse brillante, Op.54. Paris: M.Schlesinger, 1843. US:Wc.

Rosenauer, Alois

Militärisches Tonbild, Charakterstück, Op.27. Berlin: Simrock, ca.1906. US:Wc. Instructional piece. (LI/E-5)
Zigeunerleben, charakteristische Tonstücke, Op.20. Berlin: Simrock, ca. 1908. US:Wc. Instructional pieces. (LI/E-5)

Rosenecker, Johann

Menuett und 6 deutsche Tänze nebst Trios und Coda. Vienna: Cappi, ca. 1826. A:Wgm.
Polonaise und 6 deutsche Tänze samt Trios und Coda. Vienna: Cappi, ca. 1827. A:Wgm.

Rosenhain, Jakob (1813–1894)

German pianist and composer; his music was influenced by Schumann and Mendelssohn.
Fantasia appassionata, grand duo (g), Op.40. Leipzig: Hofmeister, 1844. US:Wc. Large-scale work in Romantic idiom, tending toward salon music in style and content. (I)
3 Petits duos, Op.38. Paris: M. Schlesinger, ca.1841; Mainz: Schott, n.d. US:Wc.

Rosenstengel, Albrecht Arthur J. (1912–)

Schlichte Weisen; Klaviermusik über deutsche Volkslieder. Cologne: Gerig, 1953. US:Wc. Six felicitously arranged German folk songs; interest in both parts. (LI)

Rösler, Gottlob Benjamin

6 *Polonoises à quatre mains pour le clavecin ou forte piano.* Leipzig: C.F. Lehmann, n.d. D-ddr:Dl.

Ross, W.B.

Tarantella. London: Augener, 1928. GB:Lbl. Bright, lively, rhythmical piece in traditional style. (LI-I)

Rossini, Gioacchino (1792–1868)

Celebrated Italian opera composer. He also wrote liturgical works, songs, and piano pieces.

Marches, from *Péchés de Vieillesse.* I:PESc—US:NYp.

2 Pas redoublés et une marche militaire. Leipzig: B&H, n.d. US:Wc. Charming light joyful works. (I)

Rott, Clemence

°*Side by side series,* Book VI (Reverie; Valsette; The Gypsies; Boat song; March; Merrymakers). London: Ashdown, n.d. (E)

Rotter, Ludwig (1810–1895)

Divertissement (A), Op.1. Vienna: J. Czerný, ca.1829. A:Wgm.

Rougnon, Paul (1846–1934)

French piano virtuoso. He composed songs, operas, and educational piano works.

°*Coucou.* Paris: Salabert, n.d.

°*Dansez, fillettes.* Paris: Salabert, n.d.

°*En promenade.* Paris: Salabert, n.d.

°*7 Pièces faciles et brillantes* (Danse bretonne; Rondo-valse; Ballade; Galop; Carillon; Menuet gracieux; Pastorale), Op.120. Paris: Hamelle, n.d. Also sold separately.

Rousseau, Jean-Jacques (1712–1778)

French philosopher; self-taught composer. He wrote operas, instrumental and vocal works, a *Dictionnaire de musique,* and articles on musical subjects.

Duo, arrangé à quatre mains pour pianoforte par Desormerie et Piccini. Paris: LeDuc, ca.1792. DK:Km.

Roussel, Albert (1869–1937)

French composer; naval officer until 1894; studied with d'Indy. He wrote operas, ballets, symphonic and chamber music, songs, and piano works.

°*Sarabande,* from the ballet *L'Éventail de Jeanne* (q.v.). Paris: Heugel, 1927. Sombre, heavy-textured work of considerable musical interest; probably intended for orchestra since the 4H setting tends to be awkward in places. (I-UI)

Rowland, Edith

Old English dance tunes. London: Joseph Williams, 1920. US:Wc. Pleasant settings of British folk melodies. (I)

Rowley, Alec (1892–1958)

Pianist, composer, and author of one of the first English-language guides to piano 4H literature—*One Piano Four Hands* (London: OUP, 1940). Alec Rowley was also an active and respected contributor to the repertoire itself. His compositions for piano duet, which reflect his experience as a distinguished music educator, range from elementary teaching pieces to serious works of moderate difficulty, all of them solid, attractive, and skilfully cast for the four-hand medium in a refined traditional harmonic idiom.

Badinage. London: Elkin, 1952; Novello, n.d. GB:Lbl.

Barcarolle (f). London: Curwen, 1947. US:Wc. (I)

Bergerettes, 4 pieces based on French folk tunes (Berceuse; Pipers; Pastourelle; Burlesque). London: Curwen, 1957. GB:Lbl. (I)

6 *Cameos*. London: OUP, 1928; Ashdown, 1956. GB:Lbl. (LI/E)

Canzonetta. London: Curwen, n.d. (E-UE)

Carillon. In collection *Thirty-two graded pieces for piano duet*. (I)

Three centuries, suite (Through the centuries). London: Lengnick, 1933. GB:Lbl. (I)

Dignity and impudence. London: OUP, 1928; Ashdown, 1956. GB:Lbl. (LI-I/E)

5 *Divergencies* (Russian dance; Hawaiian lullaby; From France; March; Valse). London: Ashdown, 1926. GB:Lbl. (UE-LI/E-5)

4 *Duets after old nursery tunes*. London: Novello, 1935. GB:Lbl. (LI)

Graceful dance. London: Lengnick, 1951. GB:Lbl. (UE-LI)

Four impressions (Robin goodfellow; The sleepbringer; The witch; The leprechaun). London: Curwen, 1955. GB:Lbl. (UE-LI)

7 *Little marches* (Sieben kleine Märsche) (Parade march; Scottish pipe march; English festive march; Solemn march; Irish regimental march; Oriental march; Quick march), Op.47. Leipzig: Peters, 1936; NEd. 1954. (I)

Morris dance. London: Curwen, 1944. (LI)

Nautical toccata. London: Curwen, 1947. US:Wc. (I-UI)

3 Noëls. London: Elkin, 1958. (LI)

Pastorale. London: Boosey & Hawkes, 1932, 1968. (LI)

Pipe and tabor/Hare and tortoise. London: Curwen, n.d. (LE)

Polka. London: Curwen, n.d. (UE-LI)

Roving jack. London: Curwen, n.d. (I)

6 Short dance impressions (Sechs kurze Tanzstücke), Op.41. Leipzig: Peters, 1932; NEd.1952. (I)

Side by side series, Book I (Flanagan keeps a-dancin'; Highland march; Jazz band; Colin Clout's come home again; Jack Tar). London: Ashdown, n.d. (LI)

Side by side series, Book V (The organ grinder; Toy band; Dance of the moths; Peep o'day; Wooden soldier). London: Ashdown, n.d. (LI)

°*Side by side series,* Book IX (Russian dance; English dance; Scandinavian dance; French dance). London: Ashdown, n.d. (UE-LI)

Tit-for-tat. In collection *Thirty-two graded pieces for piano duet.* GB:Lbl. (E)

°*Toccatina.* London: Curwen, n.d. (I)

Valse arabesque. In collection *Thirty-two graded pieces for piano duet.* (I)

Rozin, Albert (1906–)

°*Two together.* New York: Schroeder & Gunther, 1962. Eleven tuneful pieces comfortably set for both parts. (UE-LI)

Rubertis, Victor de

°*Minué.* Buenos Aires: Ricordi, 1953. Effective teaching piece in Classical style. (LI)

Rubinstein, Anton Gregorievich (1829–1894)

Russian pianist of great distinction and composer of operas, symphonies, piano concertos, and piano pieces. Most of his works, written in facile, conservative German Romantic idiom, have long since faded.

Bal costumé, suite de 20 morceaux caractéristiques, Op.103. Berlin: Bote & Bock, ca.1880. US:NYp,Wc. Tone pictures describing various historical characters at a costume ball, each character representing a different national group and historical period. Requires advanced pianism. (UI-A)

°*Character-Bilder,* 6 Clavierstücke (Nocturne; Scherzo; Barcarole; Capriccio; Berceuse; Marche), Op.50. Leipzig: Kahnt, 1859; Paris: °Hamelle, n.d. GB:Lbl–US:PHf,Wc. Elegantly turned-out piece in salon style with interest and activity in both parts. (I-UI)

°*3 Mélodies caractéristiques* (Chanson russe; Nocturne sur l'eau; La cataracte), Op.9. Vienna: Haslinger, n.d.; Paris: °Hamelle, n.d. US:Wc. Descriptive pieces in light salon style. (I)

Sonata (D), Op.89. Berlin: Simrock, 1871; Paris: Hamelle, 1871. US:Wc. Sweeping, large-scale bravura work in three movements: Allegro; brilliant Scherzo; slow movement with well-developed fugal section. In spite of its rigorously conservative, often saccharine, harmonic idiom and its general lightweight character, the entire work is structurally imposing with skilful thematic manipulation. Excitingly pianistic throughout. (A)

Rubinstein, Nikolai Gregorievich (1835–1881)

Russian pianist, brother of Anton; founder of Moscow Conservatory. He composed many piano pieces in light Romantic style.

°*Tarantella,* Op.14. London: Augener, n.d.; °NEd. Paris: Hamelle, n.d. °NEd. rev. G.Rosati, Ancona: Bèrben, 1974. US:PHf. Brilliant display piece. (UI)

Rübner, Cornelius (1855–1929)

Marche triomphale, Op.17. Leipzig: Schuberth, ca.1889. US:Wc. Instructional piece. (I)

Rüfer, Philippe (1844–1919)

Belgian-born German composer, teacher, and pianist. He wrote operas, chamber and orchestral works, piano duets, and songs.

Scherzo (g), Op.28. Offenbach: André, 1876. D-brd:OF.

Rummel, Christian (1787–1849)

German pianist, violinist, clarinettist, and conductor. He wrote operas and vocal and instrumental music in light early Romantic style.

Amusement de société, walse (Eb). Mainz: Schott, ca.1823. US:NYp,Wc.
  Salon piece. (I)

Le délivré, valse (Eb), Op.54. Mainz: Schott, n.d.

Fantaisie sur un air écossais (Eb), Op.60. Mainz: Schott, 1826. US:Wc.
  Salon piece. (LI)

Rummel, Joseph (1818–1880)

German clarinettist and pianist; prolific arranger of operatic music for piano; also wrote piano duets.

°Boléro. Paris: Consortium Musical, n.d. (I)

Ruppe, Christian Friedrich (1753–1826)

Premières leçons pour apprendre le piano forte consistant en 6 sonatines très faciles et progressives, dont le sixième est à quatre mains à l'usage des commençans, oeuvre XIII. Leiden: by composer, n.d. NL:At.

3 *Sonates* (F,D,Eb), oeuvre V. The Hague-Amsterdam: Burchard, Hummel et fils, ca.1785. D-brd:KIl—F:Pc—NL:DHgm—S:Skma.

3 *Sonates* (c,F,D), oeuvre 16. Rotterdam: Plattner, n.d. US:BE.

Russell, Olive Nelson

°Fantasy on "In Dulce Jubilo," Boston: Boston Music, 1966. Well-balanced teaching piece, with chime effects. (LI)

°Turnabout duets (A pleasant walk; Caravan; At the ball; Country fair; The clang of the anvil; Country dance; On the march; Royal procession). Melville, NY: Pro-Art (Belwin), 1965. Tunes from the classics; rhythmic bass patterns in Secondo, melodies in Primo; excellent fare for the early pianist. (E-5)

Russell, Robert

Composer of chamber music, including a trumpet sonata and a woodwind quintet.

°Places, suite (1964), Op.9. New York: General Music Publishing Co., 1968. Unusual set of refreshing descriptive pieces in contemporary dissonant, tonal idiom. Various areas of New York and environs are depicted colorfully and with great effect. New York, N.Y.: fast and busy; uses jazz elements and quotes from the popular song "The Sidewalks of New York" concealed in a "wrong-note" hurdy-gurdy accompaniment. Brooklyn Bridge: eerie, misty effect is achieved by the Primo strumming fingernails over strings inside piano while chords soundlessly pressed down on the

keyboard by the Secondo are sustained by the middle (sostenuto) pedal. Orchard Street: unusual key signature of two sharps and two flats (resulting in a scale containing two augmented seconds) and a bright, whirling 7/8 lend an exotic Middle Eastern flavor. The Cloisters: represented first by somber chords in resonant bell-like sonorities: then when the chant "Dies Irae" is softly introduced, the tolling bells fade into silence. Central Park Green: children frolicking. The Bay at Dusk: an Impressionistic tone picture. Perambulation: has a pleasant jazzy, sauntering nonchalance.

Ruthardt, Adolf (1849–1934)

German pianist and music editor; author of piano handbook; composed chamber music and piano studies.

°*Teacher and pupil* (Lehrer und Schuler). Leipzig: °Peters, ca.1893; °Kalmus. Arrangements of folk songs, operatic arias, movements of Haydn chamber music, Handel oratorios, etc. (UE-LI/E-5,UE)

Rutini, Giovanni Marco Placido (1723–1797)

Italian composer of operas, cantatas, and keyboard music in early Classical style.

12 Divertimenti facili e brevi per cimbalo a quattro mani o arpe e cimbalo (C,G,F,C,F,C,C,F,D,A,a,D), Op.18. Pub. and date missing. I:Mc, Nc. Series of short, thin-textured pieces in various forms (including menuet and rondo), set in an early, often primitive, 4H idiom with extensive use of parallel sixths and tenths. The work is undated but it is worth mentioning that in his introduction the composer alludes to the fact that four-hand music is "a style recently introduced from England." This suggests that the Divertimenti could have conceivably been written as early as 1777 or 1778, the date of the publication of Dr. Charles Burney's four-hand sonatas, to which Rutini was doubtless referring. (LI)

S., C.A.

Two duettino's for two performers on one piano forte. London: pub. by composer, ca.1796. GB:Gh,Lbl,Ob. Very simple, largely chordal three-part pieces in colorless Classical idiom by an unidentified composer. (LI)

Saar, Louis Victor (1868–1937)

Dutch-born American teacher, pianist, and composer; wrote orchestral, choral, and chamber music in lightweight Romantic style.

5 Piano pieces. Op.21. New York: Schubert, 1897. US:Wc. Instructional music. (UE-LI)

Suite (Préambule; Contredanse; Scène d'amour; Dévise noble; Marche et polonaise), Op.27. New York: Schirmer, 1899. US:Wc. Salon pieces. (I-UI)

Saint-Aulaire, Roland
°*Les contes de Grand'mère* (Riquet à la houppe; Rêverie de Cendrillon; Cendrillon au bal; Le sommeil de la belle au bois dormant; Peau d'âne; Le petit poucet et ses frères). Paris: Jobert, 1923. (UE-LI)

Saint-Juste, Édouard
Fête polonaise. London: A. Hammond, 1926. US:Wc. Bright, rhythmical display piece in Polish style. (LI)

St-Lubin, Léon de
Grand notturno, Op.23. Vienna: Mechetti, 1829. A:Wgm.
Variations faciles et agréables sur un thème autrichien favorit (D), Op.24. Vienna: J. Czerný, ca.1829. A:Wn. Five variations on a simple Austrian yodeling theme; agreeable and unpretentious without manifesting any strong musical personality. (UE-LI)

Saint-Saëns, Camille (1835–1921)
French composer of operas, symphonies, tone poems, concertos, chamber music, songs, and piano compositions. His direct, tuneful, fastidious, often brilliant style was once held in high esteem, but its standing has diminished somewhat in recent years because of its superficiality.
°*Berceuse,* Op.105. Paris: Durand, 1896. US:Wc. Ingratiating tranquil mood piece. (LI)
°*Duettino* (G), Op.11. Paris: Hamelle, ca.1861. US:Wc. Show piece, brilliant in part. (I)
°*Feuillet d'album,* Op.81. Paris: Durand, 1887. GB:Lbl—US:Wc. (I)
König Harald Harfagar (nach H. Heine), Ballade, Op.59. Berlin: Bote & Bock, 1880. US:Wc.
Marche dédiée aux étudiants d'Alger (with chorus ad lib.), Op.163. Paris: Durand, 1922. GB:Lbl—US:Wc.
Marche interalliée, Op.155. Paris: Durand, 1919. GB:Lbl—US:Wc.
°*Pas redoublé,* Op.86. Paris: Durand, 1890. GB:Lbl—US:NYp,Wc. (I)
3 Rhapsodies. Paris: pub. missing, 1880. GB:Lbl.

Salner, G.P.
Slow march; composed for three hands on the pianoforte, or accompaniment for the German flute. London: Edward Riley, n.d. GB:Lbl.

Salomé, Théodore César (1834–1896)
French organist and teacher; wrote organ, orchestral, and piano pieces in traditional style.
°*2 Pièces* (Carillon; Notre dame des flots), Op.40. Paris: Hamelle, n.d.

Salter, Lionel (1914–   )
English pianist, harpsichordist, conductor, teacher, and critic. He has composed incidental music for radio plays, orchestral works, songs, and piano pieces in conventional style.
°*A grey day.* London: Boosey & Hawkes, 1954. GB:Lbl—US:Wc. Attractive teaching piece. (UE-LI)

°*Out in the sun.* London: Boosey & Hawkes, 1954. GB:Lbl–US:Wc. Well-crafted instructional piece. (UE-LI)

Sammartino, Luis R. (1890–)

Argentine composer of orchestral and chamber music.

°*Gato,* from *De mi Patria.* Buenos Aires: Ricordi, n.d.

°*Huella.* Buenos Aires: Ricordi, n.d.

°*Zamba de Vargas,* on popular Argentine themes. Buenos Aires: Ricordi, n.d.

Samuel, Edward

2 *Esquisses* (Romance sans paroles; Scherzo), Op.6. Mainz: Schott, n.d. Scherzo is in collection *Thirty-two graded pieces for piano duet.* (UI)

Sonatines faciles (G,G,e). Mainz: Schott, 1885. D-brd: MZsch–GB:Lbl. Alec Rowley comments in *One Piano Four Hands* that these sonatinas are "three of the most remarkable works in the whole of four-hand literature; in strict sonata form with amazingly clever modulations considering the fact that both primo and secondo are in five-finger positions throughout." (UE-5)

Samuel-Rousseau, M.

French composer of operas, ballet, and incidental theater music.

°*Menuet;* °*Valse.* Paris: Lemoine, n.d.

Sandré, Gustave

°*Marche caractéristique,* Op.13. Paris: Maho (Hamelle), ca.1875.

°*6 Pièces,* Op.10. Paris: Hamelle, n.d.

°*Valses,* Op.17. Paris: Hamelle, n.d.

°*2 Pièces,* Op.18. Paris: Hamelle, n.d.

Sandström, S.D.

°*5 Duets.* Stockholm: Nordiska Musikförlaget, n.d.

Santos, Manuel Inocêncio Liberato dos

Portuguese musician.

Quinteto (pequeno) para piano a quatro mãos, dois violinos e uma flauta, 1854. Ms. P:La.

Saran, August (1836–1922)

3 *Polonaises* (Ab,E,F), Op.3. Leipzig: Leuckart, ca.1861; New York: Carl Fischer, 1905. US:NYp,PHf,Wc. Well-written salon pieces. (I)

Sárközy, Istvan (1920–)

Hungarian; has written stage works, pieces for orchestra, choral and chamber works, and piano pieces.

°*Sonatina.* Budapest: Editio musica, 1956. Impressive, single-movement piece in Hungarian modal idiom; sparkling, melodious; unusually effective. (LI)

Satie, Erik (1866–1925)

Eccentric French composer. He cultivated a cool, clear, satirical musical style, with simple melodies and harmonies, as a revolt against the lushness of the Impessionism of Debussy and Ravel. He was a significant influence on Milhaud, Sauguet, Poulenc, and "les Six."

°*Aperçus désagréables* (Pastorale; Chorale; Fugue) (1908–1912). Paris: Eschig, 1913. Three-movement work from the composer's "Classical" period following his completion of a rigorous three-year course in composition at the Schola Cantorum. Serious, often stern, pieces in weighty chromatic style, heavily interspersed with Satie's enigmatic and amusing performance directions. (I-UI)

°*En habit de cheval* (Choral; Fugue litanique; Autre choral; Fugue de papier) (1911). Paris: Rouart, Lerolle, 1911. Though full of odd harmonic shifts, naive melodies, and other compositional eccentricities associated with Satie, this serious, skilfully written suite, which also dates from the composer's "Classical" period, is uncharacteristically somber in mood and idiom. (I-UI)

°*Trois morceaux en forme de poire* (Manière de commencement; Prolongation du même, I, II, III; En plus; Redite) (1903). Paris: Rouart, Lerolle, 1911. Satie's earliest piano duet; written in response to criticism that the composer neglected form in his music. Typical of his clownish wit and full of the harmonic and melodic naiveté, the odd and often cryptic interpretive indications, the literary allusions, and the unpredictable dynamic changes so closely associated with the composer's musical rhetoric. (I-UI)

Satter, Gustav (1832–1879)
Viennese pianist and teacher; lived briefly in U.S.

Sonate (f). Hamburg: Cranz, 1854. US:Wc. Long, brilliant, demanding four-movement work in shallow Romantic style. (UI-A)

Saupe, Christian Gottlob (1764–1819)
German organist and composer of piano pieces.

°*Sonatine* (g). Leipzig: B&H, 1792. °NEd. in collection *Vermischte Handstücke*, ed. Kreutz. Two-movement work in lean-textured Classical style; well balanced technically, but with greater interest in the Primo. (LI)

Sauvrezis, A.
°*Fresque marine*. Paris: Salabert, n.d.
°*Little piece*. Paris: Salabert, n.d.
°*Petites feuilles*. Paris: Senart, n.d. (LI)

Savage, Jane (late 18th cent.)
A *favorite duett for two performers*, Op.6. London: Longman & Broderip, ca.1790. GB:Lam,Lbl,Ob.

Schäfer, Alexander (b.1866)
Russian conductor and composer of operas, ballets, symphonic and chamber music, songs, and piano pieces.

Russian dances, Op.46. Leipzig: Zimmerman, 1900. US:Wc. Skilful arrangements of six Russian folk dances; well balanced, with rhythmic variety. (LI-I)

Schäfer, R.

°*Volks- und Kinderlieder*. Vienna: Doblinger, n.d.

Schäffer, Boguslaw (1929–)

Polish; self-taught composer; has worked with Polish folk music. In recent years he has cultivated avant-garde procedures, including tape and serial techniques and graphic notation.

°*4H/1P, Music for piano:* four hands—one piano. Berlin: Ahn & Simrock, 1968. Commissioned by Milton and Peggy Salkind. Work in post-serial idiom employing contemporary notation symbols; elegantly printed in large oblong format. Demands experienced and sophisticated pianism. (A)

Schall, Claus Nielsen

Sonate à quatre mains (in *Nordens Apollo*, 3. Jhg. pp. 119–144; also contains 2 songs and 4 Écossaises by Schall). D-brd:B—DK:Kk.

Scharwenka, Philipp (1847–1917)

The Scharwenka brothers, Philipp and Xaver, contributed generously to the four-hand medium. Xaver, a brilliant pianist, was the more successful of the two, but both men were competent and resourceful composers in the late-Romantic tradition, turning out a quantity of first-rate, elegantly crafted duets in the smaller forms. (I-UI)

All'Ongarese (bb) *und Walzer* (Eb), Op.30. Leipzig: B&H, 1879. US:PHf, Wc. Bright; deftly written. (LI-I)

Heimat, 5 Phantasietänze in polnischer Art, Op.109. Leipzig: B&H, 1900. US:Wc. (I)

Herbstbilder, 6 Klavierstücke, Op.6. Leipzig: B&H, 1885. US:Wc.

Hochzeitsmusik (Hochzeitsmarsch; Walzer; Abendmusik), Op.23. Bremen: Praeger & Meier, 1879. US:PHf,Wc. Serious pieces, skilfully set; effective. (I-UI)

Intermezzi, 5 Klavierstücke, Op.48. Berlin: Bote & Bock, 1883. US:Wc.

Marsch, Intermezzo all'ongarese, und Brautreigen, Op.42. Leipzig: Rühle, 1882. US:PHf. (I)

6 Polnische Tanzweisen, Op.38. Bremen: Praeger & Meier, 1882. US:PHf, Wc. Pleasant folk-song settings; brisk, with well-balanced activity. (I)

3 Scherzi (e,F,bb), Op.91. Leipzig: B&H, 1893. US:Wc. (I)

Suite de danses caractéristiques (b,Eb,d,f♯,f,c♯), Op.78. Breslau: Hainauer, 1888. US:Wc. (I-UI)

Tanz-Novelle, 5 Tanz-poeme mit einem Intermezzo und Epilog, Op.103. Leipzig: B&H, 1898. US:Wc. (I)

Tanz-Suite (Polonaise; Mazurka; Menuett; Tarantella), Op.21. Leipzig: B&H, 1877, 1898. US:PHf,Wc. (UI)

5 Tanzscenen (Maskentanz; Lenzreigen; Pas de deux; Brautreigen; Polnischer Tanz), Op.75. Breslau: Hainauer, 1887. US:PHf;Wc. (I)

Scharwenka, Xaver (1850–1924)

See note under Philipp Scharwenka.

Aus alter und neuer Zeit, vier Tänze (Gavotte; Menuetto; Mazurka; Walzer), Op.24. Bremen: Praeger & Meier, 1875. US:Wc. (I)

Bilder aus dem Süden, Op.39. London: Augener, n.d. US:Wc. (I-UI)

Nordisches, Op.21. Berlin: Simon, 1875. US:PHf,Wc. Two melodious tone pictures on Scandinavian subjects in fluent style. (I)

°*Suite de danses* (Tanz-Suite) (Alla marcia; Gavotte; Menuetto; Bolero), Op.41. Leipzig: °Peters, 1881; New York: Schirmer, 1905. GB:Lbl—US: Bp,PHf,Wc. Attractive pieces; effectively written in tuneful, salon style. (I)

2 *Walzer* (D,Eb), Op.44. London: Augener, 1879; Leipzig: Peters, 1881. GB:Lbl.

Schaum, John W. (1905–   )

American teacher and composer; author of piano method and many instructional pieces for piano.

°*Blue boogie.* New York: Belwin, 1946. Teaching piece in jazz style. (UE-LI)

°*The "eggs pert" hen.* Melville, NY: Belwin, 1953. Teaching piece with pun-filled text to help pullet off. (E)

Schelb, Joseph (1894–   )

German composer and teacher. His works include symphonic and chamber music, an opera, and piano pieces.

°*Kleine Sonate.* Heidelberg: Süddeutscher Musikverlag (Willy Müller), 1943. Jovial rhythmical work with bright melodies. Neo-Classical style with linear textures predominating. Echoes of Hindemith in the structure and harmony, and hints of a cool French touch here and there. The first movement, Lebhaft, is lively and strongly rhythmical; the second, Ruhig, liedhaft, is lyrical and quietly flowing; and the work ends with the very fast and exciting Rasch, sehr straff. The sonata is carefully balanced and effectively set; excellent fare for the young advancing pianist. (LI-I)

Scher, William (1900–   )

American composer whose prodigious output of instructional piano music includes a quantity of bright, unpretentious four-hand pieces set in a well-worn and predictable conservative style. However, the music is useful—it is attractive, is always playable, and generates an instant, though often short-lived, appeal. (UE-LI)

°*Arabian dance.* Melville, NY: Pro-Art, n.d. Short piece employing Middle Eastern scale patterns. (LE-E)

°*At the circus.* New York: Century Music, n.d. Bright, jolly piece. (UE)

°*Blue candle light.* Melville, NY: Pro-Art, 1970. Soft, lyrical piece. (UE)

°*A Chinese fairy tale.* Melville, NY: Pro-Art, n.d. Short work employing clichés of oriental music. (UE)

Csardas rhapsody. Melville, NY: Pro-Art, n.d. Short piece featuring Hungarian folk rhythms. (UE)

Dancing mosquitoes. Melville, NY: Pro-Art, 1954. (UE)

For four hands (Campus capers; Girl with the silver baton; Gypsy camp fire; March of the giants; Music box minuet; Polka of the wooden soldiers; Spanish fiesta; Waltzing by candle light). Melville, NY: Pro-Art, 1962. (E)

Happy go lucky. New York: Carl Fischer, 1960. Also in collection *Four hands at the keyboard.*

Hobby Horse. Melville, NY: Pro-Art, 1970. Rhythmical little piece. (E)

Hungarian wedding scene. Melville, NY: Belwin, 1969. Short piece in traditional Hungarian folk style. (LI)

Jolly little Chinaman. Boston: Boston Music., n.d. The pentatonic scale provides color for this short piece. (E-UE)

Little Cossack. New York: Sam Fox, 1959. Very short piece with Russian flavor. (UE)

March of the green berets. Melville, NY: Pro-Art, 1971. Rhythmical piece on a strutting martial theme. (UE)

Movie mystery. New York: Sam Fox, n.d. Short piece using familiar haunted-house sound-effect clichés. (E)

Peasant dance. Melville, NY: Pro-Art, n.d. Lively, high-stepping, rhythmical little tune. (E-UE)

Polka dot polka. Melville, NY: Pro-Art, 1970. Lively dance. (UE)

Polka time in Vienna. New York: Schroeder & Gunther, 1964. Bustling dance tune. (UE-LI)

Rhapsody for two. Melville, NY: Pro-Art, n.d. (E)

Rocking horse polka. New York: Sam Fox, 1957. (E)

Scooter race. Melville, NY: Pro-Art, n.d. Lively piece featuring simple melody and accompaniment. (UE)

6 Sketches for two players (Cuckoo waltz; Gnomes; From a hurdy-gurdy; In the days of the covered wagon; March of the little sergeants; Sparklets). Boston: Boston Music, 1963. Short pieces in various styles. (E)

Valse Romany. New York: Century Music, 1966. Gypsy rhythms and melodic patterns are featured. (E)

Waltzing peacock. Melville, NY: Pro-Art, n.d. Short, stately waltz. (UE)

Schickele, Peter (1935–)

American composer, pianist, and musical satirist; studied with Bergsma and Persichetti.

The civilian barber, overture. Philadelphia: Elkan-Vogel, 1963. Merry, witty spoof in the style of a Rossini overture with a dash of Beethoven; cleverly set, well balanced; great entertainment. (I)

Toot suite (S212°) (1967). Bryn Mawr: Theodore Presser, 1973. Another of the composer's good-natured and wittily arranged musical stunts.

Though specifically written for steam calliope or organ, at least two of the movements, O.K. Chorale and Fuga vulgaris, can be performed quite effectively on the piano—even without the "toot" of the calliope called for in the score to punctuate the end of each phrase of the fugal subject, the first phrase of the Song of the Volga Boatmen. (I)

Schillio, Émile

°*Morning in Madrid.* Philadelphia: Presser, 1949. Salon piece in Spanish style. (LI)

Schiske, Karl (1916–1969)

Hungarian-born Austrian composer; wrote in contrapuntal, neo-Classical idiom.

°*Sonata* (1949), Op.29. Vienna: Doblinger, 1957. US:Wc. Compact, linear work; makes no excessive demands on performers. (I)

Schlechter, Mathias

3 *Marches avec trio,* Op.4. Vienna: Mollo, 1829. A:Wgm,Wn.

Schlesinger, S.

7 *Melodious duets.* Philadelphia: Presser, 1904. US:Wc. Instructional pieces. (UE/E-5)

Schloër, B. T.

La sympathie, divertissement, Op.18. Rotterdam: Plattner, n.d. US:Wc. Set of attractive variations in lightweight, early-Romantic style. (I)

Schloër, François and Jean Ancot, fils

Fantaisie. Paris: Victor Dufaut, ca.1825. GB:Lbl. Set of florid variations on a simple theme; salon in style but not without a certain charm and sparkle. (I)

Schmid, Heinrich Kaspar (1874–1953)

German pianist and teacher. His compositions are written in late-Romantic style.

°*Bayerische Ländler,* Op.36. Mainz: Schott, 1921. Attractive set of ländler cast in a tonal idiom related to those of Richard Strauss and Reger. (I)

°*Freut euch des Lebens,* 20 Volkslieder in neuem Satz, Op.93 (1937). Mainz: Schott, n.d. (LI)

Schmid, Josef (ca.1770–1828)

6 *Allemandes avec trios,* Op.9. Vienna: Cappi, ca.1810. A:Wgm.

Sonata, Op.25. Vienna: Mollo, ca.1803. US:Wc. Brief, two-movement work; harmonically thin; pedagogical in intent. (LI)

Schmitt, Aloys (1788–1866)

German pianist and teacher. He composed concertos, chamber music, and liturgical works in addition to a quantity of instructional piano music.

Grande sonate (G), No.3, Op.23. Berlin: Schlesinger, n.d.

Grosses Tongemälde, Op.45. Leipzig: Probst, ca.1824. US:Wc. (I)

Introduction et variations sur un air des matelots hollandais (Bb). Rotterdam: L.Coenen, 1835. US:Wc. (I)

4 Marches, Op.36. Mainz: Schott, ca.1822. US:Wc. (I)

Marsch den zur Befreyung des Griechen helfenden Deutschen gewidmet (Eb). Offenbach: André, n.d. US:Wc. (I)

Scherzo (Eb), Op.42. Offenbach: André, ca.1824; NEd. 1871. US:Wc. (I)

Sonata (A), No.2, Op.22. Berlin: Schlesinger, ca.1823. US:Wc. This work and Op.21 are pedagogical sonatas, rambling and academic. (I)

Variations sur un thème original (A), Op.25. Berlin: Schlesinger, n.d. US: Wc. (I)

Variations (Bb), No.4. Offenbach: André, ca.1824. US:Wc. Routine instructional work; dry, plodding, lacking in imaginative writing. (I)

Schmitt, Florent (1870–1958)

French composer; student of Massenet and Fauré. He cultivated a heavy-textured style incorporating elements of French Impressionism with Classical structures and often employed unusual rhythmical devices. His compositions include ballets, choral and chamber music, orchestral works, and piano pieces.

°*Feuillets de voyage* (Aus meinen Wanderjahren) (Sérénade; Visite; Compliments; Douceur du soir; Danse brittanique; Berceuse; Mazurka; Marche burlesque; Retour à l'endroit familier; Valse), Op.26. Paris: Durand, 1905; Berlin: Schlesinger, 1905. Suite of attractive character pieces describing the composer's travels in his younger years. (I-UI)

°*8 Courtes pièces*, préparatoires à la musique contemporaine (Ouverture; Menuet; Chanson; Sérénade; Virelai; Boléro; Complainte; Cortège), Op. 41. Paris: Heugel, 1909. Melodious, dextrously written pieces, exceptionally well set for the medium; Secondo somewhat demanding; very useful. (I-UI/UE-LI-5)

°*6 Humoresques* (Marche militaire; Rondeau; Bucolique; Scherzetto; Valse sentimentale; Danse grotesque), Op.43. Paris: S. Chapelier, 1912. Delightful, imaginative, descriptive pieces. (I/UE-LI)

°*Kermesse-Valse*, from the ballet *L'Éventail de Jeanne* (q.v.). Paris: Heugel, 1927. Rousing waltz in Viennese style. (UI)

°*Musiques foraines* (Parade; Boniment des clowns; La belle Fathma; Les éléphants savants; La pythonisse; Chevaux de bois), Op.22. Paris: Hamelle, 1901. Set of six rather long descriptive pieces in traditional harmonic idiom depicting circus subjects. (UI)

7 Pièces (Somnolence; Souvenir de Ribeaupierre; Scintillement; Souhaite de jeune fille; Promenade à l'étang; Fête septentrionale; Traversée heureuse) (1899), Op.15. Paris: Leduc, 1901. US:Wc. Tidy set of pieces in the composer's characteristic flowing and lyrical style; excellent fare for student and teacher. (LI-I)

°*3 Pièces récréatives* (Quadrille; Gavotte; Marche), Op.37. Paris: Hamelle, ca.1907. Diverting set of pieces with ingeniously written Secondo complementing the easy Primo part. (I/UE-LI-5)

°*Reflets d'Allemagne;* 8 valses (Heidelberg; Coblentz; Lübeck; Werder; Vienne; Dresde; Nuremberg; Munich), Op.28. Paris: Mathot, 1906. Bracing, rhythmical waltzes describing the composer's impressions of various German and Austrian cities. (I)

°*Une semaine de petit elfe ferme-l'oeil,* ou, les songes de Hialmar, d'après Hans Christian Andersen (La noce des souris; La cicogne lasse; Le cheval de ferme l'oeil; Le mariage de la poupée Berthe; La ronde des lettres boiteuses; La promenade à travers le tableau; Le parapluie chinois), Op.58. Paris: Durand, 1913. Suite of imaginative and skilfully arranged pieces. The composer has succeeded in creating works of great beauty and enchantment within the limited note range of the Primo part. Rich in harmonic and rhythmic variety; challenging for both parts. (UI-A/UE-LI-5)

°*Sur cinq notes,* petite suite (Ronde; Barcarolle; Mazurka; Bercement; Danse pyrénéenne; Mélodie; Pastorale; Farandole), Op.34. Paris: Max Eschig, 1907. Charming set of eight pieces; innocent and simple melodies in the Primo with sophisticated harmonic accompaniments in the Secondo. French in style and character, subtle, colorful, atmospheric. (I-UI/UE-5)

Schmitt, Jacob (1803–1853)

German pianist and teacher, brother of Aloys. He wrote a quantity of pieces, études, methods, and other pedagogical works for piano, a selection of which are listed below.

Cantabile et rondo (A), Op.63. Hamburg: Cranz, n.d. US:Wc. Instructional work in routine Classical style. (LI)

8 *Instructive Sonatinen,* Op.208 (C,F,G,G); Op.209 (F,a,a,A). Leipzig: Schuberth, ca.1845; Leipzig: Peters, n.d.; B&H, n.d. US:PHf. (LI)

Introduction et variations (F), Op.102. Hamburg: Schuberth, n.d. US:PHf. Predictable, trite. The Primo bears most of the melodic burden, often in octaves; the Secondo has largely accompanying figure. (LI-I)

Introduction et variations (Eb), Op.119. Hamburg: Schuberth, n.d. US:PHf. Similar to preceding work in structure and musical character. (LI-I)

Introduction et variations faciles (A), Op.79. Offenbach: André, ca.1825. US:Wc. Instructional work. (LI)

2 *Märsche* (Eb,E), Op.2. Offenbach: André, ca.1822. US:Wc. (UE-LI)

Rondeau facile et agréable (a), Op.92. Offenbach: André, n.d. US:NYp. Instructional. (UE-LI)

Sonate facile (D), Op.31. Offenbach: André, NEd.1868. US:PHf. (UE-LI)

Sonata (G), Op.46. Offenbach: André, ca.1828. US:NYp. Moderately long instructional work in three movements. (UE-LI)

2 *Sonatines faciles,* Op.118. Offenbach: André, n.d. D-brd:OF.

Variations (D), Op.30. Offenbach: André, ca.1826. US:Wc. Instructional work. (UE-LI)

Variations (thème original) (Eb), Op.58. Brunswick: Spehr, n.d. US:Wc.

Schmitt, Susan
*Easy tunes for two. Boston: Boston Music, n.d.

Schoberlechner, Franz (1797–1843)
German pianist, conductor, and composer; pupil of Hummel. He wrote operas, liturgical and symphonic music, chamber works, and piano pieces.
Rondeau (e), Op.5. Vienna: Pennauer, n.d. I:Nc. Long, serious work in Classical style; melodically weak; repetitious. (LI)

Schoenberg, Arnold (1874–1951)
See Josef Rufer, *The Works of Arnold Schoenberg*, trans. Dika Newlin from original German ed. of 1959 (London: Faber & Faber, 1962).
Phantasia for piano to [sic] *four hands*. Ms. incomplete (1937). Rufer catalogue II.B.7.
6 Stücke für Klavier zu vier Händen (c,C,a,E,G,c) (1896). Los Angeles: Belmont Music Publishers, 1973. Rufer catalogue II.B.1. Six short, contrasting pieces in the composer's early post-Romantic style with strong echoes of Brahms and Dvořák. Fresh and melodious, although uneven in quality. (LI-I)
These two works are included in *Arnold Schoenberg Sämtliche Werke*, Abt. II: Klavier- und Orgelmusik, Reihe A, Bd.5, ed. C.M. Schmidt. Mainz: Schott, 1973.

Schreker, Franz (1878–1934)
Austrian teacher; composed operas, chamber symphony, and a ballet, *The Birthday of the Infanta*, from which the following work is probably derived.
Der Geburtstag der Infantin, Tanz-Suite. Vienna: UEd, 1909. US:Wc. Descriptive tone pictures; skilfully set for 4H. (I)

Schroeder, Hermann (1904–)
German teacher and choral director; his compositions reflect his interest in polyphonic textures.
Rondino capriccioso (a). In collection *Spielbuch, zeitgenössischer Originalkompositionen*. Sprightly work in mildly contemporary idiom with linear texture, scale passages, and quartal harmony. (I-UI)

Schröter, C. F.
Sonate facile, Op.4. Offenbach: André, n.d. D-brd:OF.

Schubart, Christian Friedrich Daniel (1739–1791)
German organist and conductor. He composed operettas, cantatas, songs, and piano pieces; also wrote the poems of several of Franz Schubert's songs.
Sonata (C), (with three sonatas for two hands), in *Etwas für Klavier und Gesang von Schubart*. CH:Zz.

Schubert, Franz (1797–1828)
Not only was Schubert one of the most prolific composers for the four-hand medium, but his contributions to duet literature are, for the most part, of

uniform excellence. Many of them must be counted among his finest works; a few are masterpieces. Schubert was especially sensitive to the duet medium and seemed almost more comfortable writing for it than for solo piano. Schubert's abundant and astonishingly varied four-hand music is a treasury of melodic invention, emotional range, rhythmic excitement, and architectural strength, from the delicate and lyrical smaller compositions to the grand and intense major works.

The complete editions and supplementary collections of Schubert's four-hand works are listed first, followed by descriptive entries by categories: Allegros, Dances, Divertissements, Fantasies, Fugue, Marches, Overtures, Polonaises, Rondos, Sonatas, and Variations. Within each category the works are listed chronologically, and publishers are given for pieces available separately. The final listing is of collections of selected works. Opus numbers are given whenever they occur, and the designation "D" refers to Otto Deutsch, *Schubert: Thematic Catalogue of All His Works in Chronological Order* (London: J. M. Dent, 1951).

Complete Editions (with exceptions as indicated):

Franz Schubert, Complete Works, vol.4 (T1326). New York: Dover. A single-volume reprint of the Breitkopf & Härtel Critical Edition of 1884–1897, (*Franz Schubert's Werke*. Kritisch durchgesehene Gesamtausgabe) Series 9 (1885). Complete except for *Deutscher Tanz und zwei Ländler*, D.618; *Overture* (g), D.668; *Overture to Alfonso und Estrella*, D.773; and *Overture to Fierrabras*, D.798.

°Franz Schubert: Werke für Klavier zu vier Händen, 3 vols. Munich: G. Henle. Complete except for *Overture* (g), D.668; *Overture to Alfonso und Estrella*, D.773; and *Overture to Fierrabras*, D.798.

°Franz Schubert: Original compositions for piano four hands, Kalmus ed., 5 vols. Melville, NY: Belwin.

°Schubert: Original compositions. Piano four hands, 4 vols. New York: Peters.

The Kalmus and Peters editions are complete except for *Fantasias* D.1, D.9, and D.48; *Deutscher Tanz und zwei Ländler*, D.618; *Zwei deutsche Tänze*, D.783; and *Overtures* D.592, D.597, D.668, D.773, and D.798.

Supplementary Collections:

°Franz Schubert, Complete works, vol.18. New York: Dover. Reprint of Breitkopf & Härtel Critical Edition, Series 21 (1897). Contains *Overtures* D.668, D.773, and D.798.

°Ländler for four hands, ed. Kinsky. Mainz: Schott Ed. 2338. Contains *Deutscher Tanz und zwei Ländler*, D.618, and *Zwei deutsche Tänze*, D.783 (both missing from Kalmus and Peters editions); *Vier Ländler*, D.814; and *Eleven Ländler*, D.366 (which Brahms arranged for 4H from Schubert's original piano solo version). The order and key signatures of the *Eleven Ländler*, with deviations from the original Schubert numberings

and keys, are as follows: 1 (A); 2 (A); 3 (a); 4 (a); 5 (a); 6 (C); 7 [orig. 8] (D); 8 [orig. 9 in B] (b); 9 [10] (b); 10 [12] (eb); 11 [13] (bb).

Allegros:

Allegro moderato (C) and *Andante* (a), also called Sonatine, D.968 (1828, or possibly as early as 1812). °*Allegro moderato* available separately. Leipzig: VEB B&H. The authenticity of these two minor works has been questioned. However, they are ingratiating and quite easy to play; the structure of both is simple; and the themes are melodious. (LI-I)

Allegro (a) ("Lebensstürme"), Op.posth. 144 D.947 (1828). Considered by some to be part of a larger composition, this extended single-movement piece in sonata form is one of Schubert's most dramatic and exciting works, containing sharp contrasts of mood, tender lyricism, and fiery passion. The bold main theme is orchestral in character. The second subject, subdued and gently moving, is introduced and soon embellished with delicate rising and falling scale passages, triple pianissimo. The dramatic and concisely organized development section leads into a return of the two themes and to a brief, fervent coda. (A)

Dances:

Deutscher Tanz with two trios and coda (G), and *Two Ländler* (E), D.618 (1818). The first trio (G) of the *Deutscher Tanz* is identical with that of No.7 of *Seventeen Ländler* (also known as *Deutsche Tänze*) for piano solo, D.366. The second of the *Two Ländler* was originally intended as a trio to the first. The manuscript of these two fresh, charming dances was first discovered by Brahms in the library of his friend Julius Stockhausen. Unpublished until 1934, they are available in °*Ländler for four hands* from Schott, as well as in Schubert's complete four-hands works published by °Henle-Verlag. (LI-I)

Zwei deutsche Tänze (Eb,C), Op.33, D.783 (1824). Delightful, short, melodious dances also occurring in a version for 2H. Published by °Schott and °Henle only. (LI/I)

Vier Ländler (Eb,Ab,c,C), D.814 (1824). Fresh and tuneful, these four short pieces are Schubert's easiest 4H works. (UE-LI)

Eleven Ländler, D.366, arr. for piano 4H by Johannes Brahms. See °*Ländler for four hands* in Supplementary Collections.

Divertissements:

Divertissement à la hongroise (g), Op.54, D.818 (1824). Written after the composer had spent a vacation at the Esterházy estate in Zseliz, where he was first introduced to Hungarian music. Extended work in three sections: Andante; a short Marcia; and Allegretto. The music has a strong Hungarian flavor, modal at times, with pronounced Magyar rhythms, florid cadenzas, and imitations of cimbalom tremolos. According to one source the work also contains an actual Hungarian folk melody Schubert is said to have overheard a servant singing as she worked in the Esterházy kitchen.

Divertissement (à la française) (e), Op.63 and Op.84/1 and 2, D.823/1,2, and 3 (ca.1825). There seems to be no question that this brilliant, large-scale work, built on three marchlike themes, was conceived and written as one three-movement composition. However, it was divided by the publisher, apparently without Schubert's consent, and the movements were issued singly with different titles and opus numbers: 1. *Divertissement en forme d'une marche brillante et raisonnée*, Op.63. °Leipzig: VEB B&H. The dazzling, technically demanding, opening movement is in sonata form with a strong, assertive main theme and a lyrical second theme. Energetic development with brilliant passage work; exciting climaxes. 2. *Andantino varié*, Op.84/1. °Leipzig: VEB B&H. The beguiling, tranquil, jewel-like middle movement maintains its dreamy quality throughout the three exquisite variations. Contains some of the most delicate writing in Schubert's 4H works. 3. *Rondeau brillant sur des motifs originaux français*, Op.84/2, though somewhat less inspired than the other movements, is melodious and well written. A simple rhythmical pattern, introduced as part of the first theme, develops into a repeated dactylic figure that pushes its way on with relentless drive to the end of the piece. (I-LA)

Fantasies:

Fantasia (G), D.1 (1810). Rambling youthful work; long, repetitious, and lacking in formal organization but offering occasional glimpses of the more mature Schubert, especially in the Allegretto section. (I)

Fantasia (g), D.9 (1811). Discursive and naive, but somewhat shorter and more compact than the preceding Fantasia. Demonstrates greater control of the thematic and formal development. (I-UI)

Fantasia (c), D.48 (1813). Early work; impressive for its use of chromaticism and counterpoint, although there are occasional crudities in writing and in the sequence of sections. It appeared in two versions, first as *Grosse Sonate* and later as *Fantasia* with a concluding fugue. (I-UI)

°*Fantasia*(f), Op.103, D.940 (1828). New York: Schirmer. Schubert's best-known 4H work and one of the great masterpieces of the medium. Represents the composer at the height of his creative powers in its harmonic richness and orchestral color, its haunting melodies and rhythmic vitality, and especially in its structural inventiveness and cohesion. In formal design and organization the work reflects the influence of Mozart, notably the two Fantasies, K.603 (f) for organ or piano 4H and K.475 (c) for solo piano. The fantasy begins with one of Schubert's most sublime and radiant melodies; it is developed and expanded and soon progresses into a dotted-note Largo section in French overture style, which in turns gives way to a brilliant Allegro vivace scherzo and trio. A return of the first theme leads into a fugal development of the closing theme of the first section. A fiery, sonorous coda follows, and a final quiet reiteration of the first theme concludes the work. (UI-A).

Fugue:

°*Fugue* (e), for organ or piano duet, Op.posth.152, D.952 (1828). Leipzig: VEB B&H. Originally written for organ, this fugue was composed as the result of a lighthearted competition between Schubert and his friend Franz Lachner to celebrate their visit to a Cistercian abbey during a summer walking tour. Following traditional contrapuntal practice, Schubert wrote the four-voice fugue on four staves instead of two, in order to extend the range of the individual voices. Under the mistaken assumption that the work was intended as a piano duet, the *Fugue* has traditionally been included in collections of the composer's complete 4H works. As an academic exercise the *Fugue* is irreproachably correct, but its principal interest lies in its unexpected chromaticisms. (I)

Marches:

Three marches héroïques (b,C,D), Op.27, D.602 (1818). Spirited, melodious works. The first march is the most interesting; short and compact. The second and third have harmonic and rhythmic variety, though they tend to be somewhat spun-out. (I-UI) °Op.27/3, D.602/3. Ancona: Bèrben.

Three marches militaires (D,G,Eb), Op.51, D.733 (ca.1822). Begins with the familiar Marche militaire (D). Charming, lightweight marches in popular style. They have a bandlike quality but are nonetheless very Schubertian in the variety and richness of their melodic and harmonic development. (I-UI) °Op.51/1, D.733/1. Mainz: Schott; New York: Schirmer; Paris: Consortium Musical; Milan: Ricordi.

Six grandes marches and trios (Eb,g,d,D,eb,E), Op.40, D.819 (1824). Extraordinarily fine series; abundance of dynamic and harmonic shifts and ever-present lyricism. Mood ranges from brilliant and exciting in the opening march; through the Hungarian style of the third; the slow, introspective dirgelike solemnity of the fifth; to the exuberant final work of the group with its enchanting trio. (UI-LA)

°*Grande marche funèbre à l'occasion de la mort de sa majesté Alexandre I, empereur de toutes les Russies* (c), Op.55, D.859 (1825). Leipzig: VEB B&H. It is not known what prompted Schubert to commemorate the death of Czar Alexander I of Russia in the present work, or the coronation of Czar Nicholas I in the following one. Possibly he was hoping for some modest financial remuneration from the Russian court. In any case he honored both historical events with stirring, imaginative marches, written in his most refined style. The first is a solemn funeral march with dotted rhythms and a trio featuring drum-roll figures in the Secondo part.

°*Grande marche héroïque composée à l'occasion du sacre de sa majesté Nicolas I, empereur de toutes les Russies* (a), Op.66, D.885 (1826). Leipzig: VEB B&H. Similar in character to D.859, but longer and with a much more complex and advanced formal structure. The opening festive Maestoso is followed by a contrasting Trio (I), a well-developed Allegro giusto section, and a second Trio (II). The return of the full Allegro giusto gives way to the coda, with detailed references to Trio I and to the beginning Maestoso. A remarkable work, abounding in melodic variety; approaches the *Fantasia* (f), D.940, in the grand scale of its architectural design. (UI-LA)

Two marches caractéristiques (C,C), Op.posth.121, D.886 (1826). Brilliantly exciting, energetic marches in 6/8 time; similar in their joyous sparkle and dynamic drive. (UI-LA)

°*Children's march* (*Kindermarsch*) (G), D.928. New York: Schirmer. Schubert's only essay into writing for children, this is one of his easiest and, at the same time, most perfunctory works. It was written for the birthday of a friend's young son. (UE-LI)

Overtures:

With the exception of *Overture* (F), D.675, and possibly *Overture* (g), D.668, the Overtures below are four-hand arrangements made by the composer from his original orchestral versions; they are especially noteworthy for the sensitivity and creative skill Schubert used in transferring his own symphonic works to small, chamber-music proportions.

Overture "im italienischen Stile" (D), D.592 (1817), arr. from D.590. (UI)

Overture "im italienischen Stile" (C), D.597 (1817), arr. from D.591. (UI)

Overture (g), D.668 (1819). Because of its orchestral character and layout, this is most likely a 4H sketch of a lost or never-completed symphonic work. It is nonetheless charming, melodious, and effective in its duet version. (UI)

Overture (F), Op.34, D.675 (1819). Originally written for 4H. Long, diffuse, undistinguished work with engaging moments, but fails to generate very much musical interest. (UI)

Overture to *Alfonso und Estrella*, Op.69, D.773 (1822), arr. for 4H in 1823. (UI)

Overture to *Fierrabras*, D.798 (ca.1824). (UI)

Polonaises:

Four polonaises (d,Bb,E,F), Op.75, D.599 (1818).

Six polonaises (d,F,Bb,D,A,E), Op.61, D.824 (1825). Both sets of these delightful short pieces, similar in form to the marches, are fresh and rich in inventiveness, containing some of Schubert's most lyrical and engaging music; several of the trios are especially felicitous in their grace and delicacy. (I-UI)

°*Polonaise* (d), Op.61/1, D.599/1. Ancona: Bèrben.

°*Ten polonaises*, Op.61, D.824 and Op.75, D.599. Leipzig: VEB Peters.

Polonaise (Bb), D.618A, completed for practical use by Fr. Reinhard van Hoorickx, Provisory Edition (pro manuscripto), n.d. US:Wc. Competent reconstruction in Schubertian style from a manuscript in the Houghton Library of Harvard University; a curiosity. (I-UI)

Rondos:

Rondo (D) ("Notre amitié est invariable"), Op.posth.138, D.608 (1818). A work in the composer's lighter vein, this gem charmingly combines a lilting melody in the nature of a polonaise, elusive harmonic shifts, florid passages, and frequent contrasts in instrumental color. The crossed hands at the end provide an amusing diversion, perhaps a whimsical commentary on the subtitle. (UI-LA)

Rondo (Grand rondeau) (A), Op.107, D.951 (1828). One of the most direct and accessible of Schubert's 4H pieces. This extended work is instantly appealing with its haunting lyrical melodies, harmonic subtlety, and effective writing for both parts. (UI-A)

Sonatas:

°*Sonata* (Grande sonate) (Bb), Op.30, D.617 (1818). Ancona: Bèrben, 1876. An early work, this three-movement sonata is set in a broad structural framework and shows a mastery of form and skill in the manipulation of thematic materials. It is full of melodic warmth, orchestral color and harmonic variety. The opening movement, Allegro moderato, is prefaced by a short cadenza; the graceful first theme and its companion second theme in triplets are richly developed in melodious passages with unexpected modulations. The lyrical Andante con moto second movement is one of the composer's most beautiful creations. The finale is a flowing Allegretto. (UI-LA)

Sonata (Grand duo) (C), Op.posth.140, D.812 (1824). This monumental four-movement work is filled with soaring lyricism and emotional intensity; at times it is brilliant, at others delicate and tender. Although it is symphonic in scope and frequently emphasizes orchestral textures, it remains thoroughly pianistic in feeling and setting. The extraordinary structure of the sonata and the demands it makes on the performers often seem to exceed the expressive and technical powers of the piano, an impression that suggests the work may be an arrangement of a projected or lost symphony. Robert Schumann was the first to voice this opinion and was supported by a number of critics; more recently, however, the theory has been disputed. Joseph Müller-Blattau, the German musicologist, offered a reasonable compromise in "Zur Geschichte und Stilistik des vierhändigen Klaviersatzes," *Jahrbuch der Musikbibliothek Peters für 1940*, XLVII (Leipzig, 1941). He describes the work as the "first four-hand symphony," pointing to its specific pianistic effects, which are used in conjunction with other features more characteristic of symphonic style. The first movement of the Sonata, Allegro moderato, opens simply with a gentle theme in octaves; passage work in triplets and orchestral-sounding bass tremolos lead into the songlike second theme introduced in the Secondo. Free modulation and thematic imitation are effectively used throughout the movement. The tranquil and graceful Andante follows, with moments of unusual harmonic color and suggestions of Beethoven second movements. The brilliant Scherzo, a driving Allegro vivace with some dramatic biting dissonances, contrasts with the veiled quality of the enigmatic and unearthly Trio. The work concludes with an energetic Finale, exciting and forceful. One of the towering achievements of Schubert's creative life, the Sonata is a nobly inspired and prodigious masterpiece, and one of the most challenging works of the 4H repertoire. (A)

Variations:

Introduction and variations on an original theme (Bb), Op.posth.82/2, D. 603 (1818). This amiable, flowing set of four variations is an early work that alternates between tranquil and brilliant passages, and concludes with a jovial Vivace finale filled with echoes of Ländler and German dances. Nottebohm placed this work among Schubert's "spurious and doubtful" compositions when it first appeared in 1860, but subsequent scholarship has confirmed its authenticity. (UI-LA)

Eight variations on a French song (E), Op.10, D.624 (1818). Schubert's first published duet (1822). This set of genial variations was dedicated to Beethoven, who criticized the score and encouraged the young composer. The variations are set in artful Schubertian style, and while not as fully developed as later works, they are alive, interesting, and full of melodic and harmonic invention. (UI-LA)

Eight variations on an original theme (Ab), Op.35, D.813 (1825). The longest and most diversified of the composer's works in this form. Here Schubert is particularly inspired and imaginative as he subjects his theme—broad, stately, and eloquent—to the most ingenious and versatile kind of development, submerging it in florid passages, refining it into a solemn and plaintive chorale, or permitting it to burst into brilliant flashes of color and rhythmic excitement. It is a work rich in variety and invention. (UI-LA)

°*Eight variations on a theme from Hérold's opera Marie* (C), Op.82/1, D. 908 (1827). Leipzig: VEB B&H. Difficult set of variations written in the last year of the composer's life and based on a theme from a currently successful French opera. Although the work is not as absorbing or ingratiating as the other sets of variations, the writing is sure-handed and effective throughout. (UI-A)

Collections of Selected Works:

°*Children's march*, D.928; *Four Ländler*, D.814. Mainz: Schott, n.d.

°*Children's march*, D.928; *Four Ländler*, D.814; *Marche militaire* (D), Op. 61/1, D.733/1. Ancona: Bèrben, n.d.

°*Ländler und Stücke*, leichte Originalkompositionen. Leipzig: VEB Peters.

°*Marches*. Copenhagen/London: Hansen (Chester), n.d.

°*Two marches caractéristiques*, Op.posth.121, D.886. Leipzig: VEB Peters.

°*Six marches*, Op.40, D.819. Leipzig: VEB Peters, n.d.

°*Eighteen marches*. New York: Peters, n.d. *Three marches héroïques*, Op.27,

D.602; *Six grand marches*, Op.40, D.819; *Three marches militaires*, Op. 51, D.733; *Marcia* from *Divertissement à la hongroise*, Op.54, D.818; *Grande marche funèbre*, Op.55, D.859; *Grande marche héroïque*, Op.66, D.885; *Two marches caractéristiques*, Op.posth.121, D.886; *Children's march*, D.928.

°*Trois marches militaires*, Op.51, D.733. Paris: Consortium Musical, n.d.

°*Original Compositions*. International. *Divertissement à la hongroise*, Op.54, D.818; *Introduction et variations* (Bb), Op.82/2, D.603; *Andantino varié*, Op.84/1, D.823/2; *Rondeau brillant*, Op.84/2, D.823/3; *Fantasia* (f), Op.103, D.940.

°*Original-Kompositionen*, ed. Wöss. UEd. *Divertissement à la hongroise*, Op. 54, D.818; *Variations on a French song*, Op.10, D.624; *Polonaise* (d), Op.61/1, D.824/1; *Fantasia* (f), Op.103, D.940; *Rondo* (Grand rondeau) (A), Op.107, D.951; *Sonata* (Bb), Op.30, D.617.

°*Three overtures*, D.592, D.597, D.668. Leipzig: VEB Peters.

°*Six polonaises*, Op.61, D.824. Leipzig: VEB Peters.

°*Selected original compositions*. New York: Schirmer. Vol.I: *Allegro moderato and Andante*, D.968; *Children's march*, D.928; *Four Ländler*, D.814; *Marche militaire* (D), Op.51/1, D.733/1; *Marches héroïques* (b,D), Op. 27/1,3, D.602/1,3; *Marche caractéristique* (C), Op.121/1, D.886/1; *Four polonaises*, Op.75, D.599; *Polonaise* (D), Op.61/1, D.824/1; *Rondo* (D), Op.138, D.608; *Grosse Sonate* (Fantasia [c], D.48, without concluding fugue); *Grande Sonate* (Bb), Op.30, D.617; *Andantino varié*, Op.84/1, D.823/2. Vol.II: *Grand Rondeau*, Op.107, D.951; *Allegro* (Lebensstürme), Op.144, D.947; *Fantasie* (f), Op.103, D.940); *Divertissement à la hongroise*, Op.54, D.818; *Grand duo*, Op.140, D.812.

°*Neue Schubert-Ausgabe*, ed. Christa Landon. Kassel: Bärenreiter, 1972–. Vol.VII/1/2: *Sonata* (C) (*Grand duo*), Op.posth.140, D.812; *Variations sur un thème original*, Op.35, D.813; *Divertissement à la hongroise*, Op. 54, D.818; *Divertissement sur des motifs originaux français*, Op.63 and 84, D.823. Vol.VII/1/4, *Märsche und Tänze*. *Three marches héroïques*, Op. 27, D.602; *Three marches militaires*, Op.51, D.733; *Six grandes marches*, Op.40, D.819; *Grande marche funèbre*, Op.55, D.859; *Grande marche héroïque*, Op.66, D.885; *Two marches caractéristiques*, Op.post.121, D. 886; *Children's march*, D.928; *Four polonaises*, Op.75, D.599; *Six polonaises*, Op.61, D.824; *Deutscher Tanz mit zwei Trios*, D.618; *Zwei Ländler*, D.618; *Vier Ländler*, D.814.

°*Selected piano works for four hands*, reprint of selections from Breitkopf & Härtel Critical Edition, 1879–1887. New York: Dover, 1977. *Three military marches*, Op.51, D.733; *Two characteristic marches*, Op.121, D.886; *Children's march*, D.928; *Overture* (F), Op.34, D.675; *Sonata* (Bb), Op. 30, D.617; *Sonata* (Grand duo) (C), Op.140, D.812; *Rondo* (A), Op. 107, D.951; *Variations* (Ab), Op.35, D.813; *Variations* (C), Op.82/1,

D.908; *Andantino varié* (b), Op.84/1, D.828/2; *Allegro* (Lebensstürme) (a), Op.144, D.947; *Fantasia* (f), Op.103, D.940; *Four polonaises*, Op. 75, D.599; *Four Ländler*, D.814; *Fugue* (e), Op.152, D.952.

Schulhoff, Julius (1825–1898)

Czech-born German pianist and teacher; toured widely as concert pianist. He wrote prolifically for piano in Romantic style.

°*Valse brillante* (Db), No.2. Paris: Salabert, n.d.

Schultz, Edwin (1827–1901)

Six easy piano pieces, Op.202. Boston: B.F.Wood; Magdeburg: Wernthal, 1897. US:PHf. Instructional pieces. (E)

Schulz-Beuthen, Heinrich (1838–1915)

German composer; adherent of the Wagner-Liszt school.

Characteristische Clavierstücke, Op.10. Leipzig: Rieter-Biedermann, 1874. US:Wc. Salon pieces, effectively written. (I)

Schumann, Georg (1866–1952)

German choral director and composer of chamber music, orchestral and choral works and piano pieces in Romantic style.

4 Stücke (Scherzo; Menuetto; Intermezzo; Marsch), Op.37. Berlin: Simrock, 1904. US:Wc. Serious, likable pieces in Romantic style. (LI-I)

Schumann, Robert (1810–1854)

Schumann's four-hand music is full of the same vitality, charm, and warmth found in his other works. Compared with his total musical output, however, his contributions to the four-hand repertoire are minor, consisting of five collections of short pieces. Though few in number, these works reflect in style and character three phases of the composer's life: the early experimental days of his youth when he wrote the fresh, imaginative *Polonaises*, Op.III; the active middle period, which produced *Pictures from the East*, Op.66, and *Album for the young*, Op.85, at the peak of his creative powers; and the tragic, final years of waning mental strength when he composed the *Ball scenes*, Op.109, and the *Children's ball*, Op.130.

°*Robert Schumanns Werke*, ed. Clara Schumann. Leipzig: B&H, 1885; reprint Farnborough, Hants, England: Gregg International Publishing, Ltd., 1968. Complete 4H works except for *Polonaises*, Op.III.

°*Robert Schumann: Original compositions for four hands*, 2 vols. Kalmus ed. Melville, NY: Belwin.

°*Robert Schumann: Original compositions for piano four hands*. New York: International Music Co.

°*Schumann: Original compositions for piano four hands*. New York: Peters.

The Kalmus, Peters, and International editions are complete except for *Polonaises*, Op.III, and *Spanish love-songs*, Op.posth.138.

°*Album for the young, twelve four-hand pieces for big and little children*, Op.85 (1849). New York: Schirmer. Four-hand counterpart of the composer's successful solo piano *Album for the young*, Op.68. This charming set of pieces is in Schumann's most inspired and captivating style: graceful, lively, inventive, and exuberant. 1. Birthday march (Geburtstagsmarsch) (C), direct, unaffected, rather routine (LI); 2. Bear dance (Bärentanz)(a), heavy-footed Primo plays over drone bass accompaniment (I-UI); 3. Garden melody (Gartenmelodie)(A), tender, gentle theme with accompaniment (LI); 4. Garland wreathing (Beim Kränzwinden) (F), charming, simple, songlike (I); 5. March of the Croats (Kroatenmarsch)(a), brisk military march with trumpet fanfares, drum rolls; easier Secondo (LI/I-UI); 6. Mourning (Trauer)(F), expressive, mostly single-line melody in Primo against flowing Secondo accompanying figure (LI); 7. Tournament march (Tourniermarsch)(C), robust, vigorous, rhythmical, with delicate trio (I); 8. Round dance (Reigen)(G), happy melody with imitation, amiable accompaniment (UE-LI/I); 9. At the spring (Am Springbrunnen)(D), to be played as fast as possible, both parts active and constantly moving (I-UI); 10. Hide and seek (Versteckens)(F), brilliant, playful; light staccato, presto (I-UI); 11. Ghost story (Gespenstermärchen)(d), sudden dynamic changes (I-UI); 12. Evening song (Abendlied) (Db), tender, meditative; written for three hands, with Primo playing single line throughout; most famous piece in the suite (I/LI-I). Available individually: °Op.85/1, Schott; °Op.85/1, 3, 8, 9, Bèrben; °Op.85/12, Durand. °Op.85/1, 12 with *Waltz*, Op.130/2, Bèrben.

Ball scenes (Ballszenen), Op.109 (1851). 1. Préambule (G), festive, spirited, bright; 2. Polonaise (D), bold, forthright; 3. Walzer (G), bright, lilting; 4. Ungarisch (D), lively piece in Hungarian style; 5. Française (e), fast dance in 6/8 time, like a tarantella or gigue; 6. Mazurka (g), Primo more difficult; 7. Écossaise (D), pulsating beats, driving, with 16th-note passages; 8. Walzer (G); 9. Promenade (D), serious, jubilant. (I-UI)

Children's ball (Kinderball), six easy dance pieces, Op.130 (1853). 1. Polonaise (C), brisk, majestic; 2. Waltz (G), light, happy; 3. Menuett (D), slow, serious; 4. Écossaise (F), animated with fast 16th notes; 5. Française (a), flowing, gigue-like; 6. Ringelreihe (Round dance)(C), rhythmical, full of vitality. (I-UI)

The two late works, Opp.109 and 130, written just before Schumann's final breakdown, reflect the tragic decline of his creative powers and energy. Although they contain many moments of great melodic beauty, they lack the artful and fastidious development of his earlier works.

Pictures from the East, six impromptus, Op.66 (1848). In the introduction Schumann attributes his inspiration for these pieces to a reading of a free translation by the German poet Friedrich Rückert of excerpts from the *Maqamat*. This 11th-century Arabic chronicle by Al-Hariri recounts the adventures of a precursor of Til Eulenspiegel, the rascal Abu Zayd, and his friend Hareth. The composer admits he had no specific situations in mind as he wrote the work but suggests that the final, solemn piece, marked "Reuig, andächtig," might be an echo of the last *Maqama*, in which we see the hero penitent and contrite as his life draws to a close. The inspiration for these delightful lyrical character pieces may be Middle Eastern, but they are written in Schumann's solid German Romantic style, with few, if any, traces of exotic musical color. The textures tend to be somewhat thicker than in the composer's other 4H works, though No.4, "Nicht schnell," is more spare and open—one of the loveliest of all Schumann's duets. 1. Lebhaft vivace (bb), bright, lively; 2. Nicht schnell und sehr gesangvoll zu spielen (Moderato e molto espressivo) (Db), charming, romantic; 3. Im Volkston (In popular style) (Db), strong, bright, stirring, songlike; 4. Nicht schnell (Moderato) (bb), expressive melody with simple bass accompaniment; 5. Lebhaft (vivace) (f), strong, chordal first section, almost orchestral in the fullness of its texture; lyrical middle section with thinner texture; 6. Reuig, andächtig (Repentant, devout) (bb), solemn, religious in feeling. (I-UI) Available separately: °Op.66/1 (as *Impressione d'oriente*), Bèrben.

Eight polonaises, Op.III (1828), ed. Geiringer. Vienna: UEd, 1933. Published posthumously, these early pieces were obviously influenced by Schubert's polonaises. They abound in youthful freshness and energy and are of special interest for musical materials the composer was to develop and reshape the following year into his Op.1, *Papillons*, for piano solo. US: Bp,NYp,Wc. (U-UI)

Spanish love-songs (Spanische Liebes-Lieder) (1849), Op.posth.138, song cycle for soprano, alto, tenor, and bass, with an accompaniment for piano 4H. In *Robert Schumann: Various choral works*. Kalmus miniature score 1139. Melville, NY: Belwin. Vorspiel (piano 4H solo); Lied (soprano); Lied (tenor); Duett (alto and soprano); Romanze (bass-baritone); Intermezzo (piano 4H solo); Lied (tenor); Lied (alto); Duett (tenor and bass); Quartet (SATB). Also includes *Three songs*, Op.114, and *Deutsche Rhein*.

Schuster, Giora (1915–   )

Israeli composer of choral, orchestral, chamber, and piano works.

°*Mimos I* (1966). Tel-Aviv: Israel Music Institute, 1970. US:Wc.

Schuster, Joseph (1748–1812)

German church and opera conductor; composed operas, oratorios, symphonic and chamber music, songs, and piano pieces.

Recueil de petites pièces (L'assemblée; La savoyarde; Pluton et Proserpine). Dresden: Hilscher, ca.1790. °NEd. La Savoyarde only, in collection *Vermischte Handstücke*, ed. Kreutz. D-ddr:Dlb. Short descriptive pieces in Classical style; pleasant, intriguing little curiosities, crudely set at times, but with unusual harmonies and appealing melodic lines. (LI-I)

Schütt, Eduard (1856–1933)

Russian-born pianist and conductor. He wrote two piano concertos, chamber music, and piano pieces in light Romantic idiom.

Scènes champêtres, 4 morceaux caractéristiques, Op.46. Berlin: Simrock, 1895. US:Wc. Salon pieces. (I)

Souvenir-valses, 5 morceaux, Op.64. Berlin: Simrock, 1901. US:Wc. Salon pieces. (I)

Walzer-Märchen, Op.54a. Berlin: Simrock, 1897. US:Wc. Salon pieces. (I)

Schwaab, Maurice

°*Avec maman.* Paris: Durand, n.d. Instructional. (E)

°*Premières notes.* Paris: Durand, n.d. Instructional. (E)

°*Ronde.* Paris: Durand, n.d. US:Wc. Instructional. (UE-LI/UE)

Schwalm, Oscar (b.1856)

°*Young musicians,* the very easiest pieces. New York: Schirmer, 1900; NEd. Kalmus reprint. Instructional; collection of original melodies and easy folk-song arrangements. (E-UE)

Schwanenberg, Joseph Franz (late 18th cent.)

Die versprochenen rothen und blauen Krebsen, eine Belohnung durch Verwandlung, dem Talente solcher Zöglinge zum Andenken. Vienna: pub. and date missing. A:Wgm. Musical curiosity by obscure composer; music is printed in red and blue.

Schwarz, Maximilian

°*6 Kleine Stücke* (Erweiterte Tonalität; Triolen; Taktwechsel; Moll; Im Walzertakt; Fröhlicher Ausklang). Leipzig: VEB Peters, 1961. Charming collection of short, attractive pieces in refined, tonal, mildly contemporary style; folk-like melodies; linear texture; changing meters. Very worthwhile. (UE-LI)

Schwencke, Carl (1797–1870)

German cellist and pianist; lived in Sweden for many years. He composed chamber works and piano pieces, many of which anticipate later Romantic trends.

Adagio (Db). Hamburg: Böhme, ca.1851.

Trois amusemens (Tempo di marcia; Vivace; Andantino), Op.14. Leipzig: B&H, ca.1828. A:Wgm. Delightful three-part pieces, inventively set in Schwencke's individual idiom. Classical in feeling with harmonic and melodic twists relating the music to a later period. (LI-I)

Divertissemen (F), Op.12, liv.2. Leipzig: B&H, ca.1826. S:Skma. Light work of moderate length in the form of a long polonaise; set in Classical harmonic idiom with occasional mid-Romantic stylistic features. (LI)

Divertissement (A), (1821). Ms. S:Skma.

Grande sonate (Eb), Op.5 (1816). Leipzig: B&H, ca.1820. S:Uu–US:NYp.

Large-scale work in forceful, strongly individual Classical idiom; should be republished. (I)

5 *Pièces faciles* (Eb,G,a,F,A), Op.12. Leipzig: Hofmeister, ca.1825. US: NYp. Suite of short pieces; fresh, inventive, original. (LI-I)

Schytte, Ludwig (1848–1909)

Danish pianist and teacher; composed works in melodious, tasteful salon style.

Conte oriental. Leipzig: Hofmeister, ca.1907. US:PHf,Wc. (I)

Masked garden festival, suite. Philadelphia: Presser, 1910. US:PHf,Wc. (LI-I)

Musikalische Wandelbilder, Kaleidoscope, 12 Stücke, Op.112. Breslau: Hainauer, 1899. US:Wc. (LI-I)

Nordischer Carneval. Leipzig: Hofmeister, 1907. US:PHf,Wc.

Spanische Nächte, Op.114. Berlin: Schlesinger, 1899. US:Wc. (I-UI)

Zu zweien am Klavier, 5 Stücke. Münster: Bisping, 1908. US:Wc. (I)

Scott, Cyril (1879–1971)

English composer of operas, concertos, choral works, songs, chamber music, and piano pieces. He wrote in a strikingly individual idiom using bold, often Impressionistic, harmonic devices and unconventional structures.

3 *Dances.* Philadelphia: Presser, 1926. US:Wc. Attractive instructional pieces, frequently modal, with colorful harmony. (I)

Nursery rhymes, 6 pieces. London: Augener, n.d. (UE)

Scott, John Prindle (1877–1932)

°*At the Donnybrook fair.* Philadelphia: Presser, n.d. (LI)

Sebastian, Mary

°*Sleepy head.* Boston: Boston Music, n.d. (UE)

Sechter, Simon (1788–1867)

Viennese teacher, author of music texts, and one of the foremost contrapuntists of his period. Schubert, just before his death, had planned to study with Sechter. His piano compositions consist mainly of contrapuntal dances, preludes, and fugues, and other intricate polyphonic pieces.

24 *Fugen,* Op.53. Hamburg: Cranz, n.d. A:Wgm. Four books of 24 fugues based on original themes, motives from operas, Beethoven's *Septet,* Haydn's *Seven last words,* Mozart's *Requiem,* and others.

Sedlak, Adolf

°*Klavierfibel.* Kassel: Bärenreiter, n.d. Folk-like melodies with some cautious polyphony. (UE-LI)

°*Vierhändiges Musizieren am Klavier* (Vol.1: Kinder- und Volkslieder; Vol.2: Volkslieder und Volkstänze). Vienna: Doblinger, n.d.

Sekles, Bernhard (1872–1934)

German conductor and teacher; composer of operas, symphonic and chamber music, and piano works.

Lullaby; River-song; Even-song. Mainz: Schott, n.d. In collection *Thirty-two graded pieces for piano duet.* (UE)

Musikalisches Skizzenbuch für Jung und Alt, Op.4. Frankfurt: Oehler, 1909. US:Wc. Instructional pieces in pleasant style. (UE-LI)

Senft, Luigi (fl. late 18th cent.)

Concerto (D), for piano 4H, 2 violins, viola, and bass. Leipzig: Breitkopf, ca. 1770. B:Bc—D-ddr:SWl.

Serov, Aleksandr Nikolaevich (1820–1871)

Russian critic and musician; opposed nationalist musical styles, later espoused Wagnerian principles in his own music, which includes operas, orchestral works, incidental music, and small instrumental pieces.

Fugue (Eb) (1849). Moscow: State Publishing House, 1958. US:Wc (in collection *Pedagogicheskii Repertuar*). Effective contrapuntal work; well set for piano 4H. (LI)

Seshita, Kenji

°Piano duets for children (March "Chum"; Dolly's lullaby; A dream of fallen leaves; Spring waltz; Menuet "Birds"). Tokyo: Zen-on Music Publishers, n.d. (I)

Šesták, Zdeněk (1925–   )

Czech music educator and editor. He has written orchestral and chamber music, songs, and cantatas in traditional style colored by Czech folk song.

°Studentská knížka, pro klavír na čtyři ruce (The student's book, for piano four hands) (1963). Prague: Panton, 1968. Seven pieces of different character—happy, sombre, atmospheric, descriptive—exploiting the resources of the keyboard in a mildly contemporary idiom; effective; useful. (I/UE-LI)

Séverac, Déodat de (1872–1921)

French composer, student of d'Indy. His colorful works, with many allusions to life and events in his native region of southern France, are cast in a striking personal idiom.

°Danse des treilles. Paris: Salabert, n.d.

°Le soldat de plomb (Sérénade interrompue; Quat'jours de boite; Défilé nuptial). Paris: Rouart, 1906. Witty tone pictures in Satie idiom. (I)

Seybold, S. Philip

Two duets for the harp or pianoforte, Op.16 (2nd set, Duetto III and IV). London: L.Lavenu, ca.1799. GB:Lbl.

Seydelmann, Franz (1748–1806)

German conductor; Kapellmeister at Dresden. He composed masses, operas, cantatas, and instrumental music.

6 Sonaten für zwo Personen auf einem Clavier (C,F,G,Eb,D,g). Leipzig: B&H, 1781. D-ddr:Dlb—GB:Lbl. Series of short, two-movement sonatas in highly refined, compact, Classical idiom, masterfully set for the medium. Expressive and imaginative, they represent some of the finest 4H sonata writing of the period. (LI-I)

Seydl, L.W.

2 *Menuetti* (Bb,C) pour clavier ou pianoforte. Vienna: Joseph Eder, ca. 1798. A:Wn. Attractive, melodious pieces in Classical idiom by a little-known Viennese composer, identified as "a pupil of P. Struck." (UE-LI)

Seyler (Sailer, or Sailler), Joseph Anton

Deutsche samt Coda. Vienna: Mechetti, ca.1818. A:Wgm.

Shapero, Harold (1920–   )

American composer; student of Krenek, Piston, Hindemith, and Boulanger; teacher at Brandeis University. He has written a symphony, an overture, and piano pieces.

Sonata (1941). Los Angeles: Affiliated Musicians, 1953. US:Wc. Fresh, three-movement work (Very slowly—moderately fast; slowly; fast) in fastidious, tightly knit, neo-Classical idiom, characterized by rhythmical complexity and textural contrast. Clean; well written for the medium. The rousing toccata finale, with its samba rhythm, is a brilliant, driving conclusion. Very effective concert fare; should be reprinted. (A)

Shapey, Ralph (1921–   )

American conductor, teacher, and composer; studied with Stefan Wolpe. He has written for orchestra, chorus, chamber ensembles, voice, and piano; employs serial and electronic techniques.

Seven for piano four hands. Pub. and date missing. Commissioned by Milton and Peggy Salkind. Ms. available from composer, University of Chicago, Chicago, IL 60637.

Shaw, Clifford (1911–   )

°*Third street rumba.* Bryn Mawr: Oliver Ditson, 1951. Rhythmical, often flashy piece; effectively distributed for both partners. (I)

Shaw, Geoffrey (1879–1943)

English music pedagogue and organist. He wrote church music, organ and orchestral works, choruses, and piano pieces.

°*6 Black key duets.* London: Novello, 1938. US:Wc. Pleasant instructional pieces, carefully set, grateful to play. (LI/E)

°*Traditional melodies.* London: Novello, 1923. (I)

Shchedrin, P. and A. Filiarkovskii

Two polyphonic arrangements of children's popular songs (It's raining in the street; As on the grey ocean). In collection *Ansambli v Chetyre Ruki.*

Shelley, Harry Rowe (1858–1947)

American organist and teacher; student of Dvořák. He wrote symphonic, sacred music, organ, and piano music.

3 *American dances* (In B major; Creole days; Plantation echoes). New York: Schirmer, 1905. US:Wc. Large-scale work with 19th-century American dance flavor in well-crafted salon style. (I-UI)

Sherbachëv, V.

Bigarrures, petit supplément. See *Paraphrases*.

Derevenskaia Kartinka (Landscape) (I). In collection *Sbornik fortepiannikh*, ed. N.Agafonnikov.

Shifrin, Seymour (1926–1979)

American composer; studied with William Schuman, Otto Luening, and Darius Milhaud. His works include songs, piano pieces, and orchestral, choral and chamber music.

°*The modern temper*, a dance (1959). New York/Frankfurt: Litolff, 1961. Commissioned by Milton and Peggy Salkind. Single-movement, avant-garde work in serial idiom. Compact, strongly rhythmical with jazz influence; textural interest. (A)

Shostakovich, Dmitri (1906–1975)

Waltz. In collection *Sbornik Fortepiannikh*, ed. N. Agafonnikov. (UE-LI)

Shott, Michael

American.

°*Give and take* (Vol.1: Bakers kneading bread; Black key serenade; Fanfare; Friendly spooks; Saturday night blues; Singin' in the saddle; Tidbits. Vol.2: Alone; An argument; March of the escalator; Mushroom dance; Parade of the imps; Rainy day; Tag). Boulder, CO: Myklas Press, 1976. Short, compact, imaginative, descriptive teaching pieces; effectively written for 4H. °Mushroom dance from vol.2 issued separately, Myklas Press, 1978.

°*Romance*. Boulder, CO: Myklas Press, 1978. (LI-I)

Shulgin, L.

°*Two Russian songs*. Moscow: State Music Publishing House, n.d.

Siciliani, José

Senderos de la juventud, 10 piezas fáciles y originales (Pathways of youth; 10 easy original pieces). Buenos Aires: Ricordi Americana, 1953. US:Wc. Short, attractive, descriptive teaching pieces in conventional idiom. (UE-LI/E)

Siebmann, Fr.

12 Pieces, Op.83. Cincinnati: John Church, 1892. US:Wc. Instructional works. (UE-LI)

Soirées musicales, Op.79. New York: Schuberth, 1895. US:Wc. Instructional pieces. (UE-LI)

Siegl, Otto (1896–   ) ·

Austrian violinist, conductor, and composer. His contemporary musical idiom has its roots in medieval and baroque forms.

°3 *Polyphone Klavierstücke* (1963). Vienna: Doblinger, 1964. US:Wc. Attractive works employing various contrapuntal devices with great effect; in mildly contemporary style. (I)

Sigtenhorst Meyer, Bernhard van den (1888–1953)

Dutch pianist, teacher, musicologist, and composer. He adopted a national style in his piano, choral, and chamber music.

De zeven intervallen, Op.51. Amsterdam: Alsbach, n.d. NL:Ad–US:Wc. Attractive set of eight studies featuring various uses of seven different intervals and employing eight different time signatures. (UE)

Wals, Op.50. Amsterdam: Alsbach, 1952. NL:Ad.

Sigurbjörnsson, Thorkell (1938–)

Icelandic composer; studied at Reykjavík School of Music, Hamline University, and University of Illinois. He founded the group Musica Nova in Reykjavík, and is currently director of the Icelandic Music Information Centre. He has written works in all forms; in addition to conventional instruments he uses tape, synthesizer, and other electronic devices.

Dedication (1967). Ms. IS:Rmic. Commissioned by Milton and Peggy Salkind.

Šin, Otakar (1881–1943)

Czech teacher, author of theory textbooks, and composer. His musical style is influenced by Czech folk music.

Five dances, easy children's pieces. Prague: Hudebni Matice, 1925. CS:Pchf.

Zpěvem a tancem; osm nejsnadnějších skladbiček pro klavír na čtyře ruce oba party v rozsahu pěti tónů. (With singing and dancing; eight very easy pieces for piano four hands, each part in a span of five notes). Prague: Státní nakladatelství krásné literatury, hudby a umění (Artia), 1954. The eight short folk songs are tastefully set for two beginning pianists; pretty melodies and stirring rhythms. Czech words are furnished, unfortunately without translations. (UE-5)

Sinding, Christian (1856–1941)

Norwegian pianist; composed symphonies, concertos, and piano pieces in Romantic style.

Épisodes chevaleresques, suite (F) (Tempo di marcia; Andante funèbre; Allegretto; Finale), Op.35. Leipzig: Peters, 1896. US:Wc. Serious work carefully fashioned for the medium; brilliant in part. (UI-LA)

Nordische Tänze und Weisen, Op.98. Leipzig: B&H, 1909. US:PHf,Wc. Effective settings of Norwegian dances, strongly influenced by Grieg in style and idiom. Full resources of the keyboard are used; solid technical facility required. (UI-LA)

8 *Stücke* (Caprice; Ständchen; Humoreske; Altes Lied; Ländliches Fest; Nocturne; Waldesdunkel; Sonnenaufgang), Op.71. Leipzig: Peters, n.d. US:PHf,Wc. Large-scale, competently drafted genre pieces. The often

heavy-textured harmonic style skirts the salon level. Brilliant, demanding. (UI-LA)

7 *Valses*, Op.59. Copenhagen/Leipzig: Hansen, 1903. US:Wc. Suite of pleasant, flowing, tuneful waltzes. (UI-LA)

Singer, Otto, Jr. (1863–1931)

German composer of chamber music, choral pieces, and piano works in salon style.

7 *Musikalische Plaudereien*, Op.7. Leipzig: Leuckart, 1895. US:PHf, Wc. Genre pieces. (LI)

Wenn meine Kinder tanzen, allerlei Zwei- und dreivierteltakt, Op.11. Berlin: Bote & Bock, 1911. US:Wc. Melodious instructional pieces. (LI)

Sjögren, Emil (1853–1949)

Swedish organist; his compositions are in the Scandinavian Romantic tradition with both French and German influences.

Festpolonäs, Op.5 (1881). Stockholm: Abraham Lundquist, n.d. S:Sic.

Sköld, Yngve (1899–)

Swedish pianist and composer of symphonic, choral, chamber, and piano works.

Dansfantasi (1960). Ms. S:Sic.

Gavott och musett (1944). Ms. S:Sic.

Menuett (1930). Ms. S:Sic.

Tarantella (1953). Ms. S:Sic. Exceptionally long, serious work in highly chromatic, traditional harmonic style; makes extensive use of ostinato figures.

Två dansstycken (Two dance pieces) (1953). Ms. S:Sic. Long, rhythmically strong work rooted in traditional harmony; chromatic, linear. (UI-A)

Slavický, Klement (1910–)

Czech composer of film scores, symphonic works, and chamber music.

°*Suite* (Ballad; Games; Sad lullaby; Brigands' dance) (1968). Prague: Panton, 1971. Bright, dextrously written set of contrasting pieces in contemporary tonal idiom with strong Czech flavor. (I-UI)

Smallwood, William

Thoughts of springtime. London: Patey & Willis, 1891. US:Wc. 12 instructional pieces in light style. (LI)

Smit, Leo (1900–ca.1943)

Dutch composer of symphonic works, chamber music, and piano compositions in neo-Classical idiom; victim of Nazi persecution.

°*Divertimento*. Amsterdam: Donemus, 1940. Energetic, light, three-movement work with well-distributed activity between the parts; linear sections. Idiom is 20th-century French with strong jazz influence. (UI-LA)

Smith, Eric (1906–   )

Alla gavotta; Alla tarantella. London: Elkin, 1957. US:Wc. Instructional pieces in 18th-century style. (UE-LI)

Four dances (Valse; Spanish dance; Gavotte; Graceful dance). London: OUP, 1935; °NEd. 1970, as *Three Dances,* with *Graceful Dance* omitted. Useful teaching pieces in conventional idiom. (LI)

Nocturne. London: Joseph Williams, 1955. US:Wc. Instructional pieces. (UE-LI)

Three studies in contrast. London: Elkin, 1943. US:Wc. Teaching pieces. (UE-LI)

Smith, Gregg (1931–   )

°*Songs of innocence,* for treble choir and piano 4H (from *Beware of the Soldier*). New York: Schirmer, 1975. (LI-I)

Smith, Hannah

Six duets. New York: Schirmer, 1905. US:Wc. Instructional pieces. (UE-LI)

Five plantation dances, Op.22. Cincinnati: John Church, 1907. US:Wc. Amiable pieces in Black southern folk style; liberal use of pentatonic scale and syncopated rhythms. (UE-LI)

Smith, Sydney (1839–1889)

English composer of popular drawing-room piano pieces.

Maypole dance. Boston: Oliver Ditson, n.d. US:PHf. (UE-LI)

Smith, Theodore (fl.ca.1770–ca.1810)

A relatively obscure figure from the early days of duet writing, Theodore Smith was a composer of popular teaching materials, especially four-hand sonatas for harpsichord or piano. Few details of Smith's life have survived, but he appears to have been of German origin (Theodor Schmidt, perhaps) and flourished in London as a teacher and composer during the last quarter of the 18th century. His duet sonatas are light, flowing, melodious, compact works in Classical style, easy to play, useful for study, but often thin and lacking in musical substance. They were issued in sets of three, each sonata consisting of two, sometimes three, very short contrasting movements.

Three favorite duets for two performers on one harpsichord or pianoforte, Sonatas (G,C,A), Op.1, Book 1. London: Longman & Broderip, ca. 1779. GB:Cu,Gm,Lbl,LEc,Mp,Ob. Other editions: GB:BA,Bp,Lcm. As *Trois sonates en duo,* Op.1. Berlin: J. J. Hummel, ca.1775. US:Wc. (UE-LI)

A second set of three favorite duets for two performers on one harpsichord or pianoforte, Sonatas (D,Bb,F), Op.1, Book 2. London: Longman & Broderip, ca.1780. GB:Lbl,Ob. As *Trois sonates en duo,* ca.1775. D-ddr:Dlb—GB:Lbl. (UE-LI)

A third set of three favourite duets for two performers on one harpsichord or piano-forte, Sonatas (Bb,C,F), Op.3. London: Longman & Broderip, ca. 1780. GB:Lbl—US:NYp. (UE-LI)

Trois sonates en duo qui peuvent être exécutées par deux personnes sur un clavecin ou pianoforte, Sonatas (F,G,C), Op.4. Berlin: Hummel, ca.1775. D-ddr:Dlb—GB:Lbl—US:Bp. (UE-LI)

A sixth sett of three favorite duetts on one harpsichord or piano forte, Sonatas (D,C,F), Op.6. London: Henry Holland, ca.1788. GB:Lbl,Ob. (UE-LI)

Collections of Sonatas:

Three duetts for two performers on one harpsichord or pianoforte. Philadelphia: Moller, ca.1793; Moller's imprint effaced by that of G. Willig, ca. 1800. US:PHu (Francis Hopkinson coll.), Wc. Contains Op.1, Book 1/1 and 2, and Op.3/2.

A second and fourth sett of three favorite duets for two performers on one harpsichord or pianoforte. Longman & Broderip, ca.1795. US:Bp. Contains Op.4 and Op.1, Book 2).

Three sonatinas composed for two performers on the pianoforte. Baltimore: John Cole, n.d. US:PHf. Contains Op.1, Book 1/1 and 2, and Op.3/2.

Unidentified Works:

Duetto, [by] Smith, No.24 in *Bland's collection of duets for two performers on one harpsichord or pianoforte by eminent composers.* London: J.Bland, 1794. US:Wc.

Three duetts for two performers on one harpsichord or pianoforte. Philadelphia: Willig, ca.1800. US:Wc.

Favourite duets for two performers on one harpsichord or pianoforte. London: Longman & Broderip, n.d. B:Bc. Contains two collections of three pieces and a third suite.

Smith, Warren Storey (1885–   )

American teacher, critic, and composer; taught at New England Conservatory.

Festal suite (F), Op.21. Boston: A.P.Schmidt, 1915. US:Wc. Salon pieces. (I-UI)

Smolanoff, Michael

American composer and teacher; on the faculty of Rutgers University. His works include a one-act opera and piano compositions.

°Concerto for piano four hands, strings and percussion. New York: E.B. Marks, n.d.

Snížková, Jitka (1924–   )

Czech musician; has written orchestral, chamber, and piano works.

°Start (1960). Prague: Supraphone, n.d.

Söderman, August (1832–1876)

Swedish conductor; composed operettas, songs, chamber music, choral works, and piano pieces.

Swedish wedding march. Chicago: National Music Co. US:PHf.

Sohet, S.

°*Pour nous les petites mains* (Ronde; Ding-ding-dong; Valse du furet; Carillon; Mélodie; Guitares). Paris: Lemoine, n.d. (E)

Sokolov, Nikolai Alexandrovich (1859–1922)

Russian composer of orchestral and chamber music, songs, and piano pieces. *Trenis.* See *Badinage.*

Soliva, Carlo (1792–1851)

Sonate et variations (G). Vienna: Artaria, ca.1820. A: Innsbruck Musikverein.

Sommer, Friedrich Anton (early 19th century)

Grosse Sonate (Eb). Vienna: Cappi & Diabelli, ca.1820. A:Wgm. Large-scale, four-movement work in Classical style; pleasant melodies, interesting harmonic twists; some effective climaxes. Allegro vivace; melodious Andante Fantasia; dashing Scherzo Presto; Rondo Allegretto. The formal structure strongly suggests the pervasive influence of Beethoven, especially in the shape and dramatic drive of the Scherzo. Despite these noble auspices the Sonata cannot be rescued from its basic defects: weak thematic development, lack of textural contrast, and a general absence of skilful and imaginative writing. (I-UI)

Soproni, Joszef (1930–)

Hungarian teacher; his compositions include orchestral, chamber, and choral works; organ compositions; and piano pieces.

°*Öt kis negyezes zongaradarab* (Five small pieces for piano duet) (Capriccioso; Codaletta; Marcia; Barcarola: Giocoso). Budapest: Editio Musica, 1973. Capriccioso and Barcarole in collection *Album for piano duet*, ed. Váczi. These short, neatly crafted pieces are contemporary in sound: chromatic, dissonant for the most part, and set in a thin, open texture. (I)

Sorge, Erich Robert

7 *Miniaturen.* Berlin: Sirius-Verlag, 1966. US:NYp,Wc. Charming, short, epigrammatical works in mildly contemporary, predominantly linear, tonal idiom. Ingenious in the harmonic and rhythmical variety; effective. (UE-5)

8 *Veränderungen über Der Winter ist vergangen.* Cologne: Gerig, 1960. US: Wc.

Sorokin, K.

Valse. In collection *P'ecy dlia fortepiano v chetyre ruki—starshie klassy DMSh.* Moscow: Music Pub. House, 1969.

Soubeyran, E.

°*Le livre bleu;* petites pièces et Noëls variés dans le style facile, Op.18. Paris: Rouart, Lerolle, 1923. US:Bp. 12 pleasant settings of Christmas pieces. (UE-LI)

°*Pour deux petits amis*, recueil de pièces faciles (avec préface de Vincent d'Indy). Paris: Rouart, Lerolle, 1923.

Sowerby, Leo (1895–1968)
American organist and composer of symphonic and choral works, concertos, chamber music, and piano pieces.
Suite. Pub. and date missing. US:NYamc.

Spahn, C.
12 Pièces progressives, Op.24. NEd. Offenbach: André, ca.1871. US:Wc. Charming and inventive instructional pieces. (UE-LI)
Der Schmetterling, 10 Stücke, Op.21. Offenbach: André, ca.1838. US:Wc. Instructional pieces. (UE-LI)

Späth, Andreas (1792–1876)
German conductor, organist, and composer of music in traditional style.
Divertissemens, Op.92. Mainz: Schott, ca.1825. US:Wc. Six marches, waltzes, and polonaises in tasteful and appealing settings. (LI-I)
Marche, antipode et valse avec trio et coda, Op.122, liv.2. Mainz: Schott, ca.1828. US:Wc. Instructional. (I)
Récréations musicales, ou six walses progressives, Op.116. Mainz: Schott, ca.1828. US:Wc. Suite of diverting waltzes. (I)
Rondeau varié (A), Op.80. Mainz: Schott, ca.1827. US:Wc. Instructional piece. (LI-I)
Rondino, polonaise et siciliano, Op.122, liv.1. Mainz: Schott, ca.1828. US: Wc. Instructional work. (LI-I)
Six variations (air allemand), Op.123. Mainz: Schott, ca.1828. US:Wc. Instructional. (I)
12 Walses, Op.73. Offenbach: André, ca.1836. US:Wc. Instructional. (I)
Six walses de moyenne difficulté, Op.108. Mainz: Schott, ca.1826. US:Wc. Instructional pieces. (I)

Spaulding, George L.
°*Just we two*, 23 pieces. Bryn Mawr: Presser, 1917. Instructional. (E-UE)
°*You and I*, 17 pieces. Bryn Mawr: Presser, 1916. Instructional. (E-UE)

Spech, Johann (1767–1836)
3 Fugues (c,D,F), Op.39. Vienna: Diabelli, ca.1830. D-brd:B.
2 Rhapsodische Allegri im freien und gebundenen Style, Op.43. Vienna: Diabelli, n.d. D-brd:B.

Spencer, Ruth
°*Fireflies frolic*. Cincinnati: Willis, n.d. (LI)

Spiegelman, Joel (1933–)
American harpsichordist and composer; teaches at Sarah Lawrence College. He has written music for piano, chamber ensembles, chorus, and symphony orchestra, and has worked with electronic techniques.

°*Morsels* ("Kousochki"). New York: MCA Music, 1967. Commissioned by Jean and Kenneth Wentworth. Three-movement serial work featuring a variety of bell sonorities, inspired by the 12th-century monastery bells the composer heard on a trip to the Soviet Union. Widespread use of clusters, string plucking, aleatory procedures, and improvisation. Advanced pianism essential. (A)

Spindler, Fritz (1817–1905)

German pianist and composer of pedagogical works and salon music.

°*Immortelles*, Op.90. Magdeburg: Heinrichshofen, 1857; Paris: Hamelle, n.d. US:PHf. Short instructional pieces. (UE-LI)

Ländliches Fest, Op.393. Boston: A.P. Schmidt, 1897. US:Wc. Instructional piece. (LI)

°*Scènes de bal*, 6 morceaux, Op.246. Paris: Hamelle, n.d.

°6 *Sonatines* (C,F,D,a,G,e), Op.136. Paris: Hamelle, 1863. (UE/E-5)

°*Träumende Knospen* (Fleurs de printemps), Op.130. Paris: Hamelle, n.d.

°*La vie du soldat*, 5 morceaux caractéristiques, Op.140. Paris: Hamelle.

   °No.3 as "Husarenritt." Cologne: Kistner & Siegel, n.d.

Spinelli, Niccola (1865–1906)

Italian composer of operas and piano music.

Tempo di minuetto. Berlin: Bote & Bock, 1909. US:Wc. Instructional piece. (I)

Spivak, Sam

°*Boogie woogie nocturne*. New York: Belwin, 1944. US:Wc. Instructional piece. (LI)

Staempfli, Edward (1908–   )

Swiss composer of symphonic and chamber music, ballets, an opera, songs, and piano pieces. His early works are in neo-Classical style; after 1949 he began to use serial techniques.

Dialoge (1965). Ms. CH:Zma.

Sonatina (1941). Ms. CH:Zma. Attractive, serious work in three movements. The idiom is strongly linear, occasionally dissonant, and reminiscent of Hindemith. Worth investigating. (I)

Stamaty, Camille-Marie (1811–1870)

Greek-French pianist and teacher; wrote études and other instructional material for piano, sonatas, and a piano concerto.

The curfew bell. In collection *Thirty-two graded pieces for piano duet*. (UE-LI)

Stamitz, Carl (1745–1801)

German violinist virtuoso. He wrote operas, symphonies, concertos, chamber music, and piano pieces in early Classical style.

Duetts, Nos.1 and 2 from *Bland's collection of duetts for two performers on*

one harpsichord or piano-forte. London: J.Bland, ca.1790. GB:Ckc,Lcm–
US:Wc.
Sonate (F), No.3. Amsterdam: J. Schmitt, 1780–85. B:Bc.

Stanzen, Johann Ludwig (fl. late 18th cent.)
Sonate (C), Op.2. Offenbach: André, 1793. B:Bc. Though it contains pleasant melodies, antiphonal sections, and some textural variety, this three-
movement work remains generally thin and colorless. (I)

Staray, Michel, comte de (late 18th cent.)
3 Polonaises, Op.2. Vienna: Kozeluch, ca.1789. A:Wgm,Wn,Wst.
6 Polonaises, Op.4. Vienna: Kozeluch, ca.1793. A:Wgm,Wst.

Starer, Robert (1924–   )
Austrian-born American composer of orchestral and chamber music, choral
works, songs, and piano pieces. His style is tonal with frequent use of modified serial techniques.
°Fantasia-Concertante (1959). New York: MCA, 1966. Commissioned by
Lillian and Irwin Freundlich. Large-scale single movement in brilliant
style. The bold, dotted-note introduction is followed by a bright, rhythmically exciting scherzando section. The first section reappears and leads
to a strong, dramatic, driving finale. Symphonic in scope, the work is technically demanding. (A)
°Five duets for young pianists (Fanfare in five; Drizzle; Evens and odds;
Two can be lonely too; Lines, dots and dashes). New York: MCA Music,
1967. Dedicated to Jean and Kenneth Wentworth. A variety of meters,
structural devices, technical puzzles, and musical styles are the features of
this most appealing group of pieces. The language is contemporary and
frequently dissonant, and the writing idiomatic for the medium. (UE-LI)

Starke, Friedrich (1774–1835)
German musician to whom Beethoven entrusted his nephew Carl's music
education. He wrote sacred pieces, chamber music, and piano works.
Pas de deux mit Variationen, aus dem beliebten Ballet *Die Tanzsucht,* Op.
23. Vienna: Artaria, ca.1807. US:Wc. Pleasant, unpretentious set of varia-
tions carefully distributed for both parts. (UE-LI)
Pièces faciles. Vienna: Eder, ca.1816. I:MOe. Collection of short pieces in
Classical idiom; fluent and charming. (UE-LI)

Staub, Victor
°Trois pièces (En trottinant, marche, Op.19; En dansant, valse, Op.20; En
chantant, sérénade, Op.21). Paris: Durand, 1909. US:Wc. Instructional
pieces. (LI)

Stecher, Marian (b.ca.1760)
Grosse Sonate (B♭). Leipzig: B&H, ca.1795. D-brd:B.

Stecher, Melvin; Norman Horowitz; and Claire Gordon
°The pleasure of your company (Book I: The bell tower; The setting sun;

Me too; Fine feathered friend; Two for a see-saw; Crocodile creep; Tommy hawk. Book II: Pony tales; Rice paddies; Swiss music box; Ticker tocker; Dutch treat. Book III: Wheels of chance; Pastorale; Ruck-a-chuck. Book IV: A summer to remember; Fandango; Westward Ho! Book V: Rippling river; Superstars and stripes; Dmitri's dream). Minneapolis: Schmitt, Hall, and McCreary, 1974. Instructional pieces in traditional idiom, from mood pieces to dances and marches. Conventional harmony and rhythm. Excellent fare for sight-reading. (Book I: LE-E; Book II: E; Book III: UE; Book IV:LI; Book V: LI-I)

Steele, James Aloysius

Australian composer and teacher.

Six nursery tunes. Melbourne: Allans Music, 1955. US:Wc. Tasteful arrangements of folk tunes. (UE)

Stehman, Jacques (1912–)

Pastorale (1941). Brussels: Hulpiau, n.d. B:Bcdm.

Steibelt, Daniel (1765–1823)

German pianist; composed operas, orchestral works, chamber music, and piano pieces in Classical style with pre-Romantic touches.

Six sonatas, Op.1. Paris: B. Viguerie, 1798. Sonata (F), No.6. Leipzig: B&H, ca.1809. US:Wc has Sonatas (D,G), Nos.1 and 2. Two-movement works in Classical style with appealing melodic ideas, rhythmic interest, and resourceful thematic development. Texture generally spare; parts carefully balanced. (LI-I)

Steiger, Charles

°*Chemin fleuri,* 24 récréations. Paris: Lemoine, n.d.
°*25 Pièces faciles sous forme de leçons progressives.* Paris: Durand, n.d. (E)
Le vagabond. Paris: Durand, 1909. US:Wc. Instructional piece. (UE)

Stein, Carl

3 Marches, Op.46. Vienna: Maisch, ca.1823. A:Wgm.
Pièces détachées, Op.20. Vienna: Maisch, ca.1820. A:Wgm.
Six polonaises suivies d'une marche, Op.30. Vienna: Maisch, ca.1821. A: Wgm.

Steinacker, Charles

8 Walses avec introduction et coda suivis de quelques [4] *menuets et* [4] *écossaises.* Leipzig: Hofmeister, ca.1812. US:PHf. Bright, lively suite of waltzes in Schubertian form and style. The idiom is Classical and lightweight. (LI-I)

Steiner, Eric

°*Four in a rowboat.* Melville, NY: Belwin-Mills, n.d. Instructional. (UE-LI)
°*Hike on the pike.* Melville, NY: Belwin-Mills, 1963. Instructional piece using canon. (E-5)
Starting together. Melville, NY: Belwin-Mills, 1963. Collection of 15 pieces,

mostly arrangements of folk songs, spirituals, and popular tunes. (UE-5)
*Two happy farmers. Melville, NY: Belwin-Mills, n.d. (E)

Steinfeld, Albert (ca.1757–ca.1824)

12 Lieder von Herrn Röding nebst einem Andante für vier Hände mit Veränderungen. Hamburg: Meyn, 1797. B:Bc.

Stephens, Charles Edward (1821–1893)

English pianist, organist, and teacher. His works include orchestral, chamber, and liturgical music, and piano and organ pieces.
Duo brillant (G), Op.19. Mainz: Schott, 1875. D-brd:MZsch.

Sterkel, Abbé Johann Franz Xaver (1750–1817)

German priest and amateur musician; prolific composer of symphonies, choral and chamber music, piano works, and songs.
Petites pièces. Berlin: Hummel, n.d. D-ddr:SWl.
6 Stücke. Munich: Falter, n.d. A:Wgm–D-brd:Rp. As 6 Pièces faciles. Offenbach: André, ca.1809. US:Wc. A variety of ingratiating, light pieces in Classical style. (LI)
Recueil de petites pièces. Mainz: Zulehner, ca.1805. GB:Lbl.
Sonata, Op.15. London: Longman & Broderip, ca.1785. A:Wgm–GB:Lbl. Attractive, melodious work in Classical style; comfortably balanced with activity and interest in both parts. (I)
Sonata (D), Op.21. Mainz: Schott, ca.1780. A:Wgm–D-brd:SPlb–D-ddr: Bds, LEm–GB:Lbl.
Sonata (F), Op.23. Mainz: Schott; Berlin: Concha, n.d. A:Wgm–D-brd: SPlb,DO–D-ddr:LEm.
4 Sonates pour les commençans, Op.28. Offenbach: André, ca.1787. A:Wgm.

Sternberg, Constantin (1852–1924)

Russian pianist, conductor, and composer. He wrote a quantity of salon pieces for piano.
Sonst und jetzt, 2 Tänze (Menuett; Polka), Op.18. Leipzig: B&H, ca.1880. US:PHf. Salon pieces. (I)
Walzer, Op.16. Bremen: Praeger und Meier, 1877. US:PHf. Salon waltzes. (I)

Steup, H.C. (b.1775)

Sonata (G). Bonn: Simrock, ca.1807. D-brd:B.

Stevens, Bernard (1916–)

English composer of orchestral, choral, chamber, and film music as well as piano works. He tends toward a lyrical personal contemporary style.
*A birthday song (for Mary and Geraldine Pippin). London: Galliard, 1969. Enchanting, gentle little piece. The recurrent theme is based on the letters of the names of the two girls to whom the work is dedicated. (LI)
Fantasia on "The Irish Ho-Hoane," Op.13 (1950). London: Lengnick, 1953.

US:Wc. Attractive work in free style; rhythmically varied; carefully written. The contemporary idiom is musically demanding at times. (I-UI)

Stevens, Everett

°*Sugarloaf mountain.* Philadelphia: Elkan-Vogel, 1959. Imaginative teaching piece with modal melody and unusual harmonies. (E)

Stevens, Halsey (1908–)

American composer and teacher; author of *The Life and Music of Béla Bartók.* He has written symphonic and chamber music, concertos, and piano pieces. His music is characterized by solid craftsmanship, expert contrapuntal and harmonic manipulation, rhythmic variety, and flowing lyricism.

°*Sonatina* (1975). Champaign, IL: Editio Helios, 1977. Thin textures, modality, and linear writing predominate in this attractive three-movement, neo-Classical work, commissioned by the Music Teachers National Association for its Centennial Convention, 1976. Andante con moto: tranquil; begins with a graceful Dorian mode melody in 5/8, strongly reminiscent of Gregorian chant in outline and character. Alla barcarolla: slow-moving melody in the Primo part is accompanied by gently swaying figures in the Secondo; a contrasting theme, developed fugally, is followed by a return of the first melody. Allegro: bright and rhythmical, with brilliant ending. The work is solidly tonal, with free dissonance, and is engagingly written for the medium. (I-UI)

Strategier, Herman (1912–)

Dutch organist; has written orchestral, chamber, and liturgical music, organ and piano pieces, and songs.

°*Suite* (1945). Amsterdam: Donemus, 1946. Handsomely written set of seven, short, light, inviting movements. The idiom is tonal, frequently chromatic, with considerable French harmonic influence. I. Lively, bright; II. Bold, waltzlike; III. Quiet larghetto with rippling scalewise accompanying passages; IV. Strong rhythmical Allegro ma non troppo; V. Stately gavotte; occasional changing meters; VI. Light syncopated melody in popular style; VII. Rousing march. (I)

Straus, Oscar (1870–1954)

Viennese operetta composer; also wrote orchestral, chamber, and piano music.

Bilderbuch ohne Bilder; pittoreske Szenen nach Andersen, Op.38. Mainz: Schott, 1899. D-brd:MZsch. (UI)

Strauss, Johann (1804–1849)

Leaflet waltzes (Flugschriften Walzer), Op.300. In collection *Duet album,* ed. L. Mannes.

Stravinsky, Igor (1882–1971)

When Stravinsky and his family were living in Switzerland during World War I, the composer took time from his other creative efforts to enrich the four-hand repertoire with two sets of delightful pieces for piano duet. Both suites are written in the tradition of educational music with one easy and one more difficult part: *Five easy pieces*, as instructional material for his children, and *Three Easy Pieces*, for the entertainment of his artistic associates. Despite the careful distribution of parts, very little of the music from these two suites is really practical as instructional material for children. The notes may lie well under the hands but the problems of ensemble are intricate and subtle, even for mature musicians. Needless to say, the teacher's part is often very demanding.

°*Five easy pieces* (1917). Andante: the easiest of the suite, slow, deliberate, serious; Russian folk influence, in Aeolian mode. Española: in zarzuela style, difficult Secondo, thorny ensemble problems. Balalaïka: rhythmical imitation of Russian folk instrument. Napolitana: joyful tarantella. Galop: high-spirited, jubilant. (I-UI/E-LI)

°*Three easy pieces* (1915). The Secondo part is almost absurdly simple, consisting of single 2- or 3-note patterns repeated from beginning to end of each piece. March is dedicated to Alfred Casella, Valse to Erik Satie, and Polka to Sergei Diaghilev. Dry, satirical, with changing meters, wide leaps in Primo, and "wrong note" dissonances. (E/I-UI)

Both groups of pieces are charming, witty, and elegantly written, and are worth looking into. They are available in °Chester, °International, and °Omega (Sam Fox) editions, and also appear in numerous collections.

Stravinsky, Soulima (1910–   )

Swiss-born pianist and composer; appeared frequently with his father, Igor, in two-piano concerts. Teaches at University of Illinois.

°*Music alphabet*. New York: Peters, 1973. The elegantly turned music in this unusual collection is ingeniously arranged so that each of the 25 pieces is cast in a particular musical form, develops a technical device, or represents a musical instrument beginning with a different letter of the alphabet. The writing is polished, up-to-date, pianistic, and embraces a variety of styles, textures, rhythmic problems, meters, and key signatures. The results are refreshing and effective. Volume I: A. Arietta, languid melody in Primo against dronelike Secondo accompaniment; B. Barcarole; gently rocking ostinato in Secondo supports plaintive cantando theme in Dorian mode in Primo; C. Canon, succinct, ingeniously worked out; D. Danza, lively, with Spanish flavor; exploits 3/4(6/8) rhythmic patterns; E. Etude, delightful, amusing little piece with motives derived from finger exercises; F. Fughetta, neat, carefully balanced; G. Gavotte, bright, with elegant grace; H. Hymne, solemn, with vertical harmonies and 2 against 3 rhythms; I. Intermezzo (Hommage à Johannes Brahms), short piece in Brahmsian style, using harmonic, melodic, and notational devices of the composer in a charming and tender way; J. Jota, animated Spanish dance; K. Keys (Black and white), bitonal waltz; L. Lullaby, quiet, songlike.

Volume II: M. Menuet, fluent, graceful; N. Notturno, misty, restless, shadowy atmospheric piece; O. Ode, changing meters, moderately paced; P. Polka, lively, joyful dance; Q. Quodlibet, good-humored, bantering, happy piece; R. Rondo, rhythmical, fast; S. Scherzo, carefree, energetic; T. Twelve-tone, short serial piece; U. Unison, consists entirely of single-line melody in octaves between the parts; V. Valse, very short easy waltz; W. Western song, pentatonic melody in Primo, simple harmonic accompaniment in Secondo; "Primo may be divided between two players"; X-Y. Xylophone: ingenious piece imitating the xylophone; Primo plays very high and Secondo very low; Z. Zarzuela: piece in Spanish style, florid opening with contrasting rhythmical section. (LI-I)

Strelezki, Antoine (pseud. of Anton Burnand) (1859–1907)

English pianist and composer of quantity of light piano music.

Danses valaques. New York: Schirmer, 1886. US:PHf,Wc. Settings of Wallachian folk songs in agreeable salon idiom. (I)

7 *Idylles.* Breslau: Hainauer, ca.1891. US:Wc.

5 *Norwegian dances.* Boston: Oliver Ditson, 1901. US:PHf. Salon pieces. (LI)

6 *Piano pieces.* Boston: Oliver Ditson, 1903. US:Wc. Salon pieces. (I)

Russian military march. Leipzig: Kiesler, 1898. US:Wc. Salon piece. (I)

Strimer, Joseph (1881–)

Russian-born American teacher; made folk-song arrangements and wrote piano pieces.

The country holiday, 10 short pieces. London: Augener. As °*Claire journée,* dix pièces. Paris: Heugel, n.d.

Stromenger, Karol (b.1885)

Polish music critic, pedagogue, radio music commentator and author. Arranger of folk songs and composer of incidental theater music and piano pieces.

°*Chodzi baj po świecie* (The story teller). In collection *Drobiazgi,* vol.I, ed. Raube. (UE-LI)

°*Etiuda we dwoje* (Study for two players). In collection *Drobiazgi,* vol.II, ed. Raube. (I)

Strong, Templeton (1856–1948)

American, German-trained resident of Switzerland; follower of Liszt. He wrote cantatas, a symphonic poem, chamber music, and piano pieces in Romantic style.

3 *Bagatellen* (G,Eb,d), Op.21. Leipzig: Kistner, ca.1884. US:Wc. (E-LI)

Klänge aus dem Harzegebirge, Charakterstücke, Op.17. Leipzig: Kistner, 1885. US:Wc. Deftly written pieces in salon style. (I)

2 *Marches,* Op.39. Leipzig: A.P.Schmidt, ca.1892. US:Wc. Salon pieces. (I)

3 *Pièces* (Petite danse américaine; Le rêve de Cendrillon; Jack, le tueur de

géants) (1926). Geneva: Henn, 1926. CH:Zma. Occasional unexpected modulations and unusual turns of phrase add color to these three moderately long pieces written in a strongly individual musical style rooted in traditional harmonic practice. (I-UI)

Struck, Paul Friedrich (1776–1820)

Rondeau, Op.9. Vienna: Cappi, ca.1808. A:Wgm.

Studer, Hans (1911–)

Swiss teacher and composer; works include choral, orchestral, chamber, organ, and piano music.

°*Kleines Konzert*, for string orchestra, piano four hands and flute ad lib. Kassel: Bärenreiter, 1952.

Subotnick, Morton (1933–)

American composer; student of Milhaud and Kirchner. He uses avant-garde techniques including pointillism and aleatory and electronic procedures.

Sonata (1959). Ms. Available from composer, California Institute of the Arts, Valencia, CA 91355.

Suffert, J. G. (end of 18th cent.)

Sonate. Brunswick: pub. missing. 1796. A:Wgm.

Sugar, Rezső (1919–)

Hungarian composer of orchestral works, chamber music, songs, and piano pieces.

Hungarian children's songs. Budapest: Editio Musica, n.d.

Suk, Vaša (Václav) (1861–1933)

Czech violinist and conductor; student of Fibich. He composed an opera, piano music, and symphonic works.

5 Morceaux, Op.20. Leipzig: Zimmerman, 1911. US:Wc. Descriptive pieces with Czech flavor. (I)

Supino, —

°*Tic tac*. Bologna: Bongiovanni, n.d.

Suter, Robert (1919–)

Swiss composer.

Petite suite (1950). Ms. CH:Zma.

Suzin, A.

Čika Pera jaši konja bela. Sarajevo, Jugoslavia: J. Studnička i drug, 1938. US:Wc. Setting of Jugoslav folk song in conventional style. (UE)

Swift, Richard (1927–)

American composer and teacher; uses serial techniques.

Capriccio (1955). Ms. Commissioned by Milton and Peggy Salkind. Available from composer, University of California, Davis, CA 95616.

Swinstead, Felix (1880–1959)

English pianist and teacher; composed mainly instructional piano music in traditional idiom.

°*Light heart*. London: Boosey & Hawkes, n.d. Pleasant little teaching piece; carefully balanced. (UE)

°*Side by side series*, Book II (The soldiers are coming; Valse; Marionettes; Toe dance). London: Ashdown, n.d.

Sydeman, William (1928–   )

American composer; studied at Mannes College of Music and with Roger Sessions. He has written for a wide variety of instrumental combinations, including electronic devices. Among his commissions are *In memoriam, for President Kennedy*, by the Boston Symphony, and *Texture studies for orchestra*, by the Koussevitsky Foundation.

Concerto for piano four hands and chamber orchestra (1967). Ms. Commissioned by Jean and Kenneth Wentworth. Available from composer, Box 1176, Running Springs, CA 92382. The composer is quoted as follows on the jacket of the Wentworths' recording of the Concerto (Desto DC-7131): "The Concerto is conceived as a huge arch form in two large divisions. The climax of the work is the end of the first movement. The second movement, which is divided in two parts, functions as a return to serenity after the cataclysms of the first. . . . Part one sustains a sonority throughout, in which fragmented events by piano and percussion occur—part two superimposes orchestral fragments over a consistent terribly high, terribly quiet, terribly omnipresent flow of piano notes. The piece sort of floats away at the end." A version of the Concerto for 4H and tape (1969) also exists.

Szabó, Ferenc (1902–1969)

Hungarian composer; lived for a time in Russia; director of Franz Liszt Academy in Budapest. His compositions are lyrical, with open textures and fluency of expression in a traditional framework.

°*Recruiting*. Budapest: Editio musica, n.d.

Szávai, Magda and Lili Veszprémi, eds.

Let us play together. Budapest: Editio musica, n.d.

°*Nemzetek táncai és dalai; négykezes zongoradarabok kezdők számára* (National dances and songs; four hand pieces for beginners). Budapest: Zeneműkiadó (Editio musica), 1969. 38 folk songs and national dances, attractively arranged in a variety of meters, keys, and styles; excellent teaching material. (E-UE)

Szelényi, Istvan (1904–   )

Hungarian editor, teacher, and writer on musical subjects. He has composed stage and orchestral works, cantatas, chamber music, and piano pieces.

Colorit, suite (1932). Copenhagen: Hansen, 1932. US:NYp.

Piano duets by Hungarian composers. Budapest: Editio musica, n.d. US:Wc.

°Twenty easy piano duets, 2 vols. Budapest: Editio musica, 1970. The Primo part of these attractive pieces advances from simple tunes with one, two, and three fingers in Book I to more complex melodies and rhythms in Book II. The Secondo remains at the same level of difficulty throughout. Contemporary harmonic idiom. Both books are of exceptional musical and pedagogical interest. (I/E-LI)

Szeligowsky, Tadeusz (1896–1963)

Polish composer; his operas, ballets, choral and orchestral music, songs, piano pieces, and chamber works combine nationalist elements with the influence of Stravinsky and Szymanowski.

°Mr. Li-Si-Tsoa (LI), and Grymasy (Funny faces) (UE-LI). In collection Drobiazgi, vol.I, ed. Raube.

°W cyrku (At the circus). In collection Drobiazgi, vol.II, ed. Raube. (LI)

Szervánsky, Endre (1911–   )

Hungarian teacher and composer. He has written choral, orchestral, and chamber music; scores for films and stage productions; and educational music.

Folk song suite I (Mely a Tiszának a széle) (1935). Budapest: Magyar Kórus, 1938. Also in °Album for Piano Duet, ed. Váczi. Attractive, modal setting of Hungarian folk song. (UE-LI)

°Sonatina (1950). Budapest: Editio musica, 1950. Absorbing, tuneful work in three contrasting movements. Modal idiom with strong Hungarian flavor. Effectively laid out for both parts. (LI-I)

Szöllősy, András (1921–   )

Hungarian teacher and writer; has written music for stage, orchestra, and chorus as well as songs and piano compositions.

°Old Hungarian dance. Budapest: Editio musica, 1957.

Szőnyi, Erzsébet (1924–   )

Hungarian teacher, choral conductor, and author; has written stage works, choral and orchestral pieces, chamber and vocal music, and piano and organ compositions.

Playing. Budapest: Editio musica, 1946.

°Small chamber music. Budapest: Editio musica, 1964. US:Wc. Fastidiously shaped group of ten delightful pieces consisting of folk or folklike melodies in a variety of styles: linear, chordal, occasional Bartókian dissonance, irregular meters. (UE-LI)

Tag, Christian Gotthilf (1735–1811)

German composer and cantor. He wrote liturgical and choral works, songs, organ pieces, and piano compositions.

12 Veränderungen auf die Melodie des Liedes "Gaudeamus igitur," for piano four hands and flute. Pub. and date missing. D-brd:B.

Tailleferre, Germaine (1892–   )

French pianist; former member of "les Six." She has written ballets, songs, a piano concerto, and chamber music.

°*Premières prouesses,* six pièces progressives. Paris: Jobert, n.d. (I)

Takagi, Toroku (1904–   )

Japanese pianist and composer; studied in Paris and Tokyo; has written an opera, ballet, piano concertos, songs, and piano works.

°*Piano duets for the young* (Sweet home; Rondo "Morning"; Waltz for mother and child; La berceuse; Variations from "Oedo Nihonbashi"; Le farceux du rhythme; Valse pour la princesse élégante; Arabian serenade). Tokyo: Zen-on Music Publishers, n.d.

Talexy, Adrien (1821–1881)

French pianist and conductor; wrote a piano method and many instructional piano pieces.

Les noces de Jeannette, fantaisie, Op.58. Mainz: Schott, n.d. D-brd:MZsch.

Tallis, John

Prelude and fugue. London: Augener, 1956. US:Wc. Resourceful, large-scale contrapuntal work in mildly contemporary idiom; well-balanced parts. (UI)

Tanenbaum, Elias

°*Contrasts for teacher and pupil.* New York: ACE, n.d.

Tansman, Alexandre (1897–   )

Polish-born French pianist and conductor. His works include symphonic, choral, and chamber music, ballets, and piano pieces written in an individual lyrical style influenced by Chopin, Szymanowski, Ravel, and Stravinskian neo-Classicism.

°*Les jeunes au piano,* 4 vols. Paris: Max Eschig, 1951. Four books of progressive difficulty, consisting of mood and descriptive pieces, national dances, and (terminating in) four fugues. An impressive collection of fine teaching material. 1er recueil, *En tournant la T.S.F.* (1939–1940): Radio-France; Radio-Angleterre; Radio-Pologne; Radio-États-Unis; Radio-Russie; Radio-Hongrie; Radio-Espagne; Radio-Italie. (UE) 2ème recueil, *Pièces de fantaisie* (1939–1940): Chant lointain; Air d'Espagne; Le berger de Pologne; Choral; Plainte d'Orient; Le régiment passe. (LI-I) 3ème recueil, *Feuillets d'album* (1939–1940): Habañera; Carillons et cloches; Fileuse; Pièce chromatique; Alerte; Sicilienne. (LI-I) 4ème recueil, *Quatre pièces fuguées* (1937). (I)

°*Nous jouons pour maman,* 12 morceaux très faciles (°Noel; Air solonnel; °Rêverie; Air à bercer; °Choral; °Valse; °Chanson; °Arietta; Tempo di

minuetto; Air populaire; °Petit conte; °Final). Paris: Max Eschig, 1939.
Single items with °also issued separately. Very easy, short pieces in large
notes. Light, tuneful, excellent teaching material. (LE-E)

Tarenghi, Mario (1870–1938)

Italian pianist; composed over 600 piano pieces of wide popularity.

°*Bozzetti dal vero* (six pieces), Op.71. Milan: Ricordi, 1918. Descriptive
and mood pieces carefully set in pleasant, traditional style. (I)

La fileuse, Op.45. Leipzig: A.P.Schmidt, 1909. US:Wc. Instructional piece.
(UE-LI)

Out of the past; Star of Italy, from Op.76. Boston: A.P.Schmidt, 1920. US:
Wc. Instructional pieces. (UE-LI)

Tarp, Svend Erik (1908–1953)

Danish composer of chamber and orchestral works, ballets, film music, and
piano pieces in a fresh, melodious style. He often made use of Danish folk
music.

Cirkus, ti smaa klaverstykker for to og fire haender (Circus, ten little piano
pieces for two and four hands), Op.47. Copenhagen: Engstrøm & Sødring,
1947. Nos.1 and 10 for four hands. US:NYp.

Tate, Phyllis (1911–   )

English composer; has written operas, song and folk-song arrangements,
chamber and choral music, and piano compositions.

°*Hampstead Heath*, rondo for roundabouts, arr. David Stone, for strings,
woodwinds, brass, percussion and piano four hands. (Music for amateur
orchestras.) London: OUP, 1964. See *Notes* 23 (1966): 157.

°*Let's play duets*. London: OUP, 1940. Six short, attractive descriptive
pieces, capably set for the medium. (UE-LI)

°*Lyric suite*. London: OUP, 1975. The language of this intriguing work is
basically tonal with frequent polychords and other dissonance punctuating
the predominantly open linear texture. The parts are well balanced, and
the writing is effective and idiomatic. "The five sections of this work are
continuous. I. Aubade. The first subject is made up of three motifs, and
the development of these provides the material of the middle section.
Then a recapitulation, with a coda based on an extension of the first motif,
gradually leads into: II. Lullaby. This is on two levels: the secondo part
plays a 'crooning', rocking figure. . . . alternating with the primo part playing a well-known nursery rhyme. These two contrasting features are subse-
quently shared by the two performers and played backwards, inverted,
backwards-inverted, and finally combined. III. Arabesque. Phrases from
the Lullaby are interspersed with anticipations of the Ländler. IV. Ländler. This comprises a refrain separated by three waltz fragments which are
frequently overlapped by a cadential interruption. At the end a violently
articulated high 'C' prepares the way for: V. Dirge. Based on a 'tear drop'

scale descending by 9ths and paralleled by rising 7ths, distributed among the four hands. In addition there is a melodic line which develops and merges into a rather richer interlude. These ideas work up to a chordal climax before subsiding into the Coda which ends with a sudden, foreboding (ff) Middle C, with overtones" (from the Composer's Note). (UI-LA)

Taubert, Ernst Eduard (1838–1934)

German composer, teacher, and music critic.

4 Tänze, Op.37. Leipzig: Siegel, 1881. US:Wc. Instructional pieces.

Unter fremden Musikanten, Op.22. Leipzig: Leuckart, 1872. US:Wc. Salon pieces. (I-UI)

Taylor, H.J.

5 Miniature duets. London: Collard Moutrie, 1918. US:Wc. Instructional pieces. (UE-LI)

Taylor, Raynor (1749–1825)

English organist and singer; immigrated to America in 1792, settling in Philadelphia. He composed a ballad opera and other stage works, songs, instrumental pieces, and piano compositions.

An easy and familiar lesson. . . . Philadelphia: B.Carr's Music Repository, ca.1795–1797. US:NYp.

•*Gavotte and Fandango; Minuetto; President's march*, arr. In collection *Duets of Early American Music*, Anne McClenny and Maurice Hinson, eds. Melville, NY: Belwin, 1971. Short attractive pieces by the early American composer. (E)

Tchaikovsky, Peter I. (1840–1893)

•*Fifty Russian folk songs*. •International; •Kalmus; a selection of 36 is published by •Peters. Short melodies arranged for piano 4H by the composer in a variety of meters and key signatures. Many of the tunes are familiar themes from the composer's chamber music and symphonic repertoire; their settings in this collection are short and succinct and often have a modal character. Appealing and interesting for both partners, and especially useful for sight-reading. (UE-I)

Tcherepnin, Alexander (1899–1977)

Russian-born American pianist and teacher. He composed operas, piano concertos, chamber music, and piano pieces in an eclectic tonal style with Russian and French influences. He also made use of nine-tone scales and oriental color.

Exploring the piano (Processional; Hopscotch; Dreamy Donna; Tommy Talent; Pandora; Busy Bill; Poor Paula; Math-Whiz; Kill-Joy; Gina and Gino; Hurried Harry; Jimmy Chang). Evanston: Summy-Birchard, 1959; •NEd. New York: Peters, 1976. Entrancing set of polished little pieces for teacher and a very young student. Crisply written with a light and fanciful touch by a fine craftsman. Broad range of musical styles, mood, color, and key signature. The Secondo part, which can also be performed by an advanced student or parent, is demanding, but the student's part is very easy, consisting mostly of repeated notes or patterns. Two of the pieces require that a second piano be used or that the child sit on the teacher's lap. (I-UI/LE)

Thalberg, Sigismond (1812–1871)

Virtuoso pianist; concertized throughout Europe and the Americas. He wrote operas and many piano pieces.

°*Danza sorrentina.* Ancona: Bèrben, 1976. While most of Thalberg's 4H works appear to be arrangements of his own piano solos, this bright, energetic, and effective tarantella is carefully written and is most likely original in its duet setting. (LI)

Grandes valses brillantes, Op.47. Paris: M. Schlesinger, n.d. US:Wc.

Thiessen, Karl (b.1867)

6 *Walzer,* Op.5. Dresden: E. Hoffmann, ca.1909. US:Wc. Salon pieces. (LI)

Thiman, Eric (1900–1975)

English organist and prolific composer of choral works, orchestral pieces, and piano compositions in a light, melodious style.

°*A Sligo reel.* London: Curwen, 1948. US:Wc. Teaching piece with Irish flavor. (UE-LI)

On Brockham Green, suite (Shepherd's song; Springtime; George the fiddler). London: Keith Prowse, 1930. US:Wc. Instructional pieces in pleasant, flowing style. (UE-LI)

Thomé, François (1850–1909)

French composer of songs and piano pieces in salon style.

°*Six valses.* Paris: Hamelle, n.d.

Thomson, Virgil (1896–   )

American critic and composer of operas; ballet, choral, and orchestral works; film music; songs; piano pieces; and chamber music. His style is simple, direct, and tonal, with clarity of expression.

Synthetic waltzes, for piano four hands or two pianos (1925). Pub. missing. US:NYamc.

Thuman, Herman

Svenska folktoner lätt sätta för pianoforte fyra händer (Swedish folk melodies in easy four hand arrangements). Stockholm: Bagge, ca.1887. S:Sim.

Thurm, Joachim

°*Europäische Volkslieder.* Leipzig: VEB Peters, 1964. Inviting series of folk songs in imaginative settings; exceptional harmonic interest. (LI-I)

Tibbits, George (1933–   )

Australian musician.

Variations (1969). Pub. missing. AU: Samc.

Tinel, Edgar (1854–1912)

Belgian pianist, teacher, and author. He composed sacred choral music, organ pieces, religious music dramas, chamber music, and piano works.

Sonata (g), Op.15. Leipzig: B&H, 1889. US:Wc. Long, four-movement work competently set in Romantic style, influenced by Mendelssohn. Lacking in strong thematic ideas or sustained harmonic interest, though brilliant at times. (UI-LA)

Tischler, F.

5 *Variations sur un thème de Himmel*, Op.3. Vienna: J. Czerný, 1829. A: Wgm.

Toch, Ernst (1887–1964)

Austrian-born American teacher and composer. He wrote in a highly individual post-Romantic chromatic style. His compositions include operas, orchestral works, chamber music, and a quantity of film and radio music.

°*Sonata*, Op.87. New York: Mills (Belwin), 1963. Pleasant, sunny, tidy three-movement work in urbane, neo-Classical idiom; thin-textured, mildly dissonant, tonal. Allegretto: tuneful and witty. Andante espressivo: deliberate and lyrical. Allegretto amabile, leggiero: bright and spirited. Proficiently set for 4H. (I-UI)

Tomaschek, Wenzel Johann (1774–1850)

Ouvertüre (Eb), Op.38. Prague: Berra, n.d. D-brd:B.

Tomkins, Thomas (1572–1656)

English composer, pupil of William Byrd; composed church music, madrigals, and music for viols and virginals.

°*A fancy for two to play.* See *Elizabethan Keyboard Duets* and the collection *Style and interpretation*, Vol.V, ed. H. Ferguson.

Torjussen, Trygve (1885–1977)

Norwegian composer and music critic. His works include chamber music, an orchestral suite, and music for organ and piano.

Carnival suite, Op.68. Boston: A.P. Schmidt, 1947. US:Wc. Three descriptive pieces; instructional. (I)

Torrá, Celia (1889–)

Argentine violinist, conductor, and composer; studied with Jenö Hubay, Kodály, and d'Indy.

°7 *Pequeñas piezas fáciles* (Sobre el puento de Aviñon; Arroz con leche; Arrorró; La torre en guardia; La hora del té; El cochecito; Canción de Navidad). Buenos Aires: Ricordi, n.d.

Tours, Berthold (1838–1897)

English organist and violinist of Dutch birth; composed hymn tunes, anthems, songs, and piano pieces.

Intermezzo, Op.1. Rotterdam: Vletter, ca.1857. US:Wc. Instructional piece.
(LI)

Suite de pièces. New York: Schirmer, 1893. US:Wc. Salon pieces. (I)

Tovey, Donald Francis (1875–1940)

English pianist, musicologist, and teacher; best known for his scholarly essays on Bach, Beethoven, Schubert, Gluck, and others. He composed an opera, choral and orchestral works, chamber music, and piano pieces.

Balliol dances (Oxford Tänze), Op.17. Mainz: Schott, 1906. GB:Lbl–US: Wc. Suite of sixteen waltzes in Romantic style, modeled after Brahms, Op.39. Melodious, graceful, pleasant to play; well balanced for both parts. (I-UI)

Townsend, Douglas (1921–)

American composer and musicologist; leading expert on piano four-hand music. He has written an opera, orchestral and chamber music, a ballet, and piano pieces.

°*Four fantasies on American folk songs* (Follow the drinking gourd; The new river train; Johnny has gone for a soldier; Two in one [Old Joe Clark and Sourwood Mountain]). New York: Peters, 1960. Suite of diverting arrangements of four American folk songs, freely set in a tidy, refined, traditional idiom; frequently modal with occasional complex rhythms. Ingenious, well balanced, and thoroughly enjoyable. There is an informative introduction by Oscar Brand on the backgrounds of the folk songs. (I-UI)

Trnka, Wenzel Joseph (1782–ca.1849)

6 Danses villageoises (C), Op.37. Vienna: Diabelli, n.d. A:Wgm.

Rondino (A), Op.35. Vienna: Diabelli, n.d. A:Wgm.

Trojelli, A.

°*Cantilène; Chasse; Villageoise*. Paris: Consortium Musical, n.d. (I)

Truzzi, Luigi (1799–1864)

La gioia delle madri (D), Op.66. Milan: Ercole Bonolini, n.d. I:Bsf.

Türk, Daniel Gottlob (1756–1813)

German theorist and composer; best known for his pedagogical material including a piano method, *Klavierschule*, and an instruction book on figured-bass playing. He also composed piano music.

[120] *Tonstücke*. Leipzig/Halle: pub. by the composer, ca.1807–1808. A: Wn–D-ddr:Mbs–US:Wc. °NEd. *Tonstücke*, ed. Doflein, 2 vols. Mainz: Schott, 1933; and °*30 Tonstücke*, ed. W. Serauky. Leipzig: Litolff (Peters), n.d. The 120 pieces of this distinguished collection of early teaching material were originally published in four volumes of 30 pieces each and appeared in progressive order of difficulty. They are not only excellent technical studies but are first-rate music as well. Both the Schott and Litolff editions provide useful selections of the original pieces. (UE-I)

Tutschek, Franz
°*Frühlingsmarsch*, Op.37. Leipzig: Siegel, 1867.

Twardowski, Romuald
Polish composer; has written three operas, ballets, orchestral and choral works, and compositions for various instrumental combinations.
°*Dwa Michały* (Joe and Jack) (LI); and *Japoneczka Miki* (Miki, the Japanese girl) (UE-LI). In collection *Drobiazgi*, vol.I, ed. Raube.
°*Dzwony* (The bells); and *Perpetuum mobile* (Perpetual motion). In collection, *Drobiazgi*, vol.II, ed. Raube. (I)

Twinn, Sydney
°*First year duets*. London: Lengnick, n.d. (I)

Twinning, Walter L.
Four short duets. London: Collard Moultrie, 1926. GB:Lbl. Bright, tuneful teaching pieces. (UE-LI)

Umlauf, Ignaz (ca.1746–1796)
Austrian conductor and violinist; wrote Singspiele, church and stage music, and chamber works.
Grande sonate (c). Vienna: Wiegl, n.d. A:Wgm.

Urspruch, Anton (1850–1907)
German pianist and composer.
Deutsche Tänze, Op.7. Hamburg: Cranz, 1877.
3 Marches, Op.18. Hamburg: Cranz, 1883.
Sonate (quasi fantasie) (A), Op.1. Leipzig: Kistner, 1871. US:Wc. Long, rambling single-movement work in Romantic style; extensive contrapuntal development, but weak in thematic interest. (UI-LA)

Vaňhal, Jan Křtitel (Johann Baptist) (1738–1813)
Czech composer of the Viennese School, contemporary of Haydn and Mozart. His four-hand music, written in skilled Classical style, is light, flowing, and tuneful. Most of his piano duets, however, have long been out of print, but, because of their charm, melodic appeal, and clarity of expression as well as their practical value as pedagogical material, many of these fine works deserve to be republished. In the absence of a comprehensive thematic index of the music of Vaňhal, the following compilation of his four-hand works has been assembled from a variety of sources: library catalogues, general and national encyclopedias, late 18th- and early 19th-century publisher's cata-

logues, and Margerethe von Dewitz, "Jean Baptiste Vanhal, Leben und Klavierwerke," diss. Ludwig Maximilians Universität, Munich, 1933. An examination of Vaňhal's music in several American libraries and of photocopies of similar material from European libraries aided in the accurate identification of a number of doubtful works and facilitated the classification of many others. The composer's 15 four-hand works are listed in roughly chronological order of publication.

Divertimento, avec accompagnement de flûte, violon, et vlcelle ad lib. (Eb). Vienna: Hoffmeister, ca.1785 (i. Allegro [Eb], ii. Adagio [c], iii. Allegro [Eb]). A:Wn–B:Bc–CS:Pnm–GB:Lbl. Other editions published as *Divertissement* and *Grande Sonate:* GB:Lbl–I:Mc,Nc–US:NYp,Wc. (LI)

2 *Sonates* (F,A), Op.32/1 and 2. Vienna: Artaria, 1785 (No.1: i. Allegro moderato [F], ii. Adagio-Andante [F], iii. Allegretto [F]; No.2: i.Adagio alla Francese [A], ii. Variazioni alla Italiana, thema: Andante moderato [A], iii. Rondo alla Tedesca [A]). A:Wst. Other editions and single movements of the sonatas at: CS:Pnm,Pu–GB:Lbl,Lcm. (I)

Sonata [w.o.n.] per il clavicembalo o fortepiano (Bb). Vienna: Hoffmeister, ca.1787 (i. Allegro [Bb], ii. Adagio [F], iii. Allegretto [Bb]). A:Wn–GB: Lbl. Other editions published as *Sonata* or *Duetto* at: B:Bc–US:Wc. (LI)

Une sonate très facile (C), Op.64. Vienna: Kozeluch, 1799 (i. Allegretto [C], ii. Adagio [F], iii. Allegro [C]). A:Wn. °NEd. [Sonata, Op.64 complete] Nos.8, 9, and 10 in *Album of four hand compositions by old Czech masters,* ed. Kleinová, Fišerová, and Müllerová. Other editions at: CS: Pnm. (LI)

2 *Sonates* (*sonatines*) (C,F), Op.46. Mainz: Schott, ca.1800. (No.1: i. Allegretto [C], ii. Adagio [F], iii. Allegro [C]; No.2: i. Andante, Allegro moderato [F], ii. Tempo di menuetto, moderato [F], iii. Allegro [F]). D-ddr: Bds. (UE-LI)

Sonate (F), Op.65. Vienna: Kozeluch, 1802 (i. Adagio [F], ii. Allegro moderato [F], iii. Allegro [F]). CS:Pnm. °NEd. [Op.65/iii (Allegro)] No.6 in *Album of four hand compositions by old Czech masters,* ed. Kleinová, Fišerová, and Müllerová. (LI)

3 *Sonatines* (F,C,Bb), Op.8. Hamburg: Böhme, ca.1804 (No.1: i.Adagio [F], ii.Andante [Bb], iii. Allegro [F]; No.2: i. Adagio–Allegro [C], ii. Adagio [F], iii. Allegro [C]; No.3: i. Andante [Bb], ii. Andante molto [Eb], iii. Allegro [Bb]). CS:Pnm. Other editions at: CS:Pnm–US:Wc. °NEd. [Op.8/2/ii (Adagio in F)] No.7 in *Album of four hand compositions by old Czech masters,* ed. Kleinová, Fišerová, and Müllerová. (UE-LI)

[13] *Pièces agréables.* Rotterdam: Plattner, ca.1805 (Vol.1: C,C,F,C,C,C,C; Vol.2: F,C,C,C,F,C). US:Wc. Other editions published as *Petites Pièces; Kurze und leichte Clavier Stücke; Duettini;* and 12 *Drobnyck Skladbiček*

at: B:Bc—CS:Pnm—D-brd:B,OF—GB:Lbl. °NEd. Nos.3, 4, and 8 in
Album of four hand compositions by old Czech masters, ed. Kleinová,
Fišerová, and Müllerová. (UE-LI)

3 *Neue Sonaten*, sehr leicht (—,F,Bb) [w.o.n.] Vienna: Cappi, 1805 (No.1
missing; No.2: i. Adagio [F], ii. Allegretto [F], iii. Allegretto [F]; No.3:
i. Allegro moderato [Bb], ii. Andante sostenuto [Bb], iii. Allegretto [Bb]).
A:Wn (No.2)—CS:Pnm (No.3). (LI)

6 *Leichte deutsche Tänze* (C,F,Bb,G,Eb,C). Vienna: Cappi, 1806. A:Wst.
Other editions published as *Six walses; Six walses faciles; Six pièces*; and
Six pièces faciles at: A:Wst—CS:Pnm—GB:Lbl—US:Wc. °NEd. [No.1
(C)] No.4 in *Album of four hand compositions by old Czech masters*.
(UE-LI)

6 *Danses hongroises* (C,F,Bb,G,D,A). Vienna: Cappi, 1807. D-ddr:Bds. Also
as 6 *Ländlerische Tänze*. (UE-LI)

6 *Menuetten und 6 Ländler* (C,F,Bb,G,D,A, —). Vienna: Cappi, ca.1809.
Menuetten only; Ländler missing. D-ddr:Bds (Menuetten only). (UE-LI)

3 *Sonatines faciles* (C,G,D) [w.o.n.]. Offenbach: André, ca.1810 (No.1: i.
Adagio-Allegretto [C], ii. Andante sostenuto [F], Allegro [C]; No.2: i.
Adagio-Allegretto [G], ii. Polonaise [G], iii. Allegretto [G]; No.3: i. Al-
legro moderato [D], ii. Andante alla siciliana [D], iii. Allegretto [D]).
US:NYp, Wc. (UE-LI)

6 *Leichte Stücke* (G,C,F,C,G,D). °NEd. Walter Frickert, ed. Kassel: Bärenreiter, 1966. (UE-LI)

8 *Petites pièces faciles*. Pub. and date missing. (1. Alla tedesca [C]; 2.
Marcia vivace [C]; 3. Allegretto [C]; 4. Allegretto [F]; 5. Polonaise [F];
6. Allegretto [F]; 7. Cantabile [Bb]; 8. missing). A:Wn has *Huit petites
pièces*. Ms. (Ex Rebus Theresia Edla von Fritsch).

Unidentified or Only Partially Identified Works:

Rondo (C). Ms. A:Wn.

Sonata a quattro mani per il clavicembalo o Fortepiano. Ms. Copie de l'edition de Hoffmeister à Vienna. B:Bc.

Sonata à quatro mani per il clavicembalo o fortepiano. Vienna: Hoffmeister,
ca.1790. GB:Lbl.

Due Sonate auf vier Hände pro Piano Forte. Ms. (Josepha Pinsker, 1833.)
CS:Pnm. This handwritten collection of three sonatas and one sonatina is
introduced on the title page by the multilingual heading together with the
name of the owner (also the copyist?) and the date. Below the title and
in a much later hand is scribbled the name "Wanhal," suggesting that he
may have been the composer of the entire collection. However, the copyist
has identified only the fourth work as a Vaňhal composition, "Sonata a
quatro mani von Wanhal" (identical with the Sonata [F], Op.65, in the
above list). The three other pieces—Sonata Iª: Rondo andante (C); So-

nata II^da: Allegro (C), Cantabile, Andante (Bb); and Sonatina: Allegretto molto (C)—remain anonymous and do not correspond to any other Vaňhal works encountered in the present study.

Sonata (F). Stamp. Chimica. CS:Pu.

Sonate brillante. Vienna: Artaria, 1812. A:Wst.

Due sonate per cembalo. Ms. CS:Pnm—I:Bc.

Sonatine (C). Bonn: Simrock, ca.1813. D-ddr:Bds (?).

Sonatine (F). Bonn: Simrock, ca.1814. D-brd:B (?).

3 *Sonatines*, No.III. Offenbach: André, ca.1818. B:Bc—GB:Lbl.

Suite des sonatines (I and II) à l'usage des commençans. Vienna: Mollo, ca. 1808. D-ddr:LEm.

Van Slyck, Nicholas

°*With twenty fingers* (1970–1971), Books I, II, and III. Hastings-on-Hudson, NY: General Music Publishing Co., 1973. 45 delightful pieces, varying in length from five measures to two pages. They sparkle with wit and are attractively set in a contemporary, tonal, linear style with rhythmic vitality and structural interest. Various contrapuntal exercises are exploited, especially canon, and the pieces maintain a light and buoyant character throughout. Book I: Hello Dance—A; Hello Dance—B (with more advanced Secondo); Resting (very short); Sheep (folk tune with chordal accompaniment); Waltz; Lines and spaces (short with chromatic Secondo part); Ties (sustained, tied notes over bar lines); Canonball (simple canon between partners); Sheep No.2 (folklike melody with accompaniment); Chorale (with double thirds in accompaniment); Compass Points; Hopping (bright melody with syncopated Secondo part in seconds); Folk Tale (melody in canon between parts); Classic Way; Dance Tune (bright, rhythmical); Close Quarters (hands play close together). (UE-LI/E-UE) Book II: Rainbow; Ties and Dotted Notes; Mirror; Mirror (2nd version); Scherzo (bright and fast); See-Saw (canon at the fourth); Herbs and Spices; Hommage à Béla Bartók (dissonant, rapid 16th notes); Strolling (changing meters; amiable melody and accompaniment); River Tune (smooth-flowing melody with arpeggiated accompaniment); Quasars (mysterious mood piece; slow moving); Ox-cart (heavy, plodding piece with canon at the lower fifth); Old Fashion (rippling waltz); Pitter-Patter (fast, repeated two-note patterns); Christmas Ground (ostinato). (UE-LI) Book III: Out of the Mist (Impressionistic tone picture); Double Trouble (rhythmical melody in canon at the second); Chord study (slow, deliberate, imitative); Gavotte (graceful melody with duolets and triplets); Idea Exchange (scalar melody with imitation); Icebergs (slow, sustained, dissonant); Five by Five (exercise in 5/8 time); Copy Cat (melody treated canonically, with augmentation); Ancient History (free recitative with faster middle section); Chase (Presto with repeated notes); Reflections (placid, slow-moving mirror canon); Night-ride (fast; exercise in repeated notes and alternating notes between the hands); Pieces of Eight (rhythmic study emphasizing alternating groupings of 2 and 3 eighth notes); Journey's End (Fughetta, chromatic, four-voice fugue). (LI-I)

Vargas, G.
°*A garden dance.* New York: Sam Fox, n.d.

Vasseur, Henry
°*En vacances,* suite enfantine, six pièces. Paris: Rouart, 1938.

Veal, Arthur
°*Rumba.* London: Ashdown, 1977. Bright, strongly rhythmical dance in popular style. (LI-I)

Vellones, Pierre (Rousseau) (1889–1939)
°*Une aventure de Babar* (Lududu joue de la flûte douce; Entrée et grand air d'Adrienne l'autruche; Berceuse du pays natal; Pastorale du centaure; Le lever du jour; Le temple de la justice; Marche de la reconciliation). Paris: Lemoine, 1947. Short, pleasing, descriptive pieces from the tale of Babar the Elephant. (UE-LI)
°*Invitation à la musique.* Paris: Eschig, 1938.

Veretti, Antonio (1900–   )
Italian composer; his musical style reflects influences from jazz to serial techniques.
Passepied I e II. In collection *Album di Musica Moderna,* vol. II.

Verhaar, Ary (1900–   )
Dutch composer of orchestral and chamber music, piano pieces, and works for school chorus.
°*Ballade,* Ritornel en Rondel, Op.37. Amsterdam: Donemus, 1948.

Verne, Mary
°*Duets on four Brazilian songs* (Vita; O Ceolinho; Dorme, Nenê; Na Bahia, Tem). New York: Lee Roberts, 1972. Attractive folk-song arrangements. (E)

Vieru, Anatol (1926–   )
Romanian conductor, teacher, and composer; studied with Khachaturian. He has written orchestral, choral, chamber, and piano works; concertos; and electronic compositions.
The birth of a language (1971). Ms. Commissioned by Milton and Peggy Salkind. Available from composer, Union of Composers of the Romanian Socialist Republic, Bucharest, Romania.

Viguerie, Bernard (1761–1819)
Six sonates. Paris: pub. by composer, n.d. I:Mc has Sonata No.4 only.

Vil'koreiskaia, T.

Kazach'ia (Cossack girl). In collection *Sbornik fortepiannikh,* ed. N. Aga-fonnikov. (UE-LI)

Villa-Lobos, Heitor (1887–1959)

A folia de um blóco infantil (Play-block frolic), No.8 in *Carnaval das Crianças* (Children's carnival). Rio de Janeiro: Arthur Napoleão, n.d. US:Bp. Brilliant, rhythmically exciting piece; probably the composer's only composition for piano 4H. (UI-LA)

Vitlin, V.

V tsirke (At the circus). In collection, *Sbornik fortepiannikh,* ed. N. Aga-fonnikov. (UE-LI)

Vogler, Georg Joseph (1749–1814)

German pianist, organist, teacher, and music theorist; composed prolifically in all forms. He was also a priest and was idealized by Robert Browning in the poem "Abt Vogler."

Concerto for piano four hands and orchestra, 1794. Pub. and date missing. F:Pc.

Sonata. Paris: Boyer, 1785. F:Pc.

Vogler, Johann Baptist (fl. late 18th and early 19th cent.)

12 Oberösterreichische Ländler (Eb,Eb,Eb,Bb,Eb,Ab,Eb,Eb,G,G,D,D). Vienna: Eder, 179[?]. D-brd:Mbs. Series of Ländler similar to Schubert's in structure, but more restricted harmonically and melodically; naïve and fresh charm. (UE-LI)

3 Tempostücke für Anfänger, No.1. Vienna: Eder, 1816. A:Wgm.

Vogt, Jean (1823–1888)

German teacher, concert pianist, and composer; wrote an oratorio, chamber music, and piano works.

Tscherkessen-Lied, charakteristisches Tonstück, Op.152. Berlin: Schlesinger, 1884. US:Wc.

Vol'fenson, S.

Soviet musician

Krakoviak. In collection *Sbornik fortepiannikh,* ed. N. Agafonnikov. (UE-LI)

Volkart, Hazel

A cruise on the river (Smooth sailing; Fun on deck; Stormy voyage; Homeward bound). New York: Mills, 1959. Instructional pieces. (UE-LI)

Riding along. New York: Mills, 1959. Show, lazy cowboy tune in traditional style. (UE-LI)

Volkart-Schläger, Käthe (1897–   )

Mohrentanz und Mummenschanz, Tänze. Mainz: Schott, ca.1960. Attractive dances in traditional style. (UE-LI/E)

Der Spielgarten, 14 leichte Stücke. Mainz: Schott, 1941. Charming instructional pieces. (UE)

°*Zu zweit mehr Freud'*; kleine Stücke zum Anfang, 2 vols. Heidelberg: Willy Müller (Süddeutscher Musikverlag), 1939. (Vol.1,E-UE;Vol.2, UE-LI)

Volkmann, Robert (1815-1883)

German teacher; composed orchestral, chamber, and many piano works in Romantic style.

°*Hungarian sketches* (Ungarische Skizzen; Esquisses hongroises), Op.24. Budapest: Rózsavölgyi, 1861; Leipzig: Peters, n.d.; London: Augener; Paris: °Hamelle, n.d. US:Wc. Graceful, fluent suite of seven pieces in pleasant style; Hungarian folk-song influence. (I)

3 *Märsche* (Eb,C,f), Op.40. Budapest: Heckenast, ca.1860; London: Augener, n.d. US:Wc. (I-UI)

Musikalisches Bilderbuch, 6 Stücke, Op.11. Budapest: Rózsavölgyi, 1852. US:PHf,Wc. Charming gems, imaginatively set; excellent study pieces. (LI-I)

Rondino & Marsch-Caprice, Op.55. Budapest: Heckenast, 1867. US:Wc. (I)

°3 *Serenades*, Opp.62,63, and 69. Leipzig: VEB Peters, n.d. (I-UI)

Sonatine (G), Op.57. Mainz: Schott, 1868. US:Wc. Melodious, well-constructed three-movement work in flowing Schumannesque style. (I)

°*Die Tageszeiten* (La journée), 12 Klavierstücke, Op.39. Mainz: Schott, 1915; °Paris: Hamelle, n.d. Graceful, descriptive pieces. (I)

Visegrád, 12 musikalische Dichtungen, Op.21. Budapest/Leipzig: Rózsavölgyi, n.d.; Vienna: UEd, ca.1908; London: Augener, n.d.; Leipzig: Peters, n.d. US:Wc. Tastefully fashioned suite of tone pictures. (I)

Vorlová, Sláva (1894–1973)

Czech teacher and composer of cantatas, symphonic and chamber music, concertos, choruses, songs, folk-song arrangements, and piano pieces.

°*Happy intervals*, Op.54. Prague: Panton, 1965; °Hastings-on-Hudson: General Music Co. This series of eight pieces, written as interval studies, has exceptional musical and pedagogical merit and displays masterly compositional skill as well. Although limiting herself to the use of one specified interval in both the Primo and Secondo parts throughout each piece, Vorlová succeeds in producing compositions of charm and vitality. Musical interest is also sustained by the carefully balanced activity between the parts. (I)

Vuataz, Roger (1898–   )

Swiss organist, conductor, and composer. His works include oratorios, songs, piano pieces, chamber music, and orchestral works.

Les cloches, Op.47/4 (1935). CH:Zma.

Vueillemin, Louis (1879–1929)

French music critic and composer; his style was influenced by Breton folk music.

°3 *Bluettes faciles*. Paris: Durand, n.d. (UE-LI)
°*Pour se distraire*. Paris: Lemoine, ca.1908. (UE-LI)

Wachs, Paul (1851–1915)

Les archers du roy. London: Hatzfeld, 1908. US:Wc. Instructional piece. (LI-I)
°*Bébé et sa maman*, petit morceau très facile. Paris: Hamelle, n.d.
°*Canzonetta rusticana*. Paris: Consortium Musical, n.d. (I)
Capricante. Philadelphia: Presser, 1913. US:Wc. Instructional piece. (LI-I)
°*March of the flower girls*. Paris: Hamelle, n.d.
°*Mes petits concerts*. Paris: Salabert, n.d.
°*Les petits inséparables*, duo enfantin. Paris: Hamelle, n.d.
°*Six pièces dans le style ancien* (Gavotte; Madrigal; Menuet; Passacaille; Passepied; Pavane). Paris: Lemoine, n.d. (E)
°*Shower of stars*, caprice. Philadelphia: Presser, 1909. (I/UI)

Wagner, Richard (1813–1883)

German composer, conductor, essayist, and philosopher. He expanded the operatic form into large-scale stage works, which he termed "music dramas" and for which he wrote the libretti and the music. Wagner exerted a strong influence on the course of nineteenth- and twentieth-century music. His four-hand works date from his student days.
Largo maestoso [introductory movement]; *Allegro con brio* [beginning only] (C). Ms. GB:Lbl.
°*Polonaise* (D), Op.2 (1831). NEd. London: Curwen, 1954 (ed. T.A. Johnson), and in collection *Meister der Romantik*.
Sonata (Bb), Op.1 (1832) (lost). Originally pub. together with *Polonaise*, Op.2 by B&H, Leipzig. Later arranged for orchestra.

Walker, Ernest (1870–1949)

English pianist, author, composer, critic, and teacher. His compositions are written in fastidious, often chromatic, Romantic style.
Six duettinos. London: OUP, 1927. (UE-LI)
Fantasia-Variations on a Norfolk folk song, Op.45 (1929). London: OUP, 1930. GB:Lbl–US:Wc. Large-scale, heavy-textured rhapsodic piece in the idiom of Vaughan Williams. (LI-I)
Rhapsody and fugue, Op.57 (1934). London: OUP, 1934. US:Wc. Virtuoso work in chromatic idiom; free fantasy introduction followed by a bold, brilliantly worked-out fugue. (UI-LA)
A West African fantasia, Op.53 (1932). London: OUP, 1934. US:Wc. Colorful settings of various Central African native melodies collected at or near Albert Schweitzer's hospital at Lambaréné, Gabon. This edition of the work was sold for the benefit of the hospital. (I)

Walker, George (1922–   )

American pianist and composer; teaches at Rutgers University, Newark. He has written orchestral and choral works, chamber music, and piano pieces.

°*Five fancies for clarinet and piano, four-hands.* Hastings-on-Hudson, NY: General Music Publishing Co., 1975. Set of short variations on a theme in dissonant idiom; compactly written and skilfully set for the instruments. (A)

Walsh, Mary

°*Black hawk waltz* (Eb). Cincinnati: Willis, n.d. (UE)

Walter, — (fl. ca.1800)

3 *Sonates*, (G,D,Bb), par Walter, élève de Michel Haydn. Paris: Érard, ca. 1800. GB:Lbl. Short works in pallid Classical style. Undistinguished except for occasional spurts of harmonic and melodic interest. (LI-I)

Walton, William (1902–   )

English composer. His lyrical musical style is generally tonal with detailed harmonic and contrapuntal writing and rhythmical drive, showing influences of jazz, Elgar, and Stravinsky. He is best known for *Façade*, suite for declamation and instruments. He has also written choral and orchestral works, songs, and chamber music.

°*Duets for children*, arr. Herbert Murrill (Book 1: The music lesson; The three-legged race; The silent lake; Pony trap; Ghosts; Hop-scotch. Book 2: Swing-boats; Song at dusk; Puppet's dance; Trumpet tune). London: OUP, 1940. Although arranged from the original orchestral suite, *Music for children*, these alluring, tidy little pieces have been included here because of their polished 4H setting, sparkle, and effectiveness. (UE-LI)

Wansborough, —

°*Hopi wigwam dance.* Philadelphia: Presser, n.d. (UE)

Ward, Lela Hoover

°*Twenty fingers*, 24 folksong arrangements in 2 vols. Boston: Boston Music, n.d. (UE)

Warlock, Peter (pseud. of Philip Heseltine) (1894–1930)

English author and composer of songs, choral works, chamber pieces, and orchestral music. His individual style shows the influence of his friend Delius and of Elizabethan composers.

°*Capriol suite* (Basse-danse; Pavane; Tordion; Bransles; Pieds-en-l'air; Mattachins) (1926). London: Curwen, 1928. Based on dance melodies from Arbeau's *Orchésographie* (1588); better known in its orchestral version, but attractive and satisfying in its 4H form. (I-UI)

Webbe, Samuel (the younger) (ca.1770–1843)

English composer of glees, motets, songs, and piano pieces.

Duett for two persons on the piano-forte. London: Birchall, ca.1824. GB: Lcm,Ob—US:Wc.

Weber, Ben (1916–1979)

American composer; wrote ballet music, works for orchestra and chamber groups, and piano compositions; developed an individual, compact, serial idiom.

Suite. Ms. Commissioned by Milton and Peggy Salkind. US:NYamc.

Weber, Carl Maria von (1786–1826)

In recent years, the many solo piano works by Weber, which were once held in high esteem, have waned in popularity. But his twenty piano duets are still very much alive and waiting to be discovered. Appearing in three sets, Op.3 (6 pieces), Op.10 (6 pieces), and Op.60 (8 pieces), they are in progressive order of difficulty and show the development of the composer's harmonic and melodic style and mastery of form. The arrangements of the suites and the nature of the individual pieces have suggested to critics that Weber might have patterned them after the multi-movement Viennese serenade as cultivated by Mozart in his lighter works and by Beethoven in his *Septet*, Op.20. In groups or individually, these short, small-featured, fluent pieces, masterfully designed for the medium, are appealing and satisfying.

Weber's complete works for four hands are available in *International, *Peters, and *Ricordi editions. Opp.3 and 10 are issued in one volume by *Bärenreiter and *Hansen.

Six pièces, Op.3 (1801). 1. Sonatine (C): pleasant, flowing work in truncated sonata form. 2. Romanze (F): slow, melodious. 3. Menuetto (Bb): fast, bright. 4. Andante con variazioni (G): slow, theme with three variations. 5. Marcia (C): light, stirring, rhythmical. 6. Rondo (C): happy, rapid-paced. Available separately: Op.3/1, *Bèrben; Op.3/3, *Bèrben; Op.3/5, *London: Associated Board of the Royal Schools of Music.

Six pièces, Op.10 (1809). 1. Moderato (Eb): flowing, pleasant melodies; in sonata form. 2. Andantino (Eb): gently moving siciliano. 3. Andante con variazioni (G): theme with three variations. 4. Mazurka (C): lively, strongly accented. 5. Adagio (Ab): slow, lyrical. 6. Rondo (Eb): long, rhythmically active. Available separately from *Schott: Op.10/1 and 3.

Huit pièces, Op.60 (1818–1819). 1. Moderato (D): elegant and charming minuet. 2. Allegro (C): strong, assertive; in sonata form. 3. Adagio (F): broad, melodious. 4. Allegro, tutto ben marcato [All'ungharese] (a): bold, rhythmical, in Hungarian style. 5. Alla siciliana (d): delightful, flowing. 6. Tema variato "Ich hab' mir Eins erwählet" (E): short, amiable folklike melody with seven brief charming variations. 7. Marcia (g): powerful, rousing. 8. Rondo (Bb), lively.

Weckerlin, Jean-Baptiste (1821–1910)

French teacher, scholar, music editor, and composer; published editions of early French songs and folk songs.

Carmencita, 3ème romanesca. Paris: Durand, n.d.

°*Les cigognes,* suite de laendler alsatiens. Paris: Durand, n.d. (UE)

°*Noëls.* Paris: Consortium Musical, n.d.

°*La valse des amours.* Paris: Durand, n.d. (UE)

°*Valse des canards.* Paris: Consortium Musical, n.d.

Wehrli, Werner (1892–1944)

Swiss composer of comic opera, orchestral and chamber works, songs, and piano pieces.

Kleines musikalische Spielzeug, Op.23 (1927). Zürich: Hug, n.d. CH:Zma.

Nachlese, 9 kleine Stückchen, Op.46. Zürich: Hug, 1938. CH:Zma.

12 Variationen über das Lied "Im Aargäu sind zwöi (zweü) Liebi," Op.45. Zürich: Hug, 1938. CH:Zma.

Weihnachtsmusik, Op.50/II. Zürich: Hug, 1939. CH:Zma.

Weiner, Leó (1885–1960)

Hungarian composer; his works include chamber and orchestral music, concertos, and piano pieces. He followed nineteenth-century German musical techniques rather than the Hungarian nationalism of Bartók and Kodály.

°*Three little pieces* (Három kis négykezes zongoradarab), Op.36. Budapest: Zenemükiadó Vállalat, 1950, 1969. Attractive little pieces in Hungarian folk style. The conservative harmonic idiom is effective. A few rhythmic difficulties. (LI/E-UE-5)

°*Suite on Hungarian folk dances,* Op.18. Budapest: Zenemükiadó Vállalat, 1965. Graceful arrangements of Hungarian folk tunes. (UI)

°*Tündérek tánca* (Dance of the elves). Budapest: Editio musica, 1968. Brilliant work in moderately contemporary idiom. (UI)

Weingartner, Felix (1863–1942)

Distinguished Austrian conductor, author of books on conducting, and composer.

Lustige Ouvertüre, Op.53. Leipzig: B&H, n.d. CH:Zma.

Weis, Karel (1862–1944)

Czech organist, conductor, and composer; collector of Bohemian folk songs.

Böhmische Tänze, Opp.8 and 9. Berlin: Bote & Bock, 1886; Prague: Burzik & Kohoüt, 1889. CS:Pchf. (I)

Weismann, Julius (1879–1950)

German composer of works in Romantic harmonic style with strong neo-Classical formal elements.

°*Sonatine* (1943). Leipzig: VEB Peters, 1957. Lyrical two-movement work in traditional harmonic idiom: pleasant, rhythmic Allegro and flowing Allegretto. Linear in part. Well distributed for both partners. (I)

Wells, Elsie

°*Sea pictures;* 15 easy piano duets. London: OUP, 1977. Set 1: Summer breezes; The fishing boat; The sparkling sea; Donkey ride; A stormy day;

March of the sea urchins; The mystery ship; The seashell's lullaby; Dancing waves; Sand castles. Set 2: Sailor's dance; Chinese lanterns; Dolphins; Ebb tide; Coral island. Attractive pieces in traditional instructional style; well balanced for both partners. (UE)

Welsch, Ulrich

°3 *Fröhliche Tanzweisen*, Op.1. Leipzig: Peters, 1938. Bright, effervescent dances in conventional harmonic idiom with a variety of rhythmical-interest. (UE-LI)

Wendel, Ernst (1876–1938)

German conductor, violinist, and teacher. He wrote choral and orchestral works, songs, and piano pieces.
Walzer, Op.12. Leipzig: Kistner & Siegel, 1911. US:Wc. Salon pieces. (LI)

Werdin, Eberhard (1911–   )

German composer of music for young people.
°*Slawische Tanzweisen mit Variationen* (Ketuša; Durdevka; Kozačko). Mainz: Schott, 1953. Three Serbian melodies expertly and imaginatively set. (I)

Werner, Jean-Jacques

°*La boîte à jeux*, pièces enfantines (Mikado; Bilboquet; Diabolo) (1961). Paris: Edition musicales transatlantiques, 1961. Short, ingratiating pieces in mildly contemporary idiom. (LI)

Werner, Johann Gottlob (1778–1822)

German teacher and organist. He wrote an organ method, a harmony text, and piano pieces.
Leichte vierhändige Uebungsstücke. Leipzig: Hofmeister, n.d. A:Wgm.

Wesley, Samuel (1766–1837)

Distinguished English organist. He composed church music, orchestral and chamber works, songs, organ and piano pieces, and harpsichord lessons.
Andante (D). Ms. GB:Lbl.
Duet (G) (1791) (Larghetto; Allegro spiritoso; Largo; Comodo; Presto). Ms. GB:Lbl.
2 Duets (F,D), from *Four sonatas and two duets*, Op.5. London: L. Lavenu, 1800. GB:Lbl. Short, three-movement works in Classical style. Antiphonal, spare-textured, with rhythmical interest and harmonic variety. Writing tends to be thin in spots. (LI)
Easy duet (G) (1832). Autograph. GB:Lbl.
Fragment [F ?] Ms. GB:Lbl.
"*God save the King*" *with variations* (1834). Copy. GB:Lbl.
Grand duet. London: J.E. Dean, n.d. US:Wc. Large-scale work, linear, in classical style; written for organ or piano; the setting and texture suggest organ, with emphasis on four-part writing. (I)
°*March* (D). London: W. Hodsoll, ca.1807; 1823. °NEd. Basil Ramsay, ed.

London: Novello, 1958. US:Wc. Short, dashing little march in classical style. (LI)

Wesley-Smith, Martin (1945–)

Australian composer. His works include an opera, theater songs for children, choral pieces, orchestral and chamber music, piano works, and educational music. His style influenced by jazz, popular music, and electronic music.

To noddy man, for high voice and piano four hands. Pub. missing, 1969. AU:Samc.

Westenholz, Carl Ludwig Cornelius (1788–1854)

Adagio et polonaise. Pub. missing, 1813. D-ddr:SWl.

Andante et rondo. Pub. and date missing. D-ddr:Swl.

Westenholz, Eleonore Sophia Maria (1759–1838)

One of the few women composers of the time.

Sonata (F), Op.3. Berlin: Werckmeister, 1806. B:Bc. Thin four-movement work. Has some pleasant melodies, a few chromaticisms, arresting modulations, and a general stylistic consistency but is long and repetitious. (LI-I)

Weybright, June

°*Another duet book* (10 pieces). Melville, NY: Belwin, 1971. Instructional pieces including folk song arrangements. (E)

°*Double play*. New York: Mills (Belwin), n.d. Instructional. (UE)

°*In the saddle*. Melville, NY: Belwin, n.d. Instructional. (UE)

°*Valse bleue*. Melville, NY: Belwin, n.d. Instructional. (UE)

Whitefield, Bernard (1910–)

°*Boogie woogie*. Boston: Boston Music, 1944. US:Wc. Teaching piece in popular idiom. (LI)

°*Easy boogie woogie duets*. Boston: Boston Music, 1947. US:NYp. Eight instructional pieces in popular style. (LI)

Whiting, Arthur Battelle (1861–1936)

American pianist and early expert on harpsichord and clavichord music. He composed piano concertos, orchestral and chamber music, vocal works, and piano pieces.

Fantasy waltzes, Op.13. Boston: Boston Music, 1897. US:Wc. Pleasant works in late Romantic style. (LI)

Wickenhauser, Richard (1867–1936)

German choral conductor, teacher, and composer.

°*Twelve dance melodies*, Op.32. London: Novello, n.d.

Widdicombe, Trevor

°*Circus parade*. London: Curwen, 1954. (I)

Widdoes, Lawrence L. (1932–)

Antique shop (Highboy; Pewter; Spinning Wheel). Photocopy, 1960. Available from composer, The Juilliard School, Lincoln Center, New York, NY 10023. Dissonant; in free style. (I-UI)

Widor, Charles Marie (1844–1937)

French organist, composer, and teacher. He composed operas, symphonies, and organ works.

Sérénade (A). Mainz: Schott, ca.1906. D-brd:MZsch.

Wihtol, Joseph (1863–1948)

Latvian composer and conductor; student of Rimsky-Korsakov. His compositions often employ Latvian folk themes.

Été. See *Badinage*.

Wijdefeld, Wolfgang (1910–   )

Dutch pianist and composer. His works include film scores, chamber music, ballets, orchestral compositions, and piano pieces.

•Piano piece (1970). Amsterdam: Donemus, n.d.

Wijker, Henk

Dutch musician.

•Poco moderno, une petite suite facile (Valse; Sérénade; Danse rustique). Utrecht: J.A.H. Wagenaar, 1965. US:Wc. Pleasant group of instructional pieces. Strongly tonal with mild dissonance, polytonality, and use of the whole-tone scale. (LI)

Wilkinson, Philip G.

•Country carillon; Marche humoreske. London: Curwen, 1961. (LI)
•Two country sketches. London: Novello, 1958. Instructional. (I)
The gentle stream; Pony ride. London: Elkin, 1959. US:Wc. Instructional pieces. (UE)
•Two idylls. London: Curwen, n.d. (UE-LI)
•The playful pixie. London: Augener, 1960. Refined, well-balanced instructional piece. (UE-LI)
•Rural scenes. London: Augener, 1961. Instructional. (UE-LI)

Willfort, Egon Stuart (1889–   )

17 Duos für Jedermann. Vienna: Österreichischer Bundesverlag, 1953. US: Wc. Short, diverting teaching pieces in progressive order of difficulty; imaginatively designed in traditional harmonic framework. (LI-I/E-5)

Waldsuite (G). Vienna: Österreichischer Bundesverlag, 1948. US:Wc. Pleasant, effective teaching pieces. (LI)

Williams, —

•Graduation grand march. New York: Sam Fox, n.d.

Williams, David Russell (1932–   )

American composer and teacher at the Eastman School of Music.

Concerto for piano four hands and orchestra (Buoyantly; Ponderously;

Brightly), 1963–1964. US:PHf Fleisher Collection. Three-movement work in conservative contemporary tonal idiom. Brilliant, rhythmical. (A)

Suite for piano. US:NYamc.

Williams, Jean

*Dance Johnny! New York: Schroeder & Gunther, 1949. Lively Irish jig. (UE-LI)

Williamson, Malcolm (1931–   )

Australian organist and pianist; resident of England. He has written operas, orchestral and chamber music, piano works, and organ pieces in eclectic style.

*The happy prince, for chorus, strings, percussion and piano four hands. London: Joseph Weinberger, n.d.

Travel diaries (in part for piano four hands). London: Chappell, 1962. US: Wc.

Wilm, Nicolai von (1834–1911)

Russian composer; studied at Leipzig Conservatory and lived in Germany after 1875. Prolific, capable composer of fastidiously written, often descriptive, four-hand works and chamber music in resourceful, fluent salon idiom. The following works are all (I-UI) unless otherwise specified.

4 Charakteristiche Klavierstücke, Op.147. Vienna: UEd, ca.1900. US:Wc.

3 Charakteristische Märsche (D,d,Eb) Op.70. Vienna: UEd, 1888. US:Wc.

6 Deutsche Volkslieder, Op.178. Berlin: Simrock, 1901. US:Wc.

Im russischen Dorfe, Op.37. Berlin: Ries & Erler, 1883. US:Wc.

4 Klavierstücke, Op.152. Leipzig: Forberg, 1897. US:Wc.

6 Leichte Charakterstücke, Op.143. Magdeburg: Heinrichshofen, ca.1896. US:Wc.

3 Leichte melodische Klavierstücke, Op.255. London/Mainz: Schott, 1912. US:Wc.

Musikalische Federzeichnungen, Op.28. Berlin: Ries & Erler, 1882. US:Wc.

Paraphrasen nordischer Volkslieder, Op.140. Magdeburg: Heinrichshofen, 1895. US:Wc. (I)

Suite (e), No.7, Op.180. Leipzig: Forberg, 1900. US:Wc.

Suite (A), No.8, Op.199. Leipzig: Kahnt, 1903. US:Wc.

Vom Gestade der Ostsee, Op.169. Leipzig: Forberg, 1899. US:Wc.

Walzersuite (C), No.1, Op.86. Munich: Aibl, 1890; New York: Schirmer, 1890; Vienna: UEd, 1890. US:PHf, Wc. (I)

Wilms, Jan Willem (Johann Wilhelm) (1772–1847)

Dutch pianist and organist; in addition to writing the Dutch national anthem he composed chamber music, orchestral works, piano pieces, a flute concerto, and other music.

Sonata (C), Op.31. Leipzig: Hofmeister, ca.1812. NL:DHgm or DHk.

Sonata (Bb), Op.41. Leipzig: Peters, ca.1813. NL:DHgm or DHk.

Wilson, Mortimer (1876–1932)

American teacher; composed orchestral and chamber works and film music.
Images of an artistic infant; miniature tone pictures, Op.9. New York: Composers Music Corp., 1919. US:Bp,NYp. 17 jocular little pieces, many based on nursery jingles, in progressive order of difficulty. Occasional rhythmic irregularities and chromatic surprises punctuate the traditional harmonic idiom. (LI-I/E-UE)

Wilson, Samuel

°*Easy for me,* eight duets (Country hike; Ghost in the attic; Night prayer; Oriental dance; Starry night; Two black pups; Waltzing autumn leaves; Water ball). Boston: Boston Music, 1960. Pleasant instructional pieces for beginners. (E-UE-5)

°*Either part* (Chasing chipmunks; A cold day; Happy holiday; Lullaby for a baby Indian; Walking to school; Waltz for a peppermint stick). New York: Schroeder & Gunther, 1960. Tidy little pieces with interest and activity carefully balanced between the parts. (E-UE-5)

°*Five duets for twenty fingers.* New York: Mills, n.d.

°*For me and my teacher;* six duets. Boston: R.D. Row, 1958. Well fashioned little teaching pieces. (UE-LI/E-5)

°*Twelve fun tune duets* (Country carnival; Dance in the garden; Lullaby; Cotton patch; Little lost lamb; At the puppet show; To a china doll; The pirate's ghost; Party polka; Wild horses; For a lost sheep; Plantation dance). Boston: Boston Music, 1964. Short, melodious pieces; well harmonized with unusual sonorities; rhythmically varied; features some infrequently encountered key signatures. (LI/E-UE)

Winding, August Hendrik (1835–1899)

Danish pianist; director of Copenhagen Conservatory. His works include orchestral and choral pieces, songs, a piano concerto, chamber works, and piano music.
Aus jungen Tagen, Op.32. Breslau: Hainauer, 1868. US:Wc. Salon pieces. (I)

4 Clavierstücke, Op.6. Hamburg: Cranz, 1864. US:NYp. Salon suite competently set for piano 4H. (I)

Wineberger (Winneberger), Paul Anton (1758–1821)

German cellist and organist; wrote piano works, chamber music, an opera, and cello concertos.
Gavotte (C); *Marsch* (F). Ms. copy. D-ddr:Bds.

Sonates faciles. Hamburg: Cranz, ca.1815. D-ddr:Bds.

Variations sur l'air "God save the King." Rotterdam: Plattner, n.d. US:Wc. Instructional work. (LI)

6 Walzer (G,D,Bb,G,F,G); *6 Walzer* (C,F,A,D,Bb,F); *6 Walzer* (Eb,Bb,G, D,Bb,D). Contemporary ms. D-ddr:Bds. Instructional pieces; thin, trivial. (LI)

Winkler (Winkhler), Charles Angelus von (d.1845)

Polonaise mignonne (E), Op.32. Vienna: Diabelli, ca.1809. A:Wgm.

Rondeau (f). Vienna: Mechetti, ca.1819. A:Wn. Passage work and thin musical ideas dominate this work. Set in traditional Classical harmonic idiom. (LI)

Wodniansky de Wildenfeld, Antoine

3 Grandes Marches, Op.16. Vienna: Mechetti, ca.1828. A:Wgm.

12 Valses, Op.5. Vienna: Maisch, ca.1822. A:Wst.

Wohlfahrt, Heinrich (1797–1883)

German piano teacher and composer. Like his sons, Robert and Franz, he wrote a quantity of instructional piano music, including studies, folk-song arrangements, and original pieces in dry, pedagogical style.

°*The children's musical friend* (Musikalischer Kinderfreund), 50 easy and melodious pieces in progressive order for beginners, Op.87. °Carisch; °Durand; °Heugel; °Kalmus; °Peters; °Ricordi; °Schirmer. Instructional pieces. (E-LI)

Wolf, Ernst Wilhelm (1735–1792)

German composer; Kapellmeister at Weimar. Prolific writer of works in refined Classical style, including cantatas, oratorios, symphonic and chamber music, piano concertos, songs, and piano pieces.

Sonata (C). Leipzig: B&H, 1784; °NEd., in *Zwo Stücke für Vier Hände*, ed. Alfred Kreutz. Schott, 1940. B:Bc. Delightful piece in lean Classical style, beautifully set for 4H. (UE-LI)

Wolf, Georg Friedrich (ca.1782–ca.1814)

German organist and composer of motets, songs, and piano sonatas. He also wrote piano and singing instruction books and a musical dictionary.

Sonata (F), pour les amateurs. Leipzig: B&H, 1794. B:Bc—US:NYp. °NEd., in collection *Sonaten für Liebhaber*, ed. Frickert. Attractive, bright, four-movement work in Classical idiom. (LI)

Sonata (C). Leipzig: B&H, 1796. B:Bc—US:NYp.

Wolf, Johann Conrad Ludwig (1804–1859)

Variations über "Brüderlein fein," Op.3. Vienna: Maisch. A:Wgm.

Wolff, Bernhard (1835–1906)

German pianist and teacher; student of Hans von Bülow. He wrote instructional piano material.

Der erste Erfolg, 10 Vortragsstücke in leichte Spielart, Op.192. Leipzig: Steingräber, n.d.; Philadelphia: Hatch Music, 1898. US:Wc. (UE-LI)

Wolff, Christian (1934–   )

French-born American composer and teacher. His style developed from association with Cage and Feldman and includes the use of prepared pianos and aleatory techniques.

°*Duet I.* New York: Peters, 1962. US:Wc. Avant-garde work. (A)

Wölfl, Joseph (1773–1812)

Austrian pianist; student of Leopold Mozart and Michael Haydn. He composed orchestral and chamber music, piano concertos, and piano pieces.

3 *Duos*, avec flûte ou violon, ad lib., Op.45. London: Goulding & Co., 1806–1813. GB:Lbl.

Sonata (C), Op.17. Leipzig: B&H, 1803; Hoffmeister & Kühnel, ca.1803. Probably same as *Grande Sonate*, Op.69, and *Sonate favorite*, Op.62, Offenbach: André, ca.1815. A:Wgm—B:Bc—D-ddr:Bds,LEm. Four-movement work in Classical style. The first movement introduces some unusual harmonic relationships in the development section that point toward early Romantic tendencies, but the work is flawed by generally thin and colorless thematic material, structural weakness, and extended stretches of passage work. (I)

Sonate (g), Op.42 (with optional flute or violin). Leipzig: B&H, ca.1807. D-ddr:Bds.

6 *Walzer*. Leipzig: B&H, ca.1807. D-ddr:Bds.

Wolfsohn, K.

Six *duettinos faciles*, Op.35. Offenbach: André, ca.1868. D-brd:OF.

Wollenhaupt, Hermann Adolf (1827–1865)

German pianist. Established himself in New York as a teacher and toured widely as a concert artist in U.S. and Europe. He wrote many piano pieces.

Bilder aus Westen, 4 charakteristische Stücke, Op.48. Leipzig: Kahnt, 1859. US:NYp. Salon pieces. (LI)

Wolters, Klaus

°*Erstes Spiel zu vier Händen;* 34 alte Volkslieder in sehr leichten Sätzen. Kassel: Bärenreiter, n.d.

Wood, Charles

A *favorite duetto for two performers on the piano or harpsichord.* London: Longman & Broderip, ca.1790. GB:Lbl,Ob.

Woollen, Russell (1923–   )

American composer; studied with Walter Piston. He has written songs, choral and organ works, chamber and orchestral music, and piano compositions.

°*Sonata* (1950). New York: Peer International, 1955. Engaging, three-movement work in tonal, dissonant, chromatic, neo-Classical idiom. Clean and open-textured. Linear counterpoint. Allegro: bright, active. Adagio: lyrical, in gently swaying siciliano style. Rondo: intensely rhythmical finale with driving jazz figures and exciting climaxes. (UI-LA)

Woollett, Henry Édouard (1864–1936)

French composer of orchestral and chamber music, songs, and piano pieces.

°*En barque*. Paris: Senart, n.d.

Wormser, André (1851–1926)

French composer of operas, orchestral works, choral music, and piano pieces.

°*Six pièces pittoresques.* Paris: Lemoine, 1902. (LI)

°*12 pièces pittoresques.* Paris: Lemoine, 1876. (I)

Wörner, V.

Polonaise (D), Op.1. Offenbach: André, ca.1824. US:Wc. Instructional piece. (LI)

Wranitzky (Vranický), Paul (Pavel) (1761–1820)

Czech violinist, active in Vienna. As a composer he was known to Mozart and Haydn. He wrote symphonies, concertos, chamber music, and piano pieces in great abundance.

Polonaise (F). Ms. CS:Pnm. Short instructional piece in Classical style. (LI)

Sonata (C). Leipzig: B&H, ca.1796. B:Bc–USSR:Ml(ms.). Bright, attractive, vigorous three-movement work in Classical style. Well-defined melodies, often folklike; rhythmical variety; frequent sequential repetitions. Well written for the medium, with Primo slightly favored in importance. (LI-I)

Wray, John (1915–   )

Tarantella. London: Augener, 1951. US:Wc. Lively, melodious dance. (LI)

Wrede, Ferdinand (1827–1899)

German pianist, teacher, and composer. He is best known for his songs and men's choruses; also wrote piano pieces in salon style.

Deutsche Walzer, Op.23. Berlin: Schlesinger, 1884. US:Wc. (LI-I)

Wright, N. Louise

°*Echoes of Vienna.* Philadelphia: Presser, n.d. (LI)

Wuensch, Gerhard (1925–   )

Viennese-born Canadian. He writes in both dissonant-chromatic and traditional styles; often light and witty.

°*Valses nostalgiques,* Op.61 (1972). Ms. C:Tcmc. Chain of pleasant Viennese waltzes in conventional harmonic style; parts are well distributed. (I)

Wuorinen, Charles (1938–   )

American pianist, conductor, and composer. His works include orchestral and chamber works, piano concertos, and pieces for organ, harpsichord, and piano. He uses serial and electronic techniques.

°*Making ends meet.* New York: Peters, 1970. Commissioned and recorded by Jean and Kenneth Wentworth.

Wurm, Marie (1860–1938)

English pianist and composer. She wrote an opera, chamber and orchestral pieces, and piano compositions.

Tanzweisen (Walzer; Allemande; Ländler; Tyrolienne; Sequidilla), Op.28. Leipzig: B&H, 1892. US:Wc. Tuneful salon pieces. (LI-I)

Wurmser, Lucien
°Six pièces (Caline; Dolente; Menuet; Barcarolle; Tristesse; En forme de czardas). Paris: Consortium Musical, n.d. (I)

Wyk, Arnold van (1916–   )
South African pianist and composer; studied at the Royal Academy of Music, London. He has written symphonic and chamber music, a cantata, songs, and piano works.

Three improvisations on Dutch folk songs (To the market; Prayer for the homeland; The silver fleet). London: Boosey & Hawkes, 1944. US:Wc. Impressive settings of folk material; imaginative use of the full resources of the piano; demanding in part. (I-LA)

Yevlakhov, Orest Aleksandrovich (1912–   )
Soviet teacher; has written music in all forms and articles on music education.

Detskii tanets (Children's dance). In collection *Sbornik fortepiannikh*, ed. N. Agafonnikov. (EU-LI)

Young, Irene Harrington
°A merry dance. Boston: Boston Music, n.d. (UE)

Young, Percy Marshall (1912–   )
5 folk song duets (Barbara Allen; The ash grove; Wi' a hundred pipers; A lullaby; Christmas piece). London: Forsyth, 1938. US:Wc. Melodious settings of English folk songs. (UE-LI)

Young, Stuart
°Boats on the lake. London: Curwen, n.d. (UE)
°The cuckoo clock. London: Curwen, n.d. (UE)
The gay companions. London: Curwen, 1948. US:Wc. Instructional piece. (UE)
°Wee two at play. London: Curwen, n.d. (E)

Yudina, Yelena Alekseyevna
To the children of Dagestan; collection of piano pieces on Dagestan folk songs, for two and four hands. Makhach-kala, Dagestan (USSR): Dagestan State Music Publishers, 1927. US:NYp.

Yuyama, Akira
°Fireworks. Tokyo: Kawai Gakufu Co., 1969.
°The flower laughed. Tokyo: Kawai Gakufu Co., 1969.
°The school of killifishes. Tokyo: Kawai Gakufu Co., 1969.

Zagwijn, Henri (1878–1954)

Dutch composer of orchestral, choral, chamber, and piano works written in a refined contemporary style influenced by Debussy and Schoenberg.

°*Lichte klanken* (Soft sounds). Amsterdam: Alsbach, 1921.

Zander, Heinz Joachim

Schwarzwälder Schlittenpost. Hamburg: Hüllenhagen & Griel, 1965. US: Wc. Lively melodious march. (I)

Zaninelli, Luigi (1932–)

American composer; works include choral, orchestral, and chamber music.

°*A lexicon of beasties.* Delaware Water Gap, PA: Shawnee Press, 1968. Using adaptations of Edward Lear's *Nonsense Alphabet,* these imaginative and witty pieces are written in a mildly contemporary idiom and are intended for teacher and pupil. The teacher's part is sometimes below, sometimes above the student's, and, in a few instances, both; occasionally the teacher stands behind the pupil. Sparkling, attractive suite. (I-LA/E-LI)

Zanni, G.

°*Impressioni infantili* (Vacanze; L'uccellino è ammalato; A caccia nel bosco; Canzonetta; Lacrimette; Pagliacetto). Milan: Carisch, ca.1938.

°*Impressioni marini,* 6 pezzi facilissimi (Alba marina; Piccola barca; Onde marine; Vele addormentate; Luna sul mare; Mareggiata). Milan: Carisch, n.d.

Zaranek, Stefaniia Anatol'evna (1904–1962)

Soviet composer of ballets, operettas, orchestral and film music, and piano pieces.

7 Children's pieces (Cradle song; Music box; Fairy tale; Return from the fields; Waltz; Chinese music; Railroad train). Moscow: State Music Publishers, 1927. US:NYp.

Zarembski, Jules (Juliusz) (1854–1885)

Polish pianist, student of Liszt. His compositions show a strong Polish folk-song influence.

Danses polonaises, Série I, 3 danses galiciennes, Op.2; Série II, quatre mazurkas, Op.4. Berlin: Simon, 1880. US:PHf. Bright, rhythmically vigorous Polish national dances and folk melodies in effective 4H settings. (I)

Zecchi, Adone (1904–)

Italian conductor. Makes use of pandiatonic harmony and other contemporary resources as part of his highly personal musical idiom.

°*La bella addormentate;* favole di Massimo Dursi; tre piccoli pezzi (Gavotta dei due re; Il principe e la principessa; Valzer degli sposi). Bologna; Bongiovanni, 1949. US:NYp.

Zemlinsky, Alexander (1871–1942)

Austrian conductor; wrote operas, oratorio, symphonic works and piano pieces in post-Romantic style.

[*Four pieces for four hands*] (Eine Morgendämmerung; Der Polinchinell; Zwei Nonnen; Das Hindumädchen [incomplete] (May 1903). Ms. US: Wc. In Lawrence A. Oncley, "The Works of Alexander Zemlinsky: A Chronological List," *NOTES* 34 (1977):298–302.

Zenger, Max (1837–1911)

German conductor and composer.

Sonate (A♭), Op.33. Munich: Wilhelm Schmid (Richard Janke), 1879. US: Wc. Large-scale work in Romantic style. (UI-LA)

Ziegler, Johannes

First piano duets, Op.50. Boston: Oliver Ditson, 1908. GB:Lbl–US:Wc. Series of 12 instructional pieces in progressive order of difficulty; attractive, melodious, useful. (LI-I/UE-LI)

4 Melodious duets. Boston: A.P.Schmidt, 1907. US:Wc. Instructional. (UE)

Zilcher, Hermann (1881–1948)

6 Kleine Stücke, Op.8. Leipzig: B&H, 1904. US:Wc. Descriptive tone pictures in salon style. (UE-LI)

Zilcher, Paul (1855–1943)

4 kurze Klavierstücke, Op.62. London: Augener, ca.1908. US:Wc. Easy, tuneful instructional pieces. (UE-LI)

Side by side Series, Book XIV (On the march; Waltz; Cradle song; The brook; Tarantella). London: Ashdown, n.d.

Zipp, Friedrich (1914–   )

German teacher and conductor; has written cantatas and instructional works.

Canzona e sonata, Op.22. Mainz: Schott, 1947. Attractive works in traditional tonal idiom; modal, lyrical, with occasional chromaticism; rhythmic and textural variety. (I)

Zöllner, Heinrich (1854–1941)

German teacher and conductor; composer of operas, choral and symphonic works, and chamber music.

Am Bodensee, eine ländliche Geschichte in 12 Walzern, Op.27. Leipzig: Siegel, ca.1886. US:Wc. Light, melodious waltzes in salon style. (I)

Zolotareff, Vasili A. (b.1873)

Russian professor; composer of orchestral and chamber music, songs, and piano works.

30 Piano pieces (Ukrainian folk songs), rev. A. Siloti, Op.15. Moscow: State Pub. House, 1930; *NEd. 1970. US:NYp,Wc. Exceptionally fine folk-song settings in progressive order of difficulty, using a variety of meters and key signatures. (UE-UI/E-LI)

Zuccaro, Antonio

La danza del diavolo, polca-galop. Milan: Ricordi, 1955.

Zutphen, H. van

Caroussel, 11 easy piano pieces. Amsterdam: Broeckmans & VanPoppel, n.d.

Appendix I
Collections of Four-Hand Music

The following list of collections of four-hand music includes currently available anthologies as well as many that have long been out of print. In keeping with the policy of this volume, the collections are restricted to original four-hand compositions. However, in several anthologies a few duet arrangements of solo piano or orchestral pieces appear, and they are identified as such. There are also a number of collections of just four-hand arrangements—some of them skilful adaptations of solo piano pieces arranged by competent composers—but they are beyond the scope of the present list.

Agafonnikov, Nikolai, ed., *Sbornik fortepiannikh p'yes sovietskikh kompozitorov* (Collection of four-hand piano pieces by Soviet composers. For students of advanced grades at children's music schools). Leningrad: Sovietskii Kompozitor, 1957. US:Wc. Sherbachёv, V.: *Derevenskaia Kartinka* (Landscape); Liubarskii, N.: *Ukrainskii Tanets* (Ukrainian dance); Makalov, V.: *Medved' na Progulke* (The bear out for a walk); Manevich, A.: *Pokhodnaia pesnia kitaiskikh soldat* (March song of the Chinese soldiers); Balkashin, Iu.: *Echo*; Agafonnikov, N.: *Russkii Tanets* (Russian dance), *Waltz* and *Polka*; Vil'koreiskaia, T.: *Kazach'ia* (Cossack girl); Vitlin, V.: *V tsirke* (At the circus); Vol'fenson, S.: *Krakoviak*; Yevlakhov, O.: *Detskii tanets* (Children's dance); Chernov, A.: *Negritanskaia Melodia* (Negro melody); Shostakovich, D.: *Waltz*; Dunayevskii, I.: *Galop.* Pleasant, well-written pieces in traditional harmonic idiom by contemporary Soviet composers. Some may be arrangements. (LI-I)

Album di Musica Moderna per Pianoforte a Quattro Mani. Milan: Ricordi, 1932. US:Wc. Vol. I. Bartoccini, Mario: *Vilanella e canzone*; DePaolo, Domenico: *Pastorale* and *Berceuse*; Ferrari Trecate, Luigi: *Il Prode Anselmo*; Masetti, Enzo: *Nei giardini di villa Strà*; Mortari, Virgilio: *Mar-*

cetta. Vol.II. Parodi, Renato: *Danza* (in forma di fuga); Parrachio, Luigi: *Scherzetto;* Petrassi, Goffredo: *Siciliana* and *Marcia;* Pilati, Mario: *Entrata alla ciaccona;* Staffeli, Attilio; *Tempo di minuetto* and *Giga;* Veretti, Antonio: *Passepied* I and II. Attractive duets by Italian composers of the first quarter of the 20th century. (I-UI)

Album pour piano à quatre mains. London: Augener, n.d. US:Wc. Vol.1. Moszkowski, M.: *Volkslied;* Rubinstein, A.: *Barcarole,* Op.50; Volkmann, R.: *The knights,* Op.24/6; Ourville, Léon d': *Chant des chasseurs;* Mayer, Charles: *Galop militaire;* Schumann, R.: *Abendlied,* Op.85/12; three arrangements. Vol.2. Hiller, Ferdinand: *Huntsmen's chorus,* from Op.106; Rubinstein, A.: *Nocturne,* Op.50/1; Jensen, A.: *Scherzo,* Op.18/1; Reinecke, C.: Fragment from *Nussknacker und Maus?könig;* Volkmann, R.: *Under the linden,* Op.24/7; Gade, Niels W.; *Nordische Tonbilder* No. 2; one arrangement.

*Altberg, E., ed., *The little French fan.* Warsaw: PWM, n.d. Aubert: *Confidence,* from *5 Pièces enfantines;* Caplet: *Une petite berceuse* and *Une petite danse slovaque,* from *Un Tas de Petites Choses;* Inghelbrecht: *Les chevaliers du roy* and *Où vas-tu petite boîteuse,* from *La Nursery;* Fauré: *Berceuse,* from *Dolly,*Op.56; Orban: *Près du petit lit,* from *Pour les petits.* (I)

*Altberg, E., ed. *Selected works of French composers.* Warsaw: PWM, n.d. Bizet: *Trompette et tambour,* Op.22; Debussy: *Menuet,* from *Petite Suite;* Debussy: *Pour invoquer Pan, dieu du vent d'été,* from *Six épigraphes antiques;* Ravel: *Laideronette,* from *Ma Mère l'Oye;* Schmitt, F.: *La cigogne lasse,* from *La Semaine du petit elfe Ferme l'oeil,* Op.58; Schmitt, F.: *Dresde,* from *Reflets d'Allemagne,* Op.28. (I-UI)

Ansambli v chetyre ruki (Ensembles for four hands), Piano music for children's music schools, fifth grade. Moscow: Sovietskii Kompozitor, 1970. Goedicke, A.: *Barcarolle,* Op.12/2; Rakov, N.: *Protiazhnaia;* Shchedrin, P., and A. Filiarovskii: *It's raining in the street* and *As on the grey ocean* (polyphonic arrangements of popular children's songs); Glière, R.: *Bravura mazurka,* from ballet *Taras Bulba* (prob. arr.); Tchaikovsky: *Three Russian songs;* Grieg: *Norwegian dance,* Op.35/2. (I)

*Balogh, Erno, ed., *Eighteen original piano duets.* New York: Schirmer, 1953. Bizet, G.: *La poupée* and *Petit mari, petite femme,* from *Jeux d'Enfants,* Op.22/3, 11; Dvořák: *Slavonic dances,* Op.72/10 and Op.46/2; Glière: *Etude,* Op.48/5, and *Scherzo,* Op.48/11; Rachmaninoff: *Russian song,* Op.11; Saint-Saëns: *Pas redoublé,* Op.86; Mussorgsky: *Sonata* (1860); Stravinsky: *Three easy pieces* and *Five easy pieces;* Fauré: *Berceuse,* from *Dolly,* Op.56/1. (I-UI)

Bassford, W. K., ed. *Album for piano four hands.* New York: Schirmer [1895]. Contents identical with *Album pour piano à quatre mains,* q.v.

*Beer, Leopold J., ed., *Vier Hände spielen. Tunes for four hands.* Vienna:

UEd, 1939. Vol.1. Mozart: *Andante*, from *Sonata* (D), K.381(123a)/ii; Mozart: *Molto presto*, from *Sonata* (B♭), K.358(186c)/iii; Beethoven: *Allegro molto*, from *Sonata* (D), Op.6/i; Beethoven: *March* (C), Op.45/1; Schubert: *Allegro molto* (C), D.968; Schubert: *Kindermarsch*, D.928; Schubert: *Vier Ländler*, D.814. Vol.2. Weber: *Sonatine*, Op.3/1, *Mazurka*, Op.10/4, *Rondo*, Op.10/6; Schumann: *Birthday march*, Op.85/1, *Garden melody*, Op.85/3, *Evening song*, Op.85/12, *Waltz*, Op.109/3; Brahms: *Waltzes*, Op.39/1,2,15,16, *Waltz*, from *Liebeslieder*, Op.52/5, *Hungarian dance* No.6; Reger: *Waltzes*, Op.22/1,5,6. (I-UI)

Classic four-hand collection, vol.1. Boston: Oliver Ditson, 1918. US:Wc. Behr, Franz: *Witches' frolic*, Op.252/6; Bohm, Carl: *Charge of the Uhlans*, Op.313, *The dance queen*, polonaise, Op.305; Hoffmann, B.: *The dragon fighter*, polonaise, Op.1; Krause, Anton: *Serenade*, Op.6/1; Löw, Joseph: *Minstrel's serenade*, Op.330/3; Moszkowski, M.: *Spanish dances*, Op.12/1, 2,3,4; seven arrangements.

°*Classical album*, twelve original pieces. New York: Schirmer, 1895. Haydn: *Il maestro e lo scolare*; Mozart: *Sonata* (D), K.381(123a), *Sonata* (B♭), K.358(186c), *Fantasy* (f), K.594; Clementi: *Sonata*, Op.6/1/i; Kuhlau: *Sonata* (G); Weber: *Sonatina* (C), Op.3/1, *Romanza*, Op.3/2, *Menuet*, Op.3/3, *Mazurka*, Op.10/4, *Adagio*, Op.10/5. (I-UI)

Classische und moderne Pianoforte-Musik, originale und arrangements, Leipzig: B&H, n.d. US:Wc. Vol.1. Mozart: *Fantasy* (f); Beethoven: *March*, Op.45/1; Schubert: *Rondo*, Op.138, D.608; Reinecke, C., *Christmas Eve* from *Nussknacker und Mausekönig*; Bargiel, Woldemar: *Suite*, Op.7; five arrangements. Vol.2. Mozart: *Andante and variations* (G), K.501; Weber, *Moderato*, Op.60/1; Schubert: *Marche caractéristique*, Op.121/1, D.886; Schumann: *Waltz* and *Minuet*, from Op.130; six arrangements. Vol.3. Beethoven: *Six variations on the song "Ich denke dein,"* WoO74; Weber: *Rondo*, Op.60/8; Schubert: *Hungarian march*, from *Divertissement hongrois*, Op.54, D.818; Krause, Anton: *Serenade*, Op.6; Hofmann, Heinrich: *Ständchen*, from *Italienische Liebesnovelle*, Op.19. Mendelssohn: *Allegro brillant*, Op.92; four arrangements. (I-UI)

°Diller, Angela and Kate Stearns Page, arr., *The green duet book*, thirty folk tunes (E); *The brown duet book*, thirty folk tunes (UE). New York: G. Schirmer, n.d.

°Diller, Angela and Elizabeth Quaile, arr. *First duet book*, 50 duets (E); *Second duet book*, 33 duets (UE); *Third duet book*, 23 duets (UE-LI). New York: G. Schirmer, n.d.

Both the Diller-Page and Diller-Quaile series of duets consist of tasteful 4H settings of folk melodies, carefully arranged in progressive difficulty.

°Eckard, Walter, ed., *Forty-four original piano duets*. Bryn Mawr: Presser, 1968. André: *Sonatina* (C), Op.45/1; Arensky: *The cuckoo*, Op.34/2, *Waltz*, Op.34/4; Beethoven: *Allegro molto*, from *Sonata*, Op.6/i; Bizet:

Merry-go-round, Op.22/4; Brahms: *2 Waltzes*, Op.39/11,12; Bruckner: *2 Little pieces*; Czerny: *Allegretto*, Op.824/18, *Allegretto vivace*, Op.824/ 38; Debussy: *En bateau*, from *Petite Suite*; Diabelli: *Allegro*, Op.149/10; Dussek: *Rondo*, from *Sonata* (F), Op.67/2; Fauré: *Kitty waltz*, from *Dolly*, Op.56/4; Fuchs, R.: *Viennese waltz*, Op.42/12; Gretchaninoff: *March of the tin soldiers*, Op.98/3, *The little general*, Op.98/15, *In the meadows*, Op.99/1; Gurlitt, C.: *German dance*, Op.136/15, *Peasant's dance*, Op.211/17; Haydn: *Two minuets*; Köhler, H.: *The wanderer*; Moszkowski, M.: *Spanish dance*, Op.12/2; Mozart: *Rondo*, from *Sonata* (C), K.19d; Reger: *Waltz*, Op.22/1; Reinecke, C.: *Variations on the C major scale*, Op.122b/5, *Rustic dance*, Op.122b/6; Schubert: *Two Ländler*, D.814/3, 4, *Allegro moderato*, D.968; Schumann: *Waltz*, Op.130/2, *Birthday march*, Op.85/1; Stravinsky: *Andante* and *Balalaïka*, from *Five easy pieces*, *Valse* and *Polka*, from *Three easy pieces*; Türk, D.G.: *Rondo*; Volkmann, R., *The cuckoo and the wanderer*, Op.11/5, *The Russians are coming*, Op.11/3; Weber: *Sonatina* (C), Op.3/1, *German dance*; Wohlfahrt, H.: *Moderato*, Op.87/44. This excellent anthology of duets, representing various styles and periods from Haydn to Stravinsky, is geared to students of the earlier grades, but is equally useful to adult amateurs of limited technical and reading facility as an introduction to 4H literature. (UE-I)

°Ferguson, Howard, ed., *Style and interpretation*. London: OUP, 1971. Vol. 5, Keyboard Duets, 17th and 18th centuries. Tomkins, Thomas: *A fancy for two to play*; Haydn: *Menuet*, from *Partita* (F), Hob.XVIIa/2; Bach, J.C.: *Rondo*, from *Duetto* No.5 (G); Clementi, Muzio: *Allegro*, from *Duetto* (G), Op.3/3; Mozart: *Andante and variations*, K.501; Beethoven: *Sonata* (D), Op.6; Weber: *Adagio*, Op.10/5. Vol.6, Keyboard Duets, 19th and 20th centuries. Schubert: *Andantino varié*, D.823/2; Schumann: *Versteckens*, Op.85/10; Brahms: *Three waltzes*, Op.39/2,14,15, *Hungarian dance* No.18; Bizet: *La toupie*, Op.22/2; Dvořák: *By the dark lake*, Op.68/2, *Slavonic dance* No.16, Op.72; Debussy: *Pour remercier la pluie au matin*, from *Six épigraphes antiques*. Two handsome, beautifully annotated and fastidiously edited collections by an eminent British pianist, composer, and musicologist. In addition to presenting a small selection of the choicest 4H masterpieces, Ferguson has written a delightful Preface and Introduction. These absorbing remarks should be especially useful to amateur and professional musician alike, both for their practical suggestions for performance and for their general observations on 4H music. (LI-A)

Four-hand exhibition pieces for the pianoforte. Philadelphia: Presser, 1919. US:Wc. Berwald, W: *Danse caractéristique*; Brahms: *Hungarian dance* No.7; Moszkowski, M.: *Hungary*, Op.23/6; Grieg: *Norwegian dances*, Op. 35/2,3; Dvořák: *Polonaise* (E♭), *Slavonic dance*, Op.46/1; eight arrangements.

°*Four hands at the keyboard,* 12 easy duets. New York: Carl Fischer, 1965. Lake, Genevieve: *Czech dance;* Kolinsky, M.: *Around the maypole, At the court of Old King Cole, By the campfire;* Greim, Helen A.: *Dutch dance, Jig, Mazurka, Twilight;* Keenan, Gertrude: *Off to Donegal and back, Prancing pony;* Scher, W.: *Happy go lucky;* two arrangements. (UE-LI)

Fraemcke, August, comp., *Popular duets,* suitable for two equally advanced players. New York: Schirmer, 1910. US:Wc. Book I. Biedermann, A.J.: *Impromptu,* Op.81; Bohm, C.: *Blonde Locken,* waltz, Op.208; Enckhausen, H.: *Allegro moderato,* Op.72/12, *Polonaise,* Op.72/20; Encke, H.: *Galop,* Op.8/3, *Funeral march,* Op.8/6; Fuchs, R.: *Maestoso,* Op.28/7, *Un poco lento,* Op.28/11; Grenzbach, E.: *Gondellied,* moderato espressivo; Gurlitt, C.: *Vivace, Moderato,* and *Tarantella,* Op.102/9,10,12; Kleinmichel, R.: *Der kleine Postillon;* Kontski, Antoine de: *The awakening of the lion;* Loeschhorn, A.: *Two tone pictures,* Op.51/2,6; Reinecke, C.: *Romance, Waltz,* and *Polonaise,* Op.54/3,6,7; Gael, Henri van: *Rope dance,* Op.85; five arrangements. (UE-LI) Book II. Behr, F.: *Victoire,* polka élégante; Bohm, C.: *Rondo,* Op.84/1, *Intermezzo,* Op.250a; Hofmann, H.: *Schneeflocken;* Kleffel, A: *Cossack dance;* Klein, B. Cecil: *Slow waltz* and *Spanish serenade;* Loeschhorn, A.: *Allegretto,* Op.88/3; Ourville, Léon d': *Gondoliers;* Schubert: *Marche militaire,* Op.51/1; Spindler, F.: *Immortelle,* Op.90/5; two arrangements. (I)

°Frickert, Walter, comp. and ed., *Zu Zweit am Klavier (Two at the Piano).* Wiesbaden: Cranz, 1961. US:Wc. °Vol.I. Giordani, Tommaso: *Rondo* (D); Sterkel, J.F.X.: *Polonaise* (a); Mozart: *Menuet,* from *Sonata* (C), K.19d; Türk, D.G.: *Greetings to my charming piano* (Eb), *Belinda, cease thy wrath* (D); Beethoven: *Sonata* (D), Op.6; Weber: *2 German dances* (Eb,D); Schubert: *2 Ländler* (Eb,C), D.814/3,4; Schumann: *Birthday march* and *Evening song,* Op.85/1 and 12; Brahms: *2 Waltzes* (d,A), Op.39/9,15. (LI) °Vol.II. Weber: *Sonatine* (C), Op.3/1; Schubert: *Marche militaire* (D), Op.51/1; Schumann: *Reigen* (G), Op.85/8; Volkmann: *The cuckoo and the wanderer,* Op.11/5; Kirchner, T.: *Albumleaf,* Op.7/5; Bruckner: *Two little pieces;* Brahms: *Two Liebeslieder waltzes* (E,G), Op.52a/9,10; Jensen, A.: *Abendmusik* (G), Op.59/1; Bizet: *Soap-bubbles,* Op.22/7; Tchaikovsky: *2 Russian folk songs;* Dvořák: *Silhouette,* Op.8/8; Herzogenberg, H.von: *Waltz,* Op.53/1. (I-UI)

°Frickert, Walter, ed. *Sonaten für Liebhaber.* Mainz: Schott, n.d. Bach, J.C.: *Sonata* (A), Op.18/5; Hässler, J.W.: *Sonata VI* (c); Haydn: *Partita* (F), Hob.XVIIa/2; Wolf, Georg F.: *Sonate für Liebhaber* (F).

Für alle Welt, 24 ausgewählte Salon- und Charakterstücke. Leipzig: Portius Musikverlag, 1932. US:Wc. Vol.I. Wenzel, H.: *Deutsche Reichsadler Marsch* and *Ein lustiger Ritt;* Gänschals: *Mein Täubchen* and *Abendstille;* Fröhlich: *Das Kärtnerland;* Blüthner: Mauerblümchen. Vol.II. Wenzel: *Das Laiserlocke zu Speyer* and *Neuer Husarenritt;* Gänschals: *Alpenveilchen* and *Herzblättchen;* Fröhlich: *Festmarsch;* Blüthner: *Capriccio.* Vol.

III. Wenzel: *O frage Sterne* and *Nach dem Manöver;* Gänschals: *Schorle-Morle* and *Herzklopfen;* Blüthner: *Beim Mondenschein;* one arrangement. Vol.IV. Wenzel: *Aschenbrödel* and *Ich denke dein;* Gänschals: *Zither-klänge;* Aletter: *Meteor Waltz;* Gruber: *Heiterer Sinn;* Spindler: *Kaskade.* Collection of assorted salon pieces. (I)

*Goldstein, Michael, ed., *Brother and sister* (*Bruder und Schwester*), a collection of Soviet piano music. Leipzig: VEB Peters, 1965. Nazarova, T.: *Khakassian folk dance;* Grinfeld, G.: *Estonian folk dance;* Berkovich, I.: *Ukrainian dancing song, Romanze,* and *March,* Op.30/6,9,10; Feinberg, S.: *Chuvash melody;* Makarov, E.: *Who is faster?;* Goldstein, M.: *Merry dance;* eight arrangements. (UE-I)

Herrmann, Kurt (1900–1975), ed., *Primo und Secondo;* leichte Klavier-stücke. Wiesbaden: Steingräber, 1941. Part 1 (UE-LI/E) Part 2 (E/ UE-LI)

*Herrmann, Kurt and Otto Sonnen, eds. *Vierhändiges Klavierbuch* [classical duets]. Mainz: Schott, 1955. Beethoven: *March* (C), Op.45/1, *Gavotte* (F) [Leopold Koželuh, but erroneously attributed to Beethoven]; Bizet: *Merry-go-round,* Op.22/4; Brahms: *Liebeslieder waltzes,* Op.52a/9,11,15; Dvořák: *Waltz* (g), Op.54/5 [arrangement]; Kuhlau: *Menuett,* from *Sonatina* (F), Op.44/3; Schubert: *Marche militaire* (D), Op.51/1, D.733/1; Schumann: 2 pieces from *Pictures from the East,* Op.66/2,4; Sterkel: *Allegro* (C); Tchaikovsky: *Five Russian folk songs;* Volkmann, R.: *Ländler* (e), Op.39/7; Weber: *Moderato,* Op.10/1. (UE-LI)

*Hillemann, Willi (1903–), ed., *Sonatinen und leichte Stücke aus der Frühzeit der vierhändigen Klaviermusik.* Wilhelmshaven: Noetzel, 1962. Türk, D.G.: *Sonatina* I (G), II (C), III (D), IV (F), from *30 Tonstücke;* Sterkel, F.X.: *Allegro* (C); Seydelmann, Franz: *Menuets* (C, Eb), from *Sonatas* II and IV; Vaňhal, J: *Adagio* (C), *Allegro* (C), *Andante* (C); Just, Johann: *Andante* (G), *Menuetto* (D). Unusual collection of early 4H music. (UE-I)

Hock, Agnes, ed., *Neues Spielbuch,* zeitgenössisches Musiziergut. Cologne: P.J. Tonger, n.d. US:Wc. A collection of piano 4H music by German composers of the 1930s. Contains works by Cesar Bresgen, Helmuth Jörns, Armin Knab, Ernst Lothar von Knorr, Hans Lang, Walter Rein, and Karl Schäfer.

*Jonas, Oswald, ed., *Piano for two,* Book 2, a unique collection of original duets by Schubert and Schumann. Evanston: Summy-Birchard, 1958. Schubert: *Four Ländler,* D.814, *March,* from *Divertissement à la hongroise,* D.818, *Polonaise* (D), Op.61/4, D.824/4; Schumann: *Birthday march,* Op.85/1, *Garden melody,* Op.85/3, *Pictures from the East,* Op. 66/4, *Waltz,* Op.130/2. (LI-I)

Jonas, Oswald, ed. *Brahms and Dvořák for two.* Evanston: Summy-Birchard, 1961. Brahms: *Waltzes,* Op.39/4,5; *Hungarian dances* Nos.2 and 9; *Lie-*

beslieder Waltz, Op.52a/3; Dvořák: *Slavonic dance* (Ab), Op.72/8, *Legend,* Op.59/1. (I-UI)

°Kleinová, Eliška; Alena Fišerová; and Eva Müllerová, eds. *Album of four-hand works by old Czech masters* (Album čtyřručních skladeb starých českých mistrů). Prague: Editio Supraphon, 1972. Dušek, F.X.: *Allegretto,* from *Sonata* (G); Vaňhal, J.K.: *Allegretto, Andantino,* and *Andante,* Nos.4,3,8, from *Kurze und leichte Clavierstücke, Tempo giusto* No.1, of *Six valses faciles, Allegro* and *Adagio,* from *Sonata* (C), Op.65, *Allegretto, Adagio,* and *Allegro,* from *Sonata* (C),Op.64; Koželuh, L.: *Andante* and *Rondo,* from *Duo* (F), Op.19 (Poštolka XI:3), *Allegro, Andante,* and *Presto,* from *Sonata* (C) (Poštolka XI:5); Bečvařovsky: *Adagio* and *Allegretto,* from *Sonatina* No.10; Dusík (Dussek), J.L.: *Polonéza, Rondo,* from *Sonata* (F), Op.67/2. (E-LI)

°Kreutz, Alfred, ed. *Vermischte Handstücke für zwo Personen auf einem Clavier aus dem 18. Jahrhundert.* Mainz: Schott, 1938. Beck, Christian F.: *Minuetto* (G); Schuster, Joseph: *La Savojarde* (e); Geyer, Johann E.; *Andante grazioso* (G); Anonymous: *Sonatina* (C); Neefe, Christian G.: *Petite pièces,* from *Die Zauberflöte;* Geyer: *Andante* (F); Saupe, Christian G.: *Sonatina* (g); Scheidler, Johann David: *Tempo di menuetto* (E) and *Minuetto moderato* [both for three hands]. An especially attractive and valuable collection of unusual late 18th-century duet music. (E-LI)

°Kreutz, Alfred, ed., *Zwo Stücke für vier Hände.* Mainz: Schott, n.d. Bach, Wilhelm Friedrich Ernst: *Andante* (a); Wolf, Ernst Wilhelm: *Sonata* (C). (LI-I)

°Lubin, Ernest, comp. and ed., *Teacher and student.* New York: Amsco Music Publishing Co., 1976. Cui, César: *10 Pieces for five fingers,* Op.54/1–4; Diabelli, A.: *Melodious pieces,* Op.149/1–8; Haydn; *Il maestro e lo scolare* (*Teacher and pupil*); Moscheles, Ignaz: *Daily studies on harmonized scales,* Op.107 [excerpts]; Reinecke, Carl: *Easy four-hand pieces,* Op.54/4–6; Stravinsky, Igor: *Five easy pieces,* Nos.1,3,5; Tchaikovsky: *15 Russian folk songs,* from *Fifty Russian folk songs,* selections from *Paraphrases* on "Chopsticks"; Liadov, A.: *Galop;* Rimsky-Korsakov: *Tarantella;* Borodin, *Mazurka.* Delightful and unique collection featuring some of the less-familiar masterpieces of the 18th- and 19th-century 4H literature.

°Lyke, James, ed., *Ensemble music for group piano.* Champaign, IL: Stipes Publishing Co., 1965. Diabelli: *Rondo* and *Andantino,* from Op.163/1; Beethoven: *Allegro molto,* from *Sonata,* Op.6/i; Brahms: *Waltz* (Ab), Op.39, Theme from *Variations,* Op.23; Bizet: *Little husband, little wife,* Op.22/11; Debussy: *Minuet* and *Ballet,* from *Petite Suite;* Dello Joio, Norman: *Play time,* from *Family Album;* Dussek: *Rondo,* from *Sonata,* Op.67/1; Haydn: *Andante,* from *Il maestro e lo scolare;* Persichetti, V.: *Serenade* No.8, Op.62/i; Ravel: *Pavane,* from *Ma Mère l'Oye;* Schubert: *German dance with two trios, 3 Ländler* (arr. Brahms); Stravinsky: *Andante* and *Balalaika*, from *Five easy pieces*; Tchaikovsky: *3 Russian folk songs*; Türk, D.G.: *The storm* and *Sonatine* (D); Walton, W: *Pony trap*, from *Duets for Children*; Weber: *Sonatina* (C), Op.3/1; arrangements and pieces for two pianos.

°McClenny, Anne and Maurice Hinson, eds., *Duets of early American music*. David Carr Glover Piano Library. Melville, NY: Belwin-Mills, 1971. Taylor, Raynor: *Minuetto, Gavotte and Fandango, President's march* (arr.) (E); Mason, William: *French melody* and *Honest old miller*, Op.26/1,7, from *Duos for instruction and recreation* (E-UE); Foote, Arthur: *Reverie* and *Waltz*, from *Twelve duets on five notes* (UE/E-5).

Mannes, Leopold, comp., *Duet album*. New York: Music Press (Presser), 1948. US:Wc. Vol.2. Mozart: *Andante and variations*, K.501; Schumann: *Pictures from the East*, Op.66; Brahms: *Waltzes*, Op.39; Dvořák: *Legends*, Op.59; MacDowell, E.A.: *Three poems*, Op.20; Strauss, Johann: *Leaflet waltzes*, Op.300. (I-UI)

°*Meister der Romantik*, Originalstücke. Leipzig: Peters, 1944. Brahms: *Waltz* (a), from *Neue Liebeslieder Walzer*, Op.65a; Bruckner, A.: *Piece* (F), from *Three little pieces*; Grieg: *Norwegian dance* (G), Op.35; Herzogenberg, H. von: *Three Lithuanian dances* (C,Eb,G), from *Dainu Balsai, Litauische Volkslieder*, Op.76; Kirchner, Theodor: *Elegie* (e), from *Albumblätter*, Op.7; Liszt, F.: *Altes provençalisches Weihnachtslied* (B), No.8 of *Weihnachtsbaum*; Schumann: *Reigen* (G), from Op.85; Wagner, R.: *Polonaise* (D). (I)

°Mirovitch, Alfred, ed., *Original eighteenth century duets*. New York: M. Witmark (Warner Bros), 1957. Book I. Colizzi, J.A.: *Arietta* and *Rondoletto*; Giordani, Tommaso: *Trumpet call* and *Polonaise*; Weber, C.M.v.: *Minuet* and *Sonatina*. Book II: Giordani, Tommaso: *Air* and *Allemande*; Weber: *Romanza* and *Rondo*.

Miscellaneous duets (special collection), vol.1. US:Wc. Mayseder, Joseph: *Kronungs-Rondo*, Op.49; Wörner, V.: *Polonaise*, Op.1; Czerny, C.: *6 Rondos mignons*, Op.90; Schmitt, Jacob: *Introduction et variations*, Op.48; Herz, Jacques Simon: *3 Polonaises*, Op.15; Ries, Ferdinand: *Air national de Moore varié*, Op.108/2; Labitzky, Joseph: *Eine Sommernacht*, waltz, Op.210; four waltzes by Joseph Lanner, arr.

Moy, Edgar, ed. and comp., *The royal road*. London: A. Lengnick, ca.1935. GB:Lbl. Book 1, Primary. Moy, Ed.: *Berceuse* and *Carillon*; Zilcher, P.: *Memories, A little dance, Merry wanderer, Teasing*; Gurlitt, C.: *Morning light, Hide and seek*; Hunt, E. Ernest: *Ye banks and ye braes, Avenging and bright, A-hunting we will go*; Lee, E. Markham: *O where is my little dog gone, Oranges and lemons*; Marston, S.: *Slumber song*. Book 2, Elementary. Gurlitt, C.: *Playfulness*, Viennese waltz, Op.178/19; Zilcher, P.: *Idyll, March, Barcarolle*; Marshall, M.E.: *Sprites at play*; Hunt, H.E.: *The Bay of Biscay*; Lee, E.M.: *In Switzerland*. Book 3, Lower. Zilcher, P.: *Alla polacca*; Barbour, F.N.: *March burlesque*; Rowley, Alec: *Valse triste*;

Thompson, Roy: *Fantastic dance;* Lee, E.M.: *Norwegian dance;* Behr, F.:
La revue; one arrangement. Book 4, Higher. Brahms: *Waltz,* Op.39/1;
Austin, E.: *The Campbells are coming;* three arrangements. Book 5, Intermediate. Dvořák: *Slavonic dances* Nos.1,8; Brahms: *Waltzes,* Op.39/3,
15; Lee, E.M.: *Romance.* (LE-UI)

°Oesterle, Louis, ed., *Four-hand collection.* 42 Melodious and instructive
piano duets for elementary and first grades. New York: Schirmer, n.d.

Oesterle, Louis, ed., *Oesterle's graded four-hand collection.* New York:
Schirmer, 1910. Four-volume collection of original and arranged pieces in
salon style. US:Wc. (E-LI)

Oesterle, Louis, ed., *Recital pieces,* original pieces. New York: Schirmer,
1900. US:Wc. Bargiel, W.: *Ländler,* Op.24/1; Dvořák: *Slavonic dance,*
Op.72/10; Fuchs, R.: *Dream-Visions,* Op.48/4; Gade, N.W.: *Piece in
march-form,* Op.18/1; Godard, B.: *Au village,* Op.46/4; Jensen, A.: *Notturno,* Op.45/4; Moscheles, I.: *Little gossip,* Op.142/1; Moszkowski, M.:
Hungarian dance, Op.11/3; Mozart: *Andante and variations,* K.501; Pa-
derewski, I.: *Polish melody,* Op.12/2; Rubinstein, A.: *Toréador et Anda-
louse,* Op.103/7; Schumann: *Am Springbrunnen,* Op.85/9; Wilm, N. von:
Gavotte, Op.30/3; two arrangements.

°Olson, Lynn Freeman; Louise Bianchi; and Marvin Blickenstaff, eds., from
piano course *Music Pathways.* New York: Carl Fischer. *Ensemble three*
(1975). Diabelli: *Allegro* (e), from Op.149; André, J.A.: *Andante,* Op.
44/1; Rollino, J. and P. Sheftl: *Canon* and *Double cross,* from *Festivities;*
Köhler, L.: *French folk song* (Au clair de la lune); Bishop, Dorothy, arr.:
Frog went a-courting; Spindler, Fritz: *Immortelle;* Bruckner, Anton: *Moderato;* Gretchaninoff, A.: *On the green meadow,* Op.99/1, *Russian song,*
Op.98; Türk, D.G.: *Step lively, Susannah.* (UE-LI)   *Ensemble four*
(1976). Kohn, Karl: *A dance* and *The knights and ladies enter,* from *Castles and Kings;* Schubert, F.: *4 Ländler;* Arensky, A.: *Fugue on a Russian
theme;* Türk, D.G.: *The raging storm;* André, J.A.: *Sonatina* (F), Op.
45/3; Reinecke, Carl: *Variations on the C major scale,* Op.125b/5. (LI)
Ensemble five (1976). Debussy: *En bateau,* from *Petite Suite;* Ran, Shul-
amit: *A game* and *Rag doll valse,* from *Children's Scenes;* Schubert, F.:
Military march, Op.51/1; Schumann: *Pictures from the East,* Op.66/4;
Türk, D.G.: *Rondo.* (LI-I)

O'Toole, William J. and Felix Gunther, comps. and eds., *Classic masters and
we too,* original piano duets by J. Chr. Bach, Haydn, Mozart, Beethoven,
and Weber. New York: Creative Music Publishers [1948]. US:Wc.

P'esy dlia fortepiano v chetyre ruki (Pieces for piano four-hands, for intermediate grades of children's music schools). Moscow: Muzyka, n.d. US:
Wc. Schubert: *Polonaises,* Op.61/3,6, D.824/3,6; Schumann: *Impromptus,* Op.66/4,5; Balakirev: *4 Russian folk songs;* Arensky: *Tears,* Op.34/3;
Goedicke: *March,* Op.12/3. (I)

°*Piano for two,* Book 1, a unique collection of original duets. Evanston, IL:

Summy-Birchard, 1954. Arensky, A.: *The cuckoo*, Op.34/2; Bizet: *Carousel horses*, Op.22/4; Chaminade, C.: *Rigaudon*, Op.55/6; Diabelli, A.: *Rondino*, Op.159/17; Moszkowski, M.: *German dance*, from Op.25; Schubert: *Children's march*, D.928; Türk, D.G.: *Rondo*, from *Tonstücke*. (UE-LI)

Piano for Two, Book 2. See Jonas, Oswald.

°*Pianoforte album*, original compositions. London: Hinrichsen, 1955. Vol.I. Weber: *Minuetto* and *March*, Op.3/3,5; Clementi: *Larghetto con moto*; Schubert: *Children's march* and *Polonaise*, Op.75/2; Schumann: *Grief*, Op.85/6. (LI) Vol. II. Grieg: *Norwegian dance*, Op.35/2; Moszkowski, M.: *Mazurka* (G), Op.55/2; Bizet: *The top*, Op.22/2; Lancen, Serge: *Cubana*, Johnson, T.A.: *Scherzino* (C). (LI-I)

°*Pianoforte Album*, Sammlung beliebter Compositionen. Leipzig: Peters [1879; 1952]. Vol.I. Haydn: *Il maestro e lo scolare*; Mozart: *Sonata* (Bb), K.358, *Sonata* (D), K.381, *Fantasy* (f); Clementi: *Sonata* (C); Kuhlau: *Sonatina* (G); Beethoven: *Sonata* (D), Op.6; Weber: *Sonatina* (C), Op. 3/1, *Romanze, Minuet, Mazurka, Adagio*. (I)

Piteriu, Iuri, comp., *Khrestomatia (Anthology for piano four hands)*, Moscow: Sovietskii Kompozitor, 1968. US:Wc. Glière, R.: *Folksong*, Op.38/5; Goedicke; *Waltz*, Op.12/1; Rakov, N.: *Protiazhnaia* and *Mazurka*.

°*Playing together for the pianoforte*. Bryn Mawr: Presser, n.d. Collection of salon and instructive pieces. (UE-LI)

°Podolsky, Leo, ed., *Duet playing*. Melville, NY: Belwin, 1954. Vol.1. Ganschals, Carl: *Big notes, Cheer up, Comic son, Hussar's galop, In double time, March, Rustic dance*; Wurzburg, C.: *Cadets*; Clark, Frederick: *Prelude*; Brunner, C.T.: *Happy thought*; Gurlitt, C.: *Pleasant event*, Op.102 [E/E-5], *Prayer*, Op.136 [E-5/E], *The mill*, Op.102 [E/E-5]; Wolff, Bernhard: *Ties, Little harmony*, Op.194; six arrangements. (E-UE) Vol. 2. Czerny, C.: *A lesson, At play, Fancy play, Quiet pool*; Maykapar, S.: *Bells, Big and little drums, Dancing doll*, from Op.29; Wohlfahrt, H.: *Dancing on the dike*; Diabelli: *Follow me, Scherzo*; Gurlitt, C.: *Gayety, Having fun, In the meadow, Knight Rupert, Springtime*; Oesten, T.: *In the haunted castle, Morning promenade, Silver bell*; Enckhausen, H.: *March* (C). (E-UE, mostly UE/E-5) Vol.3. Czerny: *Allegro, Danse slave, Polish dance, Scherzando, A study*; Volkmann, R.: *Cuckoo and the wanderer*; Gurlitt: *Evening bells*; Spahn, C.: *Follow me, Roundel, Russian dance*; Sor, Ferd.: *Galopade*; Wolff, B.: *Gavotte*; Heins, Carl: *Happy games*; Lemoine, H.: *Skating*; two arrangements. (UE-LI) Vol.4. Weber: *Andante con variazioni*; Reinecke, C.: *Gavotte, Over the waves*; Türk, D.G.: *Rondo, 'Twas rainy and stormy*; Landry, A.: *Le petit moulin*; Lemoine, H.: *Rondino*, Hofmann, H.: *Snowflakes*; Concone, G.: *The flight*; Reinecke, C.: *To the guitar*. (LI) Vol.5. Willfort, Egon: *An old shepherd's tune, Dance of the armed Montenegrins, It's raining*, from *Duos für Jedermann*; Lack, T.: *Baptismal bells for a doll, Cradle song for a doll*;

Moonie, W.B.: *Highland lullaby;* Troendle, Teodora: *In the moonlight;* Ore, Harry: *Latvian folk song;* Brahms: *Waltz* (A), Op.39. (I)

°Raphling, Sam, ed., *One piano four hands,* original duets by the masters. Everybody's Favorite Series, No.129. New York: Amsco Publishing Co., 1965. Beethoven: *Sonata* (D), Op.6; Bizet: *Trompette et tambour* and *Le bal,* Op.22/6,12; Brahms: *Waltzes,* Op.39; Debussy: *Petite suite;* Mozart: *Sonata* (Bb), K.358(186c); Rachmaninoff: *Slava,* Op.11/6; Schubert: *Fantasy* (f), Op.103, D.940.

°Raube, Stanisław, ed., *Drobiazgi* (Bits and pieces). Kraków: PWM, 1976. (Pieces marked (†) also appear in an earlier, shorter edition of *Drobiazgi,* published by PWM in 1968, now p.o.p.) Vol.I. Lefeld, Jerzy: *Dzwony* (The bells); Paciorkiewicz, Tadeusz: *Melodia* (Melody), *Sygnały* (Signals), *Zolnierzyki* (Toy soldiers); Prószyński, Stanisław: †*Pacynki* (Glove puppets); Stromenger, Karol: †*Chodzi Baj po swiecie* (The story teller); Szeligowski, Tadeusz: *Grymasy* (Funny faces), †*Mr.Li-Si-Tsoa;* Twardowsky, Romuald: *Dwa Michaly* (Joe and Jack), *Japoneczka Miki* (Miki, the Japanese girl). (UE-LI) Vol.2. Garztecka, Irena: †*Kolej* (Train ride), *Taniec muszek* (Dance of the young flies); Lefeld, Jerzy: *Marsz* (March), *Toccatina, Wariacje na temat ludowy* (Variations on a folk theme); Lutosławski, Witold: *Zasłyszana melodyjka* (A tune I once heard); Stromenger, Karol: †*Etiuda we dwoje* (Study for two players); Szeligowski, Tadeusz: †*W cyrku* (At the circus); Twardowski, Romuald: *Dzwony* (Bells), *Perpetuum mobile.* (I)   Charming collection of contemporary Polish 4H pieces for children; imaginative, beautifully written, with handsome illustrations.

°Rehberg, Willy (1863–1937), ed., *Vierhändiges Klassikerbuch* (*Classical duets,* Easy original piano duets). Mainz: Schott, 1931. Bach, J.C.: *Rondo* (F), Op.18/6/ii; Haydn: *Tempo di menuetto,* from *Maestro e scolare;* Mozart: *Sonata* (D), K.381; Clementi: *Larghetto con moto;* Beethoven: *Sonata* (D), Op.6; Schubert: *Two Ländler* (Eb,Ab), D.814, *March,* D.928, *Marche héroïque* (D), Op.27/3, D.602/3; Weber: *Andante con variazioni,* Op.10/3; Schumann: *Birthday song,* Op.85/1; Brahms: *Waltz* (A), Op.39/15. (LI-I)

Repertuar fortepiannogo ansamblia srednie klassy DSMU (Repertoire of piano ensemble for the intermediate class of children's music schools; pieces for piano four hands). Moscow: Muzyka, 1969. US:Wc. Schubert: *Two polonaises;* Schumann: *Two impromptus,* Op.66; Balakirev: *Four Russian folk songs;* Arensky: Three excerpts from *Six pièces enfantines,* Op.34; Goedicke, A.: *March,* Op.12/3, from *Six pièces.*

°Rieger, Adam, ed., *Selected little compositions.* Warsaw: PMW, n.d. Bizet: *The doll* and *Little husband, little wife,* Op.23/3,11; Brahms: *Waltzes,* Op.39/1,2,15,16; Schumann: *Écossaise, Française,* and *Waltz,* from Op. 130; *Melody* and *Evening song,* from Op.85 (LI-I)

Rowley, Alec, comp., *Études for four hands.* London: Schott, n.d. Three-volume graded selection of studies garnered from various collections.

Rowley, Alec, ed., *The path of progress*, 5 books. London: Lengnick, 1933. GB:Lbl. Book 1. Zilcher, P.: *Melody, Morning song, Over the hills, Gavotte;* Marston, S.: *The carpet, Heigh-ho, the holly, The ghost-walk;* Moy, Edgar: *Chanson, Valse;* Hunt, H. Ernest: *Early one morning, All through the night, The girl I left behind me* [arr.]; Lee, E.M.: *Little Jack Horner;* Marshall, M.E.: *Minuet;* Rowley, Alec: *Rondaletto.* (E) Book 2. Moy, E.: *Berceuse* and *Roundelay;* Porter, F.A.: *Dance by moonlight;* Hunt, H.E.: *Here's to the maiden* and *The Arethusa;* Rowley, Alec: *Sea song;* Krentzlin, R.: *Birthday march,* Op.20; Aletter, W.: *In stately measure;* Marshall, M.E.: *Haunted house;* one arrangement. (E-UE) Book 3. Lee, E.M.: *In the meadows;* Austin, Ernest: *Lass of Richmond Hill, Waltz;* Behr, F.: *Dors chéri* (Berceuse); Krentzlin, R.: *Turkish march;* one arrangement. (UE) Book 4. Rowley: *Gavotte,* No.3 of *Three Centuries;* Lee, E.M.: *Nigger dance* and *Irish tune;* Austin, E.: *St. Patrick was a gentleman* and *Sailor's hornpipe;* Brahms: *Waltzes,* Op.39/1,2. (UE-LI) Book 5. Austin, E.: *Gavotte and musette;* Jensen, A.: *Elfin dance;* Rowley, Alec: *Blues;* two arrangements. (LI) Mostly original 4H compositions, although there may be a few more arrangements than are indicated.

°*Salon-Album,* 2 vols. Leipzig/Zürich: Hug, n.d. Salon pieces by Behr, Rohde, Lange, Nagy, Giese, Pache, and Werner.

°*Salon-Album.* Sammlung beliebter Stücke. Leipzig: Peters, n.d. Salon pieces by Gade, Behr, Bungert, Raff, X. Scharwenka, Moszkowski, and Dvořák.

Scharwenka, Xaver, ed., *Modernes Vortragsalbum;* Album of selected contemporary pieces, 5 vols. Leipzig: B&H, 1916. Salon works by Moritz Vogel, A. Tuczek, J.O. Armand, Reinecke, F. Neumann, Grenzbach, Nicodé, Rohde, A. Holländer, J. Röntgen, E. Rudorff, R. Kleinmichel, Hans Huber, and Heinrich Hofmann.

°Scholz, E. Chr. (1910–   ), ed., *Die allerersten Klassiker und Romantiker.* A selection of easy original compositions. Vienna: Doblinger, 1963.

°Schüngeler, Heinz (1884–1949), ed., *Vierhändiges Vortragsbuch,* 2 books. Mainz: Schott, 1943. Book 1. Bruckner: *Three little pieces;* R. Fuchs: *Two miniatures,* Op.93/3,6; Gretchaninoff: *March of the tin soldiers* and *The little general,* Op.98/3,15, *In green meadows,* Op.99/1; Gurlitt: *Peasant's dance,* Op.211/17; Schmid, H.K.: *Three German folk songs,* Op.93/12, 15,8; Schubert: *3 Ländler;* Schumann: *Sadness and Reigen,* Op.85/6,8; Volkmann: *In the mill, The postillon, On the lake* and *Wanderer,* from Op. 11; Weber; *Sonatina,* Op.3/1. (UE-LI) Book 2. Bizet: *The doll* and *March,* Op.22/3,6; Brahms: *3 Waltzes,* Op.39/1,2,6, *Hungarian dance* (A), No.7; Dvořák: *2 Silhouettes,* Op.8/4,8; R. Fuchs: *2 pieces from Frühlingsstimmen,* Op.1/1,2; Reger: *2 German dances* (Ab), Op.10/7; Schmid, H.K.: *Bayrische Ländler,* Op.36 (excerpt); Schubert: *Military march* (G), Op.51/2, *Polonaise* (D), Op.64/1; Schumann: *Evening song,* Op.85/12, *Polonaise,* Op.109/2; Weber: *Rondo,* Op.60/8. (LI-I)

Sokolov, F., ed., *P'esy na temy russkikh pesen* (Pieces on themes of Russian songs and dances for piano two- and four-hands). Moscow: Muzyka, 1965. US:Wc. Nos. 1-7 in the ensemble section. Attractive settings of Russian folk songs by E. Shenderovich, F. Sokolov, A. Manevich, D. Tolstoi, and B. Savelev.

°*Spielbuch, zeitgenössische Originalkompositionen.* Leipzig: VEB Peters, 1957. Bresgen, Cesar: *Kuckucksuite;* Genzmer, Harald: *Langsamer,* from *Sonata* (D); Frommel, Gerhard: *Impromptu;* Brehme, Hans: *Gavotte;* Schroeder, Hermann: *Rondino capriccioso;* Raphael, Günther: *Romantisches Tanzbild,* Op.10; Kauffmann, Leo Justinius: *Bagatelle;* Lang, Hans: *Kleines Maienkonzert*—Musik über alten Frühlingslieder; Knorr, Ernst-Lothar von: *Introduktion und Allegro;* Girnatis, Walter: *Kleine Suite* (derived from *Musik zu einem Handpuppenspiel*); Weismann, Julius: *Rondo,* from *Sonatina,* Op.142; Höller, Karl: *Kleine Sonate,* Op.32/1. Appealing and varied collection of works by German composers of the pre–World War II era; identical in contents with *Strassburger Klavierbuch, zeitgenössische Hausmusik* (Leipzig: Peters, 1943), with the exception of one work, *Romantisches Tanzbild,* by Günther Raphael, which appears in the later edition in the place of *Feierliche Tanz* by Heinrich Spitta. (LI)

°Szávai, Magda and Lili Veszprémi, eds., *Nemzetek Tancai és Dalai* (38 National dances and songs). Budapest: Zeneműkiadó, 1969. Four-hand arrangements of Hungarian, Czech, Russian, German, French, Irish, and Polish folk songs; early French dances; and a few original 2H pieces for clavichord.

°Szelényi, István, comp., *Magyar szerzők négykezes zongoradarabjai* (Piano duets by Hungarian composers). Budapest: Editio musica, 1952. Járdányi, Pál: *Érik a szőlő;* Ligeti, György: *Three wedding dances;* Maros, Rudolf: *Változatok* and *Tüsköm dance;* Patachich, Iván: *Vidám dal;* Szabó, Ferenc: *Three short piano pieces.*

Thirty-two graded pieces for piano duet. London: Schott, n.d. GB:Lbl. *Very Easy* (5-note compass). Humbert, G.F.: *Dream song;* Rowley, A.: *Tit-for-tat;* Gariboldi, G.: *Fable;* Moy, E.: *Chanson;* Humbert, G.F.: *Falling leaves;* MacIntosh, S.C.: *Passing thoughts.* (E/E-5) *Easy* (Grade 2). Gariboldi, G.: *Canzonet;* Sekles, B.: *Lullaby, River song,* and *Even-song;* Bertini, H.: *Mechanical figure;* MacIntosh: *Two little impromptus;* Stiehl, H.: *2 Album leaves;* Burlitt, C.: *Tarantella;* Gretchaninoff: *Spring morning* and *Serenade;* Moy, E.: *Valsette;* Behr, R.: *Galop.* (E-UE) *Moderately Easy* (Grade 3). Rowley, A.: *Valse arabesque;* Stamaty, C.: *The curfew bell;* Kronke, E.: *Gipsy dance;* Bertini, H: *Motor race;* Guest, L.: *Phyllis and Strephon;* Volkmann, R.: *The cuckoo;* Berens, H.: *In the twilight;* Moy, E.: *March miniature.* (UE-LI) *Moderately difficult* (Grade

4). Samuel, E.: *Scherzo;* Berens, H: *Autumn song* and *Gnomes;* Jensen, A.: *Fireflies;* Moszkowski: *Romance;* MacIntosh: *Pastoral dance;* Ladmirault, P.: *Ronde;* Moy, E.: *Bucolique;* Rowley, A.: *Carillon.* (LI-I)

°Townsend, Douglas, ed. and comp., *Piano duets of the Classical period.* Bryn Mawr: Oliver Ditson (Presser), 1956. André, Johann Anton: *Divertimento* No.3; Burney, Charles: *Sonata* No.1; Clementi, Muzio: *Sonata* No.1; Giordani, Tommaso: *Duettino* No.3; Haydn: *Il maestro e lo scolare* and *Partita* (F). (I-UI)

°*Two little players,* first and second grade piano duets without octaves for equal performers. Boston: Boston Music, 1906. Pieces by Behr, Bachmann, Gurlitt, Kleinmichel, Krug, Küchenmeister, Löw, F. Hiller, Loeschhorn, Reinecke, Tschirch, Vogel, and Volkmann.

Ungdomsvännen (Friend of youth) for klaver, 4 haender, Bind 1–3. Andersson. Herning (Denmark) Centralbibliotek.

°Váczi, Károly, ed., *Album for piano duet.* Melville, NY: Belwin-Mills [1972], (joint edition with Editio Musica, Budapest, originally entitled *Piano duet music for beginners).* Bizet: *The top,* Op.22/2; Diabelli: *Rondo;* Doppler, Károly: *Csardas;* Járdányi, Pál: *Hungarian folk song* (Érik a szőlő); Kadosa, Pál: *May song;* Köhler, L.: *Moderato* and *Allegretto moderato;* Patachich, Iván: *Gay song* (1952); Poldini, Ede: *Clown;* Ránki, György: *Recruiting dance,* from *Kapuvár;* Soproni, József: *Capriccioso* and *Barcarole;* Szervánsky, Endre: *Folk song suite I* ("Mély a Tiszának a széle").

Weiner, Leó, comp., *Vierhändige Klavierstücke ungarischer Meister.* Budapest: Kultura, 1952.

°Windsperger, Lothar (1885–1935), ed., *Notenmappe des Klavierschülers,* eine Sammlung von 22 Vortragsstücken von Gurlitt, Gretchaninoff, Sartorio, etc. Mainz: Schott, n.d.

°Zeitlin, Poldi and David Goldberger, comps. and eds., *The duet books.* The CMP Piano Library. New York: Consolidated Music Publishers, 1961–76. The four books of this collection are similar in character and content to the next anthology, *Easy original piano duets,* by the same editors. A dagger (†) before an item indicates that it appears in both collections. *Duet Book I.* Cui, César: *Funeral of a bird,* Op.74; Czerny, C.: †*Melody;* Diabelli, A.: *March,* Op.149/4; Enckhausen, H.F.: *Ländler* (C); Gretchaninoff: *Sunday morning* and *Russian song;* Hoffmeister: †*German dance;* Koehler, L.: †*Christmas song,* †*French folk song,* and †*Norwegian reindeer song;* Rinck, Johann: *German dance* (e); Spindler, F.: †*Immortelle* (G); Tchaikovsky: †*I bow my head,* †*Little Vanya,* and †*Rustling pine,* from *Fifty Russian folk songs;* Türk, D.G.: †*Two chorales,* from *Tonstücke;* Wohlfahrt, H.: †*Bagatelle* and †*Waltz.* (E) *Duet Book II.* Diabelli, A.: †*Allegro* (e), Op.149/28; Gurlitt. †*Allegretto;* Czerny: †*Andantino con grazia* (Bb); Stravinsky, I.: †*Andante,* from *Five easy pieces;*

Burgmüller, J.F.: †*Dance*, from *Quadrille*; Rebikov, V.: †*Dance of the myosotis*, Op.30/2; Weber: *German dance*; Spindler, F.: *Immortelle* (d); Schubert: *Ländler* (C), D.814/4; Gretchaninoff: *Lullaby*; Türk, D.G.: †*Rondo*; Tchaikovsky: †*Sing not, nightingale*. (UE) *Duet Book III.* André, J.A.: †*Divertimento* (C), Op.18/1; Blanc, Adolphe: †*Scherzetto*; Arensky, A.: †*Tears*, Op.34/3; Cui, César: *Overcast skies*, Op.74; Gurlitt, C.: †*Scherzo* (F); Gretchaninoff, A.: †*On the green meadow* (C), Op.99; Schubert: *Ländler* (Eb), D.814/1; Tchaikovsky: †*On the meadow*; Türk, D.G.: †*The storm*. (UE-LI) *Duet Book IV.* Schubert: †*Children's march*; Tchaikovsky: *Dance*; Debussy: *En bateau*, from *Petite suite*; Bizet: †*Little husband, little wife*, Op.22/11; Dussek: *Rondo*; André: *Theme and variations*; Brahms: †*Waltz* (G), Op.39/10; Dvořák: *Waltz*. (LI-I)

°Zeitlin, Poldi and David Goldberger, comps. and eds., *Easy original piano duets*. Vol.23 of Music for Millions series. New York: Consolidated Music Publishers, 1959. See note above on duplication in *The duet books*. Arensky, A.: *Tears*, from *Six pièces enfantines*, Op.34; Bizet: *Little husband, little wife*, from *Jeux d'enfants*, Op.22; Blanc, Adolphe: *Scherzetto*; Brahms: *Waltz* (G), Op.39/10; Burgmüller, E.: *Two dances*, from *Quadrille*; Czerny, C.: *Andantino con grazia, Melody*, and *Tyrolean dance*; Diabelli, A.: *Allegro* (e), Op.149/28, *Polonaise*, Op.149/23, *Hungarian dance* Op.149/20; Grieg, E.: *Norwegian dance* (A), Op.35; Gretchaninoff, A.: *On the green meadow*, Op.99/1; Gurlitt, C.: *Allegretto* and *Scherzo*; Haydn: *Minuet*; Hoffmeister, F.A.: *Two German dances*; Hofmann, H.: *Conversation*, Op.19/4; Koehler, L.: *Christmas song, Norwegian reindeer song, French folk song, German lullaby*, and *Lithuanian song*; Koželuh, L.: *Gavotte* (F) (incorrectly listed under Beethoven); Löw, J.: *Tarantella* and *Krakowiak*; MacDowell, E.A.: *The swan*, from *Moon Pictures*, Op.21; Mozart: *Finale*, from *Sonata* (Bb); Ourville, Léon d': *The lake*, from *Soirées musicales*; Rebikov, V.: *Danse des myosotis*, from *Petite suite*, Op.30; Schubert: *Children's march*; Schumann: *Round dance*, Op.130/1; Spindler, *Two immortelles*, Op.90; Stravinsky, I.: *Andante*, from *Five easy pieces*, and *Polka*, from *Three easy pieces*; Tchaikovsky: *Little Vanya, Rustling pine, I bow my head, Oh, my green grapes, Sing not, nightingale*, and *On the meadow*, from *Fifty Russian folk songs*; Türk, D.G.: *Two chorales, Rondo*, and *The storm*, from *Tonstücke*; Volkmann, R.: *Ländler*, Weber: *Sonatina*, Op.3/1; Wolf, Georg Friedrich: *Finale*, from *Sonata* (F) (erroneously attributed to Ernst Wolf). Varied collection of predominantly 19th-century music containing a number of unusual items; useful. (E-LI)

°Zeitlin, Poldi and David Goldberger, comps. and eds., *Easy piano duets of the nineteenth century*. New York: Schroeder & Gunther, 1976. Brahms: *Waltzes*, Op.39/2,3; Bruckner, Anton: *Recital piece* (F), from *Three pieces;* Czerny: *Bagatelle* (B♭); Diabelli: *Andante,* from *Sonatina* (C), Op.24/1; Dvořák: *Waltz,* Op.54/5 (not originally for 4H); Kuhlau, Friedrich: *Arioso,* from *Sonatina* (G), Op.44/1; Liszt: *Old Provençal Christmas song;* Schubert: *German dance* (E) (Ländler No.3, D.618); Schumann: *Evening song,* Op.85/12; Tchaikovsky: *Two Russian folk songs* (B♭,E♭); Weber; *Marcia,* Op.3/5. (UE-LI)

°Zeitlin, Poldi and David Goldberger, comps. and eds., *Eleven piano duets by the masters,* for the intermediate grades. New York: Schirmer, 1964. Beethoven: Six variations on "Ich denke dein" (D), WoO 74; Bizet: *Colin-Maillard* (Blindman's buff), Op.22/11; Brahms: *6 Waltzes,* Op.39/ 1,5,3,11,15,2; Dvořák: *6 Écossaises,* Op.41 (d,C,B♭,B♭,A,F); Grieg: *Symphonic piece* (C), Op.14/2; Haydn: *Allegro,* from *Partita* (F), Hob. XVIIa,2; Hummel: *Variations on a Tyrolean theme* (F), [Op.118]; Mozart: *Sonata* (C), K.19d; Schubert (arr.Brahms): *11 Ländler,* D.366; Schumann: *3 Impromptus,* Op.66/2,3,4; Weber (arr. Czerny): *Sonata* (C) (originally for violin and piano). (LI-I)

Appendix II
Music for Piano, Four-Hands with Voice(s) and/or Other Instrument(s)

(See main listing for full reference)

Abeille, J.C.: *Grand concerto* (orchestra)
Arnold, Malcolm: *Concerto* (orchestra)
Berens, H.: *Gesellschafts-Quartets* (string quartet)
Binkerd, Gordon: *And viva sweet love* (voices)
Böhm, J.C.: *Wechselgesang* (voice)
Bois, Rob du: *Deuxième Série de Rondeaux* (percussion)
Boyd, Anne: *Rain on Castle Island* (voices, percussion)
Brahms, Johannes: *Liebeslieder waltzes* (voices)
Brant, Henry: *Ceremony* (voices, orchestra)
Britten, Benjamin: *Noye's fludde*, Op.59 (voices, orchestra)
Czerny, Carl: *Concerto* (orchestra)
Dvořák, A.: *Three men's choruses*, Op.43 (voices)
Fétis, F.J.: *Sextet* (string quartet)
Fröhlich, F.J.: *Concerto* (orchestra)
Gaertner, Marie-Thérèse: *Concertino* (percussion)
Genzmer, Harald: *Spielmusiken* (instruments)
Ghiel, T.F. de: *Sonata concertante* (intuments)
Gutchë, Gene: *Gemini*, concerto, Op.41 (orchestra)
Hastetter, E.: *Eine kleine Krippenmusik* (instruments)
Hauer, Josef Matthias: *Zwölftonspiel* (accordion)
Hauer, Josef Matthias: *Zwölftonspiel* (2 violins, viola, cello)
Hauer, Josef Matthias: *Zwölftonspiel* (violin, cello, accordion)
Hoddinott, Alun: *The silver swimmer* (voices)
Hofmann, Heinrich: *Minnespiel*, Op.42 (voices)
Hollfelder, W.: *Kleine Tiergarten* (voices, percussion)
Huber, Hans: *Walzer*, Op.27 (instruments)

Hummel, Johann Nepomuk: *Nocturno*, Op.99 (4 horns)

Imbrie, Andrew: *Concerto* (orchestra)

Jadassohn, S.: *Sextet*, Op.100 (string quartet)

Klebe, Giselher: *Szene* (4 solo violins, tutti violins)

Klink, Waldemar: *Kleines Lob der grossen Stadt* (voices, percussion)

Köhler, Gottlob H.: *Introduction et polonaise* (flute)

Koželuh, Leopold: *Concerto* (orchestra)

Küffner, Johann J. P.: *Sonate* (2 violins, 2 horns, cello)

Lahmer, Ruel: *Passacaglia and fugue* (clarinet)

Lee, Peter: *A conversation piece* (voices)

McBride, Robert: *Vocalise* (voices)

Marez Oyens, Tera de: *Ballade grotesque* (voices)

Mažek, Vincenz: *Concertino* (orchestra)

Masséus, Jan: *Gezelle liederen* (voice, percussion)

Mater, E.: *Improvisaciones* No.1 (string quartet)

Mayuzumi, Tochiro: *Sphenogrammes* (flute, alto sax, marimba, violin, cello, voice)

Meale, Richard: *Sinfonia* (strings)

Mul, Jan: *Concerto* (orchestra)

Niehaus, Manfred: *Einige Anweisungen für die Millelage* (electric guitar, viola)

Nietzsche, Friedrich: *Hymnus an die Freundschaft* (chorus)

Noskowski, Siegmund: *Fahrender Spielmann*, Op.18 (chorus)

Novák, Viteślav: *Dvě balady*, Op.19 (chorus)

Osieck, Hans: *Suite concertante* (orchestra)

Owen, Harold: *Metropolitan bas cantata* (chorus)

Pijper, Willem: *Op den Weefstoel* (chorus, wind instruments)

Randhartiger, B.: *Variations*, Op.11 (2 horns)

Regner, Hermann: *Klangspiele* (percussion)

Respighi, Ottorino: *Suite della tabacchiera* (wind instruments)

Reynolds, Verne: *Graphics* (trombone)

Reynolds, Verne: *Xenoliths* (flute)

Rogalski, Theodor: *Two dances* (winds, percussion)

Santos, Manuel I.: *Quintet* (2 violins, flute)

Schumann, Robert: *Spanish love songs*, Op.138 (voices)

Senft, Luigi: *Concerto* (2 violins, violin, bass)

Smith, Gregg: *Songs of innocence* (chorus)

Smolanoff, Michael: *Concerto* (strings, percussion)

Studer, Hans: *Kleines Konzert* (instruments)

Tag, Christian T.: *12 Veränderungen* (flute)

Tate, Phyllis: *Hampstead Heath* (Woodwinds, brass, percussion)

Vogler, Georg Joseph: *Concerto* (orchestra)

Walker, George: *Five fancies* (clarinet)
Wesley-Smith, Martin: *To noddy man* (voice)
Williams, David R.: *Concerto* (orchestra)
Williamson, Malcolm: *The happy prince* (strings, percussion, chorus)

Select Bibliography

Chang, Frederick Ming and Albert Faurot. *Team piano repertoire, a manual of music for multiple players at one or more pianos.* Metuchen, NJ: Scarecrow Press, 1976. List of four-hand music (pp.3–37), with descriptive and critical annotations.

Eberler, Max Wilhelm. "Studien zur Entwicklung der Setzart für Klavier zu vier Händen von den Anfängen bis zu Franz Schubert." Diss., University of Munich, 1922 (U23.9561). A study of the development of four-hand music, its setting, and its literature, with many musical examples; covers the period from mid-18th century to ca.1315. The second section contains lists of original duets and four-hand arrangements of other works.

Ferguson, Howard, ed. *Style and interpretation,* vols.5 and 6. London: OUP, 1971. In addition to the helpful interpretive suggestions accompanying the pieces in these two collections, the Preface and Introduction are of exceptional interest for their useful and practical discussions of the techniques and mechanics of duet performance. Also contains chronological list of duets.

Friskin, James and Irwin Freundlich. *Music for the piano: a handbook of concert and teaching material from 1580 to 1952.* New York: Holt, Rinehart, and Winston, 1954; reprint New York: Dover Publications, 1973. Useful section on piano four-hand repertoire with terse critical evaluations of the music.

Ganze, Karl and Ludwig Kusche. *Vierhändig.* Munich: Heimeran, 1937; reprint 1954. Attractive, entertaining, and practical introduction to the piano duet. The carefully annotated index of four-hand works is worth looking into, despite its unfortunate Nazi bias in the heavily German choice of composers and the conspicuous omission of Mendelssohn and Moscheles.

Georgii, Walter. *Klaviermusik.* Zürich-Freiburg: Atlantis, 1950. The brief discussions of four-hand literature, while not comprehensive, are thorough.

Kanwischer, Alfred. "Aspects of performance practices of four-hand one piano music illustrated by works taken from the period 1850–1900." Document, D.M.A., Boston University, 1967. Contains an analysis of the Debussy *Petite suite* and the Dvořák *Legends,* and a selected list of four-hand music written between 1850 and 1900.

Lubin, Ernest. *The piano duet: a guide for pianists.* New York: Grossman, 1970. Attractive, practical introduction to four-hand literature and its performance. Written with great warmth, affection, and breadth of experience by a sensitive musician; includes critical studies of the major works with copious musical examples and helpful performance suggestions. A major work on the subject.

Miller, Hugh M. "The earliest keyboard duets." *Musical Quarterly* XXIX (1943): 438. A discussion of the two *Fancies* of Thomas Tomkins and Thomas Carlton; both works are written out in full.

Müller-Blattau, Joseph. "Zur Geschichte und Stilistik des vierhändigen Klaviersatzes." *Jahrbuch der Musikbibliothek Peters für 1940*, XLVII:55–58. Leipzig: Peters, 1941. Analysis of Mozart's, Beethoven's, and Schubert's approaches to four-hand writing.

Rowley, Alec. *Four hands—one piano: a list of works for duet players.* London: OUP, 1940. One of the first English-language surveys of duet repertoire: general works, the "classics," special lists of English and French compositions, graded lists of educational pieces, and études; many out-of-print items.

Ruthardt, Adolf. *Wegweiser durch die Klavier-Literatur*, 10. Auflage, pp. 261–300. Leipzig/Zürich: Gebrüder Hug, 1918–. Brief descriptions of works in graded lists. Good commentaries; best for instructional music, studies, and exercises. Good coverage of European music, mostly German but with some French and English listings.

Sonnedecker, Donald I. "Cultivation and concepts of duets for four hands one keyboard, in the eighteenth century." Diss., Indiana University, 1953. A critical study of the duet from its early stages to 1800. Investigates the development of musical form, style, and harmonic idiom of the four-hand works of the Viennese, German, and French schools, and of English and American composers.

Townsend, Douglas. "The Piano Duet." *Piano Quarterly*, Fall 1967; 15–18. Excellent study of the historical background of the rise and development of four-hand music, with brief list of works.

Webb, John Elliott. "Compositional features of original music for one piano, four hands." Diss., University of Rochester (Eastman), 1957. Analysis of the music and discussion of technical features including textures, sonorities, doublings, imitations, sequences, repetitions, integration of melodic material, rhythms, and ensemble problems of: J. C. Bach: *Sonata*, Op. 18/5; Mozart: *Sonata* (F), K.497; Beethoven: *Sonata* (D), Op.6, *Marches*, Op.45; Schubert: *Fantasy* (f), Op.103; Mendelssohn: *Allegro brillant;* Schumann: *Bilder aus Osten*, Op.66/4 and 6, *12 Pieces*, Op.85/9 and 12; Brahms: *Variations on a theme by Schumann*, Op.23, *Waltzes*, Op.39; Debussy: *Six épigraphes antiques;* Poulenc: *Sonata;* Casella: *Pupazzetti;* Hindemith: *Sonata;* and Constant Lambert: *Trois pièces nègres.*